Maynard Brichford

EUROPE
1492 to 1815

EUROPE

1492 to 1815

A Social, Cultural, and Political History

CHESTER PENN HIGBY

Professor of History

University of Wisconsin

Edited by **WALTER CONSUELO LANGSAM**
President, Wagner College

J. B. LIPPINCOTT COMPANY

CHICAGO · PHILADELPHIA · NEW YORK

To

Captain John B. Higby

PREFACE

The state and its fortunes have long been the major interest of historians and the writers of historical textbooks. This conception of history has led to the narration in great detail of the actions of rulers and their ministers and favorites and the successes and failures of the state in war, diplomacy, and administration. Since the days of Voltaire, halfhearted efforts have been made to include in historical narratives some account of economic and social institutions and conditions and even some of the artistic and literary achievements of mankind. In spite of these concessions to other phases of history, however, the main interest of historians has continued to be political, military, and diplomatic events.

The author of this textbook believes that such a conception of history is misleading. At best, political, military, and diplomatic history give only a part of the picture. They do not reveal man's original ignorance of the universe in which he lived, the world which he occupied, and himself; or his great conquests in the art of living, science, art, literature, and philosophy. To dwell at great length on the petty wars for Italy, the amours of Louis XIV, or the witty, madcap indecencies of the court of Charles II and to omit the splendid achievements of the scientists, artists, and literary men of the successive periods is to distort history.

As a result of this belief, the author has included much material that does not usually find its way into a textbook of European history. He has tried to emphasize the achievements as well as the failures of Europeans. He has endeavored to make European Man rather than the states of Europe the center of attention. At the risk of trying the impossible, the author has inserted in his narrative, in addition to the traditional material, an unusual amount of material on the lives and achievements of the European scientists, artists, writers, and inventors. He believes that only such an approach to history will reveal European man and the society which he has developed in a true perspective.

The author is deeply indebted to many people. They include the scholars whose work forms the foundation of all textbooks; the author's wife, who has corrected the diction and the style of the manuscript; and the editor, whose knowledge of history, fidelity, and sense of humor have done much for the work. The author owes the sections on vaccination and the optical telegraph to the researches of two of his former graduate students, Dr. R. G. Dunbar of Colorado State College and Dr. Duane Koenig of Miami University.

The sections on science have been carefully read by Professor Robert C. Stauffer, Department of the History of Science, at the University of Wisconsin, but he is in no way responsible for any mistakes that may be found in the text.

The chapters on religious history have been read by Father Leo Rummel of the Norbertine Order, but he must not be held accountable for their contents.

The maps owe much to the pioneer work of Tschan, Grimm, and Squires.

CONTENTS

Part 1: European Society about 1492

Part 2: The Sixteenth Century

Part 3: The Seventeenth Century

Part 4: The Eighteenth Century

Part 5: The Revolutionary Period

PART 1

European Society about 1492

CHAPTER 1

The Background of Modern European History

The historian of modern times has the task of telling a story that began at a much earlier period. He must mention individuals who already have played their parts and disappeared from the stage of life. He has to allude to events that already have taken place. He must refer to institutions that were created many years before the opening of the modern period. He has to speak of movements that have been long under way. Yet, some knowledge of these actors, events, institutions, and movements is necessary to one who would understand modern times. It is the aim of this chapter to give enough of this indispensable background to make the subsequent narrative intelligible.

The Geographical Background

Modern European history cannot be understood without a considerable knowledge of the geography of Europe. The islands along its shores, its straits, channels, and coastal seas, its rivers, mountains, and peninsulas have all deeply influenced the course of European history. Its surrounding waters have lured men to fish, to travel, and to attack other groups. The physical features of Europe have isolated peoples and caused the growth of distinctive cultures. They must, therefore, be learned by the student of history.

The Peopling of Europe

Europe, however, became only gradually the settled continent that we know today. At one time, much of present-day Europe was heavily forested and such inhabitants as there were roamed from place to place. Men had to be on guard against wild animals. Only in the lands bordering the Mediterranean Sea had men settled down and adopted civilized ways of living. All who lived north of the Rhine and Danube rivers were counted barbarians. Those living between the Rhine and Elbe rivers were called Germans or Teutonic peoples. Those east of the Elbe were known as Slavs. In time, the Germans broke into the western provinces, and the Slavs forced their way into the eastern provinces of the Roman Empire. From the seeming chaos caused by the barbarian invasions arose the present peoples

3

of Europe. From the wreckage of the Roman Empire came the so-called Latin peoples: the Italians, the French, the Spanish, the Portuguese, the French-speaking Swiss, the Belgian Walloons, and possibly the Rumanians. The Teutonic peoples broke up into the Germans of today, the English, the Flemish people of Belgium, the Dutch, and the three Scandinavian peoples. The Slavs became divided into three groups: the Eastern, Western, and Southern Slavs. The first included the peoples known as Great, Little, and White Russians; the second, the Poles, the Czechs, and the Slovaks; and the third, the Croats, Serbs, Slovenes, and the Bulgars. The last group may be designated by the name of the province in which they reside. In that case they may be known as Bosnians, Montenegrins, Dalmatians, and the like. There are, too, a few peoples in Europe that are neither Latin nor Teutonic nor Slavic peoples.

The Heritage of Europe from the Ancient Past

These modern peoples of Europe owe much to the past. From the peoples who once flourished in Western Asia and the valley of the Nile River, Europeans received their religious ideas and a great body of practical knowledge. From the Greeks, they inherited the systems of philosophy associated with the names Plato and Aristotle, the beginnings of science and mathematics, various forms of literary expression, and several important types of architecture. From the Romans, who welded the lands around the Mediterranean into a single empire, they obtained the Latin tongue—which is still the medium of expression for the Roman Catholic Church and, until lately, for governments and the learned world, a political terminology, Roman law, a useful calendar, a system of weights and measures, an architectural vocabulary, and the Christian Church.

The Christian Church

The Christian Church started among the Jews of Palestine. By the fourth century it had ceased to be a despised and persecuted Jewish sect. As the result of the work of missionaries, it had become rich, powerful, and highly organized—the religion of the Roman state. Its changing fortunes, however, had profoundly transformed it. Like the State, the Church developed a hierarchy of administrative districts—parishes, bishoprics, archbishoprics, and patriarchates. Its prelates became great figures in Roman society. The Church acquired great powers and privileges.

During the invasion of the Roman Empire by the Germans and the Slavs, the Christian Church was the sole Roman institution that survived. While other institutions were breaking down, the

Christian Church increased its powers and privileges and gained new provinces for Christendom. On more than one occasion its prelates overawed the rude and simple barbarian invaders. It took the weak and defenceless under its protection. It acquired many civil and political powers and privileges. It sent missionaries all over Europe.

It was almost inevitable, however, that the Christian Church should become divided. Before the barbarian invasions, the Roman world had broken into the Eastern and Western Roman Empires. Quite naturally, the people of the Western Empire came to look to Rome for leadership; those of the Eastern Empire tended to look to Constantinople as a center. In time, there developed some differences in doctrine, ritual, and organization in the two parts of the Empire. Finally, in 1054, the Christian Church definitely separated into two distinct churches: the Roman Catholic Church and the Eastern Orthodox Church. Thenceforth, religious differences tended to hold apart the peoples of Western and Eastern Europe.

The Heritage of Europe from Medieval Times

The invasion of the Roman world by Germans and Slavs transformed Europe. Temporarily, the breakdown of the Roman government threw Europe into political and social chaos. The rude kingdoms set up by the invaders inside and outside of the limits of the Roman Empire by no means took the place of the Roman government. For a time, there was a marked decline in all that constitutes civilization.

In time, this confusion was increased by other invasions. Early in the eighth century the Arabs overran the Iberian Peninsula. In the ninth century the Magyars swept through Central Europe and finally settled down in the Danube Valley. At the same time the coasts of Western and Southern Europe were being harried by Northmen from Scandinavia.

From these attacks the terrified inhabitants of Europe sought protection where they could find it. The unprotected tillers of the soil put themselves and their little holdings of land under the protection of some strong man of the neighborhood, an official of the Church, or the head of a monastery. These, in turn, put themselves under the protection of some still stronger individual. This process resulted in the development of two important institutions. The humble folk of Europe, for the most part, became attached to big estates and became tenants, on some sort of terms, of great landlords. Thus arose the institution known in England as the manorial system and on the European continent as the seignorial system. This institution, in turn, formed the foundation for a complex hierarchy of

5

landlords that largely took the place once held by the Roman government. These peculiar relationships of lords and their vassals constituted the institution known as the feudal system.

In theory, the members of the landlord class were known as lords and vassals. A lord granted his vassal land in return for homage. This relationship obligated the lord to protect his vassal and the vassal to give his lord military service. The land granted to the vassal was known as a fief. In theory, all landlords were vassals of the king or vassals of the royal vassals.

In reality, the situation was quite different from the theory. Vassals acted as independently as they dared. Everyone felt himself to be the equal of other lords. There were constant disputes and wars between lords and their vassals. In practice, Europe consisted of isolated estates and warring lordships.

In spite of the turmoil, however, a new and different civilization gradually developed. Embracing much more of Europe than Roman civilization, it fused the Roman and German worlds and the Christian religion into a new civilization. At first, it was almost wholly an agricultural society. In time, though, as men became somewhat more settled, towns and cities developed within the agricultural framework. Sometimes the harassed inhabitants sought the protection of ancient walls. At other times they settled near popular shrines, at the fords of rivers, and at the intersections of routes of travel and trade. Kings, moreover, consciously founded towns to increase their revenues. As a result, towns and cities arose all over Europe.

At first, the inhabitants of even the towns and cities supported themselves largely by agriculture. Later, petty industries and local trade grew up. Still later, commerce between regions developed. In the end, the inhabitants of the towns and cities were largely engaged in trade and industry.

In time, those in the urban centers engaged in commerce and industry felt the need for organization. At first, they organized merchant gilds. Later, those engaged in the various trades formed craft gilds. Out of the exchange of goods between town and country developed the weekly market held in the open square of the town or city. Out of the exchange of commodities between regions grew the medieval fairs.

In the beginning, the inhabitants of the towns and cities, like those of the open country, were under the rule of the feudal lords: a king, a noble, an officer of the Church, or the head of a monastery. The interests of the landlords and their urban tenants, however, soon conflicted. As a consequence, the townsmen sought a larger and larger measure of self-government. As a result of their struggles with

6

their lords, some towns and cities gained more and more self-government. Others acquired complete independence and became, particularly in Germany and Italy, little city-states. Town and country thus
became differentiated. The successful townsmen became a middle
class, characterized by their occupations, their prosperity, and their
political freedom. The inhabitants of the countryside, on the other
hand, remained peasants.

The new society that developed in Western Europe gave rise to a
new and striking style of architecture. It is known as Gothic. It
expressed itself particularly in magnificent cathedrals and churches.
The building of these ecclesiastical structures often took generations.
Their adornment monopolized the time and skill of masons, sculptors, painters, and wood carvers for centuries.

Though most people of Europe could not read or write, some
schools arose in connection with the cathedrals and the monasteries.
In time, some of these schools developed into universities that
attracted to their lectures thousands of students. Some of the more
famous professors at these universities elaborated systems of thought
that aimed to give reasonable answers to the natural queries of men
and that still influence the thinking of the modern world.

As times became more settled, men and women became more
cultivated. The lords and ladies of the time developed chivalry, a
way of life which aimed to promote courtesy and good manners,
a pattern which still influences the conduct of men and women. For
the entertainment of the upper classes, bards composed songs about
heroic deeds. For the amusement of the middle classes, romances,
tableaux, and narrative verses were written which described ordinary
life with great realism. Men, too, made some effort to write history.
First in rude chronicles and later in prose narratives of some literary
and historical value, they told the story of the society in which they
lived. Such memoirs as Villehardouin's *The Conquest of Constantinople* and Joinville's *Life of St. Louis* are still read with pleasure.

Men of the Middle Ages, however, felt particularly the need for
order. Their longing for peace made them look back to the Roman
Empire as an ideal and strive for a restoration of order. This made
them value the work of Charlemagne, set up the Holy Roman
Empire, and, finally, develop states comparable to our modern
states.

CHAPTER 2

The Economic and Social Organization of Europe

The first chapter of this book attempts to sketch the history of the complex civilization inherited by the modern world from the past. The aim of the next three chapters is to describe the society that Europe had developed by 1492, the traditional date of the beginning of modern times. Such a survey will give the reader a standard by which to measure the significance of subsequent events.

The Economic Organization of Europe

Then as now, European society depended largely on its natural resources as an economic base. The peoples of Europe supported themselves mainly by extractive industries. A few, like the Dutch and the Norwegians, dwelt near the sea and lived, to a large extent, by fishing. Some were engaged in small-scale mining. These, however, were the exceptions. Most people in Europe tilled the soil or raised flocks and herds of domestic animals. As a result, the organization of rural life must be studied by those who wish to understand European society at the beginning of the modern period.

Rural Organization

Wherever grain constituted the principal crop, big estates were the chief rural unit. They gave the European countryside a far different appearance from a typical American rural scene. If in imagination we could climb to some point that overlooked a big European estate about the beginning of the modern period, we would be struck by its large size, the arrangement of its buildings, and the organization of its lands.

Instead of living in detached farmhouses as in America, the inhabitants of a typical great European estate lived in a village. The dwelling of the landlord, which varied from a castle or chateau to a habitation hardly distinguishable from the huts of the peasants, tended to dominate the other buildings. In most parts of Europe it was built for protection rather than for comfort. If we were to look further from our point of vantage, we would perhaps notice the church, the rectory, and the mill. Lastly, we should see the huts of the peasants who tilled the estate. Fear of wild animals and of law-

8

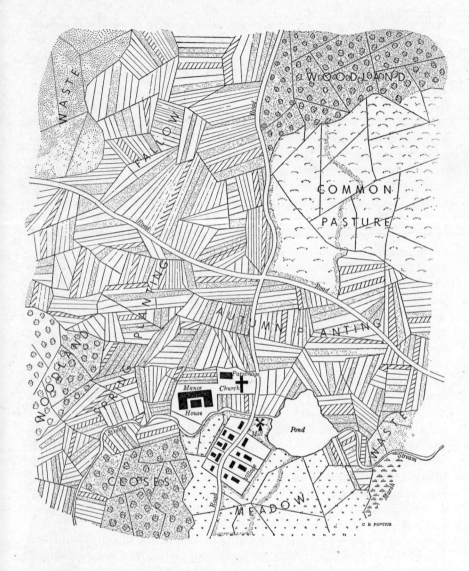

WASTE

WOODLAND

COMMON

PASTURE

FALLOW

SPRING PLANTING

AUTUMN PLANTING

WOODLAND

Parsonage

Manor House

Church

Mill

Pond

Stream

Village

CLOSES

WASTE

Stream

Marsh

MEADOW

C B PONTIUS

▓ DEMESNE ▨ PARISH PRIEST'S ARABLE LANDS
PEASANT'S TYPICAL HOLDING-10 STRIPS PER FIELD

Manor House and Parish Lands

9

less individuals still dominated the countryside and caused men to live in compact villages.

If we were to look further, we would note that the land in the estate was arranged in a manner that differed greatly from that which prevails in present-day America. We should find two or three great unfenced fields and a smaller piece of meadowland that stretched away from the village toward the horizon. If we were to look still further, we would see that the meadow and the arable fields were surrounded by common pasture land, stretches of forest, and wastelands. It must be remembered, though, that in reality there were no typical estates. They were often very irregular and varied greatly in size and arrangement.

If we should descend from our point of vantage and enter the village, we would find much that would seem strange to an American. The village might be surrounded by a stockade. The dwellings of the villagers would differ greatly in material and plan according to the region in which they were found. Some would be fairly comfortable. Others would be mere huts. In some cases the dwelling of a peasant and his barn and sheds formed an enclosed court. In others, the peasant and his farm animals all lived under one roof.

If we were to enter some of the peasant cottages, we would continue to find great differences. In England, France, the Netherlands, and parts of Germany we might discover signs of considerable prosperity. In most parts of Europe the peasants would be found living in miserable huts. The roofs would be thatched, the floor would be merely the hard-packed earth, and the windows would be mere openings in the walls.

In most peasant cottages, life centered in one large room that served as kitchen, dining room, and general gathering place. Meals would be cooked in the open fireplace. At best, the room would be furnished with a handmade table, some chairs or stools, a chest or two, strange beds designed to exclude every breath of the supposedly dangerous night air, a cupboard, a spinning wheel, and a few pots and pans. Usually, only the head of the household and his wife would have separate sleeping quarters. In many cases, the children and the servants slept in the loft over the oxen and cattle. At worst, we might find little or no furniture and the peasant and his family sleeping on a pile of straw.

If we wandered into the arable fields surrounding the village, we should find them arranged in a very peculiar manner. The two or three large fields would have somewhat the appearance of an old-fashioned crazy quilt. Each field would consist of a great number of long, narrow, irregular strips of land, called acres and divided from each other by balks of unploughed land, a line of stones, or merely a furrow. The strips would be arranged in groups, and some groups of strips would run one way and some another. The meadowland, we should find, had a similar arrangement.

If we should inquire about the ownership of the land, we should learn that the landlord reserved for himself part of the lands, possibly some especially desirable piece, or, more likely, some of the strips in the arable fields and in the meadowland. This was known as the demesne of the landlord. The rest of the arable strips would be held by the peasant tenants of the landlord. A typical holding for a peasant was thirty acres. The holdings of the landlords, the parish priest, and the peasants were scattered and intermingled in such a way that a third of each holding was to be found in each of the three arable fields, and the strips of each tenant were irregularly dispersed over the different fields. The holding of the parish priest was known in England as the glebe.

Landlord, parish priest, and peasant tenants carried on agriculture in a very primitive way. Much of the work on the manors or seigniories, as the big estates were called, was done cooperatively. Several tenants furnished the eight or twelve oxen that were used to pull the rude, cumbersome, wooden plows, and the plowing for the whole estate was done all at one time. The seed was strewn by hand. In any one year we should find that one of the three arable fields was planted with a winter crop such as wheat or rye. Another was sowed with a spring crop such as oats, barley, beans, or peas. A third was allowed to lie fallow. At harvest time, everybody again cooperated in the cutting of the grain with a sickle or a scythe and in the gathering of it. Finally, the peasants threshed the grain with a flail; or they spread the grain on a hard-packed floor, drove oxen round and round over it to loosen the kernels, threw the grain and chaff up into the air to separate them, and finally scooped the winnowed grain up into containers.

Both landlord and tenants had rights of pasture in the harvested fields, the common pasture, the forests, and the wasteland. The cattle, sheep, pigs, and poultry used them in common. At certain times of year they would be pastured on the stubble of the arable fields; at other times, in the common pasture. Consequently, no careful breeding of farm animals was possible. They were, accordingly, incredibly light, small, and scrubby. Both the landlord and his tenants obtained firewood from the forest.

The relationship between the landlord and his tenants was usually a peculiar one. Most tenants were bound to the land. They owed the landlord services and payments in return for protection and the right to till a plot of ground. They were expected to work for the landlord for a certain number of days a week and at certain times during the year. They owed him certain payments in money or in kind. At the time of the death of a tenant, his successor paid a heavy tax for the right to succeed him. Furthermore, the tenants were expected to have their grain ground in the landlord's mill, to have their grapes pressed in his wine press, and to bake their bread in his oven. In some places the landlord claimed the right to dictate the tenant's marriage and demanded for a number of years the services of the tenant's children. In other words, most of the rural inhabitants of Europe at the beginning of the modern period were serfs.

By 1492, however, particularly in England and France, changes were taking place in this manorial or seignioral system. Many landlords were ceasing to farm their demesne lands. Instead of having them tilled for their own benefit by their peasants, they were beginning to lease them to enterprising persons and were becoming merely collectors of rents and seignioral dues. After this, the landlords were less insistent upon the payment of dues and services by their serfs and other tenants. The landlords, consequently, often sold to their serfs their freedom. This did not free the former serfs, however, from all the troublesome dues that they had been paying.

In England many landlords were making another change in rural organization. They were "enclosing" their estates or manors. This meant that they were rearranging the various holdings in such a way as to enable the landlords to exchange their scattered strips for compact holdings that they could manage without regard to what their tenants were doing. Unfortunately, many landlords were unscrupulous and simply deprived tenants of their lawful holdings. This process resulted in the dispossessed tenants becoming either agricultural laborers, or even beggars. In some parts of Europe, it must be remembered, just the opposite process was taking place. In Bohemia and Russia, for example, free peasants were sinking into serfdom.

Even where these changes were taking place, many things tended to mark off the landlords from the rest of the population. They retained their castles, chateaux, and manor houses. Their tenants paid them many signs of deference. The landlords had special seats in the parish church. They often appointed the parish priests. When they died, they were buried within the walls of the church instead of in the churchyard where the rest of the parishioners found a last resting place.

The landlord class at the beginning of the modern period must not be confused with the polished, elaborately dressed, memoir-writing nobles of a later time. They were still rude, uncouth, illiterate men who thought of themselves primarily as fighting men. Most of them could neither read nor write. They hated the merchants of the towns for their prosperity and thought themselves within their rights when they made a foray against the merchants. They even felt themselves the less fortunate equals of the kings.

Landlords and peasants sought only to produce what they ate and used. They grew their own food, made their own clothes, and fashioned their own tools, utensils, and furniture. There was, therefore, little demand for a surplus. As a consequence, the landlords and their peasants lived, for the most part, isolated from the rest of the world and seldom went beyond the confines of their own estates. They needed and had no roads except a few well-nigh impassable tracks through the countryside. Few travelers passed their doors. No automobiles swished by their cottages. No trains thundered through their villages. No telephones rang shrilly. No letters, telegrams, or newspapers came to them. When the landlord or villager did venture forth, he had to trudge on his own feet, mount a horse or burro, ride in a cumbersome, jolting cart or wagon, or go by boats that were dragged slowly by men or horses or were driven by capricious winds.

For the mass of the villagers life was hard. Their sweat and toil extorted a scanty and monotonous fare from the earth. They suffered much from hunger and famine. They were ill-clad and poorly sheltered. They knew little about the past or the distant. They were at the mercy of the weather, terrifying pestilences, brutal marauders, and fears born of their own ignorance and superstition. They were exploited by their landlords.

The Organization of Cities and Towns

In spite of the many obstacles placed in the way of their growth, some towns and cities developed in medieval times. In contrast with the manors and estates found in rural regions, the inhabitants of the growing towns and cities of Europe lived, for the most part, by trade and the exchange of goods. They sought to free themselves from the restrictions imposed on them by the feudal and seignioral systems. They wanted to get rid of the control which kings, church prelates, and secular lords exercised over them. They fought against tolls and customs duties. They defended themselves against plundering and extortionate lords. As a result of their efforts, they gradually established trading relations with other regions.

Medieval towns and cities were not characterized by the wide boulevards, extensive parks, pleasant suburbs, and swift transportation systems of present-day towns and cities. If in imagination we could again climb to some point of vantage that would permit us

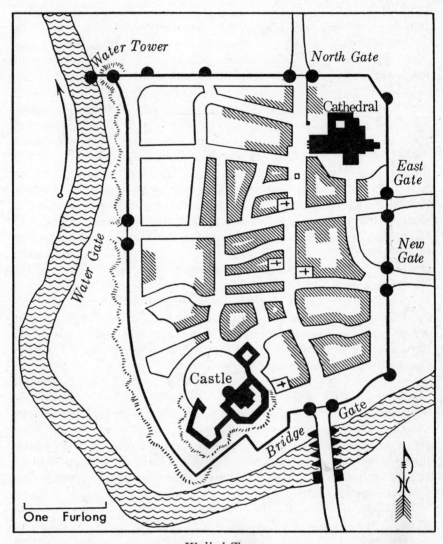

Water Tower

North Gate

Cathedral

East Gate

New Gate

Water Gate

Castle

Bridge Gate

One Furlong

Walled Town

14

to overlook a typical European city or town at the end of the medieval period, we should see much that would seem strange to us. In the first place, the city would appear quite small. At best, most of the cities and towns had only a few thousand inhabitants, who lived crowded together. London probably had not more than a population of sixty thousand, and a city of twenty thousand people was counted large. In the second place, the city or town would be built in some easily defended place, on a hilltop, or at a bend of a river. If we should next look at our typical city or town attentively, we should find that it was surrounded by a high wall and perhaps by a moat. The wall would be studded with towers and pierced at a few places with gates. Above the top of the wall and the roofs of the houses would tower the steeple of a cathedral or important church, perhaps the battlements of a castle or the top of a watchtower.

If, however, we should come down from our imaginary high point, approach the town, cross the moat, and enter one of the gates, we should find ourselves in even stranger surroundings. We would discover a tangle of narrow, dark, often crooked, and indescribably dirty, unsanitary, and malodorous streets, alleys, and passageways, that swarmed with beggars, peddlers, and scavenging dogs. In the streets and passageways we should discover no sidewalks, no signs at street corners, no street lights, and no numbered houses. Instead, the streets would be lined with tall, gabled houses with overhanging stories that cut off most of the air and light. Here and there, we should see bits of carving ornamenting the exterior of the houses and many signs to inform the illiterate where an inn or a shop was to be found. Upon inquiry, we should find that many of the streets were named after the crafts that worked in them. In the center of the city or town, we should probably find an open space where the weekly market was held and the inhabitants gathered on pleasant evenings to see and to gossip. Around the central square, we should discover the principal church, the municipal building, possibly a belfry, and perhaps some gild halls and the houses of some of the prosperous merchants.

In order to understand the life of a typical town or city, we ought to enter some of the principal buildings. We should go into some of the tall, gabled houses and see the petty shops opening on the street and the quarters behind and above the shop where the craftsmen, their families, and their apprentices worked and lived. We should visit the principal church, the pride of the city and the product of its highest skill. We should look up at the lofty vault of its nave and transept, enter its many chapels, visit its treasury of holy relics, priceless vestments, and sacred objects, and stand before its ornate choir and glittering altar. We should go into some of the larger, prisonlike houses of the more prosperous merchants. There we should discover in the basement, storehouses; on the first floor, busy counting rooms; and on the upper floors, apartments for the merchant and his family. In the latter we should find large, heavy pieces of furniture, fine plate and glassware, and perhaps even a cannon for protection against a possible mob. Lastly, we should visit the castle, built for the purpose of overawing the city or serving as a last place of refuge for a hard-pressed garrison. We should enter the dungeons and vaulted storerooms in the basement, the gloomy guardrooms and courtyards on the first floor, and the dark baronial hall and governor's quarters of the second floor. Such a visit would give us some insight into the life of the town.

In every town some inhabitants still were engaged in agriculture and merely lived in the urban center for protection. This was particularly true of the towns in southern Italy. Most of the urban population, however, was engaged in either trade or industry. In Italy, particularly, a small portion of the population of the towns might be nobles.

Such inhabitants as were engaged in trade and industry were organized into gilds. Those who worked at the same craft or industry were organized into a gild. In theory, a boy who wished to learn a craft worked in the shop of a master of that craft for a number of years as an apprentice. He lived with the master and supposedly learned the secrets of the trade. After serving some years as an apprentice, he became a journeyman. That meant that he knew the craft but did not as yet have a shop of his own. Finally, he would become a master. In practice, the masters dominated the craft gilds. They made it very difficult for an apprentice or journeyman to become a master. The easiest way to attain a mastership was to be the son of a master or to marry the daughter or widow of a master. Some gilds were counted more important than others; therefore, gilds were known as greater and lesser gilds. Only the former would have a voice in the government of the town. Each gild had its own officials and managed its own affairs.

The gilds performed many functions. Their avowed primary purpose was to insure good and honest workmanship. With this end in view, they regulated the number of journeymen and apprentices a master could employ, the supply of raw material, the hours of labor, and the quality and prices of goods. The gilds, however, were social and religious as well as economic organizations. They gave banquets. They took part in civic processions and festivities. Their members attended baptisms, marriages, and the funerals of members of the gild. They paid for Masses for the souls of departed gildmen. The real aim of the gilds was not to gain wealth but a comfortable, assured living for their members.

The gilds, however, must not be looked upon as fixed and stationary organizations. They constantly underwent important changes. There came to be a distinction between the masters who could afford the livery worn on ceremonial occasions and those who could not. There was a tendency for the former to gain control of the gilds. There was, too, a growing tendency to hedge the acquisition of the mastership so round with requirements that journeymen could no longer produce the required "masterpiece" or pay the fees demanded from candidates for the mastership. In self-defense the journeymen attempted to organize gilds of their own or moved into rural areas to escape the gild restrictions.

The towns and cities of Europe usually had some sort of political organization. The real objective of most towns and cities was full self-government. Some of the German and Italian towns actually achieved full political independence. These towns, with a little of the surrounding countryside, constituted city-states. In Germany, they were known as free imperial cities. In the stronger, monarchical states of Western and Central Europe, the towns and cities never achieved more than a considerable measure of autonomy.

Not everyone who lived in a town or city had a voice in its government. In most cases, there was a comparatively small governing class. This class was likely to include the nobles (particularly in Italy), the prosperous merchants, and the masters of the greater gilds. In Italy, especially, the governing class was likely to be divided into hostile parties that destroyed the power of the state by civil strife.

Medieval man, living in towns and cities, put up with many conditions that would seem intolerable to people today. He had a strong stomach and an insensitive nose. Medieval men threw their slops and refuse into the never-cleaned streets. The resulting filth bred fearful plagues and deadly diseases that decimated the urban populations. Only the steady drift to the towns and cities from the rural areas enabled the urban centers to maintain and increase their population. At night, the dark unlighted streets were haunted by prowling criminals who made it unsafe for honest men to be abroad. In Southern Europe, especially, assaults and assassinations were looked upon almost as natural phenomena and accepted as a part of life.

In spite of these conditions, urban life was considered more attractive than rural life. There was excitement in the ebb and flow of the inhabitants through the public squares and the narrow streets of the towns and cities. On the occasion of royal weddings, the reception of ambassadors, and great feast days of the Church, townsmen had holidays. Then they decorated the streets and squares with pennants, hangings, and tapestries. They took part in or at least witnessed brilliant processions. At all times there was contact with their fellows. For the successful merchants and gildmen there were comforts and opportunities that even the feudal lords lacked.

Trade and Commerce

In describing rural and urban life, many hindrances to the development of commerce have been mentioned. The ideal of the tenants of a manor or big estate was self-sufficiency. As a consequence, those engaged in agriculture bought comparatively little. Though the upper clergy, the nobility, and the prosperous townsmen purchased somewhat more, they confined their purchases largely to luxuries. Merchants found many obstacles in the way of their activity. The roads were poor, few in number, and infested with highwaymen. There were few bridges and ferries. Highways and rivers were studded with toll and customs stations. Trade was hampered by gild restrictions and by staple rights, i.e., the right of the citizens of a town to purchase the stock of a passing merchant. Those engaged in trade had to contend with coins that had been clipped and debased and with many different kinds of currencies. As a result of these hindrances to commerce, whole countries then had less trade than many a small American city of the present day.

As a result of its small bulk, commerce then had quite a different organization from that of today. As the inhabitants of the towns and cities abandoned agriculture for trade and industry, a petty trade between town and countryside sprang up. Townsmen and peasants exchanged their products at the market held in the town square.

For trade between regions, peddlers, traveling on foot or on horseback with packs on their backs, largely took the place of the present-day store. They were supplemented by the institution known as the fair. At certain fixed times, under the protection of some noble or prelate, merchants from distant and widely scattered places would assemble at some point and set up booths. Here, the peasant bought the salt and the iron that he needed for the coming year; the lords, the upper clergy, and the prosperous townsmen, their luxuries—textiles, jewelry, drugs, spices, leather, skins, furs, and food and drink. For the amusement of those attending the fair, there came also a motley throng of musicians, clowns, trained dogs, wild animals, and monstrosities, as well as poets and actors. The various fairs of

18

Europe waxed and waned in popularity, but the institution itself lasted far into modern times.

In time, certain special centers of commerce arose. One such center was Italy. Such commodities as pepper, spices, drugs, perfumes, sugar, precious stones, textiles, and dyestuffs found their way by sea and by caravan to the ports of the Levant, i.e., the Eastern Mediterranean region. There, they were picked up by Italian ships, particularly those from Genoa and Venice, and taken to Italy, where they were sent north of the Alps to various parts of Europe. By 1492 the city-state of Venice had come to dominate this trade with the Levant and had built up a considerable state that included Venetia, much of the Eastern Adriatic coast, and trading posts and colonies in the Eastern Mediterranean. To Venice, accordingly, came merchants from Lombardy, Tuscany, Hungary, France, and Germany. They came not only for the commodities brought by the Venetians from the Levant but also for the glass, cloth, silk, leather, paper, and soap manufactured in Venice. Incidentally, they carried back to their homes to be incorporated in their own languages many Italian commercial terms. As a result of its flourishing trade and manufactures, Venice, though only a city-state, was counted almost as a great power in Europe.

Another important center of European trade was the Baltic. As early as the opening years of the thirteenth century, German knights and merchants began to make their influence felt along the shores of the Baltic Sea. The semireligious, semimilitary order, known as the Teutonic Knights, became dominant on the eastern coast of the Baltic Sea as far north as the Gulf of Finland. At the same time, enterprising merchants began to establish trading posts in the region. They carried to the Baltic the products of Europe and Asia and exchanged them for dried and salt fish, honey, butter, salt meat, furs, pitch, tar, copper, and iron. In the fourteenth century the trading cities of northern Germany began to organize for the protection of their commercial interests. Their merchants had a monopoly of the trade with Russia and Scandinavia and an important position in the trade of London, the Netherlands, and the Bay of Biscay. By 1492, however, this so-called Hanseatic League was beginning to decline as a result of the competition of other merchants and the restrictions being placed upon them by the rising states of Northern Europe.

Another important center of commerce and industry was the Netherlands. This region was a natural point of exchange and transshipment between England and the Rhineland and Northern and Southern Europe. Merchants came to its commercial cities from

19

all over Europe. Its fishermen supplied a large part of the European continent with the fish that good churchmen were supposed to eat on Fridays. It was a center for the manufacture of cloth and fine tapestries. Its cities and provinces, accordingly, had succeeded in winning a large measure of self-government.

The Opportunity to Rise in the World

In spite of the many obstacles placed in the way of the ambitious by gild restrictions and the existence of fixed social classes, there was some opportunity to rise in the world. In Florence, for example, the Medici family rose to a position of great power and wealth. It started as a middle-class family. Under the leadership of such men as Cosimo I (1389–1464) and Lorenzo the Magnificent (1449–1492), it established business connections over all Western Europe and became practically master of its native city.

In Germany the Fugger family illustrates in another way the fact that it was possible to rise to a position of wealth and power. The first known member of the family was a weaver. In the fourteenth century he moved to Augsburg, where he began to deal in textiles and engage in banking. In time, the Fuggers came to have agents over most of Europe. These kept the Fuggers informed through newsletters of economic and political developments. These newsletters have now been printed and can be found in many large libraries. Eventually, the Fuggers were ennobled. In the early years of the modern period the family acted as papal bankers and financed the campaign of Charles V for the Imperial title. As a pledge for repayment of these loans they took control of certain valuable mining properties that brought them added wealth.

Banking

In the early Middle Ages there was little money and there were no banks. When people feared for the safety of their valuables, they sometimes put them under the protection of some church or monastery. In Italy, where trade developed earliest, the merchants had to exchange the currency of one region for that of another. For this service they charged a fee. Later, these so-called Italian bankers established themselves in other commercial centers and began to make loans. For the latter, because of the risk involved, they charged a high rate of interest. Toward the end of the Middle Ages, regular banks were established, banks that served as places for deposit as well as centers for the exchange of currencies and the making of loans.

This survey has shown that European society at the opening of the modern period was mainly agricultural. Towns and cities were rather the exception than the rule. In rural areas the chief social and economic unit was the big, self-sufficing estate. In the towns the aim was self-government and moderate, assured comfort. They sought the latter objective through the organization of gilds. There were many hindrances in the way of the development of commerce. Such as there was, was carried on through peddlers, weekly markets, petty shops, fairs, and merchants like the Fuggers who carried on relatively large commercial operations. In the end, however, rather important trading centers arose in Italy, the Baltic Sea, and the Netherlands. That there was some opportunity for the ambitious to rise was proved by the career of the Medici and the Fugger families in Italy and Germany.

CHAPTER 3

European States and Governments

As we have seen, the breakdown of the Roman Empire was followed by a period of chaotic political conditions. The rude barbaric kingdoms that grew up in Europe by no means took the place of the orderly Roman government. After the invasions of the Arabs, the Northmen, and the Magyars, political power, for the most part, fell into the hands of feudal lords. The feudal lords organized little armies, maintained petty courts, coined money, and obtained revenues through the collection of fines, tolls, and feudal and seignioral dues.

The feudal system, however, contained the seed for its own destruction. Each feudal lord sought to extend his power. Some of them, usually the nominal kings, were more successful than the rest. They first gained real control over their own vassals. By force, purchase, or inheritance they then acquired other fiefs. They compelled their subjects to obey the royal officers, to be tried in the royal courts, to use the royal money, and to speak the royal language. With some groups, national feeling developed as a result. This was the case in England, France, Spain, Portugal, Hungary, Poland, and Russia. In other cases, they tried to create states from ethnic elements too diverse to be welded into a single nationality. In still other instances, as, for example, in Italy and Germany, political power fell almost completely into the hands of the feudal lords and no strong central government developed.

As a result of this process, a great variety of states and governments developed in Europe. Most of the states were monarchies. At the head of such a state there might be a king, a prince with a less exalted title, or an ecclesiastical dignitary—an archbishop, a bishop, an abbot, or an abbess. An exception was the city-states of Italy and Germany. As we have seen, they were usually controlled by an oligarchical patriciate. In any case, the head of the state was held in check somewhat by a body known as the estates. These bodies were composed of nobles, ecclesiastical dignitaries, and sometimes of representatives of the towns. They were usually divided into two or three houses. In spite of their differences, it is possible to make some

22

generalizations about governments at the beginning of the modern period.

Some Generalizations about Governments

As a result of their unproductivity, all states were poor at the opening of the modern period. In earlier times the idea had prevailed that kings and other lords should live on their own resources. This meant that they must depend on their own estates. Only gradually had they been able to force or persuade their subjects to pay taxes. For a number of reasons, even taxes were relatively unproductive. The primitive methods in vogue prevented agriculture from being productive. Commerce and industry were only beginning to develop. The feudal lords and the Church were largely exempted from taxes because of the services that they supposedly rendered. As a consequence, the revenues of government were then quite small.

For this and other reasons, governments attempted to do much less than they do today. For example, European states were just beginning to develop a foreign service. In Italy the balance between the states was so precarious that the governments of the peninsula felt that they must watch each other carefully. Most of the larger states of Europe, however, still scorned the idea of having diplomatic representatives in other capitals. None of the states had large armies and navies. As a rule, they made no provision for the carrying and delivery of mail or packages. They contributed nothing for the support of schools, did nothing for agriculture, assumed no part in the relief of the poor, entirely neglected public health, and built no roads or bridges. In short, governments did much less for their subjects then than they do today.

The result of this situation was that there was much less governmental machinery than at the present time. In most states the rulers had only a few ministers. Most of them were dignitaries of the Church, as only churchmen had sufficient education to fill such posts. The feudal estates or parliaments which acted as a check on the kings were not like modern legislative bodies. They did not enact laws. The issuing of the few laws and decrees of the time was the prerogative of the king. Local administration was largely in the hands of the feudal lords. They were inclined to put their own interests before those of the king. As a result, the character of his landlord was of far more concern to the ordinary peasant than that of his distant sovereign.

In the fifteenth century the central governments began to organize small, permanent armies. Earlier kings had depended on feudal levies composed of the royal vassals. As such troops were not very dependable, kings began to hire mercenaries to take their place. A majority of these were pikemen, armed with long pikes and capable of withstanding cavalry charges. An increasing proportion of the infantry, however, was armed with slow-firing, short-range, highly inaccurate hand guns.

At the beginning of the modern period, the most famous pikemen came from the Swiss cantons. In their efforts to defend their Alpine homes, the Swiss developed military tactics that for a time were irresistible. Arranged in serried rows, with pikes eighteen feet long extended before them, they advanced and presented a forest of sharp points to the enemy. From 1477 to 1525, the Swiss mercenaries were the most sought after troops in Europe. The Swiss guard maintained by the Pope is a relic of the time when the Swiss sent their surplus young men abroad to serve as mercenary troops.

The artillery of the time was just at the beginning of its development. For a long time men had used catapults and battering rams in warfare. In the fourteenth century there began to be reports of cannon that could throw, with the aid of gunpowder, stones of considerable size for a hundred yards. At first, they had mainly a moral effect. They were valued more for the noise they made than for the damage that they wrought. By the end of the fifteenth century two types of cannon had developed, ponderous cannon capable of throwing stone shot weighting as much as six hundred pounds and lighter ones that could be used in the field. Armed with the new cannon, kings were in a position to hold in check their domestic and foreign enemies.

Navies, too, were just beginning to develop. In the Western Mediterranean the most important naval power was Genoa. Its galleys were rowed by criminals, vagabonds, and slaves. In the Atlantic sailing vessels were in use. England, Portugal, and Spain each had made a beginning toward the development of a naval force. In England some ships were built by the king and others were furnished by his subjects. They were manned by a sort of naval militia.

In 1492 governments were just beginning to assume the task of conveying letters. As most people could not read or write there was not so much need of a postal system as at present. The literate depended on travelers, ship captains, and special messengers for the carrying of letters. Toward the end of the thirteenth century the University of Paris felt the need of establishing some sort of contact between its students and their homes and developed a system for the transmission of letters. Later, it was used to carry letters for private individuals as well as for students. Then, in 1487, Louis XI,

24

king of France, established a postal service for the conveyance of government messages. This system was soon used to carry the letters of private persons, provided the government was permitted to read the letters. About the same time the Taxis family seem to have developed in northern Italy a network of post stations where messengers could get the fresh horses that they needed.

The States of Europe

By the opening of the modern period of history, Europe was characterized by a system of states that had developed out of the feudal system. As they differed greatly in size, power, and organization, some account of the separate states will be given in the following pages.

The Holy Roman Empire

The strangest of these European states was the Holy Roman Empire. In theory, it claimed to be a continuation of the Roman and the Carolingian empires and to have jurisdiction over much of Europe. On ceremonial occasions its emperor actually took precedence over other rulers. In reality, the Holy Roman Empire embraced little outside of modern Germany. The Swiss cantons, the Netherlands, and northern Italy were no longer really parts of the Holy Roman Empire. These limits gave it a population of perhaps twenty million inhabitants.

Nominally, the Empire had a central government, but it possessed little real power. In contrast to the kings of France and England, the Holy Roman emperors failed to centralize authority. As a consequence, they had very few rights or prerogatives. They could grant titles and collect a few fees and dues. They had no Imperial treasury, no staff of administrative subordinates, and no army and navy. From this time they were invariably chosen from members of the Habsburg family. They were elected each time by seven of their important vassals known as the Electors. Besides the emperor there was an Imperial diet of three houses: the Electors, the princes, and the representatives of the free imperial city-states. This body, likewise, had little real authority. Just at the beginning of the sixteenth century, an effort was made to reform the Empire by the establishment of an Imperial court, the levying of a general tax, and the creation of new administrative divisions called "circles," but little came of the attempt.

Political authority had fallen into the hands of the states composing the Empire. These varied greatly in size, importance, and form of government. In the Danube Valley there was the group of provinces which we might for convenience call Austria. It was ruled by the Habsburg family. It had a population of perhaps two million people and was able to play a part in international affairs. Then there were somewhat smaller states like Brandenburg, Bavaria, Württemberg, and Electoral and Ducal Saxony that were large enough and strong enough to follow an independent policy and to exercise considerable political influence. Then there were many states so small and weak that they were hardly as big as a typical American college campus. Consequently, they were mere pawns in the politics of the time.

Some of the states composing the Empire should be described a little more fully. Austria started as a mark, or border district, of the Empire. Later, it came under the control of the Habsburg family. By 1493 the Habsburgs had acquired a whole group of provinces that included Upper and Lower Austria, Tyrol, Styria, Carinthia, and Carniola. The inhabitants of Austria did some mining, raised grain, and cultivated vineyards. In 1477 Maximilian of Habsburg, heir to Austria, married the heiress of the Burgundian state, and thus, in time, became ruler of his wife's as well as his own state.

The Burgundian state had been built up by the Dukes of Burgundy, a branch of the French royal house. They were given by the kings of France the duchy of Burgundy as an appanage. They had added to their original territory certain lands of the Holy Roman Empire—the Free County of Burgundy or, to give it its French name, *Franche Comté,* and most of the seventeen provinces of the Netherlands. From these French and Imperial fiefs Charles the Bold, who came to power in 1467, tried to create a new and independent kingdom. In 1477, however, he was defeated by the Swiss and killed on the field of battle. His death precipitated a struggle for the hand and the lands of his daughter and heiress, Mary of Burgundy, which was won by Maximilian of Habsburg. His defeated rival, the aging Louis XI of France, consoled himself by seizing the duchy of Burgundy, Artois, and Picardy. After the death of Mary of Burgundy in 1482, Maximilian ruled the Burgundian state as regent for her son, Philip the Handsome.

The Swiss cantons were closely connected with both Austria and the Burgundian state. In 1291 three of these Alpine cantons had formed themselves into a confederation. From time to time, neighboring cantons had joined the alliance. Some of the cantons spoke French and others German. Politically, they varied in organization from simple democracies to narrow oligarchies. The confederation had to defend itself from attacks of the Habsburgs and the Dukes of Burgundy. In the course of these struggles they had made them-

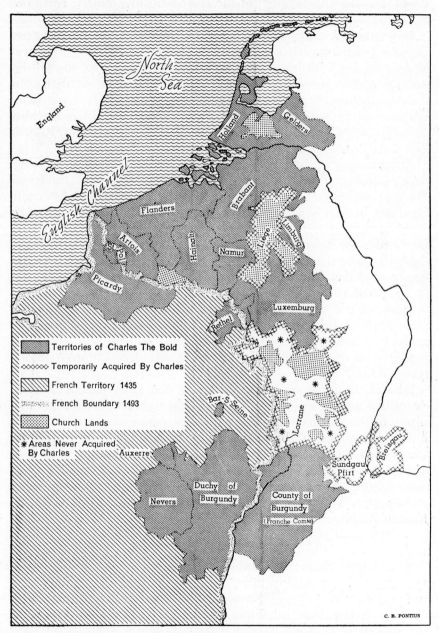

North Sea

England

English Channel

Holland

Gelders

Brabant

Flanders

Limburg

Artois

St. Pol

Hainault

Liege

Namur

Picardy

Luxemburg

Rethel

Bar-s-Seine

Lorraine

Breisgau

Sundgau
Pfirt

Auxerre

Nevers

Duchy of
Burgundy

County of
Burgundy
(Franche Comte)

Territories of Charles The Bold
Temporarily Acquired By Charles
French Territory 1435
French Boundary 1493
Church Lands
* Areas Never Acquired
By Charles

C. B. PONTIUS

The Burgundian State in the Time of Charles the Bold

selves virtually independent of the Holy Roman Empire. This position was not formally recognized, however, until 1648.

In northern Germany, the Hohenzollern state of Brandenburg as yet gave little indication of the role it was to play later as the rival of Austria. Like Austria, it had developed out of one of the border districts of the Empire known as marks. Though as yet there was little to distinguish it from other states of the Empire, its rulers had built up in the valleys of the Elbe and Oder rivers a considerable state. Its ruler was one of the seven electors of the Holy Roman Empire.

Another state of the Empire that should be mentioned is the kingdom of Bohemia. It consisted of the three provinces of Bohemia, Moravia, and Silesia. It was inhabited by three different peoples: the Czechs, a branch of the Western Slavs, who constituted the largest element in the population; the Germans, who were to be found on the borders of Bohemia and Moravia and in the cities; and, lastly, the Poles, who lived in Upper Silesia. In 1492 its ruler was a Polish prince who had been elected king of both Bohemia and Hungary. It was soon to fall under the control of the Habsburgs. At the opening of the modern period certain social changes were taking place in the Bohemian kingdom. The nobles were growing in power at the expense of the monarchy, the towns, and the peasantry. The peasants, on the other hand, were losing their freedom and sinking into serfdom.

Besides the more usual secular states, the Holy Roman Empire comprised a large number of ecclesiastical states ruled by some dignitary of the Church. The ruler of such a state might be an archbishop, a bishop, an abbot, or even an abbess. Such an ecclesiastic was at the same time a prelate of the Church and a political head of a state. While these ecclesiastical states tended to be small in size, some of them were large enough to give their rulers positions of some power. The rulers of three of them were electors of the Holy Roman Empire.

France

The strongest state in Europe was France. By a combination of political skill and good fortune, the kings of France had gained control of the feudal fiefs of France and welded them into a state of about sixteen million inhabitants. After they had almost completed the process of creating a French state, however, they undid their work by granting to their younger sons huge portions of the royal domain as appanages. In a generation or two, the holders of these appanages were only distantly related to the reigning sovereign and were concerned mainly with their personal interests. By the end of the fifteenth century, however, most of the appanages had been regained by the kings of France.

At that time France already had a good deal of the political machinery that was to characterize it until the French Revolution. At the top of the administrative system was the Royal Council, composed of various sections: a privy council, a secret council that really governed the state, a judicial committee, and a council of finances. Below the Royal Council were the great officers of state, the governors who represented the king in the provinces, and their subordinates. In addition, there was a system of courts, the seven parliaments, and a confusing number of inferior and special courts. There was also the advisory body, known as the estates general, consisting of three estates: the clergy, the nobles, and representatives of the third estate.

The king of France was considered by contemporaries to be relatively rich and powerful. He had nearly absolute power over a country comparatively fertile and productive by reason of its grain-growing and its vineyards. He had been successful in depriving the nobles of much of their power, but they continued to enjoy some power and many privileges. He also had acquired power at the expense of the Church. By the Pragmatic Sanction of Bourges (1438) he gained from the Pope the right to name candidates for French benefices and to collect annates, an important source of papal revenue. He had at his disposal the largest permanent military force in Europe, a force composed largely of Swiss and German mercenaries. These gains put the sovereign of France in a strong position.

Spain and Portugal

The second state of Europe from the point of view of power and importance was Spain. It was cut off from the rest of the continent by the lofty Pyrenees Mountains and occupied the greater part of the Iberian Peninsula. During the Middle Ages it had had a unique development. After being a part of the Roman Empire, it had been overrun at first by Teutonic and later by Moslem invaders. Somewhat later, when written records are again available, the surviving Christian inhabitants of the peninsula are found to have formed on the southern slope of the Pyrenees Mountains a series of petty states, Castile, Leon, Navarre, Aragon, and the county of Barcelona. During the rest of the Middle Ages they devoted their attention to the reconquest of the peninsula from the Moslems, the unification of the peninsula, and the centralization of authority. By 1492 these objectives had been largely achieved. The Moslems had been driven back to their last foothold in the peninsula, to the kingdom of Granada in southern Spain. Most of the provinces of the peninsula had been united in the kingdom of Spain by the marriage in 1469 of Ferdinand, heir of the kingdom of Aragon, to Isabella, heiress of the kingdom of Leon and Castile. Only the comparatively small states of Portugal and Navarre had not as yet been acquired. The new Spanish kingdom constituted a state of seven million inhabitants.

At first, the states composing the new kingdom retained their identity and their separate institutions. They were united only by the personal ties between the two sovereigns. From the first, however, Ferdinand and Isabella followed a common policy that eventually welded the separate provinces into a single kingdom. They put down brigandage, quelled the factious nobles, reorganized the royal council, established greater control over local government, ended the independence of three powerful military orders, followed a common foreign policy, and carried to a successful conclusion a war (1481–1492) for the conquest of the kingdom of Granada. These policies did much to unite the kingdom of Aragon and the kingdom of Leon and Castile.

In fact, the disunion in the peninsula was originally even greater than has been indicated. Not only did the two states of Aragon and of Leon and Castile at first retain their identity but Aragon, for example, was itself composed of six smaller kingdoms—the little states of Aragon, Valencia, Majorca and Roussillon, Sicily, Sardinia, and the principality of Catalonia. Each of the six subordinate kingdoms had its own institutions. Before the peninsula could really be unified, these separate institutions had to be suppressed and replaced by new ones common to the whole new Spanish kingdom.

In addition to those it had in common with all states, the new Spanish kingdom had certain problems that were peculiar to the peninsula. The very fact that many Spaniards were of dubious ancestry made the inhabitants of the new Spanish kingdom profess great zeal for Christianity and the Medieval Church. They were more than usually hostile to foreigners, Jews, and the Moriscos, i.e., the descendants of the Moslem invaders. They felt that the Spanish kingdom must be unified at all costs. To meet this situation Ferdinand and Isabella founded, with the consent of the Pope, the terrible institution known as the Spanish Inquisition. It was created for the purpose of enforcing political and religious uniformity. The ultimate result of this fanaticism was the expulsion of both the Jews and the Moriscos, the most industrious elements in the population of Spain, and the creation of the tyrannical institution that the monarchy itself could not control.

The other large independent state of the Iberian Peninsula was Portugal. It had started as a sort of offshoot of the kingdom of Castile. Like the other medieval states of the Iberian Peninsula, it had expanded at the expense of the Moslem invaders. After the completion of this task, it had turned its attention to the sea. One result of the new direction taken by Portuguese policy was the establishment in 1294 of an alliance with England that has survived until the present day. In the fifteenth century, it led, under the remarkable leadership of Prince Henry the Navigator (1394–1460), to a series of voyages of exploration down the west coast of Africa which laid the foundation of a great Portuguese colonial empire.

This remarkable prince, gathering around him at Sagres in southern Portugal a group of learned men and skilled seamen, sent out exploring expeditions year after year. By the time of his death in 1460, these voyages had gone down the west coast of Africa as far as Guinea. After his death, the royal family continued his work. By 1492 Portuguese explorers had rounded the Cape of Good Hope and had become convinced of the possibility of reaching India by that route. These voyages of exploration opened up some trade with Africa. One of the most profitable branches of the new trade was the inauguration of the slave trade, a form of commerce that ultimately gave rise to many grave social problems.

England, Scotland, and Ireland

In the British Isles the political situation was quite different from the present one. At that time there was no state known as the United Kingdom of Great Britain and Ireland. In the largest of the islands there were two separate kingdoms, England and Scotland. The kingdom of England was a state of two million inhabitants, and of far less relative importance than at present, which claimed rule over the whole island of Ireland but in reality controlled only a comparatively small district around Dublin, known as the Irish Pale; Scotland was poor and small, but it was an independent and intensely national state. At that time there seemed little or no reason to expect the later unification of England, Scotland, and Ireland into a single state.

In England significant changes were taking place. A devastating civil war, the War of the Roses (1455–1485), had just ended. It had decimated and greatly weakened the turbulent nobles and had placed on the throne Henry VII (1485–1509), the founder of the Tudor line of kings. The new ruler quickly proved himself to be a strong, shrewd sovereign who was keenly aware of the real interests of the dynasty, the state, and the English people. In foreign affairs he followed a cautious policy that was characterized by a strengthening of dynastic alliances rather than by wasteful wars. In international politics England was significant for the part it could play in maintaining the balance of power between France and Spain. In domestic affairs Henry VII gradually increased his personal power. He favored the rising middle class which was developing a town life of some importance, engaging in manufactures, and taking the place hitherto held by foreigners in foreign trade.

England already had developed distinctive institutions that later were to be of great importance. Out of an institution brought to England by its Norman invaders, the English people had gradually developed the modern jury system. Out of the royal council that gave advice to the king had grown both the privy council and parliament. Unlike the medieval estates of the continent, which usually had three or more estates of unequal authority, the English parliament had developed into a bicameral body of two strong houses with some control over finances and legislation. This development was the result of the lesser vassals of the king, the knights of the shire, throwing in their lot with the representatives of the towns to form the House of Commons. Under Henry VII and his Tudor successors, the parliament was always consulted, but it seldom ventured to oppose the sovereign resolutely. Under later kings it was to win a position of great power and to become a model to be imitated by other nations. Finally, in striking contrast with the usual practice on the continent, only the eldest sons of noble families inherited the titles of nobility and the family property. This custom made for fewer but stronger nobles.

In northern Britain, as we have seen, Scotland was a small but entirely independent state. It was very poor but intensely national in feeling. It was characterized by a weak line of sovereigns—known as the Stuarts, by perpetual feuds among the nobility, by a policy of alliance with France, and by great hostility toward England.

In Ireland, England's real control was limited to the restricted area around Dublin known as the Pale. The rest of the island was characterized by the clan system, internecine strife, and backward political, economic, and social conditions. The Irish people looked upon the English as foreigners and conquerers.

Italy

Italy was only a "geographical expression." Since the days of the Roman Empire, there had been no political unity in the peninsula. The Holy Roman emperors never won recognition of their claims to rule over all Italy. Instead, there arose many comparatively petty states; in northern and central Italy, city-states. In the latter there was a tendency for the lower classes to rise to political power under the leadership of captains of the people. This development was followed by two others. The citizens of the city-states finally became tired of the almost continuous civil strife and left the fighting to their leaders and the mercenaries whom they employed. Then in time, these captains of the people gradually developed into sovereigns of their states. Once in power they maintained their rule by corruption, the embellishment of their cities, the conquest of lesser, neighboring towns, the protection of the trading classes, the provision of posts in the administration and the diplomatic service, and the patronage of the arts and literature.

As a consequence, the peninsula had come under the control of six states. All of them were small in comparison with such great powers as France and Spain. In the northwestern part of the peninsula, on both slopes of the Alps, the Dukes of Savoy had built up a state which included the duchy of Savoy and the county of Nice on the French side of the Alps and much of the province of Piedmont on the eastern slopes of the same mountains. Their state was important because of its control of several Alpine passes of strategic importance. East of the territories belonging to the Dukes of Savoy was the duchy of Milan, which gradually had come to include the whole province of Lombardy. By 1492 it had fallen under the rule of the Sforza family. Still farther east, in northeastern Italy, was the aristocratic republic of Venice. It was built on an island just off the mainland at the head of the Adriatic Sea. For a long time it was satisfied with this easily defended position, but eventually it had extended its authority over the mainland until it included Venetia, Istria, Dalmatia, and various points in the Balkan Peninsula. It owed its power to the wise rule of its oligarchy of nobles and to the importance of its commerce and manufactures. In central Italy the former republic of Florence had fallen, as we have seen, under the control of the Medici family. Under their leadership it had gained rule over all Tuscany and had become the artistic and cultural center of the Italian Peninsula.

In central Italy, likewise, the head of the Roman Church had built up a considerable principality. This made its ruler at the same time the spiritual head of Western Europe as Pope and the petty sovereign of a small Italian state. The two positions were difficult to coordinate. As a result, at the end of the fifteenth century the popes were inclined to forget their religious duties and to devote their attention to secular affairs. Some of the popes of the time seemed to look on the papacy as a lucrative sinecure that made possible a comfortable life, the collection of rare books, valuable manuscripts, and fine objects of art. As a consequence, they became known primarily as patrons of great sculptors and famous painters. Other popes sought to play a significant role in the politics of the Italian peninsula. They strove to advance the interests of the members of their families and to subjugate and extend the territory under their rule.

In southern Italy there was the kingdom of Naples, the largest state in Italy. During much of its history it had been connected with the island of Sicily under the name of the Kingdom of the Two Sicilies. By 1492, however, the island of Sicily had fallen under the rule of Aragon.

The development of Italy into six nearly equal states had a number of important consequences. Each state was afraid of its neighbors. Out of this mutual jealousy grew the custom of maintaining ambassadors at the courts of rival states. The reports of such ambassadors, particularly those of Venice, constitute one of the principal sources of our knowledge of European politics of the time. The rivalries and divisions of the six Italian states, too, soon opened the way for the invasion of the peninsula by France, Spain, and Austria.

Hungary

The Hungarian state was the creation of the Magyars, a non-European people. In the ninth century they had come into the Danube basin. For a time they had terrified Western Europe by their terrible invasions. In the latter part of the tenth century they at last had been defeated by the Germans. After that defeat they had settled down in the Danube Valley. There, eventually, they established a kingdom which included Slovaks, Carpatho-Russians, Rumanians, and Southern Slavs. They adopted the Roman Catholic form of Christianity. This state of Hungary was characterized by an elective monarchy, by the privileges enjoyed by its prelates and nobles, and by the wretchedness of its peasantry. These conditions were soon to cause the disastrous defeat of the Magyar state at the hands of the Turks.

The Ottoman Empire

The so-called Ottoman Turks first attracted attention in Asia Minor. By the middle of the fourteenth century they had acquired a foothold in Europe. By the beginning of the sixteenth century they were north of the Black Sea and were threatening the Danube Valley. They, however, did not exterminate the Christian peoples of the peninsula. They came among the Serbs, the Greeks, the Albanians, the Croats, the Bulgars, and the Rumanians like an invading army. In the thoroughly conquered provinces they organized a hierarchy

34

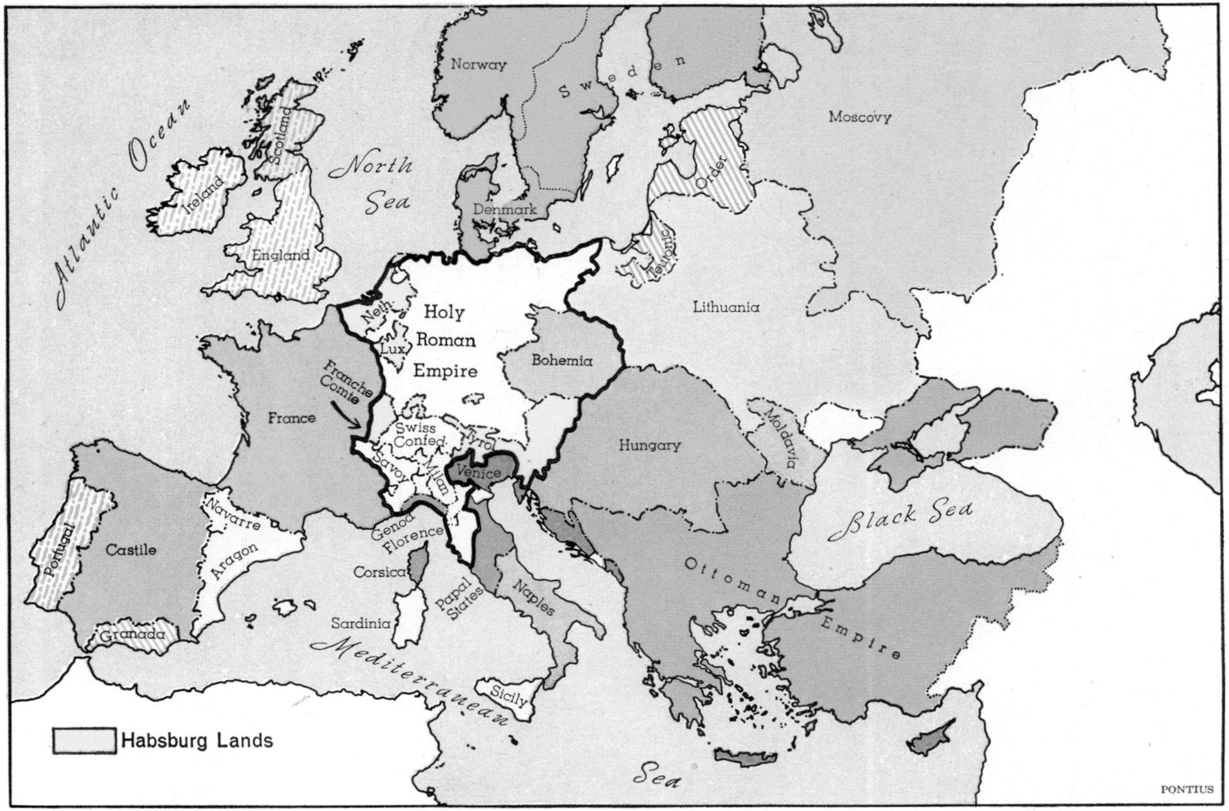

Europe in 1490

Habsburg Lands

Moscovy

Lithuania

Black Sea

Moldavia

Ottoman Empire

Hungary

Sweden

Order

Prussia

Norway

Denmark

North Sea

Bohemia

Naples

Holy Roman Empire

Tyrol

Venice

Papal States

Sicily

Neth.

Lux.

Swiss Cantons

Milan

Savoy

Genoa

Florence

Corsica

Sardinia

Mediterranean Sea

Scotland

Ireland

England

Atlantic Ocean

France

Franche Comté

Navarre

Aragon

Castile

Granada

Portugal

PONTIUS

of administrators and distributed among the victors the land as fiefs. However, they left control of religious affairs and local government in the hands of their Christian subjects. Outside Europe the Ottoman Turks had an extensive empire that included Asia Minor, Palestine, and Northern Africa.

The Duchy of Muscovy

For a long time the inhabitants of the Great Russian Plain were hardly considered Europeans. They were cut off from Western Europe by geography and by their culture. Western Europe had been Christianized by missionaries sent out from Rome; the Russians, by missionaries sent out from Constantinople. This gave rise to differences in language, in religion, in customs, and in tradition. Then from 1240 until 1480 the inhabitants of the Great Russian Plain had been subject to the Tatars. This had tended to make them still more oriental. As a result of these influences, the peoples of Western Europe and those of the Great Russian Plain had little in common for a long time.

In the Middle Ages the Great Russian Plain had been divided between a number of principalities. Among these, the rulers of Muscovy proved to be the strongest. Toward the end of the fifteenth century they had firmly established their rule in their own state, they had begun to free themselves from the rule of the Tatars, and they had started to conquer the neighboring principalities. By the close of the century they had conquered much of the Great Russian Plain, they had begun to develop an administrative system, and they had organized the Russian Orthodox Church. After the fall of the Byzantine Empire in 1453, the Duke of Muscovy married the niece of the last Eastern emperor. He then took the title of Autocrat of All the Russias and adopted many of the customs of the Eastern Empire.

Poland

In the valley of the Vistula River there had grown up the state of Poland. It had suffered from invasion at the hands of the Tatars and from the division of its territory into small states. The resulting wars had tended to depopulate the country. As an inducement to immigration, the Polish authorities had offered self-government and exemption from taxes to prospective immigrants. In response to this appeal, many Germans and Jews settled in the rising state. In the thirteenth century the Teutonic Knights, a semimilitary, semireligious order, composed of the younger sons of German nobles, established themselves along the Baltic and cut Poland off from the sea.

This German threat to the Polish state had important results. It led to a marriage between the heiress of Poland and the heir of the neighboring state of Lithuania. Though there was much subsequent friction between them and at times they were actually separated, this marriage laid the foundation for the permanent union of the two states into an enlarged Poland.

In the course of the development of Poland, however, conditions arose that ultimately were to cause the downfall of the Polish state. The external pressure gave rise to a military caste that put its own interests before those of the state. The Church had won exemption from most of the burdens of state. Even more than in other countries the support of the nobles, the clergy, and the state fell on peasantry. As a result, the Polish peasants were even more impoverished than those in other countries. Poland, too, lacked defensible boundaries.

In spite of these weaknesses Poland was still expanding. In 1466 it had defeated the Teutonic Knights and incorporated the province of West Prussia into the Polish state. At the same time it compelled the province of East Prussia to acknowledge Polish suzerainty. Twenty years later it came in contact with the expanding Ottoman Empire. As a consequence of its expansion, by the end of the fifteenth century Poland was counted an important power of Western Europe.

The Scandinavian States

In Northern Europe, in the Danish and Scandinavian peninsulas, there eventually developed the three states of Denmark, Norway, and Sweden. From 1397 an attempt was made to unite these three kingdoms, but in 1459 the effort ended in failure. For a long time thereafter, however, Denmark controlled not only the Danish Peninsula and the adjoining islands but the whole of Norway and the southern part of Sweden. The rest of Sweden formed a separate Swedish state that was weakened by the strife of a Danish and an anti-Danish party. Economically, the whole region was dominated by the Hanseatic League. There was a tendency for the three Scandinavian kingdoms to hold aloof from the politics of Western Europe.

From this survey it is evident that at the beginning of modern times governments and states were quite different from those we know today. Governments were poorer, had far less machinery, and attempted less than they do now. Some of the states of the present day were beginning to emerge. On the other hand, some of the states of that day have since disappeared. Italy was only a geographical expression. Poland and the Ottoman Empire were powers of the first rank. The duchy of Muscovy was just beginning to develop into a strong state. None of the states had as yet the boundaries and organization that they have today.

36

CHAPTER 4

European Culture

After the breakdown of the Roman world, the people of Europe had the task of creating a new civilization. To this new culture the ancient world, Christianity, and Teutonic and Slavic society all contributed. By the end of the fifteenth century much progress had been made toward the creation of a new civilization. Much of the earth's surface and the universe had been discovered. Schools, a considerable body of knowledge, and new languages and literatures had been developed. A new ecclesiastical and administrative architecture had been created. Works of art of a high order had been produced. Some account of these achievements must be given in order to understand Europe at the close of the Middle Ages.

The Conception of the Universe

At the beginning of modern times Europeans had only begun the discovery of the universe in which they lived. In ancient times men had made some progress toward revealing its secrets. They had made many acute observations of the heavens and had catalogued such stars and planets as they could see with the naked eye. In the second century, A.D., an Alexandrian scholar named Ptolemy had summed up in a book the ideas of the ancient world concerning the universe. During the entire Middle Ages this book was accepted as an authority on astronomy.

This work of Ptolemy gave the men of the fifteenth century quite a different conception of their place in the universe from that held by men of the present day. Instead of thinking of themselves as living on a relatively small planet in an immeasurable universe, they thought that they lived at the very center of creation. They believed that the sun, the moon, the planets, and the stars revolved around the earth on which they lived. Being without telescopes, they had no conception of the vast immensity of the universe.

By the fifteenth century, however, the learned were becoming somewhat puzzled about the Ptolemaic system. The Arabs and other schools were discovering bits of information that did not fit into the accepted ideas of the time. As a result, the learned were trying to make a place for the new knowledge in the system of Ptolemy.

One of the reasons for this backwardness of the science of astronomy was the general belief in the false science of astrology. Even the most learned men of the time believed that the stars and the planets had a determining influence on the lives of men and that their characters and futures could be foretold by careful observation of the position of the stars and planets. As a result, the men of the time collected a great body of useless lore and neglected the true path to knowledge.

The Known World

The Europeans of the fifteenth century were almost as ignorant about the earth on which they lived as they were about the universe around them. They still knew comparatively little about the greater part of the earth's surface. Though a few Norsemen had a faint tradition about some voyages to land in the West, Europeans in general scarcely suspected the existence of three of the continents. They knew nothing about North and South America or Australia. They knew only a little more about most of Asia and Africa. Even Russia was an unknown land to most Europeans. For most of them, the known world included only the greater part of Europe, Western Asia, and Northern Africa. They paid little attention to the reports of European travelers in Asia and Portuguese explorers along the African coast.

The Science of Navigation

One reason for the ignorance of Europeans concerning the earth was the backwardness of the science of navigation. During the Middle Ages, the Mediterranean Sea was the main highway of travel and commerce. As yet, men hardly dared to venture out of sight of land onto the ocean. The coast was the only means that they had of determining either their location or their direction. They had no instruments to aid them in navigating.

Not until about 1400 did European navigators begin to have the aid of instruments. About that date the compass began to come into use. This gave sailors an idea of the direction in which they were going. About the same time, navigators began to make use of the cross-staff and the astrolabe. These instruments enabled them to calculate the declination of the sun and the latitude of their ships. They still lacked even the crudest methods of determining longitude. They could tell something about the position of a ship by its speed in relation to a floating object and about the passage of time by using a sand glass or saying certain sentences.

The vessels of the time were so small that they could easily be

38

stowed away on the deck of a modern steamship. In the Mediterranean the prevailing type of vessel was the galley. A typical galley was a vessel about one hundred and thirty feet long, twenty feet or so wide, and shallow in draft. Such a craft was propelled by a single bank of oars rowed by sixty or more men. Each oar was at least fifty feet long. In the Atlantic Ocean a small sailing vessel known as the caravel had been developed. These craft were usually about one hundred and twenty feet long and twenty-six feet wide. In the bow these vessels had a high, clumsy-looking overhanging forecastle. Aft, they had towering half and quarter decks. In spite of their small size, they were soon to be used in making the greatest voyages of geographical discovery of all time.

In the fifteenth century those who ventured on the sea lacked many modern aids. They lacked docks and powerful cranes. They had no trained pilots waiting to guide them into harbors. From the headlands of Europe few lighthouses flashed warnings of dangerous rocks and shoals. Both trade and travel was far more uncomfortable and dangerous than at the present time.

Man's Knowledge of Himself

The men of the period knew as little about themselves as they did about the earth on which they lived. The human mind and body were as yet unknown territory. Men accepted as knowledge the shrewd guesses of the Greeks. The great anatomists had not yet begun their work of exploring the human body. The doctors of the time, for example, knew nothing about the nervous system or the circulation of the blood. They had not even named and described some of the most common diseases. Most of the children who were born at this period died in infancy. Those that survived were often sickly and short-lived. Virtually every adult had had smallpox. Leprosy was a very prevalent disease. From time to time, bubonic plague struck down great numbers of people.

The Conditions of Life

At the opening of the modern period, the population of Europe was much smaller than it is today. As a result, not so much land had been cleared as now. The forests were larger and more numerous. Wild animals were more plentiful. Bandits often lurked in the forests. Pirates swarmed on the seas. Most people went armed. The peasants often built stockades around their villages. The nobles, with the exception of those in Italy, lived in castles and fortified manor houses. Merchants and travelers went in armed bands. All seagoing vessels carried cannon.

The Attitude of Europeans toward their Fellowmen

The men of the fifteenth century had very little of the humanitarian spirit. This was shown by their treatment of the poor. They gave alms to the poor because the giving of alms was supposed to be one of the cardinal virtues. They did little or nothing toward the permanent cure of poverty. They discriminated very little between the worthy and the unworthy. As a result, the towns and the countryside swarmed with beggars. At times, the beggars were a positive menace.

The lack of a humanitarian spirit was shown by the treatment of criminals. There were no judges or juries striving to give the accused a fair trial. The rack was used to gain, by torture, confessions of guilt. The penalty for hundreds of petty cases was death. The convicted were hanged, drawn, and quartered. They were often broken on the wheel. Heretics were burned at the stake. Such an occasion was considered a gala affair and attracted great crowds of people. The prisons of the day were places of torture and breeding spots of crime and disease.

Education

In 1492 the educated man was the exception and not the rule. In the early Middle Ages only a few churchmen made any pretense to education. Even some of the famous kings could not read or write. Most of their subjects were equally illiterate. Quite early in the Middle Ages, however, some need of schools began to be felt. In response to this demand, a variety of educational institutions grew up. Cathedrals, collegiate churches, and monasteries started schools for the training of priests and novices and soon began to admit laymen. Parishes, gilds, and chantry priests, likewise, established schools. As commerce grew in importance, efforts were made to prepare young men for business. Out of some of these early schools universities were developed. Certain university centers became famous. Salerno, for example, became noted for the study of medicine; Bologna, for law; and Paris, for theology. In time, these universities, as they came to be known, usually had five faculties. At first, students enrolled with the faculty of liberal arts. If they went further they took canon law, Roman law, theology, or medicine. Each faculty had its own rules and organization. By the end of the fifteenth century such universities were to be found in most parts of Western Europe.

The universities of Western Europe drew to their lectures crowds of students. These ranged in age from boys of fourteen to men of maturity. As a usual thing, students were counted as members of the clergy. The students had their own organizations. As a rule, these took the form of colleges. Founded as a result of the generosity of some donor, these institutions were designed to give food and shelter to a certain number of students. University students were often accused of being unruly and given to excesses. These outbreaks frequently took the form of battles between students and townsmen and sometimes resulted in the death of some of the participants.

The curriculums of the various schools and universities varied greatly in content. Some of the schools taught little beyond reading and writing. Most of them taught in some fashion the so-called seven liberal arts. These included the trivium—grammar, dialectics, and rhetoric; and the quadrivium—geometry, arithmetic, music, and astronomy. Grammar included the form and content of the known works of Latin literature. Rhetoric was the art of speaking and writing persuasively. Arithmetic was limited to simple calculations. Geometry included geography and natural history. Dialectics comprised logic, ethics, and metaphysics.

In the universities, the faculties of arts or philosophy gave advanced work in the seven liberal arts. During the greater part of the Middle Ages, dialectics, particularly logic, was especially emphasized. In this field of knowledge, the great authorities were the writings of the Church Fathers and the works of Aristotle. The method used by medieval thinkers was known as Scholasticism. The various Scholastic philosophers built up elaborate systems of thought. By the end of the fifteenth century, however, they were under attack. The students were abandoning the lectures of the Scholastics for those of the Humanists.

The teaching methods of that day differed greatly from those of today. The professor lectured in Latin. He read from some treatise and commented upon it. In later times, the professor commented as well on the comments of earlier professors. The students took notes. They often repeated a course to impress it upon their memories.

The medieval universities must not be thought of as institutions with large physical plants. They had no spacious campuses and no regular buildings. The classes were held wherever space could be found for them. Books were scarce and expensive. So the universities of the time had no libraries. There were no museums or laboratories. The medieval universities got along without most of the things that are now thought to be indispensable.

Universities, then as now, recognized the progress of students by the conferring of degrees. Often as early as the age of fifteen, students sustained theses in a public disputation. If they were successful in passing this test, they became bachelors of arts. Later, at about the age of twenty, they had to undergo a more severe examination. If this was met successfully, they became masters of arts, or doctors. This degree entitled them to become professors.

In the curriculum of medieval universities, theology held a very important place. Professors and students sought to interpret the doctrines of the Church. Taking the statements of the Bible and a book known as Peter Lombard's *Sentences* as foundation they built up great systems of thought. This process reached its culmination in the work of a great Italian teacher, Thomas Aquinas (1226–1274). The most famous of the medieval theological faculties was that of the University of Paris.

In the opening years of the sixteenth century, Roman law was another very popular subject in the universities. There were a number of reasons for its popularity. Roman law seemed to the students of the period so superior to the crude bodies of customary law developed by the Germans. The rulers of the day, too, found support in Roman law for their pretentions to power. As a result, ambitious young men crowded into the lectures on Roman law.

Medicine was not yet a science. The medical faculties of the day did little more than repeat the empiric conclusions of the Greeks. There were hundreds of textbooks in medicine, but their authors knew little about the human body, the laws of health, or remedies for the ills of men and women. In spite of their unscientific attitude, the doctors of the period had come to recognize such diseases as smallpox, measles, typhus, plica, scurvy, syphilis, and whooping cough. For the cure of these diseases, they placed great reliance on drugs and bleeding. At the close of the fifteenth century, the doctors were hotly discussing the proper method of bleeding a patient.

Universities first developed in Italy. As early as 1100 A.D. the writers began to speak of Italian universities. In the next century a similar institution was founded at Paris. In the thirteenth century universities were started in England and in Spain. In the following century such institutions were established at Prague, at Vienna, at Cracow, and at various German cities. By the fifteenth century the movement reached Scotland, Denmark, and Sweden.

The Renaissance

In the closing years of the fifteenth century, a new way of looking at life had been gaining ground for some time in Western Europe. Medieval man had believed very firmly that life on earth was only a prelude to a better and eternal world. This conception of life explains the importance attached to theology, to personal asceticism, and to prayer to the saints. For this reason, men devoted their treasure and their artistic skill to the building and decorating of churches, monasteries, and cathedrals. They tended to let religion dominate their lives.

Toward the close of the Middle Ages, this situation began to change. Men, particularly those in the towns and cities, tended to become more interested in their earthly life. More and more they devoted themselves to commerce, industry, and the making of money. They commenced to enjoy the luxuries money would buy. They built fine houses and stately municipal buildings. They took pleasure in paintings and statues. They became secular in their outlook on life.

The period in which this new viewpoint was being adopted is called the Renaissance. It extended from thirteen hundred to the end of the sixteenth century. It was marked by a declining interest in theology and by a revival of interest in ancient times. Renaissance men discovered that ancient man had had the same point of view as themselves. They sought, accordingly, to learn all they could about the culture and life of Greece and Rome. They began a search for the literary, artistic, and material remains of these early civilizations. They attempted to write like the men of classical times. They tried to make their own languages the mediums for the expression of their thoughts and emotions. They sought to discover more about their own world. They expressed their new point of view in their architecture, their painting, and their sculpture. They abandoned Scholasticism in favor of Humanism.

Italian Humanism

It is usually asserted that Humanism began in Italy with Petrarch (1304–1374). In fact, it was the work of many men who for the most part are now forgotten. They lived in Italy, France, England, and Germany. In Italy, however, the Humanist movement found a particularly favorable soil and grew rapidly. There, town life and the secular tradition were farther advanced than elsewhere. Conditions were ready for a gifted leader.

Italian Humanism found this leadership in Francesco Petrarch. He was born in Tuscany, the son of a notary. In 1312 he went to Avignon, at that time the seat of the papal court. Later, at the insistence of his father, he studied law at the universities of Montpellier and Bologna. Upon the death of his father in 1326, however, he abandoned law for literature. In the latter he early won fame through his sonnets. These poems were written in the Tuscan dialect and were addressed to a certain Laura whose identity is not definitely known. Petrarch, however, was much more proud of his epic poem, *Africa*, and his letters, verses, and biographies, that were written in

43

Latin. He had the greatest admiration for the classics and searched enthusiastically for the lost works of Latin authors. In the end he was rewarded by the finding of two speeches of Cicero and the letters of that celebrated orator to Atticus. For these achievements, he was finally crowned poet laureate both at Rome and at Paris. During the greater part of his life, he enjoyed the patronage, homage, and friendship of all kindred spirits.

From that time on, the Humanist movement steadily grew. Among the contemporaries of Petrarch the name of Boccaccio (1313–1376), the author of the famous collection of tales known as *The Decameron*, should be mentioned. He broadened the scope of the Humanist movement by studying Greek, a language which he considered superior to the Latin. In 1396 Manuel Chrysoloras, a Greek, began to teach his native language at Florence. Meanwhile, the followers and successors of Petrarch continued the search for the works of lost classical authors and for coins, medals, statues, inscriptions, and other remains of ancient civilization. They also opened libraries and founded chairs for the study of the classics.

By the fifteenth century the rulers of Italy were vying with each other as patrons of the Humanists. At Florence, for example, Cosimo de Medici (1309–1463) found places for many Humanists in the service of the state. He aided in the search for coins, manuscripts, and inscriptions. He collected and opened for the public a fine library. He organized an academy for the study of Plato. He established the first modern ornamental garden. The grandson of Cosimo, Lorenzo the Magnificent (1449–1492), generously patronized scholars, architects, sculptors, and painters. Soon the Humanists began to find places at the papal court and were even elected popes. These popes started the priceless, present-day collections of the Vatican and built many of the architectural monuments of present-day Rome. Other Italian rulers, likewise, did much to favor the Humanists.

Early Italian Renaissance Architecture

The enthusiasm of the men of the Renaissance period for the past affected Italian architecture, sculpture, and painting. The Italian Humanists had found the writings of Vitruvius, a Roman author, on architecture. Their reading of this work led to a study of the remains of Roman buildings. The ideas which they gained from these studies were soon embodied in a variety of structures. The rulers, nobles, and municipalities of the period began to erect churches, palaces, and public buildings of various sorts in a new style. In their construction the architects employed cornices, pilasters, and capitals.

They enclosed doors and windows in richly carved frames. They made much use of flat surfaces. They employed horizontal mouldings. They constructed great domes and cupolas. They embellished gates, chapels, tombs, and fountains with friezes, mouldings, wreaths, and scrolls.

The men of the Renaissance were great builders. One of the most famous architects of the period was Brunelleschi (1377–1446). He was a Florentine by birth. He first spent long years studying the remains of Roman architecture at Rome. In 1417 he successfully competed in a contest held in his native city. He presented plans for the completion of the cathedral. As a result of his success, he was authorized to construct a great octagonal dome. Later, he supervised the building of other edifices at Florence. These included two churches and the famous Pitti Palace.

In other Italian states similar building enterprises were undertaken. In Venice, for four generations, members of the famous Lombardi family supervised for its rich merchants the construction of churches, palaces, and public edifices. At Rome the popes, cardinals, and nobles were great builders. The most famous of the Roman architects was Bramante (1444–1514), who drew the original plans for St. Peter's Church, for many years the largest church in Christendom. In many other Italian cities there were architects of great ability.

Early Renaissance Sculpture in Italy

The activity of the Italians in the construction of new buildings stimulated a demand for sculpture. The Renaissance sculptors of Italy worked in marble, bronze, and terra cotta. At first, they found their subjects in the Bible and in the lives of the saints. Later, they turned to classic themes.

Most of the important early Italian sculptors were Florentines. Their work was characterized by a close imitation of nature and a masterly treatment of perspective. One of the most noted of these early Renaissance sculptors was Ghiberti (1378–1455). His most famous work was the doors of the Baptistery in Florence. Another important sculptor was Donatello (1386–1466), who designed tombs for people of wealth and rank, ornamented churches, and carved statues of both historical and living personages. Another important sculptor was Luca della Robbia (1399–1482). For three generations members of his family continued to fashion from enameled terra cotta lunettes for doorways, bas-reliefs for tombs, and medallions and statues. Many other sculptors, only a little less famous than those who have been mentioned, worked in other Italian cities.

45

Early Renaissance Painting in Italy

The new interest of men of the Renaissance period in nature and in ancient times affected their painting as well as their sculpture and architecture. In the early Middle Ages Italian artists strove to teach religion through the pictures that they painted on the walls of churches. Their pictures, however, were little more than religious symbols. They were flat and had only two dimensions. The painters of that time knew comparatively little about the proportions of the human body, perspective, and the use of colors, tones, and shadows. They knew only the mediums of fresco and tempera.

About 1400 the Italian painters commenced to be somewhat less religious in their choice of subjects and to find solutions for various technical problems. They adopted a new medium of expression, namely, painting in oil. They studied anatomy, nature, and classic models. As a result, their pictures started to show a third dimension, their figures commenced to look like real people, and they introduced landscapes into the background of their pictures.

The early Italian painters were so numerous that not even a catalogue of their names can be given. The founder of modern painting is usually considered to be a young man, Tommaso Guidi (1401–1428), who went by the nickname Masaccio because of his slovenliness. During his short lifetime, he painted pictures on the walls of churches and chapels in Florence, pictures which were almost unnoticed by his contemporaries. After his death, people slowly began to realize that he had far surpassed his fellow painters in ability. His great contribution to painting was atmospheric perspective. A contemporary of Tommaso Guidi, Paola Ucello (1397–1475), made a somewhat better use of perspective and flattered his Medici employer by introducing into his pictures battle scenes and other historical events. Andrea del Castagno (1390–1457) and Antonio Pollaniolo (1429–1498) embodied in their paintings the results of a more thorough study of anatomy. A young Sicilian, Antonella da Nessina (1430–1516), learned about painting in oil from a Flemish painter working in Italy. He carried his discovery to Venice, where Giovanni Bellini and his students perfected the new medium of expression. These painters, with many others that for lack of space cannot even be mentioned, prepared the way for the great masters of Italian painting.

Social Effects of the Renaissance in Italy

The movement known as the Renaissance had an important effect on society in Italy as well as on Italian art. Men of great activity rather than the saints were held up as models of conduct. The upper classes of Italy, at least, strove to be ladies and gentlemen. They tried to be courteous, refined in language, acquainted with the rudiments of scholarship, capable of writing and speaking well, and appreciative of artistic things. On the other hand, they became very irreligious and even pagan in their outlook on life. Many an Italian gentleman of the period was quite capable of poisoning a rival or stabbing him to death.

The Early Renaissance North of the Alps

From Italy the movement known as the Renaissance spread to the countries north of the Alps. In 1492, however, Humanism was just getting under way in Germany, France, the Netherlands, and England. The relations maintained between Italy and Germany made it inevitable that the latter country should in time be affected by developments in Italy. On the one hand, Italians, steeped in the new learning—like Aeneas Silvius, the later Pope Pius II, who found employment from 1442 to 1455 with Emperor Frederick III—made their way north of the Alps. On the other hand, many German students studied and traveled in Italy.

Among the Germans there was no one dominant personality like Petrarch. Rudolf Agricola (1443–1485) is usually credited with being the pioneer German Humanist. For a long time Conrad Celtes (1459–1508) wandered about Germany giving lectures and founding groups of Humanists. Later in life he became librarian of Emperor Maximilian, for whom he made a notable collection of Greek and Latin manuscripts. John Reuchlin (1455–1522) introduced the study of Hebrew into Germany.

In contrast with those in Italy, the German Humanists were deeply religious. They loved the ancient languages because these helped them to understand the Bible and the Church Fathers. The German Humanists were, of course, opposed to Scholasticism. They considered its methods an obstacle to the study of ancient languages. This point of view often brought them into conflict with the partisans of Scholasticism. A little later, this conflict was to culminate in a famous quarrel which centered around John Reuchlin and divided Germany into two hostile camps.

In Germany as in Italy, the Humanists found influential patrons, among both secular and ecclesiastical princes and among the rich burghers and important officials of the towns. In Germany, however, the Humanist movement was diverted and interrupted in its development by the Protestant Revolt.

47

The Invention of Printing

The most important contribution to culture of the German people during the period of the Renaissance was the invention of printing from moveable type. During ancient and medieval times books were written by hand. Writing materials were scarce and expensive. The principal makers of books were the monks. For the most part, they wrote on vellum or parchment. When they wished to make an especially fine book, they took great pains with illuminated initial letters and illustrated their books with marginal pictures. In making these so-called illuminated manuscripts, they made much use of gold leaf and fine colors. After the development of universities, the making of textbooks became a business. Secular scribes arose to meet the demands of students for books. Even by this method, comparatively few books were produced and they continued to be scarce and expensive.

Toward the close of the Middle Ages, this situation was changed. People commenced to use paper made from fibrous materials instead of the more expensive vellum and parchment. The art of making paper seems to have been discovered by the Chinese as early as the second century B.C. From them it passed in some way to the Arabs and on to Western Europe. Paper seems to have been introduced first into Spain and Italy. From these two countries it passed into France (1189), Germany (1356), England (1450), and Austria (1513).

A second important step in revolutionizing the making of books was the discovery of the art of casting and using moveable type. The story of its development is not well known. Many cities have claimed to be the birthplace of the new art. The two strongest claimants for the honor of inventing printing seem to be Laurens Janzoon Coster (1370–1440) and John Gutenberg (1397–1468). To the latter certainly belongs the credit of bringing printing with moveable type into general use.

This famous printer belonged to a patrician family of Mainz. For some years, apparently, he lived at Strasbourg. About 1445, he seems to have returned to Mainz, where he gained the aid of John Fust, one of the rich burghers of the city. About 1455, with the help of Fust, Gutenberg brought out a printed book. It is now known as the Mazarin Bible. Gutenberg, however, does not seem to have been successful financially, and the firm soon became known as Fust and Schoffer.

The new art of printing from moveable type spread quickly. By the end of the fifteenth century there were at least twenty-five German printers. From Germany the art was diffused rapidly. It is said to have reached Italy about 1464; Paris, 1475; Hungary, 1473; England, 1477; Denmark, 1482; Portugal, 1487; the provinces later known as Rumania, 1508; and Russia, 1564. By 1500 about twenty-five thousand books are believed to have been published.

Early Renaissance Painting North of the Alps

In most of the regions north of the Alps, the new developments in architecture and painting were just getting under way or were not yet started. In the Netherlands, however, the new artistic movement had already produced some masterpieces. The brothers, Hubert (1366–1426) and Jan (1385–1440) van Eyck, had already painted in the new oil medium altarpieces and portraits for the Dukes of Burgundy and the rich burghers of Flanders. They put into their pictures a wealth of exact detail without losing sight of the main theme. During the fifteenth century, also, Roger van der Weyden (1399–1464) had become a famous portrait painter, and Hans Memling (1430–1494) had painted pictures that expressed a deep religious spirit and great delicacy of feeling.

By the end of the fifteenth century, accordingly, Europe was in the midst of an important cultural movement. For some time the Italians had abandoned the ideas about learning, art, and the meaning of life which had prevailed during most of the medieval period. In their place they had gone back to ancient times and to nature—in education, painting, and architecture—for inspiration and for their point of view in life. About 1500 the new cultural ideals were noticeably on the point of spreading north of the Alps.

PART 2

The Sixteenth Century

CHAPTER 5

The Beginning of European Expansion, 1492–1598

The year 1492 is undoubtedly one of the most significant dates in European history. Until that time, as we have found, the peoples of Europe lived in a restricted world. In that year began a movement that led to the discovery by Europeans of most of the earth's surface, to the colonization by them of three hitherto unknown continents, and the extension of European influences to two other continents. This expansion of the peoples of Europe and their culture did more to revolutionize European conditions than any other movement of modern times.

Causes for the Expansion of Europe

In the closing years of the fifteenth century, forces were at work that were to push adventurous Europeans beyond the confines of their own continent. They had finished some of the tasks which had long absorbed their energies. In 1492, for example, the reconquest of the Iberian Peninsula from the Moors was just being completed, and the veterans of the Moorish wars were not likely to be contented to settle down to a humdrum existence in some sleepy Spanish village. Some of the states of Europe had become sufficiently strong and centralized to enable their governments to undertake new enterprises. By their recent voyages down the west coast of Africa and around the Cape of Good Hope, the Portuguese had revealed a hitherto unknown world, started a profitable trade with new regions, and roused hopes for the establishment of direct and cheaper commercial relations with India. Also, improvements in navigation and shipbuilding had made possible long voyages of discovery in new seas.

Spanish Explorations and Settlements

Many European peoples have claimed the honor of discovering America. Most of these voyages, however, even if they really took place, did not make Europeans generally really aware of the existence of the New World and of the advantages to be gained by its exploration and settlement. From this point of view, the decisive voyages were made under the auspices of the Spanish government by the man known to Italians as Christoforo Colombo, to Spaniards as Christobal Colon, and to English-speaking peoples as Christopher Columbus (1451–1506). His four voyages of discovery did start a movement for the exploration, settlement, and exploitation of North and South America.

The obscurity which surrounds Columbus' early life has given rise to a number of theories concerning his origin and early career. It seems certain, though, that he was born at Genoa, the son of a comparatively humble family. In his early years he seems to have sailed to many Mediterranean ports in the interest of Genoese merchants. About 1483, apparently, he was sent to Portugal by the firm for which he worked. In Portugal he married into a family established in the Azores. Finding himself on the edge of the known world, it is not surprising that he began to speculate about the unknown regions beyond these islands. It is known that he owned and made notes upon some of the books that discussed the subject. One of them was a book that related the travels of Marco Polo, a Venetian, who spent many years in the Far East. As a result of his reading and reflections, Columbus became convinced that the earth was smaller than it actually is, that Asia extended farther east than it really does, and that it could be reached by sailing west.

In all probability, the conclusions reached by Columbus were not particularly novel. Many of his contemporaries were speculating about the same problem. The great merit of Columbus lies in the fact that, in contrast to other speculators on the subject, he set to work to obtain the help necessary for putting his ideas to a practical test.

He turned for aid, naturally, to the sovereigns of some of the new states which were developing in Europe. After some rebuffs in other quarters, he turned about 1485 or 1486 to the two Spanish sovereigns, Ferdinand and Isabella. As was to be expected, he had a great difficulty in persuading the two rulers and their advisers of the feasibility of his plans. He was a comparatively unknown adventurer, an advocate of an expensive and a hazardous voyage. Money was scarce and needed for many other things. In addition, the attention and the resources of the two sovereigns were fully engaged in an arduous and expensive campaign against the kingdom of Granada, the last foothold of the Moors in the Iberian Peninsula.

After the conquest of Granada in 1492, however, the two rulers finally decided to authorize an expedition to test the theory of Columbus. With the aid of the royal government and of some merchants of Palos, the port of embarkation, Columbus fitted out three small caravels: the *Santa Maria,* the *Pinta,* and the *Nina,* manned by crews that numbered less than one hundred men. On the morning of August 3, 1492, accordingly, Columbus and his little expedition set sail from Palos, a port in southwestern Spain, for the great adventure.

Columbus first sailed southwestward to the Canary Islands, the farthest outpost of the known world. Upon his arrival there, he turned westward into the pathless, unknown Atlantic Ocean. From the diary which he kept during the voyage, it would seem that the most difficult problems of the commander arose from the ignorance and fears of his crews rather than from the sea and the weather. There seems to have been a real danger that the attitude of his crews would force him to turn back.

As the expedition approached the as yet unknown American continent, the members of the crews began to see such evidences of land as plants, birds, and a carved stick, and, finally, on October 11, at two o'clock in the morning, a sailor on the *Pinta* saw at some distance from his ship a light which rose and fell as though carried by someone walking. The next morning, the rising sun revealed to the astonished sailors a small island which its discoverers named San Salvador, one of the group of islands now known as the Bahamas. Thereupon, Columbus and many of his crew landed. Surrounded by naked, trustful, and wondering natives they took possession of the island in the name of Ferdinand and Isabella. Heartened by this discovery, Columbus continued his explorations and discovered Cuba, Haiti, and a number of other islands before he turned back.

Events, however, finally warned him that he must return to Spain. One of his three small vessels deserted him and another struck a sand bar and had to be abandoned. On January 3, 1493, accordingly, Columbus sailed for Spain in his remaining vessel. On the way he overtook the truant *Pinta*. Both of the tiny ships were badly buffeted by storms. After almost giving up hope of reaching home, the two vessels finally reached Spain.

After he landed, the Spanish people gave Columbus a great reception. He was treated almost as a royal personage by both the sovereigns of Spain and their subjects. Though he brought little actual wealth, his voyage aroused the greatest expectations. Hundreds and even thousands of Spaniards began to dream of obtaining fame and wealth in the newly discovered world.

The success of Columbus, however, alarmed the Portuguese. By reason of certain papal bulls and a treaty concluded with Spain in 1480, they considered themselves entitled to all the non-European lands that might be discovered. Quite naturally, the voyage which Columbus had just completed greatly disturbed them because the Spanish sovereigns felt, of course, that these lands should belong to them. The Portuguese, consequently, appealed to the Pope, a natural arbiter of difficult problems, for a decision of the question. On May 3 and 4, 1493, the Pope disclosed his decision. He tried to settle the dispute between the two claimants by dividing the non-European lands that might be discovered. All the lands beyond a line running north and south one hundred leagues west of the Azores and the Cape Verde Islands were to belong to Spain. All east of this demarcation line were to be under the jurisdiction of Portugal. A subsequent papal bull and treaty moved this dividing line to a point three hundred and seventy leagues west of the Cape Verde Islands, a decision which eventually gave Portugal a claim to Brazil and the right to explore it. By virtue of these decrees and agreements and their various explorations, Spain and Portugal asserted their right to monopolize the non-European world.

The successful voyage of Columbus inaugurated an era of discovery. In a little more than half a century, European navigators, most of them sailing under the auspices of Spain, traced the greater part of the coast line of the two American continents and began their settlement. Not even a catalogue of their names can be given. At first, the explorers thought that they were tracing the coast line of Asia. Gradually, the discovery of land in unsuspected places, the crossing of the Isthmus of Panama by Balboa (1513), and the circumnavigation of the earth by the expedition led by Magellan led to a realization that Columbus had reached a new world.

Only a few of the more noteworthy territorial discoveries can be mentioned. Columbus made three more voyages to the New World. In 1493 he returned to the West Indies with a large expedition, took the first steps toward the settlement of America, and discovered Puerto Rico, Jamaica, and other islands. In 1498 he found Trinidad and touched the mainland of South America in the vicinity of the Orinoco River. Finally, from 1502 to 1504, he was at the head of a fourth expedition that reached the coast at a point within the limits of the present Honduras.

In 1497, John Cabot (1451–1498), another Genoese navigator (employed by the English), sailed westward and probably discovered the coasts of Newfoundland and Labrador. In the following year he seems to have traced the coast of North America from Labrador to Cape Hatteras. These voyages gave England a basis for her subsequent claim to the whole continent.

Other navigators discovered South America. In 1499, Vincent Pinzón (1460–1524), a member of the family which aided Columbus on his first voyage, sailed along the northeastern coast of South America for a long distance. In 1508 Pinzón and Diaz de Solis explored the eastern coast of South America as far as the Plata River. In 1513, Balboa, a capable Spanish adventurer, struggled through almost impenetrable forests and over lofty mountains across the Isthmus of Panama to the Pacific Ocean. Six years later, Magellan (1480?–1521), sailing under the auspices of Spain, pushed down the west coast of Africa, entered the strait which now bears his name, crossed the Pacific Ocean in spite of incredible hardships, and discovered the Philippine Islands. Although Magellan was killed in a skirmish with the natives, his companions completed the circumnavigation of the earth, perhaps the greatest feat of navigation in history. These voyages and expeditions revealed the existence of the new continent, South America.

In the meantime, a number of expeditions had revealed more about North America. In 1519, a Spaniard, Ponce de Leon, discovered Florida. In 1534, Verrazano (1480–1527), and ten years later, Cartier (1494–1552) made explorations that gave France a basis for claims to Canada. These various voyages of exploration gave Europeans a fair idea of the outline of North and South America.

By a peculiar quirk of fate, the new lands were not named after their discoverer. Instead, they were called America in honor of a comparatively obscure adventurer, Amerigo Vespucci (1451–1512). This Florentine, an employee of the Medici family, established himself at Seville. In some letters writen to his former employer, he boasted, just as many another man has done in similar circumstances, of the part he was playing in the startling events of the time. He told (in his letters) of having made several voyages, the first of which had taken place as early as 1497, and of having discovered a new world, the continent now known as South America. These letters happened to be seen by a German geographer, Martin Waldseemüller, who was trying to incorporate the new geographical knowledge into maps and books. Taking the claims of the boastful Amerigo Vespucci at their face value, the German geographer suggested in 1507 that the new continent be called America. The suggestion met with favor. In time, the new name was applied to North America as well as South America.

The Settlement of Spanish America

As soon as they had discovered the New World, the Spaniards tried to make settlements in the new lands. On his first voyage, Columbus built a fort on the island of Haiti and left in it a garrison of forty-three men. On his return to the island next year, however, he found that the fort had been deserted and that the garrison had vanished. The garrison had been the victims of disease, hostile Indians, or their

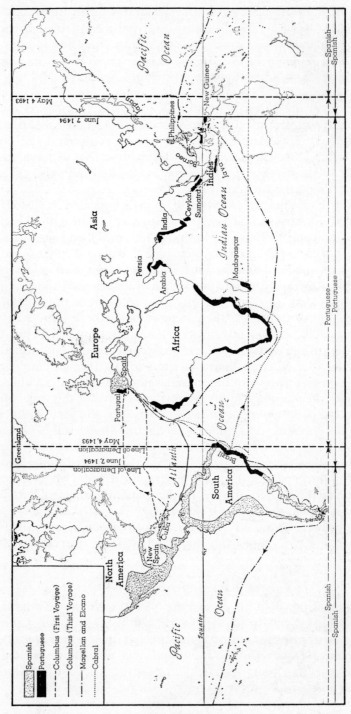

The Great Discoveries of the Sixteenth Century

own rashness. Consequently, the permanent settlement of the New World began during Columbus' second voyage. The first settlements were established in Haiti or, as it was called by the Spaniards, Hispaniola. In 1508, Ponce de Leon led a band of colonists to the neighboring island of Puerto Rico. The year following, Esquivel conquered Jamaica. In 1511, Velasquez, a companion of Columbus and one of the leaders in the Hispaniola colony, led three hundred settlers to Cuba where within a year they founded six settlements. The first colonies of the New World were thus in the West Indies.

Adventurous Spaniards soon pushed on to the mainland. On the continent they first tried to establish a settlement on the Isthmus of Panama. The story of this colony is too long to be given here, but it illustrates the hardships, hazards, and difficulties encountered by the early settlers of America. In 1502, Columbus made an unsuccessful attempt to found a colony on the Isthmus of Panama. Eight years later, two Spanish adventurers, Ojeda and Nicuesa, were authorized by the Spanish government to make another effort to found a settlement. They had to contend with sickness and hostile Indians and lost hundreds of their followers. The survivors were plagued by mutinies and dissensions. In spite of these difficulties, the colony survived and became a center for further colonization. From there in 1513 started the expedition of Balboa across the Isthmus of Panama that led to the discovery of the Pacific Ocean. From this colony in 1519 left the expedition that founded the city of Panama, the first permanent settlement on the mainland and the point of departure for various expeditions along the western coast of North and South America.

The Conquest of Mexico

During the course of their explorations, Spaniards had touched Yucatan and other points along the coast of Mexico. They returned to the West Indies with exciting reports about the country that they had sighted. These reports finally caused the governor of Cuba to prepare an expedition for the exploration and conquest of Mexico. He selected as its commander his brother-in-law and one time secretary, Hernando Cortes (1485–1547), a poor Spanish noble with considerable military experience, who had attracted the attention of the Cuban colonists by his successful completion of some important tasks and by some madcap adventures.

At the last moment, just when the expedition was ready to start, the governor of Cuba became alarmed lest the bold and energetic Cortes escape from his control. The governor, accordingly, tried to recall Cortes, but the latter refused to give up his great opportunity for wealth and adventure. He eluded the first messenger sent by the

59

governor and ignored later ones. On November 18, 1518, Cortes sailed for Mexico. He took with him some five hundred soldiers, some Indians, and a few Negroes. He also had sixteen horses and a few cannon.

In the spring of 1519 the expedition reached Mexico and made a settlement where the city of Vera Cruz now stands. In order to prevent the fainthearted from turning back, Cortes is said to have burned his ships. Thereupon, he set out for the unknown interior. From the messengers sent to him by the ruler of the country, he had learned that the Aztecs had built up in Mexico a great empire. Cortes accordingly made the bold decision to march on its capital near the site of the present-day Mexico City.

To many of the four hundred men of the expedition, it must have seemed a formidable undertaking. Lofty mountain ranges lay before them, and many hostile Indians lived along their proposed line of march. With great skill, Cortes overcame all difficulties and turned many of the vassals of the Aztec Empire into allies.

By November, 1519, Cortes reached the capital. In achieving this remarkable feat, he had been greatly aided by a strange tradition. The ruler of the Aztec Empire believed Cortes was a god whose coming had long been foretold. Accordingly, he regarded any struggle against Cortes as useless. On the contrary, Montezuma, the Aztec emperor, received Cortes and his four hundred companions as guests.

At the Aztec capital the Spaniards discovered much that impressed them. They found themselves in the midst of a society that possessed a relatively high civilization. They were surrounded by a people of some learning and considerable mechanical ability. They saw around them great temples, pyramids, fine aqueducts, broad causeways, and public buildings of various sorts. They discovered that they were at the center of a great empire, built up by the Aztecs, that extended to such distant points as Yucatan and Guatemala and that possessed a highly organized government with armies, administrative officials, and courts of justice. These marks of civilization were offset in part by a religion that demanded human sacrifices.

Having reached the capital by a stroke of good fortune, Cortes acted with great skill and boldness. Disregarding justice and common decency, he seized his host, Montezuma, in a most unscrupulous fashion and held him as a hostage. For the time being, the Aztecs hesitated to take hostile action against the Spanish intruders.

At the end of six months, however, disturbing news reached Cortes. He learned that a large expedition had reached Vera Cruz with orders to arrest him. Confronted by this dangerous situation, Cortes acted with his usual skill and boldness. Leaving a garrison of one hundred and forty men at the captial, he hastened back to Vera Cruz with the remainder of his little force. Upon his arrival at the coast, by a skillful intermixture of surprise and bribery, Cortes overpowered the commander of the new expedition and incorporated into his own forces the troops of his rival. This success enabled him to return to the Aztec capital.

Upon arriving there, Cortes found the Spanish garrison in a bad situation. By their unwise conduct during his absence, the Spaniards had finally driven the Aztecs to revolt. The situation was so serious that Cortes decided for the moment to abandon the capital. He and the little band of soldiers under his command had to fight their way out of the city over a long narrow causeway. Many of the Spaniards foolishly tried to take with them the gold they had wrested from the Aztecs. Many of them were killed or drowned, and much of their equipment was lost. Only a battered remnant of the original Spanish force finally took refuge with their Indian allies.

In this place of refuge Cortes made preparations for a new attack on the Aztec capital. In October, 1520, he began the march back to the center of the empire. By August, 1521, he had retaken the city. Thereupon, the victorious Spaniards set to work to destroy the Aztec Empire. They captured the successor of the unfortunate Montezuma and gradually took his chief followers prisoners. Thereafter, the victorious Spaniards occupied the place hitherto held by the Aztecs.

This great victory, however, did not solve all the problems confronting Cortes. He was still legally in rebellion against the angry governor of Cuba. Faced by this situation, Cortes took a bold course. Ignoring the irate governor, he appealed directly to the sovereign of Spain, Emperor Charles V. In a series of five letters, Cortes told his master the story of his amazing victory and described the great wealth of the conquered country. His policy proved effective. Always hardpressed for money, Charles V accepted Cortes' explanation of his conduct and made him captain general of the newly conquered province of New Spain. In 1529 the Emperor made Cortes a marquis.

The Conquest of the Inca Empire

The astonishing feats of Cortes fired the imagination of other Spaniards. Dreaming of finding similar wealth, various Spanish leaders led exploring expeditions into many parts of the New World. Some, like De Soto (1496–1542) and Coronada (1500–1545), wandered fruitlessly through the forests and swamps of the southeastern United States or over the trackless plains of the West. Others, like Pizarro (1471–1541), found treasures that equaled those of Mexico.

To Pizarro and the colony of Panama had come reports of both the success of Cortes and of the existence, south of the Isthmus of Panama, of another rich and powerful empire. These accounts stirred Pizarro and two companions, Almagro and an influential priest named Lucque, to action. From 1524 onward, under the leadership of Pizarro, they explored the west coast of South America. For seven years, undaunted by physical hardships, the lack of money, terrible diseases, and the timidity of their followers, they searched for the rumored empire. They found enough signs of wealth and civilization to cause them to continue the search. Finally, in 1531, after two expeditions had failed, a third set sail from Panama City, followed the west coast of South America southward, and finally landed about the latitude of the present city of Quito. With only one hundred and eighty men and thirty-seven horses, Pizarro hoped to conquer a great empire.

After landing, the little expedition began the long and difficult march from the low and infected coast to the lofty plateaus of the interior. Finally, after a difficult march, it reached the Indian capital of Cajamarca. Pizarro arrived at a moment when two brothers were struggling for possession of the throne. One appealed from prison to Pizarro for aid. The other believed like Montezuma that the Spanish leader and his followers were supernatural beings against whom it was useless to fight. This situation enabled the Spaniards to occupy the capital without hindrance and pose as deliverers of the Indians from tyranny. Hence, as had been the case in Mexico, they were courteously received by the Indian sovereign and his followers.

The Indians were repaid for their courtesy by a daring act of treachery. Through a priest, Pizarro demanded that the Indians should promptly accept the Christian religion and recognize the authority of the king of Spain. When the Indian sovereign refused the Spanish demand, Pizarro unscrupulously gave a signal to his followers, stationed at strategic points, to attack the Indians without warning. The ensuing attack was a massacre. The cannon balls of the Spaniards plowed through the crowded ranks of the Indians, and from three sides the cavalry bore down upon them. The battle ended in the complete victory of the Spaniards. The Indian sovereign became a prisoner, and two thousand of his followers lay dead or dying in the great square and the adjoining streets of the capital.

After they had gained the capital by this treacherous action, the Spaniards turned their attention to the conquest of the whole Inca Empire. Although the Indians lacked leadership, they continued their resistance against the Spaniards for several years. In 1533, Pizarro made a long march southward against them and captured Cuzco. In the same year, three other expeditions marched into what is now Ecuador. Two of them were led by followers of Pizarro. The third allowed itself to be bought off and withdrew from the country. These expeditions into Ecuador led to the founding of the present-day cities of Quito and Guayaquil. Two years later, a brother of Pizarro led a force of sixty men into what is now known as Bolivia and founded the city of Sucre.

After their conquest of these parts of the Inca Empire, the Spaniards turned their attention toward Chile. In 1535, Almagro, one of the associates of Pizarro, led an unsuccessful expedition into that region. Five years later, Valdivia, another lieutenant of Pizarro, commenced the conquest and settlement of Chile.

The conquerors of the Inca Empire were hard, bold, and unscrupulous men. For years they kept the Spanish settlements in South America in turmoil by their rivalries and dissensions. In 1537, for example, Almagro, feeling that he had been cheated by Pizarro, declared war against his former associate. He was defeated and executed by Pizarro. Then the son of Almagro continued the struggle and revenged his father's death by assassinating Pizarro. Finally, the younger Almagro was defeated and put to death by a brother of Pizarro. In 1548 the Spanish government intervened in the civil war and sent a representative to put an end to the strife.

The Settlement of Other Parts of Spanish America

The Spaniards were rather slow about establishing themselves in the northern part of South America. In 1527, however, they did found a settlement at Coro on the coast of Venezuela. In the following year, Charles V turned the management of the new colony over to the Augsburg banking firm of the Welsers, who retained control of the region for the next eighteen years. Their failure to find precious metals prevented the rapid growth of the colony in population.

In 1536, Quesada led an expedition from the coast of Colombia up the valley of the Magdalena River to the present site of Bogotá. Upon his arrival there, he started a settlement. By his rapid march, Quesada forestalled expeditions that had started from Ecuador and Venezuela. He was thus the founder of the present state of Colombia.

The exploration and settlement of the Plata region was the work of many men. In 1537, after a number of leaders had failed in their attempts to found colonies there, Irala succeeded in making a permanent settlement near Asuncion in the state of Paraguay. In 1581 emigrants from this colony founded Buenos Aires in Argentina. Montevideo, the present capital of Uruguay, was not settled until the eighteenth century.

Settlement of the Philippine Islands

Magellan, as we have seen, discovered the Philippine Islands for Spain. Subsequent investigation revealed that the archipelago was located on the Spanish side of the demarcation line drawn by the Pope. In 1564, accordingly, Philip II, king of Spain, ordered that an expedition should be prepared in Mexico for the purpose of occupying the Philippine Islands. As a result of this order, an expedition was organized under the command of Legaspi. It consisted of one hundred and fifty-eight sailors, two hundred soldiers, and five friars.

After reaching the Philippines, Legaspi showed himself to be a commander of tact and skill. The task of occupying and exploring the islands was made easier by the fact that he found there no organized states. Legaspi made his first settlement on the island of Cebu. In 1571 he founded Manila, later the capital of the Philippines. By the time of his death in 1572, Legaspi had explored and pacified the islands, won the good will of the natives, and driven out the Portuguese. While doing this, he had to contend with famine, mutiny, and neglect by the home government.

After the death of Legaspi, the islands vegetated for a long period. The Spaniards found nothing in them to exploit. For the first twenty-five years, the only contact of the Philippine Islands with the outside world was through two small ships sent out each year from Mexico.

The Effect of the Expansion of Europeans into Spanish America

The exploration and settlement of Spanish America affected both Europe and the Americas. As a result of this movement, two peoples were brought into contact with each other. A relatively small number of white men found themselves settled in the midst of a large Indian population. This contact of the two peoples was bound to have a deep influence on both races.

In the West Indies the coming of the white man brought widespread depopulation. The rapacious Spanish colonists killed off the gentler Indians by overwork and the diseases that they communicated to them. They destroyed the fierce Caribs in battle. This destruction of the natives was not the purpose of the Spanish government. The Spanish authorities had the best of intentions toward the native population. In her zeal for the salvation of the Indians, however, good Queen Isabella permitted the establishment in the West Indies of the encomienda system. By this action, in spite of excellent regulations, the Spanish government gave certain favored white colonists the power to exploit the Indians. As a result, in spite of all that the devoted fathers of the Church did to protect the In-

64

dians, the Spaniards caused a rapid decline of the native population.

In their efforts to save the Indians, the Fathers of the Church resorted to a peculiar expedient. Europeans had been familiar with the institution of Negro slavery for at least half a century. In the hope of sparing the Indians, Las Casas and other Spanish missionaries suggested the substitution of Negro slaves. As a consequence, very early in the history of the West Indies, Negroes were transported to the islands and sold as slaves. In 1516, Charles V sold the privilege of importing four thousand Negroes a year into the islands to a Flemish speculator. Thus was introduced into America Negro slavery, a system destined to cause untold human suffering and to create some very difficult social problems.

On the American mainland the coming of the white man had quite different results. The Spaniards did not go to the American colonies in large numbers. Probably not more than a thousand or fifteen hundred persons emigrated from Spain to the colonies in a single year. Most of the emigrants were single men. The Spanish government did eventually require colonial officials to take their families with them but did little or nothing to encourage the emigration of single women. After the discovery of gold and silver in Mexico and Peru, the colonists tended to abandon the plantations in the West Indies and to rush to the new mining regions where they became, for the most part, merchants, planters, and stock raisers, rather than miners. By 1574 it is estimated that there were about one hundred and sixty thousand Spaniards in America and some two hundred chartered Spanish towns.

On the American mainland the Spanish conquest did not result in the extermination of the thinly scattered Indian population. The Spanish authorities, though, did grant favored individuals the right to exploit the Indians. These persons were granted tracts of land and the custody of a larger or smaller number of Indians. The favored individuals were supposed to group the Indians into villages and towns, provide them with the services of a priest, and protect and civilize them. In return, they were authorized to demand labor services from the Indians.

Nevertheless, on the mainland, the impact of white civilization upon that of the Indians was not so disastrous as it was in the West Indies. It is true that many natives, particularly in the vicinity of the mines, were killed off by overwork, diseases, and wars. In other regions a sufficient number of Indians survived for them to form the dominant strain in the population.

By the end of the first century of emigration, Spanish American society already had assumed its future pattern. At the top of the social scale in Spanish America were the officials sent out from Spain. Next to them in importance were the Creoles, the descendants of Spanish emigrants. The more fortunate members of this class were landholders. For the most part, they lived in the towns, scorned manual labor, and often indulged in degenerating vices. The less successful Creoles were merchants and professional men. The officials and the Creoles seldom constituted as much as ten per cent of the population. The rest of the population was, in the main, partly or wholly Indian. The presence of Spaniards, Negroes, and Indians together had led to their intermarriage and the formation of three distinct classes: mestizos, mulattoes, and zambos. They were considered inferior to the officials and Creoles and constituted the soldiers, the laborers, and the idlers of Spanish America. In many regions, though, the population was almost pure Indian and had been hardly touched by the Spaniards and Negroes.

From the first, the Spanish colonists tended to implant in the New World the civilization they had known in Spain. There was a tendency for the early adventurers to do as they pleased, but the Spanish authorities even then made some effort to establish orderly government in the New World. In this, they had as an incentive the wish to protect the fifth of the revenue which was reserved for the royal government. In 1511 they began to create *audiencias*, a judicial, administrative, advisory institution, which corresponded directly with the Spanish authorities at home and served as a check on the representatives of the royal government in the colonies. In 1535 they set up in Mexico a viceroy, armed with all the authority of the crown. Seven years later, a second viceroy was set up in Peru. On the frontiers were to be found captains general who were higher in rank than the provincial governors. In the towns, local government was in the hands of *cabildos*, or councils. At first, the members of these bodies were appointed; later, they were elected; and finally, they became self-perpetuating bodies. Thus the Spaniards set up in the new world, as in the old, an absolutism.

The Spaniards also transferred from Spain to the New World the all-powerful Church. By the side of the Spanish explorers and conquerors marched brave priests of the Church. Fathers of the Church, too, took a prominent part in the making of settlements. They were able and devout men and endeavored to bring the comforts of religion to both the colonists and the Indians. They did all they could to check the rapacity of the Spanish colonists and to convert, protect, and civilize the Indians. As the settlement of the country progressed, the Church authorities set up bishoprics and monasteries.

On the frontiers the founding of missions kept pace with the establishing of presidios.

In Spanish America the clergy were the guardians and promoters of culture. Although they did found some schools for the Indians, in the main they confined education to the upper classes. In 1553, more than a half century before the founding of the first permanent English settlement in America, the Spaniards established universities at Mexico and Lima. In these institutions they offered courses in the Bible, canon law, profane law, the arts, rhetoric, and grammar. Later, they added medicine to the courses which were given. The clergy attempted to protect the morals of their students by forbidding them to smoke, wear arms, or use colored socks.

The Establishment of a Portuguese Colonial Empire

While the Spaniards were exploring and settling the new western world, the Portuguese were founding a commercial empire in the Eastern Hemisphere. During the greater part of the fifteenth century, they had been feeling their way down the west coast of Africa. In 1486 these discoveries had culminated in the rounding of the Cape of Good Hope by a Portuguese captain named Diaz. This voyage virtually established the fact that India could be reached by sailing across the Indian Ocean. For a decade, however, the Portuguese failed to test this hypothesis.

The success of Columbus stirred the Portuguese to further action. In 1498 the king of Portugal sent Vasco da Gama (1469–1524) with a fleet of ships to see whether the proposed route to India was feasible. Rounding the Cape of Good Hope, he skirted the east coast of Africa to Malindi, and then, under the guidance of an experienced pilot, he struck out boldly across the Indian Ocean to the port of Calicut in India. After staying about six months in Indian waters, Vasco da Gama returned to Portugal with a cargo that paid many times over the cost of the expedition. For his success in carrying out the epoch-making voyage, he was richly rewarded with titles and money.

As they had progressed down the coast of Africa, the Portuguese had occupied points of strategic importance. After reaching India, they continued this policy of occupation. In 1505 they sent out Pedro da Nhaya to found a colony in Sofala in what is now known as Portuguese East Africa. By 1510, the Portuguese had gained control of the sultanates which the Arabs had established in East Africa. After they had acquired control of the region, however, the Portuguese tended to neglect it. They failed to get possession of the gold mines in the interior. They suffered much from native attacks. As a result, the Portuguese never settled in the colony in large numbers.

At first, the Portuguese had no intention of creating an empire in Asia. The Asiatic continent was already densely populated and, consequently, was not suitable for colonization. Therefore, at the beginning, the Portuguese only strove to establish trading relations with the Asiatic continent. But very soon they found themselves forced to adopt a different policy. Before the coming of the Portuguese to India, the Arabs had monopolized the trade of the region. They naturally regarded the Portuguese as intruders. Their hostility forced the Portuguese to win naval supremacy in the Indian Ocean and to fortify their factories or trading posts.

Within a few years, accordingly, the Portuguese had gained control of a series of posts of strategic and commercial importance stretching from Madagascar to China. In 1506 they seized Socotra. This gave them command of the route through the Red Sea. In 1511 they made the port of Goa in India the seat of the viceroy for Portugal and captured Malacca, a post which gave them control of all trade between the Far East and the Indian Ocean. In 1512 they opened up direct trade with the Molucca Islands, the center of the spice trade. In 1515 they took possession of Hormuz at the mouth of the Persian Gulf. In 1517 a Portuguese captain visited Canton and started trade with China. In 1542 three Portuguese accidentally discovered Japan. These exploits gave Portugal, for the time being, a monopoly of trade with Asia and the East Indies.

At its greatest extent, the Portuguese Empire included one important colony in the New World. In 1500 the king of Portugal sent a second expedition to India. For some reason not definitely known, possibly to avoid unfavorable winds and currents off the Guinea coast or perchance in the hope of discovering some new land, Cabral (1460?–1576?), the commander of the expedition, sailed much farther to the west than Vasco da Gama had gone. By doing this, he touched the coast of what is now Brazil. Later, it was established that Brazil lay on the Portuguese side of the papal demarcation line. These two facts gave Portugal a basis for claiming the newly discovered territory.

For many years the Portuguese neglected their colony of Brazil. At first, as the Portuguese posts in India, the East Indies, and the Far East were far more profitable, only a few criminals or an occasional merchant went to Brazil. By 1531, though, the Portuguese felt that they must do something more to establish their claim to the territory and prevent it from falling into the hands of the French and Spanish. In that year, accordingly, in the hope of promoting the settlement of Brazil, the Portuguese government introduced a system which had worked successfully in the Azores and in the Madeira Islands. It gave certain individuals large grants of land. These grants usually included ten leagues of coast line and ran back into the interior for an indefinite distance. The holders of the grants were given extensive powers. In return for these concessions, they were expected to finance the settlement of Brazil.

The plan did not prove to be a success. Some of the holders of grants lacked the needed resources or encountered misfortunes. The greatest defect of the plan was its failure to provide a central authority for the guidance of the new settlements. Each holder of a grant had to struggle independently against hostile Indians and intrusive foreigners. In 1548 the Portuguese government revoked the political power of the holders of grants and sent out a governor. Under this new plan the colony was more prosperous. A succession of governors founded new settlements, established a militia, defeated the Indians, and thwarted the efforts of foreigners, the French particularly, to get a foothold in Brazil.

The Union of the Two Colonial Empires

In 1581 the vast Spanish and Portuguese colonial empires came under one ruler. The union of Spain and Portugal had long been dreamed of by both royal families, but local pride and dynastic interests had, up to that time, prevented its realization. In 1578, however, the situation changed. The king of Portugal died. His successor was a sickly, elderly ecclesiastic. As a result, a host of claimants arose who commenced to intrigue for the succession. The most successful of the claimants was Philip II of Spain. In 1581 he succeeded in crushing those who opposed his rule. This success gave him the difficult task of defending two great colonial and commercial empires.

The Attack on the Spanish Colonial Monopoly

Neither Spain nor Portugal could expect to maintain their claim to monopolize the non-European world unchallenged. Other powers would not be likely to remain mere spectators while Spain and Portugal grew rich and powerful from their overseas possessions. Almost from the first, rival powers sought to participate in the discovery and exploitation of the newly discovered lands in Africa, Asia, and America.

During the sixteenth century, France sent out a number of explorers. In 1524 the king of France instructed Verrazano to find a northwest passage to India. In carrying out his instruction, he seems to have sailed along the coast of North America from New York Harbor to Newfoundland. Ten years later the French sovereign sent out Cartier, who sailed up the St. Lawrence River to the site of the present city of Quebec. In 1541 the king of France entrusted Robeval with the task of founding a settlement at that point.

Somewhat later than the French, the English began to attack the Spanish monopoly. In 1563, Captain John Hawkins (1532–1594) of the port of Plymouth obtained three hundred Negroes on the west coast of Africa, crossed the Atlantic, stopped at Haiti, sold his human cargo as slaves, and loaded his ships with colonial produce. Before he could get away, however, the Spanish authorities seized two of his ships. This experience and those undergone on two subsequent voyages made Hawkins and his even more famous nephew, Francis Drake (1535–1595), implacable enemies of Spain.

The two men became leaders of a group of sea captains who waged continuous war on Spain and Spanish ships and colonies. Their most famous exploit was the circumnavigation by Drake of the earth for a second time. In 1578 this famous captain sailed with several ships across the Atlantic, passed through the Strait of Magellan, skirted the western coast of South America, crossed the Pacific, came around Africa, and returned to England. During the voyage, Drake plundered many Spanish ships and did some trading in the East Indies.

In the last quarter of the sixteenth century, the English took a more active part in the exploration of America and made unsuccessful efforts to found settlements there. Many almost forgotten captains took part in the exploration of the American coast. Sir Humphrey Gilbert (1539–1583) and his half brother, Sir Walter Raleigh (1552–1618), made important attempts to found settlements. Though they failed, these attempts made Englishmen more conscious of the problem of colonization and the difficulties that must be overcome.

The Effect of European Expansion on Europe

The expansion of Europe overseas affected European society in many ways. For one thing, it greatly changed the commerce of Europe. It widened the field of European commerce, opened up new routes of trade, and introduced new commodities to the marts of Europe. The discovery of large stocks of gold and silver brought into general use among the upper classes cloth of gold, silver, taffeta, rings, silver plate, watches, and chains. The wearing of such jewels as emeralds, turquoises, opals, and pearls became more common. New foods and drinks were introduced that greatly changed the diet and the social customs of Europeans. These foods included potatoes, tomatoes, maize, sugar, molasses, peanuts, chocolate, cocoa, sassafras, rum, and lime juice. From America the early explorers brought back tobacco and the custom of smoking.

The conquest of Mexico and Peru and their great stocks of gold and silver profoundly changed the value of money. Much more money rapidly came into circulation. This decreased the buying power of the coins in use and raised prices two, three, and even four hundred per cent and changed the economy of European society. Seignioral dues, for example, that had formerly supported the nobles, declined so much in value that they impoverished the nobles and became little more than a source of irritation to the peasants. The fact that the purchasing power of money varied from country to country only made the situation worse.

The new discoveries caused a shift of the economic center of Europe. Before the voyages of Columbus and Vasco da Gama, the lands around the Mediterranean Sea had been the center of European trade and finance. The Atlantic coast was on the outskirts of Europe. After the completion of these epoch-making voyages, commercial centers like Venice, Genoa, and Florence tended to stand still or actually to decline in importance, while ports along the Atlantic coast, such as Seville, Lisbon, Antwerp, Amsterdam, London, Bristol, Hamburg, and Bremen, gradually became the most important centers of European trade and industry.

The new discoveries, too, had the effect of strengthening the rising monarchies, especially those of Spain and Portugal. The central governments of these states demanded a share of the revenues derived from the new colonies. The Spanish government, for example, received a fifth of the yield of the mines of Mexico and Peru. With the royal fifth and other fees received from the colonies, the king of Spain could employ reliable mercenary troops instead of uncertain feudal levies and loyal officials instead of feudal nobles who put their own interests first. These changes tended to strengthen the monarchies.

In the case of Portugal, it is generally conceded that the acquisition of a colonial empire had on the whole a bad effect on the country. The opportunity to acquire wealth in colonial service tended to discredit manual labor and ordinary occupations at home. Townsmen sought positions in the colonies. Peasants abandoned agriculture and crowded into the towns. Slaves and large estates replaced the peasants and small holdings. Those who went overseas died in large numbers from wounds, shipwrecks, and tropical diseases. The general effect of the acquisition of colonies was a depopulation of Portugal.

Both the Spanish and Portuguese governments tried to supervise carefully the exploitation of their colonial empires. As early as 1503, the Spanish government established in Seville the famous *Casa de Contratacion*. This institution became a school of navigation and map making, issued licenses to emigrants, registered merchandise, collected duties, took charge of the royal revenues, arranged for the sale of colonial products, and kept a record of the courses followed and the places visited by ships sailing to the colonies. These records kept by the *Casa de Contratacion* have been preserved and constitute an important historical source for the history of expansion of Europe. In 1511 the institution was placed under the supervision of a Council of the Indies. This administrative body proposed to the sovereigns of Spain the names of prospective viceroys, generals, captains, judges of *audiencias,* bishops, and other officials; attended to matters of colonial finance; served as a court; and attempted, at least, to supervise Indian affairs.

These Spanish institutions and the corresponding ones in Portugal carefully regulated colonial commerce. From the first, trade with the colonies was limited to subjects and such foreigners as the two governments might license. Even authorized traders were most carefully regulated. After 1566, Spanish ships engaged in colonial trade always sailed in fleets. Usually, they went to the colonies and returned to Spain only twice during the year. In America the ships of these fleets came only to a few specified ports. Usually, the fleet sailed from Seville to the West Indies. Upon its arrival there, one part of the fleet went to the Isthmus of Panama and another to Vera Cruz. Upon their return, the ships assembled at Havana and then went back to Spain. These cumbersome regulations hampered the economic development of the colonies and gave rise to much dissatisfaction.

Another important result of the new discoveries and settlements was the growth of the middle class in Western Europe. This was not so true in Spain and Portugal as in France, England, and the Netherlands. In Spain and Portugal the increased trade was too hedged around with regulations and made too little appeal to the average Spaniard and Portuguese to permit much growth of the middle class. The new commerce, consequently, fell largely into the hands of foreigners. In France, England, and the Netherlands the ultimate effect of the new trade was the development of the middle class. The speculative character of the new trade called for the rise of a class that specialized in banking and the exchange of goods. It grew as the volume of commercial transactions increased.

The new discoveries, likewise, affected profoundly the minds and imaginations of Europeans. They brought to their attention new lands and unknown peoples. They offered the adventurous prospects for bold and possibly profitable undertakings. They offered the religious the opportunity to promote the salvation of many new peoples. They gave the studious the material that led some to religious skepticism and others to the study of comparative religions.

The voyages of discovery made in the fifteenth and sixteenth centuries thus had a great influence on Europe and on the newly found lands. They led to the discovery of two new continents and to a greater knowledge of Africa, India, the East Indies, and the Far East. Spain and Portugal attempted to divide the non-European lands between them and to monopolize them. Spain gained for the time being the greater part of the two Americas and the Philippine Islands; Portugal acquired Brazil and a series of strategic posts in Africa, India, the East Indies, and the Far East. This expansion of European peoples overseas had many results. In America it led to the colonization of Brazil and Spanish America by Europeans and the transfer of many of the institutions of Europe to the American colonies. In Europe it led to a widening of the area of commerce, the opening of new routes of trade, the introduction of new commercial products, great changes in the value of money, a shift of the economic center of Europe, a strengthening of the rising monarchies, and a growth of the middle class. Toward the end of the sixteenth century the two empires, which had come under the sovereignty of Philip II, found their monopolies seriously challenged by the Netherlands, France, and England.

CHAPTER 6

European Politics, 1494–1559

For a long time the political leaders of Europe did not fully realize the importance of the discoveries being made by the navigators sailing under the auspices of Spain and Portugal. While whole empires were being won and lost overseas, they continued to center their principal attention on Europe. There, the rulers and their advisers were engaged in the interesting task of building the modern European states. By the end of the fifteenth century, the sovereigns of France, Spain, England, and Austria had made great progress toward this objective. This made them rivals for the acquisition of desirable border provinces and plunged them almost unwittingly into the fascinating game of international politics.

The French Invasion of Italy

The most advanced of the rising European states was France. In 1493 its young sovereign, Charles VIII, had just come to the French throne. He was not so astute as his crafty father, Louis XI, or as his sister, who had acted as royal regent during his minority. If he had been, he would have stayed at home and continued to build up the royal power and rounded out his territories. He was, however, young and intrigued by the idea of playing a leading role in international politics. He was surrounded by youthful and ambitious nobles who were eager for the glory to be gained in a foreign war. Before him lay the Italian Peninsula, weakened by its division among a number of small and jealous states. Accordingly, Charles VIII abandoned the task of the further building up of the French state and embarked on an invasion of Italy. By his action he involved France and the other states of Western Europe in a long series of international wars.

Charles VIII had little trouble in finding an excuse for his interference in Italy. He discovered most easily that he had dynastic claims on the kingdom of Naples. He bought off his rivals, Ferdinand of Aragon and Henry VII of England, by important concessions and then led into Italy an army, composed of Swiss pikemen, German *Landsknechte,* and French heavy cavalry and supplied with one hundred and forty of the newly invented cannon.

In the Italian Peninsula, Charles VIII and his army met almost no

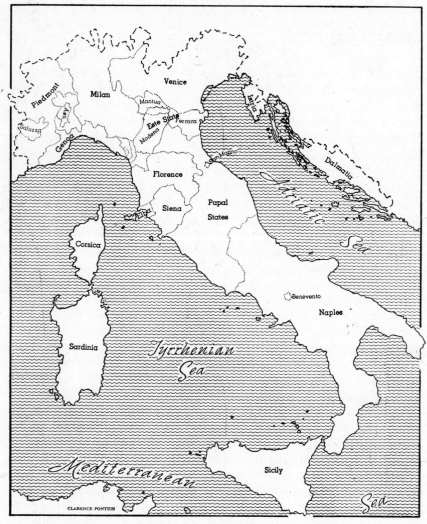

Italy on the Eve of the French Invasion—1494

armed opposition. Their march southward through Italy was an almost bloodless military parade. The prestige of the Swiss pikemen, of the French army, and of the new French artillery was high, and the little states of Italy felt that resistance was useless. As a result, Charles VIII and his army soon mastered the kingdom of Naples.

The very ease of the French victory, however, caused widespread alarm. The other Italian states began to fear that they might meet the same fate as had just overtaken the kingdom of Naples. The rivals of Charles VIII in Western Europe, especially Ferdinand of

Aragon and Maximilian I of Austria, felt that the success of the French endangered their interests. Aragon had for some time been following a policy that would eventually gain for it control of the Western Mediterranean. Austria had shadowy claims to most of northern Italy and especially to the duchy of Milan. Within three months, consequently, Charles VIII and his victorious army found themselves in a precarious position. With the aim of expelling the French from the peninsula, the republic of Venice, and the duchy of Milan, the Pope, Ferdinand of Aragon, and Maximilian of Austria formed a league. Their action forced Charles VIII and his army to abandon the kingdom of Naples and return to France.

While Charles VIII had nothing to show for his expenditure of blood and treasure, his invasion of Italy had a malign influence on his successors. Each of them thought that he could invade Italy with ease and gain important conquests. In 1498, Charles VIII was killed in an accident before he could undertake another expedition. His cousin and successor, Louis XII, however, was intrigued by the Italian political situation. In 1499 and again in 1500 he undertook expeditions against both the kingdom of Naples and the duchy of Milan. In conquering the Neapolitan kingdom, he had the cooperation of Ferdinand of Aragon. Almost immediately, through the treachery of his ally, Louis XII lost his hold on the kingdom of Naples, but he retained possession of the duchy of Milan for fourteen years. For the moment, it seemed as if France and Spain were going to share the hegemony of the peninsula between them.

In 1503 a new factor entered the Italian political situation. In that year Julius II (1443–1513) was elected pope and occupied the papal throne for the ensuing decade. He proved to be far more concerned with the temporal than the spiritual interests of the Church. His political ambition brought him into conflict with the various states of Europe. As a result, he organized leagues composed of states that for the time being shared his views concerning Italian affairs. Aided by these temporary combinations of powers, Julius II attacked in turn Venice and France. In 1513 his policy culminated in the crushing defeat of the French by Swiss mercenaries and their expulsion from Italy.

This defeat of France was followed almost immediately by the death of Louis XII of France and the accession of his cousin and son-in-law, Francis I (1494–1547), to the French throne. The new sovereign of France was only twenty, but his subjects and contemporaries considered him well-fitted to rule France. In reality, he was more interested in the prestige and privileges of his position than in the true good of his state. He began his reign, therefore, with an attack on the duchy of Milan. In 1515, at Marignano in northern Italy, his troops crushed the hitherto invincible but insubordinate Swiss pikemen. This victory gave the young monarch control of the duchy of Milan, the key to the Italian Peninsula, and seemed to stabilize Italian politics. The Swiss concluded a peace with France that proved permanent. France and Spain divided Italy between them. Europe seemed to have entered upon a period of peace.

The Threat of Universal Monarchy

The political calm that seemed on the point of settling down over Europe was soon broken. In 1516, the very year after the great French victory at Marignano, Ferdinand of Aragon died. Three years later, Maximilian I of Austria died. The death of these two important rulers threatened Europe with the rise of a universal monarchy. In playing the game of international politics, the sovereigns of Spain and Austria had arranged a series of marriages that suddenly made a young man of nineteen ruler of four important European states. First, the marriage of Ferdinand and Isabella had paved the way for the union of the kingdoms of Aragon and of Castile and Leon into the kingdom of Spain. Then the marriage of Maximilian I of Austria and Mary of Burgundy provided for the cooperation of those two states. Finally, Philip the Handsome, heir of Maximilian I and Mary of Burgundy, and Joanna, heiress of Ferdinand and Isabella, were married and had two sons, Charles and Ferdinand. This series of marriages made the older of these sons, known in history as Charles I of Spain and Charles V in the Empire, the prospective heir of the four states of Aragon and its dependencies, Castile and Leon with their great colonial empire, Austria, and Burgundy. The death of his two grandfathers, Ferdinand of Aragon and Maximilian I of Austria, brought him to actual power.

Although he was already ruler of four powerful states by hereditary right, Charles coveted still another title. Since 1438 it had been customary for the seven electors of the Holy Roman Empire to choose a member of the Austrian royal house, the Habsburg family, as emperor. Accordingly, upon the death of his grandfather, Maximilian I, the young Charles put forward his claim to the vacant Imperial throne on the ground that he belonged to the Habsburg family. At the same time, two competitors for the honor, Francis I, king of France, and Henry VIII, sovereign of England, appeared and inaugurated campaigns for the votes of the seven electors. In the ensuing contest, bribery played almost as great a part as historical tradition.

The three candidates for the Imperial title had youth in common, but they differed greatly in character and circumstances. As later events were clearly to show, Prince Charles, the Habsburg candidate, was grave, cold, tenacious, ambitious and calculating, simple and modest in manner, and master of himself on all occasions. In a sense he was religious, but the religious strain in his character scarcely affected his personal conduct. His French rival, Francis I, spoiled by an admiring mother and sister, was gay as long as his affairs went well, was brave but thoughtless, ready to flirt, at least, with new Protestant doctrines, and genuinely anxious to promote the spread of arts and letters in France. In most things he was rather superficial. The third candidate for the Imperial title, Henry VIII, was in his youth considered by his contemporaries an attractive figure. He, too, was gay, given to athletic exercises, well educated for a sovereign, and fond of music. In addition, he was the beneficiary of his father's wise and careful administration. All three claimants seemed to have the world before them.

In the end, Prince Charles was the victor in the struggle for the Imperial title. Historical tradition combined with a free use of money made him Holy Roman emperor under the title of Charles V. His accession to the Imperial throne, however, gave him prestige rather than power. He was strong, not because he had been elected Holy Roman emperor but because he had inherited the resources of his four hereditary states. As emperor he had little additional income or authority.

The Early Years of Emperor Charles V in Spain

The new ruler of Spain was not a Spaniard. He was born at Ghent and grew up in the Netherlands. As a result, his subjects in the Low Countries felt that he was one of themselves; the Spaniards, that he was a foreigner. After the death of his father, Philip the Handsome, in 1506, he had ruled nominally both Castile and Leon and the Burgundian state, but, in reality, his grandfather, Maximilian I, ruled the Burgundian state and his grandfather, Ferdinand, Castile and Leon. Prince Charles did not come to Spain until 1517.

Upon arriving there, the new Spanish sovereign found himself confronted by a difficult situation. He knew neither the language nor the condition of the country. There was, in fact, as yet no Spanish state. There were, instead, still the two separate states of Aragon and of Castile and Leon. Each of these states had its own separate institutions. As long as Ferdinand and Isabella had occupied the thrones of the two states, they had followed a common policy. After the death of Isabella in 1504, however, there was a great deal of trouble over the question of who should exercise the royal authority in Castile and Leon. Queen Isabella had intended that the royal authority should be wielded by her husband, Ferdinand of Aragon, as regent for her mentally incapable daughter, Joanna. This plan, however, was not carried out. Philip the Handsome, the husband of Joanna and the son-in-law of Ferdinand and Isabella, insisted on acting as regent for his wife in Castile. As a result, after 1504, there were again the two entirely separate states of Aragon and of Castile and Leon.

This arrangement, however, lasted only two years. In 1506, Philip the Handsome suddenly died. This left Castile and Leon without an actual ruler. There seemed to the leaders of the kingdom nothing to be done except to invite Ferdinand of Aragon to assume the regency of Castile and Leon. From 1506 until the death of Ferdinand in 1516, therefore, the two states of Aragon and of Castile and Leon, again, as in the days of Queen Isabella, followed a common policy. Under the able rule of Ferdinand, the royal power continued to increase, the turbulent nobles were held in check, the Spanish holdings in North Africa were extended, Aragon increased its territorial possessions in southern Italy, and the part of Navarre on the Spanish side of the Pyrenees Mountains was conquered and occupied.

Prince Charles, the successor of his grandfather, made a very bad beginning in Spain. In reality, he was not the lawful sovereign of Castile and Leon but only regent for his mentally incapable mother, Joanna. Upon his arrival in Spain in 1517, however, he promptly demanded that the rights of his mother should be disregarded and that he should be recognized as the legal sovereign of both Aragon and Castile and Leon. His brusque demand shocked the punctilious Castilians.

The new sovereign of Spain, too, came surrounded by courtiers from the Netherlands. Soon after he had landed on Spanish soil, Charles began to turn over to these rapacious foreigners the offices and revenues of the country. This policy first led to protests and finally to still more vigorous action. In 1520, accordingly, after the new sovereign had left Spain to be crowned in Germany as emperor, many of the Spanish cities rose in revolt. They objected to the mounting cost of government and demanded more autonomy. Their revolt reached serious proportions but was finally repressed.

The Beginning of the Rule of Charles V in Germany

Upon his arrival in Germany, Charles V was confronted by a delicate international situation. There were many causes for tension between Charles V, with his widely scattered possessions, and Francis I, king of France. The French monarch was naturally bitter over the outcome of the recent Imperial election. There was, also, the old quarrel over the seizure of the Burgundian border provinces by Louis XI of France after the marriage of Maximilian I of Austria and Mary of Burgundy. Then in 1512, Spain had seized the part of the little kingdom of Navarre on the southern slopes of the Pyrenees Mountains. Lastly, there was the danger that France would be encircled by the possessions of a ruler who threatened to dominate Europe.

The international situation demanded great wisdom and caution on the part of the young Emperor. During his journey by sea from Spain to the Netherlands, therefore, Charles V stopped in England in the hope of winning the support of Henry VIII in the approaching struggle. In this quest, the young Emperor was successful. For this achievement there were economic and personal reasons. For one thing, the Netherlands was the chief market for English wool. Then, too, the wife of Henry VIII was the aunt of Charles V. Lastly, Wolsey, the chief adviser of Henry VIII, felt that the emperor could further the English minister's ambition to be pope better than could the king of France. For all these reasons, Henry VIII finally allied himself with Charles V.

Upon his arrival in Germany, the Emperor found many problems awaiting him. As his predecessors, he hoped to transform his position of merely nominal power into one of substantial authority. This would involve him in a struggle with the princes of the Empire in whom most of the political power was vested. In addition, at this time a religious revolt threatened the unity of the Empire. Then, too, both as emperor and as heir of Ferdinand of Aragon, Charles V was interested in Italian affairs. Finally, the Turks, by their advances, were menacing the Danube Valley.

The first act of Charles V upon reaching Germany was the summoning of an Imperial diet. It convened (1520) at Worms on the Rhine River. It was an imposing assemblage. It brought together the Emperor, his principal advisers, the heads of the German states, and great prelates of the Empire. In spite of its membership, however, it accomplished almost nothing.

At this time, though, Charles V took one important action. He handed over to his younger brother, Ferdinand, the actual administration of the original Habsburg lands in the Danube Valley. This relieved him of a part of the many problems facing him.

The Turkish Menace and the Development of the Habsburg State

The chief problem of Ferdinand proved to be the Turks. As early as the fourteenth century, the Ottoman Turks had gained a foothold in the Balkans. After that success, they exerted increasing pressure on Christian Europe. After establishing themselves in the Balkan Peninsula, they had captured one strategic point after the other. In 1432 they had invaded Hungary for the first time. They found that country ill-prepared to withstand their repeated attacks. The king, a sovereign of Polish extraction, who was also king of Bohemia, had no real authority. Political power was really vested in a small body of nobles and prelates, who were mainly intent on the continuance of their privileges and were too ignorant to see the dangers threatening them. They maintained swarms of armed retainers that were dangerous only to the weak and to each other. They were of little value against a well-armed and disciplined invader. Many of the Hungarian lesser nobility had even fled to Turkey in order to escape the tyranny of the governing clique. A number of the Hungarian towns were involved in feuds with the nobility. As a result, they had lost their charters and were declining in prosperity. The royal troops were unpaid and neglected. The frontier fortresses were falling to pieces through lack of attention.

In 1521, the Turks began a new campaign against Hungary. They opened their military operations by capturing the city of Belgrade. In 1526 they won a victory that decided the fate of Hungary for nearly two centuries. At the battle of Mohacs the Turkish forces attacked the king of Hungary and a small ill-prepared army. The struggle ended in the death of the king and most of his followers. This defeat gave the Turks control of the greater part of Hungary.

The years following the battle of Mohacs were a troubled period for the kingdom of Hungary and its peoples. Deprived by the battle of Mohacs of their legitimate sovereign, one of the leading nobles, John Zapolya, voivode of the semi-independent district of Transylvania, convoked a diet. The diet elected him king of Hungary. This action, however, did not settle the question of who was to rule Hungary. There was another claimant for the royal title. Archduke Ferdinand, brother of Charles V and brother-in-law of the slain king of Hungary, also put forward claims to the thrones of both Bohemia and Hungary. In Bohemia, Ferdinand had little difficulty in gaining recognition of his asserted rights. In Hungary he only succeeded in having his claim to the throne confirmed by a diet that in reality represented a very small part of the kingdom of Hungary.

As a result of having elected two kings, Hungary was plunged into a devastating civil war. In 1529, the Turks, who supported the claims of Zapolya, marched up the Danube Valley to the very walls of Vienna and almost captured the city. In 1538 the two claimants for the Hungarian throne finally reached a temporary settlement. This agree-

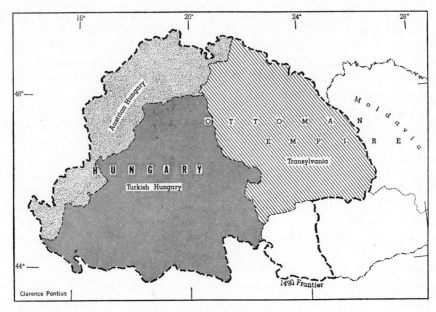

Hungary after 1526

ment gave the royal title and control of about two thirds of the kingdom of Hungary to Zapolya and assigned the remaining third of the kingdom to Archduke Ferdinand, the Habsburg claimant. This decision gave Ferdinand control of the original Habsburg lands, as regent of Charles V, and of the kingdom of Bohemia and one-third of the kingdom of Hungary, as king in his own right. The union of these three territories in the hands of Prince Ferdinand laid the foundations of the modern state of Austria.

The peace established by the agreement of 1538 did not last long. Two years later Zapolya died. This led to a renewal of hostilities. Disregarding the agreement of 1538, Zapolya had attempted to leave the kingdom of Hungary to his son. This caused Ferdinand of Habsburg to attack the younger Zapolya, and the Turks to invade Hungary again. The revived civil war did not end until 1547. By an agreement effected at that time, Hungary was divided into three parts. Ferdinand, the Habsburg claimant, was given a strip of territory along the western border of Hungary contiguous to his other possessions. The younger Zapolya received Transylvania in northeastern Hungary and sixteen additional counties. The Turks obtained southeastern Hungary, the largest share. This division of Hungary lasted about one hundred and fifty years.

82

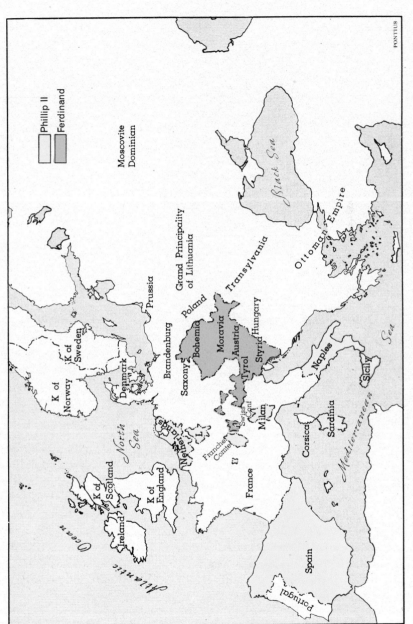

PONTIUS

Phillip II

Ferdinand

Moscovite
Dominian

Atlantic Ocean

Ireland

Scotland

K of
Norway

North
Sea

K of
Sweden

Denmark

K of
England

Netherl.

France

Franche
Comté

Swiss
Conf.

Milan

Spain

Portugal

Mediterranean
Sea

Corsica

Sardinia

Naples

Sicily

Brandenburg

Saxony

Poland

Prussia

Bohemia

Moravia

Austria

Tyrol

Styria

Hungary

Grand Principality
of Lithuania

Transylvania

Ottoman Empire

Black Sea

The Division of the Empire of Charles V, 1555

The Struggle of France against Encirclement

In the meantime, Charles V had been carrying on a struggle with France. The conflict began in 1520 and continued intermittently for forty-nine years. Involved in the struggle at various times were the hereditary possessions of Charles V, France, England, the German princes, and the little states of Italy. Out of the welter of incidents, three important facts now stand out. Charles V was struggling for predominance in Europe. France was fighting for its national existence. England was merely trying to play an important role in international politics.

The war began with invasions of northern and southern France by the troops of Charles V. These invasions were soon repulsed. They were followed by a rash French attack on northern Italy that culminated in 1525 in a disastrous defeat of the French at Pavia. This defeat had important consequences. Francis I, the king of France, was captured and taken to Spain. In order to obtain his freedom, he made important concessions to his captor, Charles V, which the French sovereign never actually carried out. Then, in order to rally all the influential elements of the French nation around himself in the crisis, Francis I abandoned the flirtation which he had been carrying on with the French Protestants and the religious reformers and became an orthodox supporter of the Church. These concessions were embodied in the Treaty of Madrid (1526).

This agreement did not, however, end the war. The striking success of Charles V alarmed Europe. Both the allies and the enemies of Charles V rose against him and formed the so-called Holy League (1526). In the succeeding struggle, as always, Charles V was hampered by his lack of money to pay the mercenary troops under his command. In 1527 his unpaid mutinous soldiers took matters into their own hands. They marched on Rome and sacked the city. Their action only eliminated the Pope from the conflict. Released because of certain promises, the faithless Francis I, as soon as he was free, continued the struggle for two more years. On the whole, though, the remaining fighting was indecisive.

By 1529 the Emperor was ready to make peace. In that year he concluded with France the Treaty of Barcelona and with the Pope the Treaty of Cambrai. For taking this action, he had a number of reasons. England and France were drawing together. His brother Ferdinand was so engrossed with his personal policies in Bohemia and Hungary and with the threat of Turkish attack that he could give little support to Charles V. As a sign of the general reconciliation, the Pope placed the Imperial crown on the head of Charles V at Bologna.

In the latter part of the reign of Charles V, the war between the Emperor and Francis I of France was twice renewed. In the years from 1536 to 1537 and from 1542 to 1544, the ever-present tension broke out again into open warfare. The two later wars were destructive but not decisive. In the main they left the political situation unchanged. The duchy of Milan and northern Italy, therefore, remained in the hands of the Emperor.

Thus, Charles V never established the universal monarchy that his contemporaries feared. In spite of his vast possessions and his great revenues from the mines of Mexico and Peru, two conditions hampered and upset his plans. The Emperor was chronically short of money, and he never could really settle any of the problems created by his large and widely scattered possessions before others arose that demanded immediate attention. As a result, he was constantly moving from one part of his dominions to another and never was able to solve completely any of his almost innumerable problems.

The Campaigns against Africa

Another of the problems that plagued Charles V was Northern Africa. The Moslem inhabitants of this region lived largely by piracy and constantly harassed the southern shores and the shipping of Western Europe. In an effort to ward off these attacks, the coast line of Western Europe was studded with fortified towers. In spite of these defences, however, the Moslem pirates every year captured and enslaved hundreds of Christian Europeans.

This situation became even worse upon the rise of Barbarossa II to power. This redoubtable pirate chieftain gained control of Algiers and Tunis, put himself nominally under the suzerainty of the sultan of Turkey and intensified the attacks on Christian ships and towns.

Finally, Charles V felt that something must be done about this situation. In 1535, accordingly, he organized an expedition against Northern Africa and attacked Tunis. The principal result of this campaign was the freeing of a great many, some say twenty thousand, Christian captives.

The German Problem

During the greater part of his reign, Charles V was unable even to attempt to settle the problems pressing for attention in Germany. After the conclusion of peace with France in 1544, however, the Emperor thought that the moment had at last come when he could do something decisive about the German situation. He felt that he could at the same time crush the Protestant Revolt and get real control over the German princes.

The chief obstacle to the realization of his plans was the German princes. In 1547, however, a number of ambitious Protestant princes, Maurice of Ducal Saxony being the most prominent, turned temporarily to the side of the Emperor. Without any warning, Maurice invaded the territory of his relative, the Elector of Saxony. The opponents of Charles V, on the other hand, failed to cooperate with each other. As a result, they were forced one by one to make their peace with the Emperor. The Elector of Saxony was even forced to surrender his electoral title to the treacherous Maurice. Other rulers were punished by fines and imprisonment.

Before much time had passed, however, the German princes commenced to realize the danger of the policy they had adopted. Fearful of putting too much power into the hands of Charles V, they began to range themselves again against the Emperor. As a consequence of their new policy, they refused to choose Philip, son of Charles V, as emperor-elect. In his place they chose as heir to the Imperial throne the son of Ferdinand of Habsburg. In 1552 the treacherous Maurice placed himself at the head of an open revolt against the Emperor. This put Charles V in a position of great peril.

The danger of the Emperor's situation was increased by the policy of France. Henry II, the son and successor of Francis I, joined the ranks of the enemies of Charles V. In return for his military aid, the German princes, hostile to Charles V, allowed the king of France to occupy the three important border fortresses of Metz, Toul, and Verdun.

In the end, Charles V was forced to admit that his plans could never be carried out. The treacherous Maurice just missed capturing the Emperor at Innsbruck. With considerable difficulty, the sick and weary Emperor escaped from Innsbruck, made his way through the Brenner Pass, and reached safety at Villach. Hopeless about improving his position, he authorized his brother Ferdinand to open negotiations with the German princes. These negotiations resulted in the conclusion of the preliminary Peace of Passau (1552). By the terms of this agreement, Charles V consented to liberate one important German prince from captivity, to restore the freedom of the German nation, to eliminate Spanish influences from Germany, and to conclude a perpetual peace between the warring religious factions.

The settlement of the details of the religious agreement were left to a diet. The proposed diet, however, did not meet for three years because of the unwillingness of some of the German princes to accept the Treaty of Passau and the difficulty of compromising the demands of the various religious factions. In 1555 an agreement known as the Peace of Augsburg was finally reached. Its provisions will be given in the next chapter.

The Plans of Charles V for His Son, Philip II

The failure of all his plans discouraged Charles V. He felt worn-out by his many campaigns and by his excesses at the table. Though he was only a little over fifty, he thought of himself as an old man. He began, therefore, to transfer his hopes and his offices to his son, known in history as Philip II. In 1553, consequently, he arranged a marriage for his son that gave promise of advancing his political interests and of solving one of the most troublesome problems of his widely scattered empire. In that year Mary Tudor, oldest daughter of Henry VIII, ascended the English throne. If Charles V could arrange a marriage between his son Philip and the new English queen, he saw an opportunity to strengthen his power, to assure the sea route from Spain to the Netherlands, and to aggrandize the Habsburg family. As Mary was a close relative and a Catholic, the Emperor had comparatively little trouble in bringing about the proposed marriage.

Though Mary herself raised no objections to his proposals, her shrewd advisers drove a hard bargain with the Imperial negotiators. They extorted from Charles V a promise that in case Mary should die without issue Philip would make no claim to the English succession, that any child born to the marriage should inherit both England and the Netherlands, and that Philip should not involve England in his wars with France. By these provisions, the English negotiators hoped that they had safeguarded English interests.

After he had made this rather brilliant provision for the future of his son, Charles V decided to retire from public affairs. In 1555 he began his withdrawal from his various offices by abdicating the crown of the Netherlands. In a moving scene, made famous by Motley, the American historian, he handed over to his son his authority in the Low Countries. After this beginning he quickly abdicated his other hereditary thrones. This gave Philip rule over Spain and its dependencies in Italy and the New World and over the Burgundian kingdom.

Charles V was unable to bequeath one of his titles to his son. The Imperial title was elective. The German princes were unwilling to make Philip ruler of the Empire. Their attitude forced Charles V to leave to his brother Ferdinand the succession to the Imperial title and the original Habsburg possessions in the Danube Valley which he had long ruled as regent. This division of the lands of Charles V created two Habsburg dynasties, the Austrian and the Spanish Habsburgs.

First Measures of Philip II

Philip II, the head of the Spanish Habsburgs, had been born in 1527. He was, therefore, twenty-eight years of age when he took the place of his father as ruler. In contrast to his father, he was a Spaniard in all respects save looks. He was not very well-educated. At a time when most sovereigns spoke several languages, he knew only Spanish. He impressed most of those whom he met as being cold and grave. On the journeys that he had made to various provinces of his father's great empire, he had made a poor impression. Though he was slight in build, he was very dignified and he often disconcerted those presented to him by his piercing glance. Like most Spaniards of the time, he was an intolerant Catholic. He was very suspicious of those around him. In the conduct of public affairs he was very diligent but procrastinating. If one can judge from the pictures he gathered to ornament his famous palace, the Escorial, he would seem to have had some taste in artistic matters. At the time of his accession to the various thrones of his father, he had already been married twice. At the age of sixteen he had been united to a Portuguese princess, but she had died within a year and a half in giving birth to a son, Don Carlos, who was destined to give his father much trouble. Then in 1554, as we have seen, he had married his cousin, Mary Tudor.

His contemporaries differed widely in their judgments concerning him. His subjects loved and admired him greatly. Foreigners feared and hated him. His subjects liked him because he was a typical Spaniard. Foreigners based their judgments of him on highly prejudiced and unreliable sources. In reality, he had the faults and virtues of the Spaniards of his own time.

Though devoted to the interest of his church, the new ruler of Spain started his reign by quarreling with the Pope, the head of his own church. This strange development had a number of causes. The Pope was a personal enemy of Philip and Spain and had no intention of allowing himself to become a puppet in the hands of the Spanish sovereign. On the other hand, Philip II, in spite of his orthodoxy and zeal for the Church, did not have any intention of allowing the Pope to encroach on his temporal prerogatives. This situation easily gave rise to a quarrel.

The Pope promptly put his highly placed opponent under the ban of the Church. In no uncertain terms he denounced him as "engendered in iniquity, Philip II of Austria, son of the so-called Emperor Charles, pretended King of Spain, following in the footsteps of his father, competing with him in infamy, and qualifying himself as perjurer, schismatic, and rebel." Unperturbed by this blast, Philip II defended himself as best he could and finally forced his opponent to retract his statement.

The death of Francis I in 1547 and the abdication of Charles V in 1555 did not end the struggle between Spain and France. The forces that had caused a series of four devastating wars between the two sovereigns continued to influence events under their successors, Henry II of France and Philip II of Spain. Accordingly, in 1557 war broke out again between the two powers. The conflict was marked by a number of important military events. In Italy a significant campaign was waged between the French forces led by the Duke of Guise and the Spanish troops commanded by the Duke of Alba. In northern France there was a decisive campaign which ended in a great Spanish victory at St. Quentin, that the procrastinating Philip II failed to follow up by a march on Paris. An incident of this campaign was the English loss of Calais, the last English foothold on the continent. Notwithstanding the stipulations made at the time of their marriage, Philip II had succeeded in persuading his wife Mary to bring England into the struggle between France and Spain.

By 1559, both sides in the conflict were again ready for peace. France had warded off the threat of universal monarchy and had even occupied the border fortresses of Metz, Toul, and Verdun. In 1558 Mary Tudor died brokenhearted at the coldness of Philip II, the loss of Calais, and her unpopularity with her own subjects. She was succeeded by her half sister, Elizabeth, who by birth and other circumstances was a Protestant and a potential enemy of Philip II. To the rulers of Catholic France and Spain, it seemed as if they should stop fighting and unite against the rising tide of Protestantism.

As a result, the two powers concluded in 1559 the important Treaty of Cateau Cambresis. By its terms, France and Spain agreed to wage war against Protestantism, especially in France and the Netherlands. This agreement was the occasion of much rejoicing and many festivities. In the course of them, Henry II, king of France, was accidentally killed in a tourney. The accession to the French throne of his three weak sons in turn had disastrous results for France and for all Europe. Philip II, on the other hand, sailed for Spain and never again left Spanish soil. The Treaty of Cateau Cambresis thus brought to a close the era of wars inaugurated by the expedition of Charles VIII to Naples.

In 1494, therefore, the rising states of Europe commenced to play the fascinating game of international politics. In that year France inaugurated a new period of history by an invasion of Italy. By its action it alarmed other powers and initiated a series of wars that troubled Europe until 1559. In 1519 the struggle spread from Italy to Western Europe. In the years from 1516 to 1520, the young Charles V gained control of four states by inheritance and of the Imperial title by election. This threatened France with encirclement and Europe with universal monarchy. The situation led to a series of five disastrous wars. They proved to be indecisive. In 1559, as a consequence, France and Spain ceased to attack each other and agreed to fight together against the rising tide of Protestantism.

CHAPTER 7

Religious Revolt and Reform in German and Scandinavian Lands

During ancient and medieval times, Europe had become Christianized. Christianity had first spread from Palestine as a center over the Roman Empire and in 325 A.D. had finally been adopted by it as the state religion. Then from Rome and Constantinople as centers, Christian missionaries had gone out to the Germans and the Slavs. By the sixteenth century all Europeans, except the widely scattered Jews and the Moslems of Southwestern Europe, considered themselves to be Christians.

In time, the Christians of Western and Eastern Europe differed about some matters of organization, beliefs, and doctrines and came to be recognized as two distinct churches, the Roman Catholic and the Eastern Church. Communicants of the Eastern Church rejected the supremacy of the Pope, thought that the Holy Ghost proceeded from God the Father alone, denied the doctrine of Purgatory, and differed from the western Church in their beliefs about the Virgin. They had, too, a different calendar, used the old Greek or the old Slavonic language instead of Latin in their services, and made no use of preaching or images. They rarely confessed their sins, were baptized by immersion, and took both bread and wine at communion time. The Eastern Church likewise permitted the ordinary clergy to marry. These ideas about the organization, beliefs, and service of the Church came to be generally accepted in Russia and by the Christian subjects of the Turks in the Balkans.

Organization, Beliefs, and Service of the Eastern and the Roman Catholic Churches

The two churches, however, closely resembled each other in organization. Each had a hierarchy of officials, known as secular clergy, for the government and administration of the church. At the bottom of the hierarchy were the parish priests, each in charge of a parish. They were supposed to care for the religious needs of the laity entrusted to them. They offered Requiem and Nuptial Masses and presented the Holy Sacrifice on Sundays and feast days. They baptized the new born, catechized children, heard confessions, supervised the morals of their parishioners, and administered the last rites for the dy-

90

ing. They were paid for their services by tithes and fees. They usually lived in a rectory provided by the parish. In rural regions they had their own acres in the arable fields and their own rights in the meadow, pasture, and forest land of the estate. The parish priests obtained their "livings" from a patron. He might be the chief proprietor of the parish or a neighboring prelate. Contemporary satirists said much about the ignorance of the parish priests but less about their morals.

The parish priests were under the supervision of bishops. They were in charge of districts known as bishoprics or dioceses. The bishops supervised the education of candidates for the priesthood, ordained them, approved or opposed their appointment as parish priests, and admonished and disciplined them after they had been installed in office. The bishops inspected the religious edifices in their dioceses and saw to it that Church property was properly used. The bishops visited the monasteries and nunneries of their dioceses except in cases where these institutions had been granted exemption by the Pope. They also had courts which had jurisdiction over Church property, the clergy, and the laity. The bishops, likewise, usually had palaces in which to live.

Each bishop had an exceptionally fine church known as his cathedral. During the Middle Ages, the bishop, the clergy, and the laity of each diocese had the ambition to make their cathedral as fine as possible. Architects, sculptors, wood carvers, painters, and glass makers lavished their skill on these edifices. They made the altar, the choir, and the chapels of their cathedrals veritable museums of painting, sculpture, wood carving, tapestries, and the art of the gold and the silver smith. They amassed in the treasury of the cathedral relics of the saints, jewels, chalices, crucifixes, and priceless vestments. By these means they sought to glorify God and increase the fame of the city.

In addition to his spiritual duties, a bishop might have secular obligations of various sorts. He might serve as landlord of estates and other property owned by the Church. He might be a minister of the State. He might sit in a parliament, estates general, Cortes, or diet. In the Holy Roman Empire many of the bishops were heads of states. Because of the way in which they lived and the extensive revenues which were attached to the offices, the greater number of the bishops were recruited from the younger sons of the nobility.

Above the bishops were the archbishops. This title gave the holder prestige rather than power. The archbishops had special insignia and precedence over the other clergy on ceremonial occasions, but they did not control or supervise the bishops under their jurisdiction. They performed the duties of a bishop in one of the bishoprics of their archdioceses. Their administrative district, consisting of a group of bishoprics, was known as an archbishopric, archdiocese, or province. Like the bishop, the archbishop had a palace and cathedral and might be a minister of state or member of the representative body and act as a landlord or head of a state.

At the top of the hierarchy, in the Roman Catholic Church, stood the Pope. In many ways he resembled a secular monarch. He was both head of the Roman Catholic or Medieval Church and of the petty kingdom known as the Papal States, which was located in central Italy. He was assisted by an army of officials. The whole body of officials was known as the *curia*. The most important of them were known as cardinals. In case of a vacancy in the papacy, the college of cardinals elected a new pope, usually a member of their own body and an Italian. As head of the Church, the Pope issued decrees for the guidance of both the clergy and the laity. He also had a considerable revenue derived from various sources. Among these were Peter's pence, a payment made by the faithful in many countries; first fruits or annates, the first year's revenue from an ecclesiastical office; and fees paid for judicial and administrative services. He sent representatives, known as legates, to the courts of secular sovereigns. He had fine palaces like the Vatican and the Quirinal in which to live.

Besides the secular clergy which has just been described, there was the regular clergy. In contrast to the secular clergy who lived out in the world, the regular clergy lived in monasteries and nunneries apart from ordinary men. They were called regular clergy because they lived according to rules. They were grouped into orders. Each order had its own rules. All monks and nuns took vows never to marry, to have no property, and to obey their superior. In other matters the various orders differed greatly. Each order had a distinctive dress. Some orders allowed their members to have a comparatively easy life. Others bound them to a simple fare, prescribed uncomfortable clothing, and admonished them to fast and pray frequently and to maintain an absolute silence. Their members were supposed to abandon all thought of the world and to devote themselves to God and his service.

An important branch of the regular clergy was the friars. They took the same vows of chastity, poverty, and obedience as the monks and nuns. They lived, however, in the world. They were likely to be found in crowded quarters of the towns instead of in the country. The two oldest orders of friars, the Franciscans and the Dominicans, dated back to the thirteenth century. Later, such orders as the Carmelites and the Augustinians were established.

Each monastery and nunnery had a head. A monastery had an abbot or prior; each nunnery, an abbess or a prioress. The head of a monastery or nunnery enjoyed much prestige and authority. Like the bishops, an abbott or prior might be at the same time a head of a monastery, the administrator of a great estate, and minister of a state. He might be a member of parliament or provincial diet. As representative of the power and wealth of the monastery, he lived apart from the ordinary members of his order, maintained a large establishment, and entertained lavishly. Because of the power and revenues enjoyed by them, the heads of monasteries and nunneries were usually recruited from younger sons and daughters of the nobility. This was detrimental to the religious life of the regular clergy.

The monasteries and nunneries in which the regular clergy lived varied greatly in size, power, wealth, and the number of inmates. A monastery might consist of a single, shabby building or an imposing collection of edifices. In the latter case, it would very likely include a church, a chapter house for the transaction of business, a dormitory, a refectory, a house in which to lodge guests, a school building, a bakery, a wine press, and the buildings needed for the administration of a large estate. It might eke out precarious existence or be supported by rich estates. Around the whole establishment there was likely to be a wall which excluded the secular world.

The purpose of this elaborate organization in the two churches was the salvation of souls. Both believed that the Church was the sole agent of God in the important task of saving men from everlasting punishment for their sins. It guarded and interpreted the two great sources of truth, the Bible and the unrecorded traditions of Christianity. Through its theology it pointed out the way of salvation. By means of its clergy it mediated between God and sinful man. Through its sacraments it initiated the individual into the way of salvation and increased his righteousness.

In this work of the Church, the seven sacraments of baptism, confirmation, the Eucharist (communion), penance, extreme unction, marriage, and holy orders played a vital role. Baptism freed the child from the portion of original sin with which he was born. Confirmation made the one receiving it a full member of the religious community. The Eucharist identified the individual with the person of Christ, for, according to the doctrine of transubstantiation, the officiating priest transformed the bread and wine into the body and blood of Christ. Contrition, confession, and penance removed the guilt of the penitent sinner. Extreme unction put the sick and dying soul in harmony with God. The sacrament of marriage gave the institution of the family a religious character. Ordination or holy orders endowed the priest with power to mediate between God and man. The bishops administered confirmation and ordination; the parish priest dispensed the five other sacraments.

The doctrine of penance, as taught by the Roman Catholic Church, calls for a fuller explanation. According to the belief of the Church, the sinner could scarcely hope for salvation unless he received absolution from a priest endowed with the power to forgive sins. To obtain forgiveness, the sinner must feel truly sorry for his sins and confess them openly to the priest, for the priest could not pass judgment on sins about which he knew nothing. By absolution, however, the priest only freed the sinner from the danger of everlasting punishment. It did not exempt him from temporal penalties. These might be expiated in this world by such acts of penance as fasting, praying, pilgrimages to holy places, and making gifts to pious causes or in the next world by suffering for a time the cleansing fires of Purgatory.

The religious services developed by the two churches were designed to stir the emotions of the hearer. This was especially true of the services of the Roman Catholic Church. Its central ceremony was not a sermon as in Protestant churches but the Mass. In this rite Christ was believed to be sacrificed anew. The ceremony accordingly tended to arouse the holiest emotions. Attendants at Masses assumed an attitude of great reverence and bent the knee and made the sign of the cross upon passing in front of the altar. Masses were said on Sundays, at weddings, for funerals, for the souls of the dead, and in commemoration of saints' days. In the larger churches Masses were said daily and even hourly. Instead of merely attending Church on Sundays, the devout and zealous Roman Catholic was likely to begin each day by attending Mass.

Everything possible was done to make the services of the Church impressive. They were held in churches on which had been lavished the wealth of the laity and the skill of the artists. The altars were rich and ornate. The doorways, windows, walls, and chapels told the Christian story and expressed man's religious aspirations by architecture, paintings, carvings, stained glass, and rich hangings. In the services of the Church the clergy used incense, candles, and vestments, all calculated to appeal to the senses and stir the emotions of the worshiper.

In the sixteenth century, much more than now, religion and the daily life of men were closely interwoven. The Church intervened at the most crucial times in the life of men, women, and children. The most popular holidays were the sacred days of the Church. Many popular customs had a religious side. Roadside shrines reminded the passerby of his spiritual duties. Religious pilgrimages were frequently made.

Criticism of the Church

By the opening years of the sixteenth century the Roman Catholic Church was subject to considerable criticism. One cause of attack was the existence of actual abuses within its organization. The officials of the Church were human beings living in a society with relatively low standards of conduct. There was, consequently, a natural tendency for them to sink to the level of the society around them. In some cases, as a result, the clergy led lives that invited attack. Even some of the Popes of the time brought down criticism upon the Church. Nicholas V, for example, surrounded himself with skeptics and scoffers who mocked the papacy, poked fun at the monks, attacked the Bible, and exalted the pagan spirit of antique times. Sixtus IV nearly exterminated the Colonna family by a series of judicial murders in order to advance his own family. Innocent VIII obtained the papacy through bribery, sold offices of the Church to the highest bidder, and stopped a crusade in return for the payment of tribute by the sultan. Alexander VI surpassed these popes with his own crimes and vices and those of his children. Sometimes the lower clergy forgot their vows and maintained wives. In some cases the priests were so ignorant that they were unable to repeat correctly The Creed or the Lord's Prayer or to understand the words of the service. In spite of these conditions, however, it must be remembered that the clergy had higher standards of conduct than the laity and included many men and women of saintly character.

The abuses existing in the Roman Catholic Church do not explain by any means all the attacks made upon it. The new centralized states developing in Europe resented the great powers exercised by the Church. Since the early years of the fourteenth century, the kings of France and England had been waging a determined struggle against the appointive power of the papacy in respect to bishops, archbishops, and the heads of monasteries. Many sovereigns disliked the extensive jurisdiction of the church courts, the interference of the popes in the internal affairs of their states, and the exemptions enjoyed by the clergy in taxation. The kings and their nobles coveted the property which the Church had gradually accumulated through the centuries by pious gifts and bequests. The commercial classes objected to the immobilization of capital needed by the rising commerce and industry. The devout, especially in Germany, criticized the greedy officials of the Church for selling for the sake of financial gain offices, pardons, and indulgences.

Another cause of criticism of the Church was its attitude toward the new learning. The intellectual classes in Western Europe, as we have seen, had been profoundly stirred by the Renaissance. In Italy this movement had tended to paganize society. North of the Alps, the Humanists had shown more piety. They directed their attention to such things as better texts of the Bible and the Church Fathers and a clearer understanding of the doctrines of the Church. They encountered stubborn resistance from the conservative clergy, particularly from those in charge of the universities.

In the opening years of the sixteenth century, this opposition culminated in an attack on the famous Humanist and student of Hebrew literature, John Reuchlin. From about 1507 onward, a renegade Jew named Pfeffercorn, encouraged by some friars at Cologne, attacked the Jews in a series of pamphlets and urged the seizure and destruction of all Hebrew books. Shocked by the proposal, at the same time foolish and dangerous to learning, Reuchlin raised his voice in protest. As a result of this defence of scholarship, Reuchlin was tried for heresy. The trial attracted much attention.

In the dispute the Humanists naturally took the side of Reuchlin. They heaped on their opponents invectives and ridicule. In 1514 these attacks culminated in the publication of an anonymous work known as the *Letters of Obscure Men*. The writers of the letters pretended to be former students of a Cologne professor. They wrote a barbarous mixture of Latin and German which disclosed the supposed ignorance, superstition, immorality, and lack of scholarship among their opponents. The Humanists thought the letters were exceedingly amusing and they did much to discredit their opponents.

The more spiritually minded Humanists found leaders in a number of different countries. In France, Jacques Lefévre d'Etaples (1455–1536) published in 1512 a revised Latin version of the *Epistles of St. Paul*. In England, John Colet lectured on the same subject. In addition, there were a number of mystics whose lives and teachings had important effects. These leaders taught that the Church was too materialistic, too much given to meaningless formalism, and too neglectful of personal piety.

The Humanists found their ideals realized to a surpassing degree in another scholar. He is known to history as Desiderius Erasmus (1469–1536). He was born at Rotterdam but lost his parents at an early age. His guardians then put him in a school at Deventer in Holland, where he learned to love the ancient classics. Later, somewhat against his will, as was sometimes done in those days, they placed him in a monastery. He very much disliked monastic life and in 1492 freed himself from living as a monk by becoming secretary to a bishop. In 1495 this patron made it possible for Erasmus to attend the University of Paris. He did not like either the living conditions or the instruction that he found at the University of Paris, but he did enjoy the contact with the young Humanists whom he met there. His patron, however, was not always prompt about paying Erasmus the promised pension. This forced him to supplement his income by tutoring other students.

One of these students, Lord Mountjoy, an English noble, invited Erasmus to visit England. While there, he met many of the English Humanists, Colet, Moore, Grocyn, and Linacre among others. His contact with these men really set him on the course that in the end made him the most famous scholar of his age. They showed him what could be done by the application of Humanistic methods to the field of theology. They inspired him to do for the Christian literature what other Humanists had been doing for the Greek and Roman classics. This necessitated a study of a subject untouched by him up to this time, the Greek language. He hoped to lessen the ignorance and superstition of the world without controversy by applying reason and scholarly methods to the problems of life.

For the achievement of this end, Erasmus depended mainly on his writings. He first attracted the attention of the learned world through his *Adages*. This work was a collection of familiar quotations from the classics. From time to time, new and enlarged editions of the *Adages* were published. The work was long used to embellish the speeches and writings of less gifted men. Some years later Erasmus really established his reputation as a man of letters by his *Praise of Folly*. This satire exposed the follies of scholars, the superstitious, theologians, monks, and even princes and popes. The contemporaries of Erasmus found the book highly amusing. To modern readers, much of it appears dull and humorless. In 1516 Erasmus published his famous Greek *New Testament*. This work was supposed to give scholars a better text than the Latin version which had long been in use. By this time, Erasmus was an international figure. He lived in a number of places and visited various countries as an honored guest. His constant aim was to improve the Church. With this end in view, he gave a large part of his time in his later years to the editing of the writings of the Church Fathers. He finally came to think of himself as a citizen of the world. Throughout his life he fought ignorance, superstition, the spirit of controversy, and wars in the name of religion and the rising tide of nationalism. His later years were saddened by the failure of the world to realize his ideals. When he died, all those things which he had struggled against seemed to be in the ascendant.

97

The Lutheran Movement

In 1517, while Erasmus was at the height of his influence, an event occurred that proved to be a turning point in the history of the Church. The Pope, like many a bishop before him, decided to build a great church, now known as St. Peter's, at Rome, the largest and finest religious edifice in Christendom. The construction of the large church entailed the raising of vast sums of money. In his efforts to get the needed money, the Pope and his agents used methods of doubtful propriety. The Pope granted indulgences,[1] the monetary side of which caused a scandal. The privilege of handling the indulgences in Germany was entrusted to Archbishop Albert of Mainz, a prelate who had just obtained office by borrowing from the Fuggers. For handling the indulgences, he was allowed to retain half of the money collected.

In turn, the archbishop entrusted the actual campaign for the disposal of indulgences to an ecclesiastic named Tetzel. Given the whole situation, it is not surprising that Tetzel often seemed more interested in the financial returns of the campaign than in its possible effect on the people of Germany. Many persons felt that the buyers of indulgences were being given a false idea about them and that the real interests of the Church were being seriously disregarded.

One of these critics of the campaign for the sale of indulgences was an Augustinian friar named Martin Luther. He came from substantial peasant stock. He never entirely freed himself from the hardships, the simple religious faith, the stern upbringing, and the superstitions of his early life. In 1501, after having attended a number of schools, Luther entered the University of Erfurt. In this institution he seems to have been interested mainly in studies of the older type rather than Humanistic subjects. In these studies he seems to have done rather well and to have impressed people favorably with his personality. As, later in his career, his enemies never attacked his life in the university, it must have been above reproach. In 1502, after having received both a bachelor's and a master's degree, Luther took up the study of law, a very natural step for an ambitious young man of that day to take. After two months, however, for reasons that are not entirely understood, Luther suddenly gave up the study of law and entered an Augustinian monastery.

As he later looked back on his life in the monastery, Luther felt that he had spent much of his time struggling with the problem of his personal salvation. After a long effort, he seems finally to have found peace of mind in the idea of justification by faith. In reality, he by

---

[1] According to Rome, an indulgence is a remission of the temporal punishment due to sins, after the guilt of sin has been remitted by sincere repentance.

no means spent all of his time wrestling with the problem of his personal salvation. In 1508 he was sent by his order to teach in the newly founded University of Wittenberg. In this community he became a figure of local importance. He attracted students to Wittenberg by his lectures. He preached with success to both students and townsmen. In 1515 his order even made him provincial vicar over eleven of its monasteries.

As a leader of the local community, it was natural and even a duty for Luther to take a stand on the question of indulgences. Accordingly, when Tetzel came near Wittenberg and commenced to dispose of them by questionable methods, Luther felt that the people of his community were being misled and denounced the sale of indulgences. As a result, Luther unexpectedly inaugurated one of the most significant movements of history. On October 31, 1517, at a time when the edifice was sure to be crowded with visitors, Luther posted ninety-five theses on the door of the church at Wittenberg. In doing this, he was merely employing a very usual academic custom, designed to arouse discussion of questions of public interest.

By his action, however, Luther quite unexpectedly brought before an open forum ideas that were stirring all Germany. Within two weeks after they had been posted, the ninety-five theses of Luther had been printed and distributed all over the country. They set all Germany to asking troublesome questions. Why, men asked, does not the Pope, if he really possesses the power to free men from the torments of Purgatory, exercise his power for charity instead of for money?

Although the ideas of Luther seemed to enlist the support of the whole German people, the Church still had defenders. At first, Pope Leo X was inclined to regard the whole affair as a squabble among some German monks. But many partisans of the Church saw more quickly the implications of Luther's ideas. These defenders of the Church finally persuaded the Pope to summon Luther to Rome. The question, however, was deeply enmeshed in politics. Out of deference to his sovereign, the Church authorities did not insist on Luther's going to Rome. Instead, the Pope finally sent a legate to Germany to investigate the troublesome friar. When he was summoned before this official, Luther boldly defended his point of view. As a result, the discussion of religious questions continued.

In spite of all this, Luther still regarded himself for some time as a good member of the Church. In 1519, however, two years after the posting of the theses, an important debate took place at Leipzig between Doctor Eck, a skillful, well-trained Catholic theologian, and Carlstadt, a friend of Luther. In the course of this debate, Luther, who took part in it, was forced to make some unexpected admissions.

In discussing the primacy of the papacy, Luther was compelled to concede that, if his own views were correct, those of the famous Bohemian heretic, John Hus, who had been burned at the stake in the previous century, were also good Christian doctrine. This admission made Luther a heretic and leader of a revolt against the Church. Thenceforth, Luther and his followers were referred to as Lutherans. In self-protection, Luther was compelled to rally Germany, if he could, to his point of view. With this end in mind, Luther wrote three pamphlets. They were entitled "Address to the Nobility of the German Nation," "Babylonian Captivity of the Church," and "Freedom of a Christian Man." These pamphlets gave the Lutherans a program. They denied certain claims of the Pope and the clergy. They advocated the abolition of annates, pilgrimages, festivals, indulgences, monasteries, the papal court, and Masses for the dead. They advised priests to marry. They proposed that the mendicancy of monks and friars be stopped and the number of Masses be greatly decreased. They maintained that the only God-ordained sacraments were baptism and communion. They argued that the laity should be given both bread and wine at communion time. They substituted the special doctrine of consubstantiation for the Catholic doctrine of transubstantiation. They set forth the idea that man was justified by faith and not by works. These stirring appeals gained for Luther, for the time being, the support of all the discontented elements in the German nation.

In reply, the Pope condemned the three pamphlets in a papal bull. He censured forty-one of the statements found in them, ordered them to be burned, forbade Luther to preach, and demanded a recantation of his views within sixty days. The writings of Luther, however, had had the desired effect. Many of the German princes refused to allow the publication or circulation of the papal bull in their territories. By December 10, 1520, Luther felt strong enough to defy the Pope publicly. Surrounded by a large crowd of professors, students, and townsmen, he burned the papal bull at the town gate of Wittenberg.

This was the religious situation that confronted Emperor Charles V upon his arrival in Germany in 1521. He promptly summoned Luther to appear before the diet convened at Worms. Upon arriving there, Luther was asked to recant. For a time the black-robed friar seemed humbled by the brilliant gathering of princes and prelates. On the following day, however, he regained his courage and composure and defended himself in a bold but respectful speech in which he declared, "Unless I am convinced of error by the testimony of

100

Scripture or plain reason . . . I cannot and will not retract anything, for it is neither safe nor right to act against one's conscience." Thereupon, Luther hastily left the diet and the city of Worms, and that assembly pronounced against him the ban of the Empire. The Emperor, however, felt compelled to turn his attention to the impending war with France rather than to his troublesome German subject.

As Luther made his way back to Wittenberg, he was seized by his friends and hidden in the castle of Wartburg. In this place of refuge he lived and worked for ten months. It was a decisive period in the history of the revolt against the Church. While the people of Germany speculated as to his whereabouts, Luther wrote an exposition of the Psalms, a treatise on monastic vows, and a tract on the Mass and began a translation of the Bible into the speech of the people, an event of great importance in the history of German literature.

This series of events set all Germany in motion. Luther had criticized many things about the organization, beliefs, and services of the Church. He had not been so definite about what should be put in their place. He had seemed to put the authority of the individual conscience in place of that of the Church. As a result, while Luther remained hidden in the castle of Wartburg, his followers took affairs into their own hands. Colleagues at Wittenberg, princes, priests, monks, and nuns began to make religious innovations. This was particularly true at Wittenberg and in the surrounding country. Critics of the Church began to denounce monasticism, celibacy of the clergy, veneration of images, and the Mass. Priests began to give wine as well as bread to communicants. Two priests openly married. Several monks left their monasteries. A crowd did some damage to church property and ridiculed the old ritual. Three so-called prophets arose who preached radical doctrines. This movement was only checked by the sudden appearance of Luther.

Up to this time, the whole German nation seemed favorable to Luther and his ideas. With the passage of time, however, Luther began to alienate some of those who appeared ready to follow him. Among those unwilling to follow the leadership of Luther were Erasmus and Humanists of his type. Erasmus hated strife and controversy and sought to improve conditions by reason. Luther, in contrast, seemed to enjoy intellectual battles. Erasmus was a reformer; Luther, a revolutionist. So in the end Erasmus and the Humanists remained communicants of the old church.

The German knights, too, sought at first to use Luther in rescuing their declining order. Led by Ulrich von Hutten, they were struggling against both Church and State. When Luther refused to be drawn into their futile fight against the economic and political forces of the time, they too lost interest in the Lutheran movement.

The most serious defection, however, came from the peasants of Germany. They felt that they had legitimate cause for complaint about their condition and that the new gospel preached by Luther authorized them to take matters into their own hands. In 1525, consequently, they rose in revolt. To modern people their demands seem very reasonable. To the upper classes of their own time they appeared impious and outrageous. Their revolt put Luther in a very difficult position. During the past eight years of controversy, he had actually said many things that justified such a rising. If he approved the action of the peasants, though, he stood in grave danger of alienating the powerful princes of the German states and the landlords of Germany. In the light of all this, Luther could not avoid taking a stand on the great social question raised by the revolt.

In the end, Luther took the side of the upper classes. To him it probably seemed a question of law and order. As a consequence, he finally denounced the peasants in language of great violence. He told them that they had no right to attempt to correct their situation. He called them "robbing and murdering bands of peasants." He urged the princes and landlords to strike down the rebels like mad dogs. The princes and landlords were quite ready to follow his advice. They put down the rising, therefore, with great savagery. As a result, the peasants, particularly those in southern and western Germany, decided that the new gospel was not for them and turned against Luther and his movement.

In spite of these defections, the Lutheran movement continued to spread. Many of the clergy went over to the side of the reformers. Usually, the last Catholic priest became the first Lutheran minister. Many of the regular clergy welcomed the opportunity to escape from monastic life. The nuns adopted the new doctrines more slowly.

For the success of the Lutheran movement, however, the action of the princes and the free imperial cities was more important than that of the clergy. In 1525, Electoral Saxony, Hesse, and Prussia became officially Lutheran. In the following year, the Diet of Speyer declared that for the time being each prince of the Empire should decide for himself the question of his religious allegiance. Within a few years after this decision, nearly all the states of northern and central Germany revolted from the Roman Catholic Church. The states of southern and western Germany, for the most part, remained loyal to the old church. The Germans who had settled in Bohemia, Poland, Hungary, and Transylvania tended to follow the example of Germany.

The German princes and the free imperial cities were not moved wholly by conviction. It was also to their interest to adopt the Lutheran religion. They might not understand clearly the doctrines of Luther, but they realized fully the advantages to be gained by their adoption. By embracing the Lutheran doctrines, they increased their power and their revenues. The Catholic hierarchy could then no longer interfere with the internal affairs of their states. The Lutheran clergy became submissive servants of the secular authorities. The ecclesiastical states came into the possession of the secular princes. The monasteries and their lands and other pious foundations also fell into their hands. The secular courts no longer shared jurisdiction with the church courts.

Throughout the revolt, it must be remembered, Luther had no official position. Throughout his life he continued to be a respected professor at the University of Wittenberg. He was, at best, an unofficial adviser of his followers. The princes and their subjects sought his advice on religious matters. The princes consulted him about the organization and services of the new churches which they were setting up and about the care of the poor and the education of ministers. Former monks and nuns sought his opinion on personal problems. The final decision in all these matters, however, finally rested with the princes.

Among those profoundly affected by the religious revolt was Luther himself. First, he ceased to be a friar. In 1525 he took a far more radical step. He tried to advise a young nun of noble birth, named Catherine von Bora, about her future. He suggested to her a number of possible husbands but ended up by marrying her himself. His action shocked the conservative, but the young lady seems to have made Luther an excellent wife. After their marriage, the couple lived in an abandoned monastery which was given to them by their sovereign, the Elector of Saxony. In this domicile the wife of Luther supplemented his rather meager salary by cultivating a garden, keeping pigs and chickens, and taking in student boarders. Some of the latter were wise enough to record Luther's "Table Talk," one of the important sources for our present knowledge of the reformer. Besides boarders, Luther's family came to include three sons, two daughters, an aunt, two orphaned nieces, and a grandniece.

As a consequence of the direction of religion falling into the hands of the secular princes and the city governments, ecclesiastical affairs in each state became a branch of the government. Each state set up machinery for the administration of church matters. The sovereign, directly or indirectly, decided ecclesiastical matters. As a result, there developed as many Lutheran churches as there were Lutheran states.

The general dependence on Luther for advice, however, did establish a certain uniformity in religious matters. The Lutheran ministers all used German instead of Latin in the service. They gave up the saying of Masses, since they thought them discredited by the doctrine of justification by faith. They put the sermon in place of the Mass because of the emphasis that they placed on the authority of Scripture. They ceased to require confession and the giving of absolution. They condemned fasts, asceticism, prayers to the saints, and pilgrimages. They no longer considered relics and shrines sacred.

The organization of the new churches usually came later. The princes ordinarily appointed consistories or ecclesiastical commissions, composed partly of members of the clergy and in part of laymen, which took the place of the court of the bishop. They had the power to excommunicate, to punish, and to suspend from office. In place of the bishops, the princes generally appointed superintendents to watch over the parish clergy.

For some time the Lutheran movement lacked a full and definite statement about its beliefs. Luther never seemed to feel the need for such a declaration. In 1529, however, he did publish his longer and shorter catechisms. In the following year his close friend and colleague, Melanchthon, drew up for presentation to the Emperor the Augsburg Confession, which is still used by the various Lutheran churches. Even this document lacks somewhat in clarity and fullness as a statement of their faith. It sought to show that the views of Luther and his followers were not at variance with the writings of the Church Fathers, that they accepted the greater part of the doctrines of the Medieval Church, and that they repudiated the ideas of Zwingli, the Swiss reformer, and those of the Anabaptists. As a consequence, it did state well enough the Lutheran doctrines concerning justification by faith, good works, the Eucharist, confession, and the sacraments, but it was silent on such matters as the priesthood of all believers, predestination, indulgences, the power of the papacy, the indelible character of the priesthood, Purgatory, and the sacraments which might give offence. In the services, organization, and doctrines of the church, Luther changed only such things as he considered contrary to the Scripture.

Throughout his reign, Charles V expected to reach a point where he could settle the religious dispute that was splitting Germany. His wars with France, however, prevented him from devoting much attention to the religious affairs of the Empire. From time to time, he convened diets in the hope of effecting a settlement of the ecclesiastical situation. In 1529, the Emperor made such an attempt at a diet at Speyer. Though the Emperor was not able to be present, he instructed the diet to enforce the edict promulgated against Luther at the Diet of Worms. The diet, accordingly, decreed that there was henceforth to be no preaching against the Mass and no one was to be prevented from attending such a service. The Lutheran princes found themselves in a minority and could only protest against this action of the diet. As a result, they came to be known as Protestants. In time, the name came to be applied to all who rejected the claims of the Pope and the Roman Catholic Church.

The Diet of Augsburg (1530) failed to restore religious peace in Germany. In spite of the conciliatory tone of the Augsburg Confession, the majority of the diet voted that the Edict of Worms should be enforced and that all confiscated property must be returned to the Church. In reply, the Protestant princes formed the League of Schmalkald. Germany, consequently, continued to be divided into two hostile religious parties until the Emperor finally arranged peace with France in 1544.

After the conclusion of peace with France, it looked for a short time as if the Emperor was at last in position to enforce a religious settlement in conformity with his own ideas. Before he could act decisively, however, the situation changed again. The ambitious but treacherous Maurice of Saxony deserted him; Henry II of France formed an alliance with the Protestant princes of Germany; and the Emperor was forced to permit his brother, Ferdinand, to negotiate first the preliminary Treaty of Passau (1552) and finally the definitive Peace of Augsburg (1555).

The latter treaty defined the legal status of Catholics and Protestants in Germany from 1555 to 1648. It gave the German people a very limited degree of religious toleration. It accorded to each prince the right to choose for himself and his people either the Catholic or the Lutheran religion. If a subject did not like the choice of his sovereign, he could either conform or emigrate to a state of his own faith. In the free imperial cities the agreement permitted both factions to continue to reside. The treaty did not state clearly what should be done about the ecclesiastical states and the church property which had been confiscated. It gave the followers of Zwingli no legal protection. Instead of bringing lasting peace, it merely postponed the impending civil war over religion.

The Zwinglian Revolt

Although he must be credited with having started the new religious movement, Luther was never the leader of all the Protestants of Europe. In other parts of the European continent, other critics of the Church arose. One of these was Ulrich Zwingli (1484–1529).

In order to understand his role in the religious affairs of the time, something must be said about conditions in the Swiss cantons in which he lived and worked.

In the Middle Ages, the Swiss peasants, aided by their native Alps, had wrested their political freedom from the Habsburgs and maintained it in spite of the frequent aggressions of surrounding princes. Under these conditions, they had developed a loosely organized league of thirteen cantons that left to each canton a large measure of autonomy. The cantons varied considerably in form of government, wealth, and influence. They derived considerable revenue from the hiring of their young men as mercenaries. Then, too, the prestige of the Swiss troops was still great enough for foreign governments to bribe and pay pensions to influential men in the cantons.

Amid such conditions, Ulrich Zwingli lived and worked. He came from a family of some prominence. In his native village of Wildhaus in the Toggenburg Valley, his father was the chief magistrate and his uncle was the parish priest. After attending two Swiss secondary schools, Zwingli took work, in turn, at the Universities of Basel, Berne, and Vienna. In 1506 he assumed charge of a parish. Thirteen years later, he was called to an important post at Zurich, one of the principal cities of the Swiss cantons. In the beginning, Zwingli was more a Humanist than a religious reformer. He was not above reproach in his personal conduct and was more interested in political than in religious questions. Until 1520 he continued to accept a pension from the Pope. He first attracted attention by his criticism of the practice of hiring the young men of the cantons to foreign sovereigns as mercenaries.

In his later years, Zwingli always claimed that he commenced his attacks on the Church before he ever heard of Luther. At any rate, he did not become a public critic of the Church until two years after Luther posted his theses on the door of the church at Wittenberg. He began, as Luther had done, by attacking the sale of indulgences at Zurich by a certain Friar Sampson. In the following year, from his influential position as people's priest in the Cathedral of Zurich, he commenced to preach against such things as prayer to the saints, Purgatory, monasticism, and tithes, and simplified to some extent the service of the Church.

After 1522, the town council intervened in the controversy. In that year it forbade further sale of mercenaries and settled a dispute over the eating of meat in Lent. In 1523 the Great Council of Zurich held a public debate over the religious questions troubling the city. In the discussion, Zwingli maintained such points as the priesthood of the individual, the authority of the Bible, and the

106

right of secular rulers to have a voice in church matters. He declared against the power of the Pope, the Catholic hierarchy, the Mass, invocation of the saints, the doctrine of Purgatory, fasting, and clerical celibacy. At the close of the debate, the burgomaster declared in the name of the council that Zwingli was not guilty of heresy and that he should continue to preach the gospel. His action committed the city and canton to religious reform.

Further religious innovations quickly followed this decision. On Christmas Day (1523), Zwingli administered both bread and wine to the laity in the communion service and substituted a sermon for the Mass. Early in 1524, the authorities abolished indulgences, pilgrimages, celibacy of the clergy, and the sacraments of penance and extreme unction; destroyed sacred pictures, statues, and relics; and confiscated the property of the Church. As in Lutheran countries, the monks and nuns began to leave their monasteries and nunneries. The property and revenues of the cathedral chapter were devoted to the poor and to the maintenance of schools. By the end of 1525, Zurich had broken completely with the Church.

Zwingli and Luther differed somewhat in their religious ideas. Zwingli did away with everything that in his judgment was not sanctioned by the Bible. Luther retained all that in his opinion was not contrary to Scripture. As a result, Zwingli kept fewer of the ceremonies of the Medieval Church and his followers worshiped in churches that were simple and plain. The two leaders differed especially in their interpretation of the communion service. To Zwingli, it was merely a commemoration of Christ. To Luther, Christ was actually present in the bread and wine. These differences not only kept the followers of the two leaders separate but made them bitterly hostile to each other.

The example of Zurich was soon followed by other cities in the Swiss cantons and in southern and western Germany. In 1528, after a public debate, Berne went over to the Protestant side. In the following year, Basel, Mühlhausen, Schaffhausen, Saint Gall, and other places in the German-speaking cantons and the cities of Augsburg, Ulm, Mainz, Frankfort, and Strasbourg in Germany turned to the Protestant cause. Five of the rural Swiss cantons, however, remained loyal to the old church.

This division of the Swiss into two religious parties led to two civil wars. The Protestant cantons organized the League of Christian Civic Rights and tried, at the urging of Zwingli, to force Protestantism on the Catholic cantons. In self-defence, the Catholic cantons organized with Austria the Christian Union. The first conflict between the two leagues, which occurred in 1529, resulted in the establishment of the principle that each canton should be free to choose its own religion. Two years later, as a consequence of the activities of Zurich, a second conflict took place that resulted in the death of Zwingli. Fortunately for the ill-prepared forces of Zurich, the victors did not press their advantage.

The Anabaptists

Luther and Zwingli were relatively conservative reformers. While advocating changes in the Medieval Church, they left a large part of the doctrine, organization, and service of the old church untouched. In the heat of their agitation for reform, however, they made statements which seemed to justify more radical changes. As a result, there arose, both at Zurich and in Germany, reformers who wanted to go farther along the road of reform than either Luther or Zwingli felt that it was wise to go. To some of them, historians apply the name of Anabaptists.

Those called by this name varied widely in their beliefs. All of them professed that they wanted to restore primitive Christianity. They usually were inclined to oppose the taking of oaths, capital punishment, and the exercise of civil authority. They rejected completely infant baptism. They took the Scriptures as their sole guide in life. They sought a new kingdom where men would have all things in common. Some of the Anabaptists were sober, quiet, scholarly men. Others were fanatics who went to great extremes in both their beliefs and conduct. For the most part, however, the Anabaptists were humble, obscure men who left an imperfect record of their beliefs and their activities.

Their contemporaries felt that the Anabaptists were a great menace. Luther, as we have seen, fought against them at Wittenberg. Zwingli, too, came into conflict with them. When they were driven out of cities like Wittenberg and Zurich, they swarmed over the country districts. There, they had a considerable part in stirring up the peasants to revolt. Both for this and their radical views, the authorities persecuted them savagely. Their leaders, for the most part, were either killed or driven into exile. Many of them died at the stake. Others were thrown into prison. In spite of all that was done to them, they survived and became the founders of several modern sects.

The Anabaptists at Münster

In 1534 a group of Anabaptists were involved in an extraordinary episode. At Münster in Westphalia some members of this sect gained control of the city. They thought that they were on the point of setting up the ideal kingdom of which they dreamed. Gradually, they drove out of the city the more moderate elements and drew to themselves religious radicals from all parts of Germany and the Netherlands. Led by a fanatic called John of Leyden, the group gathered at Münster went to fantastic extremes. Their leader claimed royal powers and advocated polygamy and other practices condemned by the conservative and moderate elements in society. In 1535, in spite of a heroic defence of the stronghold, the forces besieging Münster took the city and tortured and put to death its Anabaptist defenders.

The Anabaptists did not found a permanent religious body, but they deeply impressed subsequent religious thinking. Out of their midst grew such present-day religious bodies as the Baptists and the Mennonites. They stood for the separation of church and state and advocated religious freedom. They opposed the baptism of infants. They emphasized the responsibility of the individual to God, the freedom of the human will, the symbolical character of communion, congregational self-government, and simplicity of service. Some of them refused to bear arms and to take oaths.

The Spread of the Lutheran Movement to Other Lands

From Germany the ideas of Luther traveled to other lands. They crossed the mountains separating Bohemia from Germany and were taken up by the Germans settled in the Bohemian towns and border districts. They spread northward to the Germans living along the Baltic coast under the rule of the Teutonic Order. They took hold in the various Scandinavian lands.

In Sweden, which at the time included Finland, the adoption of the ideas of Luther was largely the work of Gustavus Vasa (1523–1560), who had just led his people in a struggle which freed Sweden from its political ties to the rest of Scandinavia. He employed the Lutheran movement as a means of breaking the power of the hostile clergy. He introduced the new religion gradually. At first, he supported the Lutheran preachers who entered the country. Next, he permitted the circulation of a Swedish translation of the *New Testament,* suppressed the Roman Catholic printing presses, commenced to attack monasteries, and appropriated two-thirds of the tithes of the Church in order to reduce the national debt. A year later, Gustavus Vasa hanged two hostile bishops, transferred all Swedish ecclesiastical property to the crown, and broke the tie between the Swedish church and Rome. He made no change in the ritual until 1531. He did not do away with the office of bishop. The revolt in Sweden was thus to a large extent the work of a strong ruler.

In Denmark, which also controlled Norway, the Lutheran movement was introduced more gradually even than in Sweden. As early as 1518 it looked for a moment as if the reigning king of Denmark was going to set up in his territories an independent church. By 1525, the Lutheran doctrines had made much progress. For a time, both Lutherans and Catholics were tolerated. Finally, in 1537, upon the ascension to the throne of an ardent Lutheran, the king of Denmark, with the assent of the diet, broke off relations with the Pope, introduced a Lutheran organization and service into Denmark, and confiscated the property of the Church.

The preceding survey shows clearly that Europe never gave its allegiance to a single form of religion. During most of the medieval period, the continent was divided between two branches of Christianity. Western and Central Europe recognized the authority of the pope at Rome; Eastern Europe, that of the Eastern Church. Set apart from the Christians were the Jews and the Moslems. Early in the sixteenth century, the unity of Western and Central Europe was further broken. After 1517, three religious movements arose that resulted in a further breaking up of the religious harmony. In an effort to reform certain practices of the Church, two rather conservative religious leaders, Luther and Zwingli, started movements that finally resulted in the formation of two new churches, the Lutheran and the Reformed. The Lutheran movement won the allegiance of the greater part of Germany, particularly eastern and central Germany, the three Scandinavian countries, the Germans along the eastern coast of the Baltic Sea and in Bohemia and Hungary, and the Swedish dependency of Finland; the Zwinglian movement, that of some of the German districts in the Swiss cantons and some of the towns of western and southern Germany. There was, however, a more radical religious movement, the Anabaptist movement, that won many adherents in the Swiss cantons, Germany, and the Netherlands among the common folk. In general, they were considered a menace by Catholics, Lutherans, and Reformed and were savagely persecuted by both Catholics and Protestants.

CHAPTER 8

The Calvinist and Anglican Revolts against the Medieval Church

The Teutonic lands were not the only regions affected by the revolt against the Medieval Church. The movement started by Luther eventually set in motion religious revolts in the French-speaking Swiss cantons, France, the Netherlands, Hungary, England, and Scotland.

The Early Reform Movement in France

In France the first steps toward a reform of the Medieval Church were taken by a group of Humanist priests and scholars at Meaux. They had no thought of breaking relations with the Church. They merely strove to spiritualize the Church by deepening their knowledge of Christian principles. Unintentionally, however, they started a movement that ended in an open break on the part of some of the French Humanists and many humbler folk with the Medieval Church.

The acknowledged leader of the group was Jacques Lefebre d'Étaples (1455–1536). In 1513 he began to publish studies on the Bible, and in 1523 and 1525 he put out a French translation of the Scriptures. In his writings he taught that the Mass, confession, fasts, pilgrimages, and other practices of the Church were not as important as most people had commonly regarded them. He found support for his views from the bishop of Meaux and from Margaret of Angouleme, Queen of Navarre and sister of Francis I, king of France. In spite of the mildness of these views, the ecclesiastical authorities attacked the group at Meaux and, about 1525, forced most of its members to take refuge in Strasbourg. This stopped the work of this particular group in France, but other Humanists and many of the common people of France continued the religious agitation which they had begun.

Among those that sympathized with the ideas of Jacques Lefebre d'Étaples and his followers was a small group of scholars at the University of Paris. In the light of history the most important member of this group was John Calvin (1509–1564). He was born at Noyon in northern France, a city where his father was a lawyer and often employed by the ecclesiastical authorities. John Calvin was educated and grew up in close association with the sons of the most influential family of the district. At the age of twelve, as was often the case in those days, he began to receive the income without fulfilling the duties of a chaplain in the cathedral. Later, on the same terms, he obtained a curacy in the diocese of Noyon. These sinecures freed him from financial worry. In 1525, at the age of sixteen, he went to Paris in company with the sons of his noble patron in order to continue his education. Later, he studied at Orleans and Bourges. In these various places of learning he came in contact with excellent teachers and formed friendships with some influential scholars. In this way he received a training that made him at first a prominent young Humanist and later a religious reformer.

About 1533 the young reformers associated with Calvin were invited by the king, Francis I, to set forth their ideas about reform. Accordingly, one of their numbers, Nicholas Cop, rector of the University of Paris, made a public defence of their views. Because of the delicate political situation, the king could not openly favor religious reform. As a consequence, the bold statement of Nicolas Cop led to the flight of the little group of reformers from Paris. During the next three years, Calvin stayed in a number of places. For awhile he remained at Angouleme with a friend who had an excellent library. Out of his studies during these years grew a work that made Calvin, at the age of twenty-five, a marked man among the reformers and ultimately won him a place in the reform movement comparable to that held by Luther.

This famous book is known as the *Institutes of the Christian Religion*. It is one of the great masterpieces of Protestant theology. In the work, Calvin set forth his ideas about God, Man, and salvation. Here, the famous reformer eloquently stressed the omnipotence of God and the impotence, helplessness, and inability of Man to save himself.

In spite of being all-powerful, God, according to Calvin, made himself known to men through the Scriptures. These were written at the dictation of the Holy Spirit. Man, on the other hand, is guilty and corrupt. He can be saved only through faith in Christ who became incarnate in order to redeem men. The redeemed, however, include only those predestined by God to be saved. The book owed its importance to the fact that it was the first full, clear, and logical statement of the Protestant point of view in matters of religion. The first edition of the *Institutes of the Christian Religion* appeared in 1536. Subsequently, the work was reprinted many times. Later editions contained much new material but never changed the fundamental ideas of the book. It owed much to Scholasticism and the writings of Luther and Zwingli.

In spite of the fame which his work brought him, Calvin as yet had no thought of being a professional reformer. He still hoped to lead the life of a peaceful scholarly Humanist. While in search of a place suitable for such a career, he came to Geneva, then a small city nestled in the Alps. Located just at the point where the Swiss cantons, France, and the duchy of Savoy met. Geneva was at the time an independent, French-speaking town of about fifteen thousand inhabitants. It had long been at odds with its bishop and its former overlord, the Duke of Savoy. A few years before the arrival of Calvin, influenced by Berne, it had admitted preachers who advocated religious reform and separation from the Medieval Church. These developments had been responsible for the freeing of the city from outside control but had divided its citizens into two hostile parties.

At the moment when Calvin reached the little city, the leader of the reform movement within its walls was William Farel, a former Christian Humanist who had once lived at Meaux. As soon as Farel learned of the presence in the city of the distinguished author of the *Institutes of the Christian Religion,* he was determined to enlist his aid in the struggle against the supporters of the Medieval Church. After much hesitation, Calvin finally yielded to the pleas of the fiery Farel. Only his strong sense of duty, however, persuaded Calvin to abandon his plans for a scholarly life and to become a professional reformer.

The decision once made, the two reformers had very definite ideas about what they wanted to do. Neither had the slightest intention of establishing religious toleration at Geneva. They intended to make of the city and its citizens a state dominated by their own conception of religion. Accordingly, they promptly drew up for the government of Geneva a document of twenty-one articles and compelled the citizens in groups of ten to swear allegiance to them. For the training of the youth of the city, they drew up a catechism. In this way, they introduced into the city a regime marked by austere religious services, repression of display in dress, suppression of amusements, and many other severe features. It is not surprising, therefore, that within a year and a half the two leaders of religious reform were at odds with the majority of their fellow citizens. Their differences at last culminated in a quarrel over the use of unleavened bread at Easter time in the communion service. When they found that they could not have their own way in religious matters, the fiery Farel and the irritable Calvin left the city. Farel never returned to Geneva. For three and a half years, Calvin acted as a pastor of the little congregation of French refugees living at Strasbourg.

The departure of the two reformers, however, did not bring religious peace to Geneva. The city continued to have trouble over religious matters. In 1541 the authorities invited Calvin to return to the city. With some reluctance he finally decided to comply with their request. From this date until his death he had, in the main, his own way at Geneva. By the ordinances which he drew up in 1541 and again in 1561, he made the city a sort of theocracy. There was a very close connection between the three councils which governed the city and the consistory, composed of preachers and elders, which governed the church. The lives and conduct of the citizens were controlled to a large extent by the power of the religious authorities to excommunicate the disobedient. This situation led to two important developments. Many of the opponents of Calvin left the city. Many persons persecuted in other lands for holding religious views similar to those advocated by Calvin flocked to Geneva. In time, Geneva became the recognized capital and Calvin the acknowledged leader of those holding similar views in the Swiss cantons, France, the Netherlands, Scotland, England, and Hungary.

For the rest of his life, consequently, Calvin was busy. He is said to have preached every day in alternate weeks and to have left behind him at the time of his death twenty-three thousand sermons. Three days a week he taught theology in the academy which he founded, an institution that became in time the University of Geneva. Every week he attended the sessions of the consistory, the governing body of the church. Unofficially, he was the adviser of his numerous followers in France, the Netherlands, and Scotland and carried on a voluminous correspondence with their leaders. In addition, he wrote much on religious subjects.

Since he was a man of strong convictions, Calvin was involved in many controversies. The most famous of these centered in a Spaniard, known to history as Servetus. After having differed with Calvin on the subject of religion, he foolishly ventured to go to Geneva. In doing this, he made a fatal mistake. As a rule, no one yet thought of religious toleration. Largely through the influence of Calvin, accordingly, Servetus was arrested, tried, and burned at the stake. Contemporaries of the two men thought that his fate was a perfectly natural one, but later generations have regarded the episode as a serious blot on the record of Calvin.

From various sources we know something about the appearance and private life of Calvin. He seems to have been of middle stature, somewhat pallid and dark, and with clear, lustrous eyes. He was apparently simple in dress, direct in speech, sparing in food, and severe and dignified in demeanor. Early in life, he developed a dyspepsia that made him henceforth irritable. In his dealing with others, Calvin appealed to the minds rather than to the emotions of men. In 1540, while at Strasbourg, he married the widow of a former Anabaptist. She died in 1549. All his life, probably because of his sedentary habits, Calvin had been sick. In 1564, after being ill for some time, the reformer died at the comparatively early age of fifty-five.

Recognition of the Leadership of Calvin in the Swiss Cantons

The work of Zwingli and Calvin made the Swiss cantons the headquarters of two prominent reformers. Zwingli, as we have seen, was recognized as a leader by several of the German-speaking cantons. Calvin was acknowledged as head of the reform movement in the French-speaking cantons. As the two leaders stood for about the same ideas in religion, the followers of both began to make efforts to join forces and formulate a common statement of their beliefs. After much discussion they drew up and generally adopted common confessions of faith in 1549 and in 1562–1566. The followers of the doctrines set forth in these two documents are generally known as the Reformed Church.

The church founded by Calvin and Zwingli differed in many ways both from the old Medieval Church and the Lutheran Church. The church, known on the continent of Europe as the Reformed, retained only two of the seven sacraments—baptism and communion. It regarded the bread and wine used in the communion service as merely symbols and not as the actual body and blood of Christ. Its members worshiped in plain, unadorned buildings. It abandoned the use of altars, images, the crucifix, and other ecclesiastical ornaments. It substituted pastors for priests and ceased to regard the clergy as having peculiar and indispensable powers. It made the sermon, supplemented by prayers and singing, the principal feature of its services instead of the Mass.

The Development of a Reformed Church in France

In France, Calvin came to wield an especially strong influence. Protestantism there began for the most part with humble artisans and shopkeepers. At first, the adherents of the new faith were known as Lutherans. Later, they became known as Huguenots. The origin of the name is not known with absolute certainty. It is said to have been first used derisively by a monk who was preaching against them and called them by that name because they met for worship at Tours outside King Hugo's gate. At first, the king, Francis I, seemed inclined to toy with the new movement. In the end, because of pressing political considerations, he turned against the Protestants. The change in his attitude was owing to his crushing defeat at the battle of Pavia in 1525. He no longer felt free to defy such important forces in the state as the University of Paris and the French clergy. As a result, Protestants began to be persecuted. In 1534, after the partisans of religious reform had boldly put placards in various public places, including the door of the king's palace, the persecution became more severe and forced many of the Frenchmen to emigrate. Many Protestants, however, stayed in the country.

In 1546 a group of Protestants living at Meaux formed the first Protestant church in France. In the next few years, other groups of Protestants organized congregations. In 1559, fifteen of the seventy-two congregations in France sent representatives to a synod held at Paris. This body drew up a confession of faith and a permanent organization for French Protestants. As the French government was hostile, the Huguenots had to organize themselves somewhat differently from the Protestants of the Swiss cantons. In accordance with this plan, each French congregation chose its own elders and ministers. A group of congregations held local councils and provincial synods composed of the ministers and lay delegates. This system of organization tended to become a model for other Reformed and Presbyterian churches.

After 1559, the French government seemed to be unable to stem the Protestant movement in France. As a result of an unexpected turn of events, the religious revolt became a political issue. In the later years of the reign of Henry II of France, the Guise family, led by the Cardinal of Lorraine and the Duke of Guise, steadily grew in influence. A sign of their power and importance was the marriage of Mary, Queen of Scots, a niece of the two leaders of the family, to the sickly heir of the king of France. When in 1559 this prince inherited the kingship because of the death of Henry II in a tourney, the Guises became for the time being the real heads of the French state. Their position, however, was soon challenged. Since the Guises were staunch supporters of the old church, their opponents sought the help of all the discontented elements in the state. These included the French Protestants. After forty years of loyalty in the face of persecution, they at last felt strong enough to demand better treatment. They found a large part of the French nobility ready to turn Protestant. In doing this, they were actuated in part by political motives and in part by religious convictions. As a consequence of this addition to their party, the Protestants were strong enough in 1561 to obtain liberty of conscience and in the following year an edict of toleration.

This decree, however, was not really enforced by the French government. Since 1560, the machinery of government had been in the hands of Catherine de' Medici, the neglected queen of Henry II, who ruled France in the name of her weak son, Francis II. In the face of the two strong religious factions, she found herself powerless to enforce her own edicts. The tension between the two religious parties was so great that any incident might precipitate a civil war.

The Establishment of the Reformed Church in the Netherlands

Early in the sixteenth century, the seventeen provinces of the Netherlands began to be affected by the revolt taking place in neighboring lands against the Medieval Church. Some of the Dutch Humanists were soon in touch with Luther and Zwingli. Many Netherlanders visited Wittenberg. Merchants, monks, and preachers carried the new religious ideas to cities and towns in the Low Countries. Many, particularly among the humbler folk, became followers of either Luther or the Anabaptists. By 1519 the authorities commenced to imprison the heretics. Upon the arrival of Charles V in the Netherlands in 1521, action was taken against the writings of Luther, and a lay inquisition was entrusted with the task of carrying on a campaign against those who accepted the new religious ideas. In 1523 the penalty of burning at the stake began to be inflicted. By 1530 most of the leaders and teachers of prominence in the new movement had been driven out of the country. These developments took place particularly in the northern provinces of the Netherlands.

After the rise of the Calvinist movement in France, the French-speaking Walloons of the southern provinces of the Netherlands commenced to be affected by the new religious ideas. Thereafter, the Calvinist ideas spread rapidly in both the southern and the northern provinces. By 1560 many congregations of Calvinists had been formed in the Low Countries. Before long, the Calvinist ideas had largely supplanted the earlier Lutheran and Anabaptist doctrines. In 1571 the first national synod was held. In 1574 an academy, the beginning of the University of Leyden, was founded for the purpose of preparing preachers for the new movement.

The Establishment of Presbyterianism in Scotland

Calvinism also became deeply rooted in Scotland. In the sixteenth century, this state was small, weak, and backward. In domestic affairs it was characterized much of the time by turbulent factions among the nobles. In foreign affairs it was distinguished by a tenacious fear of being absorbed by England. This hostility toward the English had caused the Scottish kingdom to form an alliance with France against that country. One of the results of this alliance had been a marriage in 1538 between James V (1513–1542), the reigning sovereign of Scotland, and Mary of Guise, a daughter of the famous French family of that name. Upon the death of the king in 1542, his queen, Mary of Guise, became regent for her daughter, the later Mary, Queen of Scots (1542–1587). In accordance with Scottish policy and her own natural ties of country and family, Mary of Guise arranged a marriage between her daughter, Mary, titular Queen of Scots, and Francis, son of Henry II, king of France. In 1548, accordingly, the young queen sailed for France where she was to be educated for her future royal duties.

In the meantime, in spite of the strong Catholic bias of the royal family, Protestantism was getting a foothold in Scotland. Little is known about the story of its introduction into the country. By 1557 the Protestant party was strong enough in Scotland to take action publicly against the old church. In that year the Protestants drew up, under the inspiration of the absent John Knox, a covenant against the ancient Catholic religion. In 1560 the Protestant party caused the Scottish parliament to abolish the Mass and papal jurisdiction. In place of the Catholic forms of worship, there was introduced into Scotland a Protestant confession of faith, a book of discipline, and a service based on the one in use at Geneva.

The revolt had been made under the unmistakable leadership of John Knox. Not much is known about his early life. He was the son of a small farmer, had attended one of the Scottish universities, had become a priest, and finally had broken with the old church. Before he became prominent in the Scottish religious movement, he had had varied experiences. He had been captured by the French and forced to serve in the French galleys. He had played a part in the religious changes taking place in England. He had spent some time with Calvin at Geneva. Finally, he became the chief adviser of the leaders of the Scottish revolt against the Medieval Church.

In 1559, Knox returned to Scotland. He immediately started a campaign against the old forms of religion. Although he was at once declared an outlaw by the regent, he preached in many of the Scottish cities. In his sermons he attacked such things as the Mass and advocated the abolition of monasteries. His preaching paved the way for the action of the Scottish parliament against the old church and its forms but divided Scotland into two religious parties. Lowland Scotland was gradually won over to the new religion and looked to Elizabeth, the Protestant queen of England, for support. The Highlands tended to remain Roman Catholic and to look to the French monarchy for help.

Knox had great plans for the Scottish people. As rapidly as possible, Protestant congregations were organized which elected their own ministers. Once selected, the ministers were supposedly subject to no earthly authority. The Word of God, of course, as interpreted by Knox, was to prevail in all matters of conduct and doctrine. The council of the realm was supposed to put down all other forms of religion. That there should be a general assembly composed of representatives of the various congregations was taken for granted. There was to be a noble scheme of general education and a system of generous stipends for the clergy.

Knox, however, never was able to carry out fully his great plans. Queen Elizabeth gave her help to the Scottish Protestants very grudgingly. For this, Knox was himself partly to blame. As a means of defeating the efforts of Mary of Guise in behalf of the old religion, the Scottish reformer had written a work entitled *The Monstrous Regiment of Women*. Being a woman, the queen of England resented the sweeping attack on women and gave only enough aid to the Scottish Protestants to prevent the triumph of the Catholic party in Scotland. The plans of Knox were also thwarted in part by the Scottish nobles. In 1567, the Scottish parliament reintroduced the institution of patronage. This gave the noble landlords instead of the congregations the power of appointing ministers. The church property, too, went for the most part to the nobles and prevented the fulfillment of the plans of Knox for education and stipends. Finally, in 1572, the nobles set up for their own benefit a sort of episcopacy over the Scottish church.

At the time of Knox's death in 1572, the Presbyterian system of church government, as it is now known, was not fully established. The completion of the Presbyterian system in Scotland was largely the work of Andrew Melville (1545–1622), who came from Geneva about this time. Under his leadership the office of bishop was abolished; pastors, doctors, elders, and deacons were recognized as the proper officers of the church; the general assembly fixed its own time of meeting and declared its actions were not subject to review; and presbyters were set up. Quite contrary to the usual practice, however, the state church in Scotland stood for the freedom and rights of the middle and lower classes against the monarchy.

The Spread of Calvinism to Poland

For a time, the Calvinist movement also affected Poland and Lithuania. Since the country had only one university, many Polish nobles studied at German universities. There, they came into contact with the new currents in religious thought. They were inclined to look with suspicion at the Lutheran movement because of its German origin, but they tended to regard as allies the Calvinists, the Bohemian Brethren, and other Protestant sects who fled from persecution because of their attacks on the powerful Polish clergy. After 1545, reports of crowded conventicles, the seizure of churches, the dissolution of monasteries are frequent. By 1550 a majority of the Polish diet favored Protestantism, and the Protestant nobles demanded the right to hold a national synod, religious toleration for Polish Protestants, and equality of treatment. They were strong enough to wrest from their sovereign a policy of toleration which lasted for a decade. Calvinism, however, never affected to any great extent the mass of ignorant and poverty-stricken peasants.

The new religious movement was one of the causes for the acquisition by Poland of an important territorial addition. Since medieval times, the lands along the Baltic coast from East Prussia to the Gulf of Finland had been held by the German crusading order known as the Teutonic Knights. When, in 1526, the grand master of this order secularized East Prussia and placed it under the suzerainty of Poland, the Teutonic Knights in the other lands held by the order refused to follow his example. By 1561, however, the remaining Teutonic Knights were in a bad situation. Sweden had plans for the conquest of their lands in order to make the Baltic a Swedish lake. Both Russia and Poland were cut off from the sea by the lands of the order and desired to conquer them. In that year, accordingly, the head of the Teutonic Knights struck a bargain with the king of Poland. The agreement was the signal for important political changes in the Baltic lands. Sweden obtained Estonia by military force. Poland acquired Livonia, which became an integral part of Poland, and Courland, which came under the suzerainty of Poland but retained a considerable amount of autonomy. The former head of the Teutonic Knights became a Protestant and the first duke of the new duchy.

The annexation of these territories soon led to a reorganization of the Polish state. Hitherto, Poland had, in reality, consisted of two separate states—Poland and the Grand Principality of Lithuania. In the efforts of the Polish king to annex the new territories, both states had shown a lack of patriotism and cooperation. In the years that followed, the king brought about the complete union of Poland and Lithuania. After 1569, accordingly, they were really one state.

The Spread of Protestantism to Hungary

At first, the revolt against the Medieval Church made little progress in Hungary. Only the so-called Saxons, the German immigrants in Hungary, who lived mainly in the towns, welcomed the Lutheran doctrines. After the national disaster at Mohacs in 1526, the situation changed. After that overwhelming defeat, it should be remembered, Hungary became divided into three nearly equal parts—one ruled by the Habsburg family, one headed by the Zapolya family under Turkish suzerainty, and a third annexed outright to Turkey. After this event, conditions favored the Roman Church only in the part of Hungary ruled by the Habsburgs. In the other two parts of the country, the government gave no support to the Roman Church, the nobles were inclined to seize its property, and education declined in a very marked way among the clergy. In Transylvania and the provinces of Hungary proper, ruled by the Zapolyas, Calvinism made great progress, particularly among the nobles, in spite of the efforts of the authorities to suppress it. In 1564, Calvinism gained for a time complete toleration. In Turkish Hungary the supporters of the old church were mostly carried off, killed, or forced to fly. The place left vacant by the Roman Catholics was filled by Serbian immigrants. The Christian churches, for the most part, were transformed into Moslem mosques. This continued to be the situation in Hungary until the Roman Church, reformed and reinvigorated by its own efforts, began a campaign for the reconquest of the ground it had lost.

The English Revolt against the Medieval Church

In England many conditions favored the spread of the new religious ideas. In the Middle Ages the protests of Wiclif and the Lollards against certain features of the old church had left a permanent mark on the religious life of the country. More recently, the Humanist movement had penetrated the country and prepared the way for the introduction of religious changes. More important still was the fact that the developing monarchy found the power and privileges of the Church increasingly irksome. These conditions prepared the English people for a break with the old church under the leadership of their young and headstrong sovereign, Henry VIII.

The father of this young king had greatly strengthened the monarchy. Although he had obtained the kingship through the civil struggle known as the War of the Roses, he had subsequently put down opposition to the monarchy through a wise mixture of conciliation and repression. He had avoided long and costly foreign wars and built up the financial resources of the crown. He favored the rising middle class in many ways.

The English people, though, welcomed the change of sovereigns, as they had grown tired of the aging Henry VII. His successor, Henry

VIII, seemed to possess many attractive traits. He was only eighteen. He was considered good-looking. He was strong and agile. He had some knowledge of music, books, and foreign languages. The English people did not see as yet that he, too, had many of the qualities of a tyrant.

Immediately after his accession, however, Henry VIII began to show his determination to have his own way. Assisted by his powerful minister, Cardinal Wolsey, he commenced to dabble in international politics. He proved, however, to be no match for his more experienced rivals. Finding himself duped by the two older and craftier kings, Louis XII of France and Ferdinand of Aragon, Henry VIII turned his attention more, for the time being, to domestic affairs.

About 1520, a problem developed which was to harass the king and his subjects for the remainder of the reign. In 1501 the two astute rulers, Henry VII of England and Ferdinand of Aragon, had arranged for the marriage of Prince Arthur, heir to the English throne, and Catherine, the daughter of Ferdinand and Isabella, joint sovereigns of Spain. Within a few months after the marriage Prince Arthur died. This turn of events threatened to upset the plans of the two shrewd politicians. Accordingly, they promptly took steps to avert the danger. With the consent of the Pope, they arranged that the young widow should marry the new heir to the English throne, the future Henry VIII.

About 1520, it commenced to be whispered around the court concerning the possibility of a divorce of the young and apparently happily married couple. No one can say with certainty the exact motive for the desire of Henry VIII to dissolve his marriage. He may have really had genuine and increasing doubts about the validity of a marriage which had failed to result in the birth of a male heir. He actually may have feared to leave the rule of the country to a woman, his daughter, Mary Tudor. England had had nineteen years of anarchy as the result of the accession of one woman to the throne and had no wish to repeat the experience. After 1522, a different and more powerful motive spurred the king into determined efforts to get rid of Catherine. About that time he fell violently in love with a bright-eyed girl, Anne Boleyn, who came to his court. As a consequence, he decided to get rid of his faithful and upright Catherine and to marry the attractive young woman who had caught his fancy.

In spite of his position and power, Henry VIII soon found that there were many obstacles to the execution of his plans. As a first step toward separation, Cardinal Wolsey, the king's chief minister and the representative of the Pope in England, summoned his master to appear in his ecclesiastical court to answer the charge that he was living unlawfully with his late brother's wife. The plan, however, failed because of the stubborn opposition of Catherine. As the injured and innocent Catherine was about to make an appeal to the Pope, the baffled cardinal referred the whole question to the papal authorities. The Pope, however, was in no position to accede to the request of the English sovereign. If he did, he would go against the traditions of the Church and offend the powerful Charles V, who was a nephew of Catherine. Finding himself in this dilemma, the Pope adopted a policy of drawing out the negotiations as much as he could. This failure to obtain a divorce cost Cardinal Wolsey his political power and finally his life. His impatient sovereign was in no mood to brook delay.

In place of the unfortunate Cardinal Wolsey, two new royal advisers rose to power, the young and gentle Archbishop Cranmer and Thomas Cromwell. These advisers urged the king to take matters into his own hands. The first action of the impetuous Henry VIII was to refer the question of a divorce to the universities of Europe. This measure, however, proved to be no more satisfactory than the application to the Pope. The answers of the different universities proved to be based on politics rather than ethics or religion. As a consequence of this failure, the king started to bring pressure where he could force a favorable answer. In 1531 he bullied the convocation, the assembly of his English clergy, into granting him a large sum of money, into promising to make no ecclesiastical laws without royal assent, and into submitting existing Church laws to a committee of the clergy for revision. Somewhat later, he extorted from this submissive body a declaration against his marriage to Catherine. Thereupon, Cranmer allowed himself to be persuaded into making a declaration against the validity of the king's first marriage, and Henry VIII secretly married Anne Boleyn.

Having wrung from the clergy approval of his plans, Henry VIII next brought pressure upon the English parliament. In 1533 he extorted from that body an act of appeals which provided that all spiritual cases (such as his suit for divorce) should be decided within his own jurisdiction. He likewise obtained acts that forbade all further payments to Rome and an act that declared the king himself to be supreme head of the Church of England. These measures gave Henry VIII far more power than any of his predecessors had had and made him master of both state and church. The king promptly used his new power to have Catherine deprived of her position as queen.

Though in the main Henry VIII was in agreement with the old church in regard to matters of doctrine, organization, and services, he used his new power to make some further ecclesiastical changes. One of his most important measures was the destruction of the monasteries. His first action against these long-established institutions was a campaign of propaganda that represented the monasteries in a most unfavorable light. Doubtless, many of the charges made against them had elements of truth in them, but the real reason for the attack was the king's desire to fill his depleted treasury and to gain the support of the influential classes in the state by sharing with them the property of the Church. By sermons, caricatures, and pamphlets the monasteries were accused of waste, corruption, and mismanagement. By 1536 the king and his advisers felt that it was safe to suppress the smaller monasteries. These were defined as the establishments with incomes of less than two hundred pounds a year or with fewer than twelve inmates. This measure affected about four hundred monastic establishments. During the next three years, the larger monastic houses, including those of the friars, were destroyed.

In order to be sure that their charges against the monasteries were never refuted, the authorities destroyed as much of the evidence as they could lay their hands on. Such evidence as escaped destruction, however, indicates the charges made against the monasteries were grossly exaggerated.

This destruction of the monasteries worked a revolution in the social life of England. For centuries, the monasteries and convents had been deeply enmeshed in English society. Many families were represented in the membership of the different chapters, and many links bound the monasteries and the surrounding regions together. All this was changed by the abolition of the monasteries. The property formerly owned by the monastic establishments fell into the hands of new owners. One third became the property of the king. The rest came into the possession of the nobles. How deeply these changes affected England is clearly shown by the uprising in northern England known as the Pilgrimage of Grace.

Besides abolishing the monasteries, the king introduced certain other changes. In 1538 an English translation of the Bible was published. This was a step towards putting the Bible in the hands of the people. In 1536 and again in 1539, statements were made which set forth what the English people were expected to believe in matters of religion. In 1538, too, the various religious shrines, many of them very rich, were demolished, and wagonloads of gold, silver, precious stones, and fine vestments were seized. The service used by the Church was put into the English tongue. The general effect of the innovations introduced by Henry VIII was to separate the English church from all allegiance to the Pope but left untouched much of the doctrine, organization, and service of the old church.

Effect of the Religious Policy of Henry VIII on Anglo-Irish Relations

The religious policy of Henry VIII made the task of England in Ireland more difficult. Since the invasion of Ireland by the Anglo-Norman barons in 1166, the English authorities had been trying to control Ireland. In the time of Henry VIII they exercised real control in the island only around Dublin in the so-called Irish Pale. This was owing to the fact that the Irish looked upon the English as alien invaders and only gave allegiance to the English sovereign when they were compelled to do so. The religious policy of Henry VIII gave the Irish people a new grievance against the English. From that time onward, the Irish looked upon the English not only as invaders but as heretics.

The Protestant Extremists in Power in England

In 1547, Henry VIII died. He was nominally succeeded on the English throne by his son, Edward VI, a boy ten years of age. The accession of so youthful a sovereign meant that the royal authority for some time would be exercised actually by the young king's advisers.

At first, the council of regency which had been named by Henry VIII put Hertford, under the title of Lord Protector and Duke of Somerset, at the head of affairs. He proved to be a man who was greedy for power but who wished well for the country. In religious affairs he went much farther toward Protestantism than Henry VIII had gone. He repealed some of the savage laws against heretics that had been put on the statute books by the predecessors of the young king. The duke authorized the seizure of the property of the crown chantries, hospitals, and gilds. Some of the seized wealth was used for the founding of new schools. Much more of it went to enrich the members of the council. In 1549 the duke pushed through Parliament an Act of Uniformity, designed to force on the clergy a form of service in English that would be alike for all parishes and that did away with various ceremonies repugnant to Protestants. By these and other measures, the duke had aroused much opposition. By 1549 the discontent was so strong that the council of regency had little difficulty in depriving him of his power and throwing him into prison.

In reality, the religious affairs of the nation were in a state of

125

anarchy. Each parish did as it pleased in matters of religion. Foreigners pressed into the country preaching Lutheran, Calvinist, Anabaptist, and Zwinglian doctrines. It looked for a moment as though England was about to fall into the hands of religious extremists.

This was the situation that faced Warwick, the new master of the state. Although he was really indifferent in matters of religion, he pretended to be a very zealous Protestant. He filled vacant bishoprics with leaders of the reform party. He continued the policy of plundering the property of the Church. In 1552 he obtained from Parliament another Act of Uniformity, which made still greater concessions to Protestant sentiment in the service of the Church, and an official statement of faith in forty-two articles. In 1553, in spite of an effort to continue in power, Warwick fell from office as a result of the death of Edward VI.

The Swing of England to Catholicism under Mary Tudor

In accordance with the arrangements made by Henry VIII for the succession to the throne, Mary, the half sister of Edward VI, succeeded him. Some of the Protestant extremists attempted to prevent her accession, but the English people generally rallied to her support. The new queen came to the throne with the best intentions, but, nevertheless, she soon alienated her subjects. One of the things that made her unpopular was her marriage. In accordance with the plans of Charles V, she married, in 1554, his son, Philip II of Spain. The marriage brought no satisfaction either to the queen or her people. The new royal consort never loved his plain, unattractive wife who was eleven years his senior. In spite of his efforts to ingratiate himself with the English people, they looked upon him as a dangerous foreigner. As soon as he could, he absented himself on the continent and only reutrned to England when he needed English help in the carrying out of his continental plans. In 1557, as a consequence of his influence over the queen, England became involved in the war with France and lost Calais, the last English possession on French soil.

Another cause for the estrangement of the English people from the queen was her religious policy. As the daughter of Catherine of Aragon, she had remained faithful to her mother and the Roman Church. As soon as she came to the throne, accordingly, she began to take steps to bring the English people back to the Catholic fold. Immediately after her accession to office, she issued a proclamation urging all men to return to the old faith and ordered the restoration of much of the plate that had been stolen from the Church in the reigns of her two predecessors. In the same year, 1553, Parliament repealed all the laws affecting religion which had been enacted during Edward VI's reign and restored the church service that had been in use in the last year of her father's reign. The Lutherans, Zwinglians, Calvinists, and Anabaptists were ordered to quit the kingdom. Married priests were forced to give up their wives or their benefices. Altars were erected in the parish churches. In 1554, the English sheriffs were admonished by the government to return to Parliament men of a wise, grave, and Catholic sort. Later in the year, the new parliament petitioned for the admission of the English people again into the unity of the Catholic Church, repealed all laws regarding religion passed since the twentieth year of Henry VIII, and restored all the old laws against heresy. Accordingly, Cardinal Pole, the recently arrived papal legate, after assuring Parliament that the Pope would make no demand for a restoration of confiscated Church lands, solemnly received the realm again into the Roman Catholic fold.

The passage of this legislation was the signal for four years of severe persecution for those who refused to conform. Nobody in that day advocated toleration. The reformers, for their part, were abusive. The queen regarded it as a duty to extirpate heresy. Ministers faithful to the reform movement, humble artisans, and tillers of the soil were burned at the stake. Even two bishops, Latimer and Ridley, suffered martyrdom. The victims of the four years of persecution numbered nearly three hundred, a larger number than had suffered persecution in the thirty-eight years of the reign of Henry VIII. They finally included the perplexed and fearful Cranmer. The names of the victims were later enshrined in the vivid but not always accurate pages of Foxe's *Book of Martyrs*. At last, in 1558, the death of the unhappy queen put an end in England to the religious persecution of Protestants by Catholics.

The Elizabethan Religious Settlement

Mary Tudor was succeeded on the throne of England by her half sister, Elizabeth. The new queen is one of the most puzzling characters of history. She was vain and uncertain of temper. She could be both prudent and rash. She was often unscrupulous. She was remarkably vigorous and capable of unremitting toil. At times she was petty, and at other moments she was more farseeing than the wisest of her ministers. She had been schooled by years of hardship and danger and by disillusioning experiences. She gathered round her a crowd of worthless favorites and a group of ministers of unusual excellence. For forty-five years she outwitted the shrewdest diplomats of Europe by a series of courtships that never terminated in marriage.

Though the new queen seems to have had little genuine religious feeling, she was forced by political considerations to be a Protestant. In no other way could she maintain her right to the English throne. One of her first measures, accordingly, was the regulation of the religious affairs of her kingdom. By the Act of Supremacy, Parliament, after a hard struggle, repealed the ecclesiastical legislation of Mary Tudor and re-enacted the antipapal laws of Henry VIII. By a new Act of Uniformity of Common Prayer, the same body established a common form of religious service for all English parishes. This measure provided severe penalities for ministers who refused to adopt the new prayer book and for laymen who failed to attend church. It made submission to the established church a test of loyalty to the state. Somewhat later, Elizabeth forced through Convocation, the chief assembly of the English church, a statement of doctrine in thirty-nine articles which is still the official statement of the beliefs of not only the established Church of England but of the Episcopal churches of the British Empire and the United States. The legislation of Parliament and Convocation together is commonly called the Elizabethan Religious Settlement.

The religious policy adopted by Elizabeth put the English state in a somewhat dangerous position. As Catholic countries, both France and Spain were at least potential enemies. At the same time, Mary, Queen of Scots and her party were hostile and might push the claims of the Scottish queen to the English throne. The danger of a Catholic alliance against England became more acute after France and Spain made peace in 1559, but the danger was averted for the time being by the cautious policy followed by both Philip II and Elizabeth and by the preoccupation of France with the Wars of Religion. This situation, however, gave rise to many plots against the English queen and made her an unwilling ally of Protestant parties and powers on the continent.

The Elizabethan Religious Settlement did not satisfy all the queen's subjects. Many Englishmen, particularly in northern England, clung openly or secretly to the ancient faith of England. After the defeat in Scotland and the flight of Mary, Queen of Scots to England in 1568, there was much plotting against Elizabeth which centered in the Scottish queen. In 1569 a rising, headed by the northern earls, was caused by a mixture of religious, political, and economic causes.

The English sovereign strove to meet the danger from the Roman Catholics in two ways. She sought to stir up revolts among the Protestant subjects of rulers that might intervene in English affairs. She imposed restrictive legislation on her own subjects, designed to compel their outward conformity to the service of the Church of England.

In 1571, however, the so-called "Ridolfi Plot" came to light and clearly showed the danger of the English queen's position. The instigator of the plot was a Florentine merchant who tried, with the aid of the Duke of Alba, Philip II, and the Pope, to liberate the Scottish queen and marry her to an English nobleman, the Duke of Norfolk. There were two attempts also to stir up Ireland against English rule and to regain Scotland for the Catholic cause. Earnest Jesuits like Edmund Campion and Robert Parsons, trained at the English college at Rome and the seminary at Douay in northern France, risked their lives in a determined effort to regain England for the Catholic Church. The only result of these attempts was the execution of the ringleaders and the imposition of still more severe measures. The repressive policy culminated in 1586 with the execution of the Scottish queen herself.

On the other hand, many of the subjects of Elizabeth were more Protestant than the English queen herself. These Protestant extremists may be divided into three classes. They include Puritans, Presbyterians, and Separatists or Brownists. All held conventicles or private meetings in which they held services according to their own ideas instead of those of their sovereign. The Puritans wanted the service of the state church purified from forms and ceremonies that resembled those of the Roman Church. They objected to the prescribed vestments, the observance of saints' days, the use of the cross in baptism, and the playing of church organs. The Presbyterians objected particularly to employment of bishops. The Separatists insisted on the right of each congregation to govern its own affairs. Somewhat later, they came to be known as Independents, Congregationalists, and Baptists because of their opposition to a state church and because of differences in their beliefs.

The Protestant revolt against the Medieval Church destroyed the religious unity which had previously prevailed in Western and Central Europe. Southern Europe remained, for the most part, Roman Catholic. The rest of Western and Central Europe renounced the allegiance to the Pope at Rome and made changes in the doctrines, organization, and service of the Medieval Church. Central and Eastern Germany and the Baltic and Scandinavian lands became Lutheran. Some of the Swiss cantons, an important minority in France, Poland, and Hungary, the seven northern provinces of the Netherlands, and the greater part of Scotland adopted Calvinism. The English government made the Anglican Church the legal church in England but failed to force it on a Roman Catholic minority on the one hand and a substantial body of Protestants on the other. It made the Anglican Church also the official church in Ireland but failed to win for it the allegiance of the Irish people. On the continent many humble folk became Anabaptists in spite of savage persecution.

While all the churches of Europe retained a substantial body of common beliefs and practices, the Protestant churches differed from the Medieval Church and from each other in various ways. The Roman Catholics held that the chief authority in matters of religion was the Bible as interpreted by the Church. The Protestants professed to believe that it was the Bible as interpreted by the individual but, in practice, often forced people to conform to beliefs and practices established by state churches. The Roman Catholics believed in the necessity for the intervention of the clergy. The Protestants professed to believe in the priesthood of all believers. In regard to salvation, the Roman Catholics believed in the need of faith and works, the Lutherans in justification by faith, the Calvinists in justification by election, and the Anglican Church left the whole matter somewhat in doubt. All Protestants abandoned the use of Latin and put the service into the vernacular used by the people. The Anglican Church retained most of the forms used by the Medieval Church. The Calvinists abandoned the Mass, adopted a service consisting of a sermon, prayer, and hymns, and worshiped in plain churches. All three Protestant churches gave up invocation of the saints and veneration of relics. They all, too, renounced their allegiance to the Pope, and, wherever they were a majority, they came under the control of the state. The Anglican Church retained bishops and archbishops. The various Lutheran churches differed greatly in regard to their machinery of government, and the Calvinists worked out a hierarchy of presbyteries, synods, and assemblies that gave the laity a voice in the government of the church. The distinguishing mark of the Anabaptists and some of the Separatists in England was their belief in the necessity of baptism by immersion. The Protestant Revolt thus substituted a great diversity of beliefs and practices for the uniformity of the Medieval Church.

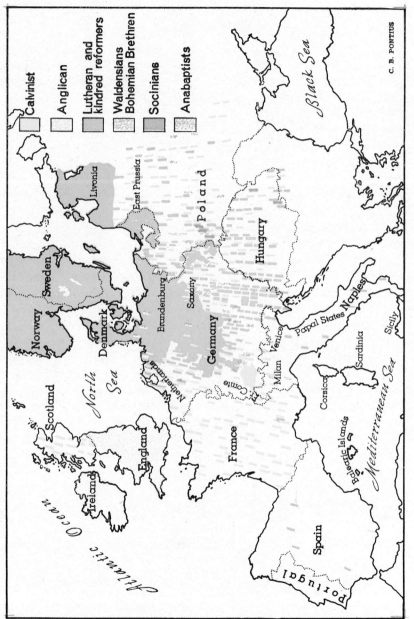

Legend:
- Calvinist
- Anglican
- Lutheran and kindred reformers
- Waldensians Bohemian Brethren
- Socinians
- Anabaptists

Progress of the Protestant Revolt by 1560

C. B. PONTIUS

Atlantic Ocean

Scotland

Ireland

England

North Sea

Norway

Sweden

Denmark

Netherlands

France

Franche Comté

Germany

Brandenburg

Saxony

East Prussia

Livonia

Poland

Hungary

Milan

Venice

Papal States

Naples

Corsica

Sardinia

Sicily

Balearic Islands

Mediterranean Sea

Spain

Portugal

Black Sea

CHAPTER 9

The Catholic Reformation and Spanish Imperialism

By the middle of the sixteenth century it must have looked to many contemporary observers as though the Medieval Church was on the verge of dissolution. Many earnest men who had started out as reformers of the Church had in the end become leaders of a revolt against that institution which had deprived it of half its communicants. Northern and Central Europe had been almost wholly lost by the Church, and Southern Europe seemed to be supinely awaiting destruction. About the middle of the century, as acute an observer as the Venetian ambassador at Rome wrote to his government that the situation was desperate.

The Medieval Church, however, was not destroyed. While some of the reformers became rebels, others remained loyal to the ancient faith and worked for its reform. Their efforts finally gave the Church a different leadership, a new faith in its mission, a reorganization of its institutions, and a determination to regain what it had lost and to win new peoples to its allegiance. From that time forward, consequently, Protestantism found itself in conflict with a militant church.

The New Papacy

One of the most important signs of the new spirit at work in the Church was the accession to leadership of a new type of pope. For a long time, the heads of the Church had lacked a consciousness of its spiritual mission. They had devoted their attention to the interests of their families, to Italian politics, or to the Renaissance. Alexander VI (1492–1503), for example, had used his position to advance the interests of his relatives. Julius II (1503–1513), an extraordinary man in many ways, devoted himself to the restoration of the independence of the Papal States, the liberation of Italy from French rule, the collection of art treasures, the building of the cathedral of St. Peter, and the beautification of the Vatican and the city of Rome. His successor, Leo X, had many excellent qualities. He was mild and courteous in manner, a generous patron of art, liberal to the poor, and even pious in an external fashion. He did not, however, make a good pope. For some time he thought the movement set in motion by Luther was a mere squabble of German monks. While the Church was visibly going

131

to pieces, he spent the resources of the papacy on music, hunting, expensive banquets, and theatrical performances. Clement VII (1523–1534) was timid and irresolute. He misjudged very greatly the political forces of his day and did little or nothing to save the Church.

The successors of these popes were men of a very different stamp. They included Paul III (1534–1549), in whose reign the Church began to put its house in order and to strike back at its Protestant opponents, Marcellus II (1555–1559), who continued to follow after his election the rules of the Dominican order, and Paul IV. These leaders of the Church and their successors appointed men of ability and piety to the college of cardinals and to other posts in the hierarchy of the Church. They encouraged the founding of new orders. They convened the great Council of Trent.[1] They sent devoted men to regain, if possible, the regions that had gone over to Protestantism and to convert the peoples in the lands being discovered by Spanish and Portuguese navigators. The new leaders, however, had the same limitations as other men of their age. They couldn't conceive even the idea of religious toleration. They thought that men must be compelled by force to do what the Church thought was right. As a consequence, they felt justified in using the inquisition and censorship of the press and in urging Catholic sovereigns to use their temporal powers for the extirpation of heresy. As yet, few understood the principle of religious toleration.

The Founding of New Religious Orders

Another sign of the new spirit at work in the Church at this time was the founding of new religious orders. Almost from the beginning, the Church had met grave religious crises by the establishment of new religious orders. Almost instinctively, therefore, the Lutheran revolt was followed by the organization of new monastic orders. In southern Italy the bishop of Chiete founded in 1525 the Theatines. Their objective was the recall of the clergy and the laity to a more edifying life. The new order spread quickly over Italy and made its way into other countries. In 1532, Jerome Emiliani, who at the time was engaged in military and administrative work and later was canonized, established in northern Italy the Somaschi, an order devoted to the care of the sick, the orphaned, and the abandoned. In 1525, in central Italy, a movement was started for the restoration of the Franciscan order of friars to its original principles. This resulted in the organization of the Capucin order. In 1530, the Barnabites were organized, an order which took a special vow never to strive for office.

---

[1] *See* page 135.

Ten years later, the Pope sanctioned the organization of the Society of Jesus, the later famous order commonly called the Jesuits.

The Society of Jesus

The founder of the Jesuit order was an extraordinary man, Igantius Loyola (1491–1556), the son of a Spanish noble family. Prior to 1521, he was in turn a page at the court of Ferdinand of Aragon, a courtier, and a soldier. In 1521 he was seriously wounded at the Siege of Pampeluna. A cannonball tore open the calf of his left leg and broke his right shin. Although he was captured as a result of the accident, his French captors sent him home to his family castle. There he made heroic but unsuccessful efforts to overcome his wounds and return to military life. Unaided by any anaesthetic, he endured to no avail the agony of having his wounded leg broken and set again and of having a protruding bone sawed off. In an effort to make the long hours of convalescence pass more quickly, he read the lives of Christ and some of the saints, the only books in the castle. As he read, he became fired with the idea of becoming a soldier of Christ instead of the king. For some time he was vague in his own mind as to how his resolve was to be accomplished. In the end he found peace for his soul through certain spiritual exercises which are still used by Roman Catholics. Although he was a mature man, he also went to school for eleven years in order to become educated. He studied Latin at Barcelona with mere boys and then attended in turn the Universities of Acala, Salamanca, and Paris. At the French capital he finally gained six followers among his fellow students. In 1534 the seven associates took a historic vow in a church on Montmartre, a lofty quarter of Paris. Later, they went to Italy and, ultimately, to Rome, where they offered their services to the Pope. In 1540, accordingly, the head of the Church authorized the little band of earnest men to organize a new order, the Society of Jesus. Its members soon came to be known as Jesuits.

The members of the new order felt that they were soldiers of Christ. They considered themselves enlisted in the service of Christ in the same way that secular soldiers of the time belonged to their captains. In the years following the founding of their order, the Jesuits worked out a distinctive organization. They took not only the three vows ordinarily taken by monastic orders but a special vow of obedience to the Pope. They gave their order a military organization and elected their founder, Ignatius Loyola, as their first general. They selected their novices carefully and trained them to combine wide learning with deep piety. They had no special garb, accepted no offices, and had no choirs. From the beginning, the order was prepared for great achievements.

133

Almost immediately, the new order became the spearhead of the revived Church. Its members were assisted by the secular clergy and other orders, but they were always in the forefront of the attack carried on by the Church against Protestantism in the last half of the sixteenth century. Bold members of the order risked their lives by going to work in the countries threatened by the Protestant movement. Wherever the cooperation of rulers made it possible, as in Bavaria, they carried on campaigns marked by preaching, catechism, the founding of schools, and the building of churches. They supplemented these measures by the use of force. In their campaign to regain territory which had been lost by the Church, they met with great success in Germany, Hungary, and Poland but failed in England.

The new order took a place of equal prominence in the missionary work of the Church. This side of their work may be illustrated by the mission of Saint Francis Xavier. Born in 1506 in Navarre, he was one of the seven founders of the Jesuit order. In 1541, at the request of the king of Portugal, he sailed from Lisbon for India to work in the Portuguese colonies. After reaching India, he spent five months at Goa, where he preached, taught the children, and ministered to the sick. Next, he spent three years in Southern India. In 1545 he went to Malacca and then on to the Spice Islands. Three years later, he returned to Goa for a brief visit and arranged to have missionaries sent to various points in India. Thereupon, he set out for Japan, a country of which he had heard while at Malacca. He spent two and one half years there and started a mission that finally claimed to have made three hundred thousand converts. He then set out for China but died before he had really started a mission among the Chinese. Ever since his death, he has been considered a symbol of wholehearted religious devotion.

The Jesuit order, too, worked in America. The career of one of their number, Jean de Brebeuf, may be used as an illustration of their work among the Indians. Coming to America in 1625, this cultured, sensitive man lived for five months in Indian wigwams and then made an unsuccessful effort to found a mission near Georgian Bay. After a short visit to France, he returned to Canada and worked for sixteen years of hardship, suffering, and danger among the Huron Indians. In 1649 hostile Iroquois captured Brebeuf and a companion. Their captors treated the captives with the greatest cruelty. The Iroquois lighted fires under the heroic missionary, slashed him with knives, poured scalding water over him in mock baptism, and forced a red hot iron down his throat. Finally, his torturers handed him over to the Dutch. As soon as he was able, however, Brebeuf returned to Canada, where he soon was put to death by the hostile Iroquois.

In South America, the Jesuits were responsible for the establishment of the so-called Reductions of Paraguay. In 1586 these Fathers of the Church began their work among the conquered and enslaved Indians of this region. At every turn, the Jesuits were hampered by the rude frontiersmen of the Spanish and Portuguese colonies. As a result, the fathers of the order began to establish the reductions. By 1630 they had settled some ten thousand Indians in twelve of these establishments. Finding that the colonial authorities would not or could not protect the Indian converts, the Jesuits moved their reductions to the region of the Parana and organized their protegés into an effective military force. From that time until the eighteenth century, the reductions flourished. By 1670 their number had grown to thirty reductions.

These Indian settlements were established in healthy spots. Their Indian inhabitants lived separate from the white colonists under the supervision of members of the order. They dwelt in stone or adobe huts, fifteen by eighteen feet in size, ranged around a public square. There, the Jesuits taught the Indians under their care to live in a civilized manner. The settlements, in large part, met their own needs. They had their own tile kilns, mills, and tanneries. They made their own thread, yarn, and cloth. The inhabitants of the reductions were loaned the tools and the draft animals which they needed and were assigned plots of ground to till. They raised crops of maize, cotton, tobacco, indigo, sugar cane, and Paraguay tea. In addition, they raised great herds of cattle and large flocks of sheep. The success of the Jesuits with the reductions, however, only increased the enmity of the colonists against the society.

The Council of Trent

Another clear indication of the new spirit animating the Church was the Council of Trent. For a long time there had been a feeling that such an assembly should be held. After the revolt from the Church by Luther and other reformers, it had been hoped that a council of the Church might bring unity again in Christendom. In addition, it was generally recognized that there were abuses in the practices of the Church which needed correction and doctrines that required definition.

The holding of such a council, however, was a delicate matter. There were so many conflicting interests that had to be taken into consideration. These included the rivalry of Protestants and Catholics, the danger to the authority of the Pope, the interests of warring rulers, and the jealousy of Germans and Italians.

In 1545, after long negotiations, a council finally was convened at

135

Trent, a city in southern Germany near the Italian border. This place of meeting gave both the Pope and the Emperor a chance to exercise some influence over the deliberations of the council. In the papal bull that convened the council, the Pope assigned the assembled representatives of the Church three tasks—the pacification of the religious dispute, the reform of abuses, and a crusade against the infidels.

The Council of Trent did not complete its work until 1563. In 1547, using an outbreak of the plague as an excuse, the Pope attempted to move the council to the Italian city of Bologna where it would be entirely under his domination, but, following the instructions of their temporal master, the bishops of Charles V stayed behind. As a result, it was not until 1551 that the council was able to continue its deliberations. In 1552, however, the political situation caused another break in the proceedings. Finally, in 1562, the representatives of the Church met again and completed their work.

The council accomplished only one of the three tasks assigned to it. No Protestants came to its sessions, and, consequently, nothing was done about pacifying the dispute between Catholics and Protestants. Likewise, no crusade against the infidels was set in motion. Nevertheless, the Council of Trent was one of the most important religious assemblies that was ever held. It devoted its sessions to the definition of the doctrines of the Church and the correction of abuses. It gave the Church a clear-cut statement of its beliefs and improved the discipline of the clergy and the laity, appointments to ecclesiastical positions, and the practices and adminstration of the Church. In the debates of the assembly, two Jesuit theologians took a prominent part —Laynez and Salmeron, two of the founders of the order.

When the Council of Trent dissolved, it left some matters in the hands of the Pope to be finished. Under his supervision, accordingly, there came out in the next few years the Tridentine Profession of Faith, which summed up in twelve articles the cannons and decrees of the Council of Trent, the Roman catechism for the instruction of the clergy, a new breviary or devotional guide, a new missal, and a new edition of the Bible used by Roman Catholics. The Council of Trent thus prepared the Church to take the offensive against the Protestant world.

The Inquisition

In its conflict with Protestantism, the Church did not hesitate to use two weapons which shock many present-day people—the Inquisition and the *Index of Prohibited Books*. The Inquisition, however, must not be judged by modern standards. On the contrary, the student must take into consideration contemporary ideas and practices.

The Inquisition was a court. Like all courts of the time, it was by modern standards unfair, unjust, and inhuman. It threw around the accused no safeguards of any sort. It used torture to extract confessions. It punished its victims with great severity. Few, if any, understood the idea of toleration. Nearly everyone thought heresy was treason against the state as well as the church.

As early as Roman times, there had been legislation against heresy. In the thirteenth century, the Pope appointed inquisitors to travel around and ferret out heretics. The early Inquisition, however, was desultory and intermittent in its action. For minor offences it imposed fines, fasting, pilgrimages, and imprisonment. More serious cases it handed over to the State for execution in order that the Church might not be charged with shedding blood.

When the institution of the Inquisition is mentioned, however, most people have in mind the Spanish Inquisition. In Spain, the Christian Spanish waged a long-drawn-out struggle for the reconquest of the peninsula. They were not sure of the loyalty of either the Jews or the Moors living in the regained territory. They feared that the heretics were also traitors. In 1480, accordingly, the inquisition in Spain assumed a new form. The secular government extorted from the rather reluctant Pope the right to establish the Spanish Inquisition. As a result, Ferdinand and Isabella appointed a Grand Inquisitor and a Council of Inquisition and set up in various cities subordinate tribunals. Nobody escaped from its jurisdiction. In time, it freed itself from the control of both Church and State. In its zeal against Jews and Moslems, it did much to destroy the prosperity of the peninsula. From Spain, it was introduced into the Spanish colonies (1516) and into the Netherlands.

The Index

The Index was the remedy chosen by the Church for the misuse of the new invention of printing. As long as books were scarce and few people could read and write, the printed page created no problem. With the multiplication and wide diffusion of books and pamphlets after the invention of printing, the situation changed. Ever since, both secular and Church authorities have felt that some supervision of the press was necessary on either moral or doctrinal grounds. They differ only about the amount of supervision necessary. The first papal list of prohibited books appeared in 1551. Ever since that date, the Church has attempted to regulate the reading of its communicants. The prohibition of the Church may affect the entire writings of the author listed; sometimes, a single book or only certain passages of an author's work are affected.

The Struggle for the Reconquest of Protestant Lands

The rise of better leaders, the foundation of new orders, the clarification of the teachings of the Church, and the correction of abuses prepared the Church for a struggle with Protestantism. Virtually everywhere, the Church was finally successful in stopping the advance of the Protestants. In some regions it won back territories that seemed irreparably lost.

One of the recovered regions was in Germany. In the middle of the sixteenth century the Rhineland, southern Germany, and the Habsburg lands seemed on the verge of becoming Protestant. These regions, however, were finally regained by the old church. In Westphalia, the bishoprics of Münster and Hildesheim were saved for the Church. In the Rhineland, the archbishopric of Cologne, which seemed likely to become Protestant because of the apostasy of its ruler, was regained as a result of the so-called Cologne War (1582–1584). In Bavaria and the Habsburg lands, the energetic support given by the secular authorities enabled the Church to stamp out Protestantism and turn those regions into strongholds of the Church. Because of these developments, there were henceforth in Germany two religious parties.

In Poland the revolt against the Church had never affected the mass of population. It had made converts mainly among the great magnates of Poland and Lithuania. The gentry and the peasants had for the most part remained loyal to the old faith. After 1572, Protestantism gradually ceased to be fashionable, and the Church carried on a campaign that in the end regained the great magnates for the Church.

In Hungary the fortunes of the Church were inextricably intertwined with those of the Habsburg family. After the disastrous battle of Mohacs, as we have seen, Hungary had been divided into three separate parts. These might be called Royal or Habsburg Hungary, Transylvania, and Turkish Hungary. In Royal Hungary, the Habsburg rulers continued to support the Roman Catholic Church. In Transylvania and the Hungarian counties attached to it, after 1557 everyone was permitted to worship God as he pleased. To a large extent, the Magyars became Calvinists, Unitarians, or Anabaptists, and the nobles confiscated the property of the Church. In Turkish Hungary the secular authorities tolerated all religions, but they were not at all friendly toward the Roman faith. After the Church became infused with a new spirit, the authorities in both Royal Hungary and Transylvania inaugurated a policy of severe persecution against Protestants. After 1593, the religious question in Hungary became inextricably mixed up with the political struggle known as the "Long War." This conflict caused Transylvania to be overrun and ravaged by Imperial troops. The cause of Protestantism seemed lost.

Just at that moment, however, the Habsburg emperor blundered. He transformed one of the most prominent men in Transylvania, Stephen Bocskay (1556–1606), into an enemy. Under the leadership of the latter, the Protestants won a great success. In 1606, as a result, Transylvania and the adjoining counties gained political autonomy and religious liberty for Lutherans, Calvinists, and Catholics; the Magyars of Royal Hungary were conceded amnesty; and the nobles of both regions regained their confiscated estates. This settlement brought peace to Hungary for twenty years and gave Transylvania a period of great prosperity.

Philip II, the Champion of Orthodoxy

While many rulers aided the Church in its struggle against Protestantism, the greatest champion of the interests of the Church was Philip II (1527–1598), king of Spain. His position as ruler of Spain, the Netherlands, important states in Italy, and large portions of North and South America made him the most important figure in Europe, not only to his own subjects but to other countries as well, and enabled him to wield great influence both within and outside of Spain. In contrast to his father, Charles V, Philip II was born and educated in Spain. He was Spanish in everything except appearance. The portraits of him, painted by Titian and doubtless somewhat flattering, show Philip II to have been a man of medium height, well-formed, regular in features, and elegant in dress. He learned from his none too faithful tutor to read and write Latin, French, and Italian, but he spoke only Castilian. His father assumed the task of training the young prince to rule over his great empire. As a result of his training, Philip II was dignified in bearing, grave in demeanor, and mistrustful of those around him. He was less licentious than most of his contemporaries. As a ruler he showed a veritable passion for work. He spent a large part of his forty years of rule, undeterred by sickness or weariness, at his desk reading an endless stream of dispatches from his ambassadors and administrators, making notes on the margins of the documents, and dictating replies. This very virtue, however, was his principal fault. He attempted the impossible. He insisted on giving his personal attention even to minute details of administration and diplomacy. The most pressing matters often waited days and weeks and months for the industrious but hesitant ruler to give them his personal attention and to make up his mind about them.

139

Philip II and Spain

In 1559, after the close of the long conflict with France, Philip II returned to Spain. He never again left its soil. In contrast to his father, Charles V, who spent his life in journeys and campaigns, Philip II did little traveling. He felt the need of a capital and a residence. Accordingly, he made the hitherto unimportant town of Madrid the political center of Spain. West of the new capital, on the slopes of the Guadarama Mountains, at some distance from Madrid, he built a palace, known as the Escorial, which became his favorite and principal residence. It was a unique structure. It was at the same time a palace, a monastery, a mausoleum, and a library. Constructed of granite, the vast, rectangular building had a very plain exterior. On the contrary, most of the interior was rich with tapestries and the paintings of Spanish and Netherland artists. For himself, however, Philip II reserved three bare rooms. In these he lived and worked.

Upon his arrival in Spain, Philip II turned first to the Mediterranean where the pirates of Northern Africa continually harassed the shores of Spain, France, and Italy. Behind the pirates, giving them support, loomed the Turks who dominated the Eastern Mediterranean. In 1560 and 1564, Philip II sent expeditions to attack the pirate strongholds along the northern coast of Africa. In 1565 his viceroy at Naples went to the aid of the Knights of Malta who were being hard-pressed by the attacks of the Turks. These measures checked the danger to the Western Mediterranean. In order to meet the Turkish menace in the Eastern Mediterranean, Philip II then formed an alliance with the Pope and the hard-pressed Venetians. In 1571, consequently, these allies formed a great fleet of one hundred and sixty-four galleys, manned by seventy-nine thousand soldiers and sailors, and commanded by the brilliant Don Juan, an illegitimate half brother of Philip II. In the Gulf of Lepanto, off the shores of Greece, the allied fleet won a great victory that averted the Turkish menace to Western Europe. Philip II, however, as on more than one other occasion, failed to reap all the advantages that might have been derived from this success.

The aggressive policy pursued by Moslems outside of Spain aroused the suspicions of the Spanish authorities in regard to the Moriscos, the inhabitants of Spain of Moorish ancestry, who were or had been Moslems. The Spanish lower classes disliked them on religious and economic grounds. Their very industriousness made the Spanish lower classes envy and dislike them. In 1567, accordingly, the Spanish government began to enforce a series of repressive decrees. Some of the Moriscos fled to Africa. Others rose in revolt and appealed for help to the king of Fez. The Spanish government, hampered by lack of money and troops, had considerable difficulty in quelling the revolt. Not until 1571 did the Spanish authorities succeed in defeating the Moriscos. In the end they uprooted the vanquished survivors from their homes and scattered them around Spain.

Another serious problem was Don Carlos, the son and heir of Philip II. Almost from birth the young prince had displayed alarming physical and mental defects. In spite of them, Philip II had hoped for a long time that Don Carlos might succeed him on the Spanish throne. As the young prince grew older, however, his unfitness for the position grew more and more apparent. He would without cause fly into rages, mistreat his servants, and display the greatest hostility toward his father. Finally, Philip II felt compelled to imprison his son. Some time after his incarceration, Don Carlos died. The episode is one of the causes for the bad reputation of Philip II outside of Spain. In spite of all that he put up with and had done for his son, his enemies hinted that Philip II was responsible for the death of Don Carlos. After his son's death, Philip II always wore black. The novelists and dramatists, however, disregarded the facts in the case and made a romantic and mistreated figure out of the miserable Don Carlos.

Another member of the court circle also did everything possible to blacken the reputation of the Spanish king. From 1567 onward, Philip II had among his secretaries a certain Antonio Perez who gradually won the confidence of his master. In 1578 the enemies of the secretary accused him of having been responsible for the assassination of the secretary of Don Juan, of Austria, the half brother of the king. In 1590, accordingly, Philip II finally ordered the arrest of his secretary. Perez managed to escape and fled to Aragon where he could take advantage of the provincial privileges and defy the royal officials. The king disregarded the constitutional rights of Aragon and crushed by force the defenders of the privileges of the province. This action forced Perez to fly from the country. He spent the rest of his life in defaming his former master. His writings are responsible for much of the prejudice against Philip II which exists outside of Spain.

Philip II and Europe

Although he was thoroughly Spanish in his outlook on life, Philip II was forced by his political position and religious interests to be a European figure. In addition to Spain and its colonies in America, he had inherited the Netherlands, the Free County of Burgundy, Sardinia, Sicily, Naples, and Milan. His championship of the Church led him to adopt a policy in the Netherlands that stirred that country to revolt and forced him to intervene in the internal affairs of France.

Both religion and politics finally involved him in a war with England.

Many developments thus explain the improvement in the position of the Roman Church during the last half of the sixteenth century. The Church acquired new and better leaders. It developed new orders devoted to its interests. It defined its beliefs and corrected abuses. It received aid from many rulers. As a result of these factors, it regained some territories temporarily lost to Protestantism and won new communicants in India, the Far East, and the New World.

CHAPTER
10

The Protestant Resistance to the Catholic Reformation and the Imperialism of Philip II

The preceding pages have shown that Philip II of Spain stood for certain ideas. They might be summarized as Spanish imperialism, the dominance of Spain in European politics, uniformity in religion, and political and economic monopoly overseas. These ideas aroused the armed resistance of his subjects in the Netherlands, of the Huguenot party in France, and among Elizabethan Englishmen. This chapter attempts to tell the story of their resistance.

The Revolt of the Netherlands

Throughout his long reign, Philip II was compelled to devote much of his attention and a large part of his resources to the seventeen provinces known as the Netherlands. Rule over them had been acquired gradually by his Burgundian ancestors. The last of the seventeen provinces had only just been gained by his own father, Charles V. Though their Burgundian and Habsburg rulers had tried to centralize authority in the seventeen provinces and get it into their own hands, the provinces and even the cities of the Netherlands had succeeded in retaining considerable political power.

Their rulers had developed a central government consisting of a regent, three councils, and a States-General, but the provinces had at the same time wrung from their sovereigns recognition of their rights and privileges. Accordingly, Philip II's regent in the Netherlands, when taking office, had sworn to observe not only the Great Privilege of the seventeen provinces but the "privileges" of each single province. These documents imposed on the rulers of the Netherlands the duties of asking the consent of the provinces in case of a declaration of war, the contraction of a royal marriage, and the levying of taxes, of employing only natives in the service of the government, and of using only the national language in the conduct of public affairs.

As long as Charles V had been their ruler, the inhabitants of the seventeen provinces had tolerated without too much protest some disregard of their rights and interests. He was born at Ghent and had grown up in their midst. They looked upon him as one of themselves. Upon the accession of his son, Philip II, however, the situation changed. They regarded him as a foreigner and had no interest in his imperial plans. As a consequence, their protests against his policies grew steadily stronger. The nobles, like William of Orange, resented the placing of all political authority in the hands of three councillors, known as the *consulta*. They disliked particularly one of the three because he was a foreigner. The people of the Netherlands opposed the plan to create new bishoprics because they would strengthen the hold of Philip II on the States-General. They were beginning to be shocked by the persecution and execution of Protestants by the central authorities. They feared that the king was planning to introduce the Spanish Inquisition into the Netherlands. They opposed the publication of the edicts of the Council of Trent in the Netherlands. They disliked the presence of Spanish troops in the provinces. As a result of these developments, there was a steady increase of tension between Philip II and the seventeen provinces.

The protests of the provinces took various forms. There was a general tendency among officials, like William of Orange—who was stadholder in the Free County of Burgundy and in three of the seventeen provinces, to refuse to enforce the edicts against heretics. In 1566 the lesser nobles assembled at Brussels, the capital of the seventeen provinces, and presented to the regent a solemn protest. Because of a derisive remark made to the regent by a courtier, the makers of the protest and, later, all who rebelled against the policies of Philip II became known as "the beggars." In 1567, mobs, composed of fanatics and the rowdy elements in the towns, attacked the churches. They systematically destroyed the priceless stained glass windows, the ornate altars, and all the symbols used for adornment and worship in the churches. As a result of these protests, many of the timid, the prudent, and the proscribed began to leave the country. One of those who emigrated was William of Orange, who had at one time been one of the most trusted advisers of Charles V. The only effect of these protests was a strengthening of the determination of Philip II to maintain at any cost his political authority and his church in the Netherlands.

A sign of his resolve to remain master of the seventeen provinces was the appointment in 1567, as his representative in the Netherlands, of the Duke of Alba, one of the greatest nobles in Spain and one of the king's most trusted advisers. With him came an army of ten thousand Spanish veterans—since the battle of Pavia, the most renowned troops in Europe. The duke came with the intention of setting himself up as a military dictator and of stamping out all opposition to the policies of Philip II. As a consequence, he instituted a

144

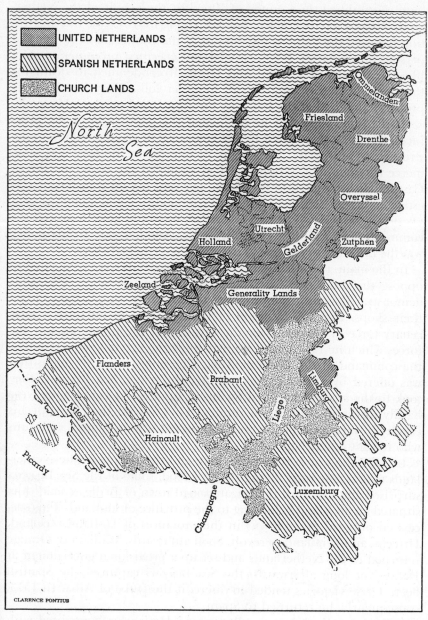

Legend:

- UNITED NETHERLANDS
- SPANISH NETHERLANDS
- CHURCH LANDS

North Sea

Friesland
Ommelanden
Drenthe
Overyssel
Utrecht
Gelderland
Zutphen
Holland
Zeeland
Generality Lands
Flanders
Brabant
Limburg
Liege
Artois
Hainault
Picardy
Champagne
Luxemburg

CLARENCE PONTIUS

The Netherlands at the Time of the War for Independence, 1567–1809 veritable reign of terror. He set up the Council of Troubles which soon was dubbed the Council of Blood by the people of the Netherlands because of its cruelty. For six years (1567–1573), this institution harassed the helpless inhabitants of the Netherlands. It attacked persons of all classes. It imprisoned and executed prominent nobles like the Counts of Egmont and Horn. It condemned to death for the crime of heresy hundreds of humbler folk. They lost all their property and died at the stake, by the sword, and on the gibbet.

At the same time that he decimated the population of the provinces, the duke threatened by his ignorance of economic laws to destroy their prosperity. He sought to impose on industry and commerce a system of taxation that had strangled the economic life of Castile. He attempted to levy a five per cent tax on transfers of real estate, a ten per cent tax on sales of commodities, and a one per cent tax on all property. If he had succeeded, he would have destroyed the commerce and industry of the country. Another side to his policy was the building of citadels to overawe the principal cities.

In the main, the inhabitants of the Netherlands were compelled to oppose the duke and his policies by passive resistance. The gilds demonstrated against the proposed taxes and the shopkeepers closed their shops. In 1568, William of Orange tried to organize a mercenary force in Germany for the invasion of the provinces, but the forces which he raised were no match for the veteran soldiers under the command of the Duke of Alba. The only successful opposition was offered by Dutch seamen. Under the name, Sea Beggars, they took to the sea and harassed Spanish shipping. At times, they were hardly distinguishable from pirates. They repaid the duke for his cruelty by terrible reprisals on the innocent priests, monks, and nuns who fell into their hands.

In 1572 the war between the duke and the people of the Netherlands took a new turn. Being short of food, some of the Sea Beggars surprised and captured the ungarrisoned town of Brille, a small fort situated on an island belonging to the province of Holland. This success encouraged other towns in the provinces of Holland, Zeeland, Utrecht, and Friesland to revolt. Soon afterwards, William of Orange returned to the Netherlands and set up a provisional government at Delft. Not long afterwards, the Sea Beggars captured the Spanish fleet. These victories tended to discredit the Duke of Alba. In 1573, consequently, he returned to Spain.

In place of the duke came Requesens. He is usually credited with good intentions, but he met with no more success than his predecessor. He was hardly prepared for the task of subduing the revolt. He could speak none of the three languages—Dutch, Flemish, and

Walloon—spoken in the Netherlands. Neither he nor his master, Philip II, understood the real character of their chief opponent, William of Orange. They thought of him still as the once gay, luxury-loving courtier. They did not realize that responsibility had gradually transformed him into a serious statesman and a deeply religious Protestant. They still cherished the idea that he could be bought. They were not willing to grant demands of William of Orange for religious freedom and provincial privileges.

The war, consequently, dragged on from year to year. It was a struggle mainly of sieges. The troops raised by the patriot party were no match for the seasoned veterans of Spain. They could only hope to offer effective resistance from behind fortifications around cities. As a consequence, the cities were besieged and the country districts were ravaged.

The most famous of these sieges was the investment of Leyden. The Spanish forces adopted the usual tactics of cutting off the supplies of the beleagured city. As a result, Leyden was threatened with starvation. The Dutch authorities tried to raise the siege by cutting the dikes and submerging the country around the city. For some time, however, the water was not deep enough to drive away the besieging forces. Finally, a northwest wind drove the sea to the walls of the city and enabled vessels with supplies to reach the starving inhabitants. The heroic resistance of Leyden encouraged other cities to continue the unequal struggle.

The position of the Spanish masters of the seventeen provinces grew steadily worse. In 1576, Requesens died. In spite of the great resources at their disposal, the Spanish authorities were unable to pay their troops. The Spanish troops, for their part, grew increasingly lawless. Finally, they took matters entirely into their own hands and began to seize and sack neighboring cities. These attacks culminated in the capture of the greatest commercial center of the Netherlands, the city of Antwerp. Many of the inhabitants were brutally murdered. Homes and storehouses were recklessly looted. The terrible event is known as the Spanish Fury. The attack on the great port greatly damaged its commercial prosperity.

The sacking of Antwerp and other cities by the undisciplined Spanish soldiers had important political consequences. Earlier, the provinces of Holland and Zeeland had formed a political union. Now, all seventeen of the provinces signed an agreement known as the Pacification of Ghent (November 8, 1576). By this document they promised to form a more intimate union. Nominally, they still recognized Philip II as sovereign, but, in reality, they repudiated his policies in the Netherlands. They annulled the decrees issued by the

Duke of Alba and returned the property that had been confiscated by him and his successor. For the moment, it looked as if the seventeen provinces were on the verge of forming a united and independent state.

In the hope of coping with the desperate situation in the Netherlands, Philip II sent as his representative in the provinces his famous, illegitimate half brother, Don Juan of Austria. The latter came to the Netherlands with all the prestige that his great naval victory of 1571 in the battle of Lepanto had given him. He hoped to play an even greater role in the Netherlands. He even thought of the possibility of freeing Mary, Queen of Scots and marrying her. Upon his arrival in the Netherlands, however, he found himself hampered at every turn. His brother, Philip II, did not give him adequate support. He found himself compelled to recognize the Pacification of Ghent and to dismiss the Spanish troops. His subsequent policy, though, soon caused the rebellious provinces to repudiate him.

In an effort to gain outside support, the seventeen provinces then invited Mathias, a Habsburg and brother of the Emperor, to become titular head of the government. With the title of Lieutenant General, William of Orange continued to be the real head of the provinces. These arrangements, however, failed to bring harmony among the rebellious inhabitants of the Netherlands. The root of their troubles was the failure of most of them to understand or practice the principle of religious toleration. The ten southern provinces were still predominantly Catholic. The seven northern provinces were, in the main, Protestant and Calvinistic. The inhabitants of both groups of provinces were intolerant. The confusion was increased by the intervention of the brother of the king of France, the rather weak and unprincipled Duke of Anjou, on the side of the rebellious provinces; by the encouragement given rather reluctantly by Queen Elizabeth to the rebels; and finally, in 1578, by the death of the brilliant but unfortunate Don Juan of Austria.

To take the place of his unlucky half brother, Philip II sent to the Netherlands the ablest man he had ever appointed, Alexander Farnese, Duke of Parma. Under his skillful leadership, the situation of Philip II in the Netherlands began to improve. The first sign of the skill of the new representative of the king of Spain was the organization in 1579 of an independent and separate Union of Arras by some of the predominantly Catholic provinces in the southern Netherlands. By May of that year, the movement had grown to a point where the ten southern provinces became reconciled to Philip II. By this agreement, the king of Spain promised to respect their Catholic religion and their political privileges and to remove the hated foreign troops.

At the same time that he was gaining this diplomatic success, the Duke of Parma was meeting with considerable military success. If Philip II had only furnished more adequate financial support and had not diverted his resources to England and France, the efforts of the Duke of Parma might have met with complete success.

The situation in the seven northern provinces was so very serious that it required all the skill and courage of their leader, William of Orange, to continue the struggle. Faced by the threatening dangers, he followed a skillful but confusing course. In 1579 the seven northern provinces formed the Union of Utrecht. In the following year, still feeling the need of outside support, the Dutch provinces made the Duke of Anjou, brother of the king of France, their titular leader. In 1581 they deposed Philip II as sovereign and virtually declared their independence. The reply of Philip II to this action was to declare William of Orange a traitor and to offer a reward for his assassination. The Duke of Anjou, however, soon discredited himself. Dissatisfied at his position in the country, he tried to increase his personal power by a treacherous attack on Antwerp, but the attack failed. In 1584, the Dutch patriots suffered a blow that seemed irreparable. An assassin, inspired by religious zeal and an offered reward, shot and fatally wounded William of Orange. Only the international situation saved the seven northern provinces from complete reconquest.

The English Attack on the Overseas Monopoly of Spain

From the time of the accession of Elizabeth to the English throne in 1558, there was tension between England and Spain. During the revolt from the Medieval Church, Spain had remained Catholic while England had become Protestant. After Elizabeth ascended the throne, she reversed the policy of her half sister, Mary, and imposed on England the Elizabethan Religious Settlement. With the death of his wife, Mary Tudor, Philip II saw that all the shrewd planning of his father and his own personal sacrifice for protecting the route from Spain to the Netherlands had come to naught for want of an heir. In addition, Englishmen, particularly the rising middle class, were determined to have a share of the plunder that Spain was deriving from the New World and to avoid being swallowed up by the imperialism of Spain. Both powers hesitated, however, to precipitate an armed struggle.

In 1568, the English began to attack the Spanish monopoly in America. In that year, an English sea captain, John Hawkins, tried to get a share of the profitable slave trade between the coast of Guinea and the colonies in America. Other attacks on Spanish treasure fleets and Spanish colonies followed. On one occasion, the English queen

149

calmly seized some Genoese ships, destined for the Duke of Alba and laden with treasure. She excused herself by asserting that she was entitled to keep what she had saved from falling into the hands of English privateers. The most famous of the English sea captains was Francis Drake. First, he accompanied his uncle, Sir John Hawkins, to Spanish America but, later, led expeditions of his own that repeatedly attacked Spanish forts and Spanish shipping. In the years from 1577 to 1580, he performed the difficult feat of circumnavigating the earth. For this deed he was knighted by his sovereign. There was, nevertheless, no open break between Spain and England until 1588. The Spanish king had to remember that England flanked his sea route from Spain to the Netherlands. The English queen hesitated to imperil her security on the throne by adopting a policy that would entail heavier taxes and cause popular unrest.

Self-interest, however, compelled her to give enough encouragement to the movements directed against Philip II to keep them alive. After the assassination of William of Orange in 1584, she felt that she must take a somewhat more active part in the conflict in the Netherlands to prevent the collapse of the revolt. The Dutch leaders, headed by the astute John of Oldenbarneveld, wanted to make the English queen sovereign of the Netherlands, but she refused to assume so great a responsibility. She did, however, furnish a small force to assist the Dutch patriots. She sent to the Dutch provinces her favorite, Leicester, with 1000 horses and 5000 foot soldiers. This intervention turned out badly. The English queen liked neither the independent spirit displayed by the Dutch leaders nor the airs assumed by Leicester. The Dutch, for their part, very much disapproved of the policies of the English leader. In 1586, consequently, Leicester returned to England.

In the end, the English by their official and unofficial policies goaded Philip II to action. In 1588 the aggressiveness of English seamen and the English intervention in the Netherlands precipitated an avowed military struggle between England and Spain. Using Spain and the Netherlands as a base, Philip II planned to attack England. Convoyed by a great fleet of Spanish galleons, the Duke of Parma with troops from the Netherlands was to be transported to English shores. After he had landed, he was to unite with the English Catholics to depose Queen Elizabeth and to free the imprisoned Mary, Queen of Scots, marry her, and seat her on the English throne.

The Spanish king failed completely in his attempt to execute his plans. In 1587, before he could act, the terrible Sir Francis Drake carried out one of his most daring exploits. Sailing out of Plymouth harbor, he plundered the town of Cadiz in southern Spain and destroyed a vast amount of stores and shipping; then, he pounced upon the fleet being prepared in the port of Lisbon; next, he intercepted off Cape St. Vincent a squadron of transports coming from the Mediterranean; and, finally, he sailed to the Azores where he captured a Spanish East Indiaman laden with treasure. This exploit forced Philip II to postpone his attack until the following year. In the meantime, the discovery of the so-called Babington plot furnished the English authorities a pretext for the execution of Mary, Queen of Scots. This deed changed the status of Philip II considerably. He could pose as the avenger of the unfortunate queen, but as a claimant for the English throne he had little hope of rallying even the English Catholics to his side. In spite of these discouragements, Philip II kept doggedly on at the task of preparing for the great attack.

Finally, in 1588, the great Spanish fleet started from Spain. Notwithstanding the mishaps that had befallen it, it greatly outnumbered the fleet gathered for the defence of England. The Spanish fleet numbered 130 ships and carried twice as large a crew and material equipment as the opposing fleet. The English fleet consisted of only 34 regular naval vessels and some 163 subsidiary ships contributed by nobles, members of the gentry, and port towns. The English vessels, however, were far easier to maneuver and were manned by better seamen. The critical struggle took place in the English Channel. The English captains did not permit the Spaniards to come close enough to board their ships with superior numbers but raked instead the clumsy Spanish galleons with their guns. Finally, the so-called *Spanish Armada* broke and fled northward. The Spanish fleet hoped to round northern Scotland and to proceed home by way of the west coast of Ireland. Scarcely half of it, though, reached Spain. The rest of the Spanish vessels were sunk in the fighting or wrecked on the Scottish, Irish, or Norwegian coast by the great storm which overtook them. The victory of English skill and courage marked the beginning of the end for Spanish maritime supremacy.

The Struggle of the French Protestants for Recognition

After 1559, Philip II felt compelled to watch developments in France. There, the accident which caused the death of Henry II had radically changed the political situation. After years of patient suffering, the Protestant minority had about reached a point where its members were ready to fight for the right to worship God as their consciences dictated. The country swarmed with restive, unemployed young nobles who were veterans of the Italian Wars and anxious for a military career. From 1559 to 1589, the French state had in succession three young and weak rulers, all sons of Henry II: Francis I

(1559–1560), Charles IX (1560–1574), and Henry III (1574–1589). This situation precipitated a struggle for control of these sovereigns among the queen mother (Catherine de' Medici), the Duke of Guise and his brother (the Cardinal of Lorraine), the leaders of the Catholic party, and the ambitious but incapable Antoine de Bourbon (king of Navarre and titular head of the Protestant party). Partly from conviction and in part for political reasons, many of the nobles became converts to Protestantism in the hope of obtaining help in their struggle against the monarchy.

During the short reign of Francis II, the Guises had the upper hand in France. The young sovereign was married to a niece of the two powerful Guises, the celebrated Mary, Queen of Scots. This put the two brothers in a position to dominate the weak, young sovereign.

In 1560, the death of Francis II changed the political situation again. The Guises lost their dominant position. The hitherto neglected queen of Henry II, Catherine de' Medici, persuaded the incapable king of Navarre to allow her to assume the regency. Thereupon, she tried to impose on the rival factions, the Catholics and Protestants, a policy of freedom of conscience (1561). The decree, however, satisfied neither faction. The Catholic party wanted everyone to conform to Catholicism. The Protestants demanded liberty of worship. Both sides were ready to take up arms for the enforcement of their ideas. In spite of this situation, the regent issued in 1562 an edict of toleration.

With the tension between the factions steadily increasing, any incident might have started civil war. In March, 1562, such an event occurred. Either by the orders or at least by the permission of the Duke of Guise, two hundred Protestants, assembled at Vassy in northeastern France for a religious service, were barbarously massacred. The episode started a conflict that devastated France for thirty years.

In theory, each side professed respect for the royal authority. In practice, each did as it pleased. The fanaticism of both religious parties made the struggle a terrible one. The conflict consisted largely of surprise attacks and seiges. Both parties in the civil war called in outside assistance. The Protestants were aided by German and English forces; the Catholics, by Italian, Swiss, and Spanish auxiliaries and, in the latter part of the struggle, by the troops of Philip II. Neither party could crush the other. From time to time, the combatants from sheer exhaustion signed truces that were poorly observed. For this reason, historical specialists distinguish by name eight separate wars of religion. Each was followed by a greater or less number of concessions to Protestants. The treaty signed in 1570

152

at the end of the third war was the most favorable to the Protestant cause. In this treaty, the Protestants extorted from their Catholic opponents a recognition of their right to freedom of conscience and worship and permission to fortify and garrison four strongholds as places of refuge. In reality, the struggle was a continuous conflict that lasted from 1562 to 1594.

The cruelty and intolerance of the time is well illustrated by the episode which occurred in 1572, known as the Massacre of St. Bartholomew. This terrible event was the result of a complicated situation. The regent, Catherine de' Medici, was afraid that one of the Protestant leaders, Admiral Coligny, might supplant her in the favor of her weak, young son, Charles IX. She was fearful, too, lest the rise of Coligny might lead to war with Spain. At the same time, the agents of Philip II were inciting her to deliver a decisive stroke against the French Protestants. As a result of this situation, the regent and some of the Catholic leaders plotted an attack on the Protestant leaders. The approaching marriage of the regent's daughter to Henry, the young king of Navarre and the son of Antoine de Bourbon, gave the conspirators the opportunity for which they had been looking. The event had drawn the heads of both religious parties to Paris. On the morning of August 24, 1572, after an attack on Coligny alone had failed, armed bands of Catholics surprised the Protestant leaders in the palace or in their lodgings, killed them without mercy, and threw their bodies into the streets below. At the capital the victims numbered some two thousand. In the provinces similar scenes took place. The young king of Navarre, the later Henry IV of France, escaped at the time of the massacre by temporarily abjuring Protestantism. This slaughter of the Protestant leaders, of course, settled nothing.

From the time of the Massacre of St. Bartholomew onward, the country was in an anarchical condition. In 1574 the third son of Henry II mounted the throne, the weak, feeble, and effeminate Henry III. He and his worthless favorites soon became highly unpopular. Political power fell into the hands of the Catholic League which had been organized to combat Protestantism more effectively, and which in the end had the support of Philip II and Spanish troops from the Netherlands. The leader of the League, the Duke of Guise, virtually supplanted Henry III as ruler of the country. This development had important consequences. For a time, the weak, young king was compelled to renew the war against the Protestants and, in 1585, even to issue a decree suppressing Protestantism in France. When, however, the Duke of Guise and the League began to consider the advisability of deposing the king, Henry III conspired to assassinate his rival. Pretending a reconciliation, the king appointed the duke lieutenant general of the realm; but after his arrival at Blois, the duke was stabbed to death by eight members of the royal guard. Henry III did not long survive his victim. The representatives of the League at Paris organized a revolutionary government; declared Henry III deposed on the ground that he was a perjurer, an assassin, sacrilegious, an abettor of heresy, a squanderer of the public treasure, and an enemy of the country; and appointed the Duke of Mayenne, the brother of the murdered Duke of Guise, regent of the kingdom. Their action forced Henry III to reconcile himself with the king of Navarre, who in 1576 had fled from the court, turned Protestant again, and become once more leader of the Protestant party. While the two kings were besieging Paris in 1589, however, a fanatical monk assassinated Henry III.

This deed, if the ordinary laws governing the succession had been followed, would have made the king of Navarre the king of France. The majority of the French people, however, were not ready to recognize a Protestant as king. The League, which still had a large following in France and, likewise, the support of Philip II of Spain and his money and soldiers, had recognized as king the elderly Cardinal of Bourbon, an uncle of Henry of Navarre. As a result, the king of Navarre had to win by some means recognition of the title of Henry IV, which he had assumed.

Henry IV finally won this recognition of his right to the title of King of France by a mixture of force and concessions. The leader of Protestant France, he succeeded in maintaining himself in northern France by gaining the two victories of Arques (1589) and Ivry (1590). After that, the war dragged on for three years without either side being able to crush the other. In other respects, however, the position of Henry IV improved. In 1590, the Catholic claimant of the French throne, the old Cardinal Bourbon, died. As candidate for the vacant position, Philip II put forward his daughter, a grand-daughter of Henry II of France. The Spanish plans roused French national sentiment. Only a handful of Catholic extremists was ready to accept a Spanish sovereign.

By his ambition, Philip II aided Henry IV to overcome all remaining opposition. In 1593, the former Protestant leader, recognizing the wishes of the majority of the French people, again abjured the Protestant faith and became a Catholic. By this act he won the allegiance of the greater part of the French people. The support of the rest was obtained by the judicious use of money and the granting of titles. In 1594, therefore, he was able to enter his capital without firing a shot, and the civil war was permanently ended.

By 1594, Philip II was coming to the end of his long reign. Everywhere—in France, in England, and in the Netherlands—his policies were being defeated. The war between France and Spain dragged on for four more years. Each power was too exhausted to strike the other a decisive blow. In 1598, accordingly, they signed the Treaty of Vervins, which really only confirmed the Treaty of Cateau Cambresis (1559).

The maritime war between England and Spain continued until 1604, six years after the death of Philip II and one year after that of Elizabeth. After the defeat of the *Spanish Armada* in 1588, a new and younger generation of courtiers overrode the older and more experienced advisers of the aging Elizabeth. Under the leadership of Essex, a nephew of Leicester, and the famous Sir Walter Raleigh, they pressed the attack on the overseas monopoly of Spain. In 1589 they organized an expedition designed to wrest the throne of Portugal from Philip II but failed almost completely. The Portuguese did not rise, and attacks on Lisbon and Coruna failed. In 1596, in cooperation with the French and the Dutch, the English sacked the Spanish port of Cadiz and destroyed the shipping found in its harbor. In that year, Philip II sent another fleet against England and, in the following year, one against Ireland. In the final years of the reign of Elizabeth, the peace party in England again gained the upper hand, but the war did not come to an end until the year after her death.

In the Netherlands, the plans of Philip II also went badly. After the assassination of William of Orange in 1584, the frightened people of the seven Dutch provinces sought without much success the help of Elizabeth of England and Henry III of France. They were saved more by the diversion of the resources and troops of Philip II to the civil war in France and the struggle being waged between England and Spain than by the grudging help extended by Elizabeth.

In time, the Dutch found new leaders worthy of their great traditions. Maurice of Nassau, a son of William of Orange, proved to be a military leader of real genius. Under his leadership, the Dutch forces took one fortified city after another and gradually cleared the seven northern provinces of Spanish troops. At the same time, one of the trusted advisers of William of Orange displayed great skill in the conduct of both civilian and foreign affairs. As the struggle dragged on, the Dutch assumed more and more the role of an independent power.

In spite of the war, the seven northern provinces of the Netherlands were becoming prosperous. The Dutch seamen preyed on the

Spanish shipping and took rich prizes. As a result of the central location of the provinces, Dutch captains and sailors did a large part of the carrying trade of Europe. After 1580, they transformed a serious threat to Dutch prosperity into a great achievement. In that year, Philip II established a claim to Portugal and the Portuguese Empire and forbade a continuance of the hitherto highly profitable Dutch carrying trade in spices between Lisbon and Northern Europe. Prohibited from entering the port of Lisbon, the Dutch navigators soon began to go to the East Indies and the Far East in their own ships. Before long, they had supplanted the Portuguese in the Eastern Hemisphere and laid the foundation of a great colonial empire.

A continuance of the struggle to retain the seven northern provinces of the Netherlands therefore seemed useless. Spain was exhausted. A considerable peace party had grown up in the Netherlands. In 1609, consequently, eleven years after the death of Philip II, the two contestants succeeded in negotiating a twelve-year truce which virtually recognized the independence of the Dutch provinces.

Death of Philip II

Undeterred by the failure of his plans in France, England, and the Netherlands, Philip II had toiled on at his desk in the Escorial. Tortured by the gout for years, he had worked long hours with his leg stretched out on a chair before him. Finally, in 1598, the same year as the disappointing Treaty of Vervins, the aging king was forced to take to his bed. Though in agony, he continued to read, annotate, and reply to dispatches until death put an end to the work. He died unshaken in his belief that he was a good servant of his state and his church.

This survey of the history of Europe during the last four decades of the sixteenth century shows that Philip II, the champion of Spanish imperialism and Catholic orthodoxy, met stout resistance to his plans in France, England, and the Netherlands. The resistance sprang in part from provincial feeling, in part from religious prejudice, and in part from a desire to share in the exploitation of the newly discovered lands overseas. Unintentionally and unwittingly, the Protestant opponents of Philip II contributed to the establishment of certain features of the modern world. In France they won temporary recognition of the idea of limited religious toleration. In the Netherlands they created a new nation. On the seas they broke by their very greed and wild cruelty the political and economic monopoly of Spain and laid the foundation of the later Dutch and English colonial empires.

In modern times an increasing amount of attention has been paid to science. In medieval times, as a general rule, men do not seem to have been as curious about the world in which they lived as are their modern descendants. Only the exceptional persons sought to increase the stores of human knowledge by careful observations, exact experimentation, and scientific thinking. The ordinary man paid little or no attention to the physical phenomena around him.

In modern times the situation has been different. Modern man has been characterized by a growing interest in science. While the majority of people still have been quite unscientific in their thinking, an increasing number of persons have devoted their attention to the observation of physical phenomena, experimentation under known conditions, the collection of accurate data, and the formulation of the laws of nature. They have thought less about a future world and more about the one in which they live.

The New Astronomy

Some of the most important contributions of the sixteenth century to science were made in the field of astronomy. During this period, man's idea of the universe in which he lived was revolutionized. Medieval man thought of himself as living at the center of a relatively small universe. According to medieval ideas, the earth was a fixed center around which revolved the moon, the planets, the sun, and the stars. They were placed in the sky to light the path of the earth's inhabitants. These heavenly bodies were supposed to be held in place by crystaline spheres.

In the sixteenth century, astronomers began to abandon the medieval idea that the earth was a stationary body and the center of the universe. This revolutionary idea was the discovery of Niklas Koppernigk, known usually as Nicolaus Copernicus (1473–1543), the son of a well-to-do family which lived at Thorn in Poland. After studying at the University of Cracow for three years, he went to Italy where he attended in turn the universities of Bologna, Padua, and Ferrara. From these institutions he carried back to Poland the idea that the medieval theories were not an adequate explanation of the universe. In Poland, through the influence of an uncle, he became canon of the Cathedral of Frauenburg. This appointment enabled him to live very much like a nobleman. For a while, he stayed at the episcopal court of his uncle at Ermeland in the capacity of physician and courtier. The last thirty-one years of his life, however, he spent mainly in a little tower on the wall of his cathedral close. From this retreat, he quietly observed the heavens and measured the altitudes and longitudes of the heavenly bodies. Quite early, he formulated a new explanation of the universe. He spent his remaining years in gathering proofs of his new theory. His ideas were entrusted only to a few friends until just before he died. On his deathbed he received a printed copy of his "On the Revolutions of the Heavenly Orbs."

According to this new explanation of the universe, the earth was merely a planet like Mars or Venus. Instead of being the fixed center of the universe, it revolved both on its own axis and around the sun. People were asked to accept the idea that the supposedly solid earth, with its houses and people and its seas and mountains, was spinning like a top and at the same time rushing round the sun in an annual course at the rate of nineteen miles per second. The sun, the moon, and the stars ceased to be lights set in the heavens for the benefit of man. The universe broadened out illimitably.

After Copernicus advanced his theory of the universe, the great need of astronomers was additional data to verify the new hypothesis. The supplying of such data was the great work of a Danish astronomer, Tycho Brahe (1546–1601). Most of his life, he was a pensioner of the king of Denmark. For twenty-one years he worked in an observatory on an island in the sound between Sweden and Denmark, making careful observations and constructing astronomical instruments. After the death of his Danish patron, he became for a short time a protegé of Emperor Rudolf. He died, however, shortly after he moved to Prague. His importance lies in his collection of accurate data. He never accepted the theory of Copernicus.

The man who perfected the Copernican system was Johann Kepler (1571–1630). During his earlier years, he encountered serious obstacles and difficulties. He started life with the handicap of being prematurely born. Shortly after his birth, his father, a soldier of fortune, entirely deserted his family. His mother, according to all reports, was undisciplined and uneducated. At the age of four, Kepler had smallpox. This disease permanently crippled his hands and impaired his eyesight. After working for a while as a field hand, he gained admittance first to a seminary and later to the University of Tübingen. In the latter institution he was privately introduced to the Copernican theory by one of his professors. In 1594 he reluctantly took the chair of astronomy at Graz in Styria. As his salary there was very inadequate, he, like many other astronomers of the time, constructed prophesying almanacs to supplement his income. After 1597, he got along somewhat better as a result of his marriage to an heiress.

Not long after he married, he was appointed successor of Tycho Brahe at Prague. Though he continued to draw horoscopes and write on astrology to please his patrons, first the Emperor and later Wallenstein, the famous general of the Thirty Years' War, he devoted his main attention to astronomy. From 1609 onward, he published various works which explained and defended the theory of Copernicus concerning the universe. In these writings he supplemented the theory of Copernicus by three laws of his own. First, he advanced the idea that a planet moves in an elipse around the sun and not in a circle as Copernicus had believed. Secondly, he asserted that a planet moves more rapidly when near the sun and more slowly when farther from it. From this, he deduced the principle that a planet's speed in all parts of its orbit is such that the area of all segments swept in equal times by a radius drawn from the sun to the planet is equal. These two laws were contained in a work published in 1609 "On the Motions of the Planet Mars." Ten years later, he published his third law, namely, that the squares of the periodic times are proportional to the cubes of the mean distances of the planets from the sun.

The popularizer of the Copernican theory was an Italian professor, Galileo (1564–1642). His father was an impoverished descendant of a noble Florentine house. In spite of the efforts of his father to prevent it, Galileo learned a good deal about mathematics. In 1588 he became a lecturer on the subject at the University of Pisa at a very modest salary. Later, he lost the favor of the grand duke and moved to Florence. By 1610 he was already well known throughout Italy by reason of his discovery of certain physical laws and because of his inventions. Eventually, we are told, he had audiences of two thousand people at his lectures.

In 1608 an obscure Netherlands optician of Middleburg invented a telescope. Galileo soon heard of the invention. Without ever seeing a telescope, he made an instrument that magnified distant objects threefold. He kept improving the telescope until he had increased the magnifying power of the instrument thirty-two times. With this telescope, Galileo was able to study the configuration of the moon, to increase the number of recognized stars tenfold, to discover that the milky way is simply a mass of stars, and to see the moons of Jupiter, the waxing and waning of Venus, and the satellites of Saturn. Orders for the new telescopes soon began to pour in from all the countries of Western Europe.

As is usually the case with new ideas, the Copernican theory was accepted slowly and reluctantly even by the intellectual class. Almost without exception, the Protestant theologians attacked the new hypothesis. Luther called Copernicus a fool who wished to reverse the science of astronomy. Melanchthon, the friend and colleague of Luther, deduced nine proofs that the earth can be nowhere if not in the center of the universe. Calvin thought that he had settled the argument by quoting from the ninety-third Psalm, "the earth also is stablished that it cannot be moved." The Catholic theologians attacked the new theory only after it began to be taught as a fact rather than a hypothesis.

As a result, the universities were slow to accept and teach the new astronomical theories. In 1600, after he had been hounded for years from one university to another in both Protestant and Catholic Europe, the rash Giordano Bruno (1548–1600) was seized at Venice and imprisoned for heresy by the Inquisition, and, upon his refusal to recant his teachings concerning religious matters, he was finally burned at the stake by the authorities at Rome. In 1633, after friendly ecclesiastical authorities had made repeated efforts to silence him on the subject of the Copernican theory, Galileo was cited before the Inquisition and forced to recant. The authorities felt that his ideas about the sun and the diurnal motion of the earth were out of line with the plain teaching of the Bible. For the remaining nine years of his life, Galileo lived under surveillance but not under arrest. In judging the action of the Church, it must be borne in mind that many enlightened men like Francis Bacon and William Shakespeare clung to the old theory of the universe. In fact, the Copernican theory was not wholly accepted even by the intellectual class until the days of Newton (1642–1727).

The New Geographical Knowledge

The discoveries of the Spanish and Portuguese explorers were disseminated more rapidly than the new ideas about the universe. The new geographical knowledge must have passed quickly from mouth to mouth. It became embodied in books, maps, and globes somewhat more slowly. As early as 1500, Juan de la Cosa, a companion of Columbus, made a map that recorded the discoveries which had been made up to that time in the New World. Two years later, a map was published which showed the Portuguese discoveries. Most of the early maps which embodied the new geographical knowledge were published as a sort of supplement to the twenty-seven maps of Ptol-

160

emy. Gradually, however, the geographical works depended less and less on Ptolemy and more and more on the new data being supplied by contemporary explorers. In 1585, a Dutch map maker published the first collection of marine maps. By this date, Antwerp and Amsterdam had become the centers of the map-making industry. In time the new maps affected popular thought.

The Discovery of the Human Body

Another of the great advances of the early modern period was a series of discoveries about the human body. As was the case in so many other fields of knowledge, the ancient Greeks had considerable knowledge about anatomy. They knew the bones of the head, the vertebrae, the ribs, the sternum, the muscles, the veins and arteries, and something about the brain. They did not know, however, the function of these various parts of the body. The tendency of the Middle Ages had been to discourage such investigation. In the fourteenth century Italian pioneers began to dissect human bodies, in spite of great popular prejudice against the practice. About the beginning of the sixteenth century, a school of anatomists began to develop in France.

Until nearly the middle of the sixteenth century, the work of these early anatomists was not well publicized. The old need for secrecy was still felt. About that time, however, a Flemish scientist, Andreas Vesalius (1514–1564), published a work on the subject. He studied first in France and then went to Italy. Later, he taught at the universities of Padua, Bologna, and Pisa and attracted students from all over Europe. By the time he was twenty-eight, he had worked out a new system of anatomy. In 1543 he published an illustrated work on the *Structure of the Human Body* which is one of the famous books of history. Finally, he became the personal physician of Charles V and Philip II. He had to contend, though, with the opposition of the advocates of traditional views and with the Inquisition. The opposition of the latter institution finally forced him to make a pilgrimage to the Holy Land. On the way home he was shipwrecked, and, as a consequence, died in Greece. He is credited with having corrected many errors and with having carefully described the sphenoid bone, the sternum, the veins, the spleen, the colon, the pylorus, the pleura, and the brain.

Vesalius shared with two other scientists the merit of having created modern anatomy. One was Bartolomeo Eustachi (1500 or 1510–1574), an Italian who in 1549 followed a member of the Rovere family to Rome and through his influence soon became a member of the medical college there. He is credited with important studies of the

161

internal ear and the teeth and is the author of a valuable set of anatomical engravings that were not published until 1714. The other anatomist, also an Italian, was Gabriello Fallopius (1523–1562). After becoming a canon of the Cathedral of Modena, his native city, he became a professor first at Pisa and later at Padua. He is credited with a considerable number of anatomical discoveries and with having named some of the most important organs of the human body. He had as clients a number of prominent contemporaries.

The new knowledge concerning the human body did not have so great an immediate effect on the practice of medicine as one might expect. Something that might perhaps be described as a campaign was waged against medieval and Arabian medical works. There was, however, a new interest in the medicinal qualities of plants and a somewhat more rational knowledge of drugs.

Advances in Other Sciences

In some of the other sciences, advances were also made in the sixteenth century. Among these disciplines was the science of botany. Plants have always attracted more or less attention. In ancient times, the elder Pliny had described about a thousand different plants. In the sixteenth century, scientifically inclined men again took up the task. In 1530–1536, Otto Brunfels published a "Herbarium," at Strasbourg, that described a large number of plants, chiefly those of Central Europe. It was illustrated with beautiful wood cuts. During the sixteenth century, a number of similar works appeared which gradually worked out a crude system of classification based on the external appearance of plants.

Just at the end of the sixteenth century came the development of an instrument that opened the door to great advances in a number of sciences. The first microscope was probably the invention of a Dutch lens grinder, Johann Zacharias Janssen, in 1590. The new instrument made many of the subsequent scientific discoveries possible.

In the meantime, important developments were taking place in the basic science of mathematics. As was the case in many other fields of knowledge, the discovery of the work done in the field of mathematics in ancient times led to a renewed interest in mathematical subjects, particularly in algebra. During the sixteenth century, important improvements were made in this field of knowledge. Among the new developments were the solution of cubic equations, the introduction of the signs now used for plus and minus and for square root, and equality and revival of the practice of denoting unknown quantities by letters of the alphabet. To whom these and other advances should be credited is not so certain. The scholars of the period were inclined to be mysterious about their methods, and at times they published the discoveries of other men as their own.

Among the famous mathematicians of the time was Jerome Cardan (1501–1576). His works on arithmetic (1539) and on algebra (1543) soon gave him a European reputation. Later, he wrote on such subjects as astrology and the explanation of natural phenomena. In later years, he had much trouble of various sorts. These difficulties finally unhinged his mind. Before this occurred, however, he wrote his own biography, a work second only to that of Benvenuto Cellini as a revelation of the times.

Somewhat later in the sixteenth century, Francois Vieta (1540–1603) became famous as a mathematician. Starting life as an advocate, he rose high in the service of Henry IV of France. This enabled him to publish in 1591 the results of his work in a treatise on algebra. His work made customary many things that had previously been used occasionally or exceptionally. He also applied algebra to trigonometry.

Contemporaneously, some pioneer work was being done in the field of physical science. In the Netherlands, Simon Stevin (1548–1620), a Flemish engineer, discovered some of the most important laws of hydrostatics and mechanics. At the same time, in Italy, Galileo was discovering the laws of moving bodies and of inertia. Although the stories told concerning some of his demonstrations may be of doubtful authenticity, he nevertheless proved such laws as the idea of uniform acceleration of falling bodies and that a body once in motion continues to move with the same velocity and in the same direction unless some force acts upon it.

Changes in Military Science

Throughout historic times, military methods have been constantly changing. In the sixteenth century, the infantry retained the important position which it had won as a result of the prowess of the Swiss pikemen. Though the Swiss lost some of their prestige after their defeat in the battle of Marignano in 1516, the infantry recruited in other parts of Europe were still highly valued. These other mercenaries included the German *Landsknechte* and the Spanish infantry. In 1525, at the battle of Pavia, the latter won a position of prestige which they retained for more than a century. Just at the close of the century, the Dutch, trained by Maurice of Nassau, showed themselves able to compete on equal terms with the Spanish infantry.

At the beginning of the century, the European soldier still wore armor, particularly plate armor. As the century progressed, the infantry found heavy armor an obstacle to marching and gradually gave it up. In the end, the pikeman wore merely a bassinet, a breastplate, and a backplate; the musketeer, only a bassinet. At the beginning of the century, military combats were decided by the push of the pikemen. The Spaniards, however, discovered the value of firearms. At first, they posted a few arquebusiers at each end of the phalanx of pikemen. As the century progressed, however, weapons with greater firepower were introduced—early in the century, the wheellock and, later, the flintlock. The muskets used by the Spanish infantry were so heavy that the soldier armed with one of them had to place it on a rest in order to fire it, and its range was comparatively short. As time passed, the proportion of musketeers increased. Both pikemen and musketeers were often flogged, and armies carried gallows with them upon which to hang the unruly.

Cavalry was still much depended upon to win battles. At first, the cavalryman was armed with a lance and a sword. About 1540 the pistol, probably named after Pistoia, Italy, was introduced. After its adoption, the cavalryman trotted up to a point near the infantry, fired his pistols, wheeled, retired to a safer position, reloaded his pistols, and again advanced toward the opposing infantry. Contemporaries thought that the new method constituted an important advance in military science.

During the sixteenth century, the importance of artillery steadily increased. The cannon of the time were of many different calibres and were loaded through the muzzle. Improvement in the powder used and the adoption, about 1545, of iron cannon balls made them more effective. Strangely enough, they were not the property of the king or the state but were owned by a civilian master gunner and were fired by civilians.

At the beginning of the century, armies had no such thing as a service of transport and supply. They obtained food, forage, and other things needed for the soldiers by ravaging the country which they occupied. Few districts could support an invading army more than a few days. This system inflicted untold suffering on regions occupied by hostile troops. Only toward the end of the century did the Spanish authorities establish the depot system for feeding and recruiting their armies.

The improvement of artillery meant the end of medieval fortifications. The lofty walls and battlements of the Middle Ages could not withstand the fire of the improved cannon. New methods of defence had to be devised. The military engineers of the time gradually developed bulwarks in front of gates, dug moats, piled the excavated earth into ramparts before and behind the lowered walls, and strengthened the whole position with counterscarps and bastions that protected the walls.

The scientists of the sixteenth century achieved some astonishing results. They revolutionized man's conception of the universe. They made important discoveries about man himself. They began to know more about the earth on which they lived. They made important advances in mathematics and some of the other sciences. When one realizes how little the average man of today, with all the present-day apparatus and works of reference at his disposal, knows about the universe, the world, and himself, it is astonishing what men of the sixteenth century accomplished without these aids.

During the course of the century, military science was also greatly changed. This was largely owing to the increased use of gunpowder. An increasing proportion of the infantry used firearms and gradually dispensed more and more with the armor it had hitherto worn. The cavalry adopted the pistol as a weapon. The development of gunpowder forced military engineers to change their whole system of stationary defence.

CHAPTER 12

Advances in Education, Art, and Literature

At the opening of the sixteenth century, the human spirit seemed to be on the verge of a period of great achievements in education, art, and literature. The Humanist movement had advanced to a point where it seemed about to revolutionize the educational programs of the schools. The artists of Italy had made much progress toward the mastery of the arts of painting, sculpture, and architecture. The writers of the time had the stimulus of the newly discovered literary forms of ancient times. There seemed to be no reason why the new century should not be one of marked achievement along all these lines.

The Development of Court Life

The stimulus toward achievement in education, art, and literature came largely from the rulers of the time. In Italy, particularly, the political life of the peninsula had developed numerous small but brilliant courts. The rulers—men like Lorenzo the Magnificent at Florence, Pope Julius II and Pope Leo X at Rome, Ludivico Sforza at Milan, and many others—had an appreciation of education, art, literature, and civilized living. They gathered around them courtiers, artists, and writers. The artists planned and decorated for their patrons' and masters' churches and palaces. The writers entertained the rulers and their courtiers by reading aloud to them their literary works. The ideals of these small but highly cultured court circles are set forth clearly and fully by the famous book, *The Courtier,* of Baldassare Castiglione (1478–1529), a member of the brilliant court of Urbino. Though they often fell far short of the ideal set forth in this book, the members of the various court circles at least tried to act like cultured ladies and gentlemen. They sought to know and appreciate art and literature. At times, they themselves even tried to write. In response to this stimulus, the architects of the time built structures which still arouse admiration, the painters painted pictures that have never been surpassed, and the writers wrote poems and histories which are still landmarks of literature and historiography.

Beyond the Alps, also, some courts played a similar role. In France, after 1513, Francis I became a patron of education, art, and literature. He himself was a cultivated man and had a sincere love of arts and letters. He, therefore, created a court. He transformed the rough feudal lords into gentlemen and drew them into his service. He made intimates of scholars like Budé and poets like Clement Marot. While engaged in the Italian campaign, he bought a large collection of antique statues and ordered paintings from such Italian masters as Raphael, Leonardo da Vinci, and Andrea del Sarto. He persuaded a number of Italian artists to come to his court. This group included Leonardo da Vinci, Andrea del Sarto, Primaticcio del Rosso, and Benvenuto Cellini. At the same time, Marguerite of Angouleme (1492–1549), sister of the king, and queen of Navarre, was maintaining a similar but smaller court at Nerac and Pau in southern France.

Education in the Sixteenth Century

The Humanist movement gradually revolutionized education in Western Europe. The introduction of the new studies, though, was stubbornly resisted by most of the schools and universities. At first, the new subjects and their teachers held a subordinate place in the schools of various grades. Here and there, some enthusiastic head of a school or some young professor sponsored the study of the classic authors. In the Netherlands and Germany, the Brethren of the Common Life were the pioneers. By 1520 many schools were started in this region or were so reorganized as to emphasize the study of the classical authors. In Poland, before the end of the fifteenth century, the University of Cracow offered lectures on the new subjects. In France, the new learning found a patron in Francis I. In England, a few powerful nobles and great ladies took the Humanists under their protection. They included such men as Sir Thomas More, Colet, Linacre, and Grocyn. In 1509, Colet founded at St. Paul's a school in which the new learning was taught. After the turn of the century, Humanist colleges were set up at Oxford and Cambridge.

In the schools and universities which introduced Humanistic studies, the students devoted their attention to a mastery of the Latin language and read the principal Latin historians, poets, and prose writers. They practiced Latin composition and learned to speak Latin. Greek was taught only occasionally. In the end, the new learning drove medieval Scholasticism out of most of the schools and universities of Western Europe.

North of the Alps, the Humanist movement was cut short by the Protestant Revolt which grew out of it. This latter movement had a mixed effect on education. Its immediate result was to throw into confusion such education as existed. The reformers were antagonistic toward Church schools. Property which had been used in support of education was secularized. The Peasants' Revolt reduced the number of scholars and destroyed many schools. Some of the Anabaptists depreciated all culture. Later, the Protestant Revolt tended to stimulate education. Luther and other Protestant leaders urged the support and spread of education in order that their movement might have trained preachers and an intelligent laity. Some of the confiscated church property was turned over to the new schools.

Luther threw all his influence behind the movement for the stimulation of education. It was for this purpose that he translated the Bible into the language of the day. In 1524 he wrote to the burgomasters and councillors of all towns in German lands urging the establishment of Christian schools. He later preached on the duty of sending children to school. He advocated state support of schools, compulsory attendance, and the establishment of separate schools for girls.

The call of Luther met with a ready response, particularly in the universities and the higher schools. The supervisor and leader of the movement was the collaborator of Luther, Philip Schwarzerde, known in history as Philip Melanchthon (1497–1560), a grandnephew of the famous scholar, John Reuchlin. In 1518, after receiving a master's degree at the University of Tübingen, he was called to the University of Wittenberg. His coming marked an epoch in German education. He first made Wittenberg the center of Protestant studies by his own lectures on the classics and theology. Thereupon, his advice was sought by others interested in schools. He established the school systems of several towns, particularly in Saxony. In all, his advice and help was sought by fifty-six German cities. His aid was solicited, too, in the reorganization of the University of Heidelberg and the founding of the universities of Marburg, Königsberg, and Jena. His work for education won him the title of the teacher of Germany.

The universities and higher schools, however, touched the lives of only a select few. More popular schools were founded very slowly. In 1559 the state of Württemberg began to make some provision for the so-called German schools. The example of Württemberg was soon followed by Saxony. At best, these popular schools were very poor institutions. The teachers were often selected because of their unfitness for other occupations and usually combined the duties of schoolmaster with those of some other trade. The schools themselves were more often than not held in the shop or home of the teacher instead of in a building especially designed for them. The curriculum frequently included only reading, writing, and religion. Arithmetic was omitted as being too difficult for most teachers.

Like Luther, Calvin also recognized from the beginning the importance of education. For some years he was unable to carry out his educational ideas. In 1559, however, he succeeded in establishing at Geneva an academy, headed by Theodore de Beza, which in time became the educational center of Calvinism. Later, Calvin's ideas were copied by the Huguenots of France, the Reformed Church in Holland, the Puritans in England, and the Presbyterians of Scotland. In the last country John Knox hoped to have a school in every parish and a college in every notable town. He succeeded in making his countrymen the most generally educated nation of Europe.

Other forces, also, cooperated to increase the demand for education. The confiscation of church property and the growth of administrative and judicial work impressed on the princes their need for educated subjects. In response to this demand, they began about the middle of the century to found princely schools. These institutions took promising boys from twelve to fourteen years of age and gave them their board and tuition free. About the same time, there arose in Germany and France the so-called courtly academies. They offered instruction in arms and gymnastics, Latin and modern languages, practical mathematics, and natural philosophy. Great emphasis, too, was placed upon law and theology, and a number of new universities were founded. The growing cities, likewise, felt the need for education and commenced to found schools. In 1551, Venice, for example, ordered that each section of the city should have a grammar school. Such schools gave instruction in correspondence in the language of the region, accounting, notarial work, and the various mercantile operations. So education became somewhat more diffused during the course of the century.

The so-called Counter Reformation gave rise to the Jesuit order and its extraordinary work for education. From the first, the order gave great attention to the training of the young. In the time of St. Ignatius, the Jesuits founded colleges in Italy, Germany, and Spain. After his death many others were founded. Quite early, the Jesuits took steps to give their methods a definite shape. They created a committee, composed of able school men representing six different countries of Europe, to study the question. In 1586, after a year of study, the committee sent a report to the various provinces for criticism. Finally, in 1599, the so-called Ratio Studiorum was drawn up. It drew its content from many sources. It contained rules for provincial superiors, rectors, and individual teachers. As in other schools

169

of the time, Latin and Greek constituted the main branches of study. History, geography, and antiquities were taught as accessories. The Jesuits used graded textbooks. They early made provision for the professional training of teachers. In the conduct of their schools, they employed a comparatively mild discipline, encouraged the playing of games, and paid attention to the physical condition of students. They urged teachers to take an interest in students and helped many needy, talented students. In their teaching, the Jesuits employed lectures; daily, weekly, monthly, and annual reviews; compositions; disputations; contests; and examinations. As a result of their zeal and the excellence of their schools, the Jesuits almost dominated the field of education in Western and Central Europe until the time of the French Revolution.

Architecture, Painting, and Sculpture in the Sixteenth Century

In most cases, the Italian artists of the sixteenth century were versatile and many-sided men. At the same time, they were often painters, sculptors, architects, and engineers. With them, Italian art reached its highest and fullest expression.

During this period, Italy continued to be the artistic center of Europe. In the peninsula the new civilization, composed of Latin, Greek, Hebrew, and German elements, had had fewer obstacles to overcome and had developed to a higher point than elsewhere. The popes, the secular rulers, and the important Italian families vied with each other in building and decorating churches, ducal palaces, municipal buildings, private residences, and country villas.

In the churches of the peninsula, rulers and men of wealth built and adorned with statues and paintings, innumerable chapels that served ultimately as burial places and monuments of the builders. The popes were engaged in the construction of the collection of buildings known as the St. Peter's Cathedral and the Vatican Palace.

Some secular structures, too, were built. Popes, secular rulers, cardinals, and nobles had learned to build residences designed for comfortable living rather than for protection. This activity in building gave the architects and artists of the time unrivaled opportunities for the development and display of their skill.

Architecture

In the main, palaces and villas rather than churches were the characteristic buildings of the period. Some churches, though, and many chapels were built. Among the churches was St. Peter's at Rome, long the largest church of Christendom. The dominant feature of the churches of the period was the great dome erected where the nave and the transept met. That of St. Peter's Cathedral measures one hundred and forty feet across and rises to a height of four hundred and five feet. The church architects of this period used the round instead of the pointed arch. In the main, however, the building of the period was dominated by the construction of palaces and villas, gates and fountains, chapels and tombs. Great attention was paid to the facades of the buildings constructed. They were marked by string courses, cornices, ranges of windows, pilasters, panels of glazed terra cotta stucco work in relief, and marvellously carved doors. Ceilings and interior walls were ornamented with paintings. Most of the new palaces were built around interior courts, the walls of which rested on columnar arcades. Often, the palaces were surrounded by elaborate gardens which were ornamented with gates, fountains, and marble statues. The villas erected in this pleasure-loving age gave more freedom to the imagination and skill of the architects, decorators, and the landscape gardeners.

The establishments of the time comprised a dwelling, amusement houses (casinos), summer houses, and arcades and were set usually in extensive grounds, laid out in terraces, cascades, and shaded alleys. The whole breathed a spirit of beauty and comfort.

From Italy, the new style of architecture spread to other countries in Western Europe. The kings and nobles returning from the Italian Wars introduced the new Renaissance style into France. And in the reign of Louis XII they began to build, particularly in the valleys of the Loire and Cher rivers, chateaux that in a general way were imitations of the palaces they had seen in Italy. These buildings were characterized by lofty roofs, pierced dormer windows, and tall chimneys, and were provided with circular or square towers at the angles, squareheaded windows, and mullions and transoms. They were, however, far from being exact copies of the architecture of Italy.

In other countries of Western Europe, the Renaissance influence arrived much later than in France or only slightly affected the native architecture. In England the architects were mainly occupied with the construction of vast country mansions for the nobility and the wealthy members of the middle class. In these residences they used at first a degenerate form of Gothic known as the Tudor style, a type of architecture well suited both to residences and collegiate buildings. Only after the accession of Queen Elizabeth in 1558, did the architects show the influence of the Renaissance in their work. The English buildings of this period are characterized by open balustrades instead of medieval battlements; by the decoration of doors, windows, and chimneys; by elaborate mantels; and by an increasing use of interior woodwork. The Spanish Netherlands did not begin to be affected by the new style until after 1530. Except for the construction of some town halls, the Dutch Netherlands was not much affected by the new architecture. In Germany, princely castles, gild and town halls, and the private residences of wealthy individuals began to show the effect of Renaissance architecture after the Peace of Augsburg was signed in 1555. The Germans showed a considerable liking for the quaint and the fantastic. In Spain the architects, trained in the new style, devoted special attention to the decoration of exterior surfaces, a tendency which won for the new style employed in Spain the name, plateresque.

Painting

In painting as in architecture, Italy was still the chief artistic center during the sixteenth century. In the Italian peninsula, Florence continued for a long time to be the chief nursery of painters. In many cases, however, they found encouragement, commissions, and patronage in other Italian centers. Under the leadership of a succession of able Italian artists, the art of painting continued along the lines marked out by Giotto and Masaccio and reached almost perfection in the skillful brushes of Leonardo da Vinci, Raphael, and Michelangelo and the Venetians—Bellini, Titian, and Giorgione. They introduced and developed the art of showing things in perspective. They gave their pictures the appearance of having a third dimension and studied the effect of light and shade. They learned to represent truthfully both the human body and objects of nature. They drew inspiration from classical models as well as from religion. Finally, the artists of Italy, and particularly those at Venice, learned to work in the new medium of oil and canvas.

Some Great Artists of the Sixteenth Century

Even a list of the important artists of the sixteenth century would fill many pages. Nevertheless, the student of history should know something about at least a few of the great artists of this period. Among these, Leonardo da Vinci (1452–1519) has always fascinated later generations because of the extraordinary fertility of his mind and the diversity of his interests and achievements.

Leonardo da Vinci was the illegitimate son of a Florentine lawyer. As he grew up, he displayed in an ever increasing degree personal beauty, charm and tact of manner, energy, and curiosity. These qualities soon won him the favor of Lorenzo the Magnificent, the master of Florence. About 1478, he began to receive independent commissions for paintings. In his own work, he showed himself to be a close student of nature. His work was accurate and precise and showed freedom and fire. At the same time he was learning to paint, he was busy learning the laws of mechanics, hydraulics, architecture, and engineering.

About 1487, he went to Milan to work for the famous Ludovico Sforza. His patron kept him busy investigating the possibility of a more sanitary arrangement for Milan, drawing plans for the completion of the Milanese cathedral, entertaining the court, and studying methods for improving the irrigation and waterways of Lombardy. In 1494, he began for his patron and one of the monasteries of Milan his celebrated painting, *The Last Supper*.

About 1499, he left Milan because of the disturbed political situation. After that, he was for short periods in Florence, in Mantua, in Venice, in Milan again, and in Rome. In each place he found patrons and began ambitious projects which in many cases he failed to complete. During this period of his life, however, he did finish his celebrated picture, the *Mona Lisa*. In 1515 he accepted the pressing invitation of Francis I, the reigning French sovereign, to come to France. He died in that country in 1519. He had a veritable passion for knowledge and was probably the most versatile and gifted man of his generation.

Another famous artist of the period was Bramante (1444–1514). In contrast to Leonardo da Vinci, he was primarily an architect. About 1500, after long years of apprenticeship and study, he went to Rome. There, he was commissioned by a cardinal to rebuild a cloister. As a result of the speed and skill he displayed at this task, the cardinal introduced him to Pope Alexander VI (1492–1503). From this time on he was consulted about most of the building projects at Rome. Under Julius II (1503–1513) he was appointed first architect of St. Peters, the monumental church, which the Pope planned to build. His various successors, however, greatly altered the original plans of that structure.

Another of the great artists of the age was Raphael (1483–1520). He was born in Urbino, one of the artistic and intellectual centers of the peninsula. He was trained to be a painter by his father and Perugino but quite early began to execute independent works. About 1504 he went to Florence, the oldest and greatest artistic center of Italy. There, he did some of his finest work. In 1508, like many other artists, he went to Rome, where the construction of St. Peters, the Vatican, and other palaces offered the artists and craftsmen of the period unsurpassed opportunities to display their skill. He immediately began to paint pictures for the Pope as well as for private patrons. In 1514 he became architect for Saint Peter's, but the work of erecting the great church progressed too slowly for him to leave many traces of his work on the finished structure. As an artist, he was a master of drawing, coloring, and composition. As a man, he was charming, kindly, and modest. In his lifetime he was treated as an equal in the courts of Julius II and Leo X. Since his death, his fame has been steadily maintained.

His great rival was Michelangelo (1475–1564). He was born near Florence. In spite of his father's opposition he decided to follow an artistic career. At first, he seemed more inclined toward sculpture than painting but received training under good masters in both branches of art. In 1496, after having worked some years at Florence, he went to Rome. Some time after his arrival there, Julius II planned to have him work on a memorial to himself, but Michelangelo was soon diverted to the task of decorating the famous Sistine Chapel. His four and one-half years spent in this work is now his chief title to fame. Constantly harassed by critics and the failure of the busy Pope to pay him promptly, he finally, in 1522, went to Florence and remained there for the next twelve years. In 1534, however, he returned to Rome, where he lived for the remainder of his life. After 1544, afflicted by a bodily infirmity and saddened by the loss of a beloved and honored patroness, he became more accessible, tenderer, and more human. By this time he had become the first citizen of Rome. Almost to the end of his long life, he was busy with such tasks as plans for buildings on the Capitoline Hill, the Farnese Palace (built for Pope Paul III), and the great dome on St. Peter's Cathedral.

Another of the great artists of the period was Titian (1477–1576), the Venetian painter. He studied painting with the famous Bellini family of painters. By 1518, he was at the height of his fame. After he had painted his portrait of the emperor, Charles V made Titian a count of the Empire. Titian made Venice his headquarters but painted pictures for several of the rulers of Italy. He is noted as a master of color and was the first painter to appreciate mountains as a background of his pictures.

Titian was only one of the many painters that made Venice an artistic center. Among the latter was Jacobo Robusti (1518–1594), nicknamed Tintoretto because his father was a dyer. After a hard struggle, he became recognized as a great painter. He probably painted more pictures than any other artist, but his work was very unequal. As a result, opinions differ as to his merit. All critics concede that he had an exuberant imagination and grand conceptions, that he was a hard and conscientious workman, and that he was a master of composition, drawing, and color.

Still another distinguished member of the Venetian school was Veronese (1528–1588). After working some time at Verona (his birthplace) and at Mantua, he came to Venice, where he quickly gained wealth and reputation. His work was much influenced by a visit to Rome. His designs were generally noble. His fertile imagination made him almost inexhaustible in inventing details. As a result, he often overloaded his pictures with ornaments. He was given to inserting architectural backgrounds in his pictures.

Meanwhile, Albrecht Dürer (1471–1528) was founding modern painting in Germany and making great contributions to the arts of copper etching and of making woodcuts. There was a market in Germany for devotional paintings and for woodcuts for illustrating books. Nuremberg, the native city of Dürer, was the center of this trade. By 1520 his paintings, engravings, and woodcuts had made him a European reputation. In this period of his life he won the patronage of Charles V and painted portraits of a number of noted men. Included in this group were Frederick the Wise (Luther's sovereign), Melanchthon, and Erasmus.

A famous contemporary of Dürer was Hans Holbein (1497–1543). Though born at Augsburg, Germany, he spent most of his working years at Basel and in England. At Basel he illustrated Erasmus' *Praise of Folly* and did the title pages and initial letters for various classics and an edition of the Bible. After 1526, he went to England, where, as yet, there were no distinguished painters. After 1537 he was attached to the court. In England he made portraits of such important people as Thomas More, Cromwell, Jane Seymour, Henry VIII, his son Prince Edward, and Anne of Cleves, one of Henry's six wives. In spite of these commissions he died, like many ordinary men of the time, of the plague.

Another important German painter of the period was Lucas Cranach (1472–1553). In 1495 he became painter to the famous Frederick the Wise, Elector of Saxony, and ruler and protector of Luther. For nearly fifty years he painted for the Electors of Saxony. He was an intimate friend of both Luther and Melanchthon and painted portraits of both men. He was ably assisted by his son of the same name (1516–1588). The work of the latter so strongly resembled that of his father that it is often difficult to tell which of the two artists was responsible for a picture.

Music

The invention of printing had almost as great an influence on music as on letters. Before the discovery of moveable type, musical scores were made one at a time by hand and were scarce and expensive. With the invention of printing, they became cheaper and more numerous.

The publishing and selling of music soon became a business. At first, the staffs and notes were printed at different times. After 1525, however, both were printed at the same time.

In the sixteenth century, Italy became a musical center. In the Italian Peninsula, Venice became a leader in music. The lucrative trade of the city with the Levant brought wealth, and wealth made possible a high degree of musical culture. The rich and ornate cathedral, known as St. Marks, became famous for its church music. In 1527, the Doge of Venice invited Willaert (1490–1562) to become choirmaster at the cathedral. For thirty-five years his influence predominated not only at Venice but throughout northern Italy. He is credited with having introduced antiphonal singing and with having trained a long list of talented students. His influence was not confined to church music. He contributed to the popularization of the madrigal.

The other great musical center of the Italian Peninsula was Rome. The existence in the city of such famous churches as the Sistine Chapel, St. Peters, and St. John Lateran stimulated the development of church music. The music at the Sistine Chapel, in particular, became a feature of the papal court. Election to its choir was considered a great honor. It enlisted the services of a long succession of great masters. The most famous of them was Palestrina (1525–1594). After serving for twenty years in various Roman churches, he was called to St. Peter's in 1571 and remained there until his death. He was a very prolific composer. He is credited with having produced ninety Masses and many other pieces of music.

North of the Alps, music found patrons at a number of courts. Many of the sovereigns of the period felt that the dignity of their courts demanded the maintenance of elaborate, royal chapels and a considerable musical establishment. Among the more famous of these musical centers were the Imperial chapel at Vienna, Munich, the royal chapel of Francis I at Paris, and the royal chapels maintained by Charles V and Philip II.

The Protestant Revolt, however, also had an important influence on the development of music. One of the Protestant leaders, Martin Luther, was well versed in music and realized the part congregational singing might play in the church service. With the aid of Johann Walther and other musicians, Luther made important changes in the services of the church. He himself composed several of the favorite hymns of Protestantism and gave many other hymn writers an opportunity to have their compositions used. The first Protestant hymnbook was published in 1525.

The Reformed Church, too, finally made use of congregational singing in the vernacular. Zwingli was not a musician, but Calvin, like Luther, appreciated the part music might play in the church service. The French court poet, Clement Marot, set some of the Psalms to music. In the end, the singing of Psalms and other hymns spread to France, the Netherlands, Scotland, and England.

In the spread of Lutheran ideas in Germany, the so-called Meister singers took an important part. In the fourteenth, fifteenth, and sixteenth centuries, groups of German popular poets had organized themselves into gilds for the revival of national minstrelsy and met weekly in the town hall or the principal church of the various cities. Their most famous singer was Hans Sachs (1494–1576), who became converted to Protestantism and did much to diffuse the Lutheran doctrines among the German people.

Italian Literature

Among those stimulated to write by the court life of Italy in the sixteenth century was Ariosto (1474–1533), who belonged to the court of Urbino. While he tried his hand at several forms of literature, he made himself famous by his epic poem, *Orlando Furioso*. It was really the sequel to an earlier poem on the same subject which many poets had sought to write. It obtains a certain unity from the love story which it narrates. It finds diversity and interest in the varied episodes and adventures which are held together by the love story. The action ranges from the Atlantic Ocean to the China Sea.

A generation later came Torquato Tasso (1544–1595). Though brought up at Naples, he found patronage and encouragement first at Ferrara and then at Urbino. His fame rests upon his epic poem, *Jerusalem Delivered*, which tells the story of the conquest of Jerusalem by the Crusaders. It narrates the story not only of the actions of Christian and Saracen knights but of their supernatural allies. In later years, the poet's life was most unhappy. His health did not very well withstand the life at court. People began to doubt his sanity and shut him up for a time in a monastery. His final years were spent in wandering from place to place.

In the meantime, important contributions had been made to the writing of politics and history by two citizens of Florence. One of these writers was Niccola Machiavelli (1469–1527). He came of a family of some local distinction and property. Entering the service of his petty state in 1494 as a clerk, he gradually rose to a position of considerable power and importance. During these years he observed men and things with unusual care, became acquainted with the classic authors, and developed a vigorous style of writing. He watched with particular interest the work of Cesare Borgia (1476–1507), the nephew of Pope Alexander VI, who by a mixture of audacity, diplomatic prudence, and self-reliance, gradually built up for himself a state in central Italy. In 1512, Machiavelli's friends fell from power, and he was driven into exile.

He used the remaining years of his life in writing various works. In 1513, he published *The Prince* and, somewhat later, the *Discourses.* In these works he really founded the science of politics for the modern world. He discussed such questions as how an ambitious man may rise to power and the genesis and maintenance of states. He proposed the unification of Italy under a powerful despot and the creation of a national army as the means of saving Italy from the dangers threatening it. In 1520 he published *The Art of War* in which he emphasized the superiority of national troops, the inefficiency of fortresses, and the importance of infantry as compared to artillery. During the last seven years of his life he worked on his *History of Florence,* the first historical account of a modern state.

Machiavelli had a famous friend and contemporary, Francesco Guicciardini (1483–1540). Though born at Florence, he was educated at the universities of Ferrara and Padua and entered the service of the Pope. While in the employ of the papacy, he held various posts of importance. He spent his last years in writing his famous *History of Italy,* which covers the history of the peninsula from 1494 to 1532.

French Literature

The contact with Italy, in the years following the campaign of Charles VIII, affected French literature as well as many other phases of French life. Frenchmen tried to imitate what they had seen and heard during the Italian wars. They used as models Italian literary works or the classics in the original languages or in Italian translations.

French writers of the sixteenth century experimented with many literary forms. Among these, poetry took a prominent place. The poets of the period experimented with many poetic eclogues, odes, elegies, epigrams, and other forms, but the dominant theme in all their poetry was gallantry.

Among the outstanding poets of the century were Clement Marot (1496–1544) and Ronsard (1524–1585), the most prominent member of the group known as the Pleiade. The former was a Huguenot. During his early life, he enjoyed the patronage of Francis I and his sister, the queen of Navarre, but in his later years Marot suffered considerably from religious persecution. His poetry, which fills five stout volumes, is characterized by an easy and polished style, a light and graceful wit, and a certain elegance of expression. He had many imitators. He was finally pushed into the background by Ronsard and his group. The avowed object of the Pleiade was to bring the French language in vocabulary and construction on a level with the classical languages. The poetry of Ronsard alone fills ten volumes. All in all, the group attained a large measure of success.

During the century there were also important developments in the drama. The first half of the century saw the end of religious mysteries. In their place arose a new class of subjects, new modes of treatment, and a different type of performers. The first French dramatic tragedy was called *Cleopatra*. Antoine de Monchretien (1576–1621) was the first dramatist to use a contemporary subject. He wrote a play based on the life of Mary, Queen of Scots. The first comic writer of any great merit was Pierre Larivey (1550–1612), an Italian by descent, who used Italian subjects and models freely.

The achievements of French prose writers during the sixteenth century were greater even than those of the poets. In many ways the poetry of the Middle Ages equaled that of modern times. In prose, the Middle Ages had produced only chronicles and romances. Latin was the language for literary expression. French was only the language of daily life. As yet, it lacked the terms of art and science and had not been used to express sustained eloquence and logical discussion.

In Francois Rabelais (1490–1553), however, France produced a writer whom critics have agreed to give a place of primary importance. Very little is known about his early life. His father, who was evidently not rich, decided to make a monk of his son. In 1511, Rabelais seems to have become a priest as well. As often happened in such cases, the son disliked monastic life and soon abandoned his monastery. After traveling around France for some time, he settled down at Lyons as head of a hospital. About 1532, he began a work which ultimately grew into a great book of five volumes. In its final form the work narrates the life and adventures of a giant, Gargantua, a popular figure in the folklore of the period, and of Gargantua's son, Pantagruel. Incidentally, it treats of feasts and the pleasures of eating and drinking, compares the schools of medieval times with those of the Renaissance, follows the hero through a great war, criticizes the monastic system, and describes a voyage that took Pantagruel to strange and distant places. The whole is told with many digressions, much satirization of politics, society, and religion, and a great display of erudition. It is a commentary on the thoughts, feelings, aspirations, and knowledge of the time but is told with a licence that would not now be tolerated. Ever since its publication, readers have differed greatly as to the author's real purpose. He has been called in turn a reformer, an advocate of sound education and rational religion, and merely a jovial good fellow without any purpose beyond amusing his readers. Whatever his aim may have been, he certainly succeeded in holding up a mirror to the century in which he lived.

Somewhat later in the century, another of the masters of French prose began to write. He was Michel de Montaigne (1533–1592), the son of a rich merchant of Bordeaux. He was carefully educated. In due time, he had some experience with judicial affairs, military life, and the life of a courtier. In 1571, however, he retired from active affairs and lived on his estate. There he studied, read, and wrote. Gradually, as a result of his meditation and reflection, his essays began to take shape. He was really the inventor of a new literary form, the essay. In their final form the essays numbered ninety-three. They touch many subjects and do not lend themselves to analysis. They treat the human comedy completely. They reflect the trend of the century which started so brilliantly and ended so miserably. The essays and their writer have been more appreciated by recent generations than they were by contemporaries.

The sixteenth century had, too, its political writers. Among these, the greatest name is probably Jean Bodin (1530–1596). Originally a lawyer, he later turned to writing. Among the topics upon which he wrote was the subject of prices. He was the first to explain the revolution in prices that resulted from the discovery of gold and silver in Mexico and Peru. He saw that there had been a rise of prices. He realized that the amount of money in circulation did not constitute the wealth of the community. He saw, too, the necessity of prohibiting the export of precious metals. He was thus an early example of what today we should call an economist. In 1576 he represented with distinction the third estate in the estates general. At considerable risk he stood for freedom of conscience, justice, and peace and withstood the efforts of the king to alienate the public and the royal demesnes. In the same year, he published his chief work, which is entitled *Six Books of the Republic*. It was the first modern attempt in France to construct an elaborate system of political science. It was based upon the ideas of Aristotle and on the author's own experience and knowledge. He approved of absolute governments but thought that they should be controlled by constitutional laws. He defended the idea of private property and accepted mercantilist views. He believed in government intervention in business, high taxes on foreign goods, and low duties on food and raw materials. He emphasized the importance of population. He was one of the first to see that the gain of one state was not necessarily the loss of another. He realized the importance of the correct adjustment of taxation. He thus called the attention of his contemporaries to a number of important principles.

Sixteenth-century France likewise produced some notable works of history. They include a history of Louis XII by Claude de Seyssel (1450–1520), a history of France by Bernard de Girard (1537–1610), and the work of Pierre de Bourdeille, lord of Brantome (1540–1614). The latter deserves a somewhat more extended notice.

Pierre de Bourdeille, Lord of Brantome, grew up in the court of Marguerite of Angoulême and then became a soldier. In these years he met most of the military leaders of the time and visited most of the countries of Western Europe. In 1589, a fall from a horse forced him to retire to private life. He spent the last years of his life writing accounts of the lives of the famous men and women he had known. They do not constitute either a great or an absolutely trustworthy history, but they do give an admirable account of the court life which he had known with all its undisguised profligacy.

Besides these formal histories, some notable French memoirs were written during this century. These include the works of Robert de la Mark, du Bellay, Marguerite de Valois, Villares, Tavannes, La Tour d'Auverge, Francois de Lanoue, Agrippa d'Aubigne, and Blaise de Monluc. They show the loose dependence of the French nobles and even the lesser gentry on the central authority, the rapid changes in the political situation, and the appetite of the French gentlemen of the day for pleasure, business, learning, and war. They can be found in the two important collections of French memoirs, those of Petitot and Michaud.

The religious reformers also fashioned the French language into an instrument of polemical discussion. The first great composition of argumentative French prose was Calvin's *Institutes of the Christian Religion*. Without any model to guide him, he made his book an example of severe logic and careful arrangement. He was not, however, the only reformer to make use of the vernacular. Lefevre d'Etaples, William Farel, and Theodore de Beze all realized the importance of reaching the French people by their own daily language.

German Literature

As far as literary activity was concerned, Germany, in comparison to France, was sterile ground in the sixteenth century. The opponents of the Lutheran movement composed some powerful and virile satires but often employed extremes of scurrility and gross personalities. There were some attempts at dramatic writing. Hans Sachs (1494–1576) of Nuremberg used every popular literary form. The literary activity of German writers (of the sixteenth century) was not, however, very great.

The one outstanding German literary monument of the sixteenth century was Luther's translation of the Bible. Its publication was the culmination of the eclipse of the medieval knight by the burgher. In this translation, Luther took great pains to make the Bible comprehensible over as wide an area and to as many people as possible. He took as a basis of his work the language of the German Chancellery. The completed translation exercised a profound influence on modern German. Luther's work as a translator was effectively supplemented by his work as a hymn writer.

Spanish Literature

In Spain the modern literary age hardly begins before 1550. After that date the genius of the nation expressed itself particularly in the drama and the novel of manners. The latter starts with the *Life of Lazarillo de Tormes,* a rare rogue who experienced many adventures. This work found many imitators.

Portuguese Literature

The Renaissance movement finally reached Portugal. While all forms of literature were cultivated in Portugal in the sixteenth century, Portuguese letters were particularly distinguished by its accounts of Portuguese explorations and travels. The great exploits of the explorers and travelers of Portugal gave the writers of the country stimulating and interesting subjects.

Out of this literature there came also a great epic poem. It was the work of Camoens (1524–1580), a relative of the great explorer, Vasco da Gama. Although Camoens was the son of an impoverished family, he seems to have received an excellent education at the University of Coimbra. He then made his way to Lisbon where, though penniless, he had some connection with court circles. About this period of his life there is much uncertainty. In 1553 he sailed to India as a common soldier and served at various points in the East until 1570.

After his return to Portugal, he published his masterpiece, *Lusiad.* The title really means "the Portuguese." The nominal hero of his poem is his kinsman, Vasco da Gama. Into his verse he wove much of the history of his country. Critics rank its author as one of the world's great poets.

English Literature

In England we do not encounter a sustained literary movement until the reign of Elizabeth. In 1516, it is true, there did appear Sir Thomas More's *Utopia,* but it proved to be an isolated example.

Its author (1478–1535) was one of the most charming Englishmen of the Renaissance period. Although he served Henry VIII as ambassador, as member of Parliament, and as chancellor, he strongly opposed absolutism. In his unique book he compares conditions on an imaginary island, which he pretends to know through the accounts of a sailor whom he met at Antwerp, with those of the time in England. He exposes in this manner the poverty of the laboring classes, the idleness and luxuriousness of the rich, the licentiousness and greed of those in office, the evils of enclosures, the cruelty of the criminal law, and the proneness of rulers to engage in war. Over against this, he describes a society in which all goods were held in common, meals were taken together, education was provided for all, the working day was only six hours, punishment was designed to prevent crime and reform the criminal, wars were fought only in self-defence, and religion was rational and tolerant. The book has been the model for most of the utopian schemes which have been drawn up since it was written. In 1535 the author was executed for his loyalty to the Medieval Church and his opposition to the religious policy of Henry VIII.

Among the few literary works of the period, a special place must be assigned to Cranmer's *Book of Common Prayer* which was published in 1549. The commission in charge of the project based its work on the form in use in medieval England but couched the service in some of the simplest yet noblest prose ever written. It is still in use in the Church of England and all the churches overseas which are derived from the Anglican Church.

It was not until about 1580 that the Elizabethan Age in literature really got under way. Before this time, classical and Italian authors began to be translated into English, and an occasional work of some merit appeared. Among these should be mentioned, because of its influence on the religious controversies of the day, John Foxe's *Book of Martyrs*, published for the first time in 1563. Then suddenly, a galaxy of great writers began to publish their works. The group included Sir Philip Sidney, Shakespeare, Spencer, Bacon, Hooker, Ben Jonson, and many others.

The greatest achievements of this group were in the field of drama. While a large group wrote plays of great merit, they are completely overshadowed by William Shakespeare (1564–1616). Not a great deal is known about his personal life. He was born at Stratford-on-Avon, was married, and had children. About 1586 he went to London, became an actor, and began writing plays. He seems to have prospered enough to be able to help his father out of serious financial difficulties and to have been able to retire from the stage five years before his death. He left behind him, though he made no provision for its publication or preservation, the priceless heritage of his nearly forty plays, his sonnets, and his other poems. In some plays Shakespeare told Englishmen their history. In others he reflected the whole life of his age. They portray every human mood and every class of society.

The poet Edmund Spencer (1552–1599) had quite a different career. After receiving a good education, he was fortunate enough to meet Sir Philip Sidney, who introduced him at court and put him in the way of preferment. As a consequence, Spencer was appointed secretary of the Lord Deputy of Ireland in 1580 and took part in the efforts to pacify Ireland after Desmond's rebellion. In this capacity he wrote a state paper on conditions in the country that showed him to be a shrewd, energetic public official. As a reward, he was finally granted an Irish estate of large extent.

During these years he found time to write a considerable amount of poetry. His most important work was his *Faery Queen,* an allegory which he never finished. It is filled with knightly adventures, the slaying of monsters, the capture of strong places, and the release of the innocent, achievements that are greatly hindered by the action of wizards and sorcerers. The episodes reveal at the same time a moral and a political meaning. They are events in a war between good and evil, England and its enemies, and Queen Elizabeth and those who wished to usurp her throne. Before his death, Spencer had completed over forty thousand lines of his great poem.

Richard Hakluyt (1553–1616) made his mark by salvaging the stories of the great English navigators of the period. Very early, he showed an interest in geography. This brought him to the attention of Lord Howard of Effingham, through whom he obtained in 1583 the post of chaplain of the English ambassador at Paris. In this position he occupied himself with collecting information about Spanish and French movements. He was later one of the principal promoters of the Virginia colony. He is remembered particularly for his *Principal Navigations, Voyages and Discoveries of the English Nation.* The definitive edition of this important historical source appeared in the years 1598 to 1601.

The sixteenth century thus owed much to the court life of the time. Small but brilliant courts patronized, employed, and encouraged the scholars, artists, and literary men of the age. The movement started in Italy but spread to France, Germany, England, Spain, and the Netherlands. It revolutionized education, greatly changed the architecture of the period, reached as great heights as painting has ever attained, and produced a wonderful literature.

CHAPTER 13

Social and Economic Developments

In order to understand a period of the past, we need to understand many things. We must know not only the great movements of history but how people dressed, their customs and institutions, general conditions, and changes in their ways of living. It is the purpose of this chapter to describe some of the things which characterized European society in the sixteenth century. Though not so important as the building of great states, the discovery of new lands, and changes in religious institutions, they still contribute to an understanding of the past.

European Man at the Close of the Middle Ages

We must not think of the men and women of the sixteenth century as being in physique exactly like those of the present day. Since that time, man himself has changed somewhat. From romantic accounts of past times, we are apt to picture the men and women of past ages as exceptionally strong and powerful. Sober investigation does not confirm this idea. In reality, the men and women of the past were neither so large nor so strong as their modern descendants. A modern man of average size, for example, would have great difficulty in getting into an ordinary suit of medieval armor.

Dress in the Sixteenth Century

The men and women of the sixteenth century, furthermore, dressed quite differently from their modern descendants. The men of each country and each class in society could be readily identified by the clothes which they wore. Most people made little change of style in their clothing. The peasants, for example, wore the same styles and even the same clothes from generation to generation. Often the actual clothes were handed down from father to son and from mother to daughter. Clothes were relatively expensive. Changes in style were for those who could afford them. As a result, the inhabitants of a given region could easily be recognized by their dress.

Some people, of course, did change from time to time their style of dress. They included the upper classes in the various countries, spendthrift mercenary soldiers, and, much more slowly, the comparatively small middle class. Though styles differed somewhat from country to country and from time to time, people of fashion quickly copied the new style.

In the sixteenth century, the upper classes, particularly the members of the various courts, usually wore brocade or velvet. The middle class could be distinguished by its woolen clothes. The lower classes made a brave show on Sundays and holidays but wore coarse materials on ordinary days.

In this period the men of all classes wore as an outer garment either a gown or a cape. The gown was a loose-fitting garment with sleeves that came down to the ankles and was caught in at the waist by a narrow belt from which was suspended the indispensable sword. The cape was thrown over the shoulders and was lined with satin of a contrasting color. Underneath the gown or cape was worn a loose-fitting jerkin or jacket (the forerunner of the modern waistcoat), breeches, that were usually very short and never came lower than the knee, and close-fitting tights that encased the legs from the hips to the feet. Under the jacket was worn a doublet, a close-fitting garment, with or without sleeves, which hung from the neck to just a little below the waist. These articles of clothing were likely to be slashed in such a way as to show in the slashes a different material. Shoes were made of velvet or soft leather and had no heels. The hat or cap usually had a low crown and was nearly flat. The hair was cut squarely about the neck.

The women of the period also had a distinctive dress. It was characterized by a full flowing skirt and a tight bodice. The skirt was divided in front and revealed a petticoat of a contrasting color. Noble and royal ladies wore under the skirt a farthingale that gave it the general effect of a hoop skirt. Usually too, the skirt had a long, flowing train.

During the sixteenth century, there were three marked changes in styles. From about 1493 to 1510, styles, particularly those of men, were much influenced by Italian models. The soldiers of Charles VIII and his successors imitated what they had seen in Italy. During the years when Charles V dominated the scene, German styles were in the ascendancy. Clothes, therefore, tended to be cut square and broad. The tights were shortened into stockings. The breeches were lengthened. The legs of the breeches were sometimes different in color. The German styles seem to have been popularized by Swiss and other mercenary troops. In the latter half of the century, styles reflected the important position held in European politics by Spain. It was a period of wasp waists, padded hips, high collars, and large ruffs, and the doublet virtually became a corset. Men wore their hair close-cropped.

The Ravages of Contagious Diseases

The men and women of the sixteenth century suffered greatly from diseases from which at present Europeans are almost free. One of the worst of these was smallpox. Practically the whole adult population of Europe was made up of survivors of this disease. It was as prevalent among children as measles are at the present time. At a time when London had a population of a half million people, it is estimated that each year one thousand persons died of smallpox and that about one fifth of those who had it died. In Europe as a whole, several million persons are estimated to have been killed each year by smallpox. Many of those who survived went through life horribly disfigured. Only about seven per cent of the population escaped this terrible disease.

The plague ravaged Europe even more than smallpox. Since the science of statistics was not yet born, it is difficult to be exact as to the havoc wrought by this or any other disease. In all countries, however, the plague was probably endemic. From time to time, terrible epidemics carried off large numbers of people. In 1563 and 1564 it was estimated that a thousand persons died in London every week from the plague. In 1570, it was thought that two hundred thousand people died in Moscow, and that, in 1575, seventy thousand persons died in Venice from the dread disease. The great number of victims gave rise to the idea that some diseases like the plague might be contagious.

At the beginning of the modern period, European society did not provide much care for the sick and infirm. In the Middle Ages, monasteries and cathedrals had established along the principal routes hospitals for the care of the poor and infirm and especially for the benefit of pilgrims and travelers. The funds for them were provided by kings, lords, bishops, and wealthy townsmen. At the close of the Middle Ages, most of these institutions were still in existence. Some of the larger cities, like Paris and Milan, had large establishments for the care of the sick. In addition, every town of any size had buildings for the isolation of lepers and smallpox patients. Italy seems to have made better provision for the care of the sick than was made by other countries of Western Europe. There, religious orders had been founded for this very purpose. In Italy a writer of the time reports that the Italian hospitals furnished their patients a white shirt, a good bed, adequate bed linen, and food and drink, as well as diligent care.

Even in Italy, though, the provision for the sick must have been inadequate. The principal aim of the regulations of the time seems to have been to protect the well rather than to cure the sick, who were, in fact, often supposed to have incurred the wrath of God, and were thus punished for their sins. Contemporary writers frequently speak of fearful conditions in the hospitals. The sick, the dying, and the dead were frequently huddled together, and often each bed had several occupants.

The insane were treated particularly badly. They were not considered to be sick but to be possessed by devils. As a means of exorcizing the demons, torture and the cruelest forms of punishment were used. The most violent were scourged, chained in dungeons, and even burned to death. The milder cases were cared for at shrines or allowed to wander about the country. The prisons came to be filled with insane persons who were naked or only covered with rags, and deprived of air, water, and almost all the other necessaries of life.

The Adoption of Tobacco in Europe

The discoverers of America saw in the new lands many things that they had never seen before. One of the unusual customs was the smoking of tobacco. Soon after the discovery of America, some sailor seems to have brought back to Spain and Portugal both the plant and the custom of smoking. From the latter country, some grains of tobacco were carried to France by the French ambassador to Portugal, Jean Nicot. As a good courtier, he sent some of the tobacco raised in his garden to Queen Catherine de Medici, who used it as snuff—which was supposed to be good for the headaches from which she suffered. The courtiers were quick to imitate their sovereign. So the use of tobacco became an established social custom.

Improvements in Transportation

In the sixteenth century one important improvement in transportation was gradually introduced. Up to that time, monarchs and nobles who wished to travel rode on horses; their servants, on mules. For a long time the leaders of public opinion insisted that this was the correct way for men to travel. In spite of popular disapproval, however, the use of carriages was gradually established.

This means of transportation seems to have originated in Hungary. From there, its use appears to have spread to Italy, where it was generally adopted. From there, the young Catherine de Medici probably brought it into France, where it came into use rather slowly. As late as 1550, contemporary reports speak of there being only three

188

carriages at Paris, and of the king being unable to go some place because the queen had the family carriage. In 1555, the first coach made its appearance in England. By the end of the century, carriages had come into general use. For a long time, the new coaches encountered a great deal of opposition. At Milan, a decree of 1578 forbade their use even by women unless they happened to be the wives of senators or nobles. At Rome, more than one pope exhorted the cardinals to leave coaches to women. In 1601 there was introduced into the English parliament a bill against the excessive use of coaches. The carriage, however, won a place for itself in spite of all the opposition which it aroused.

Improvements in Communication

In the sixteenth century there was also some improvement in communications. In 1502 a member of the Taxis family, which had had some experience in Italy, was called by Maximilian I to run a postal service throughout the Habsburg dominions. This involved the establishment of stations where fresh relays of horses could be obtained by couriers. The main purpose of the new postal system was the carrying of state communications. The Taxis family was compensated for its outlay by the concession of a monopoly for the carrying of private letters. The new system was rapidly extended from the Netherlands, where it started, as far as Naples and Spain.

In England, likewise, some improvement in communications took place. As early as the fourteenth century, there is evidence of the existence of relays of men and horses which were maintained by the government. For the supervision of these messengers, a postmaster general seems to have been appointed. In 1533 there is record of the existence of such an officer. In 1591, Queen Elizabeth prohibited the carriage of letters to and from abroad by any except government messengers.

The Status of Jews

Almost from the foundation of Christianity, Jews have been unpopular in most Christian countries. From time to time, the Jews have been mistreated in most regions of Europe, and, frequently, their property has been confiscated without just cause. By the end of the Middle Ages they had been expelled from most of the countries of Western Europe. They were to be found in considerable numbers only in Italy, Spain, Portugal, Germany, and Poland.

Wherever they were found, life was made difficult for them. Since they were usually immigrants, Jews went at first into commerce. When the rise of a merchant class among Christians tended to crowd them out of that occupation, they found themselves almost forced to enter the unpopular calling of moneylending. Later, the rise of Italian moneylenders pushed the Jews into pawnbroking. After 1200, Jews were required to wear an identifying badge, and Christians were forbidden to lodge them.

The fortunes of the Jews varied from one period to another and from country to country. In the Iberian Peninsula disaster overtook them just at the moment that the new discoveries were opening up new vistas of trade. For a time in the latter half of the fifteenth century, the position of Jews was favorable in Spain and Portugal. In some cases, Jews held important posts at both courts, and they often collected taxes for the two states. In 1492, however, in Spain, they were ordered to be converted to Christianity or go into exile. If they chose the former horn of the dilemma, they were under continual suspicion and often fell into the hands of the Inquisition. If they chose the latter alternative, they were forbidden to take with them gold, silver, or money and were subjected to many hardships. Although estimates vary greatly, it is thought that at least two hundred thousand Jews were affected by the cruel order. Many of the exiled settled in Turkey.

Ferdinand and Isabella of Spain forced their Jewish policy on Portugal. They made the expulsion of the Jews a condition for a much desired marriage alliance between the Spanish and the Portuguese royal houses. By a ruse, however, the king of Portugal managed to retain about twenty thousand Jews in Portugal. He ordered all Jewish children between the ages of four and twenty to be taken from their parents and brought to Lisbon. There, they were forcibly baptised and the older ones were offered inducements to become Christians. In spite of the king's action, those who could do so emigrated; and, by the use of bribes, many persons of Jewish faith bought their way out of Portugal.

In modern times there have been comparatively few Jews in France. As early as 1394 they had been expelled from the central provinces. They were put out of the border provinces as soon as they were annexed by the French state. In the sixteenth century, Jews who were nominal Christians began to return to the country. By a decree of Louis XII, however, Christians were forbidden either to shelter Jews or even to converse with them.

In Germany the lot of the Jews was very hard long before the time of Hitler. In the Empire the Emperor claimed the right of protecting Jews. This asserted claim had two important results. The Emperor protected the Jews in order to be able to tax them himself and to sell the pretended right of taxing them to other princes. In reality, the German Jews suffered all sorts· of indignities and injustices in spite of the alleged protection of the Emperor.

In Italy and Germany, the decrees against the sheltering of Jews by Christians led to the establishment of the institution known as the ghetto. In other countries the segregation of Jews was never complete. Where the ghetto prevailed, the Jews were compelled to live apart from the other inhabitants in a specially designated district. Usually, it was surrounded by a wall. At night and on certain Church festival days, the gates of the ghetto were locked. When outside the ghetto, a Jew had to wear a badge or special hat which would identify him. Within the ghetto the Jews usually had considerable autonomy. As a general thing, they were not permitted to own real estate.

In the Netherlands, the Jews were badly treated until 1581. After 1522, Charles V repeatedly issued edicts against them. In 1593 many Jews from Spain and Portugal commenced to enter the country. They settled particularly at Amsterdam. They tended to be people of ability and wealth. Many of them were physicians. They became supporters of the House of Orange. Even in the northern Netherlands, however, they were not allowed to practice law or become members of the trade gilds.

In the sixteenth century Jews were better-treated in Turkey than any other country of Europe. They held important posts in the government. They could engage in any trade that they wished and could live where they pleased. They could have their own schools and synagogues. The head of the Jewish community sat in the divan.[1] The ranks of the Jewish colony in Turkey were greatly increased during the course of the sixteenth century by immigrants from Spain and Portugal.

The Mercantile System

At the close of the Middle Ages, the rising states of Europe developed an economic theory that profoundly affected their economy for several centuries. The new theory made money and wealth identical. The objective of each state became the conduct of its affairs so as to attract the largest possible share of the stock of precious metals. Each state, accordingly, sought to export as much as possible and to import as little as it could. It would then have what was known as a favorable balance of trade and would receive the difference in gold and silver. This supposedly would increase the wealth of the state.

In order to achieve this goal, the governments of the time resorted

---

[1] The Turkish council of state.

to many devices. They prohibited the importation of some articles. They placed high duties on the bringing in of other commodities. They offered bounties for the export of some goods. They placed restrictions on the sending of money out of the country.

This widespread acceptance of the mercantile theory caused some economic activities to be emphasized more than others. Foreign trade was considered more important than domestic commerce. Industry was exalted because it made the raw material which it worked up more valuable. Great emphasis was laid on the growth of population. After the discovery of the non-European lands, colonies were looked upon as estates to be worked entirely for the advantage of the mother country. Each state tried to achieve these objectives by goverment action and worked by economic as well as political means to increase its own power. The larger states, furthermore, continued to strive for predominance.

The efforts of the various governments were really somewhat effective. They encouraged technical skill. They gave rise to new forms of production. They led to improvements in commerce and transportation. They quickened the tempo of life, favored the growth of cities and a greater density of population, and caused movable property to be more valued.

The Slave Trade

The new geographical discoveries and the subsequent settlements in the New World resulted in the development of the small Negro slave trade of the time into a terrible institution which lasted for more than three centuries. The beginning of the Negro slave trade, as far as Europeans are concerned, goes back to the year 1442. At that time, a Portuguese captain in the employ of Prince Henry the Navigator brought back from Africa ten black men. This aroused the cupidity of the Portuguese. Recognizing the opportunity presented by the sale of Negroes, the Portuguese began to fit out vessels and to build forts on the west coast of Africa for the purpose of conducting a trade in Negro slaves.

Upon the discovery of the West Indies, the demand for Negro slaves increased. Las Casas, as we have seen, made the unfortunate suggestion that Negroes instead of the Indians should be used as a labor force in the New World. In 1516, Charles V granted one of his courtiers the exclusive right to supply Negroes to the number of four thousand annually to the four islands of Haiti, Cuba, Jamaica, and Puerto Rico. These concessionaires bought their Negroes at the port of Lisbon.

The slave trade inflicted great suffering on the Negroes, and the traffic worked havoc and devastation in Africa. During the voyages from Africa to America, the loss of life among the captured Negroes was very great. On an average, nearly a quarter of the captive Negroes must have died on shipboard. Then after their arrival in America, perhaps a third of the Negroes died in the seasoning process. Certainly not more than half of the Negroes seized in Africa became effective laborers in America.

The Spanish Regulations for Trade

Spanish policy in regard to trade is hard to define. The government of Spain issued innumerable regulations, but they reveal few general principles. From the first, however, the Spainsh government took a paternalistic attitude toward trade with America.

For a time, the Spanish authorities seemed to have no settled policy. They decreed that the profits of the first two voyages of Columbus should be divided so as to give Columbus one tenth of the profit and the crown the remaining nine tenths. During the next few years, the trade with America was thrown open to all Spanish subjects provided they obtained a license to trade. After his accession to office, Charles V allowed his subjects in his other dominions to participate in the profitable traffic. Finally, Philip II limited trade with America to his Spanish subjects.

From an early date, the regularly licensed merchants were permitted to send their own vessels and factors to the colonies. In practice, the trade with America became a monopoly of a few wealthy commercial houses of Seville. The conditions imposed by the government made it impossible for small traders to participate in it. The system adopted led to the exploitation of the public and the restraint of legal trade.

As a protection against pirates and privateers, it became the custom for the vessels engaged in the American trade to go together under the convoy of warships once or twice a year. The first such fleet seems to have sailed in 1537. After 1543, the sailing of the fleets was regulated by law.

On the whole, the results of the American trade were disappointing. This was owing in part to the springing up of a large clandestine trade. Some outsiders escaped the Spanish authorities by loading Spanish vessels in the harbor before they sailed for America. Others carried on commerce with America under the name of some Spanish subject. Still others were simply interlopers who defied the Spanish monopoly. As early as 1527, there are reports of an Englishman being engaged in such trade.

Portugal developed a somewhat similar system for the carrying on

193

of trade with the East Indies. From the first, the trade in spices was declared a royal monopoly. The king then sold his rights to groups of merchants.

The Growth of English Trade

Down to the fifteenth century, English commerce was almost entirely in the hands of foreigners. About the middle of the century, this situation began to change. Town governments or individual merchants engaged in more or less extensive commercial voyages. England, too, began to export finished cloth instead of raw wool. The change in English commerce is shown by the statistics of the period. In the middle of the fourteenth century, a list of the substantial English merchants contains only one hundred and sixty-nine names. At the beginning of the sixteenth century, there were at least three thousand English merchants engaged in foreign trade. At the close of the century, there were 3,500 English merchants trading with the Netherlands alone. This growth of English commerce was greatly aided by the decline of the Hanseatic League, the rise of the Burgundian state, and the friendly relations maintained with Portugal.

English merchants soon saw the advantage to be gained by their organized cooperation. The greatest of these organizations came to be known as the Merchants Adventurers. This company was composed of the English merchants trading with the Netherlands and adjacent countries. Early, its members began to acquire privileges in the Netherlands. In 1564 they were formally incorporated. During the sixteenth century, this company controlled the larger part of English foreign commerce.

As a result of the success of the Merchants Adventurers, the chartered company became the usual means for the achievement of large enterprises such as the conduct of trade with distant countries and the colonization of new lands. During the latter half of the sixteenth century, the Muscovy or Russian Company (1554), the Levant or Turkey Company (1581), the Barbary or Morocco Company, and the Guinea Company (1588) were formed. In the seventeenth century, chartered companies were the usual instrument used by England, France, and Holland for the settlement of America and the exploitation of Asia and the East Indies.

PART 3

The Seventeenth Century

CH₃
CH₃—C=
O

HCH=CH—CH₂

CHAPTER  *Development of French Absolutism*
14   *1598–1661*

In the years before the Wars of Religion, the French monarchy had gradually strengthened its position at the expense of the Church and the nobles. That religious conflict destroyed much that had been done toward the centralization of authority during the preceding centuries. The Wars of Religion devastated, depopulated, and impoverished France, weakened the royal power which had been exercised by such kings as Francis I and Henry II, and even imperiled the unity of the French state. The government was bankrupt. On the surrounding seas, pirates plied their trade without much interference. In the rural areas, disbanded mercenaries made life unsafe. Many cities had been captured and sacked. As a result, the fields were devastated and unploughed, the farm animals were killed or driven off, the peasants had turned into crafty outlaws, and commerce and industry were at a standstill.

The central government had virtually ceased to function. The governors of the provinces were comporting themselves as sovereigns and were attempting to transform their revocable governorships into hereditary offices. They raised troops, levied taxes, and rendered justice as though they were independent rulers. The members of the *parlements*[1] had adopted a policy of hostility to the royal power. The cities had rid themselves of their appointed, royal officials and had begun to elect their own officers and to conduct their own administrations. During the Wars of Religion, the idea had even been advanced by some persons that the nation was superior to the king.

After the close of the ruinous Wars of Religion, the rulers of France set to work at the task of re-establishing the monarchy, reconstructing the administration, and restoring the prosperity of the country. The work went on under a succession of able rulers. This series of sovereigns and ministers gave France and French institutions the bent which has characterized them ever since.

Henry IV and the Restoration of Order

The first of these rulers was Henry IV, known during the Wars of Religion as Henry of Navarre. At the time of the signing of the

---

[1] *Parlements* were certain important French law courts.

peace treaty of Vervins (1598) with Spain, he was forty-five years of age and had been nominal ruler of France for nine years. In the Wars of Religion he had gained a reputation for simplicity of manner, bravery, good nature, and ability. After the close of that struggle, he displayed many of the qualities of a great man. He cherished no rancors. He judged men quickly and well and gathered around himself men of all parties. He was inclined to give his orders the appearance of a request and to thank those who obeyed him. Behind this mild exterior, though, was a firm will that intended to be heeded. He had not been educated for the throne and had little formal learning. In his appetites and pleasures he was gross and even vulgar. He was somewhat boastful. He was thrifty, shrewd, and cunning. He worked rapidly. He had the art of making himself liked. All in all, he made an impression on his subjects that has made him the most popular of all French kings.

As soon as peace had been restored, Henry IV began to re-establish absolutism. He carefully refrained from convoking the estates general. He excluded the princes of the blood and the great nobles from the council and other positions of political importance. Both had to content themselves with positions that gave more prestige than power. He limited the authority of the governors to military matters and withdraw from their jurisdiction the finances and courts of justice. He disciplined provincial estates that showed any tendency toward independence and took away from the cities the freedom which they had been exercising. In a few years these measures had restored to a considerable extent the royal authority.

The past history of Henry IV, his tolerant spirit and sense of simple justice demanded that something should be done to improve and protect the position of the Protestants in France. In 1598, accordingly, the king issued the Edict of Nantes. The articles of this measure gave French Protestants the right to worship according to the forms used by Calvinists in five cases. Nobles and gentlemen possessing the right of high justice in their lands could hold Protestant services for their families and others of their faith. Those who did not possess this right could only have the right of holding Protestant service for themselves and their families. Cities and other places where Protestant worship had been established in the years 1596 and 1597, or where it had been conceded in 1577, could continue to use Protestant forms of worship. In addition, Protestants could exercise their own religious forms at one place in each of the districts known as baillages. Protestants, on the other hand, were expressly excluded from using their forms of service at the court, in the city of Paris, at the seats of Catholic bishoprics, or in the army. They were not to be discriminated

198

against in schools, hospitals, or in the assignment of offices. In order to protect the Protestants, the edict further provided for the creation of special courts which were to be composed of both Catholics and Protestants. The Edict of Nantes was a first step toward the establishment of religious toleration in Europe.

In his effort to satisfy and protect his former partisans, Henry IV made further concessions in another document. By this additional agreement, most of the places, cities, and chateaux held at the end of August, 1597, which had been garrisoned by the Protestants, were to remain under their control. The king even obligated himself to contribute to their maintenance. Henry IV, in addition, permitted the Protestants to maintain a political organization. The main feature of this body was an assembly of seventy members which was to meet every three years in the presence of a royal commissioner. These military and political concessions made the French Protestants virtually a state within a state.

The restoration of prosperity in France was largely the work of Henry IV's trusted adviser, the Duke of Sully (1559–1641). He had entered the king's service when the latter was merely leader of the Protestant party. As early as 1597 the provincial governors were instructed to suppress the bands of mercenaries terrorizing rural France and the thieves swarming in the cities. More effective than these direct measures was the adoption of policies designed to re-establish French prosperity. Sully quickly restored order in the finances but did nothing to remedy the fundamental injustices of the French financial system, such as its discrimination between classes and between regions. He merely administered the existing system well. He met regularly all expenses of the government, put aside a surplus in the dungeons of the Bastille, forbade the seizure of animals or implements from peasants unable to pay their taxes, required financial officials to observe the ordinary rules of bookkeeping, and redeemed the royal domain. He caused orders to be issued forbidding the nobles to hunt over vineyards and grain fields. He lightened somewhat the burden of the taille, one of the principal taxes. He did something, particularly in the neighborhood of Bordeaux, toward the drainage of swamps. He stimulated commerce to some extent by the building of roads, the repairing of bridges, and the conclusion of commercial treaties. He made efforts to restore such decadent industries as the manufacture of cloth and tapestries and to start such new manufactures as those of silk and velvet. This, it was hoped, would prevent money flowing from France to Italy.

Henry IV furthered one of the most persistent trends of French history, the extension of the boundaries of France toward what

Frenchmen considered as their natural frontiers—the Rhine River, the Alps, the Mediterranean, the Pyrenees Mountains, and the Atlantic Ocean. Practically, but not technically, the accession of Henry of Navarre to the French throne brought to France the little kingdom of Navarre. The actual formal union of the two states took place only in 1620. In 1601, as a result of a short war, France acquired, at the expense of the Dukes of Savoy, four small districts (Bresse, Bugey, Valromey, and Gex). These acquisitions advanced the boundaries of France toward the Alps and the Pyrenees.

Until 1609, Henry IV followed a pacific and prudent policy. In that year, however, he intervened vigorously in German affairs and began to prepare for war against the Emperor and the king of Spain. To the intolerant, it seemed as if the former Huguenot was planning to make war on the Pope. These reports stirred to action a Catholic fanatic, Ravaillac. He went to Paris with the intention to kill the king. Two days before Henry IV was to leave to take command of his troops, he started by carriage through the narrow, winding streets of Paris to pay a visit to Sully, his great minister. His carriage was stopped by a cart loaded with hay. This gave Ravaillac the opportunity for which he had been looking. He approached the royal carriage and stabbed the king twice. The stricken soverign murmured that it was nothing, but in a few moments he was dead.

The Regency of Marie de Medici and the Rise of Richelieu

The assassination of Henry IV brought to power, nominally, the nine-year-old son of the king, known to historians as Louis XIII. His youth made necessary the appointment of a regent. As a consequence, promptly after the death of her husband, Marie de Medici, the rather neglected queen of the late king, hurried to the *Parlement de Paris,* the chief judicial authority of the realm, and obtained from it the regency.

Marie de Medici was born in Italy and was a member of the famous Medici family of Florence. In 1600, when she had reached what contemporaries regarded as the advanced age of twenty-seven, she was married to Henry IV. The transaction had the double advantage of providing the lighthearted monarch with a second wife and of extinguishing a rather heavy debt of the French government to the famous Medici banking house. On the whole, she proved unfitted for the role of regent. On the one hand, it is true, she was responsible for a few wise measures. She avoided the threatened war with Austria, kept Sully for a time in office, and reassured the Protestants. On the other hand, she was accountable for a policy that undid much of the work of Henry IV. At the time of her marriage, she had brought to France a crowd of greedy, impecunious, Italian adventurers, and upon her rise to power she virtually entrusted the task of governing France to two of them, Leonora Galigai, her childhood companion, and the latter's husband, Concini.

For the moment, the chief problem of the government was the great nobles. They thought the time favorable for regaining the position which they had lost under Henry IV. At first, the incapable Concini attempted to solve the problem by paying the rebellious nobles generous pensions. When later the surplus accumulated by Sully was gone and Concini tried to stop the plundering of the treasury, the nobles took up arms and demanded the convocation of the estates general. In place of sending troops against the rebellious nobles, Marie de Medici tried to bribe them into submission by the payment of money, the distribution of offices, and the summoning in 1614 of the estates general. These measures proved of no advantage to the state. The third estate, representing the commoners, demanded the suppression of the ruinous pensions. The deputies of the nobles demanded the abolition of hereditary offices. The regent terminated these quarrels by sending all the deputies home.

The dissolution of the estates general by no means terminated the troubles of the regent and her favorites. The rebellious nobles continued to plunder the treasury, and the Protestants, alarmed by the marriage of Louis XIII with a daughter of the Catholic house of Austria, joined the opposition. The monarchy and the state appeared to be on the verge of ruin.

In 1617 the rule of Concini and his wife came to an end. They had held the young Louis XIII isolated from everyone for several years. He increasingly resented his position and wished to show that he was master of France. Accordingly, he caused Concini to be killed and his wife to be burned as a witch.

The removal of the two adventurers helped the state very little. For the next four years, power was largely in the hands of a royal favorite, the Duke de Luynes. He was devoted to Louis XIII but was not much improvement over Concini. The queen mother, irritated at her removal from power, stirred up trouble. The Protestants reconstituted the organization which they had had during the Wars of Religion. In 1621, the Duke de Luynes died without having solved any of the problems troubling the state.

It was not until three years later that the situation of the monarchy began to improve. There was, however, one significant development during these years of intrigue and turmoil, namely, the rise of Richelieu. This later famous minister was the third son in a noble but impoverished family. In his earlier years he received the education of a gentleman and looked forward to a military career. The decision of an older brother to enter a monastery changed the future minister's plans. Some member of the Richelieu family usually occupied the post of bishop of Luçon, a poor and relatively unimportant diocese in Poitou. Accordingly, Richelieu gave up his plans for a lay career and made preparations to fit himself for the bishopric of Luçon. About 1602 he went to the University of Paris, applied himself to the study of theology, and began to cherish dreams of becoming a pulpit orator. In 1606, at the age of twenty-one, he was actually made Bishop of Luçon. For the next eight years he devoted himself to the administration of his bishopric and acquired something of a reputation as a reformer.

In 1614 he got a chance to distinguish himself politically. By the part he took in the sessions of the estates general, he caught the attention of the regent. The regent made him her almoner. In 1616, Concini, the favorite of Marie de Medici, made him Secretary of State for War. Upon the fall of Concini soon afterwards, Richelieu followed the regent into exile.

In spite of this apparent setback, Richelieu really continued his march toward power. In exile, he played a very difficult role. Apparently, he was merely the adviser of the exiled regent. Secretly, he was at the same time representative of the Duke de Luynes. In this difficult position he is credited with having contributed toward the reconciliation of Marie de Medici and her son, Louis XIII. In 1622, as a recompense, Richelieu was made a cardinal. Two years afterwards, he became a member of the council of state. Four months later, having found Richelieu the only man capable of managing the state, Louis XIII made him, at the comparatively early age of thirty-nine, in fact chief minister of France.

The Rule of Richelieu, 1624–1642

Richelieu's new position was entirely dependent upon the royal favor. Louis XIII was at this time twenty-three years of age. He had been a backward boy and his education had been neglected. He was fond of outdoor sports and the pageantry of war but was timid and indecisive in other matters. He expressed himself with great difficulty and usually concealed from those around him his real purposes. He had a realization of the dignity of his office and felt the necessity of supporting his minister. He did not love Richelieu, but he recognized his value to the monarchy and to the state. As a result, for eighteen years he consistently supported Richelieu and his policies in spite of the fact that the great minister's policies caused friction with the members of the royal family, the nobles, and the Protestants.

Richelieu was a striking contrast to Louis XIII. In outward appearance, he suggested a noble rather than a priest. He had a polished but haughty manner. In dress, he had a tendency toward elegance and display. He is reported to have had delicate features, a piercing eye, and a mocking mouth. He looked hard, determined, and unscrupulous. Physically, he was scarcely fitted to play the part of a stern minister. He was sickly most of the time. He suffered much from headaches, boils, and other maladies. In spite of his poor health, he had an iron will that pitilessly overrode all opposition.

Richelieu came to power with a clear program. He saw plainly the situation that confronted him. Later, he summed it up as follows: "The Huguenots shared the state with the king; the nobles conducted themselves as if they had not been his subjects, and the most powerful governors of the provinces, as if they had been soverigns. The foreign alliances were scorned, private interests preferred to public interests; in a word the dignity of his Royal Majesty was so debased and so different from what it ought to be, that it was almost impossible to recognize it." As a remedy for the situation, the new minister recommended to the king that the state ought "to ruin the Huguenot party, to lower the pride of the nobles, to reduce all subjects to their duty, and to raise the name of the king in all foreign nations to the point where it ought to be."

For eighteen years Richelieu struggled against all sorts of obstacles to carry out this program. The mother of the king, Marie de Medici, became one of his bitterest enemies. The king's brother, Gaston of Orleans, repeatedly put himself at the head of intrigues, plots, and even civil wars against Richelieu. The young queen, Anne of Austria, joined the opposition. The royal subjects never liked the king's first minister. The surrounding states, particularly the two Habsburg powers, Spain and Austria, threatened the security of the French state. These conditions, with the opposition of the nobles and the Protestants, made the task of Richelieu very difficult.

Upon assuming office, Richelieu made the very understandable mistake of taking up one of the pressing foreign problems. He attempted to gain control of the Valteline, a pass of the Alps that connected the possessions of Spain and Austria. Without control of this route from Italy to central Germany, there was danger of a revival of the political situation that faced France in the days of Charles V. Richelieu, however, soon found himself thwarted by the rebellious attitude of the Huguenots at home. This caused him to turn his attention to the solution of the domestic problems which he had pointed out to the king.

The center of the Protestant resistance to the monarchy was the port city of La Rochelle. The Protestants there were capably led. The city of La Rochelle was well defended. In addition, its defenders had an alliance with the English. The problem of Richelieu was to capture this Protestant stronghold.

The siege of the city lasted fourteen months. Richelieu himself, armed with a casque and a cuirass, conducted the investment of La Rochelle. On land, he surrounded the city with entrenchments. On the side of the sea, he constructed a long dike across the harbor that shut out the English ships. No one could get out of the city and no supplies could get into it. In the end, the defenders were forced to capitulate. In other parts of France, the Protestant resistance continued for some months longer.

In June, 1629, all the rebels formally submitted themselves to the royal government. This action on the part of the Protestants was followed by an extraordinary act by the royal government. By an edict known as the Pardon of Alais, the government imposed its terms on the defeated Protestants. For the times, the terms were exceedingly tolerant. They deprived the Protestants of the right to constitute a political party, to fortify certain places, and to hold general assemblies. They left them the liberty of worship and the equality with Catholics guaranteed to them by the Edict of Nantes. Thus the Pardon of Alais merely put the French Protestants on the same basis as other subjects of the king.

From this date, the Protestants ceased to be a political party. Many of the Protestant nobles gave up their religion and became Catholics again. This brought about, in turn, a considerable reduction in the number of places where Protestant services could be held. These changes were supplemented by the systematic campaign carried on by Richelieu and designed to persuade French Protestants to become Catholics.

Against the other great obstacle to the establishment of absolutism, the nobles, Richelieu was forced to carry on a struggle that continued through his whole period of power. The feudal lords of earlier centuries were gradually being transformed into courtiers. They were still greedy for power but looked upon it merely as a means to obtain offices and pensions. In order to achieve these objectives, they stood ready to plot against anyone in their way, to assassinate an unpopular minister, to engage in civil war, and even to ally themselves with the enemies of France. They were rapidly destroying their class in society by duels which they often fought for the most frivolous pretexts. They were incapable of appreciating or supporting a statesmanlike policy.

At the same time that they were losing political power, the nobles were suffering from unfavorable economic trends. They were victims of the changes produced by the influx of gold and silver from the New World. The income derived from their lands remained stationary at a time of rising prices, and this situation increased their greed and ruthlessness.

In this struggle with the nobility, Richelieu used various weapons. Without meeting with great success, he forbade duels; he prohibited the maintenance of private armies and fortified castles. He suppressed the great offices of state, which the nobles had hitherto filled to the great detriment of the central government. He deprived provincial governors of their judicial, police, and financial powers and gave these to officials known as intendants. These officials had previously been used occasionally and irregularly. As they belonged to the third estate, they owed their position and authority to the king and were much more likely to be devoted to his interests than to the noble governors.

Equally important as a means of checking the nobles was the stern punishment meted out to those of their number who plotted against the powerful minister or the state. The intrigues and plots of the period centered in the king's brother, Gaston of Orleans, one of the most contemptible figures in modern history. He owed his importance to the fact that until 1638 he was next in line in the succession to the throne. The plotters also received encouragement and support from the mother and the wife of the king, Marie de Medici and Anne of Austria. At times, as in 1630, on the famous Day of Dupes,[1] even the king himself seemed to side with the conspirators. In 1632, the Duke of Montmorency, governor of Languedoc and the first noble of the realm, attempted to lead a rebellion in his province. In his attempt he had the support of the Spaniards and the brother of the king. Again in 1642, a few months before the death of Richelieu, Cinq-Mars, an ambitious young favorite of the king, conspired against the first minister.

These and other plots of less importance were put down pitilessly. On the day following the Day of Dupes, the friends of the king's mother were in prison or in exile. A few months later, Marie de Medici herself was driven from the country. In 1632, Montmorency was condemned to death and decapitated. In 1642, Cinq-Mars met the same fate. In his ruthless struggle against the enemies of the state, Richelieu numbered among his victims a marshal of France, five dukes, four counts, and many persons of inferior rank. In every crisis that arose, the king in the end supported his great minister.

---

[1] A famous conspiracy.

In his zeal for the establishment of the power of the king in the state, Richelieu suppressed everything that might share the royal power. Although he owed his own rise to that body, he never convened the estates general during his period of power. He repressed the pretensions of the parlements to political power. He opposed the provincial assemblies. Wherever he could he took away the rights and privileges of cities and towns.

In the main, Richelieu devoted his attention to the futherance of the power of the king in France and of the place of France in Europe. He did little for the prosperity and happiness of the French people. He neither understood nor did anything for the reform of French finances. He neglected and even increased the poverty of French peasants and workers. As a result, Richelieu died generally detested.

The Rise of Mazarin

The dying Richelieu recommended to the king as his successor, Mazarin (1602–1661). The new minister had been born in Italy. His father had held a position there in the service of the famous Colonna family. At the age of seventeen, Mazarin had gone to Spain with a member of that family. During his three years' stay in that country, he learned at least two things which he used effectively in his later career. He mastered the Spanish language and the Spaniards' romantic art of making love. Upon his return to Italy, he served the Pope first as a captain and later as a diplomat. In this latter capacity, he displayed great ability and finally served two years as the representative of the Pope in France. At some time during his career, he took minor orders in the church and seems to have been ambitious to become a cardinal. In 1636 he entered the service of the French king. Soon afterwards, he became a naturalized citizen and entered the Royal Council. In 1641 he did actually become a cardinal.

The new minister was a very different personality from Richelieu. At the time that he took office he was a fine-looking man of forty. In bearing, he was mild and kind. He took off his hat to everyone and feared to draw attention to himself. Instead of being blunt and haughty, he was supple and crafty. He was not vindictive and never put his enemies to death. He was, however, avaricious and accumulated one of the greatest fortunes of his century. In his palace, now the National Library of France, he gathered a magnificent collection of books, manuscripts, and objects of art. He was, too, an unconscionable nepotist and took good care of various members of his family. Above all, he was one of the world's great diplomats.

For some time, his position as first minister was by no means assured. He had been appointed to office by a dying man and was surrounded by enemies. Seven months after he had appointed Mazarin as first minister, Louis XIII died. By his will he left the regency of his five-year-old son, Louis XIV, to his queen, Anne of Austria. Up to the time she assumed office, she had apparently been an opponent of Mazarin. To the amazement and chagrin of his enemies, however, her first act as regent was to confirm Mazarin in his position as first minister. From that day until his death he had the support and, contemporary gossip said, the affection of the regent.

The Foreign Policy of Richelieu and Mazarin

From the moment that he took office, Cardinal Richelieu undoubtedly knew what he wished to accomplish in foreign affairs. He desired to make France the dominant power in Europe. The chief obstacles to the attainment of this objective were the two Habsburg powers, the Emperor and the king of Spain. In the first years of Richelieu's rule, as we have seen, he had to proceed cautiously. He had to be content with guarding the keys to the Alps, preventing the union of the two Habsburg powers, maintaining the balance of power established in 1598 by the treaty of Vervins, and insuring a continuance of the anarchy existing in the Holy Roman Empire. As means toward carrying out these policies, he renewed the treaties with the Swiss, arranged a marriage between the sister of Louis XIII and Prince Charles, heir to the English throne, and supported the Protestant enemies of the Emperor.

In 1631, Richelieu was in a position to go somewhat further. In that year the Emperor seemed everywhere victorious and just on the verge of becoming master of Europe. Richelieu realized to the full the danger of this situation. In 1631, as a consequence, he negotiated with Gustavus Adolphus of Sweden the Treaty of Barwald, which provided for an alliance between Sweden and France and for Swedish intervention in the Thirty Years' War with an army of thirty thousand men in return for a large French subsidy. This treaty paved the way for a spectacular campaign that seemed on the point of putting Germany at the mercy of the Swedes. The death of Gustavus Adolphus in 1632 on the battlefield of Lützen brought to an end the brilliant Swedish successes. In 1634, the Swedes were disastrously defeated at the battle of Nordlingen.

This turn of events compelled Richelieu, if the hoped-for gains were to be obtained, to intervene directly in the Thirty Years' War. With great skill he drew into alliance with France, on the pretext that the European balance of power was endangered, the United Provinces, the Protestant princes of Germany, and others. He took into French service one of the armies of Gustavus Adolphus. In 1635, when all seemed ready, he declared war on the Emperor and on Spain. The conduct of this struggle was one of the problems inherited by Mazarin from his predecessor.

The ensuing struggle was long and furious. It was fought in the Pyrenees, in Franche-Comté, in the Netherlands, along the northern frontier of France, and in Germany and Italy. At first, the inexperienced French forces were no match for the Spanish veterans, who were still considered the best troops in Europe.

By 1637, though, France had begun to take the offensive and succeeded in capturing Roussillon and Artois. In 1643, at Rocroi, the French general, Condé, won an important victory that ended the dominance of the Spanish infantry in Europe. Finally, in 1648, the French general, Turenne, effected a junction of the French and Swedish armies that menaced with capture the city of Vienna, the capital of the Emperor. This success caused the Emperor to decide to make peace.

These military successes enabled Mazarin to win a great diplomatic victory at the peace congress of Westphalia. By this agreement, France acquired legal approval of its seizure, ninety-six years earlier, of the three important border fortresses of Metz, Toul, and Verdun; and she obtained, in addition, the rights of the Emperor in Alsace. This latter cession, it must be remembered, did not give France possession of all Alsace, but only the rights of Austria over two bishoprics, four abbeys, three counts, the noblesse who held fiefs of the Empire, and the prefecture of some ten Imperial cities. It did not give France any rights over Strasbourg. Suzerainty over the whole province still belonged to the Holy Roman Empire. The French acquisitions in Alsace, however, gave France a voice in the affairs of the Imperial diet.

The Fronde

Neither Richelieu nor Mazarin understood or did anything to remedy the finances of the French monarchy. By the end of the Thirty Years' War, the financial distress of the country had been greatly augmented. To meet the situation, Mazarin resorted to all sorts of expedients, many of them ridiculous. He sold new offices, revived old taxes, and invented new ones. These imposts bore with particular weight on the people of Paris and provoked them greatly. The exasperation was directed mainly against the regent and her first minister. In 1648 the discontent broke out into an open revolt, known as the *Fronde* movement. The word means a sling. The movement probably was given this name because of the childish acts of many of the participants.

The revolt was initiated and led by the judges of the Parlement of

Paris. From 1643 this body had been exercising its alleged right to refuse to register the new taxes. In April, 1648, Mazarin announced that an annual tax known as the *paulette*, inaugurated by Sully and paid by the judges of parlement in return for the privilege of transmitting their offices to their descendants, would, for an additional nine years, be imposed on both the judges and the financial agents of the government. Although the measure concerned only judges of other courts and not the Parlement of Paris, the members of that body invited the judges affected by the new measure to convene for the purpose of deliberating on the subject of the reform of the realm. The meeting resulted in the drawing up of a declaration that demanded the suppression of the new intendants and all extraordinary agents, demanded that no tax should be imposed without the consent of parlement, and that no subject was to be imprisoned more than twenty-four hours without being brought before his natural judges. It was an effort on the part of the Parlement of Paris to play the part of an English parliament and limit the absolute power of the French monarchy.

At first, the regent appeared to make concessions to these demands. Two months later, when she had troops at her disposal as a result of French military victories at the close of the Thirty Years' War, she suddenly caused the arrest of several of the members of parlement. These arrests led to a popular movement. Many barricades, built of barrels, carts, and paving stones, were erected in the narrow, crooked streets of Paris. Prudently, Cardinal Mazarin persuaded the regent to release one of the most popular judges, and with the aid of loyal troops the two heads of the government escaped from Paris. Their departure was the signal for a civil war.

There was a real justification for the revolt, but the Parlement of Paris was unfitted to play the role of an English parliament. The only similarity between the two bodies was one of names. The English parliament was composed of deputies of the nation. The Parlement of Paris was only an appointed tribunal. It tried to usurp a role that the estates general should have played. The members of the Parlement of Paris, furthermore, were compromised by their allies, the common people of Paris and the frivolous, self-seeking nobles who opposed the regent and Cardinal Mazarin.

In reality, there were two *Frondes*. In the first, the Parlement of Paris, supported by the common people of the capital and some of the nobles, assumed leadership. It lasted only about two months (1649). The hero of the battle of Rocroi, Condé, remained faithful to the regent and invested Paris with an army of fifteen thousand men. The Parisians and their noble allies, however, soon tired of the struggle, and the Parlement of Paris concluded peace with the court.

Thenceforth, the brave but arrogant Condé considered himself the savior of the monarchy. He thought no recompense was too great for his services. His demands and insolent pride exasperated the regent. In January, 1650, accordingly, she had the irritating general arrested. This action of the court caused a second revolt. The wife and sister of Condé stirred to the point of revolt the two provinces of which he was governor. The intriguing Paul de Gondi, the coadjutor of the archbishop of Paris (who was later known as Cardinal de Retz), discontented because he had not yet been made a cardinal, drew the Parlement of Paris and the common people of the capital into the new rebellion.

The strength of the opposition forced Mazarin to make concessions. For the moment, he set Condé at liberty, left the French court, and went to Germany. Upon his return to France somewhat later, he found the country in the greatest confusion. The Parisians were embroiled with Condé but refused to allow the young king, Louis XIV, to enter Paris. Condé had concluded an alliance with the Spaniards. The royal army was commanded by another hero of the Thirty Years' War, the great Turenne.

The principal episode of revolt took place at Paris. Turenne attacked Condé in a suburb of the city. Condé seemed on the point of being crushed between a hostile army and the walls of an unfriendly city. Just when Condé seemed lost, the guns of the Bastile began to fire on the royal troops and the gates of Paris admitted the army of Condé (1652). This action was the work of Mademoiselle Montpensier, a cousin of the king and a daughter of the notorious Gaston of Orleans. She was inordinately ambitious to take a great part in affairs. The discord among the supporters of the *Fronde* movement, however, continued. Weary of the war, the Parisians expelled Condé from Paris. Condé thereupon fled to the Netherlands, where he joined his allies, the Spaniards. His flight virtually ended the civil war. At the request of parlement, the young king, Louis XIV, and his mother returned to Paris (1652). Some months later, Cardinal Mazarin also returned in triumph. Long after the close of the political and military struggle, however, France suffered from the devastation, the disorder, and the sickness caused by the war.

The Ending of the War with Spain

The termination of the domestic strife did not restore peace to France. When the Emperor signed the peace of Westphalia in 1648, Spain had refused to conclude a treaty. It hoped to profit by the civil war which had broken out in France and to recover what it had lost.

As a result, the foreign war lasted for twelve years longer. In alliance with Condé and starting from the Netherlands as a base, the Spaniards cruelly ravaged northern and eastern France. In the main, though, neither side was able to win a striking victory. In 1657, in an effort to get the upper hand over Spain, Mazarin concluded an alliance with Cromwell, the commoner who had recently become dictator of England. In return for the aid of six thousand English veterans, Mazarin ceded the English government the French port of Dunkirk. This high price enabled Turenne, reinforced by his English allies, to win the decisive battle of the Dunes, which was fought at a point near Dunkirk. This battle destroyed the last Spanish army and made the Spaniards ready to negotiate a treaty of peace.

The resulting agreement is known as the Treaty of the Pyrenees (1659). It derives its name from the fact that it was signed on the frontier between the two countries which runs along the crest of those mountains. By this treaty France received on the south the provinces of Roussillon and Cerdagne and on the north the province of Artois, the duchy of Luxemburg, and some places in Flanders. The treaty thus continued the march of France toward its natural frontiers. In the light of later developments, however, the most important stipulation of the treaty was the arrangement for the marriage of Louis XIV with the eldest daughter of the king of Spain.

During the last eight years of his life the supremacy of Mazarin in France was uncontested. By his victory over the *Fronde* he had completed the domestic policy of Richelieu. By his conclusion of the treaties of Westphalia and the Pyrenees he had humbled both the Austrian and Spanish Habsburgs and carried to completion the foreign policy of his predecessor. He only survived the Treaty of the Pyrenees, however, a few months. He died in March, 1661. His death brought to power the young, pleasure-loving Louis XIV.

The Wars of Religion left France in great disorder. The central government was respected by neither its subjects nor foreign powers. From this situation, it was gradually rescued by a succession of strong rulers. As a result of their work, it became absolute at home and dominant on the continent.

CHAPTER
15

In 1661, France was ready to reap the results of the policies pursued by Henry IV, Richelieu, and Mazarin. Its wealth and population made it potentially a great power. It had just triumphed over the forces of disunion by defeating the *Fronde* and had established its supremacy in Europe by concluding the treaties of Westphalia and the Pyrenees. Its future and that of Europe lay in the hands of the young French sovereign, Louis XIV.

Louis XIV Assumes Power

Death had barely closed the eyes of Cardinal Mazarin before the Royal Court turned its attention to the question of his successor. The king seemed engrossed with the problem of amusing himself. For two generations the kings of France had reigned but had not governed. Two powerful ministers in turn had conducted the foreign relations of the state, determined its domestic policies, and distributed the offices and pensions that meant wealth or poverty, influence or disfavor to the anxious beribboned and beruffled courtiers. The court, consequently, breathlessly awaited a royal announcement.

The king astonished everyone, however, by his first measures. Some hours after the death of the cardinal, he assembled the principal persons of the court and the government. Before this assembly he forbade the secretaries of state and the superintendent of finances to sign anything without his order. He informed the president of the clergy that, henceforth, he should direct his questions concerning clerical affairs to the king himself. Even after this pronouncement, most of those who heard the king's orders must have believed that the young sovereign would soon tire of the humdrum work of presiding over the discussions of the Royal Council, holding long interviews, reading the numerous and interminable reports, and signing documents. No one foresaw that for the rest of his life the king would toil with considerable fidelity at the task of being the real ruler of his country.

The royal announcement made a young man, twenty-two years of age, master of France. Though he had many faults, his contemporaries thought that he looked and acted like a king. He was only of ordinary height, but he carried himself with a dignity that forbade familiarity. He was extremely polite even in that formal age and was usually just in matters that did not involve his personal interests. He was energetic in both work and amusements. He was prudent, spoke his words well, and took few risks. He accepted his exalted position without questioning its justification. He thought much about the impression his actions might make. He was scrupulous about observing the forms of religion but ignorant about its real spirit. Because of his power and position, these qualities were destined to have a great influence not only upon France but upon all Europe.

To aid him in his task of ruling France, Louis XIV had a galaxy of talented men such as few sovereigns have possessed. To conduct his diplomatic affairs during the first ten years of his reign, he had Lionne, the pupil and colleague of Mazarin, one of the negotiators of the treaties of Westphalia and the Pyrenees. For twenty-two years he had Colbert, who ultimately filled five posts in the royal government and struggled vainly to make France prosperous under a sovereign inclined to squander its resources in wars and display. To lead his armies, he could call on two famous generals, the careful and methodical Turenne and the brilliant and repentant Condé. To fortify his frontiers and to capture the fortresses of his enemies, he had Vauban, the most famous military engineer of the *ancien regime*. Even among his extraordinary group of advisers, however, Louis XIV was always the master.

With the aid of these excellent councillors, the young king had the unusual opportunity of choosing the sort of king he would be. He could listen to the advice of Colbert and make his country happy, great, and prosperous; or he could be the traditional great king and squander, sacrifice, and destroy the lives and property of his subjects in wars and display.

The Ideas and Policies of Colbert

At the time he became one of the principal advisers of the youthful king, Colbert was fifty-two years old. He was of middle-class origin. While in a subordinate position in the ministry of war, he had attracted the attention of Mazarin by his ability and industry. The cardinal first had put him in charge of his personal affairs and finally had recommended him to the king. Louis XIV at the beginning placed him in control of the royal finances but gradually entrusted him with other tasks. By the time of his death he had supervision not only of the finances of the state but of the royal marine, the household of the king, manufactures, public works, colonies, agriculture, and commerce.

213

In his imagination, Colbert dreamed of a France that was rich, powerful, and at peace. These objectives were to be gained by the acquisition of money. France was to devote her energies to productive work. Agriculture and manufactures were to produce enough not only for the needs of France but for sale abroad. With this end in view, the obstacles to production were to be removed by the abolition of interior tolls and customs lines, the establishment of uniform weights and measures, the better distribution of the burden of taxes, and the improvement of communications. When these aims were achieved, France would supply its own needs, have a surplus for sale abroad, acquire colonies for the supplying of raw materials, and carry and defend her foreign commerce with her own ships.

Though he never realized his dream for France, the work of Colbert left a deep impress on the finances, the economic life, and the navy of the French state. He began his work for France with a reform in the finances. He established a court to seek out abuses and punish the guilty. This court tracked down some four thousand corrupt financiers and officials and recovered large sums for the government. Colbert also suppressed many superfluous offices, recovered many lands for the royal domain, and increased the yield of the king's estates. He made some adjustments in the levying of the taille, the principal direct tax imposed by the state. He aided domestic commerce by abolishing interior customs lines in a large part of northcentral France, the region known as the Five Great Farms. He changed the character of the foreign commerce of France by raising the taxes on the export of raw materials and on luxuries.

Colbert also left his mark on the transportation facilities of the country. He believed canals were more economical than roads for the carrying of freight. He estimated that six men and four horses with a barge could transport by water as much as four hundred horses and two hundred men could move by road. With this end in view, he improved navigation on many of the rivers of France and constructed some important canals. Among the latter were the canal from Orleans to Montargis, begun in 1679 and completed in 1692, which connected the Loire and the Seine rivers, and the canal, started in 1666 and finished in 1681, which connected the Garonne and the Rhone rivers.

Colbert also devoted much attention to the stimulation of manufactures. He encouraged the growth in France of such raw materials as dye stuffs, flax, hemp, tobacco, and raw silk. By tariffs, bounties, privileges, and the concession of monopolies, he sought to revive old and establish new industries. He enticed skilled workers into France to teach French workmen how to make the fine cloths of the Netherlands, the mirrors, glassware, and lace of Venice, and the valuable products of many other regions. To prevent fraud and poor workmanship, he issued scores of laws and decrees regulating manufactures. In order to insure the carrying out of these regulations, he appointed inspectors who hounded the manufacturers and artisans and punished frauds and bad workmanship by the destruction of faulty products and the public exposure of both the workman and his goods. In his efforts to stimulate manufactures, however, Colbert met with only partial success. He succeeded in making France a center for the production of luxuries but hampered by his rigid regulations the efforts of later generations to improve French manufactures.

Because of his work for the French marine, Colbert must be counted as one of the founders of the French navy. Prior to the administration of Richelieu, France had had no effective French navy, and during the troubles of the *Fronde* period, much of the work of the great cardinal had been undone. Colbert made the creation of a strong navy one of his chief objectives. He began by making seaworthy the vessels still to be found in French ports, purchasing vessels where he could and scouring Europe for the workmen and the products needed for the repair and construction of ships. As rapidly as he could, he stimulated the production at home of arms, cannon, anchors, sails, masts, hemp, and tar. He made great naval bases at Toulon, Rochefort, Brest, and Dunkirk. By 1677 he had given France a fleet of 116 vessels of war of all classes in the Atlantic and a fleet of 40 galleys in the Mediterranean. With these forces he enabled France to gain the mastery in the Western Mediterranean and to contend on equal terms with the navies of Holland and England in the Atlantic.

Colbert, likewise, strove to increase the commerce of France. At the beginning of his administration, he found France carrying on a small amount of trade as compared with the Dutch Netherlands or even England. He hoped to establish profitable commercial relations with India and the Far East, the Levant, the struggling colonies in the Western Hemisphere, Africa, and the Baltic. For this purpose he created five great companies and urged not only the merchants of France but the court and the nobility to invest in them. Each company was given a monopoly of trade in one region. None of these commercial companies really prospered, and after a few years they all failed.

Although the commercial companies did not succeed, some progress was made toward creating a French empire overseas. While the great imperial dreams of Colbert were never realized, France commenced the occupation of India and established commercial relations with Siam and Japan. It succeeded better in America than in Asia. Great efforts were made to increase the population of the feeble colony in Canada. Important explorations were carried on in the Mississippi Valley and in western Canada. In 1662, two Frenchmen discovered James Bay but failed to interest the French authorities in the possibilities of the Hudson's Bay region. In 1673, Joliet (a trader) and Marquette (a missionary) made a famous journey of exploration that took them through central Wisconsin by way of the Fox and Wisconsin rivers and down the Mississippi to Arkansas. In the years from 1679 to 1682, the brilliant fur trader, La Salle, completed the work of Joliet and Marquette by a journey of exploration which took him through central Illinois and down the Mississippi River to its mouth. In 1699, a permanent settlement was made within the limits of what is now called Louisiana.

Louis XIV Chooses To Be the Grand Monarch

It was inevitable, however, that Louis XIV should not be the king of a rich and prosperous France as envisioned by Colbert. He was too vain, too conventional, too fond of the pageantry of life to take the advice of his great minister. He chose instead to be the traditional grand monarch. As a result, he organized a court that became the envy of every princeling in Europe, but that strained even the resources of France. He embarked on a series of wars that frightened Europe and brought some territorial gains to the French state but that exhausted France and laid the foundations of the retributive movement known as the French Revolution.

The Court of Louis XIV

The predecessors of Louis XIV had had courts which varied from the magnificent one of Francis I to the comparatively simple establishment of Henry IV. Louis XIV surpassed his predecessors and created the most elaborate court that Europe had ever seen. When it was fully organized, it is estimated that some eighty thousand persons devoted themselves to the task of supplying the needs, the service, the pleasures, and the protection of the king. They included swarms of servants, several thousand cavalrymen and infantry men, and hundreds of nobles. In drawing the latter to his court, Louis XIV had a serious purpose. He intentionally transformed the descendants of the rude, independent, feudal vassals, who had made so much trouble for his ancestors and for himself, into docile and obsequious courtiers.

The presence of so many people at court necessitated the development of elaborate rules of etiquette designed to dramatize the monarchy. The whole life of the king became a public spectacle. Every action became a rite performed before an attentive audience of courtiers.

This may be illustrated by a description of the ceremony of the royal rising. At the appointed hour, the royal valet wakened his master. Before the king got out of bed, however, the royal children, the princes and princesses, and the royal doctor and surgeon were introduced. Next came in the great officers of the palace, some of the grand seigneurs, the royal barber, the king's tailor, and valets. In their presence, the master of France washed his hands in wine, made the sign of the cross, and said a prayer. He then put on his slippers and his dressing gown, arose, and seated himself in a chair. At that point a third, a fourth, and a fifth group of courtiers in turn entered the royal chamber. In the meantime, the process of dressing the king went on. Two pages took off the royal slippers, the grand master of the wardrobe removed the king's night shirt, and other courtiers put on one by one the various articles of his majesty's apparel. Other courtiers held the mirror and the torch, and a valet brought several cravats from which the king chose one to wear. Finally, the attendants brought the royal hat, gloves, and cane; the almoner repeated a prayer; and the king was ready for the new day.

The obsequious service and devotion of the courtiers, however, was expensive for the king and for France. The courtiers confidently expected to be supported and amused by the king. If they pleased the king, he might reward them with outright pensions or lucrative sinecures. If they lost heavily at cards, he might even pay their gambling debts. For the courtiers, every day was a holiday. Their only work was taking as conspicuous a part as possible in the life of the court. They spent their time in dining, in attending parties and concerts, in gambling, or in changing their clothes for these various activities. They played while others toiled to make their idle lives possible.

Louis XIV soon felt that he needed a proper setting for his court and its pageantry. In 1664, he gave orders for the erection of a huge palace at Versailles, a spot a few miles southeast of Paris and its restless populace. From that date until 1695, swarms of workmen toiled at the task of building the great chateau. During the greater part of the time, they worked under the direction of Mansart, a famous member of a distinguished family of architects whose name has been perpetuated by the style of roof named after them. The completed structure stretched for half a kilometer along the crest of a grand terrace. It was large enough to shelter ten thousand persons. It gave an impression of flamboyant elegance and grandeur. As it was approached, one noticed its great wings, its high first story and pilasters and balustrade masking the roof. In front of it stretched away an immense garden designed by the celebrated Le Notre, who eventually received a title for his work in creating it. In contrast to the natural parks developed in England, the park at Versailles was characterized by its artificiality, its fountains, its succession of basins, its velvety lawns lined with statues, its clipped trees and hedges, and its immense perspectives. It was as artificial as the beruffled courtiers who wandered along its paths and drove through its miles and miles of roads.

After 1682, the great chateau became the chief center of court life. Many of the men and women whom we think of in connection with Louis XIV had already ceased to form a part of the court. The charming simplicity of Mademoiselle La Valliere had by that date been immured for a decade in a convent. The haughty beauty of Madame de Montespan was nearly at the end of its influence. Turenne had been killed some years before. Most of the fawning courtiers who competed for the favor of the king have been forgotten, but a visitor to Versailles in 1682 would have seen some who are still remembered. The clever, devout Madame de Maintenon was already almost imperceptibly undermining the position of the proud Montespan. A visitor might, too, have seen Racine, his muse silent, playing the inconspicuous part of royal historiographer. On great feast days of the Church, the visitor might have heard the great preachers of the period—the pontifical Bossuet, the orthodox Fenelon, or the charitable Bordaloue—in the royal chapel. On occasions, Madame de Sevigne might have been seen at court gathering material, as always, for letters to her beloved daughter. A few years later a comparatively inconspicuous member of the court circle, Saint Simon, was to write in secret his now famous memoirs which faithfully mirror the petty details of the court life of the time.

Early Diplomacy and Wars of Louis XIV

In his conduct of foreign relations, Louis XIV quickly showed his imperiousness and his determination to have a deciding voice in the affairs of Europe. In the first year of his exercise of the royal power, the young French king used a struggle for precedence in a procession between his own ambassador to London and the Spanish ambassador as an occasion for demanding a public promise before the foreign ambassadors, the royal princes, and the great officers of state at the French court that in the future the diplomatic representatives of France should always precede those of Spain on state occasions. In the same year (1662) that the king of Spain made the apology demanded of him, Louis XIV forced the English to treat the French as equals in the narrow seas in the matter of saluting the English flag. In this year (1662), too, he humiliated the Pope. As a result of a quarrel between some drunken Frenchmen and the papal guard, a page of the French ambassador was killed and the embassy fired upon. Because of this, the French king compelled the Pope to dismiss his Corsican guard, to send a cardinal to France to apologize for the incident, and to construct a pyramid at Rome with an inscription to commemorate the affair. These highhanded acts should have been a warning to the states of Europe of what they might expect from the young French sovereign.

While he was gaining prestige by these minor episodes, Louis XIV had been laying his plans for the acquisition of at least a part of the Spanish Empire. The relations of the two states, Spain and France, were very complicated. In 1659, as a result of the Treaty of the Pyrenees, Louis XIV had married the eldest daughter of the Spanish king. She renounced all claims to the Spanish throne, but her father never paid the promised dot. This situation gave the French sovereign a chance to make troublesome claims to the Spanish inheritance. In 1661, the only male heir of the king of Spain died, but five days later a new heir was born, the sickly Charles II, son of Philip IV of Spain and his second wife. In 1665, the Spanish king himself died. Louis XIV promptly demanded the immediate cession of the Spanish Netherlands and one third of Franche-Comté. The alleged grounds for the demand were the rights to these territories of his queen (the eldest daughter of the late Spanish king and a child of his first wife), in preference to the children of his second marriage. In reality, the claim had no legal or moral basis except a law of the province of Brabant governing the inheritance of private property. The real reasons for the demand were the desire of the French king to round out his territory by the acquisition of the Spanish provinces, the military strength of France as compared to Spain, and the fact that Spain had been engaged for two years in a disastrous war with Portugal.

In 1667, the refusal of the French demand brought on the so-called War of Devolution. A French army of 50,000 men, led by Turenne but under the technical command of the king, proceeded cautiously into the Spanish Netherlands and began the reduction of the badly defended Spanish fortresses. A succession of border cities were quickly reduced after short sieges. The whole Spanish Netherlands seemed about to fall into the hands of the French. Later in the year, the penitent Condé led a second French army of 15,000 men, which was also under the nominal command of the king, into the even more poorly defended Franche-Comté. The campaign was over in seventeen days. As a result, the Free County of Burgundy was also in the hands of the French.

The easy victory of Louis XIV in the Spanish Netherlands, however, had at last frightened the European powers. Both England and the United Provinces knew very well the danger of letting the Spanish Netherlands fall into the hands of the powerful French sovereign. Seizure of the Spanish Netherlands was the first step, too, toward invasion of the two countries. In alarm, England and the United Netherlands terminated the war which had been going on between them since 1664 and formed, on the initiative of the Dutch, a triple alliance composed of the two powers and Sweden, a state which felt that Louis XIV had not appreciated to the full the value of its alliance. The three allies then offered their services to the French monarch in mediating the war. As he was hardly ready to risk war with the three allies, Louis XIV hastened to conclude in 1668 the Treaty of Aix-la-Chapelle with Spain by which he returned Franche-Comté to Spain but retained some twelve border fortresses which had hitherto belonged to the Spanish Netherlands. The War of Devolution had thus brought France another step nearer the goal of its so-called natural frontiers.

The Dutch War

For Louis XIV, the part taken by the United Netherlands in checking his plans of conquest was the last straw. Although France and the United Netherlands had been allies since the time of Henry IV, the French sovereign increasingly disliked the Dutch for a number of reasons. They permitted their gazettes to discuss both the French king and his country with entirely too much freedom. They were both republicans and Protestants. Now, in addition to all that, they had dared to thwart his plans of conquest. His pride demanded that they must be punished.

For the next four years, Louis XIV made careful preparations for an attack on the United Netherlands. In spite of all the efforts of the Dutch authorities to frustrate him, he was successful in isolating the United Netherlands diplomatically. He concluded in 1670 the secret Treaty of Dover with the king of England, Charles II. In return for substantial subsidies and troops from Louis XIV which would free him from control of the obnoxious English parliament, the roistering Charles II of England promised to announce at a favorable time his conversion to the Catholic faith and to cooperate as an ally in the proposed war against the United Netherlands. In 1672, after a long struggle with the Dutch who were ready to pay well for their continued support, the Swedes finally returned to their alliance with France. Many of the German princes unblushingly sought for subsidies from Louis XIV, and even the Emperor, who was busy with the Turkish problem, signed the Treaty of Neutrality. By 1672, the French diplomats seemed to have everything ready for a military attack on the Dutch.

The Dutch, on the other hand, found themselves almost completely unprepared to withstand a French invasion. In 1579, the seven northern provinces of the Netherlands had formed a league against Spain, and, in 1581, they had declared their independence from the Spanish monarchy. The separate provinces, however, had been so jealous of their rights and privileges that they had never surrendered much authority to the central government. Their representatives in the States-General received instructions as to how they should vote, and the consent of all seven provinces had to be obtained before any action could be taken. This disunion was usually overcome to a certain extent by two facts. A member of the House of Orange was usually captain general of the military forces of the country and stadholder or governor of five of the seven provinces, and the province of Holland so surpassed the others in population and wealth that it tended to dominate the other provinces. Two parties contended for control of the political machinery. On the one hand there was the Orange party. It was supported by the poor nobles of the agricultural eastern provinces and the lower middle class and the artisans who had no voice in the government of the coastal cities of Holland. On the other hand, there was the Patrician party, composed of the men of affairs in the larger towns and cities of Holland. Since 1650, this party had dominated the United Netherlands. Under the leadership of John de Witt, it had struggled for commercial supremacy but neglected to take proper measures for the defence of the country. As a consequence, the United Netherlands did not seem prepared to withstand successfully the threatened French attack.

As soon as the French diplomats had prepared the way, the French monarch set in motion toward the United Netherlands two French armies, numbering 120,000 men—the largest military force Europe had seen in modern times, and also some troops furnished by his German allies. The invaders had little difficulty in capturing the Dutch fortresses on their route, and the fall of Amsterdam seemed imminent. The delay, caused by the reduction of the Dutch fortresses, however, gave the Dutch defenders a chance to open the dikes and stop the French advance.

The French successes inflamed popular feeling in the United Netherlands. The Orange party blamed the urbane John de Witt and the Patricians for the invasion. A Dutch mob, accordingly, seized and brutally murdered John de Witt and his brother. This crime put the task of conducting Dutch affairs in this crisis into the hands of William of Orange, a young man of twenty-two and the grandson of the famous leader in the Dutch struggle for independence.

The new Dutch leader had been only a small child when his father had unexpectedly died in 1650. The Patricians had utilized the situation, as we have seen, to seize control of the state. The young prince had grown up to be the antithesis of Louis XIV and all for which he stood. Always carefully surveilled by the party of his opponents, he had developed into a man who was silent, unostentatious, ambitious, and adept at keeping his own counsel. When the war broke out, he took charge of the small Dutch military forces. Upon the death of the de Witts, five of the seven United Provinces elected him stadholder. This made him for the time being both the military and political head of the Dutch state. From 1672 until his death thirty years later, he was the leader not only of the Dutch but of all the forces of Europe opposed to Louis XIV.

By this time some, at least, of the powers of Europe began to see that Louis XIV was a menace to their independence. The Emperor persuaded the Imperial diet to declare war, and, at the same time, Spain, fearful for the safety of the Spanish Netherlands and the Franche-Comté, entered the conflict. In 1674, England, which had carried on a naval war against the United Netherlands as an ally of France, forced its king, Charles II, to make peace with the Dutch. The English had no objection to the ruining of their great commercial rival, the United Netherlands, but Charles II's issuance of the Declaration of Indulgence, in behalf of the English Catholics, had opened the eyes of patriotic Englishmen to the dangers threatening their liberty and their religion. As a consequence, England became a neutral spectator in the conflict instead of a participant in the war. By 1674, also, even the avaricious German allies of Louis XIV had deserted the French monarch and had gone over to the side of his enemies.

These diplomatic developments broadened the scope of the war. While some of the French forces occupied and plundered most of the Dutch territory, other French armies operated in the Spanish Netherlands, along the Rhine, in Alsace, and in Franche-Comté. In 1674, the French abandoned the Dutch provinces but overran the Spanish Netherlands and the Free County of Burgundy. Louis XIV incited the Swedes, the Poles, and the Magyars to attack his enemies. On the French side, Turenne was killed while reconnoitering. On the other side, William of Orange employed all his powers as a general and a

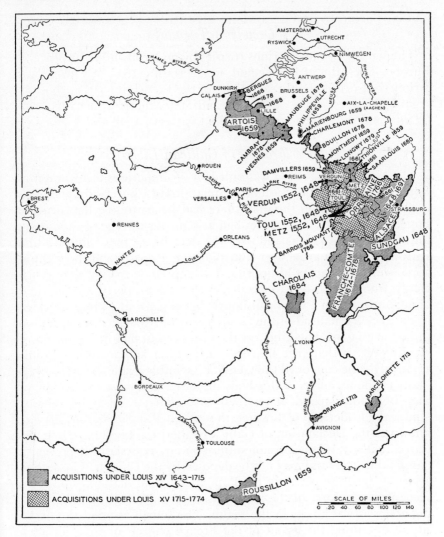

Extension of the Frontiers of France

diplomat to hold the opponents of France together and check the French monarch. From time to time, peace feelers were put out, but the war dragged on until 1678, when the weary combatants finally signed the Treaty of Nimwegen. During this and the following year, Louis XIV made peace with the various other members of the coalition organized against France. By the treaty with Spain, the French monarch gained some additional fortified cities in the Spanish Netherlands and the whole of Franche-Comté.

223

A Decade of Turmoil

The signing of these various treaties by no means brought peace to Europe. The calm of France and, to a certain extent, of Europe was seriously disturbed by three policies of the French monarch: those in regard to the relations of Church and State, the treatment of Protestants, and the interpretation of the treaties of 1648 and 1659.

The Declaration of Gallican Liberties

In a time when France was ruled by so imperious a sovereign as Louis XIV, the old question of the relations of Church and State was bound to arise. From the first, there had been trouble between the Pope and Louis XIV. Disputes had arisen over the age of candidates for ordination as priests and over the doctrine of papal infallibility. In 1673, a conflict arose over control of the property and the right of appointment in vacant bishoprics. Two representatives of the French clergy, who were hostile to the theory that the property and the right of appointment in a vacant bishopric belonged to the king, appealed to the Pope. The head of the Church naturally decided the question in his own favor. The king, on the other hand, had no intention of yielding rights that gave him so much power and wealth. In 1681, accordingly, he convoked the General Assembly of the French clergy. Many of the members of this body hesitated to oppose the Pope, but they were too dependent on their sovereign to resist him openly. Under the leadership of Bossuet, they adopted, in 1682, four articles known as the Declaration of Gallican Liberties. The first article declared that sovereigns are not subject to any ecclesiastical power in temporal matters and may not be deposed by the Church. The second acknowledged the power of the Pope in spiritual matters. The third recognized the force of the rules, customs, and constitutions governing ecclesiastical affairs in the realm. The fourth asserted the necessity of obtaining the assent of the French church in papal declarations in matters of faith. The pronouncements of the French clergy did not, however, settle the dispute. It raged for eleven more years and ended in a compromise. In 1693, the king promised to be silent on the doctrine of the declaration in return for a papal recognition of the rights of the king in vacant bishoprics.

In spite of his struggles with the Pope, Louis XIV was known as "the most Christian King" and thought of himself as a loyal son of the Church. He sought, accordingly, for an opportunity to prove his fidelity. He felt that he had found it in the persecution of the Protestant minority in France and the suppression of the Jansenists.

224

The Revocation of the Edict of Nantes

While there are no accurate statistics on the subject, students of the period think that the Protestants of France at the beginning of the reign of Louis XIV numbered more than a million persons. They were particularly numerous in the provinces of Normandy, Poitou, and Languedoc. They included famous soldiers like Turenne and many of the great manufacturers and men of finance. They are estimated to have held in their hands half or more of the personal property of the state.

Men of that age, whether Protestants or Catholics, did not understand the word *toleration*. Differences of religion within a state were considered a great weakness and something to be fought against. Each religious party really wanted to be the sole religious party in the state. To as thoroughgoing an absolutist as Louis XIV, the existence of so large a religious minority in France as the Protestants was intolerable. In addition, the adherents of the two faiths did much to keep alive religious intolerance. The Catholics, for their part, looked upon the Edict of Nantes as a temporary expedient and urged its limitation or complete revocation. Fired once again by the work of such men as Vincent de Paul, they advocated the stamping out of Protestantism. The Protestants, on the other hand, men who had seen their churches and homes destroyed and themselves disowned, vexed the Catholics in many ways. They often excluded them from membership in the gilds, feasted while the Catholics fasted, preached against them, and insulted them by showing a lack of respect for their objects of worship and their ceremonies. As a result, the fires of religious intolerance continued to burn.

Almost as soon as he assumed direction of the state, Louis XIV began to take action against the Protestant minority. By strict interpretation of the laws, limitation of rights, and actual suppression, the royal officials worked to reduce the number of Protestants in France. In 1661, royal commissioners, consisting of ardent Catholics and nominal Protestants, went out, two at a time, to inspect the Protestant establishments. They demolished all churches which had never had or had lost their legal papers. Over four hundred decrees directed against French Protestants followed. A few years later, the royal officials attempted with considerable success to destroy the machinery with which the Protestants governed their religious life. They forbade the French Protestants from holding their local colloquies and their provincial and national synods. Royal officials likewise closed the little Protestant schools and prevented Protestant artisans from rising to mastership in the gilds. The Catholics, meantime, carried on a continual campaign in favor of their own church. By these methods, many of the indifferent and fainthearted were converted.

In 1679, after the close of the Dutch War, the king decided to take more vigorous action. Royal decrees closed a long list of offices and occupations to the Protestants. Protestants who turned Catholic were for a period exempted from taxes. After 1680, rough and brutal dragoons were billeted on Protestant families and permitted to inflict all sorts of outrages upon them. After 1681, boys and girls of seven years of age were encouraged to turn Catholic in spite of the wishes of their parents. The royal authorities bought the conversion of many adults. At the time of births, marriages, and deaths, the Catholics forced their way into the privacy of Protestant families. Everywhere, the royal officials destroyed even the legally authorized Protestant edifices. By 1685, the royal sycophants around the court and in the administration told the king that Protestantism was dead or dying. In that year, accordingly, the king revoked the Edict of Nantes as a piece of unnecessary legislation. This so-called Revocation of the Edict of Nantes ordered the demolition of Protestant churches yet standing, the prohibition of Protestant religious services, the closure of all Huguenot schools, the exile of all ministers who did not accept the Catholic faith, and the punishment by sentence to the galleys of all Protestants who were caught trying to escape from the realm.

The policy pursued by Louis XIV in regard to the Huguenots was almost as disastrous for France as the earlier policy of Spain toward the Moors and the Jews. While many French Protestants stayed in France and either turned Catholic or remained secretly adherents of Protestantism, it is estimated that three or four hundred thousand French Protestants escaped at great risk by boat to England and the United Netherlands and by mountain paths to Switzerland. From these centers, in many cases, they went to Brandenburg, to America, and to Cape Colony, where their descendants are still to be found.

The War Against the Jansenists

While Louis XIV initiated the struggle against the Protestants, who had been loyal subjects all during the movement known as the *Fronde,* he found the attack on the Jansenists in full swing at the time he assumed direction of the state. The movement was unwittingly started by a theologian, Cornelius Jansenius (1585–1638), of the Spanish Netherlands, who at the time of his death was a bishop of the Church and held in high esteem. He left behind him a manuscript work, known as *Augustinus* from the fact that it dealt with the writings of St. Augustine, a famous father of the early Church. The work treated such debatable subjects as the doctrines of grace, redemption, free will, predestination, and the merit of works. The author, moreover, tried to give a practical application in the book to what he considered the evils of the time. He told his readers that the church suffered from three evils. The official scholastic philosophy, he asserted, had ceased to have any influence on popular religion; simple souls were trying to find salvation in little mincing devotions, and more robust minds were building up a natural moralistic religion. He further urged the dependence of man on his Maker and the inability of man even to wish good unless he had been born with the religious instinct. The last doctrine resembled strongly Calvin's principle of predestination.

After the *Augustinus* was printed in 1640, it found a considerable number of disciples among the theologians in the Spanish Netherlands, the United Netherlands, and in France. The new doctrines were carried to France by a wealthy disciple, Vergier, who became bishop of St. Cyran. He found followers among the members of religious orders and in many a French parsonage. Among the converts to the new doctrine were two members of a distinguished family, Antoine Arnaud, a member of an influential religious group known as the Solitaires, and his sister, Angelica Arnaud, abbess of the great convent of Port Royal, near Paris.

In 1643, the former infuriated the Jesuits by publishing a work on frequent communion, one of their practices, and by his accusation that they granted absolution too easily. This order called the attention of the University of Paris and finally of the Pope to the Jansenist movement. Both the university and the Pope condemned five propositions of the *Augustinus*. These efforts to suppress the movement only added to the heat of the controversy. Among the publications called forth by the movement were the *Provincial Letters* of Blaise Pascal, which at the same time held the Jesuits up to ridicule and displayed the possibilities of French prose.

In 1661, Louis XIV started his attack on the movement by attempting to extort a solemn renunciation from its advocates. Most of those who refused to sign went into hiding or were thrown into the prison and fortress known at the Bastille. The nuns of Port Royal (one of the most important centers of the heresy), who passively resisted the attack, enjoyed until 1679 the protection of a powerful patroness, Madame de Longueville. Throughout the reign of Louis XIV, the movement continued to trouble French society. There were attempts at compromise. Two leaders of the movement were driven

227

into exile. The adherents of Jansenism, however, kept the controversy alive by the publication of books and pamphlets of an inflamatory nature. The creeping up of old age spurred the king on to sterner measures. In 1713, the Pope, at the instigation of the king, issued a famous bull, known as Unigenitus, condemning the Jansenists. The nuns of Port Royal, who had continued the struggle throughout the reign, were finally deprived of their own convent and dispersed in a number of other religious houses. The movement lingered on, however, in various places, throughout the eighteenth century.

The Transformation of the Court

During the years of nominal peace which followed the close of the Dutch War, a decided change took place in the life of the king and his court. While he was a young sovereign, gaiety and pleasure had been the keynote of court life. A succession of mistresses had reigned for a brief space of time and then had passed out of the life of the king. By one of them, the Marquise de Montespan, the king had seven illegitimate children. By the time the pleasure-loving monarch had reached his forties, however, he began to feel that religion was more than a matter of form and that it was a question of conduct as well as ritual. This transformation was in part, certainly, owing to the growing influence of the clever woman known to history as Madame de Maintenon. As an impoverished young girl of seventeen, she had been nominally married to the comic poet Scarron, an invalid of forty-six. After his death in 1660, she stayed on as a pensioner of the court, first as a friend and later as the governess of the children of Madame de Montespan. In this way, she became known to the king, who was increasingly attracted by her beauty, her charm, her religious devotion, and her carefully concealed cleverness. About 1683, the queen having ended her little regarded life, the king secretly married Madame de Maintenon. Under her recognized but not formally acknowledged rule, the court ceased its former impiety and became devout, at least in appearance. This continued to be the tone of the courtiers until the end of the reign.

The Aggression of Louis XIV in Time of Peace

In spite of his success in the Dutch War, Louis XIV was not satisfied. The United Netherlands had successfully withstood his attack and still barred the way to the attainment of the natural boundaries of France. As a result, the king continued his policy of aggression in time of peace.

On his northern and northeastern boundary, Louis XIV had a weak power, the Holy Roman Empire, composed of several hundred states of various sizes. The sections nearest to France were occupied by small and weak principalities, relics of the feudal system and totally unable to defend themselves. The king's method of aggression against these petty states was to interpret the treaties of Westphalia and Nimwegen in his own interest. It was easy for his own courts to find that various territories in the Empire had been in feudal times dependent on the territories which he had recently annexed and to enforce the decisions of his courts by his own military forces. In this way, Louis XIV acquired additional lands in Franche-Comté, Lorraine, and Alsace. In 1681, the king seized the great city of Strasbourg without the slightest justification. This gave him control of an important bridge across the Rhine. On the same day that the great Imperial city of Strasbourg was captured, the king seized the fortress of Casale, which commanded an important route into Italy. In 1683, he forbade the Genoese to arm their galleys or construct new ones, and when they hesitated about complying with his demands, he ordered the bombardment of their city.

The inevitable result of this policy of Reunions, as the highhanded seizures of territory were called, gradually aroused Europe. The threatened powers began to form defensive alliances. Two of the diplomatic groups which they formed ultimately gained considerable celebrity. In 1686, the larger powers of western Germany organized a defensive group known as the League of Augsburg. Subsequently, its members sought the cooperation of some of the non-German powers. In 1689, after Louis XIV had brazenly invaded the Empire and wrought havoc in the Palatinate by fire and sword, the powers opposing the French king formed what was known as the Grand Alliance of Vienna. For this reason, the ensuing war is known under two names: the War of the League of Augsburg and the War of the Grand Alliance.

England Joins the Grand Alliance

In the war which broke out as a result of the aggressions of Louis XIV, the position taken by England could be decisive. In the opening years of the reign of Louis XIV, it will be remembered, the venal Charles II had persuaded the English parliament to join in the French attack on their commercial rivals, the Dutch. By 1674, however, the English people had come to see that Louis XIV was a far greater danger to England than were the United Netherlands and had forced Charles II to make peace. After that date, the English had been neutral.

During the years in which England pursued a policy of neutrality, it will be remembered, the attention of the English people was largely taken up by the struggle between the king and Parliament. Charles II and his brother and successor, James II, strove to reduce the role of Parliament. At the same time, they introduced a religious issue. Both Charles II and James II took money from Louis XIV instead of summoning Parliament, and they attempted to obtain toleration for Roman Catholics. After he came to power, James II dispensed with Parliament, appointed Roman Catholics to many important positions in the state and church in defiance of the laws, and permitted his co-religionists to open chapels throughout the country. As long as they could look forward to the accession to the throne of Mary, the Protestant daughter of James II and the wife of William of Orange (who was the great antagonist of Louis XIV), the English people did not openly rebel against their Stuart sovereign. However, when the birth of a son to James II confronted them with the prospect of a long line of Catholic sovereigns, they secretly invited William of Orange to intervene in English affairs with an armed force and to displace his father-in-law, James II, on the English throne. The ensuing campaign resulted in the overthrow of James II and the seating of William and Mary on the English throne as joint sovereigns, the confirmation of the Bill of Rights and other rights for which the English people had been struggling, and the participation of England in the Grand Alliance against Louis XIV.

The War of the Grand Alliance or the League of Augsburg (1689–1697)

The war precipitated by the French invasion of the Palatinate was fought mainly beyond the frontiers of France. Sieges, maneuvers, and naval actions went on for eight years. On land, there was fighting in the Spanish Netherlands, on the left bank of the Rhine, in Italy, in Catalonia, in Ireland, and even in America. In the main, the struggle was indecisive but put a severe strain on the resources of the participants. On the sea, England lost, for some years, control of the situation. This gave James II an opportunity to land in Ireland and rally his former Irish subjects around him. In 1696, at the battle of the Boyne in Northern Ireland, his Irish army was defeated and he himself fled rather ignominiously back to France. Contemporaneously, a rising of the Highland clans in northern Scotland, in behalf of James II, was likewise put down. In the Mediterranean, the English also gained the upper hand. During the war, there were various attempts to negotiate peace. These attempts finally led in 1697 to the signing of the Treaty of Ryswick. In this treaty, practically all the places acquired during the war were restored, but the conquests made by Louis XIV in time of peace were, in the main, retained by the French monarch. The French king, however, made other important concessions. To England he promised to cease his support of the cause of James II and to recognize the right of William and Mary to the English throne. To the United Netherlands, he was forced to make commercial concessions. So the War of the Grande Alliance was, in reality, a decided check for Louis XIV.

War of the Spanish Succession

The signing of the Treaty of Ryswick did not bring real peace to Europe. Ever since the accession of Charles II of Spain in 1665, the diplomats of Europe had been plagued by the problem of the succession to the Spanish throne. The king of Spain was hardly competent to rule. His health was wretched and his intelligence was mediocre. As the years went by, it seemed more and more likely that he would die early and leave no direct heir to the once splendid Spanish Empire in the Netherlands, the Iberian Peninsula, in Italy, in America, and in the Philippines. After the signing of the Treaty of Ryswick, the problem of the Spanish succession took first place in the chancelleries of Western Europe.

The problem seemed almost insoluble. The vocal portion of the Spanish people were proud of their great empire and anxious to maintain its integrity. The claimants to the succession, however, were numerous and included members of the royal house in France and the Imperial family in Germany. If members of either of these two houses should obtain the whole succession, it would completely upset the balance of power in Europe. Even if the inheritance should be divided, France might acquire the Spanish Netherlands and become a serious threat to England and the United Netherlands, or she might gain the parts of the Spanish Empire that would enable her to ruin the commerce of the two maritime powers in the Mediterranean or in America. The succession depended on the ability of the various diplomats to persuade the weak and sickly Charles II to decide in their favor. The results of their efforts were from time to time embodied in partition treaties that provided in one way or another for the future of the territories constituting the Spanish Empire.

After the death of Charles II in 1700, it was found that he had actually bequeathed his empire to the grandson of Louis XIV, the Duke of Anjou. This action was, apparently, in part due to the pressure put upon the dying king by the representatives of the French sovereign and in part due to the wish of the Spanish nation to preserve its vast empire. The decision of the dying monarch nullified the diplomatic negotiations of a third of a century and confronted Europe again with the problem of the Spanish succession. In the crisis, Louis XIV finally decided to accept the magnificent bequest. The other powers of Europe at first hesitated, and, for a moment, it looked as if there might be no war over the Spanish succession. Only the Emperor seemed determined to fight for what he considered to be his rights.

The imperious Louis XIV, however, by a series of aggressive acts, soon moved the powers to action. In February, 1701, the French king legally assured the new king of Spain, who had assumed the title of Philip V, his rights of succession in France. This seemed to threaten Europe with a union of France and Spain. In November of the same year, he employed French soldiers to expel the Dutch troops who had been stationed in the so-called barrier fortresses on the French border of the Spanish Netherlands as a protection against French aggression. This action seemed to threaten the security of both England and the United Netherlands. In various matters of importance, the French king began to act as if he, rather than his grandson, were the new king of Spain. Finally, the French, upon the death of James II, former king of England, recognized his son as James III and rightful heir to the English throne. As a result of this series of aggressions, England and Holland joined the Emperor, who since 1701 had been carrying on a campaign against the French in northern Italy.

This completion of another alliance against Louis XIV was the last important act of William III, who for thirty years had been the leader of the European opposition against the French monarch. His place was taken by three remarkable men. The most important of the three men was the Duke of Marlborough (1650–1722), who had started life as plain John Churchill. He had risen rapidly in the army and at the English court through the influence of the Duke of York, brother of the king. In spite of his indebtedness to the duke, he had not hesitated to desert his patron in the crisis of the revolution of 1688. For a time, William III had mistrusted him but, toward the end of his reign, put him in responsible positions. Under the successor of William III, Queen Anne, the position of the duke seemed assured by the fact that his wife was the favorite of the queen. Throughout most of the War of the Spanish Succession, the Duke of Marlborough at home virtually took the place that William III had occupied and abroad acted as commander-in-chief of both the English and Dutch forces. He had charm and tact and great military ability but was actuated by avarice and personal ambition rather than by patriotism. In his conduct of the war, he was much hampered by the chief representative of the United Netherlands, Heinsius, who reflected the fears and cautiousness of the Dutch merchants.

In Prince Eugene of Savoy, commander of the Imperial forces, the Duke of Marlborough had a remarkable colleague. Failing to obtain a suitable post under Louis XIV, Prince Eugene had gone to Vienna, where the Emperor welcomed him and entrusted to him many important posts and commands. From 1683 to 1699 he had carried on a successful campaign against the Turks. Then he had been put in charge of the Imperial forces operating against Louis XIV. In this capacity, he worked in close harmony with the Duke of Marlborough. He was cold and severe, but as a soldier he had imagination and resolution. When not on the battlefield, he displayed an unusual interest in art and literature.

The armed conflict between the European alliance and Louis XIV began in 1702. Until 1704, the armies of the French monarch were on the offensive and waged war in Italy, along the Rhine, and in the Spanish Netherlands. Then the course of events began to take an unfavorable turn for the French king. The Duke of Savoy, guardian of the Alpine passes between France and Italy and of the kingdom of Portugal, deserted Louis XIV. In 1704, too, the tide of battle definitely began to go against the French king. John Churchill, commander of the English, Dutch, and German forces guarding the Netherlands, skillfully eluded the French army watching him, marched to Bavaria, picking up various bodies of allied troops on the way, united his troops with the Imperial forces commanded by Prince Eugene, and won the splendid victory of Blenheim, which gave the allies control of Bavaria and won for the English commander great wealth and the title of Duke of Marlborough. In 1704, the English, who up to that time had been vainly trying to get a foothold in Spain, appeared with a fleet before Gibraltar, found it defended by only a small garrison of fifty men, and captured without much trouble the poorly defended stronghold. In 1705, another English fleet convoyed Archduke Charles, the younger son of the Emperor and the allied candidate for the throne of Spain, to Catalonia, where the population rose in his behalf. This gave the allies control of most of what had formerly been known as the kingdom of Aragon. In 1706, the French lost control of the duchy of Milan and the Spanish Netherlands. The loss of the latter was a result of the battle of Ramillies. In the same year, Archduke Charles entered Madrid and was crowned king of Spain under the title of Charles III. These allied successes drove the French back toward their frontiers on the northern and eastern borders and threatened to dislodge them in Spain.

In 1707, France itself was invaded and its armies had greater success in Spain. Early in the year, the forces of the French king were driven out of Naples. In Spain, however, the troops of Louis XIV and Philip V recaptured most of Aragon. Meanwhile, allied forces invaded southern France and besieged the naval port of Toulon. In 1708, English naval forces gained control of the strategic islands in the Western Mediterranean, and the allied armies in the Spanish Netherlands invaded northern France and captured the important city of Lille. By 1709, therefore, France was in great distress. An unusually cold winter destroyed all prospect of a good harvest. In the cities, white bread could no longer be obtained. In many districts, actual famine raged. Many felt peace must be concluded on any terms. The king himself began to negotiate with the allies. When the victorious allies, however, demanded that he should drive his own grandson from the throne of Spain, Louis XIV refused to make peace and appealed to the French nation for support. The appeal was successful. The king and the great nobles sold their plate in order to aid the finances of the state. The general distress made the common people readier to volunteer for military service. In the ensuing military campaign, the French fought so stubbornly in the battle of Malplaquet that Marlborough and Eugene gave up the idea of pressing further into France.

In 1710, the fortunes of Louis XIV took a decided turn for the better. In the north, the allied armies made little progress. In Spain, the bulk of the population sided with Philip V rather than Archduke Charles, the son of the Emperor. This enabled the armies of Louis XIV and Philip V to regain most of Spain which had been lost by them during the peace negotiations. The most important event for the French, however, was the political change in Great Britain.[1] The Duke of Marlborough, the skillful English general and diplomat, first lost his Whig majority, then the support of Queen Anne, and finally his position at the head of English affairs. This brought into power in Great Britain the Tory party, which was determined to make peace. As a consequence, the allies began to slacken their military pressure on France and turned to the task of negotiating a satisfactory peace.

The representatives of the warring states met at Utrecht in the United Netherlands. Their conflicting demands were hard to reconcile. Only the steady pressure of the British negotiators for peace and an allied defeat at Denain prevented a complete breakdown of the negotiations. Finally, France concluded separate treaties in 1713 with England, the United Netherlands, Portugal, the Duke of Savoy, and the king of Prussia. To England, Louis XIV conceded the rule of

---

[1] After the union of England and Scotland in 1707, the term, Great Britain, came into use.

succession adopted by the English parliament in 1701, the abandonment of his support of the Stuart claimant known to his follower's as James III, the dismantling of the French port of Dunkerque, the relinquishment of all claim to the Hudson's Bay region, Newfoundland and Acadia, and important commercial concessions. To the United Netherlands, Louis XIV ceded the Spanish Netherlands, which were then to be handed over to Austria. To the Duke of Savoy, Louis XIV promised the Spanish island of Sicily and the royal title. Philip V, the grandson of Louis XIV and king of Spain, conceded to England the *Asiento* or right to supply the Spanish colonies in America with Negro laborers, the privilege of sending to Spanish America each year a merchant ship of five hundred tons burden, and possession of the two Mediterranean strongholds of Gibraltar and Minorca.

In 1714, the Emperor signed with Louis XIV the Treaty of Rastadt in behalf of his hereditary state. By this treaty, the Emperor acquired—at the expense of Spain—Naples, Sardinia, and Milan. In 1714, the Empire concluded the Treaty of Baden. Finally, late in 1715, the Dutch signed a treaty with the Emperor which gave them the right to garrison the Spanish Netherlands and to make of them a buffer state for the protection of the United Netherlands. These various treaties were, in reality, a recognition that the long War of the Spanish Succession was in many ways a check and even a defeat for Louis XIV. His principal success, the establishment of his grandson, Philip V, on the throne of Spain, proved to be an illusory gain.

Death of Louis XIV

By 1715, Louis XIV was an old man. The closing years of his reign were marked by personal and national misfortunes. The War of the Spanish Succession had, in the main, gone badly for the king. The nation was growing tired of its elderly grand monarch. The new generation had experienced the hardships of the war but knew nothing of the early triumphs of the reign. The public discontent expressed itself in pamphlets, in street songs, and in riots. In quick succession, too, his son (the heir to the throne), his grandson (who stood next in the line of succession), and several other members of his family had died. The king's grip on the administration had weakened, and he began to show signs of serious illness. By 1715, it was evident that he had but little longer to live. As his malady progressed, the king began to arrange his affairs and took formal leave of the remaining members of his family and his close associates. Finally, on September 1, 1715, he died.

Thus, in spite of its apparent brilliance, the reign of Louis XIV weakened France. The king used the resources of men and wealth put into his hands by the policies of Henry IV, Richelieu, and Mazarin to maintain a lavish court, a large governmental machine, and four burdensome wars. He did nothing to lighten the burden of the peasant or the artisan. He took no steps toward equalizing the position of the nobility and the middle classes. He left untouched the anarchical institutions which discriminated among the various regions of the realm. With the growth of enlightenment, this situation was bound to become dangerous and even to breed revolution unless something was done to reform French society and government. This, the successors of Louis XIV failed to do. The inevitable result of their failure was the outbreak of the French Revolution.

CHAPTER 16

Development of Parliamentary Government and Religious Toleration in England

At the beginning of the modern period, England was not yet a power of the first rank. Throughout the sixteenth century her importance was owing to her potential influence on the balance of power. Both Francis I and Charles V wanted her assistance. In the reign of Elizabeth, her victory over Spain gave England for a moment a strong position. In the first half of the seventeenth century, however, she was compelled to center her attention so completely on domestic and political and religious problems that she could not play so important a part in international politics.

The Beginning of the Struggles between King and Parliament and Anglican and Puritan

Even during the reign of Elizabeth, an acute observer might have recognized that a political and religious struggle was taking shape. The Elizabethan Religious Settlement came far from satisfying all elements in English society, and, toward the end of the reign, Parliament showed a growing tendency to be restive under Elizabeth's arbitrary rule. The accession of her successor precipitated both a serious religious and an important political struggle.

As Queen Elizabeth lay dying in 1603, she designated her kinsman, James VI of Scotland, the son of Mary, Queen of Scots, as her successor. In England he was known as James I. His new subjects were not well acquainted with their new king. They knew only that he was a son of the unfortunate Mary, Queen of Scots, that he had been brought up by the Scottish Presbyterian party, and that he owed his accession to the English throne to the fact that he was a distant cousin of Queen Elizabeth. He proved to be exceedingly stubborn about some things and timid and easily led in other matters. Though he had grown up among factious, unruly nobles and plain-spoken Presbyterian divines, he really had strong views about religion and about his own power. He called his theory about the latter "the divine right of kings."

Immediately after his arrival in England, he began to create opposition. He proved to be, it is true, well informed about foreign countries, well versed in religious and political history, broad-minded and

237

good natured in matters that did not affect his own personal interests. On the other hand, he was personally unattractive. He spoke indistinctly with a pronounced Scottish accent. He shambled when he walked. He lacked tact, personal dignity, and practical wisdom.

The Religious Problem

Even before he reached London, the new king found himself confronted by the religious problem. During the reign of Elizabeth, there had grown up in the state considerable religious dissatisfaction. There were some who clung to the Medieval Church. There were many more, who came to be known as Puritans, who desired to see the English state church purged of certain Romish forms and ceremonies, a decrease in the number of holidays, a better observance of Sunday, more learned preachers, the abolition of such practices as nonresidence and the holding of several church offices by members of the clergy, and the doing away of certain oppressive customs in the ecclesiastical courts. Then there were still others, known as Independents and Brownists, who believed in the complete separation of state and church but who differed greatly among themselves about such matters as the form of baptism.

Those members of the English clergy who leaned toward Puritanism expected to find a sympathetic listener in their new sovereign. As he made his way toward London, they presented him with a petition which embodied the demands of the Puritans and was called the Millenary Petition from the fact that a thousand of the English clergy were supposed to have signed it. In the following year, as a result of the petition, James I convened a conference of Anglican and Puritan divines at Hampton Court, a royal palace just outside London. After the clergy assembled, the Puritans alarmed the king. As a result of his experiences in Scotland, he had no wish to see a Scottish presbytery set up in England. He greatly preferred the Anglican bishops, whom he found in his new kingdom, because they were inclined to be respectful and subservient. So when he thought that he had discovered a desire on the part of the petitioners to establish in England something resembling a Scottish presbytery, he ended the conference with a threat to make the Puritans conform to the Elizabethan Religious Settlement or to harry them out of the country.

This attitude taken by James I toward religious reform had some important results. Those clergymen who refused to conform to the rites and ceremonies of the Anglican Church were deprived of their livings. Some of the most irreconcilable went to Holland with their congregations. A positive result of the conference was the appointment of a group of scholars who were entrusted with the task of

238

making a new translation of the Bible. The result of their work was the King James Version of the Bible, which has had so much influence on the development of the English language and literature.

The new sovereign was also confronted with the problem of the attitude that should be adopted toward the adherents of the Pope. Under Elizabeth they had suffered persecution. All priests had been banished from the country. Children of Roman Catholics had been forbidden to study abroad. The laity had been heavily fined for absenting themselves from the services of the state church. Strangely enough, the Roman Catholics, too, looked forward to the accession of James I with hope. They thought that the son of Mary, Queen of Scots would do something for her fellow English religionists. At first, the new sovereign did give his Catholic subjects considerable encouragement. By nature kindly and by policy anxious for a Spanish alliance, he started his reign by remitting the so-called recusancy fines levied upon those who failed to attend the established church. The results of this policy, however, soon alarmed him. The Roman Catholics grew so rapidly in numbers that the king not only reversed his policy but increased the severity of the laws against Roman Catholics. One of the effects of the harsher legislation was the conspiracy, known as the Gunpowder Plot, which aimed at the blowing up of the king and the parliament, a rising of Roman Catholics, and the setting up of a new government. The discovery of the plot led to the passage of still harsher legislation against recusants.

The Political Problem

At the same time that he became involved in a religious struggle, James I's ideas about politics set him at odds with Parliament. The quarrel cannot be understood without some knowledge of the long history of that institution. In the Middle Ages, the king's council, which had started as an advisory body, had had a unique development. Upon ordinary occasions it was a relatively small body. Occasionally, when the king was desirous of strong support for his policies, he summoned all his feudal barons to meet him. As towns developed and became a possible source of new revenues, the king began to summon representatives of the towns as well. Up to this point, the history of the king's council was not unlike that of similar bodies on the continent. Now, however, its development took a unique turn. Instead of becoming a deliberative body of three or four houses, it became a parliament of two chambers—an upper house composed of the greater barons and a lower house composed of the lesser barons and representatives of the towns. The two chambers were known as the House of Lords and the House of Commons. In contrast to

239

continental bodies, the English parliament had a lower house of considerable strength, and, in time, this parliament won a recognition of certain rights, especially for the practice of obtaining its consent for the imposition of taxes and the promulgation of laws. The extent of its powers was in inverse proportion to the strength of the sovereign. Under weak kings, Parliament was insistent on its rights. Under strong rulers like the Tudors, it was inclined to be dominated by the king. So there was room for a dispute over the relative position of king and Parliament in the government.

From the very first, James I and the majority in Parliament clashed. The king, with his lofty ideas concerning his prerogatives, disagreed with the members of Parliament, who were growing increasingly conscious of their rights and privileges, over nearly every question that arose. In 1604, at the first session of Parliament in the reign, two important questions arose. They were concerned with the problem of the election of members of Parliament and the protection of members against arrest. They were both finally settled in favor of Parliament. By Godwin's Case, the House of Commons was declared the sole judge of the election of its members. By Shirley's Case, it was decided that members were free from arrest during sessions of Parliament and for forty days before and after that event. Ever since these rights were recognized, they have become widely accepted principles in free countries. In a statement, the House of Commons maintained freedom of election, freedom from arrest, and freedom of speech as inherent rights of Parliament.

During his whole reign, James I was in need of money. This situation was owing to a number of causes. In part, it was caused by the royal extravagance. In part, it was the result of rising prices. Whatever the reason, the situation gave rise to frequent conflicts over finances. In 1606 and again in 1608, the king increased taxes on his own initiative and without the consent of Parliament. In the session of 1610, consequently, Parliament refused to grant the king a permanent and fixed revenue until he had redressed this and other grievances. After an interval of four years, the question came up again. The king, however, dissolved Parliament before it had accomplished anything. In spite of this, James I continued to collect money by means which the Parliamentary party considered unconstitutional. The money-raising devices employed by the king included requests for benevolences, the sale of offices and titles, and the granting of monopolies. The resort to these devices, of course, only increased the tension between the king and Parliament.

There were, however, many other differences between James I and the Parliament party. In 1612, Parliament opposed a statesmanlike proposal of the king for the union of Scotland and England. The English feared the competition with the frugal and industrious Scots which would result from the establishment of free trade between the two countries. During most of the reign, there was much royal interference with judges. The Puritan members of the Parliamentary party disapproved of the frivolity, extravagance, and immorality of the court and the character of the men whom the king selected as favorites; and the king and Parliament differed also about foreign affairs. After the outbreak of the Thirty Years' War in 1618, the king desired to regain the Palatinate for his son-in-law through the good offices of Spain. The Parliamentary party advocated a renewal of the naval war with Spain. Then, in 1624, after the failure of his negotiations with Spain, James I arranged a very unpopular marriage for his son, the later Charles I, with the sister of Louis XIII of France. A secret article of the marriage treaty, in fact, promised a relaxation of the English penal laws against Roman Catholics. As a result of these various differences, the tension between king and Parliament steadily grew.

The Irish Problem

In the meantime, the English government had been making no progress toward a solution of the Irish problem. It had struggled with this problem during the greater part of the Middle Ages. From 1166, when Norman barons from England had first set foot in Ireland, the Irish people had looked upon the English as foreign invaders. After the introduction of religious innovations by Henry VIII, Edward VI, and Elizabeth, the Irish looked upon the English not only as invaders but as heretics. As a result of these political and religious differences, the Irish heartily hated the English.

In the reign of Edward VI, the English government introduced a new method for solving the Irish problem. Prior to that time, it had been the policy of the English authorities to remove troublesome Irish chiefs but to leave their followers undisturbed. By the new method, they confiscated the estates of rebellious chiefs, evicted their tenants from their homes and farms, and put English colonists in their place. This came to be known as the plantation system. After 1608, James employed the new method on a large scale. He confiscated the greater part of six of the nine counties in Ulster, a historic division of the island in northeastern Ireland. Then he settled English and Scottish colonists on the confiscated lands. This action still further embittered the relations of the two peoples. The plantation system gave England an outpost in Ireland, but the Irish never recognized the right of English and Scottish settlers to Irish land.

241

Charles I

In 1625, the personally unattractive James I was succeeded by his striking and attractive son, Charles I. The new sovereign was handsome, well-poised, brave, athletic, appreciative of the beautiful, and quite religious. On the other hand, he was as incapable of sensing public opinion and popular emotion as his father had been. As a consequence, the struggle between king and Parliament, and Puritans and High-churchmen continued.

Charles I chose advisers who tended to widen the gap between the king and his subjects. The royal advisers included the rash, self-confident, and incapable Buckingham; Thomas Wentworth, Earl of Strafford; Archbishop Laud; and the queen, Henrietta Maria, who was French by birth and ignorant of both the ways and the temper of Englishmen. As a result of his selection of advisers, the king pursued policies that made him even more unpopular than his father had been.

The struggle between the new sovereign and Parliament began at once. The king gave no reasons for his requests. The opposition had no sympathy with the idea of a continental war; it was determined to control taxation; it suspected the policy of relaxing the laws against Roman Catholics; and it distrusted the royal advisers, especially Buckingham. As a result of these conflicting points of view, Parliament accomplished nothing in its first session.

During the next four years, the breach between the king and Parliament steadily widened. A reckless expedition against the Spanish port of Cadiz, undertaken with the hope of relieving the royal finances, failed miserably. In 1526, the king dissolved his second parliament in order to save Buckingham from impeachment. Then Charles I imprisoned eighty gentlemen who refused to contribute to a forced loan. In 1627, an English attack on France failed. Each of these episodes increased the misunderstanding between the king and the Parliamentary party.

In 1628, the Opposition obtained from Charles I formal assent to a Petition of Right. This important document declared against further exactions without the consent of Parliament, the imprisonment of freemen without cause, the billeting of soldiers in private houses, and the issuing of commissions for punishment by martial law. Though the document failed to accomplish its immediate purpose, it has always been considered a landmark on the road from tyranny to human liberty.

The Petition of Right did not put an end to the struggle between the king and Parliament. Charles I was greatly embittered by the assassination of his favorite, Buckingham. During the ensuing year, the conflict was over the right of the sovereign to levy a tax known as Tonnage and Poundage and to introduce religious innovations of a High Church character. In the session of 1629, accordingly, the leaders of the Opposition pushed through Parliament resolutions against innovations in religion, the extension of popery, and the levying of tonnage and poundage taxes.

The Period of Personal Rule

The passage of these resolutions brought the struggle between the king and Parliament to a crisis. Charles I replied to the challenge of the Parliamentary party by ordering the arrest of the leaders of the Opposition and the dissolution of Parliament. For the next decade, he attempted to rule without Parliament. During these years, however, he did nothing toward strengthening the royal despotism or conciliating his subjects. On the contrary, he steadily increased the irritation of the vocal part of the nation. He continued to raise money in ways which they considered illegal. He alarmed both the Puritans and the ungodly by his support of the efforts of Archbishop Laud to improve morals and religion. In his efforts to please the queen, the king aroused the fears of the Puritans that the court was returning to Roman Catholicism. He maintained a rigid censorship of the press.

The royal policy led to the celebrated incident known as John Hampden's Case. This wealthy squire considered a tax known as Ship Money as arbitrary and illegal and refused to pay it. The king, however, intimidated enough judges to obtain a decision in favor of levying the tax. The incident made John Hampden a popular hero and increased the unpopularity of the royal policy.

While English resentment against the king mounted, the king's Scottish subjects acted. The Presbyterians of Scotland opposed particularly the religious policy of Charles I and Archbishop Laud. They were trying to impose new regulations for the government of the Scottish church, to make the king absolute head of the state church, and force upon it a liturgy based upon the one in use in the Anglican Church. When the king insisted on a continuance of the royal policy in spite of the opposition of the Scottish people, the latter signed the National Covenant to defend the crown and true religion. In 1638, the Scottish leaders went still further in their opposition to the royal policy. In defiance of the king, they convened an assembly which deposed the bishops who had been imposed on the Scottish church by James I, did away with the unpopular regulations and liturgy, and raised an army whose officers had been

243

schooled in the wars of the continent for the defence of their Presbyterian religion. Neither side in the dispute, however, really wanted an armed struggle, and, consequently, the two parties finally reached a compromise. By the terms of this agreement, the Scottish opponents of the royal policy promised to disband their army, and the king pledged himself to entrust the religious dispute to the Scottish General Assembly and the secular problems to the Parliament of Scotland. When, however, the king dissolved the Scottish parliament for approving the re-establishment of the Presbyterian system in Scotland, the Scottish people began to prepare for war.

The struggle in Scotland had an effect on the conflict between the king and Parliament in England. Developments in Scotland increased the royal need of money. As there was no hope of raising the required money by existing methods, the chief adviser of the king in political matters, the Earl of Strafford (the former Sir Thomas Wentworth), counseled him to summon again the English parliament. The Earl probably thought that he could control an English parliament as successfully as he had managed the Irish parliament during the six years he had been the king's deputy in Ireland. As soon as the English parliament assembled, though, it became evident that this body would grant no money to the king until its grievances had been redressed. Charles I, accordingly, dissolved it and attempted to continue his personal rule of England. He quickly found out that this was impossible, because the advance of the Scottish military forces into northern England compelled Charles I to summon the English parliament again.

The Long Parliament

In November, 1640, consequently, the body known as the Long Parliament assembled. The Opposition had in its mind a definite program for action. Under the leadership of such men as John Pym and John Hampden, it met with a determination to protect what its members considered to be their civil and religious liberties, to put an end to popery, to redress their political grievances, and to make it impossible for the king henceforth to govern the kingdom without the aid of Parliament. Almost as soon as it had convened, the Long Parliament impeached the king's chief political adviser, the Earl of Strafford. Then it took steps to curb the arbitrary power of the king. It tried to prevent another period of personal rule by passing a triennial act designed to insure a meeting of Parliament at least every three years. This measure provided further that Parliament should not be dissolved without the consent of its members. It enacted also a statute that forbade the imposition of any subsidy, customs duty, or charge without the consent of Parliament. It abolished an unpopular court, known as the Star Chamber, and restricted the jurisdiction of the Council of Wales and the Marches.[1] These measures remedied most of the political grievances of the Parliamentary party.

Up to this point, the members of the Long Parliament had been united. This situation changed as soon as that body took up the question of religious reform. In the discussions over religion, differences of opinion quickly made their appearance. At first, it looked as if the Presbyterians might win the support of Parliament, but the proselyting zeal of the Scottish preachers and the burden imposed by the maintenance of the Scottish army soon made Presbyterianism unpopular. In the end, the majority in the Long Parliament came to favor a Puritan state church, which should have an altered liturgy and no bishops. A considerable minority, known as Independents, advocated separation of church and state and control of doctrine and service by the local congregations. For a month, the Long Parliament debated the issue without reaching a decision. The discussions destroyed the unity of the Long Parliament.

In the midst of this deadlock came news from Ireland that produced a crisis. In the autumn of 1641 the chronic discontent in that island broke out into open rebellion. The peasants in Ulster, impelled by grievances accumulated through a long period of years, rose and massacred at least five thousand of the English and Scottish settlers. In addition, possibly twice this number of persons had perished as a result of the hardships imposed by the rebels on the Protestant settlers in Ulster. Rumor, of course, exaggerated the number of victims. Something had to be done about the outrage. The leaders of the Parliamentary party were determined that control of an armed force should not be placed in the hands of the king. If it were, it might eventually be used against the opponents of Charles I. Accordingly, they decided to make an appeal to the nation. They drew up a document, called the Grand Remonstrance, which set forth their case against the king and the remedial measures which they demanded. This protest divided the English parliament into two parties, namely, the Puritan-Parliamentary party and the Royalists. Familiarly, they went by the names of Roundheads and Cavaliers. The Puritan-Parliamentary party favored the proposed religious reforms and approved of the appeal to the nation. Their opponents took the opposite side.

The development of parties in Parliament encouraged the king to

---

[1] The Marches were frontier border districts.

take action. Very unwisely, he tried to arrest five of the leaders of the Puritan-Parliamentary party. He charged them with subverting the fundamental laws of England and with inviting the forces of a foreign power, i.e., Scotland, to invade the country. The attempt to seize the five members of Parliament failed, but the royal action precipitated civil war. Both parties promptly tried to get control of arsenals, fortresses, and other military establishments in the kingdom.

The Civil War

The ensuing armed struggle divided the nation. Most of the nobles and a majority of the gentry sided with the king. The trading classes favored his opponents. The English lower classes were indifferent. This left the king in control of the northern, western, and southwestern portions of the kingdom. It placed Parliament in possession of southern and eastern England. The opponents of the king had in their hands the greater part of the resources of the country.

At first, neither party was very well prepared for a struggle. They depended in the fighting on unsatisfactory, inexperienced volunteers. Neither side displayed leadership or disclosed any well-thought-out plan of campaign. Only after some bitter experiences with an amateurish soldiery did Oliver Cromwell (1599–1658) organize a well-drilled cavalry force, composed of men of substance who had serious convictions about the struggle. In 1643, the English Parliamentary party formed an alliance with the Scots. These innovations in the end had their effect. In 1644, Cromwell's Ironsides won a decisive victory over the Royalist forces. This encouraged Cromwell to form a larger force known as the New Model army. In 1645, this new military force won the decisive battle of Naseby. In 1646, after his armed forces had been virtually destroyed, the king surrendered to the Scots.

The royal action was followed by three years of tortuous negotiations, futile intrigues, and ineffective maneuvering. Throughout the three years, the king still hoped to recover his liberty and his authority. He counted on the aid of English royalists and Irish Catholics. He hoped to take advantage of the dissensions which had begun to appear among his opponents. The English parliament no longer saw eye to eye with the army it had organized. The English parliament desired to come to terms with the king and to reach an agreement with the Presbyterians. In contrast, the Parliamentary army, composed largely of Independents, asked for religious toleration, an indemnity for past acts, and the payment of arrears in pay. The Scots, meanwhile, had handed the king over to Parliament. Because of its differences with that body, the army seized the king and marched on London. Upon its arrival there, its leaders offered for consideration a plan for the pacification of the country, known as Heads of Proposals, which proved to be too statesmanlike to be accepted. In November, 1647, the king eluded his captors and fled to the Isle of Wight. Thereupon, the negotiations took a new turn. The king signed a treaty (known as the Engagement) with the Scots which ranged them on the royal side. Then, counting on Scottish as well as royalist support, Charles I adopted an uncompromising attitude toward Parliament.

This move was fatal for the king. Parliament and the army reconciled their differences, and the Puritan-Parliamentary party had little difficulty in crushing the weak risings which took place in behalf of the king or in repelling the army of the Scottish invaders. The danger, however, only silenced the discords temporarily. In 1648, accordingly, the army acted decisively. Late in that year, it drove its critics and opponents out of Parliament. Then at its dictation, the so-called Rump Parliament accused and convicted the king of treason. In January, 1649, as a result of this action, Charles I was executed.

The Commonwealth

This bold act destroyed for the time being the government of England. It left control of the country in the hands of an oligarchy that desired to maintain the forms of democracy. Its first task was to create a government to take the place of the one which it had just destroyed. Accordingly, it created the Council of State, abolished the House of Lords, and declared England to be a commonwealth. The majority of the nation, however, did not accept the new government. The greater part of the English people either transferred their allegiance from Charles I to his son, known in history as Charles II, or at least took a hostile attitude toward the domination of the country by the army. On the other hand, there were many who wished to go further along the path of reform. These desired a greater measure of individual liberty. As a result of these differences of opinion, the country was threatened with anarchy.

The new government aroused mixed feelings among Englishmen. Even its opponents admired the commonwealth's handling of foreign relations. Most Englishmen, on the other hand, disliked its domestic policies. With forces commanded by Cromwell, the new government sternly crushed the Scottish supporters of Prince Charles (1650–1651) and put down a rising in Ireland. At sea, the Commonwealth strengthened its naval forces sufficiently to hold the Dutch in check.

The army, however, still disapproved of Parliament. Finally, in 1653, led by Cromwell, it first dissolved the Rump Parliament and then the Nominated Parliament which took its place. The attempt of the oligarchy to maintain democratic forms of government had failed.

The Protectorate

In place of the commonwealth, the army set up a protectorate. Its officers drew up a written constitution known as the Instrument of Government, and, under the title of Lord Protector, placed Oliver Cromwell in power (1653). Since the opening of the Long Parliament, he had been growing in influence. When this body was convened, he had been elected to represent Cambridge. Until the Civil War broke out, he had held a respected but secondary position in the ranks of the Parliamentary party. After the outbreak of that conflict, he had steadily forged to the front as a military leader. By the time the army was at odds with Parliament, he was generally recognized as its leader and spokesman.

Cromwell had an appearance of simplicity, but, in reality, he was a complex character. Apparently, he actually felt that he was an instrument of God for the betterment of England. In spite of this deep feeling that he had a mission, he was not gloomy, morose, or ascetic. He liked to hunt, loved to jest, enjoyed playing bowls, and permitted "mixed dancing" at the wedding of his daughter. He had lofty aims and an irresistible determination to carry them out.

For five years (1553–1558) he ruled England. In matters of religion he adopted a policy of toleration. He desired that all the Protestant sects that opposed bishops and the use of the prayer book should be included in a state church. He conceded to the Independents the right to have their own edifices and forms of worship. He allowed Anglicans to have private worship. He did not try to compel Roman Catholics to attend their parish churches. He conducted the foreign relations of England in a way that aroused the admiration of even his bitterest opponents. He waged a successful war (1652–1654), as we shall see in Chapter 17, with the Dutch and concluded a peace which was satisfactory to Englishmen. In 1655, he formed an alliance with France on advantageous terms. At the same time, he carried on successfully a war with Spain that gave England possession of the important island of Jamaica (1555). He thus gave the English people a large measure of religious peace and considerably advanced their commercial and colonial interests.

In spite of the advantages which it won for England, however, the rule of Cromwell did not win the support of the majority of Englishmen. Like the commonwealth, the protectorate was imposed on the nation by a determined minority. The protector naturally differed with the parliament which had been elected and finally dissolved it. Thereafter, he attempted to rule the country through ten major generals, a system which alienated from the protectorate a still larger number of people. When, in 1657, Cromwell was made hereditary protector, only his strong hand maintained order.

In 1658, Cromwell died. He left behind him no one able to fill his very difficult position. He was succeeded in office by his son, Richard Cromwell (1626–1712), but the new protector was unfitted to carry on the work of his father. Though a worthy man and personally popular, he had neither his father's hold on the army nor his ability in affairs of state. As a consequence, things went badly from the first. The new protector failed to get along with either a new parliament or the old Rump Parliament. In 1659, accordingly, after some hesitation, Richard Cromwell resigned his office. While leaders in England debated what they should do in the crisis, General Monk, the head of the army in Scotland, unexpectedly acted. Marching south toward London, he suddenly stood forth as the champion of the authority of Parliament. As a result, he forced the Rump Parliament to recall the men who had been excluded and to re-establish the Long Parliament. Then he informed its members that they must make way for a new free parliament. He thus brought to an end the eleven-year rule of the Puritans and the Independents.

The Restoration

Monk apparently decided to forestall reaction by opening negotiations with Prince Charles, the son of the executed Charles I. Upon the recommendation of his chief adviser, the prince issued from Breda in the Netherlands a declaration in which he promised, in case he should be recalled to the throne of his ancestors, to grant a general amnesty to all his opponents except those excepted by Parliament, to concede to his subjects liberty of conscience and security of property, and to pay to the army what was due them. Upon receiving this declaration, the Convention Parliament, which had in the meantime been freely elected, decided to re-establish government by king, lords, and commons and proclaimed the long-exiled prince as king under the title of Charles II. In May, 1660, accordingly, the new sovereign landed at Dover.

The English people did not know much about the man whom they had just restored to the throne. For many years, he had been in exile. He was only thirty years old the day that he entered London as king. He seemed to be athletic, pleasant in manner, and highly intelligent.

In time, however, he revealed qualities which offset these advantages. He proved to be badly educated, disinclined to work, fickle and un-trustworthy, cynical and irreverent, selfish and desirous of comforts and amusement. As one of his boon companions put it, "he never said a foolish thing and never did a wise one."

At first, Charles II acted cautiously. He was limited in power by the Convention Parliament which remained in office. He had no wish, as he expressed it, to start on his travels again. Elected at a time of reaction against Puritanism and the rule of Parliament, the Convention Parliament proved to be more intolerant than the king. It caused the execution of thirteen regicides and issued decrees against twenty-five others who were fortunate enough to be beyond its reach. It disavowed the confiscation of Royalist estates which had been seized during the civil war. It disbanded most of the Parliamentary army but left intact a nucleus that became a standing army. It did nothing toward the establishment of religious toleration. In 1661, the Convention Parliament made way for the so-called Cavalier Parliament.

The Rise of Sects

This body found itself confronted by an almost anarchical religious situation. During the struggle of king and people (the period of the civil war, the commonwealth, and the protectorate), dissenting sects had multipled and flourished. At first, the nonconformists were all known as Puritans because they wished, as they said, to purify the state church of those things that suggested the Medieval Church. Most of the nonconformists were inclined to favor a Presbyterian form of church government. A growing proportion of the noncon-formists, however, came to believe that individuals should have the right to worship God as they saw fit without interference from the civil authorities. This wing of the nonconformists was known at first as the Independents. Later, they split into the denominations known as Congregationalists, General and Particular Baptists, Friends, Uni-tarians, and such strange sects as the Ranters and the Muggletonians.

The Congregationalists owed their name to their ideas about the organization of their churches. They believed each congregation should be completely independent of outside control and a law unto itself. At first, persecution hindered the growth of such a religious body, but, in 1616, a church composed of Congregationalists was founded at London. By the end of the protectorate, there seems to have been a large number of these churches.

Those who believed in a congregational organization of churches, however, differed considerably among themselves about forms and ceremonies. They had different beliefs, especially about the sacrament of baptism. The majority thought that baptism by sprinkling a little water on the head of the person being baptized was sufficient and that the baptism of children was proper. Others thought only the baptism of adults by immersion was admissible. In England, these ideas were derived from Congregationalists who had come in contact with the Mennonites during their stay in Holland to escape persecution. Upon their return to England, they established in London the first English Baptist church. These Baptists, however, soon divided into two bodies (the General Baptists and the Particular Baptists) over the doctrine of predestination. By 1660, the Baptists were numerous in England.

Though it appeared at one time as if Presbyterianism might supplant Episcopacy, it never took very deep root in England. Since the latter part of the sixteenth century, many Anglicans had shown a leaning toward that form of church government, and, during the Civil War, Parliament fell under the control of Presbyterians. In 1646, that body issued an ordinance for the establishment of presbyteries. Only a few, however, were actualy set up. In 1660, the Presbyterians confidently expected to have some concessions made to them and to be included in the state church.

The period gave rise to many other sects. One of the most influential was the group known to themselves as Friends but popularly called Quakers. They owed their rise to the preaching of George Fox (1624–1691), a remarkable man of humble origin, who in 1647 began to preach in churches, barns, and at market places. He emphasized the necessity of an inward spiritual experience. In contrast to the Puritans, he believed in the possibility of a complete victory over sin. He gained followers rapidly. The preachers sent out by the Friends usually conducted their campaigns with great zeal and bitterness. This brought them into conflict with other religious bodies. At first, Fox did not strive for a separate religious organization. His followers were characterized by their opposition to war, the taking of oaths, and a professional ministry; their respectful attitude towards women; their belief in the possibility of divine communion; their silent meetings; and their plain dress, language, and manners. Some of the Friends went to such extremes as going barefoot, dressing in sackcloth, and even wearing no clothes at all. Their peculiar beliefs and contentious manner caused many of them to be flogged or imprisoned.

The Religious Settlement

In spite of this development of Protestant sects, the Cavalier Parliament made no concessions to the principle of religious toleration. At once, it proceeded to re-establish a regime of religious in-

251

tolerance. In 1661, it passed the Corporation Act. This law stipulated that no one could hold office in a town unless he took the sacrament in accordance with the practice of the Anglican Church, renounced the covenant which had been drawn up in 1643 in cooperation with the Scots, and declared it unlawful to bear arms against the king. In 1662, the Cavalier Parliament passed the Act of Uniformity. This law revised the prayer book in a way to make it obnoxious to the Puritans, and it deprived of their benefices all clergymen who refused to use the new liturgy or who had not been ordained by a bishop. In 1664, the Cavalier Parliament passed the Coventicle Act which forbade five or more persons, exclusive of the members of a family, to worship in accordance with any forms that differed from those in use by the re-established state church. Finally, in the following year the Cavalier Parliament passed the Five Mile Act. This forbade any dissenting minister to teach in any school or to come within five miles of any city or corporate town. These four acts were known as the Clarendon Code. This legislation widened the breach between the Anglicans and those who refused to conform to the state church.

The Political Policies of Charles II

Until 1667, the king had an able adviser, Edward Hyde, later known as Lord Clarendon (1609–1674). Unfortunately for the royal counsellor, he became more and more unpopular. The dissolute and frivolous king, for his part, felt uneasy in the presence of such an austere adviser. The subjects of Charles II, on the other hand, disliked the royal counsellor for his arrogance; accused him of scheming for the advancement of his own family; and blamed him for the adoption of the Clarendon Code, the outbreak of the plague (which in 1665 carried off seventy thousand persons in London alone and ravaged the southern and eastern counties), the great fire of 1666 (which made two thirds of the population of the capital homeless), and for the defeats suffered in the second war with the Dutch. Though the accusations against him were unjust, the king welcomed the opportunity to get rid of his sober, sedate, and cautious adviser and dismissed him from the office. When Parliament impeached him, he fled to the continent.

Though the king seemed at first to be deferential to Parliament, he was at heart as much of an absolutist as his father and grandfather had been. Upon the fall of Clarendon, he thought conditions were favorable for increasing the royal power. As means toward achieving this end, he built up a standing army, sought to win the support of the religious dissenters by granting them the toleration that Parliament had denied them, favored the Roman Catholics, and signed in

1670 the secret Treaty of Dover. By the terms of this agreement, the king, in return for an annual grant of money, promised to join Louis XIV in his war against the Dutch, to assist him in his efforts to secure the Spanish Netherlands, and, lastly, to become a Roman Catholic. In case Charles' subjects resisted his plans, Louis XIV was to send troops to assist him. The annual grant freed the English sovereign of much of his dependence on Parliament. The royal policy was very unpopular, but public opinion was inclined to blame five of the new advisers of the king, known as the *cabal* from the initials of their names, rather than Charles II, for the new royal course. In reality, they neither dominated the king nor enjoyed his full confidence.

Two years after this treaty, accordingly, the king issued the Declaration of Indulgence which conceded to the Protestant Dissenters freedom of worship in public and to Roman Catholics the right to have private religious services. The general effect of the royal policy was to make the king much less dependent on Parliament.

In spite of the support of Louis XIV, Charles II did not have his own way entirely. Even during the administration of Lord Clarendon, Parliament had strengthened its hold on the finances. After the publication of the Declaration of Indulgence, the opposition to the royal policy was so strong that the king promised to give it up in return for a grant of money. The opponents of the king followed up this victory by the passage of the Test Act, which excluded from civil and military offices all who refused to take the sacrament of communion according to the rites of the Church of England, and by forcing the king to withdraw from the war with the Dutch (1674). The adoption of the Test Act was followed by the resignation of the group of ministers known as the cabal and the king's own brother, the Duke of York, from his various offices. The king, for his part, quietly dropped his plans for making England Catholic. Thereafter, he abandoned the Catholics. He then favored the High Anglicans and even consented to the persecution of Protestant Dissenters. Except for brief intervals, however, Charles II continued for the remainder of his reign in the pay of the king of France.

The royal policy led to an important development. Those who opposed the policies of the king finally became organized into something like a modern political party and were known as the Whigs. They employed in their campaigns such political devices as meetings, petitions, speeches, and pamphlets. Those who supported the king became known as Tories. Their numbers were augmented by an extensive use of corrupt methods. The two parties differed over the relative importance of the king and Parliament, over foreign affairs, and over the succession. In their struggles, the Whigs did gain three notable successes. In 1677, they helped to bring about the marriage of Mary, eldest daughter of the Duke of York, to William of Orange. In 1678, they forced the king to disband for a time the standing army. In the following year, they pushed through Parliament the Habeas Corpus Act. This law provided that any ordinary prisoner held on a criminal charge must, on the issuance of the writ, be brought before a judge within an interval of twenty days to decide whether he should be released on bail or held for trial, and that any one accused of treason or a felony must be tried at the next jail delivery or released on bail, unless witnesses for the crown could not be obtained. If he was not tried at the following jail delivery, he must be discharged. By this legislation, the English people made another advance on the long road from tyranny to freedom.

After these successes, the Whigs overreached themselves. In 1669, the king's brother and heir, the Duke of York, stated in the presence of his brother and a few of his most trusted confidants his desire to embrace the Roman Catholic faith and to set it up again in England. This action, since many suspected it, made the majority of Englishmen uneasy. Since the days of Mary Tudor, they had had a feeling that Roman Catholicism was a menace. This feeling had been enhanced by the plots of Philip II and by the fantastic stories about a Roman Catholic plot against England of Titus Oates, a disgruntled and repulsive former student of the Jesuits. In 1679, the Whigs took advantage of this situation and pushed through Parliament a bill to exclude the Duke of York from the succession to the English throne. In 1680 the Whigs attempted to pass a second Exclusion Bill but were thwarted by the prorogation of Parliament. They even backed up this attempt with armed bands. By their violence, however, they contributed to their own defeat, and for the rest of the reign Charles II and the Tories had the upper hand.

The king did not long survive his triumph over the Whigs. In February, 1685, he was stricken with apoplexy and died within four days. During his last days, he apologized to those around him for being such an unconscionable time in dying. In his last hours, he was received into the Roman Church by a Catholic priest.

James II

Charles II was succeeded on the throne by his brother, the Duke of York, at the age of fifty-two and under the title of James II. The new king had some excellent qualities. He had shown himself to be an able officer and a good administrator. He was brave and free of some of the grosser vices which prevailed generally at the court. On the other hand, he was dull, obstinate, and lacking in imagination and foresight. He came to power with the conviction that political concessions had been the cause of the downfall of his family and with a determination to re-establish the Roman Church in England.

The change of rulers was generally accepted without protest. The Tories manifested the most ardent devotion, and the moderate men showed a willingness to support the king. Though he openly celebrated Mass at St. James palace, the king promised his council to preserve government in church and state, and they generally believed that he would keep his word and confine his Catholicism to his own household. Parliament, accordingly, readily granted him a fixed revenue which was larger than his brother had received. He had only to conduct himself tactfully and prudently to maintain himself indefinitely on the throne.

In spite of these favorable conditions, James II succeeded in alienating the entire nation within a period of three years. After the triumph of Charles II over his opponents, many of the more embittered Whigs had fled to the Low Countries. Urged on by their hatred of James II and their desire to return to England, they persuaded the Duke of Monmouth (1649–1685), an illegitimate son of Charles II, and the Duke of Argyle, head of the great Campbell clan in Scotland, to make simultaneous attacks on England and Scotland with the aim of overthrowing the government of James II. Both attempts failed miserably, and the leaders paid for their rashness with their lives. The king was not content, however, with having suppressed the two rebellions. Instead, he took a swift and terrible vengeance on those who had participated in them. He allowed Colonel Kirke to butcher hundreds of those involved in the uprising and to enrich himself by sparing those who had money. This was followed by the series of trials, known as the Bloody Assizes, of Judge Jeffreys, which was responsible for over three hundred persons being hanged, drawn, and quartered and some eight hundred being transported. This policy naturally engendered much hatred.

James II, too, followed a foreign policy that widened the breach between himself and his subjects. Like his brother, he remained in the pay of Louis XIV. This was an even more unpopular policy at this time than during the reign of Charles II. For England was thronged with exiles who had fled there from France to escape the religious policy of Louis XIV. They felt that if Louis XIV could revoke the Edict of Nantes (1685) in France, James II might proscribe Protestantism in England. The terror that England had felt as a result of the tales of Titus Oates was revived.

Just at this moment, the king began to reveal his real intentions. He tried to achieve three objectives. He wanted to maintain the standing army which had been increased from six to twenty thousand because of Monmouth's rebellion. He attempted to have the Test Act repealed to enable him to put Roman Catholics in office. He made an effort to have the Habeas Corpus Act repealed because this act prevented him from dealing in a summary fashion with those who opposed his policies. When it stoutly opposed these projects, Parliament was prorogued by the king and never was convened again. The royal policy began to alarm even the Pope and moderate English Catholics.

James II, though, paid no heed to the increasing signs of dissatisfaction. He oppointed four Roman Catholics to the privy council. He issued dispensations that allowed other members of his faith to hold offices in the Church. He aided Roman Catholics and men who sympathized with Catholicism to invade another stronghold of Anglicanism, the universities. He revived, as a means of punishing those who refused to obey him, the Court of High Commission, which the Long Parliament had suppressed. He began to issue dispensations for the setting up of Roman Catholic chapels all over the country. He permitted the opening of a church and a school for Jesuits. Monks and friars began to appear on the streets of London. These developments steadily increased the popular discontent. Riots occurred frequently. The clergy of the Established Church preached against popery; and pamphlets defending Protestantism poured from the presses.

In Scotland, too, the policy of Charles II and James II aroused serious discontent. Charles II proved to be as arbitrary a ruler in his northern kingdom as Cromwell had been. In religious matters, he repressed the Presbyterians and favored those who believed in episcopal government. He forced through the Scottish parliament a bill which imposed heavy fines on all who avoided their parish churches. James II, first as representative of his brother in Scotland and then as king, was even more severe. He forced through the Scottish parliament a bill that punished with death and confiscation of property all those who dared to attend conventicles. He recommended, on the other hand, the repeal of the laws against Roman Catholics, an action that was very unpopular.

James II tried to offset the growing discontent by winning over the Protestant Dissenters. Since the early years of his brother's reign, they had suffered from the provisions of the Clarendon Code. In 1687, however, James II proceeded on his own authority to publish a Declaration of Indulgence which went far beyond the somewhat similar act of his brother. In 1672, Charles II had suspended the penal laws and granted his subjects the right of private worship.

James II now offered them the free exercise of their religion, suspension of the penal laws, and the abandonment of all oaths and tests for the holding of military and civil offices. It was a great temptation for Protestant Dissenters. In fear and amazement, the Tories began to make overtures to them. The Tories, however, could proffer no immediate relief, while the king offered the Protestant Dissenters prompt removal of all the galling restrictions from which they suffered. Patriotism and religious prejudice, however, triumphed. The majority of the Protestant Dissenters refused the offer of the king and remained loyal to the opposition.

In spite of his failure to win the support of any large number of the Protestant Dissenters, the king continued his unwise policies. He deprived of their offices those who refused to abet him. He attempted to force concessions to Roman Catholicism upon the greatest strongholds of Anglicanism, the Universities of Oxford and Cambridge. During 1687 and 1688, he tried to put into effect arrangements that would insure him a packed and favorable parliament. Finally, in 1688, James II issued a second Declaration of Indulgence and ordered the Anglican clergy to read it from their pulpits on two successive Sundays. This action roused to resistance even the most conservative elements in English society. Supported by a majority of the Protestant Dissenters, the Archbishop of Canterbury and six of the bishops formally presented to the king a petition which stated their inability to comply with the royal demands. In some way, the petition was printed and fell into the hands of the general public. This opposition to his policies roused the king to fury. He caused the arrest and trial of the bishops. Fortunately for the popular cause, the jury, to which the case was submitted, was not intimidated. It freed the seven bishops, condemned the so-called dispensing power, and confirmed the right of petition.

For years, the more foresighted of those discontented with the royal policy had been looking forward to the time when James II would be succeeded by his oldest daughter, Mary. She was a Protestant and married to one of the most remarkable men of the century, William of Orange, leader since 1672 of the Dutch Netherlands. He was already credited with having saved his country and of having placed himself at the head of the European opposition to Louis XIV. At first, he was inclined to hold himself aloof from English politics. In 1687, however, he sent a trusted supporter to England to prepare the way for his possible intervention. While there, his representative conducted himself with great tact. He assured the Anglicans of William of Orange's favorable attitude toward episcopacy and the Book of Common Prayer. He held out to the Protestant Dissenters

257

the prospect of toleration or comprehension. He even led the Roman Catholics to hope for a repeal of the penal laws in case of the accession of William and Mary to the English throne. On his return to the Netherlands, consequently, the representative of William of Orange took with him letters promising support from a number of prominent Englishmen.

While the nation was at a high pitch of excitement over the case of the bishops, an event occurred which dashed all hopes for a Protestant succession in England. In June, 1688, a son was born to the king. This opened up the prospect of an endless Roman Catholic succession. The birth of a son to James II precipitated a crisis. Seven leaders of both parties decided to invite William of Orange to come to England.

The Revolution of 1688

This invitation confronted William of Orange with a very difficult problem. In the first place, it was no easy task to leave the continent. William had to raise in the Netherlands a military force. This involved gaining the consent not only of the seven provinces but of each important municipality. In the second place, he had to be careful to do nothing to alienate his Catholic allies, Spain and Austria. In the third place, he had to take steps that would protect the Netherlands against attack by Louis XIV. Finally, he had to invade a foreign country without being sure how its native population would react to alien intervention.

When all was ready, William of Orange set sail for England. In order to prepare the way, he published a declaration which retold the mistakes of James II, disclaimed all idea of conquest, and promised to submit the issues at stake to a free parliament. In November, 1688, he landed on the southern coast of England at a place called Torbay, in Devonshire. He encountered little opposition to his landing but found a great reluctance on the part of the leading men of the country to break openly with James II. After a vain attempt at resistance, however, the king abandoned his army and fled to London. By this time, even those whom he trusted most turned against him. These included John Churchill, his ablest military leader, and members of his own family. Thereupon, he gave up all hope of retaining his hold on the country and attempted to escape to the continent. Thwarted at first by an overzealous subordinate, he finally succeeded in eluding his captors and getting to France.

In the opinion of the English people, the king had vacated the throne. There were several plans suggested for filling the vacancy.

Finally, after much discussion, the Convention Parliament offered the throne to William (known henceforth as William III) and Mary as joint sovereigns. In order to have clearly understood the conditions under which they should rule, the Convention drew up the Declaration of Rights. It was intended to prevent a repetition of the grievances of the two preceding reigns. After enumerating the recent attacks of James II against the Protestant religion and against the laws and liberties of the kingdom, it declared illegal the pretended power of suspending and dispensing with laws, the setting up of the Court of Ecclesiastical Commission, the levying of money and the imposition of excessive fines or bail, and the maintenance of a standing army without the consent of Parliament. It demanded freedom of election, speech, and debate. It asserted that for the purpose of amending and preserving the laws, parliaments should be held frequently. In brief, it attempted to answer in favor of Parliament and the English people the questions which had been at issue for nearly a century. In its second session, the Convention Parliament transformed the Declaration of Rights into the Bill of Rights, that contained a few new provisions. This law made it illegal for a "papist" or anyone married to a "papist" to be king of England.

The Reign of William and Mary

The reign of William and Mary was marked by other important developments. In the hurry of changing sovereigns, some safeguards had been omitted. One of the most important of these questions was the future status of the Protestant Dissenters. In the main, they had refused to be tempted by the blandishments of James II and had remained loyal to the national cause. As a matter of simple fairness, they should have been protected against the adverse legislation on the statute books. In 1689, at the earnest solicitation of William of Orange, Parliament passed the Toleration Act. This law suspended the operation of existing penal laws against those who absented themselves from the services of the Established Church and attended other places of worship, provided they took the oath of Allegiance and Supremacy and subscribed to a declaration against transubstantiation. Dissenting ministers, furthermore, were required to subscribe to most of the Thirty-nine Articles. Quakers were to escape the penalties of the law by signing a declaration, instead of taking an oath against transubstantiation, confessing their belief in Christianity, and promising fidelity to the government. "Papists" and those, such as Jews or Unitarians, who did not believe in the Trinity, were expressly excluded from the benefits of the act. William III failed to overcome the prejudice of the communicants of the Established Church against his plan for the "comprehension" of all moderate Protestants in the Anglican Church.

Several other acts which tended to safeguard the liberties of Englishmen were passed during the reign. In 1689, Parliament passed the Mutiny Act. This enabled the authorities to maintain discipline in the army without surrendering the control of Parliament. It did this through the device of granting the military leaders disciplinary power for one year at a time. In 1694, Parliament passed the Triennial Act, which limited the duration of legislative power to three years. It was thought that if its members had to give to their constituents frequent accounts of their conduct, it would check the corruption and bribery which flourished all too luxuriantly. In 1695, a long forward step was taken toward freeing the press from the censorship hitherto practiced by the government. It was effected merely by allowing the act licensing censorship to lapse. In 1701, legislation was enacted which was intended to regulate the succession to the throne. Neither William II and Mary nor the sister of the latter, Anne, had surviving children. In order to insure a Protestant succession in England, Parliament voted that upon the death of Anne the throne should pass to a distant relative, a granddaughter of James I, Sophia, Electress of Hanover, and her descendants, the nearest Protestant member of the English royal house. Several important limitations on the new line were imposed by the act. The most important of the eight was a provision that judges should hold offices during good behavior and should be removed only upon an address of both houses of Parliament.

In the reign of William and Mary, too, the English cabinet system began to take shape. Before the seventeenth century, English ministers had been dependent on the king for their appointment and retention in office and were independent of one another. During the course of the seventeenth century, several ministers were impeached and a number were forced out of office by Parliament. After the rise of modern political parties, William III found it difficult to have as ministers men who did not meet with the approval of the party in power in the House of Commons. As a consequence, he adopted the policy of choosing ministers from the party having a majority in the lower house of Parliament. William III, however, acted as his own foreign minister, and the ministers did not yet act as a unit.

In invading England, William III had been swayed by his hopes of gaining England for the alliance against Louis XIV rather than by personal ambition. The story of the conflict with France is told in the main in Chapter 15. The invasion of Ireland in 1689 by James II,

260

however, was at the same time a diversion of England from the continental struggle and an important episode of English history. Before his downfall in England, James II had planned to employ the Irish as an instrument for the carrying out of his political and religious policies in England and Scotland. After his flight from England, accordingly, he went to Ireland in the hope of enlisting the help of the Irish in regaining England and Scotland. At first, most of Ireland fell into the hands of his supporters. The Irish Protestants abandoned their property and fled for their lives. In 1690, James II and his sympathizers were defeated in the decisive battle of the Boyne. This resulted in the flight of James II and the capitulation of his supporters. They were further punished by the exile of officers, the exclusion of Roman Catholics from office, and the enforcement of the penal laws against them.

In Scotland, the situation was quite different. The Scottish parliament, dominated as it was by Lowlanders, accepted William and Mary as joint sovereigns under certain conditions set forth in a document similar to the English Declaration of Rights. The greater part of the Highlanders, on the other hand, remained loyal to James II and opposed the accession of William and Mary. They were finally defeated, but the victors marred their success by the use which they made of it. Through carelessness or indifference, the English authorities permitted the brutal massacre of the Macdonalds of Glencoe.

The Reign of Queen Anne

In 1702, William III, who survived his wife eight years, died. His death brought to the throne Anne (1665–1714), daughter of James II and sister of Mary. She was thirty-seven years of age. By nature she was meek, sluggish, and of limited understanding. During most of her life she was dominated by her girlhood friend, Sarah Jennings (wife of John Churchill, the later Duke of Marlborough), a beautiful, capable, designing, avaricious, and shrewish woman, who was devoted to the interests of her husband. Until 1711, her husband managed to stay in power. The chief problem which confronted the government throughout the reign was the war against Louis XIV which has been discussed in Chapter 15. In spite of her limited capacities, Queen Anne was inclined to take a strong stand on political and religious matters. She was devoted to the Established Church and was inclined to assert her personal rights. These traits caused her to interfere frequently in the administration appointments in church and state, and politics.

Aside from the war, the most important event of the reign was the union of England and Scotland. After the accession of James I to the English throne, the two countries had been held together by a personal union that left to each state its own institutions. While some of the leaders in the two states realized the advisability of a closer union, a mass of prejudice and even hostility had to be overcome before any union could be effected. Only the threat of retaliatory legislation and the promise to safeguard the rights of the Presbyterian Church in Scotland and those of the Anglican Church in England finally extorted the consent of the Scots and the English High-churchmen to an organic union of Scotland with England. The treaty finally signed in 1707 provided for the union of the two kingdoms under the name of Great Britain. The united states were also to have a joint parliament and to enjoy mutual freedom of trade. The union benefited both states greatly.

The struggles of the seventeenth century between the Stuart kings and their subjects gave England some of its most distinctive institutions. The political struggle gave Englishmen personal freedom and the protection of their property. It gave them, too, a voice in their own government through the development of Parliament, political parties, and the cabinet system. The struggles over religion finally ended in the adoption of the principle of religious toleration. In the eighteenth century, these developments won the admiration of visitors from France and other countries.

CHAPTER 17

Developments Overseas in the Seventeenth Century: The Rise and Decline of Dutch Predominance

In the sixteenth century Spain and Portugal were fairly successful in their efforts to monopolize the new-found lands overseas. By 1600, as we have seen, they had built up two large empires. Spain had founded new societies in Mexico, throughout most of South America, and in the Philippines. Portugal had seized a series of strategic posts along the coasts of Africa and Southern Asia and in Brazil. Until just before the close of the century, the two powers had been, in the main, successful in excluding other states from these regions.

In 1580, however, Philip II of Spain succeeded in gaining control of Portugal also. This thrust upon the rulers of Spain the enormous task of maintaining at the same time the Spanish and Portuguese monopolies in the Western and the Eastern Hemispheres. As subsequent events showed, the task was too great. Philip II and his successors found it impossible to exclude entirely other states from acquiring a share of the lands and trade to be gained overseas. After 1580, the two great colonial empires were successfully attacked by the forces of England, France, and the United Netherlands. During most of the seventeenth century, the Dutch were the predominant power in the struggle for colonies and commerce.

Reasons for the Dutch Success

There were good reasons for the success of the Dutch in building up a great colonial empire. Very early they became fishermen. In time, they became the purveyors of fish to much of Catholic Europe. From fishing to commerce was only a step. The Netherlands was by its very location a natural point of exchange. It was located at the point where the commercial routes from North to South and from East to West crossed. Very early, the Netherlands had become a place for the meeting of merchants and the exchange of goods. First, the city of Bruges, and later, Antwerp, had been the chief commercial center of the Netherlands. In 1576 the latter city was sacked by mutinous Spanish soldiers. This had convinced many merchants that they would be safer at Amsterdam. As a result, this city soon became the chief center for trade in such commodities as salt, dried fish, grain naval stores, liquors, and metals. In addition, in spite of the war with Spain, the Dutch had become the principal carriers of Europe. It is estimated that at the beginning of the seventeenth century they had 800 boats engaged in the fishing industry and 3,000 ships in commerce. Of these latter, some 800 were employed in the trade with the Baltic. The Dutch owed their supremacy to such factors as their skill in shipbuilding, the low duties which they levied on imports and exports, and to the preoccupation of their natural rivals—the French and the English—with domestic problems.

After 1580, this favorable position of the Dutch was seriously menaced. After Philip II gained control of Portugal, he closed its ports to the Dutch. This threatened destruction to their profitable business of distributing to the rest of Europe the commodities brought by the Portuguese to the port of Lisbon.

The Establishment of a Dutch Colonial Empire in the East

The Dutch merchants, however, refused to be thwarted by the decrees of Philip II. As soon as they found themselves excluded from the Port of Lisbon, they began to take steps toward establishing direct commercial relations with the points from which the valuable Eastern commodities came. First, they tried without success to reach the Eastern markets by going north of Europe. In 1592, however, they managed to obtain some maps that showed the route around Africa. They enlisted, likewise, the help of Dutchmen like Huygen van Linschoten, who had made the long voyage to the East in Portuguese ships and who had even sent a discreet agent to Lisbon to gain such information as he could about the route to India and the conditions to be found there.

By 1595 the Dutch business men were ready to attempt an expedition to the East. In that year Cornelius Houtman sailed from Amsterdam with four ships. After a voyage of fifteen months, he reached Bantam on the west coast of the island of Sumatra. His arrival at this market did not end his troubles. His expedition continued to be plagued by dissensions, sickness, and the opposition of both the natives and the Portuguese. Houtman himself fell into the hands of the natives. His largest ship burned. Before he turned homeward, however, he visited the Moluccas Islands and Sumatra. By the time he reached Amsterdam he had only eighty-nine men out of his original crew of two hundred and forty-nine.

Though the returns from their expedition to the East were comparatively small, the Dutch merchants promptly took steps to exploit the new region thrown open to Dutch commerce. The merchants of

264

the different Dutch ports desired to take part in the new trade and formed companies that promptly sent out a succession of expeditions to the East Indies. At first, these expeditions gained substantial profits. This situation, however, soon changed. The new companies competed with each other and threatened to spoil the market for spices in the East and the profits in Europe. It was soon evident that something had to be done to remedy the situation.

The remedy finally adopted was the organization of a single company for trade with the East Indies. In 1602 the merchants of the various commercial cities of the United Netherlands organized the Dutch East India Company. Each member had a certain fixed share in each expedition. For fifty years the new company was to have a monopoly of trade and the powers of a state in the region extending from the Cape of Good Hope to the Straits of Magellan.

The Dutch East India Company encountered many obstacles. The long voyages continued to take a heavy toll of lives and ships. Ship captains lacked many of the present-day instruments of navigation. Their crews suffered from scurvy and other diseases. The Dutch had to compete for the profitable trade in spices with the Portuguese, the Spaniards, and the English. Like all Europeans, they found it difficult to adjust themselves to the tropical climate. They often, too, had trouble with native rulers.

The first task of the Dutch East India Company was to establish a monopoly of the trade with the Spice Islands. This entailed much hard fighting. Hostile fleets had to be captured or driven off and fortified posts had to be taken. The alliance of petty potentates had to be gained. After some twenty years of fighting, the Portuguese were forced to abandon practically all the East Indies.

The Dutch, though, still had the competition of the English to contend with. In 1619 the Dutch and the English authorities signed a treaty which provided for the participation of both powers in the trade in spices and their cooperation in defence of their interests. This agreement, however, did not overcome the latent hostility of their subjects. In 1623, accordingly, an incident occurred that profoundly affected the situation in the Spice Islands. The Dutch thought that they had discovered through the use of torture that the English at Amboyna were planning to attack them. As a result, the local Dutch authorities took the law into their own hands and put nineteen Englishmen to death. This so-called Massacre of Amboyna led to the withdrawal of the English from the Spice Islands and gave the Dutch the monopoly at which they had long been aiming.

Meanwhile, Dutch navigators and agents had been opening up other regions in the Orient to Dutch commerce. In 1619 the Dutch governor, Coen, won a decisive victory over the Sultan, who was dominant in Java and laid out the city of Batavia which became the capital of the Dutch colonial empire. A successor of Coen, Anthonie von Diemen (1636–1645) did much to extend the sphere of the Dutch East India Company. He dispatched Abel Tasman on an important voyage of discovery that was responsible for the circumnavigation of Australia and the discovery of New Zealand and the Friendly and Fiji Islands. Other navigators also made extensive discoveries in the waters around Korea and Japan and as far north as Sakhalin Island. In short, the Dutch agents or colonies were to be found in almost all countries from the Cape of Good Hope eastward.

In 1600 a vessel from the Netherlands was wrecked on the coast of Japan. In this way the Dutch established themselves in Japan. For a time after 1609, they had the privilege of free trade with that country, and after 1639 the Dutch alone were allowed to trade with the Japanese. They were permitted to settle on the small island of Deshima in the harbor of Nagasaki, and from that date until the opening up of Japan to western trade they were the only Europeans tolerated in Japan.

The Dutch, too, tried to establish trade relations with China. In 1622 they established themselves in the Pescadores Islands, but two years later they moved to the Island of Formosa. This settlement was situated just at the crossroads between Japan, China, and Manila. From this position they carried on a flourishing trade until they were driven out by a notorious Chinese pirate.

The Dutch established themselves at a number of other strategic points. In 1641 they finally captured Malacca. This was one of the most important points in the Orient and dominated traffic between the Indian and Pacific oceans. In 1652 the Dutch made a fortified settlement at the Cape of Good Hope. This insured Dutch ships sailing between Europe and the East ample supplies of fresh food and water. In 1667 the Dutch occupied the huge island of Sumatra.

The Establishment of a Dutch Colonial Empire in the Western Hemisphere

While the Dutch were carrying on a struggle in the East with their Spanish and Portuguese enemies and other competitors, they were engaged in a similar struggle in the Western Hemisphere. At first, it took the form of contraband trade with Africa and the Spanish and Portuguese colonies in America. In these expeditions the Dutch seized and sold Negro slaves and captured, if they could, the fleets transporting to Spain the silver and gold taken from the mines of Mexico and Peru. In order to make these attacks more systematic, the Dutch authorities organized in 1621 a Dutch West India Company. At first, the principal activity of the new company was privateering, but its very successes tended to shut off this source of income. As a consequence, the Dutch West India Company turned its attention more and more to the establishment of colonies.

As early as 1609, the Dutch had begun to be interested in the region now known as New York. In that year Henry Hudson, an Englishman in the service of the Dutch, had entered the river now called by his name and had sailed up that stream as far as the site of the present city of Albany. In the following year, Dutch traders began to be attracted to the region by the fur trade. In 1623 the Dutch made a small settlement on Manhattan Island which they called New Amsterdam. The new colony grew very slowly. In an effort to promote its growth, the Dutch authorities introduced the "patroon system." By this system, enterprising men were given extensive grants of land along the Hudson River as a reward for bringing to the colony fifty or more families. In spite of these efforts, the colony did not prosper. The government was arbitrary and intolerant, and the colony had trouble with the Indians and the neighboring English settlements.

Somewhat later, the Dutch gained a considerable foothold along the coast of the Portuguese colony of Brazil. After the union of the Spanish and Portuguese Empires in 1580, Brazil became an object of attack by the French, the English, and the Dutch. In 1629 the last named power succeeded in capturing Pernambuco or Recife. In the years that followed, the Dutch conquest of Portuguese settlements continued until much of the southeastern coast of Brazil fell under Dutch control. This was a far more profitable acquisition than the colony of New Netherlands. It gave the Dutch control of a large and valuable trade in sugar and of the profits from the sale of captured ships. After Portugal regained its independence from Spain, the position of the Dutch became more and more precarious. Finally, in 1854, when a war with England made it impossible for the Dutch to send supplies to Brazil, they lost their last foothold in the country.

After 1667 the Dutch had only their holding in the West Indies and the province of Surinam. The latter was acquired during the second Anglo-Dutch War (1665–1667). Its acquisition was confirmed by the treaty concluded at the close of that struggle. The revival of the colony was largely the work of Portuguese Jews and French Huguenots.

The Establishment of an English Colonial Empire

The English, meanwhile, had been founding a colonial empire. Though their attention during the seventeenth century was largely

267

taken up by the parliamentary and religious struggles at home, English business men and administrators and people dissatisfied with conditions in England laid the foundations of the future British Empire.

In the light of later developments, possibly the most important of these overseas enterprises was the founding in 1600 of the English East India Company. Ever since 1579 the English had been interested in India. In that year an Englishman, Thomas Stephens, became rector of the Jesuit College at Goa. His letters to England seem to have aroused in that country a sentiment for the establishment of trading relations with India. The defeat of the *Spanish Armada* in 1588 permitted the diversion of attention and resources to such an enterprise. The Dutch had just demonstrated the feasibility of an invasion of the monopoly which Portugal was trying to maintain in Eastern waters. In 1601, consequently, the newly organized English East India Company sent an expedition, consisting of four ships, to the East Indies. Between 1602 and 1612, the English sent twelve other expeditions to India or the East Indies. Like the Dutch, the English traders encountered many difficulties. They had to contend with the Arabs, the Portuguese, and the Dutch. Until 1612, the subscribers to the different expeditions individually bore the cost of the voyages and reaped the profits. The latter were usually at least one hundred per cent. After 1612, the English merchants engaged in the trade organized a joint stock company. Very early they began to establish permanent trading posts in the East called factories. A little later, they commenced to fortify their establishments. In time, though, these humble factories grew into the most important division of the British Empire.

In the meantime, undeterred by the failure of the expeditions organized by Sir Humphrey Gilbert and Sir Walter Raleigh, other English business men established two companies, the London and the Plymouth companies, to exploit the opportunities for commerce and colonization in America. The London Company took the first steps toward the establishment of a settlement. In December, 1606, it sent overseas a band of one hundred and twenty men in three ships. Early in 1607 the expedition entered Chesapeake Bay, sailed some distance up the James River and established, on a small island, a settlement which its members called Jamestown in honor of their sovereign. The new colony had a hard struggle. It had to contend with the Indians, disease and hunger, as well as the disinclination of the colonists to work. For several years it was doubtful whether the struggling colony would survive. After some years, however, it began to prosper. In 1619 the colonists were finally given individual grants of land. In

Negro slaves and indented servants the colonists eventually found a needed labor force. Much against the will of James I, too, the colony was given in 1619 a considerable measure of self-government. Under the influence of these favorable conditions, the original settlement at Jamestown grew finally into the great colony of Virginia.

In 1620 a second permanent English colony was founded in America. As we have seen, many Englishmen were unwilling to conform to the established church in England. In order to avoid compliance with laws concerning religion, some of the religious dissenters fled, after the accession of James I, to Holland. They found conditions there hard and not altogether to their liking. One of these refugee congregations finally applied to the London Company for permission to establish a colony in America within the limits of its jurisdiction. In September, 1620, accordingly, with the aid of friends of some influence, one hundred and two individuals from the dissenting congregation set out from Plymouth with the intention of making a settlement in Virginia. On November 11, 1620, however, they sighted instead of Virginia the peninsula now known as Cape Cod in Massachusetts. As the captain of their small ship, which was called the *Mayflower,* refused to go south to Virginia, the members of the proposed colony finally disembarked at the spot now known as Plymouth, a point outside the jurisdiction of the London Company.

In the ensuing winter, the colonists suffered terribly. They were ill-prepared to contend with the cold weather, the hunger, and the illnesses which plagued them. During the first winter, half of their number died. Undeterred by these misfortunes, the survivors stayed in America. From time to time they were joined by other settlers. In 1621 the colonists at Plymouth received a rather unsatisfactory grant from the recently created Council of New England. This conferred on the new colony a sort of legality. In time, too, the colonists learned to wrest a living from the infertile soil of Massachusetts.

While this little group of dissenters was making a beginning toward the establishment of a second permanent English colony in America, some of those opposed to the royal policies in England began to despair over the possibility of transforming England into a country Puritan in religion and parliamentary in government. Instead of trying to convert the Old World, they began to dream of establishing in America such a society as they desired. Their planning finally led to the founding of the Massachusetts colony. As early as 1628, six of these English Puritans, one of them being John Endicott, took the first steps toward the establishment of such a colony. They secured a grant of land between the Charles and the Merrimac rivers and started the town now known as Salem. In the following year the number of associates in the enterprise was increased, and they pledged themselves to emigrate to the new colony and to take their government with them. In 1630, accordingly, led by John Winthrop, a fleet of eleven ships with nine hundred prospective settlers arrived at Salem. They ultimately established themselves in some eight different settlements. The new Massachusetts colony continued to grow until the outbreak of civil war in England stopped emigration to the New World.

Within a few years, other colonies were set up in New England. The Puritans of the Massachusetts Bay colony proved to be as intolerant of dissenting views as the Anglicans in England. As a usual thing, the Puritan authorities sent advocates of divergent ideas back to England. One of these holders of new ideas, Roger Williams, escaped from the Massachusetts Bay colony and took refuge with the Narragansett Indians. He had attracted the attention of the authorities because he preached such doctrines as the separation of church and state, that oaths should only be enforced morally, and that the soil belonged to the Indians. At what is now known as Providence, Rhode Island, he finally established a settlement which attracted other refugees from the Massachusetts Bay colony. In time, settlements were established in such neighboring towns as Portsmouth, Newport, and Warwick. From the beginning, the new colony practiced the, for the time, revolutionary doctrine of religious liberty. In 1643, Roger Williams returned to England and obtained the recognition of the Long Parliament for the colony of Rhode Island.

In 1636 the work of establishing a fourth colony in New England was begun. Both the Dutch colony of New Netherlands and the English colony at Plymouth had somewhat earlier established trading posts in the Connecticut Valley. In the year after Roger Williams fled from the Massachusetts Bay colony, the Rev. Thomas Hooker led a large part of his congregation from Cambridge to the region that came to be known as Connecticut. Other groups from Massachusetts soon followed. At the same time, still other colonists came to Connecticut directly from England. Sailing under the authorization of the Council of New England, John Winthrop, Jr. founded at Saybrook a settlement which developed rather slowly through lack of funds. In 1638 another group settled at New Hanover. After maintaining a separate existence for some time, the various settlements of the region were finally organized into the colony of Connecticut. As in Massachusetts, however, only church members had a voice in the government of these settlements.

In the meantime, the powerful Calvert family in England had been struggling to establish a refuge in America for their fellow English

Catholics. Obtaining a grant of land north of the Potomac River from his friend the king, the first Lord Baltimore took the initial steps toward founding the colony of Maryland. In 1633 his son sent out a group of about twenty Catholic gentlemen and about two hundred Protestant laborers, who established themselves at a point (which they called St. Mary's) some nine miles up a tributary of the Potomac. The new colony prospered, since the site chosen for the new settlement was healthful. The Indians were weak and friendly. From a sense of justice and liberality rather than necessity, the Calverts adopted a policy of toleration. From the first, the colonists were assigned individual holdings. The new colony, however, had its share of difficulties. The colonists attempted to seize control of the colony and to persecute Catholics. The Maryland colony had disputes with the neighboring colony of Virginia. The proprietor himself felt compelled to thwart the plans of the Jesuits. During the civil war in England, he had difficulty in maintaining himself in power.

During these years the English were busy, too, in the West Indies. In the first half of the seventeenth century they made settlements in the Barbados Islands, on the islands of St. Vincent, Antigua, Montserrat, St. Christopher, Nevis, Dominica, and the Bermudas. For the most part, the settlers in these islands became planters and devoted themselves to the raising of sugar, cotton, and other tropical products. During the civil war in England, there was a tendency for sympathizers with the monarchy to emigrate to the West Indies either from England or the American mainland.

The Anglo-Dutch Wars

For a half century after their first voyage to the East Indies, the Dutch were the most important colonial and commercial power of Europe. They could not, however, hope to maintain their position of predominance indefinitely. They owed their place of primacy in part to the preoccupation of France and England with domestic problems. The attention of the French was centered on the problem of making the monarchy absolute in France and supreme over the Spanish and Austrian Habsburgs; the English were engaged in the struggle between king and parliament. This situation could not continue indefinitely. By the middle of the seventeenth century, the English and the French were ready to challenge the Dutch position.

In 1651 the English began to attack the Dutch. Unable to compete with them by economic means, the English employed both legislation and open warfare against their rival. They enacted the Navigation Act which declared that all goods coming to England from Asia, Africa, and America must in the future come in English ships or those of English colonies and that goods coming from European countries must come either in English ships or in those of the country of origin. This was a vital blow at the profitable Dutch carrying trade.

This piece of legislation was only one of several factors increasing the tension between the two peoples. In 1623 the rivalry of the two nations in the East Indies had culminated in the Massacre of Amboyna. The English had refused to recognize the right of the Dutch to fish for herring in the North Sea. The English insisted on searching Dutch ships for Royalist arms and demanded that the Dutch recognize English supremacy in the narrow seas by lowering the Dutch flag when passing English ships. There had been trouble between the two governments over the Royalist exiles who had taken refuge in the Netherlands. The enactment of the Navigation Act simply precipitated an armed struggle between the two states.

The ensuing conflict was largely a naval war. The first clashes between the two peoples grew out of attempts of one side to intercept the convoys of the other. During the course of the war (1652–1654), both powers were defeated in naval actions, and control of the sea passed back and forth between them. English attacks interfered with the Dutch herring industry and Dutch attacks greatly disturbed English trade in the Mediterranean Sea. On the whole, however, the English had the advantage. In 1654, accordingly, the Dutch sought peace.

After the restoration of Charles II to the throne of England in 1660, the English merchants persuaded Parliament to continue the commercial policy of the Commonwealth. In that year it re-enacted and strengthened the Navigation Act of 1651. In addition to the provisions concerning the use of English ships for goods imported from Asia, Africa, and America and from European countries, it provided that tobacco, sugar, and certain other enumerated colonial products must be brought to England, Ireland, or to an English colony. The Navigation Act of 1660 was thus another severe blow to the Dutch carrying trade which for the most part neither began or ended at a Dutch port. In 1663 the English parliament supplemented the Navigation Act of 1660 by a law that required goods destined for an English colony to pass through England and to be carried to the English colonies in English ships. Ten years later, Parliament tried to put an end to evasions of the Navigation Laws by requiring every captain loading his vessel with tobacco, sugar, or one of the other enumerated articles to give bond to land his cargo in England or to pay at the colonial port of departure the stipulated English import duties. The aim of all this legislation was to make trade profitable to English importers, exporters, and ship owners at the expense of the Dutch carrying trade.

In the meantime, the English had begun to cast covetous eyes at the Dutch colony of New Netherlands, which claimed all the territory between the Connecticut and Delaware rivers and separated the New England from the southern English colonies of Virginia and Maryland. There had been friction between the Dutch and English colonists ever since the founding of the colonies. In 1654 preparations had been made for an attack on New Netherlands, which had been forestalled by the early conclusion of peace. In 1664, accordingly, Charles II, king of England, disregarded the claims of the Dutch and granted the contested region to his brother, the Duke of York, the later James II. Without a declaration of war, the new proprietor sent three English vessels with a force of troops into the harbor of New Amsterdam, later known as New York, and demanded its surrender. The expedition was aided by forces from Connecticut and Long Island. As no one but the Dutch governor was inclined to defend the interests of the Dutch West India Company, the English had little difficulty in taking the Dutch colony. The colonists were promised the liberties of Englishmen and intercourse with Holland.

These developments made a second war between the English and the Dutch inevitable. The seizure of New Netherlands and certain Dutch establishments in West Africa led to reprisals. The English, in turn, seized Dutch vessels wherever they could find them. In March, 1665, open war was declared.

The second Anglo-Dutch war was a most humiliating experience for the English. They were potentially stronger than their rivals but mismanaged the war badly. In 1666 a Dutch fleet of eighty warships attacked an English fleet while it was divided and completely defeated it. In the following year, as a result of the almost incredible folly of the king of England, a Dutch fleet sailed up the Thames River, burned the English dockyard at Chatham, and blockaded London for some weeks. This humiliating episode led to the signing of a treaty of peace.

In spite of their defeat, the English were granted relatively easy terms by the Dutch because the latter feared a French attack. The Dutch agreed to let the colony of New Netherlands remain in the hands of the English under the name of the colony of New York. In place of it, the Dutch took the colony known then as Surinam which now goes under the name of Dutch Guiana. They had begun to settle the region as early as 1613.

For some time, the Dutch had been growing conscious of the fact that they were threatened by an enemy even more dangerous than the English. From the time of their struggle for independence, the Dutch had counted on their alliance with France. After the assump-

273

tion of control over the government by Louis XIV in 1661, however, French policy took a new direction. Colbert, the chief minister of the French sovereign, adopted a policy calculated to take away from the Dutch at least a part of their profitable carrying trade. The French king was by inheritance and conviction an absolute ruler and had no liking for a republic such as the Dutch maintained nor for the freedom which it gave to the press.

In the second Anglo-Dutch war, accordingly, Louis XIV ignored the appeal of the Dutch for aid. On the contrary, they were beginning to feel that the efforts of the French to acquire the Spanish Netherlands were a threat to Dutch independence. In their desire to avert this danger, the Dutch increased the hostility of the French king to them. In 1668 they formed an alliance with England and Sweden that thwarted the plans of Louis XIV for taking all the Spanish Netherlands.

In retaliation, Louis XIV began to plan the destruction of his former Dutch ally. As a first step toward this, the French sovereign began, as we have seen in Chapter 15, to isolate the Dutch diplomatically. In 1667 he signed a treaty with the profligate Charles II which made England for the time being a dependency of France. In 1670 the two sovereigns signed a treaty which went even further. In return for military aid and a large grant that freed him from control of Parliament, Charles II agreed to aid Louis XIV against the Dutch.

In 1672, Louis XIV felt that he was ready for his long-planned attack on the Dutch. Even before a declaration of war was made, the English made a treacherous but unsuccessful attack on the Dutch Smyrna fleet. After war was formally declared, great French armies invaded the poorly prepared provinces of the United Netherlands. For the moment it looked as if there was no hope for the Dutch. Under the stimulus of the emergency, however, they rose to great heights. In the crisis they called as leader of the state a young man seventeen years of age, the youthful William of Orange, a member of a family which had always furnished them leadership in times of national crisis. Under this head the Dutch opened the dykes and flooded the country. This measure stopped the invasion. Finding themselves thwarted, the French invaders finally withdrew from the country. In the meantime, Charles II had been vainly trying to inflame English opinion against its old Dutch rival. By this time, however, the English public had come to realize that the French were a greater danger than the Dutch. Early in 1672, the English parliament refused to make further grants for the prosecution of the war. Their action forced Charles II to make peace with the Dutch.

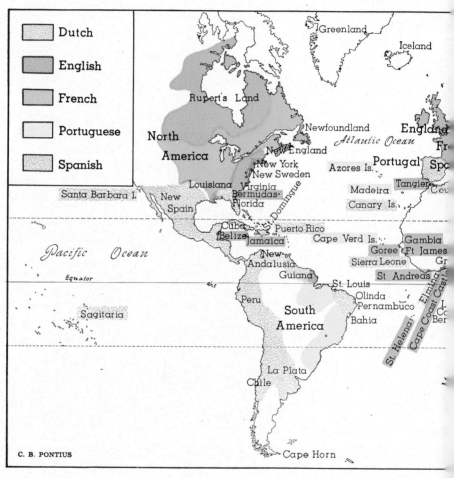

Dutch

English

French

Portuguese

Spanish

Greenland

Iceland

Rupert's Land

North America

Newfoundland

New England

New York
New Sweden

Louisiana

Virginia

Santa Barbara I.

New Spain

Bermudas-
Florida

Domingue

Cuba
Belize

Jamaica

Puerto Rico

New
Andalusia

Guiana

Peru

Sagitaria

South America

Olinda
Pernambuco

Bahia

La Plata

Chile

Cape Horn

Atlantic Ocean

Azores Is.

Madeira

Canary Is.

Cape Verd Is.

England

Portugal

Tangier

St. Louis

Sierra Leone

St. Andreas

Gambia

Goree Ft James

Fr

Sp

Ceu

Gr

St. Helena

Cape Coast Castle

Elmina

L
C
Ber

Pacific   Ocean

Equator

C. B. PONTIUS

The Colonial

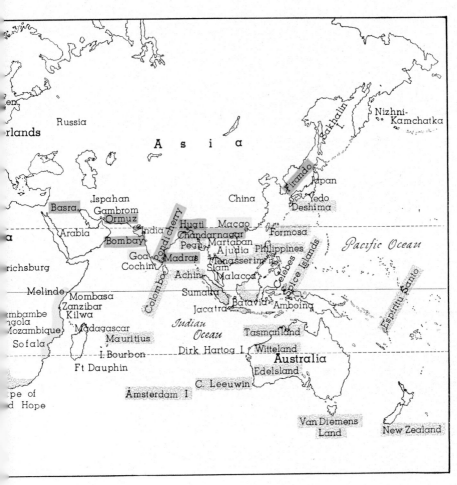

en
Russia
rlands
A s i a
Nizhni-
Kamchatka
Sakhalin
Firando
Japan
Ispahan
China
Yedo
Basra
Gambrom
Deshima
Ormuz
Arabia
India
Huati
Macao
a
Bombay
Chandarnagar
Formosa
Pegu
Martaban
Pacific Ocean
Ajudia
Philippines
richsburg
Goa
Madras
Tenasserim
Cochin
Siam
Colombo
Achin
Malacca
Pondicherry
Celebes
Melinde
Sumatra
Spice Islands
Mombasa
Espiritu Santo
Zanzibar
Jacatra
Batavia
Amboina
mbambe
Kilwa
ngola
Madagascar
Indian
lozambique
Mauritius
Oceau
Tasmanland
Sofala
I. Bourbon
Dirk Hartog I.
Witteland
Ft Dauphin
Edelsland
Australia
pe of
C. Leeuwin
d Hope
Amsterdam I
Van Diemens
New Zealand
Land

n about 1650

The Dutch continued to be one of the important European powers until after the close of the century. They hardly had the population and resources to enable them to play the role of a great power in the eighteenth century. After 1689, it became more and more evident that either England or France was to be the next predominant power in the struggles for colonies and commerce. In the latter phases of this conflict, the Dutch played the role of a junior partner in alliance with England. They ceased to show the initiative which had made them a great power, and, at a time when most other governments were becoming more centralized and more efficient, they maintained their old cumbersome political machinery which left the central government weak and the provinces and municipalities strong. In contrast with the Portuguese, the Dutch, even after their decline, managed to retain the greater part of their empire in the East Indies.

The Founding of More English Colonies

In spite of the colonizing activity of the English people in the first half of the seventeenth century, there were still great areas in North America which had hardly been touched. After the restoration of the Stuarts to the English throne in 1660, steps were taken toward the establishment of colonies in some of these regions in spite of the preoccupation of the English people with their struggle over religion and the position of Parliament. In 1663, Charles II granted to eight of his courtiers control over the territory now included in the states of North and South Carolina. The settlements which grew up in this grant, however, owed much more to the initiative of private individuals than they did to the aristocratic proprietors. Quite early, adventurers from Virginia began to explore and trade in the country. In 1663 a small band of Virginia dissenters made the first permanent settlement. In the years that followed, other groups and individuals settled in the region. They included many Baptists and Quakers who had suffered persecution in other settlements and several hundred emigrants from the Barbados. At first, the new proprietors gave the colonists a simple government suited to their needs. Later, they allowed the philosopher, John Locke, to draw up a plan of government, entirely unsuited to conditions in the colony, which called for the reestablishment of feudal conditions, a state church, and all that the colonists had sought to escape by coming to the New World. The only result of the attempt was to create in the minds of the colonists a contempt for all government.

Soon after the Duke of York seized New Netherlands (1664), he transferred the part now known as New Jersey to two of his friends. The region already had some settlers. The Dutch had spread across the Hudson from New York, and as early as 1638 the Swedes had built a fort on the lower Delaware. The new proprietors granted the colony a considerable degree of self-government, and new colonists from New England, Long Island, and England came and settled there. For a number of years, New Jersey had a rather troubled history. There were disputes between the settlers and the proprietors. In disgust, one of the proprietors sold his share in the colony to a group of Quakers who desired to create a refuge for members of their sect who were persecuted in England. In 1676 the colony was divided. Finally, in 1682 the proprietors of West Jersey purchased the interests of the other original proprietor. These transactions placed control of New Jersey in the hands of a group that included William Penn and a number of Scottish men. They organized a government that put political power in the hands of the colonists. In 1702 the proprietors, weary of disputes with the colonists, surrendered their rights to the English crown.

William Penn, however, was not satisfied with the situation in New Jersey. He desired to establish a colony to which his title was clear and in which he could establish a refuge for his persecuted fellow religionists, the Quakers, one of the many dissenting sects which had sprung up in England during the seventeenth century. In 1680, accordingly, he secured from the king a patent to the territory now known as Pennsylvania, a grant that satisfied the king's debt to Penn's father. The following year he acquired from the Duke of York the present state of Delaware in order to give his colony some seacoast.

The new colony developed rapidly. At the time of the grant to Penn there were already some English, Swedish, and Dutch residents in the territory. Other settlers quickly established themselves in Pennsylvania and in what was known at the time as the "three lower counties." In 1681 three shiploads of Quakers landed in the colony. In the following year, Penn himself came and brought about a hundred additional colonists. Within three years the colony had eight thousand inhabitants. The benevolent proprietor sought colonists even outside of England. In Germany were to be found many dissenting sects—Mennonites, Amish, Dunkards, and Moravians— which had much in common with the Quakers. Among these sectarians Penn advertised his colony rather widely. As early as 1683, a contingent of settlers came to Pennsylvania and founded Germantown, now an aristocratic suburb of Philadelphia. Later, many other Germans came to the colony. Some of them came as indentured servants; others had sufficient means to pay for their own transportation. This German element finally constituted about one-third of the population of the colony.

Pennsylvania was wisely administered. In contrast to most of the other colonies where squatters on the borders stirred up much trouble, Penn treated the Indians fairly and had little difficulty with them. The benevolent proprietor also allowed the colonists to elect their own governing bodies, a council and a lower house, which drew up a "Great Charter" for the government of the colony. Early in the eighteenth century, Delaware and Pennsylvania were divided.

For a long time the English made no attempt to settle Newfoundland. Almost from the time of its discovery by John Cabot, fishermen of various nations had haunted its waters. Writing in 1578, Hakluyt mentioned that there were 400 ships engaged in fishing in the waters off Newfoundland. In time, settlements began to be established. By the middle of the seventeenth century, it is estimated that there were some 2,000 inhabitants scattered along the Newfoundland coasts. The new settlements suffered from the attacks of the French and the opposition of the English fishermen and government.

In 1670 the great Hudson's Bay Company was chartered. It owed its existence to the initiative of two Frenchmen who found themselves excluded by monopolies from the fur trade in Canada. In some way, they learned that the rich fur-bearing regions of northern Canada could be approached from the north. They persuaded a group of English noblemen to furnish the capital to exploit the fur trade of northern Canada. In time, the company became wealthy and powerful. The rights of the English in Newfoundland and northern Canada were not recognized by France, however, until the signing of the Treaty of Utrecht in 1713.

The Founding of a French Colonial Empire

Early in the sixteenth century, the attention of France had been called by her explorers to the region now known as Canada. In 1603 a serious attempt was made to exploit the Canadian fur trade. Samuel de Champlain, one of the adventurous soldiers released by the ending of the Wars of Religion in France, was sent out to Canada. For over thirty years he represented French interests in the new country. During these years he made frequent trips back to France, made a settlement at Port Royal (now Annapolis, Nova Scotia), founded Quebec, and penetrated as far west as Lake Huron. During these years he made friends of the Indians of Canada but stirred up the lasting antagonism of the Iroquois confederacy in neutral New York.

The newly established colony grew very slowly. In contrast to the English authorities, the rulers of France allowed only the orthodox to go to Canada, and, for the most part, they showed little inclination to go to the New World. It is estimated that even as late as 1660 there were only about 2,000 French settlers in Canada. Only the fur traders and the missionaries sent out by the various monastic orders showed much interest in the new colony. None of the companies entrusted with the task of settling the new region were very successful.

In many instances, however, these missionaries and fur traders, proved to be great explorers. In 1673, for example, two Frenchmen, Joliet, a fur trader, and Marquette (1637–1675), a Jesuit missionary, set out in birch bark canoes on an exploring expedition that had important results. They pushed their way through Green Bay, up the Fox River, across Lake Winnebago, and down the Wisconsin and Mississippi rivers to the point where the Arkansas River enters the latter stream. Two years later, the intrepid missionary died while trying to found a station in Illinois for work among the Indians. Like many of these early missionaries, he kept a journal which is the basis for our knowledge of his important work.

An even more famous explorer was La Salle (1643–1687). While engaged in the fur trade, he heard reports of a great river, the Ohio, which flowed westward and which he thought might furnish a route to China. During the course of the years 1669 and 1670, he found and descended the Ohio River. He certainly reached the site of the present city of Louisville and he may have gone still further. After hearing of the expedition of Joliet and Marquette, he became convinced that the Mississippi flowed into the Gulf of Mexico. In 1678, after he had gained the support of the governor of Canada and the French authorities at home, he began to put his theory to the test of actual exploration. In 1682, after many discouragements and heroic exertions, he finally reached the mouth of the Mississippi River. He named the newly discovered region Louisiana in honor of his sovereign. A few years later, he was assassinated while making an unsuccessful attempt to colonize Louisiana.

The ambitious attempt of Philip II to maintain for Spain and Portugal a monopoly of the opportunities for trade and colonization overseas thus failed. Their resources were not great enough to exclude the English, French, and Dutch from participation in the opportunities offered by the newly discovered lands. For the first half of the seventeenth century, the Dutch were the dominant colonial and commercial power. The English and French made some efforts to found colonies in Canada, along the coast of the present United States, in Newfoundland, and the West Indies and to exploit the trade of India and in the East Indies, but their strength was largely absorbed by domestic problems. In the latter half of the century, they began to challenge the Dutch monopoly by legislation and open war.

By the end of the seventeenth century, accordingly, the English and French were firmly established in India; the Dutch held a monopoly of the profitable trade with the East Indies; the French had staked out a great but thinly populated empire in Canada and the Mississippi Valley; and the English were more or less firmly established in a line of settlements which stretched from Newfoundland to the West Indies.

CHAPTER 18

Central Europe in the Seventeenth Century

In Central Europe in the seventeenth century the Holy Roman Empire continued to disintegrate. The central government grew weaker and the states composing the empire grew stronger. Each state strove to strengthen its authority and extend its boundaries. This process was accelerated during the struggle known as the Thirty Years' War.

The Causes of the Thirty Years' War

The Treaty of Augsburg, concluded in 1555, failed to bring peace to the Empire. It gave no protection to one of three principal religious parties of the Empire, the Calvinists. All parties—the Catholics, the Lutherans, and the Calvinists—stood ready to push their own interests at the expense of other creeds and to achieve their objectives by the use of force. One fruitful cause of the resulting tension was the question of the acquisition and control of the ecclesiastical states. The Catholics naturally did not want to lose the power and revenues which possession of this numerous class of territories gave to them. The Protestant princes, for their part, seized every occasion to acquire them. The resulting tension between the religious parties led to such incidents as the seizure in 1607 of the city of Donauwörth on the Danube by the Catholic ruler of Bavaria because of a riot which grew out of an attack on a Catholic procession in the streets of the city. In defence of their interests, the Protestants were inclined to block the granting of funds for the prosecution of the war against the Turks, to form alliances with outside powers, particularly France, and to form organizations for their own defence. In 1608, as a result of the attack on Donauwörth, the Calvinists, under the leadership of the Elector of the Palatinate, Frederick IV, formed the league known as the Protestant Union. In the following year their opponents formed, under the leadership of Maximilian, Duke of Bavaria, the Catholic League. The Lutherans, however, appeared for the time being to be less bellicose than the other two religious parties of the Empire.

As later events were to show, the tension over religious questions was particularly acute in Bohemia, a province that constituted an

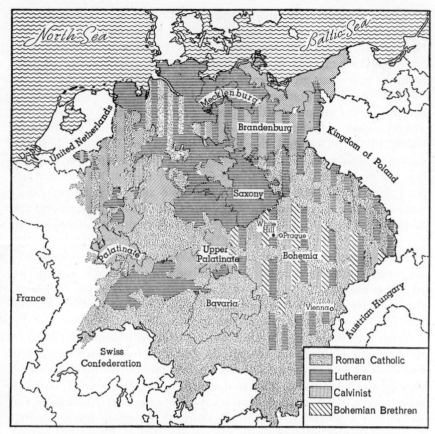

Central Europe on the Eve of the Thirty Years' War

important part of the Emperor's own hereditary state. In Bohemia
there had been political and religious dissension since the days of
John Hus (1369–1415). As a result of his efforts to reform the Church,
he had been burned at the stake. In Bohemia, where he was much
revered, the nobles refused to recognize the authority of the Council
of Constance, drove out many priests who refused to administer to
the laity at communion time both bread and wine (one of Hus's distinctive doctrines), and made preparations to resist their opponents.
The Emperor, the Pope, and the partisans of the Catholic faith carried on an unsuccessful crusade against the followers of Hus.[1] The

---

[1] These latter, on the other hand, split into two parties: the moderates, known as
Utraquists or Calixtines, and the extremists, usually called Taborites. In the ensuing
conflict the moderates were victorious, but the Taborites were nearly destroyed. In a
sense, though, the extremists survived under the name of the Bohemian Brethren or
Moravians, a very earnest sect that claimed at one time as many as four hundred
individual churches.

struggle ended in 1436 in a compromise known as "the Compacts." By the provisions of this document, the Bohemians acquired the right to receive communion according to the doctrine of Hus and to have freedom of preaching. In return for this concession, the Bohemians agreed to recognize the authority of the Emperor.

This was the situation when the Lutheran movement arose to complicate the situation still further. The doctrines of Luther found a sympathetic response among both the large number of Germans living in the cities and the border districts of Bohemia and the Czechs who constituted the majority of the population. For this reason, the Bohemians refused to aid Charles V against his German opponents. In 1567, the Compacts were done away with because they were regarded as favoring the Utraquists over the Lutherans and the Bohemian Brethren. Somewhat later, the Bohemians extorted from their ruler a verbal recognition of the Bohemian Confession of Faith, a document almost identical with the Augsburg Confession of Luther, except for the article relating to communion which was Calvinist rather than Lutheran in tone. By the end of the century, therefore, the majority of the Bohemians were hardly distinguishable from the Lutherans and were considered as Protestants.

With the rise of religious zeal among those who remained loyal to the Catholic Church, the struggle in Bohemia took a new turn. The Emperor sought to re-establish the ancient faith in all his dominions, and the Catholic nobles tried to do the same on their estates. In 1609, accordingly, the menaced Protestants demanded recognition of the Bohemian Confession of Faith, complete religious liberty, equal treatment with Catholics in the matter of political offices, and redress of some political grievances. The Emperor felt compelled to grant the Protestant demands. He formally conceded to them, accordingly, the Bohemian Confession, control of the University of Prague and the Consistory (the body in control of the Utraquists), and the right to elect certain nobles as defenders.

The Outbreak of the Thirty Years' War

The concession of this so-called Letter of Majesty did little to lessen the existing tension. Both religious factions were too aggressive for a written document to end their strife. When in 1618, therefore, the representatives of the Emperor and the Archbishop of Prague decided against the construction of Protestant churches at two points in Bohemia, the Protestant nobles of the country took vigorous counter measures. They angrily seized the representatives of the Emperor, three persons in all, and threw them out of an upper window in the royal castle at Prague. The representatives of the Emperor escaped serious injury, but this so-called "Defenestration of Prague" was the signal for a revolt which, as the years went by, broadened out from a provincial rebellion into, first, an Imperial civil war and, finally, an international struggle. The rebellious nobles elected a directory of thirty members to conduct the war and took other measures to prepare for the conflict.

The War in Bohemia and the Palatinate

At first, the prospects of the rebellious nobles seemed favorable. They had potential allies among the Protestants of the other Austrian provinces, in Transylvania, and in Germany. There was also a possibility that both France and England might intervene. The Emperor had virtually no army with which to meet the danger and had, besides, the problem on his hands of offering effective resistance to the Turks. In 1619 the Bohemian leaders took a step designed to strengthen their party still further. When their sovereign, the Emperor Mathias, died, they refused to recognize his legal successor, Ferdinand, a Habsburg archduke. They elected instead as king of Bohemia (which, it must be remembered, included not only the province of that name, but Moravia and Silesia as well), Frederick V, Elector of the important German state of the Palatinate, head of the Calvinist Protestant Union, and son-in-law of James I, king of England. This action supposedly would rally the Protestant Union and England to their cause. Buoyed up by these delusive hopes, the armed forces of the Bohemian rebels actually did force their way to the gates of Vienna.

The rebellion of the Bohemian Protestants, however, soon ended in disaster. When he found his authority defied by what he regarded as his Bohemian subjects, the new emperor placed such troops as he could raise under the command of Banquoy. He called on his Spanish kinsman, who was interested in the struggle not only by virtue of his religion but also because of the district of Franche-Comté and the ten Spanish provinces in the Netherlands which still nominally formed a part of the Holy Roman Empire. He persuaded by concessions Maximilian, Duke of Bavaria and head of the Catholic League, to come to his assistance. In order to obtain the help of this Catholic leader, Emperor Ferdinand was forced to conclude a hard bargain. Notwithstanding his Catholic sympathies, Maximilian demanded in return for his assistance a verbal promise of the transfer to himself of the electorate hitherto held by the ruler of the Palatinate. This bargain put at the disposal of Emperor Ferdinand an excellent general, Tilly (1559–1632), trained in his native Netherlands under the famous Duke of Parma. By sheer merit, Tilly had risen from a simple pikeman to commander of the excellent military forces of the League. In 1620, while the hope of help from Germany and England proved vain, these military forces drove the Bohemian Protestants back from Vienna and defeated them in battle at White Hill, a short distance from Prague. The ensuing panic of the Protestant forces made this battle decisive. The Elector, Frederick V of the Palatinate, fled from his new kingdom, where his personality and customs had made him quite unpopular. He carried with him the derisive epithet of "the Winter King," which has been associated ever since with his name. His defeated subjects made little further resistance, and the whole Bohemian kingdom fell into the hands of the victorious Catholic and Imperial forces.

The defeat of the Bohemian rebellion left a permanent impress on the country. Many of the Protestant leaders were executed and the remainder were exiled. Their vast estates were confiscated and, for the most part, fell into the hands of foreigners who were loyal to the Emperor and cared nothing about the Bohemian traditions of autonomy and independence. The Catholic Church became again the sole religion recognized in the Bohemian provinces. The Czech language became only the speech of the disregarded peasants. The promising Czech culture was suppressed. Worst of all, for the next twenty years Bohemia became the unwilling battleground of contending armies which recklessly killed and plundered wherever they went. The terrible consequences of the conflict in Bohemia are revealed in the decline of population which sank in these years from an estimated two million inhabitants to eight hundred thousand.

The victory of the Catholic party in Bohemia did not end the war. The victors naturally thought that Frederick V should be further punished for his intervention in Bohemia, and in 1621 they advanced into his own electorate; the electorate comprised two separate provinces: the Upper Palatinate, situated just north of Bavaria, and the Lower or Rhine Palatinate, an irregular province situated on both sides of the Rhine River. The forces of Tilly and the League, therefore, marched into the Upper Palatinate, and a Spanish army, commanded by the famous Spinola, entered the Rhine Palatinate. By 1622 the three armies, headed by German Protestant leaders, had all been defeated; both Palatinates had been overrun; and Frederick V had again been driven into exile. The Upper and Lower Palatinate suffered the same fate as Bohemia. They were plundered and harassed at will by the mercenary troops of both sides.

The defeat of Frederick V, Elector of the Palatinate, and the overrunning of his lands brought the war home to all the Protestant princes of Germany. They were all menaced by the requisitions and

284

pillaging of the armies which remained intact and moved from district to district as each was denuded of food, forage, and other supplies. In this connection, three things must be remembered. In the first place, each army was accompanied by a swarm of women, children, and hangers-on that outnumbered in many instances the actual soldiers. In the second place, soldiers and camp followers shortsightedly wasted more than they used. In the third place, agriculture was so unproductive as a result of the primitive methods employed that the country was much more quickly exhausted than it would be now. The Protestant princes were also seriously threatened with the loss of the ecclesiastical property and states which they had seized and which increased their revenues, gave them additional votes and seats in the diet of the Holy Roman Empire, and added to their power and prestige. Therefore, in the crisis which faced them, they began to look for aid to the powers that were interested for various reasons in the outcome of the religious war in Germany. These powers included France, England, Sweden, Denmark, and the principality of Transylvania.

The Danish Period

The first of these interested powers to act was Denmark. Its intervention in the war in Germany was owing to a number of causes. In the first place, its sympathies were naturally with the German Protestants. Then, too, its sovereign was not only head of the Danish kingdom but also duke of the two adjacent duchies of Schleswig and Holstein. As ruler of the latter, he was a German sovereign, a member of the Holy Roman Empire, and vitally interested in the fate of the neighboring ecclesiastical states of the Empire. The Danish state likewise, was being urged to enter the war by some of the outside powers. In particular, England and Holland offered it substantial subsidies if it would enter the war. In 1625, accordingly, Denmark decided to intervene in the Thirty Years' War in behalf of the hard-pressed German Protestants.

The Denmark that made this decision was not the relatively small and weak power that we now know. On the contrary, it was a great power which had to be reckoned with in all matters affecting Northern Europe. When the union of the three Scandinavian kingdoms formed at Kalmar in 1397 failed to hold together, the kings of Denmark managed to retain under their control the present kingdoms of Denmark and Norway, the duchies of Schleswig and Holstein, and the southern provinces of the present kingdom of Sweden. This gave Denmark control of the straits connecting the Baltic and North seas and enabled it for a long time to levy profitable tolls on all ships

285

passing through the Kattegat and the Skagerrak straits. The Danish state had used more wisely than most states the property of the Church which it had seized at the time of the Protestant Revolt, and this had enabled it to develop a navy and become a sea power. For a time, it was able to enforce the rule that all foreign ships must strike their topsails to Danish men-of-war. They were aided in enforcing this rule by the simultaneous decline of the Hanseatic League, which had dominated the Baltic, and by the preoccupation of the Dutch with the war with Spain. As the Thirty Years' War was promptly to show, on the other hand, the architects of the Danish state had made two serious mistakes. They crushed the lower classes instead of making them a force in the state, and at a time when surrounding states were becoming absolutisms they maintained an elective monarchy. This resulted in political power falling into the hands of a close body of nobles who failed to take the large view of affairs. As a consequence, the Danish state in 1525 was a land of declining peasants, a prosperous middle class that had no political power, and a self-seeking and shortsighted upper class that was closed against outsiders.

Upon the entrance of Denmark into the war in Germany, a strange and very remarkable man became a great factor in German affairs. He is known to history as Wallenstein (1583–1634). He was the son of an inconspicuous Protestant noble in Bohemia. After the death of his parents, he became a Catholic. He attended in turn a Jesuit college at Olmütz and the universities of Altdorf, Bologna, and Padua. In spite of his education he retained all his life a firm belief in astrology. He had visited at one time or another France, England, the Netherlands, and Italy. Early in life, he became a soldier and advanced in military rank without purchasing the positions that he held in the army. He had twice improved his situation by marriages, the first time to an elderly but wealthy widow and the second time to a woman belonging to a family which was quite influential in the councils of the Emperor. When the Thirty Years' War broke out, he was urged to throw in his lot with the Bohemian nobles; but instead of becoming a rebel, he remained loyal to the Emperor, took with him the treasure chest of the Bohemian estates, and equipped a regiment for his Imperial master. Although he did not participate in the battle of White Hill, he profited greatly by that event. He not only saved his own family lands but bought from the Emperor on easy terms extensive lands that had been confiscated from the Bohemian rebels. These territories, which included some fifty castles and villages in northern Bohemia, he formed into the duchy of Friedland, so-called from the castle of that name. He himself rapidly became in turn an Imperial count, a prince, and, finally, Duke of Friedland. At the time he became a national figure, we must think of him as being a tall, pale, thin man with reddish hair and pointed beard, brilliant eyes, and a proud and imperious manner, who seldom laughed and who worked hard, silently, and effectively, who had shown himself to be a great administrator, and who was capable of inspiring soldiers with confidence and enthusiasm.

In the crisis produced by the entrance of Denmark into the war, this remarkable man came forward with an extraordinary offer. Ever since the war had broken out, the Emperor had realized the disadvantage of having to depend for his successes on the military forces controlled by the Duke of Bavaria, at all times a potential rival. With the entrance of Denmark, this situation became not only irksome but really dangerous. In this crisis, Wallenstein came forward with an unusual offer. He promised to raise for the Emperor an army of his own without expense to the Imperial treasury. His plan called for systematic exploitation but careful expenditure of the resources of conquered provinces instead of the reckless and wasteful plundering that had hitherto prevailed; the plan included the regular payment of troops as well as the supplying of food, shelter, and equipment. The Emperor, for the moment, gratefully accepted Wallenstein's offer and soon had an army of 50,000 men at his disposal.

In the three campaigns which followed the formation of the new Imperial army, the weaknesses of the Protestant party quickly became apparent. England never paid the promised subsidy to Denmark. In 1626 the principal military forces of the Protestant party, the Danish army and the mercenaries commanded by Mansfeld, were quickly defeated at Dessau on the Elbe River and at Lutter in Brunswick by the forces of Tilly and Wallenstein. After these defeats, the Danish army slowly retreated toward Denmark and gave up one fortress after another until Jutland itself was finally occupied. Mansfeld, with the remnants of his army, withdrew through Silesia toward Hungary in the hope of joining forces with Gabriel Bethlen (1580–1629), Prince of Transylvania and leader of the Protestant party in Hungary. In this hope he was disappointed. Bethlen made peace with the Emperor, and Mansfeld took refuge in Bosnia, where he soon died.

These campaigns thus brought the war and its devastation to northern Germany. The forces of Tilly and Wallenstein occupied a vast territory from Denmark to Hungary, which for the first time suffered from the plundering and requisitions of the victorious Catholic armies. The success of the Catholic forces inspired Wallenstein with the only statesmanlike plans produced on the Catholic side by the Thirty Years' War. He hoped to use the military successes gained by the Imperial and Catholic forces to strengthen the power of the Emperor and to give him powers over Germany comparable to those exercised in their states by other rulers of the time. He also hoped to make the Emperor supreme in the Baltic. With this end in view, he occupied most of the Hanseatic cities and thus completed the destruction of that ancient league of maritime cities. His plans for supremacy in the Baltic, however, were thwarted by his failure to take Stralsund, a small Baltic port, which successfully withstood a five months' siege.

By 1629, however, Wallenstein had many enemies. Many persons resented the great powers which he exercised and the vast wealth which he possessed. By this time he had added to his personal possessions in Bohemia a large duchy in Silesia and the large state of Mecklenburg in northern Germany. In the name of the Emperor, he controlled most of Central Europe. Others appreciated his restoration of order but hated his requisitions. The Catholic princes of the league opposed his plans for strengthening the Empire just as strongly as did the Protestant leaders. In 1630 the long accumulating resentment against Wallenstein culminated in a demand of the Catholic princes for his dismissal. The alternative was a civil war. Faced by this crisis, the Emperor removed from office his great general just at a moment when, as later events proved, he needed him more than ever before.

The dismissal of Wallenstein was accompanied by an act, prompted by religious zeal, that proved to be a piece of the greatest political folly. In 1629 the Emperor issued the Edict of Restitution. The long threatened decree menaced the Protestants of northern Germany with the loss of scores of ecclesiastical estates and of many votes in the diet of the Empire. This measure tended to make the princes of northern Germany look with favor upon the intervention in German affairs of Sweden and its great king, Gustavus Adolphus.

The Swedish Period

While the Thirty Years' War was raging in Germany, the kingdom of Sweden had been carrying out its long-cherished plans for making the Baltic a Swedish lake. As early as the thirteenth century, Sweden had conquered approximately the territory now included in the Finnish state. After gaining its independence from Denmark, it had freed itself from the economic control of the Hanseatic League. When, in 1558, the independence of the Teutonic Knights was seriously threatened by the expansion of Russia, the Grand Master of the order appealed for aid to Sweden and Poland. This inaugurated a struggle that finally gave Sweden control of the provinces of Ingria, Estonia,

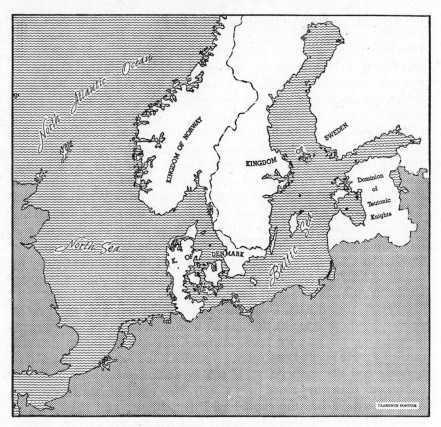

Northwestern Europe after 1620

and Livonia. This was followed by long and rather needless conflict with Poland in which dynastic and religious issues were at stake. During its course, Sweden became a military power to be reckoned with by reason of its introduction of the cantonal system of recruiting the army, a system that utilized the free peasants and made them an integral part of the Swedish state. By the truce concluded with Poland in 1629, Sweden increased its control of the Baltic by the acquisition for the time being of Elbing (the delta of the Vistula) and Braunsberg in West Prussia, and Pillau and Memel in East Prussia. With the right to occupy these places went the lucrative right to levy tolls on commerce. The next and logical step for Sweden in its Baltic policy was to gain control of the German coast line.

Much of the success of the Swedish state in making the Baltic a Swedish lake was due to its remarkable king, Gustavus II Adolphus (1594–1632). He had been carefully trained by his austere parents for his life work. He was unusually gifted in languages, as he used both Swedish and German as mother tongues; knew Latin, Italian, and Dutch by the time he was twelve; and later learned Spanish, Russian, and Polish. When he became sovereign in 1611, he found Sweden at war with Denmark, Russia, and Poland. As soon as possible, he signed advantageous treaties with the first two powers and devoted his attention and resources to the Polish conflict. This struggle was a sort of training ground for both the Swedish king and his army. Since the outbreak of that struggle, however, he had watched with increasing anxiety the course of events in the Thirty Years' War. As a Protestant, he naturally sympathized with that party in Germany; but as a Swedish ruler, he was more alarmed at the success of Wallenstein and Tilly in northern Germany and at the plans of the former for making the Emperor supreme in the Baltic. Upon the defeat of Denmark and its elimination from the war, he thought the time had come for Sweden to enter the conflict as champion of the Protestant party in behalf of Swedish national interests. The truce with Poland enabled Gustavus Adolphus to carry out this plan.

In 1630, accordingly, Gustavus Adolphus landed with an army of sixteen thousand men at the mouth of the Oder River, the natural highway for an advance into Germany. He had hoped to proceed cautiously. He needed control of provinces like Pomerania and Mecklenburg and the cooperation of the Protestant princes of northern Germany. This was gained only slowly. Not until he had threatened to bombard Berlin, the capital of Brandenburg, and the Catholic forces had stormed Magdeburg and invaded Saxony did the Protestant princes of northern Germany with the electors of Brandenburg and Saxony at their head venture to cooperate with the Swedish king. Finally, in 1631, strengthened by the forces of Protestant Germany and by a subsidy treaty concluded with France, Gustavus Adolphus was able to advance into the interior of Germany.

He marched into Saxony first with the purpose of driving out the army of Tilly. He found the Catholic forces near Breitenfeld, a short distance from Leipsig. The two armies, facing each other, represented two different principles of warfare. The mercenary troops of Tilly were a motley force, composed of Italians, Irishmen, Czechs, Croats, Danes, Spaniards, Walloons, Germans, and many others, who fought only for pay and plunder. The army of Gustavus Adolphus was, for the most part, a national army, composed of free peasants, who believed in the cause for which they were fighting. In the decisive battle which ensued, the troops of Tilly used the traditional tactics which had been followed by the armies of Western Europe since the battle of Pavia. The infantry massed together, ten rows

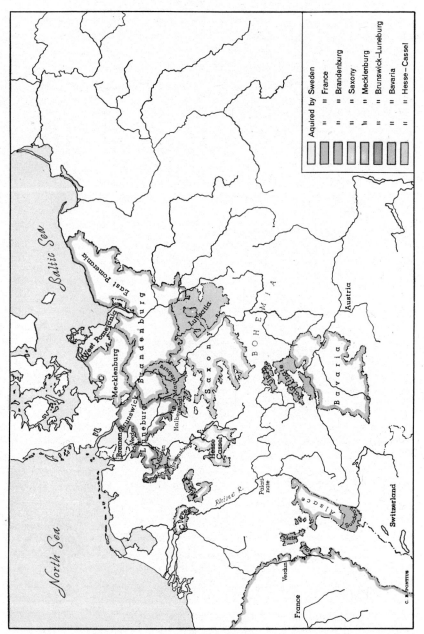

The Treaty of Westphalia

Aquired by Sweden
= France
= Brandenburg
= Saxony
= Mecklenburg
= Brunswick–Luneburg
= Bavaria
= Hesse–Cassel

North Sea

Baltic Sea

East Pomerania

West Pomerania

Mecklenburg

Brandenburg

Bremen

Verden

Brunswick

Luneburg

Minden

Schaumburg

Halberstadt

Magdeburg

Lusatia

Saxony

BOHEMIA

Hesse
Cassel

Rhine R.

Cleve

Mark

Palatinate

Austria

Bavaria

Alsace

Sundgau

Metz

Verdun

France

Switzerland

C. R. FOUNTUS

deep, still clad in pieces of heavy armor, depending mainly on the pikemen. They had some musketeers at the corners of the mass of pikemen. The cavalry was stationed on the wings. The Swedish infantry, but not those of their Saxon allies, were drawn up in two lines with a reserve. Instead of being in an oblong mass, the Swedish infantry was broken up into small, easily maneuvered brigades composed of pikemen and musketeers. The brigades of the two lines alternated like the squares of a checkerboard. The musketeers constituted a larger proportion of the Swedish than of the Imperial army and they were armed with a lighter musket, fired by a wheel instead of a match, which did not require a rest and which shot three or four times as rapidly as the musket used by Tilly.

The outcome of the battle of Breitenfeld was inevitable. The left wing of Tilly's army charged from the ridge along which the Imperial forces were drawn up but was driven off the field. Tilly's right wing had more success against the Saxons, but the victorious Swedish right wing occupied the initial position of the Imperial troops, seized their artillery, and then raked their right wing and center with their own guns. By sunset, the army of Tilly was in full retreat.

The crushing defeat of the Catholic forces at Breitenfeld put all Germany at the mercy of the victor. The advisers of the Swedish king were divided, as were later military critics, as to the use which should be made of the great victory. Some thought that Gustavus Adolphus should press on into the hereditary lands of the Emperor and take Vienna. Gustavus Adolphus, however, decided to march into southern Germany, into the lands of the princes of the Catholic League. From Saxony, accordingly, he proceeded with little opposition to Mainz, at the confluence of the Main and Rhine rivers, where he spent the winter of 1631–1632. In the following spring he advanced across the Lech, where Tilly was mortally wounded, and then pressed on to Munich, the capital of Maximilian (Duke of Bavaria and head of the Catholic League). For the moment, all Germany seemed to be at the mercy of the Protestant leader.

The decision of the Emperor to recall Wallenstein, however, promptly changed the situation. The Emperor obtained the services of the famous commander only by conceding to him almost unlimited powers. Thereupon, Wallenstein quickly raised a new army, drove the Elector of Saxony out of Bohemia, and then, instead of devastating his electorate, he offered the Saxon ruler peace on virtually his own terms. Threatened suddenly by the defection of one of his principal allies, Gustavus Adolphus abandoned Munich and hurried toward Saxony. In the Upper Palatinate he found the combined forces of Wallenstein and the Catholic League. Both of the famous commanders hesitated to bring the campaign to a decision. Each of them formed an entrenched camp and watched his opponent. At the end of two months, the lack of supplies and the threatened devastation of Saxony finally forced Gustavus Adolphus to abandon his camp at Nuremberg. This turn of events led to the battle of Lützen, which took place in Saxony.

Gustavus Adolphus came upon the army of his opponent at a moment when it was divided. A lieutenant of Wallenstein, Pappenheim, had led part of the latter's forces away from the main army. The cavalry of Pappenheim ultimately returned to take part in the battle, but his infantry were plundering a small castle when they were needed on the battlefield. This was also a battle between the traditional and the new tactics. While leading a countercharge over the fogbound battlefield, the Swedish commander was killed. In spite of this loss, however, the Swedes finally won the battle.

The defeated Wallenstein did not take as much advantage of the death of his great opponent as many thought he should have done. His motives and moves after the battle of Lützen are not entirely clear. He seems to have had plans for his own future and for that of the Empire which the Emperor neither understood nor approved. His aims can probably be summarized as religious toleration for Germany, destruction of the particularism of the individual states, unification of the Empire, and possibly some measure of personal aggrandizement such as the kingship of Bohemia. Secretly, he negotiated with all parties. Rumors concerning his plans alarmed the Emperor and the Catholic princes. The key to the situation was in the hands of Wallenstein's higher officers. Would they be willing to cooperate in his plans? When it came to a test, his officers refused to follow him. When the Emperor finally dismissed Wallenstein a second time, they allowed themselves to be won over to the idea of assassinating their former leader. In 1634, consequently, without the Emperor exactly ordering the deed to be done, some of Wallenstein's former officers killed their old commander.

In the meantime, the Swedes had tried to continue the war. Under various generals they kept up the struggle. None of these Swedish commanders, however, possessed the spark of genius which had characterized Gustavus Adolphus. His troops, too, were losing their unique character and were coming more and more to resemble the mercenary armies of the time in ideals and methods. They ceased to be invincible, and, in the same year that Wallenstein was assassinated, they suffered a crushing defeat at Nordlingen which destroyed the army of Gustavus Adolphus and lost southern Germany for the Protestant cause.

292

The French Period

The war might have ended at this point if it had not been for the direct intervention of Richelieu. For years, his subsidies had largely supported the Swedes in Germany. After their crushing defeat at Nordlingen, he felt that something more must be done if his aims were to be realized. The Habsburgs of Spain and Austria had not yet been crushed. France was not yet the dominant power in Europe. In 1635, accordingly, France declared war on Spain and actively entered the Thirty Years' War. This decision prolonged the war for fourteen years and made Germany a battleground for an international struggle among French, Spanish, Austrian, and Swedish armies.

Richelieu entered the war with plans that called for campaigns to acquire the Spanish Netherlands; the bishoprics of Metz, Toul, and Verdun; Alsace; and Roussillon. He wished also to gain control of northern Italy. At first, the raw inexperienced armies which he raised proved no match for the veterans of Spain. Gradually, however, they developed leaders of capacity, particularly Turenne and Condé, and learned the trade of war as carried on by the best armies of those times. At last, in 1643, in the Battle of Rocroy in northern France, they proved their superiority to the soldiers of Spain.

The fighting continued five more years. With the entry of France into the struggle, the original religious issues were largely forgotten. In 1635 even the Elector of Saxony not only made peace with the Emperor but entered the war on his side. The Swedes won and lost battles in northern Germany; the French, in the Rhine and Danube valleys. There was also fighting in the Netherlands, in Italy, and in Catalonia. The princes and people of Germany suffered helplessly from the plundering and murdering armies that year after year wandered through the already devastated land. In the main, the advantage in the closing campaigns was on the side of the French. Finally, in 1648, the war came to an end.

The Peace of Westphalia

For fourteen years efforts had been made by some of the states to get the representatives of the warring powers to negotiate a peace. The attempts were long thwarted in part by the attitude of Sweden and even more by that of France. The unwillingness of the Protestants to recognize the Pope in any way and questions of precedence also contributed toward delaying the assemblying of a peace congress. Finally, the powers agreed that the representatives of the Empire and France should meet at Münster and those of the Empire, Sweden, and the Protestant princes at Osnabruck, but that the two bodies of diplomats should consider themselves to be one congress, known from the name of the district in which it met as the Congress of Westphalia. The completed treaties were signed at Münster and are known as the Peace of Westphalia.

The Peace of Westphalia contained many important decisions. These included many significant territorial readjustments. Many states of the Empire acquired new provinces. Because of the skill of its new elector, Brandenburg obtained most of Pomerania, the bishoprics of Halberstadt, Minden, and Kamin, and the reversion of the archbishopric of Magdeburg. Saxony got Lusatia. Bavaria acquired the Upper Palatinate and the electorate which it had been given in 1623. The son of the unfortunate Frederick V, Charles Louis, regained the Lower Palatinate and a new eighth electorate. Two foreign powers, France and Sweden, obtained territories that gave them a voice in the affairs of the Empire. France acquired sovereignty in the three bishoprics which it had occupied since 1552 (Metz, Toul, and Verdun) and important rights in Alsace. The latter included the cession of the town of Breisack, the landgraviate of Upper and Lower Alsace, the Sundgau, the so-called advocacy of ten Imperial cities, and the right to fortify Philippsburg. By virtue of these acquisitions, France took the place of Austria in Alsace and obtained a position in the province which it was eventually to extend to complete control of Alsace. Sweden obtained Hither Pomerania, the bishopric of Verden, and the archbishopric of Bremen. These gains gave Sweden three votes in the Imperial diet, control of the mouths of the Oder, the Elbe, and the Weser rivers, and command of the Baltic and North seas. A separate treaty signed by the congress recognized the independence of the Swiss cantons and the United Netherlands. The general effect of the territorial provisions of the Treaty of Westphalia was to give the Empire an indefensible frontier.

The Peace of Westphalia also contained important constitutional provisions. It extended to the Calvinists the arrangements concerning religion concluded at Passau and Augsburg in 1552 and 1555. It bound the states of the Empire, with exception of the hereditary Habsburg lands, to permit private worship, liberty of conscience, and the right of emigration. These provisions were supposed, consequently, to apply to Alsace. The treaty annulled the Edict of Restitution which had been issued in 1629. It restored to those who held them in 1618 the Church lands, which for so long had been struggled for so eagerly in Württemberg, Baden, and the Palatinate. In other parts of the Empire, it restored them to those who had held them in 1624. These religious articles of the treaty, however, fell far short of creating in the Empire conditions similar to those which existed in England after 1689 or in France from 1598 to 1685.

The Peace of Westphalia was a long step toward that disintegration of the Empire which had been going on since the Middle Ages. It gave the states of the Empire the right to contract treaties with each other and with foreign powers. This provision made possible the growth of such powers as Bavaria, Austria, and Brandenburg, but virtually completed the destruction of the unity of the Empire.

The Effects of the Thirty Years' War

The diplomats, however, could not repair the havoc wrought by thirty years of war. Three decades of plundering and requisitions, the sacking of cities, and the raiding of villages had wrought terrible destruction throughout Germany. Tens of thousands had been killed in battle or murdered in plundering raids and the sacking of cities. Other thousands had starved to death. The population of the Empire is estimated to have declined during the long years of war from twenty million to six million inhabitants. Those who survived lost most of the things that constitute civilization. They found it useless to plant for others to reap or destroy. Much of rural Germany tended to revert to savagery. There was some cannibalism. Commerce and industry were at a standstill. The institutions of education and religion were destroyed. Germany ceased to contribute to science, art, and knowledge. Those who made any pretension to culture turned to France and often aped the worst features of French civilization.

Thus the failure of German society to reach a rational solution of its religious problems precipitated one of the most destructive wars of history. It began in Bohemia but spread to all parts of Germany. It started as a quarrel between two religious factions but grew into an international struggle of France, Sweden, Austria, and Spain on German territory. It was fought by armies that left nothing but death and destruction in their wake. After the war had ruined Germany and exhausted all the participants, the powers finally negotiated the important Peace of Westphalia which completed the destruction of the Empire and left it indefensible, gave Calvinists the same rights as Catholics and Lutherans, regulated the disposal of hotly contested Church lands, and made important territorial readjustments.

Rise of Prussia

In spite of the devastation wrought by the Thirty Years' War, some of the German states not only survived the disaster but con-

295

tinued to develop. Two of them, Prussia and Austria, became, in time, European powers of the first rank.

The kingdom of Prussia was the result of a long development. It grew out of one of the border districts established for the protection of the Holy Roman Empire, known as the North Mark. At first, it was a comparatively unimportant district situated in the flat, sandy, sparsely settled valleys of the Elbe and Oder rivers. There was little to distinguish it from other states. It slowly extended its boundaries and, in time, its ruler became one of the seven electors who chose the Emperor. His state became known as Brandenburg. In 1411, the electorate, by action of the Emperor, came into the possession of the Hohenzollern family. For several hundred years, however, there was nothing in the history of Brandenburg to attract special attention.

Early in the seventeenth century, though, the electors of Brandenburg made two important territorial acquisitions. In the years 1609 to 1614, by the threat of resorting to force, they made good their claims to the territories of Cleves, Mark, and Ravensburg, three non-contiguous territories situated in the valleys of the Rhine and the Weser rivers. In 1618 they acquired the territory known as East Prussia.

In 1226 the hard-pressed Poles had called in the Teutonic Knights, a semireligious, semimilitary order that developed in the time of the Crusades. In time, the knights had gained control of the whole Baltic coast from the Elbe River to the Gulf of Finland. In this region, the upper strata of society, the ruling, merchant, and professional classes were German; the lower classes belonged to the various Baltic peoples. In the fourteenth century the knights were at the height of their power. In the next century they began to decline. In 1466 they were forced to cede West Prussia to the Poles.

At the time that the Protestant Revolt swept over northern and central Germany, a member of the Hohenzollern family was Grand Master of the Teutonic Knights. He transformed the duchy of East Prussia into a secular state and became its hereditary ruler under the suzerainty of Poland. As was often done in Germany, the two Hohenzollern ruling houses of East Prussia and Brandenburg made an agreement later by which in case of the dying out of either line the other Hohenzollern family would inherit the territorial possessions of both houses. In accordance with this agreement, upon the extinction of the Hohenzollern family in East Prussia in 1618, the Hohenzollerns of Brandenburg inherited that duchy.

These two acquisitions had important consequences. The possessions of the electors of Brandenburg stretched clear across Germany. This forced the electors to take a wider view of German political affairs. The various territories of the electors, also, were likewise not contiguous. This dictated a policy calculated ultimately to unite their scattered territories into a single contiguous state.

It was not until 1640, however, that the electorate of Brandenburg began to attract attention. At the time he acceded to the throne, the elector, Frederick William (1620–1688), known as the Great Elector, was twenty years old. He had spent considerable time in the Netherlands, where he had attended the University of Leyden and had had a chance to observe both the policies of its ruling house, the House of Orange, and conditions in their prosperous country. He came back to his own state, therefore, with a well-stocked mind and a determination to do something for his country.

He found Brandenburg in a deplorable state. It had played a discreditable role in the Thirty Years' War. As a result, he found its population of one million and a half had been reduced to six hundred thousand, its cities had been sacked, its villages had been burned, its fields were uncultivated, its roads and bridges were destroyed, and its money was clipped and counterfeited. The whole state swarmed with foreign troops.

The first task of the Great Elector was to guide his state through the final stages of the Thirty Years' War. He cleared the state of foreign troops and obtained what advantages he could in the peace settlement. By skillful diplomacy, as we have seen, he acquired, at the time of the conclusion of the Peace of Westphalia, Eastern Pomerania, Magdeburg (1680), Halberstadt, Minden, and Kamin. These acquisitions substantially enlarged his state and reduced the distances separating his scattered territories.

Not long after the close of the Thirty Years' War, the Great Elector turned his attention to the problem of improving his situation in East Prussia. Over that part of his dominions, the king of Poland was still suzerain. This was galling to the Great Elector. In 1655 the outbreak of the Northern War between Sweden and Poland gave the Great Elector a chance to change his relations to the king of Poland. In turn, he was neutral and fought on both sides of the conflict. In the end, by playing one power off against another, he emerged from the struggle fully independent of both sovereigns.

The success of the Great Elector in diplomacy was owing in part certainly to his military policy. At the time of his accession, his army numbered only 2,500 men. Throughout his reign, he steadily built up his military forces. At the time of the signing of the Treaty of Westphalia in 1648, he had eight thousand men under arms. By the end of his reign, his army numbered twenty-four thousand men.

In medieval times, each of the territories included in the state of the Great Elector had a diet of some sort. Usually, it consisted of prelates and nobles and, in some cases, of representatives of the towns. These bodies greatly hampered the carrying out of the Great Elector's policies. In their actions, the provincial diets or estates were usually influenced by personal, class, and local interests. They opposed the wider plans of the Great Elector.

As soon as he could, accordingly, the Great Elector initiated a struggle to reduce the powers of these states and to get the political power in his various provinces into his own hands. He began the application of the new policy in Brandenburg. There, he had comparatively little difficulty in doing away with the troublesome estates. In 1653, because of the threatening Northern War, he succeeded in persuading the estates to make a money grant for the next six years. Thereafter, he never summoned them to meet again. A small committee maintained the fiction of the estates, and the Great Elector merely continued to collect the tax without authorization. At the same time, he succeeded in building up a body of loyal local officials in both town and country. In this way, he eliminated both the nobles and the towns as a check on the central government in Brandenburg.

The Great Elector did not meet with the same success in Cleves, Mark, and Ravensburg. The estates in these provinces managed to maintain a considerable amount of power and made good their contention that offices should go only to the native-born. The central government did win the right to raise and maintain garrisons in the duchies and the right of requiring regular and generous support for them.

The effort of the Great Elector to establish absolutism in East Prussia gave rise to an even more bitter struggle. In this province the estates exercised extensive privileges which deprived the elector of almost all authority. Until the Northern War the inhabitants of the duchy maintained their right to appeal to the Polish suzerain. As a result of these contentions, the province was in almost as great a state of anarchy as Poland. The ensuing struggle between the elector and the province was long and bitter. The Great Elector was forced to arrest and finally to execute some of his leading opponents. In the end, his firmness and persistence led to the disappearance of the East Prussian estates.

The Great Elector likewise did what he could to increase the prosperity of his state. Among other things, he caused the famous Frederick William Canal to be dug. The digging of this waterway connected the Oder and the Elbe rivers and made Berlin the center of water transportation between Central Europe and Hamburg. He also encouraged people from other states to settle in his state. At one time, he brought in seventy Frisian families who knew the improved agricultural methods of the Dutch. Another time, he settled eighty Swiss families in Brandenburg. He admitted Jews from Poland. After Louis XIV inaugurated his policy against the Huguenots, the Elector encouraged French refugees to come into the country. It is estimated that some 20,000 of them did come. They did much to improve economic and cultural life in Prussia.

In 1662 the Great Elector established his own postal system. The electoral system took the place of the Imperial system operated by the Counts of Thurn and Taxis. At first, the new Prussian postal system transmitted only official dispatches. Later, it carried letters and packages for other people and, finally, coach passengers. It aided much in the process of centralizing government by improving communication between Berlin and local officials.

In 1688, after many family quarrels, Frederick (1688–1713), the oldest son of the Great Elector and the third of his name, succeeded to the electoral throne. He lacked the practical sense of his father but displayed a passion for pomp and dignity and a love of the arts. The first trait finally won for him the title of king. The second characteristic led him to make Berlin a cultural as well as a political capital.

From the beginning of his reign, he strove to improve his position by acquiring a royal title. During his participation in the War of the League of Augsburg, he felt that his allies had not treated him with due consideration. He had watched with envy his fellow sovereign, the Duke of Brunswick, become Elector of Hanover and the Elector of Saxony, king of Poland. In 1700, however, a chance to improve his own position finally came. The Emperor needed troops for his intervention in the War of the Spanish Succession. Frederick III, accordingly, agreed to furnish 8,000 first class troops in return for the right to call himself king in Prussia. As a result, in the following year, he crowned himself king and was known thenceforth as Frederick I instead of Frederick III. Before long, he began to be known as king of rather than in Prussia, and the name Prussia was gradually applied to the whole state ruled by the Hohenzollerns.

As has been mentioned, Frederick I did quite a little for the arts. He did much to make Berlin one of the great European capitals. Besides fortifying it, he did something for fire protection and street lighting and opened new districts to settlement. He, likewise, founded what eventually became the great Prussian state library and the Berlin Academy. Aided by his charming but somewhat superficial wife, he brought to Berlin Dutch and French engineers, architects, painters, and musicians. He also persuaded the many-sided Leibnitz to come to live at Berlin.

The Austrian Habsburg State in the Seventeenth Century

The defeat of Hungary by the Turks in 1526 made the new state, collected by Prince Ferdinand, the brother of Charles V, a frontier district. It continued to be in this position during most of the seventeenth century. This made Vienna a frontier fortress and the inhabitants of such districts as Transylvania and Royal Hungary men with the virtues and vices of frontier men.

At the beginning of the seventeenth century, the Emperor was taking part in a long, confused conflict that became known as the Long War (1593–1606) which involved not only the Emperor but the Turks, Transylvania, and Moldavia. It ended in the defeat of Transylvania and the inauguration of a reign of terror that virtually ruined the country. The representative of the Emperor tried to make Transylvania both German and Catholic. In both Transylvania and Royal Hungary, the Imperial officers took most of the property of the nobles. In the end, no one's property was safe.

Among those unjustly threatened was Stephen Bocskay (1557–1606), a rich and powerful Transylvanian nobleman who up to that time had been a friend of the Emperor. The attempt to blackmail him turned him into a national deliverer. For a short time (1605–1606) he was Prince of Transylvania. During his brief period of rule, he concluded two important agreements, the Peace of Vienna and the Truce of Zsitvatorok. These obtained for the Hungarian people religious liberty, political autonomy, restoration of confiscated estates, the repeal of unrighteous judgments, retroactive amnesty for all Magyars in Hungary, and recognition of Bocskay as an independent sovereign of an enlarged Transylvania. The Truce of Zsitvatorok gave the Emperor and the Sultan peace for twenty years. The Treaty of Vienna was looked upon, henceforth, as the basis for Hungarian claims to political and religious freedom.

The next fifty years are looked upon as the golden age of Transylvania. During most of that time the principality had able leaders. For thirty years the attention of the Emperor was diverted and absorbed by the conflict raging in Germany over religion. The Turks ceased for a time to be a danger. This situation gave the rulers of Transylvania a chance to make their capital a Protestant Mecca. They had only to threaten an attack to bring the Emperor to observe the political and religious rights of the Magyars.

The defeat of Austria in the Thirty Years' War turned the attention of the Emperor even more from his Eastern border. For a time it looked as if the Emperor was going to gain control of the whole Empire. The intervention of Gustavus Adolphus, however, led to the defeat of the Emperor and compelled him to cede his rights in Alsace to France and his remaining Imperial authority to the states of the Empire. Henceforth, his Imperial title gave him some prestige but no power, and he and his successors devoted themselves more and more to Austrian interests.

The most important of these was the Turkish struggle. The conflict with Turkey came to a crisis in 1683. Many Hungarians had become discontented because of the Austrian attempts to persecute the Protestants of Hungary and to suppress the Hungarian constitution. In 1683, at the invitation of these malcontents, the Turks burst into Hungary and advanced to the very walls of Vienna. The city was saved from capture only by the intervention of the king of Poland at the head of a national army. This campaign proved to be the high point of Turkish achievement. A series of successes finally drove the Turks south of the Danube, and led to the signing in 1699 of the Treaty of Karlowitz. By this agreement, Austria regained all Hungary except the Banat of Temesvar.

Simultaneously with these successes, the Emperor effected certain important changes in the organization of the congeries of territories that are called Austria. In 1672 the Emperor raised troops which formed the nucleus of a standing army and were never disbanded. In a diet held at Pressburg in 1687 and 1688, the Hungarian crown was made hereditary in the House of Habsburg. Finally, in 1697, Transylvania was united to the Hungarian monarchy. In the meantime, Vienna had gradually evolved from a frontier fortress into one of the most brilliant capitals of Europe.

Like Louis XIV, however, the Emperor was tempted to try to obtain the succession in Spain for his second son, Archduke Charles (1685–1740). In 1703 he was solemnly proclaimed King of Spain. He then made his way to Spain where he acquired a considerable following in Catalonia. He stayed in Spain and contested the Spanish throne with Philip of Anjou, the grandson of Louis XIV, until 1711. In that year, his brother Joseph died, and he became emperor and ruler of the various Austrian lands. His allies, particularly England and Holland, however, had no more desire to see Austria and Spain united under one ruler than France and Spain. Accordingly, they finally forced the stubborn Charles VI of Austria to divide the Spanish inheritance with his rival. By the Treaty of Utrecht, consequently, Austria acquired the Spanish Netherlands (henceforth to be known as the Austrian Netherlands) and the duchy of Milan, Naples, and

Sardinia in Italy. These acquisitions made Austria thereafter an Italian power.

Southern Hungary, however, was somewhat depopulated and still open to attacks from the Turks. The Emperor solved the problem of defence by settling 30,000 Southern Slavs in the region. He offered them, as an inducement to immigrate, a certain degree of autonomy and recognition of the Greek Orthodox Church.

The seventeenth century thus practically completed in Central Europe a process that had been going on for a long time. In the Holy Roman Empire the Thirty Years' War transferred nearly all the remaining political authority from the Empire to the individual states. In these years, as a consequence, the comparatively small state of Brandenburg developed into the relatively large and powerful state of Prussia; and the congeries of territories acquired by one means or another by the Habsburg family became Austria, a European power of the first rank. All the numerous states of the Empire, henceforth, acted as independent powers. They concentrated their attention wholly on their supposed interests and largely disregarded the welfare of the Empire.

CHAPTER 19

Cultural Achievements of the Seventeenth Century

The seventeenth century was a period of political and religious turmoil in some of the most important states of Western Europe. It was marked by the turbulence of the French nobles up to the accession of Louis XIV, a parliamentary and religious struggle in England, and the destructive Thirty Years' War in Germany. In spite of these obstacles, it was a period of achievement in education, painting, architecture, music, and philosophy.

Education

In education the century produced at least one notable figure, John Amos Comenius (1592–1672). He was born in Moravia but was forced by the troubles of the time to move frequently from one country to another. The Thirty Years' War first drove him to Poland. There he wrote on education and compiled a series of graded textbooks. From Poland he was called to England, where he found his efforts blocked by the outbreak of the Puritan Revolution. Leaving England, he went to Sweden, where he edited a series of Swedish textbooks. By 1648 he was back in Poland. There he prepared the first, and for a long time the only, illustrated textbook for children, which may be called *The World in Pictures*. By 1650 war had driven him again from Poland. He found refuge in Holland, where he lived the rest of his life.

He saw the need of education for everyone. He considered it an essential condition for the attainment of the universal freedom which he sought. Consequently, he advocated education for even the neglected lower classes and arranged a course of study which extended from infancy to manhood. In the earlier years at least, instruction was to be given in the vernacular.

In France and Germany a new type of school arose. The new institutions were designed to educate young gentlemen and fit them for life. Not only Latin but modern languages, especially French and Italian, were taught. There was instruction in the comparatively new subjects of practical mathematics, history, geography, and jurisprudence. Attention was also paid to training in such accomplishments as fencing, riding, hunting, and dancing.

In Catholic countries education was to a large extent in the hands of the Jesuits. Their schools were generally acknowledged to be excellent. They were so good that even Protestants often sent their children to them. Their teachers were carefully trained.

Painting

In the seventeenth century Italy continued to inspire contemporary painters but ceased to produce great works of art. In most of Italy this was true as early as the middle of the sixteenth century; in Venice it was the case after 1590. The Italians had solved many artistic problems and had secularized painting. By the end of the century the artistic movement which had achieved so much seemed to have spent itself completely. Thereafter, the great painters were to be found in Spain and the Netherlands. Many of them, however, continued to owe much to Italy. Most of them traveled to the Italian Peninsula and spent some years studying the works of the great Italian masters as a necessary preparation for their own work.

In Spain the seventeenth century was characterized by the rise of three outstanding painters. Among these the greatest was undoubtedly Velasquez (1599–1660). He was born at Seville in southern Spain. He seems to have been well grounded in languages and philosophy as well as painting. We are told that he copied carefully the commonest things and made a special study of the human face. This is shown by his so-called "tavern" pieces. In this way he won for himself an assured place in the artistic circles of Seville. In 1622, armed with letters of introduction, he went to Madrid, the capital of Spain. There, he was fortunate enough to attract the attention of Olivares, for the time being the all-powerful minister of Philip IV. Through this minister, he attracted the attention of the king, who, like many other members of his family, was a bad sovereign but a good patron of art; for nearly forty years, Velasquez spent his time painting portraits of the king and other members of the royal family. From his brush we have pictures which show the pale, lackluster face, the flowing hair, the curled moustaches, and the heavy projecting Habsburg underlip of the king; the haughty, strong features of Olivares; the youthful and beloved heir to the throne, Don Balthasar Carlos; and many other members of the royal family and the court. From time to time, the monotony of court life was broken, as when in 1628, for example, Velasquez, the greatest Spanish painter, had the pleasure of showing the art treasures of Madrid to the great Flemish painter, Rubens. In 1649 Velasquez went to Italy where, at the royal command, he purchased statuary; copied, bought, and painted pictures; and studied the artistic treasures of the peninsula. He saw, but apparently did not admire, the pictures of Raphael. In 1660, at the time of the famous marriage of the young Louis XIV and the *infanta* Maria Theresa, a marriage contracted in the hope of insuring the peace of 1559, Velasquez had the honor of decorating the Spanish pavillon erected on an island in the Bidassoa River.

It has been said that Velasquez was as Spanish in the field of painting as Cervantes in the field of literature. He painted, however, only what he saw. His men and women almost seem to breathe. His horses and dogs are full of life and action. He had a mastery of expression, insight into character, and the power to place his subjects on canvas. He painted in glowing color the flesh of his subjects. He conformed to the Spanish prejudice against painting women other than queens and *infantas*. Strangely enough, Velasquez had to wait until the nineteenth century for the recognition outside of Spain which he so richly deserved. Only in the nineteenth century was he discovered by an English ambassador who had enough leisure to study the artistic treasures of Madrid.

The story of Murillo (1617–1682) is quite different from that of Velasquez. He, too, came from Seville but from a humble family. He attracted attention by his sketches and was apprenticed to a distant relative who taught him the rudiments of painting. Early thrown on his own resources, he seems to have supported himself by painting pictures which were sold at the fairs. In 1642, when he planned to go to Italy to study, he was befriended by Velasquez and was enabled to see the masterpieces of Italy and Spain without leaving the Iberian Peninsula. Returning to Seville, he began to paint pictures for the monks of a small cloister. His pictures brought him fame and, in 1648, marriage with a lady of rank and wealth. Throughout his life he found subjects among the lowly and in religion; and as a patron, the Church. He has always been one of the most popular of Spanish painters.

A third great Spanish painter, Ribera (1588–1656), spent most of his life in Italy. Quite early he made his way to Rome where he studied and painted. After spending some time in Parma and other artistic centers, he found a patron in a rich picture dealer of Naples. He spent the rest of his life there. He obtained commissions from both the Spanish viceroy and Philip IV of Spain. He is said to have collaborated with two other painters to establish a sort of monopoly at Naples to crowd out competitors. Critics term him a Spaniard in his choice of subjects and an Italian in his execution.

In the Netherlands, in painting, as in so many other things, a distinction must be made between the northern and the southern provinces. In the southern Netherlands, one of the greatest painters of all time, Peter Paul Rubens (1577–1640), lived and worked. Though of Flemish stock, he was born in Westphalia but was taken to Antwerp when only a year old. He was early apprenticed to a painter, and in 1598 he was recognized as a master by the gild of painters. The years from 1600 to 1608 he spent in the household of the Duke of Mantua. He was sent by this patron to both Rome and Spain. Returning to the Netherlands on account of his mother's health, he was forced by his sovereigns, Albrecht and Isabella, to remain there. He then entered their employ, a position which relieved him of gild restrictions. The religious struggle had stripped many of the church edifices of their sacred pictures. Rubens was employed in repairing the damage, but he did not confine himself to religious subjects. By this time, he was famous and had many pupils. In much of the work attributed to Rubens, his numerous students had a part.

Though he was to a large extent a painter of religious subjects, his pictures were more earthy than spiritual. He was fond of vast designs. His figures were the rather solid men and women of his time and of his country. His pictures, therefore, were characterized by their sensuous qualities and are full of blood, bone, and muscle. He is considered to be in painting one of the great technicians of all time.

His activity was not confined to painting nor to the Netherlands. On one occasion he was commissioned to paint twenty-four pictures for Marie de Medici and the Luxemburg palace. After 1621, he was much engaged in diplomatic negotiations which took him to Spain and England. Cambridge University gave him a master's degree, and Charles I of England conferred knighthood upon him. He was one of those delegated to meet Marie de Medici at the border of the Netherlands when she was driven out of France by the inexorable Richelieu. Until his death, Rubens retained the favor of his own rulers.

Rubens' most famous pupil was Van Dyck (1599–1641). Born at Antwerp, he was, at the early age of nineteen, admitted as a full member of the gild of painters. After working with Rubens for some time, he spent five years in Italy. After his return, he settled in London, where he found a patron in Charles I, and where he spent most of his remaining years. His facile brush has recorded in a noble manner Charles I, his queen (Henrietta Maria), and many other distinguished people of the time.

The seventeenth century produced many other excellent painters in the southern Netherlands. In a book of this compass, most of them cannot even be mentioned. One of them, David Teniers the Younger (1610–1690), almost takes rank with Rubens and Van Dyck. There are said to be some nine hundred pictures from his brush. After 1644 he found employment, both as a painter and as a keeper of his collection of paintings, with the Archduke Leopold, governor of the Netherlands. He succeeded in living as a gentleman but never obtained the noble rank which he sought. He was especially a master of open-air pictures. He was one of the first painters to find the common people of his country fit subjects for his brush.

After they obtained their independence, the Dutch blazed for themselves a new artistic path. They did not adorn their churches with great masterpieces as the Roman Catholic countries did. They seldom sought subjects in history or mythology. Instead, they took themselves as the subject of their paintings. As a result, we have landscapes and quiet interiors, portraits of private individuals and prominent officials, families and citizen soldiers, still-life and smokers, card players and drinkers. As in the case of the southern Netherlands, painters of merit are so numerous that most of them cannot even be mentioned.

One of the artists who cannot be omitted is Frans Hals (1580–1666). As an individual, he was not very admirable. He was improvident, mistreated his first wife, drank too much, and associated with low company. In 1652 a lawsuit brought him to absolute penury. As a painter, he takes rank only a little below Rembrandt. He took as his subjects all strata of society. He lacked the psychological insight of Velasquez or Rembrandt, but he was a master in his handling of light and in the portrayal of expression.

The greatest of the Dutch painters was Rembrandt (1606–1669). From childhood, he wanted to be a painter. In 1631 he was called from his native Leyden to Amsterdam. There, he had many commissions and became the first portrait painter of the city. He painted pictures of himself, his wife, and everyone around him. His wife brought him a large dowry, and for many years he was in more than comfortable circumstances and was able to gather in his large home a notable collection of paintings. Later, he became virtually bankrupt, outlived his popularity, and was forced to live in very modest quarters.

He had most of the qualities needed to make a great painter. He had an original mind, a lively imagination, and a great sympathy for his subjects. He used light and shade boldly and color subtlely. The result is a long list of great pictures. Among his more famous works are his pictures of himself, his wife, the *Lesson in Anatomy,* and the *Night Watch.*

The Dutch school produced many other excellent painters. Ter Borch (1617–1681) is well known for his portraits, especially of persons belonging to the wealthy and cultured classes and for his picture of the part of the Congress of Westphalia that met at Münster. Steen (1626–1679) is remembered for his stately interiors, tavern scenes, feasts, and festivals. Hooch (1629–1678) painted drawing rooms and cottages, housewives and cooks, clothes and furniture. Jacob Ruisdail (1628–1681) is valued for his landscapes. Paul Potter (1625–1654) is prized for his portrayal of fine animals. Each of the artists contributed richly to our knowledge of Dutch life in the seventeenth century.

In the seventeenth century, France, in contrast to the Netherlands, did not produce many first-class painters. In the reign of Louis XIII only two need be mentioned, Nicolas Poussin (1594–1665) and Claude of Lorraine (1600–1682). The former, after studying in Italy, found employment in France with Richelieu and Louis XIII, especially at Versailles and in the Louvre. The second was an indifferent painter of the human figure but achieved fame for his landscapes because of his careful study of nature.

Under Louis XIV, Charles Le Brun (1619–1690) best expressed the spirit of the age. After studying in Italy, he returned to France, where he ingratiated himself with Mazarin and Colbert. In 1648, Colbert and Le Brun founded the French Academy of Painting and Sculpture. In 1660, they purchased for Louis XIV the Gobelin plant and transformed it into a great institution for the manufacture of tapestries and furniture for the royal palaces. As director, Le Brun had great influence on the taste of the period. In 1662 he was ennobled and was given a large pension. During the rest of his life, he was busy with commissions from the king, corporations, and private individuals. He superintended the decoration of the Chateau of Versailles and other edifices built by the king.

Architecture

By the beginning of the century, the forces that had developed Renaissance styles of architecture had spent themselves. Men no longer dreamed of a literal resurrection of pagan Rome. In place of the Roman Empire arose the absolute monarchies of Western Europe and the Catholic Reformation. Absolutism made possible the development of court life and the establishment of domestic security. The Catholic Reformation inaugurated a new period of church building. These developments gave the architects an opportunity to show their skill in the designing and construction of royal palaces, villas, chateaux, and great country houses, city hotels, and innumerable churches.

To meet this demand, new architectural forms developed. The use of classic forms continued, but they were not mere imitations of the buildings of the Renaissance and ancient times. The definition of what constituted a classic form was changing. Domes and columns, cornices and string courses, and architraves and pediments were still used but in new ways. Another of the forms widely adopted is known as the Baroque style. The new style was complex and extravagant. The architects felt free to take great liberties in the planning and decoration of buildings. Facades were no longer necessarily constructed as a single plane. Cartouches were substituted for simple shields and panels. Twisted columns, colored marbles, and gilding were widely employed. Quoins were used at corners and around windows. Stucco was employed as a building material.

The new architectural tendencies are embodied in the work of certain great architects. In France, at least three should be mentioned. The first is Jacques Lemercier (1585–1660). After studying architecture for some time, he had the good fortune to attract the attention of the all-powerful minister, Richelieu, who employed him to design many great edifices. In 1624 he was commissioned to make extensive additions to the great French palace of the Louvre at Paris. Later, he designed for the cardinal the palace now known as the Palais Royal, as well as the Church of the Sorbonne (where Richelieu later was buried), and a new chateau. In order to give the new chateau the proper setting, Lemercier was commissioned to rebuild the village of Richelieu.

Another architect who left his mark on France was François Mansart (1598–1666), a contemporary of Lemercier and a member of a noted family of architects. He designed his first chateau at the early age of twenty-eight. Eventually, he drew up the plans for many chateaux and churches. His greatest monument is one of the wings of the Chateau of Blois, which he designed for the notorious Gaston of Orleans.

His grandnephew, known as Jules Hardouin Mansart (1643–1708), was also a famous architect. He designed many town and country houses and planned and supervised the erection of such famous sections of Paris as the Place Vendome and the Place des Victoires. He likewise designed the dome of the Invalides of Paris. He failed to a certain extent in the building that gave him his greatest opportunity, the Chateau of Versailles. He gave the great palace no central dominating feature, or other fine dimensions like enclosed courtyards. Neither is he responsible for the famous gardens around the chateau which are the work of Le Notre (1613–1700). Somewhat later in the reign of Louis XIV, Mansart designed for the king the Grand Trianon, a smaller palace near the greater chateau.

In England two architects left an unmistakable mark on English architecture. The first was Inigo Jones (1573–1651). He was the son of a cloth-worker, but his talent for drawing attracted the attention of the Earl of Arundel. Through the aid of his patron he went to Italy to study landscape painting but soon changed to architecture. In this branch of art he quickly won a reputation that brought him in 1604 an invitation to Denmark. There, he is credited with having designed two great palaces. In 1605 he accompanied Anne of Denmark, the new queen of England, back to his native land. He became what was then known as surveyor general of royal buildings. He designed a number of other famous English buildings.

An even more noted English architect of the seventeenth century was Sir Christopher Wren (1632–1723). After finishing his studies at Oxford, he became a professor of astronomy, first at Gresham College and later at Oxford. It is, however, as an architect that he is chiefly known and remembered. For this profession, the great London fire of 1666 gave him an unequaled opportunity. He is credited with having designed fifty churches to take the place of burned church edifices. He showed particular invention and taste in his spires. He was at the same time adept in economizing material. His greatest church was St. Paul's Cathedral. In addition to his churches, he designed many other buildings. His work brought him knighthood in 1673 and many other honors.

Music

During the century, music held first place among the arts. This period saw the development of opera and the oratorio and a wider use of musical instruments, particularly the organ and the violin. The seventeenth century, therefore, saw the development of many of the ideas on which music has since been living.

In a sense, the invention of the opera was unexpected. In the latter part of the sixteenth century, a group of cultivated men at Florence began to study the music of the ancient Greeks and its use in connection with the drama. In 1597 their study and experimentation resulted in the presentation at a private house at Florence of the first opera. This opera has been lost. The new musical form, however, proved to be so popular that an opera, which has been preserved, formed in 1600 part of the festivities at the marriage of Henry IV and Marie de Medici.

Instead of reviving Greek music, the group at Florence opened a new musical era. The new form of music spread rapidly, first over Italy, and later, into France, Germany, and England. Until 1637 operas were given only in the homes of private persons of sufficient wealth to afford the expensive costumes, scenery, and accessories required in operatic performances. At that date the first public opera house was opened at Venice. Other Italian cities quickly imitated Venice. By the end of the century all the principal cities of the peninsula had opera houses.

The rise of the opera had a number of important effects. It opened new careers to singers and managers. It fostered the rise of a large group of composers. By 1700 the latter are said to have produced seven hundred operas in Italy alone. The opera also gave rise to the development of orchestras.

Italian musicians, moreover, visited and emigrated to other countries—particularly France, Germany, and England—and took to them the new musical form. The leading figure in French opera was the Italian, Lully. Having caught the attention of the Duke of Guise, he was taken to France where he became in turn a kitchen boy, a member of Louis XIV's private band, and, finally, court composer. His development of the ballet made him a favorite of the king. After the opening of the first French opera house in 1672, he devoted his attention to the production of operas.

In Germany the opera found patronage among the ruling princes, particularly the courts of Vienna, Dresden, and Munich. In 1651 Munich erected its first public opera house. Other German cities quickly followed its example. There was no opera in the German language, however, until 1690, and no opera house in Berlin until 1742.

In England the forerunner of the opera was the masque. This dramatic form flourished under both the early and the later Stuarts. The Puritans, because of their aversion to elaborate church music and the theatre, opposed them. Many famous English writers devoted their talents to composing them. Of these, Ben Jonson was the best known.

At the same time, the musical form known as the oratorio was being developed. It was created by a choirmaster who served at churches in Assisi and Rome. At first, it differed from the opera only in subject and text. Later, Carissimi (1604–1674) put aside costume and scenery, gave the dramatic details to a narrator, and emphasized the chorus.

Up until this time, musical instruments had occupied a subordinate place. The human voice played the principal role in musical performances. From this time, however, musical instruments, particularly the organ and the violin, became more conspicuous. The organ itself underwent a considerable development. The ability to play the new instrument became more common, and this in turn stimulated the composition of music for it. In time, the organ accompaniment became a matter of course.

311

While the organ reached its highest development in Germany, the violin was a product of northern Italy. It evolved from the latter part of the sixteenth century to the early part of the eighteenth century. The chief centers of production were Brescia and Cremona. In these cities there developed famous violin makers who often handed down the fine points of the craft from father to son. Among these craftsmen, Stradivarius (1644–1737) is probably the most important.

Philosophy

In this century only a few countries made contributions toward philosophical thinking. Even in these, thoughtful men were much disturbed and hindered by the course of political events. Few had the time or the opportunity to think about intellectual problems.

In England most of the thinking of the period ran along political lines. The attention of the English people was almost wholly absorbed by the great political and religious struggles of the century. As a result, England produced at this period only three philosophers of distinction.

First in point of time was Francis Bacon (1561–1626). After entering the legal profession, he found, in spite of his influential relatives, many obstacles to his advancement. After the accession of James I, however, his position rapidly improved. He held in turn the positions of attorney general, privy councillor, and chancellor. During his rise to power, he wrote works which gave him a permanent position in both literature and philosophy. After obtaining the highest legal post in the government, however, disaster overtook him. He was charged with taking money from persons who had cases in his court, and he lost both his post in the government and his property.

There is still much debate as to the place of Bacon in the history of philosophy. To some, it appears that the two parts of his *Instauratio Magna* (1620–1623) laid the foundations of modern philosophy. In reality, he seems to have had little realization of the importance of his scientific contemporaries and little influence on the philosophers of the time. The sole exception to this is his *New Atlantis* which is credited with having led to the founding of the Royal Society nearly forty years later. His importance lies in the fact that he used his high position and remarkable personality to lead the movement against the old scholastic methods of the theologians and encouraged men to expect wonderful things from the employment of scientific methods.

He emphasized the idea that knowledge is power. He discarded religious intuition as a source of knowledge and warned of the danger of depending on books. He taught instead that knowledge should be useful and should be employed to make man superior to nature. He pointed out the significance of such discoveries as gunpowder, the printing press, and the compass in transforming society, but he thought that in the future man should not depend on chance for discoveries but on a conscious method.

In Bacon's judgment, the correct method for the attainment of knowledge had two aspects. It involved a criticism of the past undertaken with the object of getting rid of our prejudices (or idols, to use Bacon's own phraseology) and the construction of a scientific method of work. In his criticism of the past he emphasized four sources of prejudice: the presuppositions common to the human race, individual prejudices due to one's disposition or situation in life, prejudices of the form which arise from the substitution of words for ideas, and prejudices which we accept without criticism. In constructing a scientific method for the acquisition of knowledge, on the other hand, Bacon thought that there must be an exhaustive collection of particular instances, an analysis and comparison of these instances, and a discovery of the real nature of the phenomenon. By the use of these methods, Bacon foresaw a great future for the human race.

Francis Bacon once had a young secretary, Thomas Hobbes, who also became famous as a political philosopher. After attending Oxford, he became a tutor in the powerful Cavendish family, a connection which proved to be lifelong. In 1610, he made the grand tour of the continent and learned Italian and French and saw something of the new scientific methods. About 1629, he turned his attention to political philosophy. After 1640, he was much influenced by the political struggle which stirred England. He fled to Paris where he stayed eleven years. For two years of this time, he attempted to instruct the future Charles II. In 1651 he published his famous work, *Leviathan, or the Matter, Form and Power of a Commonwealth, Ecclesiastical and Civil.* It had for a frontispiece a giant made up of small human beings. This work made him at the same time the most lauded and the most decried thinker of his time and brought about his return to London. After the restoration, his ideas became fashionable and he was pensioned by his old pupil, Charles II.

To Hobbes, the physical world was a mechanism. This conception was true of the mental as well as the physical world. He taught that all that exists is body and all that occurs is motion. He did not try to deal with the supernatural. He thought there were two kinds of bodies: the natural and the artificial. The natural bodies, in his

313

opinion, belonged to the physical world; the artificial bodies are the institutions of society, like the state. He, therefore, divided his philosophy into physics, psychology, and politics.

To Hobbes, psychology was concerned with the movements of the brain. He thought that one could have no real knowledge of the external world but only of the results of external motion. Brain movements were reactions to, not copies of, the external world. The only knowledge man could have is knowledge of brain sensations. Knowledge, in other words, is purely subjective.

In the field of politics, he taught that individuals are the source of the state. In his natural state man had no other impulse than that of self-preservation. Self-interest, nevertheless, gave rise to the state. War against every man was in reality self-destructive. So man formed the political state to avoid destruction of himself. Men made a compact with each other whereby each relinquished a portion of the rights which he claimed in order to have the rest of his rights secure. To give security to this compact, man gave himself a sovereign. In a monarchy, the sovereign is represented by the king; in a republic, by an assembly. To this sovereign the people owe obedience. Might, however, makes right. Whatever the state commands is right. There was no right or wrong in nature. Even the religion of the people should be determined by the state. Any political state is better than revolution.

A third great English philosopher of the century was John Locke (1632–1704). He came of Puritan stock and studied at Oxford while that party was in power. He seems to have been alienated somewhat by the intolerance of the Presbyterians and the fanaticism of the Independents. For some years after graduation from Oxford, he was a tutor in that university. About 1666 he became secretary of Lord Ashley (the later Earl of Shaftesbury and one of the most prominent political figures of the time), a position which he was to hold for fifteen years. This brought him into contact with public men and acquainted him with the springs of political action and the duties of high office. From 1675 to 1679, after the fall of his patron from power, Locke was in France where he met many prominent men. In 1683, the fortunes of politics compelled him to take refuge in Holland, where he came in contact with other English exiles and with the future rulers of England. Upon the fall of James II, Locke followed William of Orange to England.

Until this time, he seems to have done much thinking but little writing. Then, suddenly, late in life he embodied his ideas in a series of works that made him a European celebrity. His first publication was the first of four letters which he ultimately wrote on the subject of religious toleration, one of the burning political issues of the moment. This was followed in quick succession by two *Treatises on Government,* his famous *Essay Concerning Human Understanding,* and considerable writing on education and religion. During the last fourteen years of his life, he held, at times, minor offices under the new government but made his home with a friend, Sir Francis Masham, whose family tenderly cared for Locke in his declining years.

Locke's ideas about toleration are based on his ideas about human understanding. He had a very modest estimate of man's capacity for arriving at true judgments in religion. He did not believe that man could reach more than probability in such matters, and he felt that belief must be based on evidence and that persecution merely produced hypocrites. He thought that no one had a right to control what his neighbors believed and that faith must be founded on reasonableness. Locke had no objection to a national church but thought that it should be broad enough to include most of the nation. He would refuse full toleration to the atheist and to Roman Catholics, to the latter because of their allegiance to a foreign sovereign.

In the field of education, Locke is one of the classic writers. Though his writings appeared over two hundred years ago, they have a very modern sound. He thought the main purpose of education was not the collection of facts but the formation of useful character. He felt that the part played by habit must always be kept in view. He emphasized the dependence of intelligence and character on health. He even believed that the educational process should make children happy as well as educated. He stressed the importance of having the young look for evidence rather than merely to accumulate facts.

Locke's *Essay Concerning Human Understanding* is one of the most famous works in modern philosophical literature. He felt that man's failure to comprehend himself and his environment was due to his extension of his inquiries into matters beyond the reach of human understanding. Locke, on the other hand, aimed to find only the origin, certainty, and extent of human knowledge. He knew that man fell short of a perfect comprehension of the universe but, at the same time, believed that man had sufficient knowledge for practical purposes. He felt that knowledge came through the acquisition of ideas but that no ideas were innate. He believed that human ideas were the result of experience, but that some things are true is evident from common sense. Man's ideas, even the most abstruse, though, all come from the five senses or from reflection. He thought that was the origin of ideas like space, time, personal identity, and causality.

Simple ideas, of course, are often elaborated into very complex ideas. He asserted that knowledge is based upon our perception of the relation of ideas, their agreement or disagreement. Some are self-evident, others demonstrable. God can be known only through faith. Man has no real knowledge of external things. He only knows his own consciousness.

The most influential philosopher of the century was the Frenchman, René Descartes (1596–1650). He was educated at a Jesuit school but early showed a tendency to distrust his teachers. After leaving school, he went to Paris where he became something of a recluse. In 1617, he saw military service in Holland with Maurice of Orange and, later, in the Bavarian army. Still later, he visited Hungary, Poland, Germany, and Italy. In the meantime, he had received his mother's estate, which enabled him to devote himself to philosophy. After spending some years in Paris, he went to Holland where conditions were more favorable to freedom of thought and speech. In 1637 the first of his philosophical writings appeared, his celebrated *Discours de la methode,* which presented his new views and was at the same time a sort of mental autobiography. In 1641 he published his *Meditations on First Philosophy* which expounded in more detail the foundations of his system. Three years later appeared his *Principles of Philosophy*. Throughout his twenty years' residence in Holland, Descartes maintained a voluminous correspondence that fills five stout volumes. Through a friend, who eventually became ambassador of France to Sweden, Descartes began a correspondence with the youthful and enthusiastic queen of that country, Christina. In 1649, he finally went to Sweden in order to be near and to instruct his patroness. This proved to be an unfortunate move, for in the following year, while Christina was planning to ennoble him and endow him with an estate, he became ill and died, a victim of the rigorous climate.

Descartes was the author of a philosophical system that once dominated the thinking of Holland and France particularly, and, to a lesser extent, other countries of Western Europe. The aim of his thinking was to understand man and the world in which he lived. As a means of obtaining this objective, he tried to free himself from the body of beliefs which hitherto he had accepted on the authority of others or of tradition. He doubted the validity of everything, even the evidence of the senses. In this body of accepted beliefs and sensations, however, he thought he had found one thing that could not be doubted. As he phrased it, "I think, therefore I am." After freeing himself from prejudice, he strove to analyze all problems into the simplest elements, then to ascend from the simple to the complex, and, lastly, to include all factors in the problem. By these means he thought that he could deduce other ideas that have reality. He argued at length that our consciousness of self implies a belief in God and the reality of matter. He believed, further, that the universe was a mechanism and animals, automata. He believed matter had only two properties, extension and motion. His ideas about the whole universe being in motion led to his peculiar doctrine of vortices which made the whole universe a mass of revolving whorls whose action and interaction explain its phenomena. Descartes found himself in great difficulty, though, when he tried to explain the relation of mind and body. Like those of most other thinkers of the time, the ideas of Descartes were disapproved of by the theologians, both Calvinist and Catholic.

Descartes' most important disciple was a Dutch Jew, Baruch (later known as Benedict) Spinoza. His family held a prominent place in the Jewish colony at Amsterdam. Spinoza himself received a good and somewhat unusual education from a rabbi and a German physician. Upon arriving at maturity, he broke with the Jewish community in spite of the offer of a pension if he would continue outwardly to conform. The rest of his life he spent at various points in Holland. He supported himself in the simplest fashion through his trade of lens grinder, at which he was an expert, and through a modest pension left him by a friend and admirer. During his lifetime he published only one work, his *Theological-Political Treatise,* in which he maintained that the Bible was history. This work aroused almost public horror but was widely read. By this time he was a public figure, had many visitors, and carried on a considerable correspondence. Among his close friends were the two De Witts, who played such a prominent role in Dutch history. In 1673, Spinoza declined an invitation to become a member of the faculty of Heidelberg University. After his death, certain other writings of Spinoza were published. The most important of these was his *Ethics.*

In his writings, Spinoza accepted many of the ideas of Descartes but added to them certain of his own. His great contribution was his conception of God. In fact, he has been called a God-intoxicated man. He taught that God is the only object of knowledge. He is the only substance, and finite things are but modifications of God. To know finite things truly is to know God. To Spinoza there were two kinds of things: God and all other things, or, in other words, God and the modes of God. God is, therefore, the only object of knowledge. His beliefs thus made Spinoza a Pantheist. This view seems to leave no room for freedom of the will. In the opinion of Spinoza, however, man frees and saves himself by reason and intuition. To understand a thing is to be delivered from it.

In the meantime, the soldiers and politicians of Germany had nearly destroyed all opportunity for scientific work, artistic production, and reflective thought by plunging the country in the Thirty Years' War. As a result, during the seventeenth century, Germany produced only one outstanding philosopher, Wilhelm Gottfried von Leibnitz (1646–1716). His life was quite a contrast to that of Descartes or Spinoza. His father had been a university professor at Leipzig and Leibnitz grew up in his father's study. Being very precocious, he entered the university at the age of fifteen and was a doctor by the time he was twenty. He spent a large part of his remaining years in the employ of various German rulers. For the six years following 1666, he was in the service of the Elector of Mainz and wrote at his master's request many pamphlets on religious and political questions of the day. In 1672 a diplomatic mission took him to Paris where he spent four years acquiring a knowledge of the new science. The rest of his life he spent in the service of the House of Hanover. No one book contains his philosophy or reveals his rich personality. He was at the same time a jurist, historian, diplomat, mathematician, physical scientist, theologian, and philologist. He was the author of many books and carried on an enormous correspondence. In spite of the many honors that had come to him, however, he died a rather neglected figure.

The conclusions of Leibnitz as to what constitutes the fundamental truths of knowledge are not easy to understand. He thought, however, that there were two kinds of truth which force themselves upon the mind as self-evident. There are the truths of reason which are forever true and there are the facts of experience which are true for a single instance. The first are true because the opposite is inconceivable. The opposite of the second is quite conceivable. There are thus the two worlds of reason and brute force. The world of reason is a mechanical world. Below it, however, is a world of infinite possibilities. Motion, though, is capable of being analysed into infinitely small impulses, and the ground of motion is force. The new atom of the physicists, furthermore, was capable of being divided into metaphysical atoms, which Leibnitz identifies with force. This makes nature consist of spiritual force centers which he called monads. Each monad is isolated but expresses the whole universe. Each is capable of development without changing itself. There are thus monads at various stages of consciousness. An inorganic object is a group of monads without a dominating monad or soul. An organic

318

thing is a combination of monads with a ruling monad or soul. All are tied together and dominated by God. Evil comes not from God but from the fact that man is a free agent.

The Formulation of the Principles of International Law

This century also witnessed the birth of international law. It was the work of a brilliant young scholar, known as Hugo Grotius (1583–1645). His ideas about international relations were formulated in the course of a controversy as to whether a private company like the Dutch East India Company had the right to make prizes. Later, in 1625, while in exile in Paris, he published in definite form his ideas on the subject. The work is known as *De jure belli ac pacis*. It was so complete that it left little that was new to be said on the subject.

So, when one considers the obstacles which they had to overcome, the artists and thinkers of the seventeenth century achieved much. In education, John Amos Comenius initiated some very modern reforms. In art, some of the greatest painters of all time flourished. In architecture, the architects developed the Baroque style. In philosophy, Descartes, Spinoza, and Leibnitz offered interesting explanations of the universe. In law, Hugo Grotius formulated the fundamental principles governing international relations.

CHAPTER 20

Scientific and Military Developments

The seventeenth century was a notable period in the history of science. Up to that time, the word *science* meant knowledge, and what is now called science was known as natural philosophy. In the seventeenth century the word *science* acquired its modern connotation. Henceforth, it meant a body of knowledge, systematically collected, accurately observed and measured, and bound together by general laws.

There were a number of causes for this development. It may have been due in part to the establishment of strong governments and domestic peace and in part to the accumulation of wealth and the creation of a leisure class. It also may have been partly a product of the growing secularization of society.

The Founding of Academies

At any rate, seventeenth century scientists achieved much. Some new sciences were founded. Some important advances were made in those already established. Much of this success was achieved through the organization of scientific societies and academies. As one would expect, the movement for the founding of these institutions began in Italy. At one time or another, there were few Italian cities which did not possess such a society or academy. Usually, however, these Italian institutions barely survived their founders.

From Italy, the movement spread to France and England. About 1645, some English scientists began to hold informal meetings at London. A little later a group at Oxford in close touch with the London group began doing the same thing. In 1660 the London group began to keep a record of its meetings and limited its membership to twenty-five. Two years later, this body was formally incorporated as the Royal Society, and in 1664 it began to publish its transactions. The society brought the English scientists together, stimulated experiment and discussion, published scientific treatises, maintained a museum, and promoted correspondence with continental scientists.

The beginning of the French Academy of Sciences was quite similar. A number of French scientists began to hold informal meet-

320

ings. In 1666, Colbert, the leading minister of Louis XIV, decided to give the group an official status and thus reflect glory on his master. This academy of science met twice a week in the royal library. Many of its members received pensions. In 1681, Louis XIV even attended a session of the new academy. After the death of its patron in 1683, however, the society declined for a time. His majesty, Louis XIV, had tried to shift the interest of the society from theories to practical subjects. As a result, its funds were diverted to the construction of fountains and cascades at Versailles, and its attention was directed to such useful subjects as the calculation of the chances of success in various games! In 1699, however, the academy was reorganized.

At first, the workers in the sciences tried to keep up to date through the maintenance of a vast and widespread correspondence. Later, they began to publish and support scientific publications of various sorts. Before the end of the century, such publications had begun to appear in Italy, England, France, Germany, the Netherlands, and Denmark.

Astronomy

During the seventeenth century astronomers continued to make observations and deductions of great importance. Much of this was done in observatories built and supported by governments. In the latter half of the sixteenth century, a beginning was made toward construction of public observatories. In the latter half of the seventeenth century, however, the French and English governments assumed leadership of the movement. The chief Paris observatory was completed in 1672. From that date onward, a group of brilliant scientists worked there. Each man, though, worked at the problem which interested him. No individual dominated the group. The various scientists contrived or applied to use in astronomy such instruments as the micrometer, the telescopic sight, and the pendulum clock. In 1675, Charles II appointed John Flamsteed (1646–1719) to be the official astronomical observer in charge of what later was known as Greenwich Observatory. Under the leadership of these French and English astronomers, catalogues of stars were made, the movements of such planets as Mercury (1631) and Venus (1637) were noted, and other heavenly bodies were discovered.

In the latter part of the century, however, one of the most brilliant scientific generalizations of all time was made by an English scientist. Its author was Sir Isaac Newton, the brilliant son of a small freehold farmer of Lincolnshire. Upon the advice of an uncle he was given a good education. In 1667, he was elected a fellow of one of the colleges at Cambridge and, two years later, a professor in the same institution. In 1668 he invented the first reflecting telescope. Next, he turned his attention to optics, a study in which he made discoveries of permanent value.

About 1666, Newton seems to have begun to think about the subject of gravity. Tradition says that his attention was called to the subject by the fall of an apple from a tree, and until 1820 the alleged tree from which the apple is said to have fallen was pointed out to visitors. What is certain is that it took a Newton to discover that the same force that made bodies fall to the earth made the moon stay in its orbit around the earth and the planets revolve around the sun. It is certain, too, that few other minds could have made the mathematical calculations necessary to establish the interesting hypothesis. By calculating from Kepler's laws [1] and supposing the orbits of the planets to be circles around the sun, Newton proved that the force of the sun acting upon the different planets must vary as the inverse square of the distances of the planets from the sun. He was therefore led to inquire whether, if the earth's attraction extended to the moon, the force at that distance would be of the exact magnitude necessary to retain the moon in its orbit. He found that the moon by its motion in its orbit was deflected from the tangent in every minute of time through a space of thirteen feet. But by observing the distance through which a body would fall in one second of time at the earth's surface, and by calculating from that on the supposition of the force diminishing in the ratio of the inverse square of the distance, he found that the earth's attraction at the distance of the moon would draw a body through fifteen feet and one inch. Because of this discrepancy between results, Newton came to the conclusion that his conjecture was erroneous, and he laid the problem aside for some time.

In 1679, however, Newton became involved in a dispute with another scientist over the form of a path of a falling body from a height. This led him to take up again the problem of gravity. He became convinced as a result of his calculations that gravitation was the sole influence governing the movements of the planets and their satellites. In 1684, accordingly, he sent his calculations to Halley, a fellow scientist, and Halley described Newton's discovery to the Royal Society. Three years later the Royal Society completed the publication of Newton's great work on the subject, *Mathematical Principles of Natural Philosophy*.

---

[1] *See* Chapter 11.

There were other sides to Newton's life. He took an active part in the resistance of Cambridge University to the encroachments of James II. Twice he represented his university in Parliament. After 1694, first as warden and a little later as master, he was connected with the mint, an office that gave him a much better salary than his professorship at Cambridge. From 1703 onward, he was annually re-elected president of the Royal Society. In 1705 he was knighted by Queen Anne.

Man's Discovery of Himself

During the century the work of discovering man himself continued. There were a number of causes for this. Among them should be mentioned the acceptance of the mechanical philosophy of Descartes, the contemporary progress of physics, the introduction of chemical explanations of bodily processes, the adoption of clinical instruction in hospitals north of the Alps (particularly in Holland), and, above all, the favorable reception given the discovery of the circulation of the blood. After the adoption of that idea, there was a pronounced tendency for all departments of medicine to attempt to explain the functions of the human body by scientific laws.

The discoverer of the circulation of the blood was William Harvey (1578–1657), and English physician. Like so many others who made their mark north of the Alps in the sixteenth and seventeenth centuries, he studied in Italy. He then settled in London for the practice of medicine and soon became connected with one of the large hospitals there. While meeting the demands of this position, he seems to have found time to study carefully the subject of the circulation of the blood. Before his time, even the best doctors had had the most erroneous ideas about the function of the heart and the veins and the arteries. They thought that the blood moved but slowly and irregularly like the air in a house or a crowd in the street; that one kind of blood flowed from the liver to the right ventricle and then to the lungs and another kind of blood from the left ventricle to the arteries and the general system. They had no conception of the real function of the heart.

William Harvey's refutation of these ideas was the product of long observation and careful study. He knew the anatomy of the heart better than any of his contemporaries. He observed living animals. He estimated the capacity of each ventricle and calculated the rate of the whole mass of blood through it. He demonstrated the effects of the flow of blood. His studies led him to the following important conclusions: that the contraction and dilation of the heart

323

coincides with the pulse, and that the ventricles squeeze the blood which they contain into the arteries; that the pulse is produced by the arteries being filled with blood; that the blood in the arteries and in the veins is the same blood; and that the blood propelled through the arteries to the tissues is not all used, but much of it returns to the heart through the veins. Harvey finally published his conclusions in 1628 in a treatise that fills only fifty-two pages of print. In time, this discovery revolutionized the practice of medicine.

While it in no way impaired the value of his discovery, Harvey omitted one important link in the circulatory system, the capillaries. Their discoverer was Marcello Malpighi (1628–1694), who was really the founder of microscopic anatomy. He was a rather colorless professor the greater part of his life. He was a professor of medicine in a number of Italian universities, and for twenty years he was a corresponding member of the Royal Society of London. He made his important discovery by careful observation of the lungs and the bladder.

Although the discovery of William Harvey overshadows them, other facts of importance about the human body were discovered during the century. A long line of anatomists made significant discoveries by their studies in anatomy. In 1649, Arnold de Boot and, in 1651, Francis Glisson described the disease since known as rickets. In 1646, Isbrand de Diemerbroek thoroughly investigated the plague. In 1654, Christopher Benet wrote an important book on tuberculosis. There were, too, a number of new remedies introduced in Europe. The most important of these was cinchona bark—quinine, which was brought to Spain from Peru in 1640.

To understand the seventeenth century, one must realize that a great many scientists were at work on all sorts of problems. As an illustration, we might take Anthony van Leeuwenhoek (1632–1723) of the Netherlands. Armed with a microscope, he devoted himself to the study of the minute anatomy of man, the higher animals, and insects. He confirmed and extended Malpighi's findings concerning the capillaries. He gave the first accurate description of the red blood corpuscles. He studied fleas, ants, and eels and incidentally refuted many erroneous ideas about their origin and development. Most of his discoveries were published in the transactions of the Royal Society of London.

The new discoveries affected the practice of medicine very slowly. At this time, a doctor with a scientific attitude was the exception. A few members of the medical profession, though, did excellent work. As an illustration of the better type of medical practitioner, we might take Thomas Sydenham (1624–1689). He was the son of an English country gentleman. After studying at Oxford and Montpellier, the great French medical center, he began to practice medicine in London. He won a place for himself among his contemporaries by his cooling treatment of smallpox, his use of laudanum (the first form of tincture of opium), and his employment of the new Peruvian bark in cases of the so-called quartan agues. Posterity remembers him for his important study of the variations in epidemics of different diseases according to seasons, years, and ages. He insisted that observation should have precedence over theory. He gave clear accounts of such diseases as malaria, plague, smallpox, hysteria, and gout. He was the first to diagnose scarletina and to define cholera. He regarded such diseases as fevers and inflamations as efforts of the organism to resist injurious influences. He attributed chronic diseases to errors of diet or manner of life. He is considered the founder of modern clinical medicine in England.

Developments in Mathematics

The mathematicians made the seventeenth century one of the great periods in the development of mathematics. Within these years, logarithms were invented, algebra and trigonometry were further developed, analytical geometry was discovered, and differential calculus was perfected.

The credit for the discovery of logarithms is accorded to John Napier, a Scottish baron (1550–1617). He first announced his discovery in a small work published in 1614. The book immediately attracted the attention of the two most eminent English mathematicians. One of them translated the work of Napier from Latin into English. The other calculated a part of the logarithmic tables now in use. In 1628 a Dutch mathematician published a table of logarithms that completed this earlier work.

The development of analytical geometry was the work of the French philosopher, Descartes (1596–1650). In 1637 he published his treatise on geometry. It constitutes the foundation of modern analytical geometry.

The world is indebted to Newton in part, at least, for another great discovery. In June, 1696, a European mathematician, named Bernouli, challenged the scientists of Europe to solve two problems within a period of six months. At the end of that time, Leibnitz (1646–1716), the famous German philosopher, asked for more time. In January, 1797, Newton received from France copies of the two problems. Eventually, both Leibnitz and Newton sent in solutions.

In solving the problems, both of these noted men had made use of a new branch of mathematics, differential calculus. So each considered himself as its inventor.

Developments in Other Sciences

Among the sciences cultivated at this time was botany. The botanists of the period were concerned mainly with the classification of plants. Among them was Robert Morrison, the first professor of botany at Oxford University. These early systems, of course, have long since been superseded.

In this century, too, a beginning was made toward the creation of the science of chemistry. One of the early chemists was Helmont (1577–1644), a member of a Belgian noble family. A rich marriage enabled him to spend much of his time in chemical experiments. He claimed to have invented the word, *gas*.

Much of this work in chemistry is connected with the name of Robert Boyle (1627–1691). He taught that the proper subject of the chemist was the study of the composition of substances. In his work, *The Sceptical Chemist* (1662), he criticized prevailing scientific views and advanced the idea that true knowledge could be gained only by the logical application of the principles of experiment and deduction. He asserted that matter consisted of minute corpuscles and that compounds were made by the union of corpuscles. He formulated, too, the law that the volume of a gas varies inversely as the pressure. The ideas of Boyle, though, were not generally accepted until later.

There could be little progress in geology as long as the fundamental question of the true character and history of the stratified portion of the earth's crust containing organic remains was still in dispute. Until the latter part of the eighteenth century, belief in a great general flood held the field; but even in the seventeenth century, particularly in Italy, there were some opponents of this theory. Even earlier, Leonardo da Vinci made some notable observations about the origin of fossil shells. He ridiculed the idea that they were formed through the influence of the stars and maintained that they had once belonged to living organisms and that what was then land had once been sea. A little later, Giralomo Fracastorio (1483–1553) claimed that the shells could not have been left by the flood but that the mountains in which they occur had been successively uplifted out of the sea. During the century, Nicolas Steno (1638–1686), who was born in Copenhagen but settled at Florence, discovered rocks in northern Italy that contained what appeared to be shark's teeth and that seemed to resemble closely those of the dogfish which he had recently studied. In 1669, after much hesitation, he finally published a little pamphlet on the subject. This showed that stratified formations of hills and valleys contained such materials as would be deposited in the form of sediment in turbid waters. He maintained, further, that where they contained marine productions the water must have been from the sea and that diversities in composition indicated the commingling of currents carrying different kinds of sediment.

Steno also made original and important observations on stratification. He asserted that where the strata of the earth were steeply inclined, vertical, or arched they had been disrupted by subterranean exhalations or the caving in of underground caverns. He maintained also that teeth, bones, and skeletons of many kinds of fish had been quarried out of the rock. Contemporaneously, Descartes, the French philosopher, maintained that the earth and the planets had been originally a mass of glowing material like the sun and had gradually cooled on the outside. These ideas were enlarged by the German philosopher, Leibnitz.

Many scientists of this period did not confine themselves to a single branch of science. This is illustrated by the career of Huygens (1629–1695), a Dutch scientist. He first attracted attention by his writings on mathematics. Next, he overcame certain obstacles to the advancement of astronomy by his discovery in 1655 of a new method of grinding and polishing lens for telescopes. His work in astronomy led to his application of the pendulum to the regulation of the movement of clocks (1656). The following year he exhibited the first pendulum clock to the States-General. By this time, he had a European reputation. As a reward, he was elected a fellow of the Royal Society of London and was invited by Colbert to become a resident of France. In the latter part of his career, he won fame by his researches in physical optics.

Developments in Military Science

The seventeenth century saw many important developments in military science. At the beginning of the period, the new Dutch methods were at the height of their reputation. Under the leadership of Maurice of Nassau, a son of William of Orange, the Dutch had finally developed armies able to meet the best Spanish troops in the field and fortifications capable of withstanding serious sieges. The Dutch infantry was still armed with pikes, halberts, and muskets, but the solid, cumbersome phalanxes of former days were broken up by the organization of companies and regiments that could be maneuvered.

This reorganization of the infantry was accompanied by the introduction of rigid drill. The really distinguishing characteristic of the

Dutch army was the spirit of patriotism which inspired it. In other hands during the Thirty Years' War, the Dutch methods did not meet with the same success as in the Netherlands during the Dutch War for Independence.

It was not the Dutch but the Swedes, under the leadership of Gustavus Adolphus, who introduced modern methods of warfare into Europe. The Swedish armies were raised by conscription, but the recruits left home inspired to a sense of duty by the exhortations of their preachers. Each district supplied a certain quota. A large proportion of the infantry were still armed with pikes, but the musketeers carried an improved musket that was lighter, needed no rest, and could be fired more rapidly. The greatest innovation of Gustavus Adolphus was the introduction of effective field artillery. Each regiment of the Swedish army was provided with two light, moveable, field guns, which had twice the range of the muskets of the time. Their opponents still had only heavy artillery too cumbersome to be moved rapidly. The Swedish victories of the Thirty Years' War were due to these innovations. Their failures were a result of the loss of their inspired leader and the decline of their moral fervor.

In England during the Civil War, we find a somewhat similar situation. There, two parties inspired by something more than money or the chance of plunder confronted each other. From the first, the Royalist cavalry had a sense of honor, courage and resolution. In the end, Cromwell conquered it with an army imbued with the idea of the righteousness of its cause and a strong sense of duty. The struggle, for the most part, was a war of rapid, far-reaching marches. As a result, the pikemen abandoned much of the armor which they had hitherto worn, and the artillery often reached the battlefield too late.

Toward the end of the Thirty Years' War, Europe witnessed the beginning of the rise of a new military power. In 1643, upon the field of Rocroi, the armies raised with such effort by Richelieu at last won a great victory that destroyed the prestige enjoyed by Spanish arms for over a century. By 1670, the French army was the model of Europe. The days of great causes, it is true, were over. Louvois, the great war minister of Louis XIV, attempted, however, to find a substitute for them in a regime of strict obedience and an *esprit de corps*. These objectives were achieved in part at least by better barracks and the adoption of a uniform. The improvement in equipment also went on. Louvois took the dagger of the infantryman, fixed it in the muzzle of his musket, and created the bayonet which superseded the pike. About 1680, too, the firelock replaced the matchlock as the musketeer's chief weapon. Henceforth, battles were likely to be won by the rapid volley of musketeers followed by an orderly bayonet charge.

The century, likewise, witnessed a revolution in the services of supply and transport. At the beginning of the century troops, for the most part, still lived on the country. This system reached its devastating culmination during the later stages of the Thirty Years' War. The very excesses of this struggle, however, created a revulsion of feeling and a change in the actual practice of armies. After 1648, armies were almost always supplied by magazines which were filled either by the home country or by inducing peasants by the enforcement of good conduct and the payment of cash to bring in the necessary supplies. Armies, too, had to be treated somewhat better. The cleavage between soldier and civilian was even wider than in earlier times. Soldiers were harder to obtain and demanded better treatment. If they were not well lodged and fed, they would desert. As a result, armies usually stayed within seven marches of the new magazines and within two days' march of the nearest field bakery. As much as their resources permitted, other states quickly imitated the new French system.

During the century the art of defence, too, made notable progress. At first, after the abandonment of the high walls which characterized medieval fortifications, the defensive measures were rather unsystematic. From the point of view of the defenders, the great defect of the fortresses was their inability to bring their artillery into play against attacking forces. The guns could not be depressed enough or made to sweep the approaches of the defending walls. During the Dutch War for Independence, this situation began to be met. The remedy was the bastion. Strongly defended and standing out beyond the main lines of the fortress, the artillery placed in the bastion could reach every part of the surrounding territory. It remained for one hundred years the answer of the defence to the attack.

The development of elaborate bastioned fortresses created problems of the greatest difficulty for the attack, as in some way the attackers must reach a wall of the fortress and breach it. The answer to the bastion proved to be the use of trenches supported by redoubts. This method seems to have been first used by the Turks. At first, the attackers had no clear idea of how to breach a wall, and the trenches were dug very haphazardly. Later, the investment of hostile fortresses was systematized. The first step was the complete investment of the stronghold. The second step was the placing of batteries at a range of six hundred to seven hundred yards and the provision for their protection. Under the protection of these guns, the sappers began, usually at night, the digging of a lateral trench. After its completion, zigzag trenches that prevented an enfiladating fire were dug in the direction of the fortress. At a point half way to the fortress, the advance was stopped for the time being, and a second parallel trench was dug. Finally, the sappers advanced to the foot of the fortress defences and dug a third lateral trench. That brought them to a point where the walls of the fortress could be mined and breached.

In the eyes of contemporaries, these sytems of defence and attack reached perfection under Vauban (1633–1707), the chief military engineer of Louis XIV. While he really invented nothing, he developed and modified the old ideas to their fullest extent. He is said to have repaired or constructed one hundred and sixty strongholds and to have taken part in forty-eight sieges. He is credited with many successes and no failures.

Thus, in the seventeenth century we see that the scientists continued their work in a brilliant fashion. With the help of governments, they founded academies and observatories, encouraged and rewarded scientific work, and published its results. In astronomy, Sir Isaac Newton formulated the laws of gravity. Other scientists continued to make brilliant discoveries about the human body. The mathematicians invented logarithms, analytical geometry, and differential calculus, and made improvements in algebra and trigonometry. Still other scientists made progress in botany, chemistry, and geology.

At the same time, important developments were taking place in military science. Under the leadership of Maurice of Nassau, the Dutch learned to withstand the Spaniards. In time, the Swedes, the English, and the French developed still other improvements in tactics and weapons. At the same time, important changes were taking place in the service of transport and supply and the art of defending and capturing fortresses.

In the sixteenth century, as we have seen, Italian writers established themselves as the leaders of the literary movement. In Europe they furnished the forms and often the subject matter for the literary productions of other countries. In the latter part of the century, they lost their primacy in letters. Spanish oppression and the closer scrutiny exercised by the revived Church seems to have put a damper on Italian creative power. The Italian writers had apparently exhausted the rich vein they had been working. Suspicious rulers fettered the freedom of thought. The fate of Campanella and Giordano Bruno was a constant reminder of the price that might be paid for boldness of thought. As a result, the Italian writers of the period employed exaggeration to cloak their poverty of subject matter. They became bombastic, inflated, and turgid. A few sought simplicity in imitation of ancient shepherds, but this was merely the substitution of a new artifice for an old one. As a result, only the literary historian now reads the many volumes which the Italian writers of the period produced.

Spanish Literature

The place given up by the Italians was taken by Spanish men of letters. The writers of Spain really began to make their mark before the close of the sixteenth century. They cultivated most of the literary forms known to their contemporaries, but they reached greatness particularly in the novel and the drama.

In the field of the novel, Spain produced one of the great books of all time. Its author, Miguel de Cervantes Saavedra (1547–1616), was born at Alcala. He spent some years in the household of the later Cardinal Aquaviva. About 1570, he enlisted in the Spanish army. He fought in the naval battle of Lepanto, where one of his hands was permanently maimed. He saw action in a number of other theatres of war. In 1575, he was captured by Barbary pirates and was not ransomed until five years later. In 1582, he began writing for the stage, but he was never a good dramatist. After his return from captivity, he was in the employ of the government and seems to have had financial difficulties. In 1604, the first part of his famous book, *Don*

Quixote appeared. This work brought him almost immediate fame but did little to relieve his financial difficulties. Within ten years, it had been translated into French and English. This was soon followed by another notable work, twelve tales, known as *Novelas Exemplares*. In 1614, a spurious sequel to *Don Quixote* was published. Its appearance spurred Cervantes to write the second part of *Don Quixote*. He died soon after its publication. To the end, he remained a Spanish gentleman in somewhat straightened circumstances.

It is difficult to do justice to the writings of Cervantes. By universal consent, he is regarded as the greatest Spanish novelist and one of the world's great writers. In *Don Quixote* he apparently attempted to ridicule the romances of chivalry, and he tried to show the absurdity and danger of those prejudices concerning pure blood and noble rank with which the nation was imbued and which threatened to ruin Spain. His work gives a panorama of Spanish society in the sixteenth century. Contemporaries valued it largely for its types of character and its incidents. In the first part of *Don Quixote,* some passages border on farce. The second part shows the results of criticism. There are fewer cudgelings. Don Quixote is more dignified. Sancho Panza loses somewhat in rustic cunning but gains in wit and sense. In his *Novelas Exemplares,* Cervantes also reached a high literary level.

In the drama, two writers stand out among the host of Spanish writers. First in point of time was Lope de Vega Carpio (1562–1635). He had a rather unusual career. He seems to have attended the University of Alcala. At various times, he was in the service of a bishop, a marquis, and a duke. He was a member of the *Spanish Armada.* About 1612, after the death of his second wife, he became a priest. This turn in his personal affairs, however, did not put an end to his literary output. Under the patronage of the Duke of Sessa, he continued to write until the end of his life.

Though he now is remembered as the founder of the Spanish theater, Lope de Vega Carpio really cultivated most of the contemporary literary forms. His epics, pastorales, odes, and sonnets are now forgotten. Only his dramas are still alive. In spite of the great role which he played in the development of the drama, he was always a little apologetic about his writing for the stage. This was because the Spanish stage of the day aimed to make itself intelligible even to the most illiterate classes. As a consequence, he sacrificed quality to quantity and wrote much of his work in great haste. He is said to have written eighteen hundred secular dramatic works and four hundred religious pieces. The titles of some six hundred and thirty-seven plays are still known, and some twenty volumes of plays have been preserved. For his subject matter, he drew on a wide variety of sources—the Bible, the lives of the martyrs, national traditions, and the lives of everyday men. He was best at plots dealing with middle class intrigue. During the latter half of his life, his influence was comparable to that exercised by Voltaire in the next century.

The position of leadership vacated by Lope de Vega Carpio in 1635 was taken by Pedro Calderon de la Barca (1600–1683). There is much that is not known about his life. He was educated at the Jesuit college of Madrid and the University of Salamanca. He became recognized as the foremost Spanish dramatist and was employed at the royal theatre. About 1651, he, like Lope de Vega Carpio, became a priest. Thereafter, he tended to write only religious works for the stage. In 1663 he became honorary chaplain of Philip IV. Like his predecessor, he wrote too much and too speedily. Like all his contemporaries, he plagiarized freely. He was a master of theatrical devices, and his work had depth and poetry.

French Literature

The year 1600 really marks the beginning of a new period in French literature. In poetry, the name of Francois de Malherbe (1555–1628) stands out. After 1600, he was summoned to court and spent twenty years in court circles. He rejected a good many of the importations of his predecessors, but he is responsible for some of the faults of French poetry. He sacrificed everything to correctness, and the French writers who came after him followed the path which he had marked out.

In the main, however, poetry became synonymous with the drama. In 1588 the presentation of mysteries was prohibited, and the societies of amateur actors soon disappeared. Their place was taken by strolling troupes of professional actors who created a demand for plays. The first French writers of dramatic works, like Alexander Hardy (1569–1631) who is credited with seven hundred pieces for the stage, did not reach a very high standard but were not entirely devoid of merit. They were much influenced by Italian and Spanish models.

The development of French literature, however, cannot be fully understood without some knowledge of the French Academy and its place in the intellectual life of France. It is responsible for many of the faults as well as some of the merits of modern French literature. About 1629, some eight of the intellectual leaders of France began meeting secretly at the house of Valentine Conrart, the king's secretary. They conversed on literary topics and read to each other what they had written. Some six years later, the watchful Richelieu heard of these meetings and offered to incorporate the group. The reluctant coterie did not dare oppose the plan of the all-powerful minister, for such meetings were contrary to the law of the land. The number of members of the new organization was set at forty. From the beginning, the principal object of the Academy was the purification of the French language. In 1639 the group began work on a French dictionary. The Academy tended to subordinate other forms of French literature to the drama, and to school and correct the stage. It put the greatest emphasis on the preservation of the three unities of time, place, and action. This had a more limiting effect on tragedy than on comedy. The first play criticized by the Academy was Corneille's *Cid*. The decisions of the Academy were often influenced by the personal jealousy, official pressure, and the obsequious mediocrity of its membership.

These first French dramatists were followed by three writers of the first rank. In point of time, the first of the three dramatists was Corneille (1606–1684). He came of a good Rouen family that was ennobled in 1637. Like most dramatists, he seems to have had to learn the art of writing plays. His early plays had most of the faults of those of his contemporaries but yet had some distinguishing merits. In 1635, however, six years after the appearance of his first play, his *Mocedad del Cid* was produced. Although it aroused much criticism, it was one of the epic-making tragedies of all literature. It won for its author from the jealous Richelieu a pension. Eight years later appeared *Le Menteur* which is almost equally memorable in the history of comedy. For the next three decades, new plays of Corneille appeared at frequent intervals. Unlike many writers and in spite of an unattractive personality, he won in his own lifetime recognition both from his rivals and the great men of the time. Finally, in 1662, after being twice rejected, he was welcomed into the French Academy.

In the opinion of later critics, the work of Corneille was very unequal. Some of it was fine, while some of it was dull and mediocre. He is credited with the ability to make admirable plots and to write verses of lofty grandeur. He lacked proportion and the ability to keep the interest uniform. In the opinion of many critics, his *Cinna* is his masterpiece.

Sixteen years younger than Corneille was Jean Baptiste Poquelin, known to the world by his stage name of Molière. His father was an upholsterer and had the duty of accompanying the king on his journeys in order to arrange the furniture in the various royal palaces. Not much is known about the early education of Molière, but he seems to have attended a secondary school and to have been rather well instructed in philosophy. In 1643 a group that included Molière hired a tennis court with the intention of using it as a stage. Apparently, the first dramatic efforts of Molière did not meet with great success. He became, consequently, a strolling player, and subject to all the incidents that might befall one of that profession. He had to contend with horses and mules and lumbering carts, with bad or impassable roads, with improvised theatres, and unsympathetic audiences. After spending ten years in this adventurous manner, Molière and his company found a patron in the person of the Prince of Conté. This relationship lasted four years and was terminated by the prince's sudden concern over his soul's salvation. Fortunately for Molière, just about this time he attracted the favorable attention of the young Louis XIV. At the king's command, he settled down in Paris, where his troubles changed considerably but by no means ended. With the exception of an occasional command performance in the royal camp at Versailles, Molière spent the remaining years of his life at Paris. Because of the prejudice against his profession, he was buried finally without any religious ceremony.

After settling down in Paris, Molière met with immense success. In 1662, in spite of scandalous stories told about Molière by jealous rivals, Louis XIV even served as godfather for Molière's child. His period of success really begins in 1659 with the appearance of *Les precieuses ridicules*. Other plays followed at frequent intervals. In them, he exposed the foibles of mankind, the pretensions of some women to learning, the efforts of the middle class to be nobles, the ignorance of the physicians of the day, religious hypocrisy, and many other types. His principal fault was shared by most of his rivals. He individualized too greatly a single point in a character. He made a man merely a blunderer, a lover, a coxcomb, a tyrant, or an imposter, and ignored the complexity of human character. In spite of this defect in his work, he is the greatest writer of comedies in the history of French literature.

Still a little later, the works of the third great French dramatic writer, Jean Racine (1639–1699), began to appear on the French stage. He belonged to an upper middle class family. After trying in various ways to assure himself an income, he turned in 1663 to the drama. Soon, he became a serious rival of Corneille as a writer of tragedies. For about ten years his life is the story of his plays. In the opinion of critics his *Andromaque, Phedre,* and *Athalie* are his greatest plays. In 1673, the French Academy recognized his success by electing him a member of that body.

About 1677 Racine suddenly gave up the stage and led thereafter a devout and irreproachable life. By this time he was in a position to furnish a house, collect a library, save some money, and hold a post in the state service. He seems to have been an adroit courtier, a quality which won for him in turn the good opinion of Mesdames de Montespan and de Maintenon and the position of royal historiographer.

Among the writers of French prose during the seventeenth century, there is no such group of towering geniuses as we have found among the dramatists. During this period, nevertheless, French prose underwent a great development. In the eyes of experts on language, the French prose of the sixteenth century had many defects. The ordinary writer of the period was diffuse, used poorly constructed or unformed sentences, and employed haphazard periods. The charm of even a Rabelais or a Montaigne was the result of his exuberance and naiveté. In the seventeenth century, in contrast, we find carefully planned clauses, sentences, and paragraphs with a rhythmical cadence.

The first contributor to the new prose is usually considered to be Jean Balzac (1594–1654). He had the good fortune to be befriended by an influential family and to travel some in foreign countries. This gave him a wide circle of acquaintances, many of them members of the court. With them he kept up a correspondence. They praised his letters highly, possibly somewhat more than they deserve. He became a regular member of the circle which gathered at the Hotel de Rambouillet. In 1634 he was elected a member of the French Academy. In reality, his letters are rather empty and affected but are characterized by the precision and clearness that have distinguished French prose ever since.

In the development of French literature, the institution known as the *salon* has played a great role. One of the earliest and most famous *salons* gathered around the Marquise de Rambouillet (1588–1665). She had formed her intelligence and taste by her reading in Italian and Spanish literature. About 1615, she began to gather around her a group of distinguished people. They included the great soldiers of the period, some of the most fascinating women, and many of the important writers and savants of the time. Among them were to be found the great Condé, Mademoiselle de Bourbon, Mesdames de Lafayette and de Sevigné, Corneille, Balzac, and Conrart. Though she was inclined to impose her own preferences on her guests, for over three decades the *salon* of the Marquise de Rambouillet became the model of good taste. In time, all French society imitated the standards established there. In two instances at least, guests of the Marquise finally founded *salons* of their own.

The development of such a society was calculated to stimulate the production of historical works and memoirs of merit. Mezeray (1610–1683) wrote a history of France that summarized fairly accurately the French and Latin chronicles. Incidentally, he had his pension cut by

Colbert as a result of criticizing the financiers. Louis Maimbourg (1610–1686) wrote histories of the crusades and of the Catholic League. Claude Fleury (1640–1723) wrote an erudite ecclesiastical history.

The period, however, was far richer in memoirs than in histories. After playing an important role in the actual struggle called the *Fronde,* the man known in history as the Cardinal de Retz attempted to color the opinion of succeeding generations about that conflict by writing his memoirs. Another memoir writer of the period that cannot be ignored is Madame de Motteville (1621–1689), a companion during most of her lifetime of Anne of Austria (wife of Louis XIII and mother of Louis XIV). Another is the ambitious niece of Louis XIII, Mademoiselle de Montpensier (1627–1693), the richest princess in Europe, who played a considerable role in the *Fronde,* refused to marry, at the time, penniless but charming Charles II, and failed to conclude any of the other high alliances which she sought. Another is the attractive bachelor, Jean de Gourville (1625–1713) who rose from the position of maitre d'hotel to that of the trusted diplomatic agent of Mazarin and Louis XIV. Then there was Mathieu Molé (1584–1656), a rather noble figure who essayed the very difficult part of following an independent role amid the passions aroused by the *Fronde.* The celebrated memoirs of Richelieu were not his own work but were written at his command. An almost endless list of interesting memoirs, however, might be given.

In the latter part of the seventeenth century, the authorities attempted to use the writers of France to enhance the prestige of Louis XIV. They found some difficulty, however, in regimenting La Fontaine (1621–1695). He seems to have been equally inept at managing his domestic and his business affairs but always managed to find a patron to look out for him. We are told that he was awkward in manners, silent in company, and absent-minded at all times. This has made him a convenient figure upon which to hang humorous stories. He is now remembered as a writer of fables in verse. Contemporaries valued him for his stories and other works, but changes in literary standards have outmoded his stories and caused his miscellaneous writings to be forgotten. The fables first appeared in 1668. From that time onward until his death, the position of La Fontaine was well established.

In an age when the ability to read and write was exceptional rather than universal, people prided themselves on their letter writing. Among the notable letter writers of the age of Louis XIV, Madame de Sevigné (1626–1696) by universal consent holds first place. Orphaned early and reared first by her grandparents and then by an uncle to be a learned lady, she became a member of the Rambouillet coterie.

Freed by a duel at the early age of twenty-six from a husband whom no one seems to have praised, she never married again. She used much of her freedom in writing letters, especially to her badly spoiled son and her idolized daughter. Her letters show her to have been observant of trifles, appreciative of the ludicrous, fond of amusements, and sensitive to the beauties of nature. They are, consequently, filled with interesting pictures of such things as the death of Turenne, Vichy in the seventeenth century, life at court, a fire in the house of a neighbor at Paris, the escapades of her scapegrace son, the struggles of her daughter with social competitors, and the often quoted suicide of Vatel. Like most of the nobility, she seems to have had little sympathy for those beneath her in rank. The toiling galley slaves and oppressed peasants stirred in her no chord of sympathy. As early as 1673, people began to copy and hand about her letters. Ever since her day, they have been regarded as models of good letter writing.

One of the close friends of Madame de Sevigné was the Duke of Rochefoucauld. In early life he was ambitious to play a part in affairs and became involved in the intrigues against Richelieu and the movement known as the *Fronde*. After his lack of success in intrigue, he gave up politics and won the favor of Louis XIV and of the cultivated society of the time. He is now remembered for his memoirs and his *Maxims*. These pithy sayings are based on such ideas as that *amour-propre* is the motive of all human actions and that virtues are only vices in disguise.

The intellectual life of France in the seventeenth century, however, cannot be understood without some knowledge of the movement known as Jansenism. The movement takes its name from Cornelius Jansen (1585–1638), who rose from a humble position to be bishop of Ypres. During his years at the University of Louvain, he had become a follower of St. Augustine and opposed to the Jesuits. He felt that theology had ceased to have an influence on popular religion. With a fellow student, who later became an influential French abbot, he even planned a reform for the Church. Eventually, he wrote a book embodying his views, which was published two years after his death. In his teaching at Louvain and in his writings, he urged that spiritual experience and not reason must be the guide, that man was helpless and dependent on his Maker, that no amount of going to church will save a man, and that a relation between the human soul and God could be established only through the institution of the Church.

In France, the views of the Belgian bishop finally gained a considerable following. The appearance of Antoine Arnauld's *Frequent Communion* in 1643 was the occasion of the breaking out of a violent struggle between the Jesuits and their French opponents. In 1649 the University of Paris condemned five of the propositions of Jansen. Its stand was supported by the Pope and eighty-five bishops. The French Jansenists maintained that Jansen had not meant the five propositions in the sense in which they had been condemned and that at any rate the Pope was not infallible in matters of an author's mind. Eventually, the Jesuits won outward but not inward conformity with their views. Arnauld was deprived of his degree. About 1679, after the death of a cousin and a patroness of the Jansenists, Louis XIV was very severe with them. Many of the Jansenists, therefore, ultimately took refuge in Holland.

A famous incident of the struggle over Jansenism was the appearance in 1656 of *Les letters provinciales*. They were the work of the religious philosopher and mathematician, Blaise Pascal (1623–1662). He came from a middle-class family which eventually was ennobled. In 1646 he embraced Jansenism and wrote his famous work in order to influence the popular mind. The letters are the earliest example of polite controversial literature. In them, Pascal avoids denunciation and abusive language and employs like a skillful swordsman the weapon of irony. Eight years after the death of Pascal, his *Pensées* appeared. They are alleged to be fragments of a projected apology for Christianity. They dealt with the great problems of thought and combat skepticism with skepticism. There is much controversy, however, as to the real text of the work.

Another writer who won fame in the days of Louis XIV was La Bruyere (1645–1696). He, likewise, came from a middle-class family but passed most of his mature life in the family of the great Condé or at court. Comparatively little is known about him. He is now remembered for his *Characters*. Their importance possibly has been exaggerated. They partake somewhat of the nature of a work of essays, a collection of photographic portraits, and a book of maxims. In his lifetime the book brought La Bruyere many readers and made him many enemies.

One of the features of the age of Louis XIV was the existence of a group of great preachers. At least a half dozen of the preachers of the time are still remembered. Among them, the great Bossuet undoubtedly holds first place. Sprung from a prosperous judicial family, he studied at Paris where he gained a reputation for hard work and was taken up by the coterie at the Hotel de Rambouillet. At Metz, where he came into contact with a large Protestant population, he began to dream of regaining the Protestants for the Church. With this end in view, he carefully trained himself for the pulpit. In 1670 he became tutor of the heir to the throne and was henceforth thrown into court circles. From time to time, he was called upon to preach for members of the court long and solemn funeral sermons which were considered by his contemporaries to be masterpieces. For the guidance of his royal pupil, he wrote several works. The most famous of these was a universal history designed to show God's dealings with the human race. He cherished the hope that his royal pupil would help to make France a utopia. After the end of his service as tutor, he became bishop of Meaux and continued his work of trying to transform France and to regain the Protestants. In pursuit of this, he wrote in 1688 a *History of the Variations of the Protestant Churches,* a work which made Protestant apologists much trouble.

Almost equally famous was Fenelon (1651–1715). His father was a gentleman of small estate. His son spent his early years in efforts to convert the Protestants. A favorite pupil of Bossuet, he was a natural selection for the position of tutor of the grandson of Louis XIV. In this capacity he seems to have been effective and to have won his pupil to a devout life. Like Bossuet, he did much writing. These include an interesting treatise on the *Education of Girls* and the famous *Telemaque,* which at the same time narrates the adventures of the son of Ulysses and discloses a series of hidden morals. Like his patron, Fenelon became a bishop after the end of his service as tutor.

A word should be said about a group of scholars who laid the foundation of scientific history. Writing history is not as easy an art as it seems to the layman. Documents must be collected, criticized, translated, and interpreted before history can be written. Even dates are difficult to establish. Important steps toward scientific methods in history were taken by the scholarly monks of the congregation of St. Maur in France. They found and edited some of the most valuable sources of French history. In their publication known as *De re diplomatica,* Jean Mabillon (1632–1707) at the same time crushed his critics and established the principles for handling documents. Another member of the order revised and expanded the lexicon of Du Cange, the key to the use of medieval Latin. In addition, through a cooperative work known as *The Art of Verifying Dates,* the order laid the foundations for modern chronology.

English Literature

England, too, had its share of writers in the seventeenth century. One of the first names of the period, both in point of time and of achievement was that of Ben Jonson (1573–1637). Though a friend and contemporary of Shakespeare, he did most of his writing in the seventeenth century. Unfortunately for his fame, he wrote masques, a type of play that has gone out of style. He was at the height of his reputation during the first half of the reign of James I and found employment at court. By 1616 he had produced most of his notable plays. They include *Every Man in his Humor, Volpone,* and *The Silent Woman.* The contemporaries of Jonson valued him for his learning and individuality as well as his dramatic gifts.

Jonson's contemporary, Francis Bacon (1561–1626), won distinction both in literature and philosophy. Though a nephew of the great Lord Burleigh, advancement came slowly to him. Not until the reign of James I did the desired offices begin to come to him. In 1618, however, he was made Lord Chancellor, the highest judicial officer in the kingdom. In literature he is remembered for his *Essays.* They began to appear in 1597, but in subsequent years were greatly expanded. Though brief, they contained in a pithy form the rich results of his thinking and experience. From the time of their appearance they were popular and were soon translated into French, Italian, and Latin. Though a great writer and philosopher, he had great moral defects. All his life he had been inclined to get into debt and had been given to display. This caused him to fall into the common habit of accepting what he called presents but what others termed bribes from persons interested in his judicial decisions. In 1621 this led to the loss of his high office, his imprisonment, and his financial ruin.

Most English writing of the period, however, was affected more or less by the religious and political struggle that absorbed the attention and the resources of England. Of no English writer is this truer than of John Milton (1608–1674). He was the son of high-minded, prosperous parents of Puritan affiliations. This enabled him to attend Cambridge University and, subsequently, to lead the life of a scholar at a place not far from Windsor. Almost from the first, he attracted attention by his powers as a versifier. Among his early poems are *L'Allegro* and *Il Penseroso* and a play, *Comus.* Then he traveled on the continent, but was recalled by the outbreak of the Civil War. Of this struggle he was merely a spectator until the religious question arose. Then, giving up his search for a subject of an epic poem, he plunged into the war of pamphlets. A sudden and unfortunate marriage caused him to champion the idea of divorce. This involved him in a struggle with the authorities and gave rise to his famous attack on the censorship of printing.

In 1649 he became an official of the revolutionary government. In that year he was appointed Latin Secretary to the new council of state. In this office he carried on the foreign correspondence of the government. This made him acquainted with the chief figures of the revolution on the Puritan side and caused him to continue to use his pen in the Puritan cause. Before long, however, personal misfortune overtook him. In 1652 he became blind and his wife died, leaving him to care for three small children. In the conflicts within the Puritan party, he sided with Cromwell.

Upon the restoration of the Stuarts, Milton became an outcast. In fact, it is really something of a miracle that he escaped the scaffold. Under these circumstances, he turned to literature again. The result was the appearance in 1665 of *Paradise Lost*. It was soon recognized as one of the world's great epics. The prosaic pen of this author cannot do justice to it. With an almost hallowed spirit, Milton spanned time and eternity. He sets forth the forces supposed to be at work in both the seen and the unseen world. He depicts the majesty of the Almighty, the splendors of heaven, the horrors of hell, and the significance of life. For his most famous work, Milton received small pay but great praise. He again became a celebrity. Men of every rank from home and abroad beat a path to his door. Before his death he enriched English literature with two other noble poems, *Paradise Regained* and *Samson Agonistes*. He was, as Wordsworth said of him, like a star but dwelt apart in solitary grandeur.

The fall of the Puritan regime in 1660 ushered in a new age. Starting out as a movement for religious and political freedom, Puritanism finally degenerated, at least in many instances, into a false and forbidding asceticism. It came to condemn the most innocent pleasures. In some cases at least, it clothed morality and religion in a garb of cant. It attempted to terrify men into being good. Upon the restoration of the Stuarts, the forces which for long years had been held in check by the Puritans took control both of society and the world of books and plays. They gave free reign to license and derided every virture that the Puritans had emphasized.

The greatest literary figure of the Restoration period is John Dryden (1631–1700). It is difficult to pass judgment upon him. Born into a Puritan family, he wrote in a time when England was frequently changing masters. He was inclined to court the party in power and, consequently, praised in turn Cromwell and Charles II. Yet, at moments, he showed courage and refused, as in 1688, to shift with the wind. He had great gifts both as a versifier and as a prose writer but tended to pander to the low tastes of his age. As a result, he was inclined to be influenced in his dramatic writings by French standards rather than by Shakespeare and to write passages that he himself must have blushed in his better moments to read. As a result, he does not rank with the greatest writers of English literature.

He began to write for the stage in 1663. In all, he wrote twenty-eight comedies and tragedies. Dramatic writing, however, was not his special forte. He was best at satire. Probably the most famous of his satires is his *Absolom and Achitophel*. It was written to discredit the Earl of Shaftesbury, one of the political figures of the time. In 1685 Dryden became a Catholic. His failure to revert to Protestantism after the fall of James II cost him the much needed post of poet laureate and forced him to do what might almost be called hack work to maintain himself. He continued, however, to be the literary dictator of the time.

The course of politics after 1660 gave rise to some notable work in history. In this field the work of Edward Hyde, Earl of Clarendon, stands out prominently. He first attracted attention as a supporter of the king in the struggle between Charles I and his parliament. After the execution of Charles I, Edward Hyde became guardian of the young prince who finally became Charles II. For several years after the restoration of the Stuarts to the throne, he served as chief minister of the king. He was an honorable and able man but was never really popular with either the king or his subjects. Charles II disliked his restraining influence. The subjects of the king disapproved of his display and blamed the minister for all that went amiss. So in 1767 he was driven into exile.

Like many another man in such a situation, he was eager to justify himself. With this in view, he wrote two works, *The History of the Rebellion* and an autobiography. The first, written in 1646 to 1648 during his first exile, ends in March, 1644. The second, written in his later period, covers the years from 1609 to 1660. Finally, the two works were united. They have many faults. They are marked by digressions, lengthy sentences, and a lack of proportion and are overloaded with state papers. They show that the writer had an inaccurate memory and that often he did not understand the real issues involved. In spite of these defects, however, they form a notable contribution to English historical writing.

The historian, Gilbert Burnett (1643–1715), was a Scottish clergyman, who belonged to one of the ancient and distinguished families of Scotland. He served for a time as professor of divinity at the University of Glasgow but finally went to England to live. After taking up his residence there, he showed himself to be a man of independent mind and offended Charles II. Upon the accession of the latter's brother, James II, in 1685, Burnett left the country entirely and settled in Holland, where he came in contact with the future sovereigns of England, William and Mary. After they came to power in England and Scotland, he became the bishop of Salisbury. He was a rather prolific writer. He is now chiefly remembered for his *History of his Own Time*, which was important because of his knowledge of the history of the Church in Scotland, the Catholic question in England, and the negotiations which preceded the accession of William and Mary to the English and Scottish thrones.

The Restoration period produced, also, two notable diarists—Samuel Pepys (1633–1703) and John Evelyn (1620–1706). After attending St. Paul's school and the University of Cambridge, Samuel Pepys, probably through the influence of his cousin, the Earl of Sandwich, became a clerk in the navy office. From this beginning he gradually rose to the position of chief naval official. He was also president of the Royal Society. In 1660 he began to keep a diary and continued the practice for the next nine years. As the record was intended for no other eyes than his own, he wrote in shorthand a full and honest diary. He tells how he kicked his cook, blacked his wife's eye, forced the wives of navy men to prostitute themselves, took gifts, and got drunk. After nine years, he stopped making a record of events on account of his failing eyesight. The diary was first published in 1825. Its human qualities have won it readers ever since.

John Evelyn was a far better man morally than Pepys but, in consequence, wrote a less interesting diary. He attended Oxford, traveled abroad, and took some part in the Civil War. After the Restoration, he enjoyed the favor of the court and held many posts in the government. He was a moderate politician and adhered to the Anglican Church. His diary, which covers the period from 1640 to 1706, reflects the moderation and good taste of the author. Late in his career, he made the mistake of letting his house to Peter the Great during his visit to England. His diary was not published until 1818.

So far, we have been recording the careers and achievements of men who belonged to the dominant party after the Restoration. It must be remembered that a large part of the nation suffered from legislation which restricted their religious freedom. The so-called Clarendon Code subjected the dissenters of various sorts to much persecution and many inconveniences.

An example of what the Restoration meant to the Presbyterian element in the nation is furnished by the career of Richard Baxter (1615–1691). At the age of twenty-three he was ordained and began to make a reputation for himself as a preacher. For nineteen years he was stationed at Kidderminster, which he transformed from a parish infamous for its ignorance and depravity into an orderly and peaceful community. During a part of the Civil War, he served in the Puritan army as a chaplain. About 1660 he settled in London. Two years later he lost his post as a preacher of the Established Church and began to suffer persecution. From this date until the Revolution of 1688, he was repeatedly imprisoned for preaching to unauthorized congregations, and his places of worship were closed. In 1685 he was even tried by the infamous Lord Jeffreys. During these years, however, he was author of many religious works that once brought light and comfort to his followers but which are now of only antiquarian interest. Thanks to the adoption of religious toleration in England, he spent his last years in peace and honor.

For once in the history of letters, the submerged masses had a spokesman in the famous John Bunyan (1628–1688). His father followed the humble trade of tinker. He himself never attended any educational institution except a village school. As a result of the preaching which he heard, he was haunted by religious terrors. In an effort to save himself from them, he gave up all sorts of things. Finally, he became a Baptist preacher. In 1660, after the failure of the Puritan Revolution, he was put in Bedford jail. In this environment he taught his prison companions to read works like Fox's *Book of Martyrs* and began writing for the benefit of his fellow Dissenters. His failure to emphasize the importance of baptism by immersion, however, involved him in some trouble with the stricter Baptists. In 1671, he was released from jail. At this time, he already seems to have been at work on his famous allegory, *Pilgrim's Progress,* which was published in 1678. In this work, he compared the life of a Christian to a pilgrimage in which the traveler has to contend with all sorts of obstacles: quagmires, pits, steep hills, dark glens, a gloomy castle, a wilderness, and a black river. The work won for him a great reputation among Dissenters. In 1682 he added to his fame by the publication of his *Holy War.*

Of course the party in power had little difficulty in finding a spokesman. The chief writer of the period on the Royalist side was Samuel Butler (1612–1680). His chief work was *Hudibras,* a satire. It aimed to show up the less praiseworthy side of the Dissenters. Published in installments between 1663 and 1678, the poem presents a series of ludicrous scenes which set forth the vices of the Sectaries. It brings out their hypocrisy, churlishness, ungraciousness, greed, pride, and fast and loose morality. As a consequence, the satire was highly enjoyed by their opponents.

Literature in Other Countries

In comparison with Spain, France, and England, the other countries of Europe were almost silent in this period. The exception to this statement is the new state of the United Netherlands. The rise in national feeling found expression in some literary work. As early as the sixteenth century, the national movement expressed itself in the ballads of the victorious *Water Beggars,* the *Wilhelmus Lied* of Filip von Marnix, and in various religious writings. The deeds of the

345

Dutch patriots found historians of importance in Pieter Bor, Everhard van Reyd, Emmanuel van Meteren, and Pieter Hooft. A number of other writers, Joost van den Vondel (1587–1679) being the greatest of them, produced plays of interest.

The rest of the countries of Europe produced very little in the way of literature. Most of them did something in the way of producing folk songs and ballads. Some of them did a little religious writing. Germany still cherishes its picturesque novel, *Der Abenteurliche Simplicissimus,* by Grimmelshausen, which owes its form largely to Spain and its subject matter to the disintegration and horrors of the Thirty Years' War. Norway remembers Dorthe Engelbrechtsdatter and one or two other writers. In Sweden, some plays and poetry were written. The speeches of Gustavus Adolphus have both political and linguistic importance. In Denmark, too, there were small beginnings of literary activity.

The coming of the seventeenth century thus brought notable changes in the field of literature. The Italian writers ceased to be of importance, but Italian literature continued to provide models for writers outside of Italy. Spain, France, and England seized the intellectual leadership of Europe. In Spain, Cervantes, Lope de Vega, and Calderon produced works that were much admired and imitated. In France, three of the greatest dramatists of all time wrote for the stage. In England, Ben Jonson, John Milton, and John Dryden lived and wrote. In the other countries of Europe, there was complete silence or merely the first beginnings of literary activity.

In the seventeenth as in earlier centuries, many things besides military, diplomatic, and political events and conditions must be known if one is really to understand European society. It is the purpose of this chapter to describe some of the social and economic movements and institutions which characterized the period. They will help the reader to catch the spirit of the times.

Dress in the Seventeenth Century

In all ages men and women have paid much attention to the question of clothes. The abandonment and adoption of different styles in dress is a part of history. In the period under discussion, however, it is more than ordinarily difficult to give a picture of how the men and women dressed. For a time, Spanish styles continued to predominate. In Spain, they were worn until the middle of the century. In other parts of Western and Central Europe, new styles began to be fashionable about 1620. The more conservative members of society, of course, were somewhat slower about adopting new ways of dress.

In England and France, dress depended largely on one's politics and his outlook on life. In England, the supporters of the monarchy, the so-called cavaliers, who proudly look out at us from the pictures of Van Dyck, affected long locks, used much lace, and encased their legs in a good deal of leather. They wore hats which were broad-brimmed, cocked up at one side, and decorated with great ostrich plumes. They were likely to wear their hair so long that it fell down on their shoulders. They either clipped their beards and moustaches closely or did away with them entirely. They wore around their necks a flat collar which might be of lace. The military men, especially, wore broad sashes tied in a great bow. The breast and back of the doublet might be slashed and the cloak continued to be an essential garment. Men wore high leather boots with widespreading tops and provided with spurs which were worn in the *salon* as well as on the street. Lace was used for decoration at every feasible point. The French man of fashion was, if possible, even more decorated than his English contemporary. It took a jaunty, nonchalant spirit to wear the clothes of an English Cavalier or fashionable Frenchman of the time.

The God-fearing Puritans and Huguenots dressed more soberly. The Puritan, especially, was marked by conservative colors, his steeple-crowned hat, his large white collar and turned back cuffs, and a doublet and breeches. Even Puritans and Huguenots, though, wore warmer and richer colors than many people suppose.

After 1660, fashions changed again. It was the heyday of Louis XIV and the French court. The whims of the young monarch were law for his courtiers, and the French court became the model for the rest of Europe. Thenceforth, styles originated in France.

In the latter half of the century, styles changed both frequently and fundamentally. As long as Louis XIV retained his hair, long flowing locks continued to be the style. When the French monarch commenced to grow bald, they went out of style and wigs came into use. Thereafter, heads were shaved or closely cropped and ugly, enormous wigs took the place of natural hair.

At the same time, clothes commenced to take a more modern form. When a man of fashion went abroad, he wore as an outer garment a long, close-fitting coat that fell almost to the knees and flared considerably at the bottom. It was known as a *justaucorps* and took the place of the cloak formerly worn. Beneath it, he wore a shorter coat known as a vest. This garment was the forerunner of the modern coat. After the introduction of these new styles, ribbons, plumes, and boots went out of fashion, but high heels and pointed toes came into general use. The lace collar also made way for the neckcloth. In those days, men of fashion vied with women in the matter of dress.

Early in the century, women of fashion abandoned farthingales and hip pads and adopted low necks and high waists. As a usual thing, they wore two dresses in such a way as to display an underdress of brighter colors. The outer robe usually had puffed sleeves and a short train. Fashionable ladies also carried feather fans. Later in the century, the corset came back into style.

The Introduction of Tea and Coffee into Western Europe

At the same time that the men and women of Western and Central Europe were making important changes in their dress, they were adopting new social customs. Among the most important of these changes was the general adoption of the customs of drinking tea and coffee and smoking tobacco.

Though most Europeans have come to think of tea and coffee as almost indispensable beverages, neither of these plants is of European origin, and their use as a beverage is an acquired taste. The coffee plant seems to have come from Abyssinia and the custom of drinking coffee to have spread from there to the neighboring Moslem countries. In time, institutions for the dispensing of coffee seem to have grown up in the Levant. From the Eastern Mediterranean, the café or coffeehouse finally made its way to Western Europe.

During the seventeenth century, the institution was generally adopted by the peoples of Europe. Tradition says that a café was opened in 1654 in Marseille and that soon afterwards one was established in Paris. About the same time, a coffeehouse was founded in London. Later in the century, similar establishments were opened in Vienna and other German-speaking cities. By the end of the seventeenth century, cafés and coffeehouses were very numerous in Western Europe. The new establishments served a very useful purpose. People were able to make arrangements for meeting each other at some convenient coffeehouse. For a very small charge, one could pass an evening pleasantly conversing with one's friends and watching the passing show. Every social group made one of the numerous cafés or coffeehouses its headquarters. The upper and middle classes went to them daily to hear and discuss the news. In a sense, they took the place both of the modern newspaper and of the social club.

About the same time, tea was being introduced into Europe. At first, it appears to have made its way very slowly. In 1610 the Dutch East India Company seems to have brought some to Holland, and a few years later an agent of the English East India Company referred to the plant. In 1638 a Russian embassy again called the attention of the people of Western Europe to the new beverage. The English East India Company does not seem to have brought tea to England until 1660. In that year, Pepys, in his famous diary, refers to the fact that he just had had his first cup of tea. Since the new beverage cost from thirty to fifty dollars a pound at first, only the very prosperous could afford to drink it.

The Rise of Smoking

The custom of smoking tobacco, as we have seen, came from America. The history of its introduction into Europe is not exactly known. Doubtless, adventurous ship captains and sailors tried the new stimulant in America, brought some of it to Europe, and with great relish astonished the Europeans at home with the new custom. England seems to have been the first European country to adopt at all generally the custom called by contemporaries "the drinking of tobacco." Tradition points to Sir Walter Raleigh as the man who popularized smoking in England. At any rate, in a very short time every Elizabethan gallant who made any pretention to keeping up with the fashions took up the new custom and carried around with him a

349

tobacco box, a mirror, some little tongs for lifting a live coal from the hearth to his pipe, and a case of tobacco pipes. Among all the products brought from America, none affected the social life of Europe more than tobacco.

From England, the custom of smoking was soon carried to the continent. Undoubtedly, sailors and English students carried it to the Netherlands. From the Netherlands it apparently quickly spread to other countries. Its adoption was aided by the idea, which was harbored by even the doctors of the time, that tobacco was an excellent disinfectant, particularly against plague. Its spread was further fostered by the Thirty Years' War. The motley armies of that day quickly adopted the habit of smoking and handed it on to all with whom they came into contact. The new custom was probably introduced into Russia by English sailors and into the Levant by Venetians. By the middle of the seventeenth century, at any rate, the habit of smoking tobacco had been generally adopted in Europe by all classes.

The smoking of tobacco, however, encountered much opposition. The clergy fought against it and many governments prohibited its use. All the efforts to stop it, though, proved vain. In despair, the governments started to tax tobacco. In France, Richelieu, who needed new sources of revenue, began to tax tobacco. Other governments quickly imitated him. Soon, profitable monopolies for the sale of tobacco were established in most of the European states.

Improvements in Communication

At the beginning of the century, communication between distant places was slow and uncertain. Since most people could neither read nor write, the majority still felt little or no need for intercourse with other communities. In spite of this, however, some progress was made during the century toward the improvement of postal facilities.

In England the historical investigator finds the beginning of a modern postal system. At this time, there seem to have been eight main postal routes radiating from London to provincial England. The postage paid on letters depended on the distance that they were to travel. In 1680, there was established in London what must have seemed to contemporaries to be the last word in speedy communication. There was organized what was known as the penny post. This organization carried letters and parcels provided they did not weigh more than a pound. In addition to the main office, there were seven branch offices. Mail was collected hourly. In the center of the city, letters were delivered ten times a day; in the suburbs, six times daily.

350

After 1660, the right to carry mails was farmed out, but the contract provided for the free transportation of letters of the king, the ministers, and members of parliament.

Some improvement took place also in foreign mail service. The accession of James I to the English throne led to better and more frequent mail service between England and Scotland. About 1633, mail began to be sent from London to Brussels and Antwerp twice a week. The transmission of the letters between England and the Netherlands took, ordinarily, four or five days. In 1638 an agreement about the mails was also reached with the French postal authorities.

In France, there were similar improvements in the postal service. About 1622, the couriers seem to have commenced to arrive and depart at a fixed time. In 1653, in the midst of the *Fronde* movement, a penny post similar to the one just described for London was established in Paris. In 1780, this local postal system was united with that of the state.

Travel in the Seventeenth Century

In the Middle Ages and the early modern period, society was more stationary than at present. In spite of the obstacles to movement, however, a few persons did some traveling. Ambassadors with considerable retinues passed to the capitals to which they had been accredited. Some, urged on by a natural curiosity to see strange sights and foreign countries, toured the principal states of Western Europe before settling down as the dull and gouty masters of landed estates. Merchants and students frequented foreign marts and foreign universities. There was also much travel in ecclesiastical circles. Many went to and from Rome on the business of the Church. Monks passed from monastery to monastery. Pilgrims traveled to neighboring or distant shrines.

The travelers of the period did not lack advice. Many guide books had already been written to assist them. Like most advice, much of it was somewhat theoretical. Travelers, however, were advised to provide themselves with such things as a book of prayers and hymns and a linen overall to put over their clothes in case the bed was dirty. The guide books further recommended that the prospective traveler should learn something about medicine and cooking and counseled the voyager not to travel at night and to be accompanied in the daytime by one of the official guards that many towns and cities provided. They gave very excellent advice, too, concerning investigating the life, institutions, and conditions prevailing in the various places visited. As an aid toward this, they recommended the learning of the

351

languages used in the various countries visited. Like other guides, though, they at times mislead their readers by trusting too implicitly the books from which they had copied their information.

The travelers of the period had to contend with all sorts of difficulties. Whenever it was possible, they used the waterways of Europe. Even on the water, however, there were many hardships. On the ocean, travelers were at the mercy of capricious winds. Those wishing to cross the English Channel, for example, often waited many days for a favorable wind and, not infrequently, after they had started for the other shore found themselves driven back by adverse weather. The ports often lacked facilities for landing. The boats of the day were small; their passengers frequently were seasick. They had no fixed times for departure and arrival and made no pretense of furnishing cabins. Whenever it was possible, sailors still kept close to the coast and avoided getting very far from land.

Whenever they could, travelers used the rivers rather than the miserable roads. It was a pleasanter mode of travel. Riding in the wagons of the time usually produced a sort of seasickness. Even river travel, however, had its drawbacks. The traveler had to wait until there were enough passengers to fill the boat. Where a stream was very swift, as in the case of the upper Loire, the boats went only downstream. Often the traveler was expected to do his share of the rowing. When the boats were towed, the journey was tedious. There were, besides, such obstacles as tree stumps, rocks, and mill dams. The traveler of that day could not expect speed, comfort, or conveniences.

The Heyday of Piracy

One of the greatest drawbacks to travel at this time was piracy. There has always been more or less piracy, but in the seventeenth century it reached its greatest development. There was hardly any sea except the Baltic that was not infested with pirates. They were especially strong and numerous in Northern Africa and in the West Indies.

In Northern Africa, the situation favored the growth of piracy. The country was comparatively infertile. The Moors, exiled from Spain, found little to do in North Africa. Many of them, consequently, turned to the profitable trade of piracy. They were soon joined by renegade Christians from nearly every state of Europe. In time, there were more renegades than Moslems among the pirates. At the same time, orderly government was breaking down in Algiers, Tunis, and Tripoli. The Turkish pashas sold the office of governor to incompetent purchasers whose sole ambition was to recompense themselves and to acquire as much money as possible. These governors, consequently, left the pirates practically independent as long as they turned over ten per cent of the profits to the governors. Piracy was their chief source of revenue.

At first, the pirates of North Africa harassed only the shores of the Western Mediterranean. In 1606, however, a Dutch renegade taught them to build and navigate ships like those used by Western Europeans in the Atlantic Ocean. After the adoption of vessels of this type, the pirates not only continued to harass the Mediterranean, but they ranged far into the Atlantic Ocean. They infested the waters adjoining France and England and attacked ships returning from India, the Guinea coast, and the Spanish colonies in America. No one was safe from their attacks.

The chief objective of the pirates of Northern Africa was the capture of Christians for slaves. They first sorted out of their captives those likely to be ransomed. The rest they sold into slavery. The slaves were for the most part sold to dealers who in turn sold their services. A few, like physicians, were in great demand and were treated fairly well, but most of them worked hard and died early from mistreatment and overwork.

There are no accurate statistics as to the number of captives. One source reports that between 1569 and 1616 the so-called Barbary pirates captured 466 English vessels and sold their crews into slavery. In 1634 there are said to have been forty-five thousand Christian slaves in Northern Africa, besides some eight thousand who had been converted to the Moslem faith.

Some Englishmen and Frenchmen also turned to piracy. In Elizabeth's reign, piracy was almost a respectable profession as long as the victims were Spaniards. It was difficult sometimes to tell the difference between a pirate and a privateer. After the establishment of peace with Spain, the old hostility still persisted. Many captains and sailors continued to harass Spanish ships in spite of the fact that the government no longer approved of the practice. More than one of these pirates followed piracy for a time and then made his peace with the government by the payment of a handsome sum.

The efforts of the Spanish to monopolize the trade of their colonies caused the development of the so-called Buccaneers of the West Indies. Bands of traders arose who supplied the Spanish colonists illegally with the products which Spain failed to provide for them. The first buccaneers were Frenchmen who established themselves on the island of San Domingo, which the Spaniards had almost abandoned.

At first, the pirates of this region attacked only small vessels. In the latter half of the century, however, no type of vessel was safe from them.

The Starting of Modern Newspapers

In the light of future developments, one of the most important events of the seventeenth century was the starting of the modern newspaper. This important present-day institution had, however, a rather humble origin. It goes back to the custom started after the invention of printing of publishing a single sheet which announced one item of news of general interest. The earliest example of such a publication which has been preserved was printed at Augsburg in 1609. Such sheets were soon published in other countries.

In 1631, Renaudot (1586–1653), a secretary and medical adviser of Louis XIII and a protege of Richelieu, started a publication that may justly be called a newspaper. He started out by telling his patients the news which he had learned from private letters from abroad. In some way, the idea occurred to him to print what he had been telling his patients. At first, the publication was only four pages and confined itself entirely to foreign news. Later, the new publication ventured to discuss, very discreetly, domestic news. Soon, the new newspaper was published twice a week. After 1762, it was known as the *Gazette de France*.

From France, the idea spread rapidly to other countries. Newspapers seem to have appeared in Tuscany in 1636, in Sweden as early as 1644, in Holland in 1656, in Germany in 1658, and in London in 1665. In a number of other countries, the newspaper did not appear until the eighteenth century. Newspapers seem not to have appeared in St. Petersburg until 1702, in Madrid until 1726, and in Poland until 1761. These early newspapers, it must be remembered, lacked most of the features of the present-day press.

In the latter half of the seventeenth century, another type of publication was started—the modern magazine or periodical. This seems to have begun merely as a book catalogue. In an effort to make the books listed more interesting and saleable, booksellers or their hacks added short notices to the titles of the various books. In time, the notices became the leading feature. In 1665, the *Journal des Savants* was founded. It gave full summaries of the works reviewed which appealed both to the lazy and the busy reader. In 1686, a publication, the *Universal Historical Library* (which printed critical reviews of books), appeared in France. Four years earlier, a publication known as *Weekly Memorials for the Ingenous*, which contained original contributions, made its appearance. So by the end of the seventeenth century, the forerunners of the modern magazine were rather firmly established.

Street Lighting

Until late in the seventeenth century, the streets of European cities were dark and dangerous places at night. After the Angelus had sounded, shops and houses were carefully closed, and the streets were abandoned to robbers and bandits. The only flicker of light that illumined the darkness came from an occasional candle placed before some shrine.

As early as the fourteenth century, efforts were made to remedy this situation. For a long time, however, these attempts met with little or no success. In 1558, in Paris, people were ordered to place torches in their windows from ten in the evening until four in the morning, but they often refused to do it on the ground of the expense involved. Finally, the middle class did put Venetian lanterns in their windows, and the nobles placed large torches before their houses. People, however, still felt the need of lanterns when they went abroad. In 1665, consequently, a company of lantern bearers was organized. For a long time to come, the streets of Europe were dark and dangerous places.

The Development of Public Banks

For many years, the people of Europe hardly felt the need of developing modern banks. Most people were poor and land was the main form of wealth. Such banking functions as were needed were performed by churches and monasteries, money changers, commercial houses like the Fuggers, and, in seventeenth century England, by the goldsmiths. It is difficult, however, to separate their banking functions from investments in trading ventures and other commercial transactions.

As we approached the seventeenth century, however, the situation changed. The old insecurity of life and property continued, and moveable property, particularly money, increased as a result of the influx of precious metals from America and the rise of trade. People began to feel the need of a safe place to deposit their surplus money.

In response to this demand, public banks developed. The first of these new institutions arose in Southern Europe, particularly in Italy. The most important of them was founded at Venice in 1587. In 1609, the city of Amsterdam established a public bank in order to give the merchants of the city a safe place to deposit their funds. The new institution, however, paid no interest on such deposits. During the course of the century, similar public banks were founded at other commercial centers, particularly at Hamburg in 1619 and at Stockholm in 1658.

It is in England, however, that modern banking was first fully developed. When English country gentlemen and town merchants began to hold part of their capital in cash, they turned to the London goldsmiths for a safe place to deposit their funds. From them, the depositor received a note or receipt. In time, the deposit became a fund that could be drawn upon or transferred. So almost imperceptibly, these practices led to the development of modern checks and banknotes. The first known check bears the date, 1676.

The accumulation of deposits led to the rise of another modern banking practice. The goldsmiths soon found that they could safely lend a portion of the deposits. So instead of charging depositors a fee for their services, the goldsmiths paid depositors interest on their money. By this time, the goldsmiths had become, to all practical purposes, bankers.

A new era in English banking opened with the founding of the Bank of England. During the War of the League of Augsburg, England was greatly in need of money. As a remedy for the situation, it founded in 1693 a bank. In return for a large loan to the government, it granted to the stockholders of the new bank a number of valuable privileges. The bank handled the account of the government. It was permitted to be a joint stock company with limited liability. Its notes were accepted in payment of taxes. These privileges, which were added to from time to time, gave the Bank of England a decided advantage in its competition with private banks.

PART 4

The Eighteenth Century

CHAPTER 23

Central Europe in the Eighteenth Century

In the eighteenth century, the Holy Roman Empire continued to be a loosely organized, decentralized state. Its central institutions lacked all authority. Political power had fallen into the hands of the three hundred or more practically independent states composing the Empire. These varied greatly in size and resources. Two of the states, Austria and Prussia, had come to dominate the rest.

The Continued Rise of Prussia

Upon the death of Frederick I in 1713, he was succeeded by his son, Frederick William I (1713–1740). In the case of Frederick William I, legend has been active but far from kind or truthful. He had some striking peculiarities. These, his spiteful wife and children magnified and distorted into characteristics that made him something of an ogre. Although he had a fluent command of the French language, he usually spoke a coarse, vigorous German. He abhorred the shams, the loose life, the cabals, and the extravagance that prevailed at his father's court. He did occasionally belabor with his cane the idle grafters and people who opposed him. He liked the atmosphere created by his so-called "Tobacco Parliament," a gathering of a little group of cronies who met together, smoked, drank, and exchanged stories that smacked of the guardroom. He had a fondness, too, for big soldiers. So he really was somewhat eccentric.

On the other hand, he had many excellent qualities. Beneath his gruff exterior beat a kind heart, and he was interested in all that benefited his people. He provided for poor widows and supported a large orphan asylum at Potsdam. He was as quick to pardon as he was to condemn. He worked hard himself and merely expected like service from his officials and soldiers. In his efforts to avoid taking humiliating subsidies, he enforced a rigid economy that in the end made Prussia politically an independent state. For the same reason, he avoided war whenever he could. He was an excellent administrator. He lived in about the fashion of a prosperous country gentleman.

He devoted his attention mainly to building up his state. In his eyes, one of the essential features of a strong state was a strong army. On his accession, he found an army of 40,000 men. He left his successor a trained force of 83,000 men. For the purpose of improving the officers, he dismissed many foreign adventurers, employed in their place his own nobles, and started a school for the training of officers. He replaced the wooden ramrod with an iron one. He improved the efficiency of his troops by fastening the bayonnet outside the rifle barrel instead of inside it. He built a state factory for the manufacture of guns. In 1733, he adopted the cantonal system of recruiting the army. A canton contained on an average about five thousand families, and each canton was expected to furnish the recruits for a regiment. In practice, the recruits came exclusively from the peasant class.

Frederick William I also followed in the footsteps of the Great Elector by his efforts to attract immigrants to Prussia. He sought to settle colonists on the wastelands of his kingdom. He attracted settlers from Holland, the Swiss cantons, and southern and western Germany. He is said to have brought some 30,000 colonists into his state. About half of them came from Salzburg, where the new archbishop was persecuting his Protestant subjects. Their story has been told by Goethe in his *Hermann und Dorothea*. As a result of the royal policy, Frederick William I is said to have repeopled fifty-nine royal domains, three hundred and thirty villages, and six cities. In opening his state to the persecuted and ambitious, the king increased the royal revenues. They not only paid taxes but also bought from the Prussian sovereign horses, oxen, and cows.

Frederick William I did much to improve the administration of his state. By various reforms, he nearly doubled the revenues drawn from his domains. He abandoned the showy court maintained by his father and dismissed two thirds of the court officials. He reorganized his civil and military administration. In 1723 he worked out and put into force an elaborate and detailed set of instructions for the administration of his state that became famous. It tended to increase the power of the king in the administration and organized a somewhat clumsy general directory of four departments that was a great improvement over the machinery which it superseded.

The king, however, did nothing for the cultural advancement of his subjects. He neglected the universities, kidnapped their students for his army, and heaped abuse and contempt on their faculties. He neglected the royal library and diverted its funds. He reduced greatly the royal grant to the Academy of Art; cut off entirely the pension of Leibnitz, the philosopher and mathematician; and, after the latter's death, appointed the court fool president of the Academy of Sciences.

The later years of the king's rule were embittered by his quarrel with his son and heir, Prince Frederick. The younger man liked all that his father disliked—music, literature, gay clothes, and flighty companions. He abhorred the coarse associates of his father, military life, and vigorous amusements. His father's attempt to force him into the same mould that had produced the coarse, blunt, and God-fearing king gnarled and twisted his richly endowed nature and drove him to attempt to fly from the kingdom. The king captured his son, forced him to witness the execution of an accomplice, and then set him to work as a clerk in Potsdam. During the ensuing years, Prince Frederick learned the details of administration and the maneuvering of an army. This trying period of preparation laid the foundation for his later remarkable achievements.

Events in Austria

After being disappointed in his hopes of acquiring the succession of Spain, Charles VI of Austria devoted his attention to Austrian problems during most of the remaining years of his reign. In his eyes, the most important of these questions was the regulation of the succession. As had actually happened in 1700 in Spain, Austria was threatened with the extinction of the male line of the ruling Habsburg family. In 1703 the reigning Austrian sovereign had made provision for the succession of females in default of male heirs. Then in 1713 Charles VI, in a secret document known as the Pragmatic Sanction, gave his own daughters preference over women belonging to other branches of the family. These decrees made his daughter, Maria Theresa, the potential candidate for the Austrian throne in case it should become vacant.

Charles VI spent most of his reign in efforts to obtain the acquiescence of Europe to the Pragmatic Sanction. He exacted from his nieces renunciations of their claims to the throne. He wrung from the estates of his various kingdoms and provinces promises to support the claims of his daughter. Lastly, from one European power after another, in various ways, he won the assent of the rulers of Europe to his plans for the succession. In doing this, he neglected the advice attributed to Prince Eugene that the best guarantee of the Austrian succession would be a good army and a well-filled treasury.

War of the Austrian Succession

In 1740 the question of the Austrian succession came to a crisis. Frederick William I died and was succeeded on the Prussian throne by his son Frederick II, later known as Frederick the Great. A few months later, Charles VI of Austria died and was succeeded by his daughter, Maria Theresa. The various Habsburg provinces and kingdoms recognized as they had promised to do her claims to the succession. It remained to be seen whether the rulers of foreign states would also keep their promises.

While others hesitated, Frederick II acted. He was young, ambitious, and commanded an excellent army, a well-filled treasury, and the resources of a state of two million inhabitants. Across the imaginary line that bounded his state lay the almost defenceless territories of the young and inexperienced Maria Theresa. No sense of courtesy or justice restrained him. He promptly occupied without warning the rich province of Silesia. At the same time, he offered Maria Theresa, as compensation for the province which he was taking, his support for the candidacy of her husband in the coming Imperial election and his support against all her other enemies.

The bold action of Frederick II suddenly put to the test the work of Charles VI. Would the powers of Europe keep their promises to the Austrian ruler or would they imitate Frederick II? For a moment, they hesitated to break the peace. In the end, all but Great Britain found excuses for attacking Maria Theresa. While Great Britain offered the Austrian queen support in the form of subsidies and diplomatic support, France, Spain, Bavaria, and, finally, Saxony and the Kingdom of Sardinia signed a treaty of alliance directed against her. This was followed by the conclusion of an alliance between Prussia and France.

Since the days of Henry IV and Richelieu, it had been the policy of France to oppose the Habsburgs. In spite of the reluctance of Louis XV and his aged minister, Fleury, the young and ambitious French nobles thought the occasion propitious for French intervention. Maria Theresa hoped in the coming Imperial election to bring about the election of her husband, the young Francis of Lorraine. The War party in France, on the contrary, thought the time had come to deprive the house of Habsburg of the Imperial dignity and give it to the ruler of Bavaria. In the end, they persuaded not only France but a number of the other powers to enter the war.

In Europe the war was fought in three theatres—Germany, Italy, and the Netherlands. In 1741 two French armies crossed the Rhine River. One marched north into Westphalia in order to watch the Netherlands and to compel George II of Great Britain, in his capacity as Elector of Hanover, to maintain a strict neutrality with regard to Prussia. The other army marched in support of the Elector of Bavaria. From there, the combined armies of France and Bavaria marched into Prague. This victory made certain the election of Charles Albert of Bavaria as emperor under the title of Charles VII. For a moment, the allies were jubilant.

362

The war, however, soon took a different turn. The scattered provinces of Maria Theresa finally (but not in the dramatic manner narrated by Voltaire) rallied to her support. Scarcely had Charles VII been crowned than the Austrians occupied his capital, Munich, and the new emperor found himself without a state. In the midst of these reports, the news suddenly came that Frederick II, who did not wish his allies to be too successful, had signed in 1742 a treaty of peace. By this agreement, he abandoned France without warning but acquired the recognition by Austria of his claims to the rich province of Silesia. Under the circumstances, there was nothing left for the forces occupying Prague but to retreat with great losses of men and materials. In the meantime, the British, abandoning their neutrality, intervened actively with their own troops on the continent and decisively defeated a new French army near the Main River.

In Italy, Austria, France, Spain, and some of the Italian states fought throughout the war for comparatively small objectives. Austria, supported by the British fleet, sought to defend the territory which she had acquired in 1713 and opposed France and Spain, which were trying to install Bourbon princes on Italian thrones. This gave the ruler of the new kingdom of Sardinia an opportunity. In the hope of extending his territory in the Italian Peninsula at the expense of the duchy of Milan, he, in turn, sided with the powers allied against Maria Theresa, then with Austria, and again, finally, against the Austrian ruler.

In Germany, events, in the main, were favorable to Maria Theresa. In southern Germany, the death of the emperor, Charles VII, opened the way for a new Imperial election. As a result of the victory of the Austrians in Bohemia and Bavaria, Maria Theresa had little trouble in 1745 in elevating her adored husband to the Imperial throne. In northern Germany, the wily Frederick II entered the war again with success but, alarmed at the French victories in the Netherlands and irritated at the French failure to support him, again left his ally in the lurch and at the price of Silesia abandoned the struggle.

Up to 1744, the French and the British had technically been only indirectly at war. After that date, they directly intervened in the struggle and fought each other for four years in Europe, on the sea, and in America and India. In Europe, they fought each other in the Netherlands, where the French gained a series of brilliant victories that put them in control of the Austrian Netherlands and enabled them to invade the Dutch Netherlands. For the moment, French arms seemed to have recaptured their old skill and force.

By 1748, most of the powers at war were ready for peace. In spite of the brilliant feats of his armies, Louis XV had a real repugnance toward war and was ready to be generous and even prodigal as to terms. Most of the other powers were ready to negotiate on such a basis. As a result, the peace decided almost nothing. In Germany, the powers again confirmed the Pragmatic Sanction and recognized both the right of Maria Theresa to the Austrian throne and the right of her husband to the Imperial dignity, but left Frederick II in possession of the former Austrian province of Silesia. In Italy, a new Bourbon prince was installed on the throne of Parma, and the king of Sardinia advanced the boundary of his state to the banks of the Tessino River. In the Netherlands the French monarch, in spite of his victories, restored to Maria Theresa with a grand gesture all the Austrian Netherlands. In America and India, as will be narrated in the next chapter, France and Great Britain, to the great disgust of the British colonists in America, returned all conquests. So none of the powers, except Prussia, had much reason to be satisfied with the Treaty of Aix-la-Chapelle.

The Diplomatic Revolution

Within a few years the widespread dissatisfaction of the powers of Europe with the peace led to a renewal of the war. Maria Theresa could not reconcile herself to the loss of the great and prosperous province of Silesia. Prussia, in spite of her gains, was not satisfied either with the size or the configuration of her growing state. Four years earlier, in a political testament, Frederick II had already designated Saxony, West Prussia, and Swedish Pomerania as lands that should be acquired. The French people were not in as generous a mood as their sovereign and passed from mouth to mouth the phrase "stupid as the peace." Lastly, France and Great Britain continued the armed conflict in America and India. So war on the continent was almost inevitable.

During the ensuing eight years of nominal peace, almost unintentionally a fundamental realignment of the European powers took place. For nearly two hundred years France had followed the policy of humbling the Habsburgs in Austria and in Spain, and during the War of the Austrian Succession Great Britain had been allied with Austria. In the years immediately following that war, Austria and France became allies and found themselves confronted by an alliance of Prussia and Great Britain.

This shift in the alliances of Europe came about gradually. The first step in the diplomatic revolution was the signing in 1756 of a treaty between Prussia and Great Britain. In order to understand this action of the two powers, it must be remembered that George II, king of Great Britain, was also elector of the German state of Hanover and anxious about its defense. In theory, Great Britain was not bound to defend it. In practice, she always took the interests of Hanover into consideration, and, as Maria Theresa had failed to protect it during the War of the Austrian Succession, Great Britain was on the lookout for a more dependable ally. She finally decided that the rising state of Prussia, with its able ruler and strong army, met her requirements. Prussia, on the other hand, lacked money and feared an attack from both Austria and Russia. As a result, the two powers formed an alliance for the maintenance of peace in Germany in which Great Britain contributed subsidies in return for the protection of Hanover. Frederick II of Prussia mistakenly thought he could ally himself with Great Britain without losing entirely the cooperation of her rival, France.

The king of Prussia soon found out his mistake. For some time, Maria Theresa had been bringing to the attention of Louis XV, the king of France, the idea of the abandonment of the old hostility between France and Austria and the formation of an alliance between the two countries; but up until the signing of the Anglo-Prussian agreement, Louis XV remained deaf to her pleas. The news of the conclusion of the alliance of the two powers, however, aroused the wrath of the French sovereign and his advisers, and they promptly signed a treaty promising French aid to Austria in case of attack. This action ranged Austria and France against Prussia and Great Britain.

Up to this point, the French policy had been wise. Austria was a more dependable ally than Prussia. A treaty with her guaranteed France against attack on the continent while she was at war with Great Britain over colonies and commerce. Unfortunately for France, however, forces were at work pushing her into an offensive war. Austria still wanted Silesia. Russia was bringing pressure to bear for a war against Frederick II. These factors finally brought about the formation of a great coalition of the continental powers against Prussia. In 1757, Austria and France signed a second treaty in which France promised to aid Austria in the recovery of Silesia and Austria, and Russia formed an alliance against Prussia. This step on the part of France was a great blunder. It forced France to wage war at the same time on the continent and overseas.

The Seven Years' War

In the campaigns which followed, the king of Prussia found his state surrounded by enemies. From France, two armies, those of the Rhine and of the Main, advanced toward central Germany. On the east, the Russians poured into East Prussia. On the north, the Swedes attacked from Swedish Pomerania as a base. In Bohemia, a large

Austrian army prepared to overrun the former Austrian province of Silesia. From the Prussian point of view, the situation looked grave.

During the course of 1757, the fortunes of Frederick II varied. He began the war by a bold attack on the Saxons and, before the Austrians could join them, the king of Prussia attacked and completely defeated them and compelled them to join the Prussian forces. This daring stroke was followed by a Prussian offensive into Bohemia that ended in the defeat and withdrawal of the Prussians. In the meantime, the French advanced into central Germany and defeated an army composed of Hanoverian and other troops. The Prussians apparently had lost the war. At this point, however, the situation was completely changed by two striking Prussian victories—one over the French at Rossbach in central Germany and one over the Austrians in Silesia. The first drove the French back in complete rout. The second forced the Austrians to evacuate Silesia just when they seemed on the point of reconquering it. On all sides, Prussians seemed to have the advantage.

During the ensuing years, the king of Prussia continued to be in grave danger. On all sides, the pressure of his enemies continued. Even his victories caused the loss of irreplaceable men and supplies. In the campaign of 1758, while he drove the French back across the Rhine and Main rivers, the Russians advanced into East Prussia and then into Brandenburg. They retreated only after the indecisive battle of Zorndorf. In the following year, the Russians again advanced as far as Francfort-on-the-Oder. There, they were joined by the Austrians who had advanced from Bohemia. Again, Frederick II was saved by the failure of his enemies to take advantage of their sweeping victory at Kunersdorf. Before the end of the year, he again managed to drive back the Russians, Austrians, French, and Swedes.

By 1761, it seemed as if only a miracle could save Frederick II from complete defeat. During the course of the year, he continued to experience a series of reverses. In that year, though, the needed miracle actually happened. The death of Empress Elizabeth brought to the Russian throne Peter III, a great admirer of Frederick II. On the very day of his accession, he ordered the Russian armies to stay their victorious march. A little later, the two sovereigns signed a treaty which restored East Prussia to Frederick II and guaranteed each ruler the armed assistance of the other. The new policy saved the king of Prussia for the time being but did not last long. Peter III, the enthusiastic admirer of Frederick II, was soon deposed. His successor, Catherine II of Russia, however, withdrew entirely from the conflict. This freed Frederick II from much of his anxiety and

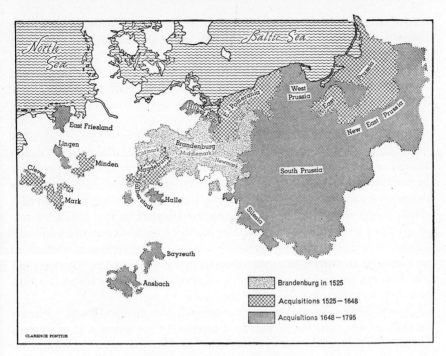

The Growth of Brandenburg Prussia to 1795

enabled him to regain his old position. All the combatants finally realized that nothing was to be gained by further fighting.

The war on the European continent ended, consequently, in the Treaty of Hubertusburg (February 15, 1763). It was signed almost at the same time as the Treaty of Paris, which brought to a close the struggle between France and Great Britain over colonies and commerce. In contrast with that treaty, the Treaty of Hubertusburg made no great changes in the map of Europe. By its terms, Frederick II kept the long-contested province of Silesia and promised to support the candidacy of Joseph II, son of Maria Theresa, for the Imperial throne. Frederick II had definitely won for his state the prestige of a great power, but he had achieved this end by ruining his subjects, exhausting his resources, and depopulating his state.

The Acquisition of West Prussia

The years following the peace of Hubertusburg were, for the most part, years of respite and recuperation from war. The ruler of Prussia and his people devoted themselves in the main to the improvement of the state. By diplomacy, however, the Prussian state, as will be shown at more length in Chapter 27, made an important

367

territorial acquisition. In 1772 the three neighboring powers of Prussia, Austria, and Russia began the partition of Poland. Prussia's share was the province of West Prussia. By its acquisition, Prussia increased its area by some 20,000 square miles, increased its resources materially, and linked together the central group of Prussian provinces with the province of East Prussia.

Frederick the Great as an Enlightened Despot

In the years of peace which followed the close of the Seven Years' War, Frederick II strove to be an enlightened despot. In the preceding century, Louis XIV and the many rulers that imitated him had thought that the state existed for the benefit of the monarch. Frederick II, on the other hand, considered himself as the first servant of the state and thought that it was his duty to work for the good of his subjects. He spent comparatively little of the revenues of the state on himself. It should be remembered, however, that the fortunes of his subjects depended on the benevolence of their ruler and not, as in Great Britain, on their rights before the law.

As a result of his theory of government, Frederick II was a hardworking sovereign. He arose at six and spent the greater part of the day at work. Only in the evening did he allow himself some relaxation. Then, he played the flute, discussed philosophy, or wrote. While he did little to change the framework of government, he actually exercised much more power than his predecessors had and left to his ministers much less freedom. He tried to give personal attention to a vast amount of business. This can be seen by examining his official correspondence which fills forty-four volumes, his collected works in thirty-three volumes, and other official publications. While he himself remained ruler, this tendency made for speedier action and for the enforcement of an honest and efficient administration. It did not insure a continuance of this sort of government.

Frederick II did little to change the fundamental structure of Prussian society. From his nobles, he merely asked unwavering loyalty, and he was even quite ready to increase their powers and privileges, particularly their local police and administrative powers. He expected the middle class to serve the state by increasing its trade and industry. To aid them in achieving these objectives, he used the usual mercantilist methods of the time. He excluded foreign manufactures by tariffs; restricted the exportation of raw materials; did away with some internal tolls, especially on the Oder (which had become a Prussian stream); established monopolies for tobacco, porcelain, and silk; stimulated mining in Silesia and shipbuilding at Stettin; and founded a Prussian bank (1765). He expected the peasants to continue to bear the burden of supporting the state. They furnished the rank and file of the army, performed innumerable services for their landlords, and built roads, transported troops, and ran errands for the state and its officials. He did do something for the peasants on his own domain lands, which included about one-third of the area of the state. He assured them heredity of tenure, limited the amount of their labor services, and freed their sons and daughters from doing menial tasks. He found the nobles too strong for him. In their case, he succeeded only in stopping the practice of *Bauernlegung* or prying the peasant from his petty holding in order to add his land to that of the lord. The ideal of Frederick II was thus what Bismarck was later to call the Christian State.

Frederick made a great effort to improve the economic condition of his state. He encouraged his subjects to make more use of clover and fodder crops, potatoes, and turnips. He introduced better methods of breeding cattle and sheep. He fostered the systematic planting of fir and pine trees. He carried out extensive drainage projects along the Oder and Vistula rivers and connected the two rivers by a canal. By these various means, he greatly increased the productivity of his state.

His greatest economic contribution to the welfare of Prussia, however, was his continuance of the family policy of encouraging the settlement of foreigners in his various provinces. As a result of the devastation wrought by the war, the Prussian state needed to increase its population materially. Consequently, Frederick II sought colonists over all Germany and in neighboring countries. They brought with them many skills and new products. They are said to have numbered 300,000. By his encouragement of colonization and the acquisition of the provinces of Silesia and West Prussia, Frederick made Prussia a state of five million inhabitants and doubled its population.

The encouragement of immigration was closely connected with another policy of the Hohenzollern rulers of Prussia. A number of factors tended to make the Prussian state tolerant of religious differences. The Prussian state needed immigrants so much that it was willing to overlook differences in religion. Lutherans and Calvinists and, finally, Jesuits and Jews were welcomed because of what they could contribute to the state. Other factors, however, made for tolerance, at least under Frederick II. Among these were the skepticism of the ruler and the influence of the times. Tolerance was being advocated by leaders of thought and literature.

Like all of his family, Frederick II devoted much attention to his army. At the close of his reign, it had the reputation of being the greatest military organization in Europe. It owed its position largely to Frederick's attention to details. The Prussian army went into battle only after long drill and with ample resources. It surpassed other armies by its precision in manoeuvers and by the superior fire power of its weapons. These qualities enabled its commanders to execute bold and unexpected tactics and strategy.

Joseph II as a Benevolent Despot

In the loosely held together state of Austria, meanwhile, a great admirer of Frederick II had come to power. In 1765 Francis I, the consort of Maria Theresa, had died. Upon the death of her beloved husband the Empress saw to it that her son, known in history as Joseph II, was elevated to the position of emperor of the Holy Roman Empire and co-ruler of the collection of provinces and kingdoms known as Austria. Upon the death of his mother in 1780, he became sole ruler of his hereditary state.

Like most other people, Joseph II was a product of his training and his times. When he was not crossed, he was an exceedingly agreeable young man, endowed with great vivacity and keen imagination. These qualities, as a result of the instructions of his solicitous mother to his tutors, had never been disciplined as they should have been. He lacked patience and understanding. Like Frederick II, he felt responsible for the good administration of his territories. In an effort to understand their needs, he traveled in Europe generally and endeavored to inquire minutely concerning the army, trade, industry, and various institutions. Absorbing from one of his tutors rationalist ideas, he prided himself on being in touch with the most advanced thought of his time. He set himself the task of reforming the customs and institutions of his hereditary territories accordingly, without much regard for their historic traditions or actual conditions.

From the time of his elevation as co-ruler of Austria, Joseph II strove to embody his ideas into reforms. He did not meet with much success, however, as long as his mother lived, since, in spite of his title, Maria Theresa gave her son a free hand only in military and foreign affairs. In domestic affairs Joseph II was unable to overcome the prudence of his mother and her attachment to her church. Only after her death in 1780 did he have real freedom in matters of reform. Upon the death of his mother, Joseph II issued in quick succession a series of reform decrees. Several of them dealt with the Church, particularly with the relations of Church and state. In order to be master in his own state, he followed the advice of a former monk who had been converted to Protestantism and strove to subordinate the Church to the state. He forbade the Austrian clergy to receive or obey papal bulls or letters from the Pope or other foreign superiors. He required pastoral letters of Austrian bishops to be submitted to the temporal authorities for approval and forbade appeals to Rome. He compelled bishops to take an oath of fidelity to himself and placed all monastic institutions under the jurisdiction of Austrian bishops.

He, likewise, reduced greatly the number of religious and monastic institutions. He bade all monastic institutions to refrain from accepting novices for a period of ten years. He abolished entirely the contemplative orders as useless but retained the teaching, charitable, and preaching orders. He used the property of the suppressed institutions for pensions of secularized monks and for the support of schools and humanitarian establishments. These provisions resulted in the suppression of 700 monastic institutions and 36,000 religious institutions. They left 324 monastic institutions and 27,000 religious institutions still functioning.

The reform measures of Joseph II, however, struck at many aspects of religious life. Other decrees attempted to regulate the decoration of churches, the use of religious relics and images, pilgrimages and processions, and burial customs. He removed marriage and divorce from the jurisdiction of the Church and made them civil matters. He introduced, also, religious toleration in his various provinces. Although he claimed to uphold and protect the Roman Catholic religion, he decreed toleration for communicants of the Protestant and Eastern Orthodox churches. Henceforth, Roman Catholics alone were to have the right of public worship, but members of other churches might worship God as they saw fit. In order to improve the education of the clergy, Joseph II suppressed the small diocesan seminaries for their education and established at Vienna, Pest, Pavia, and Louvain large general seminaries designed to give them a modern training.

Joseph II, likewise, promulgated many measures affecting economic conditions in his realm. He abolished primogeniture and serfdom. This gave the peasants personal liberty. Henceforth, they were free to marry, to make contracts, and to move from place to place. He established a protective tariff but suppressed many interior customs lines. He planned, but did not really carry out, a financial reorganization of the state that would have given the peasant 70 per cent of his income, his proprietor 18 per cent, and the state 12 per cent. By the conclusion of commercial treaties he created markets for Hungarian goods in Russia and Turkey, and promoted the establishment of commercial relations with the Levant and the East and West Indies. He fostered the construction of roads and canals.

Joseph II, too, reorganized the judicial system. He introduced a new penal code that abolished discrimination between the various orders of society. He reorganized the courts of the country. In the municipal courts, he substituted men with legal training for members of the governing class who were without legal education.

Joseph II, likewise, planned to better social conditions. He founded a hospital at Vienna, a school of military medicine, an institution for deaf mutes, and an asylum for the poor. He did much for education. In ten years the number of students in Bohemia rose from 14,000 to 117,000. He stressed, especially, agricultural and industrial education. He secularized all grades of schools. He abolished censorship of the press.

This flood of reform measures aroused opposition on all sides. The clergy led the revolt against the innovations in religion. In 1782, the Pope even went to Vienna to protest against the measures affecting the Church. Upon his arrival in the Austrian capital, he was shown the greatest courtesy by Joseph II and the deepest respect by the Austrian people, but he accomplished nothing by his visit.

In two of the territories of Joseph II, the opposition developed into armed revolt. In Hungary he had aroused discontent by not coming to the Hungarian capital to be crowned, by settling Germans in the country as colonists, enforcing the use of German instead of Latin as the official language, and imposing conscription and new taxes. In 1785, Joseph II replied to the protests of his Hungarian subjects by abolishing their ancient and long-cherished constitution and setting up a new administrative system. The peasants, particularly those in Transylvania, sided with their sovereign and burned many chateaux and villages. The nobles yielded but refused to support their king in the war against Turkey.

The Belgians, too, disliked the reforms of Joseph II. They objected to his policy of centralization and disapproved of his religious reforms. When the students at Brussels demonstrated against the reform measures, Joseph II, as he had done in Hungary, abolished the old provinces and set up a new administrative system. This stirred the protesting Belgians to armed revolt. They proclaimed the fall of Joseph II and the Independence of the Austrian Netherlands.

The outcome of Joseph II's reforms would have been disheartening even to a well man. By 1790, however, Joseph II was a dying man. In his discouragement, he annulled much of the offending legislation. Upon his accession to power in Austria, his brother, Leopold II, prudently made concessions to the protesting rebels of Hungary and the Austrian Netherlands. When this did not entirely restore order in Belgium, he firmly marched troops into the provinces. Contrary

372

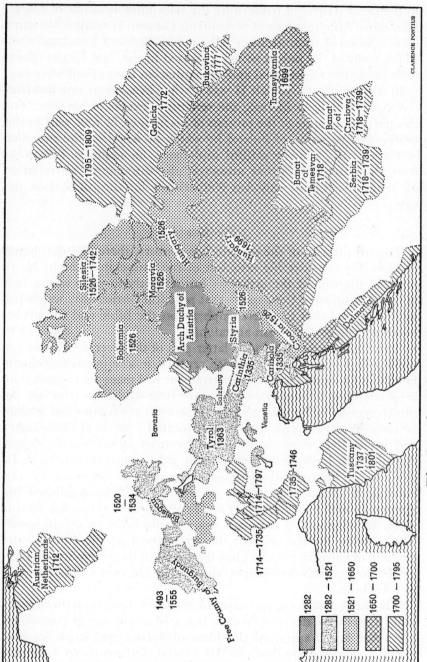

The Growth of the Habsburg Dominions to 1795

Austrian
Netherlands
1712

1520
—
1534

1493
—
1555

Free County of Burgundy

Breisgau

Bavaria

Tyrol
1363

1714—1735

1714—1797

1735—1746

Salzburg

Venetia

Tuscany
1737
1801

Arch Duchy of
Austria

Carinthia
1335

Carniola
1335

Styria
1526

Gorizia 1526

Dalmatia

Bohemia
1526

Moravia
1526

Silesia
1526—1742

1795—1809

Galicia
1772

Hungary
1526

Hungary
1699

Bukovina
1777

Transylvania
1699

Banat
of
Temesvar
1718

Serbia
1718—1739

Banat
of
Craiova
1718—1739

	1282
	1282 — 1521
	1521 — 1650
	1650 — 1700
	1700 — 1795

to the usual statement concerning the reforming measures of Joseph II, some of his reforms were permanent. Leopold II retained as much of the policy of centralization as he could. Serfdom remained abolished. Some of the public works remained in use. Not all the efforts to improve the educational and humanitarian institutions were lost.

In foreign affairs, Joseph II was neither benevolent nor humanitarian. He strove to increase the territorial extent of his state. For this purpose, in spite of the protests of his mother, he took part in the brazen first partition of Poland by which he acquired the province of Galicia. In 1775, by skillful diplomacy, he acquired Bukowina from the Turks. He strove unsuccessfully throughout his reign to exchange the distant Austrian Netherlands for the contiguous Bavaria.

Pietism

Toward the end of the seventeenth century, there had developed in Germany considerable criticism of the Lutheran Church. Many felt that the rule of the orthodox Lutheran theologians was as bad as the absolutism of the papacy, that practical Christianity was being neglected, and that the early emphasis on the Bible and the priesthood of believers had been abandoned.

This feeling gave rise, in the latter part of the seventeenth century and the first half of the eighteenth century, to a religious movement known as Pietism. Though the movement had many forerunners, its originator was Philipp Jakob Spener (1635–1705), an Alsatian. At the University of Strasbourg and at Geneva, where he spent a year, he came in contact with men who advocated a practical Christianity and whose lives were characterized by strict morality and a rigid discipline. In 1666, he became a pastor at Frankfort on the Main. In this city, he began holding religious meetings in his house for the cultivation of a Christian way of life. In 1675 he published his *Earnest Desires for a Reform of the True Evangelical Church.* In this work, he advocated a thorough study of the Bible in private meetings, a voice for the laity in the government of the Church, the practice of Christianity, the kind treatment of the heterodox and unbelievers, a greater emphasis on devotional life, and a different style of preaching.

The work made a great impression. Many Lutheran theologians and pastors were deeply offended, but a large number of pastors, on the other hand, approved the ideas of Spener and strove to give them a practical application. All central and northern Germany was deeply affected by Pietism. In some cases, it lead to exaggeration and fanaticism.

One of the important results of the Pietist movement was the founding of the church known as the Moravian Brethren. Its roots go back to the Hussite revolt. The more extreme partisans of that movement broke away from the papacy in the fifteenth century and put great emphasis on purity of morals. By 1609, they included half of the Protestants in Bohemia, but, in 1620, they were almost exterminated as a result of the battle of the White Hill. They survived as only isolated communities under the protection of some landlord.

In the early part of the eighteenth century, a number of these refugee religious groups took refuge with a pious Saxon nobleman, Count Zinzendorf (1700–1760). At first, he had no intention of founding a new church. He aimed merely to organize a Christian association for the promotion of a Christian life. Since the refugees differed greatly in religious practices, the count found himself almost forced to adopt a common order of worship and a common organization. The members of the revived church look upon the year 1727 as the date of their founding. From Herrnhut, the new church spread into many lands. It was one of the first Protestant churches to adopt the principle of carrying on foreign missions. Its missionaries found their way not only to many parts of Europe but to the West Indies, Greenland, North and South America, Egypt, and South Africa. The Moravian Church has, as a result, always exercised more influence than its numbers would seem to justify.

Transition

Thus, in the eighteenth century, Central Europe was in turmoil much of the time. After the close of the War of the Spanish Succession, there was peace for a time. Charles VI of Austria ultilized it to arrange for the succession of his daughter, Maria Theresa, to the Austrian throne. Frederick William I employed it to strengthen his state. The accession of Frederick II and Maria Theresa to power in Prussia and Austria inaugurated a long period characterized by two wars. Pushed on by ambition and invited by a favorable opportunity, Frederick II occupied the rich province of Silesia. Not until Prussia had demonstrated her strength in the two wars of the Austrian Succession and the Seven Years' War, was peace re-established. The restoration of peace gave Frederick II, and a little later, Joseph II an opportunity to play the role of enlightened despots. By following the family policy through four generations of territorial aggrandizement, military improvement, colonization, and religious toleration, the Hohenzollerns made Prussia a state of the first rank. By his disregard of tradition and actual conditions, the well-meaning Joseph II left his ramshackle empire weakened and in turmoil.

CHAPTER 24

The Struggle for Colonial and Commercial Supremacy

In the eighteenth century, the struggle for colonies and commerce continued. In this conflict, France and Great Britain played the leading roles. The Portuguese were having difficulty in clinging to the remnants of their once great empire. Spain was no longer a power of the first rank and confined her activity to the expansion of her territory in what is now the southwestern part of the United States. Holland was unable to hold the position of dominance she had once held. This left France and Great Britain as the chief contestants for colonies and commerce.

The Early Colonial Conflicts of France and Great Britain

At first, the colonies of France and England in America were too weak and too isolated to come into conflict. By 1689, however, they were strong enough to take part in the struggles which broke out between the two powers on the continent of Europe. Even by that date, though, they were hardly strong enough to wage a decisive war. The vast territory claimed by France was held by a few small and scattered fortified posts that could not raise a military force of more than twelve hundred men. The English colonies, a narrow band of settlements along the Atlantic coast, were more thickly populated but lacked unity and, in some cases, interest in the struggle of the two powers.

The first of the colonial struggles between France and England took place during the War of the League of Augsburg and is known as King William's War (1690–1697). The French, for the most part, had to content themselves with raids against the English border settlements and expeditions against Newfoundland and the Hudson's Bay trading posts. The British sent expeditions against Acadia, Montreal, and Quebec. These military actions, however, did not change the situation in the American colonies fundamentally.

Peace had hardly been concluded when the outbreak of the War of the Spanish Succession in Europe led to a new colonial conflict, known in America as Queen Anne's War (1701–1713). During its course, new raids were made on the British border settlements, and a number of expeditions were undertaken. The only decisive military action of the war was the capture of Port Royal by the British colonists. By the terms of the Treaty of Utrecht (1713), which brought the struggle to a close, Great Britain made some important territorial gains. These included the cession of Acadia by France and her recognition of the British claims to Newfoundland and the Hudson's Bay region.

The Struggle for the Coast of the Gulf of Mexico

The discovery of the Lower Mississippi called the attention of the European powers to the importance of the region around the Gulf of Mexico. Spain was already well established there in two excellent bases—Florida and Mexico. Great Britain and France both began to plan to establish themselves in the region. These plans made a struggle between the three powers inevitable.

In 1698, the French made their first attempt to establish themselves in the region that came to be known as Louisiana. Checked by the Spanish who strengthened Pensacola, they established a settlement at Biloxi which was later moved to Mobile Bay. For a number of years, the French settlement was not very successful. From time to time, other settlements were made, but actual permanent settlers came only in very small numbers. In 1718, New Orleans, named for the regent of France, was established and became the capital of the new colony. For a few years thereafter, Louisiana became the foundation on which the Scottish financier, John Law, based his schemes. During that time, colonists came in greater numbers, slavery was introduced, and tracts of land were taken up not only on the banks of the Mississippi but along a number of other rivers in the region. Finally, Louisiana came to include the Illinois country. Beyond the new French settlements, it must always be remembered, French traders ranged continually far and wide.

The advance of the French into Louisiana initiated a struggle on the part of the Spanish for control of northern Mexico and what is now southwestern United States. In Chihuahua, first a mission was founded and then in 1703 and 1704 rich silver deposits were discovered. Soon, settlements were made in the valley of the Rio Grande River. In 1706, Albuquerque in New Mexico was settled. In 1716, the Spanish established themselves permanently in Texas. Among the places settled in this region was San Antonio. From these settlements, expeditions went out in various directions. At the same time, other Spaniards, particularly Spanish Fathers of the Church, were taking the first steps toward the discovery and settlement of California.

The War Between Great Britain and Spain (1739)

Meanwhile, relations between Spain and Great Britain had grown steadily worse. The British were naturally anxious to break down the Spanish monopoly in America. By the Treaty of Utrecht, consequently, they had wrested two concessions. They obtained the right to send annually to Spanish America a ship of five hundred tons' burden and to supply the Spanish settlements with slaves. These concessions did not satisfy the British merchants. In defiance of the Spanish authorities, they carried on an extensive and growing smuggling trade. The efforts of the Spaniards to retain their monopoly led to harsh treatment of captured smugglers. This, in turn, caused a rise of the war spirit in Great Britain. By 1739, in spite of the reluctance of Great Britain's chief minister to enter a conflict, the two countries went to war.

The war was popularly known as the War of Jenkins' Ear. The name came from a certain British seaman who claimed that a Spanish coast guard captain had captured him, cut off his ear, and insolently told him to take it home to his master. Jenkins' story did much to inflame public opinion.

The ensuing struggle was indecisive. Much of the fighting took place at sea. The British sent unsuccessful expeditions against Cartagena on the Isthmus of Panama, Cuba, and the coast of Venezuela. They also sent Commodore George Anson to prey on Spanish shipping in the Pacific. On land, there was considerable fighting on the border between the Spanish settlement of Florida and the British settlement of Georgia. Each side made unsuccessful attacks on the strongholds of the other.

The Struggle for the Mississippi and Ohio Valleys

The war between Spain and Great Britain soon merged into a larger struggle. In 1740, the death of Emperor Charles VI had given rise to a conflict for control of the various provinces which he left to his daughter, Maria Theresa. Before this War of the Austrian Succession (1740–1748) came to a close, it had involved most of the powers of Western and Central Europe. By 1744, accordingly, even Great Britain and France were in open war both in Europe and in the colonies.

The fighting in America was indecisive. The New England colonies organized an expedition which took Louisburg. The French renewed their border raids from Acadia to New York. A French effort to recapture Acadia failed. There was, too, considerable fighting at sea. At the close of the struggle, however, to the great disgust

378

of New England colonies, all conquests were restored by the terms of the Treaty of Aix-la-Chapelle (1748).

The treaty signed in 1748 was hardly a truce. In Acadia, the Ohio Valley, and what is now the southeastern United States, the interests of the British, the French, and the Spaniards continued to clash. In Acadia, the French population was a source of danger. In their efforts to insure the loyalty of the conquered population, the British drove three or four thousand French-speaking inhabitants out of Acadia.

In the Ohio Valley, the interests of Great Britain and France clashed on a larger stage. By 1749, the rivalry of the two powers reached a serious point. Five years earlier, the Iroquois Indians had granted the British control of the territory north of the Ohio River. By subsequent agreements, the British acquired title to lands south of the Ohio. In 1749, steps were taken to occupy the ceded territory. A charter was granted which conveyed a half million acres of land on the Upper Ohio to some English and Virginia gentlemen. These men promptly sent out an agent to explore the region and took the first steps toward the establishment of the Cumberland Pike, as the road across the mountains was called.

This activity of the British stirred the French to action. They made considerable effort to strengthen the frontier. They established fortified posts at what are now known as Toronto, Detroit, and Sault Sainte Marie. In addition, the governor of Canada dispatched an agent to take possession of the disputed territory. Leaving Lake Erie, a French expedition passed down the valley of the Alleghany River, and then along the Ohio River. At frequent intervals, it proclaimed French sovereignty, nailed up sheets of tin bearing the arms of France, and buried lead plates which asserted that the Ohio Valley belonged to the king of France.

In 1753, the French appointed a more vigorous governor general, the Marquis Duquesne. This official promptly took steps to occupy the Ohio Valley. He sent an expedition of fifteen hundred men that built Fort Presqu 'Isle on Lake Erie, cut a road to French Creek, and built Fort Le Boeuf. The French planned to complete the occupation of the Alleghany Valley by building a fort at the point where the Alleghany and the Monongahela rivers join, but they were prevented from carrying out this part of their plans by the lateness of the season.

Realizing the significance of what the French were doing, Dinwiddie, the lieutenant governor of Virginia, obtained permission of the British home government to take countermeasures. First, he sent a message of protest. It was carried by a young surveyor, George

Washington, a member of a prominent Virginia family, who had just reached the age of twenty-one. He was courteously received but was given to understand that the French intended to keep possession of their new posts. They could be driven out only by the use of force.

Upon receiving this reply, Dinwiddie began to prepare for war. He demanded men and money from the Virginia House of Burgesses, solicited the aid of friendly Indian tribes, and appealed for help to the governors of neighboring colonies. He urged the governors of New York and Massachusetts to divert French troops from the Ohio Valley by an attack on Canada.

The outcome of his efforts was very disappointing. A small force of about three hundred provincials under the command of Joshua Frye and George Washington was actually raised. When a few backwoodsmen were sent forward early in 1754 to build a fort at the forks of the Ohio, they were captured by a body of French and Indians who then built Fort Duquesne. Washington, who by this time was in command of the British troops, then advanced as far as Great Meadows, where he built a rude fortification which he called Fort Necessity. It proved to be poorly located and badly constructed. After losing fifty or sixty men in a French attack on the new fort, Washington was forced to surrender and retreat to Virginia.

Although France and Great Britain were still nominally at peace at the time of this incident, both powers promptly began to prepare for war in America. The British sent to Virginia, Major General Edward Braddock, a stubborn, irascible man, little given to taking advice, and with him two regiments of regular troops. The French sent three thousand troops to Canada. The British had, as it proved, enough ships to dominate the sea. Upon his arrival in America, Braddock, in cooperation with a number of colonial governors, drew up a plan of campaign.

The French and Indian War (1756–1763)

In the campaign of 1755 which followed, Braddock started from Fort Cumberland as a base. He set out with about 2,000 men for Fort Duquesne. Unused to frontier fighting, the British regulars were ambushed by the French and Indians at a point about seven miles from Fort Duquesne. The French and Indians fired from behind trees. The British regulars, using the methods employed in Europe, wheeled into line and fought in the open against an invisible enemy. They displayed bravery and discipline but, in the end, broke and fled. Amid scenes of the greatest confusion, Braddock was mortally wounded. This left the command of the defeated troops to George Washington, who saved what he could of his forces. The disastrous

380

defeat left the frontier of the middle colonies open to attacks by Indian war bands who killed hundreds of British settlers.

Until 1758, the war in America was marked by a series of French successes and British reverses. For one reason or another, British campaigns against Crown Point, Fort Niagara, and Fort Ticonderoga failed. Oswego and Fort William Henry fell into the hands of French. The only British success was the driving out of Acadia of some six thousand more French colonists who were unwilling to take an oath of allegiance to the British crown. Their story has been told with some poetic license by Longfellow in his well-known poem "Evangeline."

In 1758, the coming of William Pitt into power in Great Britain brought a new vision and increased force to the campaign in America. The new minister was the first to realize the importance of the struggle in the colonies. In contrast to his predecessors, he sent capable commanders and larger forces to America. Attacks were planned against the French at Louisburg, in the Lake Champlain region, and at Fort Duquesne.

The carefully planned campaign was to a large extent successfully carried out. At Louisburg, the British destroyed a number of French vessels, captured the defences of the town, and took six thousand prisoners. The French garrison at Fort Frontenac, weakened by withdrawals, soon surrendered to a much stronger British force. At Fort Duquesne, upon the approach of the British, the French garrison destroyed the fortifications and retired. Only at Fort Ticonderoga were the British repulsed with great losses.

For the year 1759, the British authorities made preparations for another great campaign. Four expeditions were planned: one against Fort Niagara, a second against the French settlements on Lake Erie, a third against Ticonderoga and Crown Point, and a fourth against Quebec. The last was by far the most important and most dramatic operation. Led by Admiral Saunders and Major General Wolfe, thirty-nine men-of-war and twenty-six transports, manned by eighteen thousand men, moved up the St. Lawrence River to take the capital of Canada. Before them towered the almost perpendicular cliffs upon which Quebec was built, and, on the plain above, a French army of almost equal strength stood guard. For several weeks, the British fleet and expeditionary forces were baffled by the natural and military defences of the city. Finally, the British found a path up the cliffs at a point two miles above Quebec. Feinting an attack below the city, the British made their way during the night of September 12 up the path and onto the Plains of Abraham on the plateau behind the city. In the battle that followed, both Wolfe, the English leader, and

Montcalm, the French commander, were killed, but the British forces took the city, the key to the St. Lawrence. During the course of the succeeding year, the remaining French forts, including Montreal, surrendered.

The Struggle for India

When Europeans first reached India, they had no thought of establishing themselves as political powers. The peninsula had been conquered by the Moslems, and a Moslem emperor ruled over the many peoples of the peninsula. The European intruders sought merely the right to trade with India. This remained the situation until the War of the Austrian Succession.

At first, the Moslem rulers wielded great power. Their will was law over the whole peninsula. In the end, however, they only nominally ruled India. Their empire became the prey of invaders, and their subordinates gradually absorbed the power which the Moslem rulers had formerly exercised. The European traders then found their position threatened not by one great power but by numerous petty tyrants.

In 1740, at the time of the breaking out of the War of the Austrian Succession, Europeans had established themselves only at posts scattered along the coasts. The Portuguese still retained Diu and Goa. The Dutch were located at five points of which the most important was the island of Ceylon. The French had four trading posts: Chandarnagar, Pondicherry, Mahé, and Karikal. The British had established themselves at Bombay, Madras and Fort Saint David, and Calcutta. The Dutch and the French had the advantage of having a number of points of call between Europe and India.

The first European to realize the significance of the changes taking place in India was Dupleix. In 1715, at the age of eighteen, he had come out to India. In 1720, through the influence of his father, one of the large stockholders of the French East India Company, he became an official. In 1730, he became governor of the French post of Chandarnagar and is credited with stirring to new activity that indolent port. In 1741, he married a widow, born in Europe but reared in India, who had a thorough knowledge of the languages and conditions of the country. She proved to be a great help to him. His success in these subordinate positions finally attracted the attention of the French authorities and brought him the appointment to the governorship of French India.

When war finally broke out between France and Great Britain in 1744, during the War of the Austrian Succession, neither country was very well prepared for a struggle in India. This situation caused Dupleix to appeal to the local native prince, the Nabob of Arcot, for assistance in maintaining neutrality. This continued to be the situation until a French fleet, commanded by La Bourdonnais, arrived off Pondicherry. After its arrival, Dupleix hoped for its aid in destroying the neighboring British post at Madras, but the two French authorities quarreled. La Bourdonnais merely wished to sack the British post, while Dupleix desired to subjugate it completely. The quarrel made it impossible for Dupleix to fulfill his promises to the Nabob of Arcot, and he found himself at war with the local Hindu ruler as well as with the British. In the struggle which followed, the Nabob of Arcot was decisively defeated, and the French established themselves for the first time as an independent political and military power. They failed, though, to capture Fort Saint David from the British. At this point, the representatives of the two powers negotiated in Europe a peace which restored Madras to the British and its former status.

However, the peace signed in Europe by no means re-established peace in India. The posts of the two rival powers were too close together for the maintenance of peaceful relations. Even the demands of commerce made it imperative for the two powers to intervene in Indian politics. Both sides found it necessary to fortify their trading posts, to raise and maintain regular armies and native troops, and to strive for political privileges.

Struggles between the heirs of native rulers soon offered Dupleix a chance to intervene again in native politics. He was interested in the succession to two thrones in particular. One was the throne of Carnatic, the state in which Pondicherry, Madras and Fort Saint David were situated. The other was the suzerain of the Nabob of the Carnatic, the much larger state of the Nizam of Deccan.

The story of the French intervention in affairs of the two states is long and intricate and does not need to be told here. The temporary results of the French intervention is of more importance. By a skillful mixture of war and diplomacy, Dupleix gained control, for the time being, of both states. This, in turn, gave him control not only of their resources but of a number of dependent principalities. For the moment at least, he ruled over most of Southern India and a territory twice the size of France.

The impressive gains made by Dupleix, however, had a somewhat insecure foundation. The officials of the French East India Company stationed in France had no clear comprehension of the situation in India or sympathy with the ideas of Dupleix. Dupleix, moreover, was not a general. He was merely a skillful diplomat and at the mercy of subordinates for the execution of his projects. Furthermore, the British were well established in India and were almost certain sooner or later to fight the French with their own weapons. Besides this, the French position depended largely on the allegiance of native rulers and dynastic conditions liable at any moment to change.

In the end, the attitude of the officials in France brought about the downfall of Dupleix and the defeat of all his plans. They thought only of the revenues to be derived from commerce in India, and they failed to see that the plans of Dupleix gave the only assurance of a continuation of commercial revenues which they were receiving. They looked upon Dupleix, consequently, with disfavor and urged peace in answer to his requests for men and supplies. So, disregarding his pleas and without his knowledge, they entered into negotiations with the British authorities. The two parties agreed to re-establish things as they had been before Dupleix intervened in India. In 1754, a commissioner arrived from France charged with carrying out the instructions of the French East India Company. The astonished Dupleix was arrested and sent back to France where, in a few years, he died, mistreated and neglected by the company, the government, and the general public.

The British Conquest of India

The French sacrifice of Dupleix did not bring peace to India. That depended on Indian conditions and not on the wishes of European directors in France and Great Britain. Soon after the departure of Dupleix, consequently, trouble broke out in Bengal, one of the provinces that had separated itself from the authority of the former Moslem emperors of India. In this province, the British had trading posts at Calcutta and a number of other points; and the French were established at Chandarnagar. Both the British and the French were largely at the mercy of the native ruler.

In 1756, the ruling prince in Bengal was Siraj-ud-daula. Although heir to the throne, he had had no training for such a post. He was ignorant, drunken, debauched, irascible, and headstrong. He considered his own whims of the utmost importance but attached very little significance to the wishes or even lives of others. Upon ascending the throne, his first act was to persecute the other members of his family.

These qualities soon involved Siraj-ud-daula in difficulties with the British. They had given asylum to one of his victims. This heightened his instinctive hate of the British. In spite of efforts of the British authorities to placate him, he took Calcutta by a surprise attack and captured 146 British prisoners. On the night of June 19, 1756, he incarcerated his captives in a prison only twenty feet square, that has since become celebrated as the Black Hole of Calcutta. As a result of the stifling heat of the night and the lack of air, all but twenty of the captives died. The subordinates of Siraj-ud-daula had not dared to disturb the sleeping despot in order to remedy the situation. This terrible deed forced the British to abandon the policy of neutrality just at the moment the French were giving up their chance for an Indian empire.

Fortunately for the British, they found a great leader in Robert Clive. Born in 1725, he had been sent at the age of eighteen to India by his family. When war broke out there, he was a simple clerk in the employ of the English East India Company. The outbreak of the war gave him an opportunity. He gladly laid down his pen and took up the sword. In the fighting in the Carnatic, he had distinguished himself; and by the time of the Black Hole in Bengal, he had risen to the rank of lieutenant colonel in the British army, general for the English East India Company, and Governor of Fort Saint David.

Upon receiving the news from Bengal, Clive set out for that province with large powers and with a force of 900 English troops and 1,500 sepoys. Meantime, the ignorant Siraj-ud-daula had retired to his capital confident that he had disposed of the British. Upon hearing of the arrival of Clive and his army at Calcutta, the surprised ruler collected his forces and prepared for war. After some minor combats, Siraj-ud-daula, who missed the revenues he had formerly received from the British trading posts, agreed to restore to the British all their trading posts and privileges, to permit them to fortify Calcutta, and to indemnify them for the loss of their merchandise.

By this time, however, the British were ready to destroy, if possible, their French rival. After considerable negotiation, they extorted from Siraj-ud-daula permission to attack the French trading post of Chandarnagar. In the attack on that settlement which followed, the French fought bravely but were overpowered by the superior British artillery. The fall of Chandarnagar brought an end to French influence in Bengal. If the French had followed the ideas of Dupleix and allied themselves with Siraj-ud-daula, they might have saved themselves.

The defeat of the French in Bengal placed Siraj-ud-daula in a dilemma. He hated and feared the British. Sometimes, he was beside himself with anger against them. At other times, he was most servile toward them. Confronted by this situation, Clive sought to placate Siraj-ud-daula and to incite one of his subordinates, Mir-Djafer, against him. When all was ready Clive marched with 900 English troops, 2,000 sepoys, and a few pieces of artillery to Plassey, where Siraj-ud-daula had assembled a force of 50,000 footsoldiers, 1,800 cavalry, and fifty cannon. On June 23, 1757, a cannonade of the native position was followed by the desertion of Mir-Djafer to the British

385

side. There was not a great deal of fighting. The next day, Siraj-ud-daula himself was taken and put to death. This ended the conflict.

The results of this comparatively small engagement of Plassey were of great importance both to Clive and the East India Company. In return for British help in acquiring rule of the province, Mir-Djafer promised to pay the British a very large sum of money, to suppress all the French trading posts in the province, to exclude the French henceforth from Bengal, and to cede a large area around Calcutta. To Clive, the victory brought wealth and the title of Baron of Plassey. For the time being, he dominated the great province of Bengal.

In spite of their losses in Bengal, the French were still an important factor in Indian politics. They were dominant in the Deccan, where Bussy, a trusted subordinate of Dupleix, still controlled the situation with the aid of a small army of 160 Europeans and 600 sepoys. This gave the French rule over most of Southern India.

In order to save India for France, the awakened French authorities finally sent to the peninsula Lally, Baron de Tollendal, a brave officer and experienced diplomat, who brought with him a considerable number of troops. He came with the almost impossible instructions to drive out the British without mixing in Indian politics. He had the further handicap of knowing practically nothing about India.

At first, the effort of Lally, Baron de Tollendal met with considerable success. His forces attacked and captured two strongly fortified places. One of them was Fort Saint David. Almost from the beginning, however, Lally, Baron de Tollendal made enemies for himself and the French cause. In his haste to get on with the military campaign, he ignored caste distinctions and compelled Brahmins and Pariahs to work together and to take the place of beasts of burden. He recalled Bussy from the Deccan and allowed that state and all its dependencies to fall into the hands of the British. He failed to take the native state of Tandjsore, which he attacked in the hope of augmenting his resources, but increased the hatred of the Indian population by pillaging temples and cities. He quarreled with Bussy. He failed to take Madras. Finally, in 1760, his mutinous troops were decisively defeated in a battle at Wandewash. This defeat led to the fall of the remaining French posts in India. By 1761, the last French post had surrendered.

The Treaty of Paris

In 1763, the decisive defeat of France in both America and India led to the negotiating and signing of the Treaty of Paris, one of the most important diplomatic documents of modern history. It affected decidedly the situation in both America and India. In India, it brought about no territorial changes but extinguished French hopes

GREENLAND

Canada

NORTH
AMERICA

Newfoundland

BRITI
ISLE

Engl

Portug

Louisiana

Atlantic Ocean

New Spain

Florida

Cuba

Hispaniola

St. Domingue

Surinam

Peru

Pacific Ocean

SOUTH

Brazil

AMERICA

Chile

B

C B PONTIUS

The Colonial I

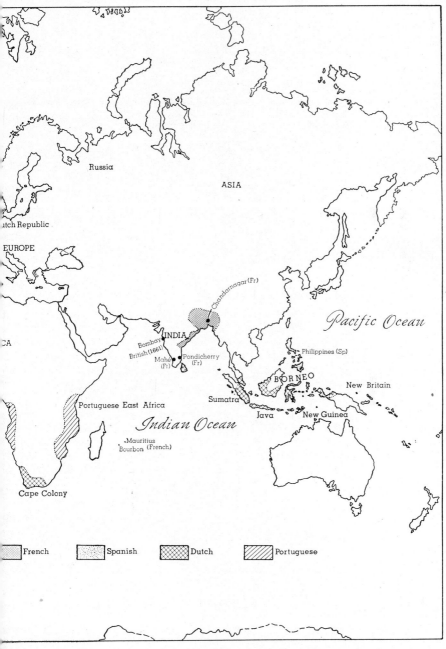

Russia

ASIA

itch Republic

EUROPE

Chandarnagar (Fr)

Pacific Ocean

INDIA

Bombay
British (1661)

Mahe
(Fr)

Pondicherry
(Fr)

Philippines (Sp)

CA

BORNEO

New Britain

Sumatra

Portuguese East Africa

Java

New Guinea

Indian Ocean

·Mauritius
·Bourbon (French)

Cape Colony

| French | Spanish | Dutch | Portuguese |

of creating an empire and gave Great Britain an opportunity to become dominant in the peninsula. It left to France her actual trading posts but deprived her of the right to fortify them or to maintain armed forces in them. In America, it changed the map decisively. France gave up all her claims to territory in North America except two small islands, Saint Pierre and Migruelon, in the Gulf of St. Lawrence. In addition, France retained fishing rights in the Gulf of St. Lawrence and in the waters around Newfoundland. She ceded Great Britain, Canada, and all French territory east of the Mississippi River. To Spain, which had intervened in the colonial war in 1762 with disastrous consequences, she ceded all her territorial claims west of the Mississippi River as compensation for her loss of Florida to the British. For the time being, consequently, Great Britain was the chief colonial and commercial power overseas.

The Struggle of the Thirteen American Colonies for Independence

The stunning defeat of France in the Seven Years' War on the continent of Europe and in India and America had unexpected consequences. Great Britain and her subjects in America had come to hold opposing views about many subjects. Great Britain, like all colonial powers, thought its colonies should be administered primarily for the benefit of the mother country. Her colonists, quite naturally, believed that their interests should be considered. From the beginning, the colonial governors appointed by the British authorities had been at odds with the colonial legislatures over money affairs and other matters. As long as the French menaced the thirteen mainland colonies of Great Britain, these differences in points of view took a secondary position. Upon the removal of the French menace, they began to take first place.

After the defeat of the French, the old differences in point of view were accentuated by the decision of the British ministers to pay more attention to their American colonies. They came to the conclusion that the growing British Empire needed more protection and that the colonies which benefited from the protection ought to contribute towards its maintenance. In 1764, in carrying out their purpose, they tried to enforce three measures. The first provided for the modification and strict enforcement of the long dormant and widely disregarded Navigation Acts. This severely interfered with the commercial relations which the New England and Middle Colonies had established with the French and Spanish Colonies in the West Indies. The second measure was the decision to maintain a British army of ten thousand men in the colonies and to maintain them in part by the strict enforcement of the Navigation Acts. To the colonists, it seemed as if the victory over the French made this measure unnecessary. The third measure was a stamp act. The new policy increased the number of customs officials, subjected the merchants of the colonies to admiralty courts without recourse to trial by jury, and led to the establishment of a permanent naval force in the colonies.

As Benjamin Franklin and other colonial agents stationed in London had warned the British authorities, the new taxes alarméd the American colonists and stirred them to action. The merchants employed every means to arouse public opinion. The colonists organized patriotic societies. Mobs took action in Massachusetts and New York. The assembly in Virginia protested against the new policy. Delegates from nine colonies met in New York and set forth their grievances in a petition to Parliament. The resulting situation, however, was not a case of Great Britain versus her colonies. Both at home and in the colonies, opinion was divided. In the colonies, there was a tendency for the moderates and the well-to-do (those dubbed by the Patriots as Tories), to oppose extreme measures. In Great Britain, many like Pitt and Burke sympathized with the colonial agitators.

The loss of trade that resulted from the new British policy finally led to attempts to repeal the obnoxious measure but to maintain the principle involved, namely the right of Parliament to tax the colonists. In 1765, after they discovered their inability to enforce the measure, the British authorities repealed the Stamp Act entirely. The joy of the colonists was soon dampened by the efforts of the British authorities to billet soldiers upon them and, in 1767, to enforce the mild direct taxes, known as the Townshend Acts. When the colonial agitation continued, the British authorities endeavored to save themselves by repealing all the obnoxious taxes save a light tax on tea.

The effort to enforce the principle of the right of Parliament to levy direct taxes failed completely. The British authorities insisted on enforcing the Tea Act of 1770. The colonists, led by Massachusetts, resorted to various devices to avoid paying the tax, such as abstention from drinking tea or dumping it in the harbor. The British authorities retaliated by attempting to punish the people of Massachusetts by closing the port of Boston, modifying the Charter of Massachusetts, threatening to try accused persons in England, and quartering troops on the colonists.

Just at this inopportune moment, the British authorities pushed through Parliament the Quebec Act. This was an effort to organize some of the territory recently taken from France. It included in the limits of the province of Quebec the region lying between the Great Lakes and the Ohio River, the Alleghany Mountains and the Mississippi River. This interfered with the claims and interests of many of the seaboard colonies. The early grants to the colonies had run from sea to sea. The colonists had long dreamed of winning wealth and prosperity by subduing the newly acquired region. These dreams were now completely destroyed by the same authorities who were already disregarding their political and commercial interests.

The colonists, for their part, had no thought of abandoning the struggle. From far and near came offers of help for the port of Boston and its poor. The colonists had come to the conclusion that the cause of one was the cause of all. Led by Virginia, the thirteen colonies decided, by 1774, to organize the Continental Congress, which met in Philadelphia. Its most important action was the adoption of an agreement neither to import British products nor to export colonial goods to any British port. Its action made war almost inevitable.

The conflict which broke out in 1775, as a result of the attempt of the British troops stationed at Boston to seize some stores collected by the patriots at Concord, was at first merely a struggle between Great Britain and thirteen of its American colonies. It was marked by the capture of Boston by the colonists, the repulse of the British before Charleston, an unsuccessful expedition against Quebec, the Declaration of Independence, the loss of New York and Philadelphia, and unexpected colonial victories at Trenton, Princeton, and Saratoga. In these campaigns, the colonists proved to the world that they were at least capable of effective resistance.

After 1778, the conflict begun in America became a European struggle. From the first, the rebellious British colonies had had hopes of obtaining aid from France, the defeated rival of Great Britain. For this purpose, they had sent Benjamin Franklin, their most experienced man of affairs, to Paris. For some time, however, the French government did not seem inclined to extend aid. The only encouragement for the colonists came from private individuals, like the young Marquis de Lafayette who went to their aid with a number of companions at his own expense. Later, the French government extended help through a dummy commercial company organized for that purpose.

The American victory at Saratoga in 1778 completely changed the situation. The people of Paris rejoiced at the news of the American success as they would at a French victory. The French government signed two treaties—one of alliance and one conceding the two parties certain commercial advantages with the American colonies, and promptly declared war on Great Britain. By 1779, the French authorities had persuaded Spain to take similar action.

Thereafter, the struggle went on not only on the American continent, but in the West Indies, on the sea, and in Europe. At first, the results of the French Alliance were disappointing in America. A French fleet appeared in American waters but failed to accomplish anything decisive. In the main, the American colonists were defeated in the operations on land. The British, through fear of the French fleet, did evacuate Philadelphia. In 1778, the colonists won the indecisive battle of Monmouth and, thereafter, invested New York. In 1780 and 1781, the British waged what seemed to be a successful campaign in the southern colonies. In 1781, through the cooperation of the French and the American colonists, however, the fighting in America finally was brought to a successful conclusion. While a French fleet prevented the escape by sea of the British forces which had been operating in the southern colonies, a combined French and American force marched south and shut the British up in Yorktown, Virginia. After thirteen days of hopeless resistance, the head of the British forces, Lord Cornwallis, surrendered to General Washington, the American commander. The victory led in 1783 to a treaty of peace that recognized the thirteen American colonies as independent.

Elsewhere, the fighting did little or nothing to change the fundamental situation of the two rival powers. The French and Spanish made an unsuccessful attack on the British post of Gibraltar. There was much fighting at sea. The main result of the war, as far as France was concerned, was the satisfaction of the French desire for vengeance and the completion of the bankruptcy of the French monarchy.

The peace settlement made some important changes in the map. After considerable delay and some disagreement between the French and American negotiators, the representatives of the American colonists and Great Britain signed a separate treaty which conceded to the thirteen American colonists their independence and all the territory between the Mississippi River and the Alleghany Mountains. The definitive treaty of peace that followed returned Florida and the island of Minorca to Spain.

By 1689, though four of the European powers were still in serious conflict, it was obvious that predominance in the colonial and commercial struggle would ultimately be wrested by either France or Great Britain. For a century, the two powers waged a contest for supremacy. Five times during the century, the two powers were at war, in part at least, over colonial and commercial issues. In the Treaty of Utrecht, signed in 1713, the French began to make important territorial concessions in America. By the Treaty of Paris in 1763, they lost practically all their remaining possessions in America and the opportunity to establish an empire in India. By her intervention in the War of the American Revolution, France obtained revenge for her losses, but she failed to change the colonial and commercial situation and completed her financial bankruptcy.

CHAPTER 25

Great Britain in the Eighteenth Century (1714–1789)

In 1714, the death of Queen Anne produced a political crisis. The succession was bound up with the principle of parliamentary government and the Protestant succession to the throne. There was, however, a large and conservative body of public opinion in the nation that still believed in the principle of succession by hereditary right. Many of these supported the claims to the throne of "James III," the son of the deposed James II and known in history as the Old Pretender. Only the sudden death of the queen and the quick action of the leaders of the Whigs, who formed the Parliamentary party, thwarted an attempt to gain the throne for the Old Pretender.

The Accession of George I

The new king, George I (1660–1727), seemed singularly unsuited to play the role of sovereign of Great Britain. He was only distantly related to the late queen and was ruler of the German state of Hanover. He had been named as successor of Queen Anne by the Act of Settlement of 1701 because he was a Protestant and, supposedly, would insure the continuance of the Protestant and Parliamentary regime in England. He loved Hanover but cared little about his new kingdom. He had not even taken the trouble to learn the English language. He scarcely comprehended the constitution or the political machinery of the English government. He was uncouth and had low tastes. He hardly seemed fitted to fill the position of great dignity to which he had been called.

His accession to power, however, was an event of constitutional importance. Because of his taking office, the English party system took a more definite form. Unable to speak English and owing the kingship principally to their party, George I turned over the management of the government largely to the Whigs. They treated the accession of the new sovereign as a party triumph and did nothing to conciliate their Tory opponents. They even went so far as to impeach the late Tory ministers. This attitude naturally increased the party feeling among both the Whigs and the Tories.

The Rising of 1715

One result of the increase of party feeling was the so-called Jacobite rising of 1715. The supporters of the Pretender, though thwarted in 1714 by the speed of events, had by no means given up hope of seating the Pretender on the throne of his fathers. The aggressive policy of the Whigs stimulated the conspirators to continue to hope for a rising. There was strong feeling against the Hanoverian succession in many parts of England, particularly in western England. The disaffection was even stronger in Scotland, especially among the Highland clans. There, national feeling, religious prejudice, and clan rivalries all played a part. The conspirators confidently counted, too, on armed support from France.

The plans of the conspirators turned out badly. The death of Louis XIV changed France from an enemy into an ally of Great Britain. The news of the French defection came too late to prevent a short-lived rising in Scotland. There, the rebellious Highland clansmen rose in considerable numbers and gained control for the time being of most of Scotland. Very shortly, however, the conspirators were defeated both in Scotland and in northern England. The clansmen were fitted only for a short dashing campaign, and most of them hesitated to cross the English border. In England, the expected numbers failed to rise. Even the belated appearance of the Pretender in Scotland embarrassed more than it helped the rising. So decisive defeats in both England and Scotland soon quelled the revolt.

The Economic Crisis

The political crisis was hardly over before an economic crisis of great violence shook the country. With the growth of material prosperity, the government had learned in times of stress to borrow money from private individuals. In this way, it had accumulated what seemed to contemporaries a huge debt, much of it the result of the War of the Spanish Succession. The interest on the debt had been put as high as seven and eight per cent. Though after the war the interest rate had dropped to as low as four per cent, much of the debt was in the form of annuities and could not be redeemed except with the consent of the investor. Naturally, the financial situation of the government alarmed many people.

Just before the close of the War of the Spanish Succession, the government had funded the floating debt of the country by creating a private concern known as the South Sea Company which assumed the debt in return for certain trading privileges. According to this scheme, the new company agreed to take a lower rate of interest, and the original creditors of the government either were paid off or accepted stock in the new company in place of their government securities. After the close of the war, the directors of the South Sea Company, anxious as they were to extend their activities, proposed to the ministry that the company should now take over the whole permanent debt in the same manner. At first, all went well. The government had one creditor instead of many and paid a lower rate of interest. The company had no difficulty about getting its shares accepted by both former holders of the debt and new purchasers of stock. Large numbers of people were anxious to obtain shares in the new company, and the price of the shares soared from one hundred and thirty pounds to one thousand pounds. So great was the seeming success of the company that all sorts of new enterprises, some of them of a highly ridiculous nature, found the general public eager to buy their shares. In their greed for gain, the public failed to use even elementary good sense.

At this point, the South Sea Company unintentionally pricked the financial bubble. Determined to monopolize all the profits, it prosecuted some of its bogus rivals. It had no difficulty in winning the suits, but its action shook public confidence in all the companies. As a consequence, the shareholders of the various enterprises began to offer their stock for sale. Their action rapidly reduced the price of the shares. The news of the failure of Law's enterprise in France contributed to the general collapse of prices. Thousands of people found themselves victims of their own greed.

The general public, however, did not recognize its guilt. It felt that someone must be responsible for the public misfortune and demanded that the government should take punitive action. The two houses of Parliament accordingly, began to make inquiries. Their investigations did bring out many things that indicated corruption and mismanagement on the part of the ministers and the company. For example, a large number of shares of stock for which nothing had been paid had been distributed by the company to ministers and royal favorites.

The general public demanded that someone should suffer for the unfortunate episode. A number of ministers were forced to resign. The directors of the company, which was still solvent, were prohibited from sitting in Parliament and were deprived of their estates for the benefit of investors. Finally, Parliament discreetly appropriated a large sum to aid unfortunate investors.

The Rule of Walpole

One political figure of the time, Robert Walpole (1676–1745), who had already held office and was a man of considerable prominence, was not implicated in the so-called South Sea Bubble. He had the good fortune to be out of office in 1720 when the South Sea Bubble burst. He had already shown ability in the management of the finances. After the collapse of the financial boom in 1720, many turned to him, therefore, for guidance.

For the next two decades, he maintained himself in office. He had many faults. He was not brilliant. He had no idealism. He was considered coarse in conversation and loose in morals in a period characterized by low standards in such matters. He was determined to have power and removed every possible rival from his path. He was unscrupulous in his methods and thought every man had his price. Yet he left an unmistakable impress on the country and English constitutional practice. He was the first English prime minister in the modern sense. For nearly twenty years, he gave the country a peace that made Great Britain prosperous and assured a continuance of Protestantism and parliamentary government. He gave the House of Commons its future place in the state. He had the art of gauging the force and direction of public opinion. He never insisted on unpopular measures. These qualities explain his continuance in power.

In 1727, it looked for a moment as if Walpole would lose his hold on public office. George I died and was succeeded by his son, George II (1683–1760). The new sovereign was a mature and brave man but vain, pompous, and fond of the trappings of power. He had long been at odds with his father and hostile to Walpole. Fortunately both for him and for the country, his wife, Queen Caroline, had great influence over him and made her husband see the importance of maintaining Walpole in power.

By 1739, the temper of the country had changed. The people were tired of a peace bought by humiliating concessions to other countries. Very reluctantly but, as events soon showed, without saving his power, Walpole gave way to public opinion and, in 1739, declared war on Spain. This action opened a new period in British history. For the next twenty-four years, Great Britain was almost continuously at war. First came the conflict with Spain over colonial and commercial questions, which will be described in Chapter 24. Before long (1740), however, in her efforts to maintain something like a balance of power on the continent, Great Britain found herself becoming involved, as an ally of Austria, in the continental struggle which was described in the chapter on Central Europe in the eighteenth century. By 1744, Great Britain had become involved in a war of its own with France over both continental and colonial questions. So in reality, the struggle, which began in 1739, continued, almost without interruption, until 1763.

By this time, a new claimant had fallen heir to the pretensions of the Stuarts to the throne of Great Britain. Encouraged by the course of the foreign war, the so-called Young Pretender, son of the Old Pretender, made an unsuccessful effort in 1745 to gain control of the British throne. Without any foreign support, he landed on the west coast of Scotland with only seven companions. His name and personal charm attracted enough of the Scottish clansmen to enable him to take Edinburgh and defeat an English force sent into Scotland to subdue him. His followers, however, were mainly undisciplined clansmen, and most of them were reluctant to advance into England. As a result, many of them went home after their initial victories. In spite of this, the Young Pretender managed to penetrate as far as Derby in England. There, the gathering English forces first brought his advance to a standstill and then forced him to retreat. In fifty-six days, the Scottish followers of the Young Pretender had marched six hundred miles. Misfortune, however, continued to follow the young prince. More followers deserted him, and those who remained loyal were forced to retreat to the Highlands, a bleak and barren region which had little to offer in the way of supplies. In the spring of the following year, the troops finally raised by the English authorities caught up with the little half-starved force of the Young Pretender and destroyed it. The defeated prince wandered around for five months longer with a price on his head before he managed to escape to the continent.

The repression of the rising of 1745 in Scotland completed a movement that had been going on for half a century. In the seventeenth century, the country had been a poor and, in the Highlands, a backward, barbaric region. The Lowlands had only a bare, rugged soil, were exposed to attacks, and were excluded from English markets. The Highlands had been inaccessible and organized into clans under petty chiefs. In the latter region, the men scorned labor and left the gathering of their scanty crops to the women and children. The men spent their time in hunting, cattle raising, and fighting.

The union with England in 1707 had been a turning point. With the removal of restrictions on trade, commerce and manufactures prospered in the Lowlands. Schools were set up. For a considerable time, the Highlands did not benefit from these changes. In 1726, however, the English authorities began to build roads in the Highlands. After the rising of 1745, many of the powerful chieftains were forced to go into exile. Then too, the government took steps to break up the old clan organization. It, likewise, disarmed the Highlanders, forbade the wearing of the National dress by any but soldiers, and organized Highland regiments for British service. In time, these measures broke down the old aloofness and created in its place a Scottish national pride. After the defeat of this latest rising among the clans, economic and social conditions began to improve in Scotland in a number of ways.

Agriculture and cattle breeding improved. Linen and stocking weaving industries were started. The Scot became known for his frugality, diligence, and stern religion.

Not all the changes in Scotland, though, were for the better. Scotland remained a comparatively poor country. There was still much in the region that was sordid and miserable, while much of the picturesqueness of the old times disappeared. In too many instances, the old chiefs were replaced by rapacious landlords who relentlessly squeezed a profit from their unfortunate tenants.

The Rule of George III

In 1760, Great Britain experienced an important change of rulers. George II made way for his grandson, George III (1738–1820). The new ruler was only twenty-two, but unlike his two predecessors he was born in England and was considered an Englishman. George I and George II had allowed others to rule the country. The Revolution of 1688 had handed the government over not to the English people but to an oligarchy of Whig nobles. The new sovereign was determined to change this situation and to be a force in the state. With this end in view, he made Lord Bute, his mother's most trusted adviser, chief minister, and he built up a group in Parliament that came to be known as the King's Friends. In their anxiety to advance the royal authority, the king and his chief adviser promptly overthrew the great war minister, Pitt, put an end to the dominance of the Whigs, and brought the war with France to a hasty close that alienated Frederick the Great and threw away many of the advantages that might have been gained.

The most important events of the reign of George III, however, did not take place in council chambers or in Parliament. Up to the eighteenth century, Great Britain, like all the other states of Europe, had been an agricultural country. Most of the people of the island lived by farming and cattle raising and carried on their agriculture in much the same way as their medieval forebears had done. In the latter half of the eighteenth century, though, this situation began to change. Great Britain gradually became an industrial state, and British agriculture experienced a veritable revolution in aims, organization, and methods.

It is always difficult to explain such changes. In the case of the British Industrial Revolution, however, there seem to have been a number of contributing causes. The religious persecutions and the devastating wars of the continent had driven to British shores thousands of skilled craftsmen who brought to their new country the industrial lore of the best artisans of the continent. In northern and western England they were themselves unhampered by gild restrictions and were free to experiment with new processes and methods. At the same time, the commercial expansion that followed the discovery of America and a sea route to India and the Far East was fostering the growth of capital. These developments favored the rise of industry in England.

The transformation of Great Britain into an industrial state was due to the development of machinery for manufacture (first of cotton, then of other textiles, and finally of other industrial products), the development of steam engines to operate the new machines, and the adoption of other new methods of manufacture. In 1733, John Kay, a skilled artisan, invented a fly-shuttle which enabled a weaver to throw the shuttle backward and forward himself and to dispense with the assistant who had been needed up to that time. This made worse a situation that was already bad. The spinners never had been able to meet the demand of the weavers for yarn. The new machine now increased the demand. This situation set a number of men to thinking about methods for increasing the supply of yarn. About 1766, James Hargreaves, an English artisan, invented a machine that became known as the spinning jenny. It was operated by hand but spun eight threads at once instead of only one. Three years later, a shrewd, alert man of humble origin, Richard Arkwright, patented another machine, known as the water frame, which really embodied the ideas of other men. Each of the two inventions had its good points. In 1779, Samuel Crompton designed his so-called spinning mule, in which were embodied the best features of both of the earlier inventions.

The new spinning machines reversed the situation of the spinners. With the new aids, they could spin yarn faster than the weavers could use it. This situation set the inventive mind of Edmund Cartwright, a clergyman, to work on the problem of a power loom. Although he had no previous training for the task, he finally contrived in 1785 a clumsy power loom that speeded up the weaving of cloth. This machine was gradually improved and brought into general use.

A number of other inventors made important contributions to the transformation of the cotton industry. In 1793, Eli Whitney, a young American, became aware of the need for speeding up the cleaning of raw cotton and invented the cotton gin. This insured a plentiful supply of raw cotton for the spinners. Other inventors perfected carding machines and cylindrical presses for printing patterns on the finished cotton cloth. Still others reduced the time required for bleaching by applying the chemical discoveries of Karl Wilhelm Scheele and Pierre Bertholet. With the aid of these inventions, Great Britain quickly became the great center for the manufacture of cotton goods.

Even earlier than the cotton industry, iron and steel manufacturing was similarly transformed. At an early date in the eighteenth century, possibly in 1709, a family of ironmasters by the name of Darby, engaged in the manufacture of pots and other cast-iron objects, succeeded in substituting coke for charcoal in the smelting process. They probably owed their success to their use of a larger furnace and a better bellows. They tried to keep their new method a secret, but it gradually became known and was adopted by other ironmasters. The more cheaply produced cast iron gradually supplanted the wood, brass, copper, lead, and malleable iron which had been used up to that time. About 1763, John Smeaton improved the smelting process still further by the invention of a blowing cylinder that greatly improved the draft of the smelting furnaces.

About the middle of the eighteenth century, Benjamin Huntsman, in search of better material for pendulums and clock springs, began to experiment with cast steel. He finally hit upon the idea of placing, in a furnace heated by coke, scraps of steel in small clay crucibles. The intense heat freed the metal from the particles of silicate or slag found in even the best iron and steel made by the former process. After it had been purified, the metal in the crucibles was removed from the furnace by long tongs and poured into molds. After the metal had hardened in the molds, it was removed and forged into bars or slit into rods of a convenient size for the manufacture of cutlery and other steel objects. In spite of his efforts to keep his discovery a secret, the competitors of Huntsman soon learned the new method of making cast steel.

A little later, the refining process was revolutionized. In 1766, two brothers named Cranage patented a reverberatory furnace which heated the metal without coming into direct contact with it. The new furnace could not be used for all purposes, but it came into general use during the next twenty years. Beginning in 1783, Henry Cort developed the puddling process. By the aid of coke, he purified the metal of dross and cinders and then rolled the glowing masses of heated metal into the desired shape. The new methods of refining saved much time and greatly increased production.

The story of the transformation of the cotton and the iron and steel industries illustrates the transformation that finally affected all branches of industry. Gradually, machines and new technical processes were introduced in all industries. By 1800, British manufacturers had increased their output enormously as a result of the new methods and had begun to undersell the hand workers of the continent in textile and in iron and steel products.

Up to the time of the new inventions, industry had for the most part been carried on in the home or in small shops. The introduction of the new machines led to the adoption of the modern factory system. Even before they began to be employed in operating the new machines, the workers in many instances had ceased to own the looms and the raw material which they worked. The introduction of the new machines generalized this situation. They were expensive and their owners felt the need of supervising them. The workers could not afford to buy the new machines or to operate them. The owners, consequently, placed them in factories under their own supervision, and the workers suddenly found themselves subjected to a discipline that they had never known before.

The new machines likewise created a demand for motive power. The early spinning factories used water power, but this motive force had some disadvantages. The streams rose and fell without any regard to the needs of the new manufacturers. Then too, factories often had to be located near water falls where labor was scarce. These conditions caused them to turn for motive power to the newly invented steam engines.

For some decades, inventors had been trying to harness the force of steam. As early as 1705, Newcomen had patented a very crude engine that could be used for pumping water from mines and for other purposes. In 1763, James Watt (1736–1819) of Glasgow, an instrument maker employed by one of the Scottish universities, commenced to work at the problem of improving the engine of Newcomen. He completed his first engine in 1765 and patented it in 1769. His contributions to the problem of motive power finally included a separate condenser, a steam jacket to keep the cylinder hot, a cylinder closed at both ends, and the use of oil and tallow as lubricants. About 1735, the improved engine of Watt began to be employed not only in the mines but in the new cotton factories and iron and steel mills.

To transform the ideas of Watt into actual engines was a difficult problem. There were as yet no steam hammers, lathes, planers, or boring mills. Each part of the engine had to be made by hand. This skill, as well as the capital for the long years of experimentation, was furnished in large part by a wealthy manufacturer of ornamental metal work named Matthew Boulton (1728–1809). The credit for the creation of the modern steam engine belongs almost equally to Boulton and to Watt.

Effects of the Industrial Revolution

The Industrial Revolution of the eighteenth century affected British life in innumerable ways. Up until the introduction of the new engines and the new machines, for example, mining had been carried on in Great Britain on a very small scale. The subsequent Industrial Revolution led to a great expansion of mining. By 1788 we are told, the production of iron ore had risen from eighteen thousand to sixty-eight thousand tons. By the end of the century, the coal mines of Great Britain had an annual output of ten million tons.

The Industrial Revolution, too, created a demand for improvements in transportation and communications. The big estates which characterized life in Great Britain and on the continent, until the eighteenth century, needed very little contact with the outside world. They were nearly self-sufficing. Weekly markets supplied most of the wants of the neighboring towns. Peddlers and yearly fairs met most of the demands of country gentlemen, peasants, and burghers. The new factories changed this situation. They demanded more raw materials than the immediate locality could produce, and they produced more goods than the neighboring region could consume. In response to these new demands came canals, better roads, the railroad, the steamship, improved postal facilities, the telegraph, the oceanic cable, the automobile, the airplane, and the radio.

Parts of the continent had long been familiar with canals. After 1759, the Industrial Revolution began to create a demand for them in England. The Duke of Bridgewater, for example, had some mines at a distance from Manchester and wanted an artificial waterway to connect his mines with the city. In that year, he commissioned James Brindley, an ingenious millwright, to construct such a canal. The two men had to overcome all sorts of obstacles but they finally succeeded in completing a waterway. The new canal made it possible to cut the price of coal in Manchester in half. The success of this first canal quickly led to the construction of a network of artificial waterways in central England.

The Industrial Revolution likewise increased the demand for better roads. The growth of cities and the two Jacobite risings of 1715 and 1745 had already called the attention of British authorities to the subject of better highways. After the Industrial Revolution got under way, the demand became insistent. The improvement which rapidly took place in British roads is inseparably associated with the names of two engineers, Thomas Telford and John McAdam. Both men emphasized the importance of thorough drainage, careful preparation of materials, and the sloping of the surface. Telford stressed the need for a good foundation. McAdam contended that proper drainage and an impervious surface would enable any sort of subsoil to bear the weight of traffic.

The Industrial Revolution had, also, many important social and political effects that did not reach their full development until the next century. One effect was a shifting of population to northern and western England. Before the Industrial Revolution, these regions were sparsely settled. They, however, offered the new industries coal, iron, and water power. As a consequence, most of the new factories were built in these sections of the country. As a result, the population of eastern and southern England stood still or went backward while northern and western England steadily grew in population. The growth of population was followed in the next century by a demand for greater representation in Parliament.

The Industrial Revolution was followed by other movements of population. New industrial towns and new manufacturing quarters in old towns rapidly sprang up. Workers crowded into hastily constructed factories and dwellings. No attention was paid to the health or safety of the workers. They lived in flimsy houses on narrow, congested, unsanitary streets. They worked long hours in factories that made no provision for ventilation or sunlight or for the protection of the worker from the moving machinery. These conditions created terrible social problems.

The Industrial Revolution, likewise, led to the development of new social classes. A few men of initiative and force and native shrewdness became owners and managers of the new industries. They swelled the ranks of the rising middle class. The majority of those connected with the new industries were recruited from the declining yeomen, agricultural laborers, mountaineers from Wales and Scotland, and poverty-stricken Irish peasants; they became a wage-earning proletariat, without property and exploited by their employers.

In comparison to modern standards, working conditions in the new mines and factories were terrible. Profits were high and labor was plentiful. Men, women, and young children crowded into the new factories. Because of their greater docility and nimble fingers, women and children were often preferred. All were subjected to brutal taskmasters. Even children of six, seven, and eight years of age often worked as high as sixteen hours a day. The new employers sacrificed everything for speedy profits.

The Agricultural Revolution in Great Britain

While British inventors were transforming England into an industrial state, British landlords and farmers were revolutionizing English and Scottish agriculture. It had become customary for the sons of English noblemen to make a tour through Western Europe as a part of their education before they settled down as British country gentlemen. After 1700, for some reason, some of them began to observe continental agricultural practices and methods. In northern Italy, Provence, Flanders, and Holland they found cultivators of the soil utilizing better implements, rotating crops, feeding cattle more scientifically, draining and fertilizing the fields, growing new crops, and farming all their land each year. When these observers returned to England, they tried to introduce the new methods and practices on their own estates.

The pioneer in this Agricultural Revolution was Jethro Tull (1674–1741). After being educated at Oxford and Gray's Inn, he made the grand tour of the continent. Even before he went abroad, he had invented a drill which sowed the seed in regular rows and covered it with earth instead of broadcasting it wastefully by hand. Upon his return from the continent, he began to pulverize the soil by frequent cultivation with the horse hoe of Languedoc. By employing this method, he thought that he could avoid the use of natural fertilizer and eliminate one of the principle sources of weeds. In reality, his ideas had the effect of delaying planting too long and subjected the growing grain to rusts. His written accounts of his methods, though, had considerable influence on English agriculture.

Another famous contemporary landlord of Jethro Tull was Charles Townshend (1674–1738). After a long career in British politics, he devoted the last eight years of his life to the improvement of his Norfolk estate. He favored the enclosure of lands and planted the clover of Spain and the turnips of Flanders. Through his warm advocacy of the advantages of planting the latter vegetable, he won for himself the sobriquet of Turnip Townshend. His work greatly raised the level of farming in one of the poorest counties of England.

The pioneer breeder of better sheep and cattle in England was Robert Bakewell (1725–1790). On a farm of some four hundred acres, he applied to sheep and cattle the methods of breeding which had long been employed in the case of dogs. He chose good stock, carefully selected the qualities that he wished to emphasize, bred within the flock or herd, and kept his animals warm and clean. By his methods, he doubled the weight of his sheep and improved their meat. His Leicestershire sheep and Longhorn cattle soon became famous.

Other members of the British nobility and gentry aided in disseminating the new ideas. The Duke of Bedford (1765–1802) maintained a model farm upon which were held under his patronage plowing contests, sheep-shearings, and exhibitions of cattle and sheep. Lord Somerville (1765–1819) bred fine Merino sheep. Sir John Sinclair (1745–1835) introduced on his Scottish estate rotation of crops and better breeding of sheep. After two of his tenants had refused leases on ridiculously low terms, Lord Coke of Holkam (1752–1842) tried his hand at farming and, by his experiments and observations, did much to transform western Norfolk.

The real leader of the Agricultural Revolution was Arthur Young (1741–1820). He wrote voluminously on the subject. In his writings he zealously advocated the abandonment of the naked fallows, open fields, and small estates which characterized British agriculture and the adoption of enclosed fields, rotation of crops, careful cultivation of the soil, and better methods of breeding. He went too far in his denunciation of commons, open fields, and small holdings, but his writings awakened an unparalleled interest in agriculture.

This new interest in agriculture expressed itself in many ways. In 1776, the first English publication for farmers, a monthly, appeared. In 1790, the first professor of agriculture was installed in the University of Edinburgh. Also, many local agricultural societies were founded.

The Agricultural Revolution transformed the English countryside. At an earlier period, many estates had been enclosed to make pastures for flocks of sheep. Now, most of the remaining estates were enclosed in order to make possible the introduction of better agricultural methods. Progressive landlords obtained authority from Parliament to enclose their estates. This meant that not only did the landlord but all his tenants exchanged their small, scattered, intermingled holdings, and their other rights in the estate for compact holdings under their complete control. After the exchange of holdings had been effected, the landlord and his tenants were free to manage their lands as they pleased. The open fields disappeared. The landlords and their tenants surrounded their new holdings with the hedgerows that now characterize the English countryside. When they had thus enclosed their holdings, they could drain, fertilize, and cultivate the land, rotate their crops, and apply the new principles of breeding.

The Agricultural Revolution, nevertheless, affected some classes of people adversely. The smaller tenant farmers and the cottagers were both too poor and too conservative to make the outlay required for surveying, hedging, draining, and fertilizing the land, and purchasing selected seed, blooded stock, implements, and material for new farm buildings. The abolition of common pastures left no place for the cow and the goose of the squatter. The small tenant farmer, the cottagers, and the squatters, accordingly, either became agricultural laborers or workers in the new factories.

The Agricultural Revolution was also marked by the introduction of farming implements. For centuries, farmers had depended on rude, cumbersome plows, the harrow, the sickle or scythe, the spade, the fork, and the flail. Now, the Dutch plow and the horse hoe were brought over from the continent. The drill, as we have seen, was invented. About 1786, Andrew Meikle, a Scotsman, contrived a threshing machine.

The Methodist Movement

For a number of reasons, the established Church of England had been losing its hold on the common people. Parishes and bishoprics had been organized while England was almost entirely an agricultural society. They were not adapted to the changes made by the growth of cities and the shifting of population to mines and factories. The rationalism of the age deprived the preaching of the time of the fervor needed to stir the common people. The landlords of England, who controlled the presentation to livings, often selected their vicars and curates without regard to their spiritual qualities. As a result, there were vast numbers of people in England in the eighteenth century who were hardly touched by the Established Church.

This need of the common people for spiritual guidance was unexpectedly met by a new religious movement. While in Oxford, a small band of students had been organized for mutual improvement which soon won for its members the nickname of "Methodists." It included two brothers, John (1703–1791) and Charles (1707–1788) Wesley, who came from a family with strong Puritan traditions, and George Whitefield, destined to become a most eloquent popular preacher. They often preached or did charitable work in the surrounding parishes.

About 1739, after the Oxford group had left college and its members had become engaged in various activities, Whitefield took the unprecedented step of preaching in the open air at Bristol. Meeting with great success in this venture, he sent for John Wesley. Up to this time, John Wesley had been a regular clergyman of the Established Church. In 1735, he and his brother had gone out to Georgia as representatives of the Society for the Propagation of the Gospel, but their efforts had met with only slight success. In 1738, however, John Wesley had had an unusual spiritual experience. Like Luther, he had been troubled with the problem of salvation. While attending a small religious service, he experienced what is known in evangelical circles as a conversion. So after some hesitation, he joined Whitefield at Bristol and began with the fervor of a new convert to appeal to others to seek a similar conversion. He still considered himself, however, a regular member of the Established Church.

Thus began a movement which gradually affected all England and eventually spread all over the world. For the remainder of his long life, John Wesley, who made himself the acknowledged leader of the movement, went around the country preaching his message. As the regular clergy looked with disfavor on his methods and closed their churches to his work, he found himself forced to preach in the open air wherever he went. At the same time, he found himself confronted with the problem of giving his converts some sort of an organization. Thus, unconsciously, he laid the foundation for the present Methodist Church. Until the day of his death, however, the founder of the new church considered himself a member of the Church of England.

The Attempt of George III to Establish Personal Government

In the meantime, a succession of ministries had been trying to carry out the ideas of George III with regard to his place in the government. They met with successful opposition both in Great Britain and in the American colonies.

The king's first prime minister, Lord Bute, had stirred up much popular opposition by his conduct during the closing years of the Seven Years' War and the ensuing peace negotiations. The agitation found a leader in John Wilkes, a profane and profligate man of fashion, who, for the sake of notoriety, employed his wit, audacity, and parliamentary skill in opposing the government. For this purpose, he founded with some assistance the *North Briton Review* and vigorously assailed the government in its pages. His attack infuriated the king, who was determined to crush Wilkes. Accordingly, George III caused a general warrant to be issued which authorized the arrest of the authors, printers, and publishers of a particularly offensive number of the *North Briton Review*. This led to the arrest of Wilkes.

Wilkes immediately protested against his arrest. He maintained that general warrants were illegal and members of Parliament could not be arrested on a civil process. The court not only freed him from arrest but awarded him damages. This did not end the matter. The government continued to pursue him in every possible way. It set spies on his track. It opened his mail at the post office. It brought suit against him for libel. It had the offending number of the *North Briton Review* burned by the common hangman. It caused the House of Peers to vote that two parodies of well-known literary works, that were intended only for private circulation, were scandalous, obscene, and impious. Finally, after Wilkes had fled to France for safety, the government outlawed him.

The exile of Wilkes did not put an end to the popular excitement. In spite of Wilkes' absence, the signs of great popular discontent continued. It expressed itself in riots and strikes and, in spite of the many limitations on the suffrage, in the election of 1768. In this election, the still popular John Wilkes was returned as a member from Middlesex. After returning to the country and voting under the protection of a popular London mob, Wilkes surrendered himself to the authorities. They, however, were not successful in their efforts to have the decree of outlawry maintained, but they managed to retain Wilkes in prison during the next two years on other charges. During his imprisonment, Wilkes succeeded in getting himself elected an alderman of London but was formally expelled from the House of Commons. Upon his re-election to that body, he was again declared incapable of sitting in Parliament. Finally, at a fourth election the court candidate, though he received fewer votes, was declared elected. This misuse of power on the part of the King's Friends made Wilkes even more of a popular hero. In 1774, consequently, he was returned to and seated in the House of Commons without protest, and in 1782 he managed to have the record of his expulsion from that body expunged.

In spite of his personal unworthiness, the agitation centering around John Wilkes was of considerable significance. Though the electors in many instances had probably been bought, it taught the House of Commons that the voice of the electors could not be defied. It likewise established two important principles—that warrants for arrest must specify the person to be arrested and that no one could be excluded from the House of Commons who was not legally disqualified. While the agitation for reform of the suffrage, started by Wilkes, was delayed for several decades by foreign war, it ultimately resulted in the reform of the suffrage.

In the meantime, the King's Friends had badly bungled their conduct of colonial affairs. The thirteen American colonies, stretching from Maine to Georgia, had been growing up. The king's minister tried, as will be shown in Chapter 24, to force the colonies back into a political and economic framework that no longer fitted them. After the close of the Seven Years' War in 1763, the situation became increasingly tense. In 1775, the tension developed into an actual revolt. In 1778, the revolt of the thirteen colonies was followed by the intervention of France. By 1781, Great Britain found herself alone facing most of Europe. In Great Britain, there was widespread dissatisfaction with the government and its policies. After the defeat of the British at Yorktown, the ministry, composed of the King's Friends, was compelled to resign. This marked the end of the royal attempt at personal rule. In place of the King's Friends, a cabinet, composed of representatives of two factions of the Whigs, took office.

The Irish Problem

In the meantime, the British authorities were making little or no progress in solving the Irish problem. The Irish still hated the English as conquerors, heretics, and despoilers. They were excluded by the Navigation Acts from all commerce that might compete with British trade. They suffered from greedy agents and middlemen and from absentee landlords. They were burdened, too, by heavy rents and their own competition with one another. Irish Catholics were still excluded from political office, the practice of law, and positions in the army; they were compelled to pay tithes for the support of the Anglican Church which they never attended and whose clergy were indifferent to their interests. Only the Protestant aristocracy were represented in Parliament.

During the War for American Independence, the British authorities found themselves forced to make some concessions to the Irish. As early as 1761, the Irish discontent had begun to find expression in a secret organization, known as the Whiteboys from the white smocks which they wore, which maimed cattle and resorted to other forms of violence in nocturnal raids. When the American Revolution broke out, the Irish leaders brought pressure on the hard-pressed British for other concessions. Some restrictions on Irish trade were removed in spite of the protests of British manufacturers. Concessions were made in regard to the leasing of land and inheritances by Catholics. Irish dissenting Protestants were freed from the sacramental test for office holding. Finally, in 1782, the Irish leaders, favored as they were by the military situation, extorted legislative independence for the Irish parliament. This did not prove to be a solution of the Irish problem.

The Rise of the Younger Pitt

The succeeding years were marked by much political maneuvering that was more interesting to contemporaries than to later generations. Out of the welter of petty politics, however, arose a figure that was to dominate the British political scene until the middle of the Napoleonic period, the man known in history as the Younger Pitt. Though he had been defeated in his attempt to rule Great Britain, the king still hoped for some measure of personal power. In his perplexity, he turned to the twenty-four-year-old son of the great popular leader, the Earl of Chatham. Entering Parliament at the age of twenty-one, the Younger Pitt had already filled the important offices of Chancellor of the Exchequer and leader of the House of Commons. Now, supported only by the king, the Chatham Whigs, and a few Tories, he assumed the responsibility of conducting the government against a majority led by the skillful statesman, George Fox, and the able Burke.

His acceptance of this task inaugurated a remarkable parliamentary battle. Motion after motion was carried against Pitt, but he refused to resign. He merely waited till his patience and courage and the violence and blunders of his opponents gradually won for him increased support. Finally, when there seemed some possibility of success, he risked his position in a general election. In this contest, he won a great victory for himself and the new Tory party. In spite of the victory, the king did not regain any measure of personal rule.

The history of Great Britain in the eighteenth century lacks unity. At home, the period was marked by the establishment of an alien dynasty on the throne, the completion of British political machinery, the domination of the country by the great Whig families, an unsuccessful attempt to establish the personal rule of the king, and the rise of the Younger Pitt and a new Tory party. Overseas, the British government was engaged in a great struggle with France and Spain for colonial and commercial supremacy that ended in the defeat of France, the gaining of the valleys of the St. Lawrence and the Ohio rivers, the opening of the door for the establishment of British rule in India, and the loss of thirteen of its most important American colonies. Real British interests and the tie with Hanover led in the middle years of the century to British intervention in two continental wars.

CHAPTER 26

The History of France in the Eighteenth Century

Louis XIV handed on to his successor two policies which vitally affected France. As a result of his own administration and those of his predecessors, Henry IV, Richelieu, and Mazarin, he bequeathed to his successor absolute power over the French state. This made the king responsible for the happiness and prosperity of his subjects. As a result of his four exhausting wars, Louis XIV left to his successor an inheritance of discontent which might eventually give rise to a revolution against the absolute monarchy. The future of France depended very largely on his successor.

France at the Close of the Reign of Louis XIV

The policies pursued for over a century by Henry IV, Richelieu, Mazarin, and Louis XIV, as we have seen, made the king in theory the center of everything in France. The nobles no longer thought themselves equal to the king. No party or institution was strong enough to resist the royal will. There were no constitutional restrictions on the sovereign, and the king's wish was the law of the land. Although he probably never said it, Louis XIV could truthfully have said "I am the state," for he had absolute power over the lives and property of his subjects.

In practice, the royal will was restricted in many ways. His power depended on his own capacity, the ability of his ministers and councillors, and the fidelity and skill of his administrative officials. The ministers included a chancellor, who appended the royal seal to all official documents, the controller general, who supervised the levying and collection of taxes, some ministers without portfolio, and secretaries of state. Most of the ministers were heads of government departments, but each minister dealt separately with the king. The ministers did not form a cabinet, and they neither took office nor resigned in a body. They did not follow, therefore, a collective policy.

From early times, the French monarchy had been aided by a council of advisers. By the beginning of the modern period, this body was displaying two tendencies. It had the propensity for growing too large and for developing special sections for the handling of definite kinds of business. By the end of the reign of Louis XIV, consequently, the advisers of the king were organized into four distinct bodies. The privy council was composed of all the councillors of the king. The so-called council of state, one of three special councils, consisted of three to five members and handled all domestic and foreign political affairs. The handling of administrative affairs was divided between the council of despatches and the council of finance. The first dealt with police affairs, the royal orders known as *lettres de cachet,* state prisons, provincial and municipal administration, and instructions to governors and intendants. The second, as its name suggests, managed the imposition and collection of direct taxes and made arrangements for the farming of the indirect taxes. The king was supposed to preside over most of the sessions of the various councils. None of the councillors of the king sat in all them. Officials known as masters of requests presented to the councils all requests, petitions, claims, and contentious cases. Thus, the different councils did a vast amount of work in the name of the king.

To carry out the decisions of the ministers and councils, there had developed during the long history of France two sets of officials. As the royal domain grew in the middle ages, it became necessary to create an administrative system. Toward the end of the thirteenth century, the kings began to appoint, in time of war, officials who were entitled lieutenants general or governors and who were given extraordinary powers. They were always either princes of the blood or nobles. During the Hundred Years' War (1337–1453), most of the French provinces came under the rule of such officials. In the sixteenth and the first third of the seventeenth century, they were the veritable masters of France. They were supposed to defend and protect the provinces under their command, to aid agents of royal justice, and to convoke *parlements,* provincial estates, and municipal bodies. They were inclined to encroach on the jurisdiction of other royal officers in matters of police, taxation, and justice. They were appointed for a term of three years but were usually reappointed. They had under them several types of subordinate officials.

From the beginning, the governors and lieutenants general had shown a tendency to put their own interests before those of the king. During the Wars of Religion, this propensity was particularly marked. They were inclined to free themselves from the central power. They raised and imposed taxes, rendered judicial decisions, and, in general, renewed the tyranny of feudal times. Under the regency of Marie de Medici, they showed the same tendency. They had proved to be very unsatisfactory agents of the royal will.

These developments led to the creation of a second set of administrative officials. Since the beginning of the sixteenth century, it had

Generalités or Intendancies of France under the Ancien Regime: (1) Flanders and Artois; (2) Hainaut and Cambresis; (3) Cous; (4) C. of Foix; (5) Perpignan.

been the custom to send out royal officials from time to time into the provinces to re-establish order and to look after interests of the king. By 1624, the system was well established. After his rise to power, Richelieu made extensive use of these intendants and put them on a permanent basis. They were entirely dependent on the king for their positions and authority and proved to be far more satisfactory royal agents than the governors had been.

As a result of the rise of the intendants, the powers of the governors declined. The office of governor became a sinecure. In spite of this development, the governorships were still much sought after. The

411

governors were paid enormous salaries. They still had duties which flattered their vanity. They represented, for example, the king at the opening of provincial estates and in other fetes and ceremonies. They had a company of guards to accompany them. Most of the governors stayed at court. They had to have special permission to visit their provinces. In the eighteenth century, there were usually about forty of them.

After the suppression of the *Fronde,* the real representatives of the French sovereign in the various parts of France were the intendants. They administered old financial districts known as *généralités.* These were often identical with the provinces and in the eighteenth century were often called intendancies. The intendants were in constant communication with one of the secretaries of state, the controller general, and the councils of despatches and finance. In the *généralités,* of which there were some thirty-three, the intendants had almost unlimited, though very precarious, power. They had the right to participate in all courts except the parlements, to supervise and suspend magistrates, and to report crimes. They issued police regulations; raised the rural militia; assigned to each parish its share of the tax known as the taille; regulated the price of provisions, carts, and billets for armies; arrested the culpable; administered cities and rural communes; supervised the royal *corvées;* and looked after the building and repair of roads and bridges. They did what they could to encourage agriculture, commerce, and industry, controlled the grain trade, and inspected factories. They aided the poor. In provinces without provincial estates, they tended to the levying and collection of the taille. They had full charge of the other direct taxes. Like the governors, they too had various subordinates.

In time, the institution known as the intendant became very unpopular. The intendants took away all local initiative. They made the obtaining of improvements, the repairing of damages, and the remedying of abuses a slow, cumbersome, and uncertain process. They crushed out all vestiges of liberty and were responsible for much tyranny. In their naiveté, the French people had come to feel that all that was good in French life came from the distant king, all that was evil, from the nearby intendants.

There were some differences in the organization of the different provinces. Twenty-four *généralités* in the heart of France were known as *pays d'élection.* In them, in spite of the name applied to them, the intendants were all powerful. In the borders of France, in some of the provinces acquired most recently, the situation was different. Some of these provinces still had provincial estates. Though they differed in organization, they usually included representatives

412

of the three orders. The clergy were represented by bishops, abbots, and deputies of monasteries; the nobles, either by the whole body of the nobility or by those nobles with titles not less than a hundred years old; and the third estate by the mayors and deputies of the towns. The three orders sometimes sat separately and occasionally as one body. The powers of the provincial estates were not extensive but were highly valued. They negotiated with the intendants over the amount of taxes which they were expected to pay and supervised their collection. They had the right of petition. They could apply their intimate knowledge of local matters to the administration of local affairs. They gave the inhabitants of a province some voice in local government.

Taxation

One of the greatest weaknesses of the administrative regime bequeathed to France by Louis XIV was the system of taxation. It discriminated among classes, individuals, and regions and was arbitrary and burdensome. The principal direct tax was the taille, which was of feudal origin and originally had been paid by tenants to their lords. In the fifteenth century, it had been diverted to the royal treasury to pay for the recently established standing army. It was paid only by the peasants. In some places, it was a land tax. In most parts of France, it was a tax on all forms of income. It was assessed and levied in a very unfair manner. The Royal Council fixed the gross amount to be raised and apportioned it among the various generalites. The intendants then did the same thing for the parishes. Elected collectors, three to seven in number, assigned to each inhabitant his share. Some districts were treated much more severely than others because influential persons often obtained favors for districts or parishes. The village collectors, who were held responsible for the share of their villages, were often ruined. Every taxpayer tried to give an appearance of poverty in order to reduce his share. The taille, therefore, tended to make France a collection of squalid villages.

There were several other direct taxes. There was, for example, a poll (capitation) tax. In reality, it was also a sort of income tax. For its collection, the inhabitants of France were divided into twenty-two classes according to their supposed ability to pay. There were also the taxes known as the tenths and the twentieths, which had been instituted by Louis XIV as a war expedient. During the eighteenth century, they increased in amount and became a permanent burden on the taxpayers. Only the clergy were exempt from them.

Another direct tax that was very much hated by French taxpayers was the royal *corvée*. At first, the landlords had exacted it from the

413

peasants. Later, the state imposed a royal *corvée* on the peasants which forced them to work for an indefinite period without pay for the king and his agents. Thereafter, the intendants and military commanders required the peasants to employ their own time and the service of their draft animals in the building and repair of roads and the transportation of military equipment and supplies. There was no equality in, nor limit to, the demands that might be made. The peasant was often subject to harsh and injurious treatment. He might be summoned at a most inconvenient time, such as harvest time. The more enlightened administrators realized the hardships and injurious nature of the royal *corvée*.

The system of collecting the indirect taxes of the *ancien regime* was also a very bad one. The indirect taxes were not gathered by government officials but by a private company, a method which goes back to Roman times. At first, many individuals, possibly as many as two hundred and fifty, were engaged in the work. They raised relatively large sums for themselves but paid ridiculously small amounts into the royal treasury. Both Sully and Colbert had made improvements in the system known as "farming of the taxes." Colbert handed over the task to a company of forty financiers who, in return for the privilege of farming the taxes, advanced a large sum to the royal treasury. They collected the customs or tariff duties, the aides, taxes on drinks, and the gabelle, or salt tax, and managed the sale of all tobacco in the kingdom. Their leases ran for a period of six years. They had an elaborate organization with offices at Paris and in each *généralité*. They made scandalous profits but had to hand over much of their gains in the form of pensions to the mistresses and courtiers of the king. The farmers of the taxes tended to add to their unpopularity by their insolence and display and by the measures to which they resorted in order to stop smuggling. As a consequence, the farmers of the taxes were among the most hated persons in France.

Two of the indirect taxes were particularly odious. One was the customs duties. In medieval times, they had been collected at the border of every fief and each province, but, toward the end of the Middle Ages, the state began to collect them. From the first, they greatly hampered the movement of merchandise. In 1664, Colbert had tried to abolish the interior customs lines, but he had met with only partial success. As a result, there were, thenceforward, three distinct tariff zones in France. A large block of seventeen provinces in north central France was subject to the tariff of 1664. Most of the remaining provinces were subject to old provincial customs duties. Lastly, a few were treated actually as foreign territory.

The other and even more dreaded indirect tax was the salt tax, or gabelle. Since it was a necessity, the government from early times had

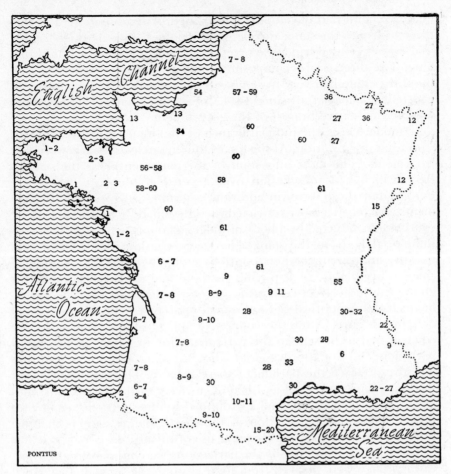

The Salt Tax and the Customs in France under the Ancien Regime

thought salt to be a good source of revenue. Most Frenchmen were required to purchase at least seven pounds of salt each year. Frenchmen would probably have disliked the tax in any case, but they hated the salt tax because of its unfairness. Some provinces were entirely exempt from the tax, while others paid as much as thirty times what was paid in other provinces. One third of the population paid approximately two thirds of the tax. This inequality made successful smuggling profitable, then measures were designed to suppress smuggling, and these measures added to the unpopularity of the tax.

The Legislative and Judicial Organization

In the eighteenth century, the French government had no modern legislative body. In the Middle Ages, an institution known as the estates general had developed. It consisted of representatives of the three orders in the state: the clergy, the nobles, and the third estate. The estates general had always met irregularly at the summons of the king. The three estates composing it had always met separately, and the third estate had very little power and influence. The estates general had not met at all since 1614. As a consequence, there was no separate legislative branch of the government.

In modern eyes, the judicial branch of the French government had a peculiar organization. At the top of the hierarchy of courts were the parlements. The most important of the parlements was the one at Paris which had jurisdiction over a considerable part of central France; but there were, in addition, a number of provincial parlements which had a more restricted jurisdiction. The business of these courts was conducted by a body of judges who formed a dignified and influential body in the state. They were considered a part of the nobility and obtained their positions either by inheritance or purchase. This method of acquiring positions had the merit, at least, of giving the judiciary a certain measure of independence. The parlements had one political right of some importance, namely, the power of remonstrance. After the council of the king had drawn up an edict, it had to be sent to the parlements for registration. In case a parlement did not approve of an edict, the king might abandon the measure or force the parlement to register it. This was done by a solemn ceremony known as a bed of justice. On these occasions, the king, seated on a throne and surrounded by the high officials of the state, commanded registration of the edict. In the eighteenth century, the parlements made frequent use of this right.

The laws administered by the parlements were numerous and confusing. They were derived from local custom, the Roman Law, and royal edicts. In the Middle Ages, each locality developed a body of local customs which had the force of law. There are said to have been two hundred and thirteen of these bodies of local customs in eighteenth century France. Educated men, however, had never been satisfied with these products of a ruder and more primitive age. From a very early period, when a doubtful question or a new situation had arisen, lawyers of Europe had struggled to solve it by applying to it the principles of the Roman law. In southern France, the Roman law was by this time dominant. By the eighteenth century, most educated men felt that the laws of France should be simplified, codified, and made uniform.

Under the *ancien regime,* the procedure of the French courts was in Anglo-Saxon eyes open to the severest criticism. In the seignioral courts, the judges were mainly concerned not with justice but with the interests of the lords who paid their salaries. In the higher courts the judges were often influenced by the solicitation of the parties to a case. The judges conducted a personal investigation behind closed doors. There were thus many opportunities for bribery and much shifting of cases to more favorable courts.

In criminal cases, the most barbarous practices still prevailed. The prisons were filthy holes that bred fevers and other dreadful diseases. The prisoner had to pay a considerable sum for even one of these private cells. The worst criminals were still sent to the galleys. Imprisoned persons might wait years for a trial that never opened. Torture was regularly used to uncover crimes. The accused were entitled to no counsel, and men and women were still broken on the wheel. Executions were looked upon as gala events, and the condemned received no sympathy from the spectators.

The Relations of Church and State

By the end of the reign of Louis XIV, the relations between church and state in France had become very close. Toward the end of the Middle Ages, there had been a revolt against the power of the Pope over the French church. Those in opposition to the papacy sought the help of the king. His response was the Pragmatic Sanction of Bourges of 1438. This document reduced to a minimum the power of the Pope over the French clergy and took away the right of the papacy to name bishops and abbots to French benefices. Henceforth, the bishops were elected by the cathedral chapters, and the abbots and abbesses were elected by the monasteries and convents. The Pope, likewise, lost important revenues and rights. The issuance of the Pragmatic Sanction was a great victory for the advocates of what became known as Gallican Liberties.

The French clergy, however, paid a big price for this victory. In their efforts to become masters of France, the kings sought to establish their power over the clergy as well as the nobles. In 1516, accordingly, Francis I had signed with the Pope a concordat that gave to the king the right to name archbishops, bishops, abbots, and abbesses. Henceforth, these dignitaries of the French church were selected by the king and were merely confirmed in their offices by the Pope.

The Concordat of 1516 thus had serious consequences for the French church. The bishops and abbots had fine residences and enjoyed great revenues. So the offices, consequently, aroused the cupidity of the nobility who sought them for their younger sons in the same manner as they sought pensions and secular sinecures for themselves. This situation obviously had serious consequences for the

French church. The upper clergy in many instances could hardly be differentiated from the nobles. They were often more interested in a pleasant life or advancement at court than in their spiritual duties. In reality, the king and not the French clergy had obtained the Gallican Liberties.

The situation of the lower and higher clergy was very different. The first were drawn exclusively from the third estate and had little chance of promotion. Some of them lived in poverty, since the bishops, monasteries, or laymen in many instances enjoyed revenues that should have gone to the parish priests. These had to eke out a living from the lesser tithes, the occasional fees, and the little pieces of land assigned to them. Often, the parish priests in the country districts had difficulty in collecting what by law was rightfully theirs. On the other hand, some advantages were attached to the office of parish priests, who, on the whole, were probably better housed than the average peasant and enjoyed a certain amount of deference and respect. In the eighteenth century, they had the reputation of being faithful shepherds of their flocks.

By the eighteenth century, public opinion was changing in regard to the regular clergy. In the Middle Ages, little doubt had been felt about the usefulness of the monastic institutions. They served as the pioneers of civilization and the refuge of the scholarly, the spiritual, and the poor. They were rewarded by grants of money and lands. By the end of Louis XIV's reign, they had come to vary greatly in wealth and spiritual zeal. Some monastic institutions had become pleasant shelters for persons of certified noble birth. In other institutions, discipline was maintained with all the severity of medieval times. By 1715, the times had changed, and many people felt that the monasteries had outlived their usefulness and had become the refuge of the ignorant and the idle. Still others coveted their wealth. As a result, the monasteries and convents were the subject of much criticism. Many people thought that both institutions ought to be done away with entirely.

The clergy, as a whole, enjoyed some privileges of importance. They had certain rights that might almost be called constitutional. They held assemblies once in ten years. These meetings granted money to the king, managed the debt of the clergy, and even made pronouncements on doctrine. The so-called Free Gift made to the king was not a very heavy burden. In return for it, the king often made important concessions to the clergy and exempted them from ordinary taxation. The ecclesiastical courts still had jurisdiction in spiritual matters. These rights made the clergy really a privileged order in the state.

In the main, France, like all other European countries, was as yet an agricultural country. French farming still functioned in the framework of the seignioral system. The country had once been a land of great estates, but, by the eighteenth century, the proprietors, in most instances, no longer conducted farming operations. Instead, they had turned over to the peasants the land which they once worked themselves. As a consequence of this development, they had become collectors of rents and dues. Some let their lands for a fixed money rent, but many others, like those of the southern part of the United States today, leased their land to share croppers, or metayers, who paid their rent in the form of a proportionate part of the crop. Sometimes these proprietors furnished the cattle and farm equipment. Their share of the crop was usually one half. There were also some proprietors who owned small farms. In many cases, the farms consisted of many bits of land instead of a single holding, since it was the custom to divide not only the farm but every piece of land belonging to it equally among the heirs of a farm.

The cities and towns of France were still largely under the control of the craft gilds. By the eighteenth century, the French called these organizations corporations. They regulated all the trade and manufactures of the country. No one could yet carry on any handicraft or trade without being a member of the appropriate gild. These gilds still consisted of all persons making a living by the same trade or craft. The masters controlled the gilds and made the acquisition of a mastership difficult. Children of masters were practically sure of becoming masters. Other persons found all sorts of obstacles placed in their paths. As a general rule, masters could take only one apprentice at a time, outside of his family; and they were inclined to lengthen the term of apprenticeship without regard to the skill of the apprentice or the difficulty of learning the craft. By the eighteenth century, the corporations had outlived their usefulness and had become an obstacle to industrial progress. They made it almost impossible to set up a new industry, and they were very jealous of their monopolies. This gave rise to frequent disputes and even law suits between gilds. The shoemakers, for example, struggled unceasingly to prevent the cobblers from selling new shoes. Also, the most minute directions had been set up for regulating manufactures. For instance, the number of threads to the inch for each variety of cloth was strictly prescribed.

Commerce, like industry, was hampered by many obstacles. At every turn, the merchant had to pay for the privilege of transporting commodities. There were innumerable customs lines, and there were still more toll stations. People were charged for the privilege of bringing certain commodities into the towns and cities. These various charges discouraged and prevented circulation of people and commodities. In spite of these obstacles, however, commerce was expanding. The products of America, Africa, and Asia were finding their way to Europe in increasing volume. This was one of the causes for the growth of the French middle class in wealth and numbers during the eighteenth century.

Social Organization

This economic foundation of France explains, in large part, its social organization. Legally, the French people were divided into three classes or orders—the clergy, the nobles, and the third estate. In reality, they were divided into two classes—the privileged and the unprivileged. The privileged consisted of the upper clergy and the nobles. The unprivileged comprised the mass of the French nation. As the upper clergy sprang from the nobility and lived much like them, they hardly need a separate description.

The privileged nobles were a comparatively small class. They comprised possibly twenty-five thousand or thirty thousand families in a nation of twenty-five million persons. A few of them were descendants of great feudal families. Some were distant collateral relatives of the king; others were the descendants of successful men in the more recent past. A large number had acquired nobility through the holding of offices that conferred noble rank. The members of this privileged class enjoyed many valuable privileges. They were given all the posts in the army and virtually all those held by the higher clergy. They held numerous sinecure positions in the administration. They escaped much of the burden of taxation, and they received many marks of deference. They were supported by the rest of the nation. So, for nobles, the *ancien regime* had many advantages.

In reality, there were many classes of nobles. The most favored section of the nobility was the court nobles. They toiled only at the occupation of being courtiers, but they spent long hours at this really most tiring task. They might have had beautiful chateaux and splendid parks in the provinces, but they seldom occupied them. Instead, they lived either at Paris or Versailles. Their chief objective was to obtain pensions and sinecures. For this purpose, they gathered around the king and sought by all means to bring themselves to his notice. They cultivated good manners and practiced bad morals. At best, they were brave, had good taste, were moderate in speech and jest, carried themselves well, and were deferential in manner. They were capable, though, of polished cruelty.

Most French nobles never saw the court. A large number of them might be characterized as provincial or country nobles. Some of them were in comfortable circumstances, but many of them were so poor that they were hardly distinguishable in appearance from the peasants. In some districts, the bond between lord and peasant was still a close one, and the proprietor took a paternal interest in his tenants. In the main, such relations were disappearing. In some cases, lords and peasants were openly at odds. The peasants complained that they could not get the pay due them for their work. As a class, therefore, the provincial nobles were dissatisfied with their lot.

The French nobility included many who had comparatively recently been members of the third estate. They had acquired the title of nobles by their occupation of certain offices in the judicial and administrative branches of the government. They frequently were richer and more capable than the older nobility. The so-called nobility of the sword, however, was inclined to look down on the nobility of the robe.

The third estate really included several classes of people. It included the middle class, the peasants, and the proletariat. In France, the middle class is known as the *bourgeoisie*. At the top of this class were the financiers, the holders of important administrative offices, and the intelligentsia. The financiers, especially, were often envied for their wealth, hated for their display, and ridiculed for their pretensions. The upper *bourgeoisie* usually struggled to acquire a title and buy landed property. The intelligentsia owed their position to their power to entertain and amuse their fellows. The middle class, of course, included other professions. There were, for example, many physicians, surgeons, and lawyers as well as masters of corporations and shopkeepers in this class. The last two classes were, for the most part, at the head of really petty establishments. The ordinary master had under him at most a journeyman and an apprentice or two. The shopkeeper depended for help mainly on his wife and was more like a huckster than a merchant. The French *bourgeoisie* was rapidly increasing in numbers.

Below the middle class, particularly at Paris, there was a large class that, for want of a better name, we might call the proletariat. It included petty artisans, journeymen, apprentices, the hawkers and vendors of all sorts that filled the streets of Paris with noise and confusion, and swarms of beggars who infested the cities and the rural districts alike. At best, they lived in one or two rooms up some narrow alley or passageway or boarded with their masters and ate a scanty and monotonous diet. At worst, they had no shelter at all and suffered from hunger. In the time of the French Revolution, they were to furnish the terrible mobs that characterized that movement.

The rise of the French middle class had not yet greatly changed French cities and towns. They still retained much of their medieval appearance. The moats, it is true, had been filled in, but the surrounding walls remained. The cities and towns were still a maze of dirty, narrow, crooked streets. Little fresh air and sunlight found its way into the tall, gabled houses. The houses still sheltered both the shopkeeper's or master's business and his family. Within this medieval framework, however, some signs of modern times were beginning to appear. In the reign of Louis XIV, public conveyances came into use. Street lights that threw only a feeble glare were being introduced. When it stormed, the streets were still veritable mires, but sidewalks were soon to appear. The houses were shortly to be numbered. The inhabitants of these cities and towns worked for longer hours than modern workmen but at a more leisurely pace. They had, besides, many holidays in which they did no work at all. At Paris, at least, the police were already well organized, and provision was beginning to be made for the putting out of fires.

The largest section of the third estate was composed of the peasants. Their mode of life had changed very little in two hundred years. They still lived in unkempt villages surrounded by open fields. Their houses, barns, and sheds, their families, farm animals and poultry were still huddled together. Most houses had thatched roofs. Many had no floors or windows. The evidence concerning their appearance and treatment is very conflicting. Probably, the greatest change in the status of the peasant was in his intelligence and in his ideas concerning himself. The boldest of them no longer accepted mistreatment and injustice without protest. All had come to hate the remaining vestiges of the seignioral system—the rent, or share of the crop, paid the lord; the heavy dues imposed when they sold their land; the labor still often demanded of them; and the *banalités* required for the use of the lord's mill, oven, wine press, or bull. They rebelled against laws which gave the lord the right to gallop and hunt over the peasant's growing crops, while they were being prohibited from hunting or fishing on their own lands. They were apt to look on the neighboring chateau as a seat of oppression and a sign of tyranny. They complained bitterly at the payments in kind which they were required to make to the parish priest, but they still believed implicitly what he taught. They worked long hours but, usually, they refused to be hurried. In the main, their own village was still their world.

422

The Regency

As a result of a series of tragic deaths in his family, Louis XIV left the French throne to his great grandson, a boy of five years, instead of to his own son. He entrusted the regency to a near relative, the Duke of Orleans. The new ruler of France was not very well fitted for his post. He was amiable, generous, and intelligent but lazy, careless, and corrupt. As a result, a prompt change took place in the tone of the court. In his later years, Louis XIV and his courtiers had been reverent and devout, at least in appearance. The regent and his friends distinguished themselves by their incredulity, their vices, and their love of pleasure.

The most pressing administrative problem was the finances of the country. The regent inherited from his predecessor a heavy debt and a revenue that met only about half the yearly expenditure. When all other expedients had failed, the regent decided to try the ideas of John Law, a Scottish banker.

The ideas of Law about public finance were based on a custom followed by private merchants. In cases where the buyer did not wish to pay cash for a purchase and was known to be honorable and solvent, he was allowed three months in which to make payment. In such a case, the buyer gave the seller a statement recognizing his indebtedness and promising to pay at an agreed date. If the seller wished to make a purchase before the arrival of this agreed date, he simply handed over the first buyer's promise to pay in place of money. The promise thus circulated virtually like money.

Law planned to establish, with the aid of a number of rich men, a large bank which would inspire similar confidence. It would accept at a slight discount the promises of merchants and keep them until payment was due. In exchange, it would put in circulation bank bills which would pass like money and be payable at sight. When these bank bills should be transformed into true money, Law proposed to use the paper money to reimburse the creditors of the state.

In 1716, the proposed bank was established as a private enterprise. The general public liked the light paper money much better than the heavy metal, and the bank prospered. In 1718, it was even transformed into a royal bank.

The bank, however, was only part of Law's system. He planned to stimulate commerce and extinguish the state debt by founding commercial companies which should be made monopolies. In 1717, accordingly, he created a West India Company which was given a monopoly for the exploitation of Louisiana. Next, he bought the French East India Company. Finally, he obtained monopolies for the coining of money, the sale of tobacco, and the collection of indirect taxes.

The capital needed for the functioning of these various companies was obtained by the sale of shares of stock which could be bought and sold on the market. They could be paid for in part by evidences of the state debt. At first, people were optimistic about the prospects of the enterprises started by Law. They thought there were mines of gold and stores of precious stones in Louisiana, and everyone wanted to purchase the stock of the new companies. The price of shares rose rapidly. By 1719, it was forty times what it had been at the beginning.

The actual returns received by share holders did not justify the prices for which the shares were being sold. So the prices of the shares began to fall and people commenced to lose confidence, first in the companies and finally in the bank. Some speculators began to sell their shares and to take in payment metallic money instead of the new paper money. One prince of the royal house alone withdrew three carriages full of specie. The bank, however, had put more paper bank notes in circulation than there was metallic money in all France and, consequently, was unable to redeem much of the paper money it had issued. In 1720, accordingly, Law fled from France.

The episode had some beneficial results for the country. It caused some of the public debt to be paid off and began the exploitation of Louisiana. It contributed to the building up of Atlantic ports like Bordeaux, Nantes, and Le Havre. On the other hand, it brought France to the verge of mob violence.

In 1723, though but thirteen years old, the king, Louis XV, was declared of age. Under the guidance of his tutor, Fleury, the king designated as chief minister the Duke of Bourbon, who stayed in power three years. His only significant act was the arrangement of a marriage between the young king and Marie Leszczinsky, daughter of the dethroned king of Poland.

In 1726, the tutor of the king, seventy-two year old Cardinal Fleury, for whom Louis XV had a real affection, became first minister of France. He was prudent and pacific both by nature and by reason of his age. For seventeen years, he gave France good government. He was economical, and partially succeeded in his efforts toward straightening out the finances of the state. In 1738 he balanced the budget. He died in 1743.

The Reign of Louis XV

At the time he assumed direction of affairs, Louis XV was thirty-three. He was a fine-looking man. Without being really well known to them, he was popular with his subjects. In 1745, when he fell ill at

Metz, the people all over France crowded into the churches to pray for his recovery. In reality, he was quite unworthy of such a demonstration. He was intelligent but lazy and left the work of government to ministers who held office through unworthy royal favorites. He occupied himself with hunting, with a succession of favorites, with making coffee in the apartment of his daughters, and with reading reports of his secret police and the intercepted correspondence of private individuals.

The most famous of his favorites was Madame de Pompadour. From 1745 until her death in 1764, this intelligent, beautiful, artistic, and literary middle-class woman, with the plebeian name of Antoinnette Poisson, was the true sovereign of France. She had her own apartment in the palace. She made and unmade ministers, gave and withdrew command over the armies of France, and shifted alliances of the state. She acquired, to be sure, a certain popularity among the writers of the day through her patronage of letters. On the whole, however, the people of France detested her for her squandering of the resources of France and for the political and military disasters for which she was held responsible.

During her period of power, the court was absorbing nearly half the revenue of the state. Part of the huge sum was spent in display, and part was expended for pensions for courtiers who did nothing in return for them. Large sums, too, were given to the favorite herself. All these expenditures contributed to the discrediting of the existing regime.

The wars of the period had the same effect. In 1740, without much reason, France joined the coalition against Maria Theresa, heiress of the Habsburg claims in Austria. The justification for French participation in the war was the old antagonism against the Habsburgs and the maintenance of the policy of supporting the lesser German states against the larger. France had as allies the Elector of Bavaria, Frederick II of Prussia, and the Bourbons of Spain and Italy. At first, France acted solely as an auxiliary of Bavaria, but in 1744 she declared open war not only on Maria Theresa but on England and the United Provinces, the allies of Austria. In the Netherlands, the French fought well against the Austrians, the English, and the Dutch; conquered the Austrian Netherlands in the great battles of Fontenoy (1745), Raucoux (1746), and Lawfeld (1748); and took the key to the United Netherlands.

In the negotiations for peace that followed, the French diplomats showed great ineptitude. They not only restored the territory just conquered, which the French had so long desired, but they even returned the materials for waging war that they had taken from the enemy. To judge from the treaty of peace, France had fought the War of the Austrian Succession and King George's War for the benefit of the king of Prussia and the Spanish Bourbons. "As stupid as the peace" consequently became a byword in France.

The Treaty of Aix-la-Chapelle did not bring permanent peace to Europe. Too many causes of conflict remained. Austria was not reconciled to the loss of Silesia to Prussia. The colonial and commercial rivalry of France and England was as yet undecided. Overseas, the war can hardly be said to have ceased at all. In Europe, the powers almost immediately began to prepare for a renewal of the conflict. France, therefore, allowed herself to become involved again in both the continental and the colonial struggle.

The opening of the Seven Years' War was preceded by an astonishing shifting of alliances. In the War of the Austrian Succession, France and Prussia, England and Austria had been in alliance. In some way, as will be shown more at length in Chapter 23, the representatives of Maria Theresa brought about a complete rearrangement of the alliances. France was dissatisfied with the conduct of its Prussian ally in the War of the Austrian Succession. The Austrian diplomats, through flattery of Madame de Pompadour, according to some, persuaded France to abandon a policy pursued for two hundred years and to join an alliance that included Austria and Russia against Prussia. One of the first results of the new alignment of the powers was the arrangement of a marriage between the future Louis XVI and Marie Antoinette, daughter of Maria Theresa. This shifting of allies was exceedingly unpopular in France, increased the dissatisfaction with the ruling favorite, and greatly injured the prestige of the French monarchy.

The ensuing war did nothing to restore the popularity of the king. In Europe, a great Franco-German army was defeated and crushed in 1757 at Rossbach in Saxony. Overseas, the French were completely defeated both in America and in India. By the subsequent treaties of peace, France gained nothing in Europe by its seven years of war, surrendered in America all its colonial possessions save four small islands (two in the Gulf of St. Lawrence and two in the West Indies), and in India gave up the opportunity to establish its rule.

As in the time of the *Fronde,* the Parlement of Paris assumed the leadership of the movement against the monarchy. Again, they claimed the right of watching over and controlling the acts of the government. They found pretexts for their opposition in religious affairs and in the wasting of the resources of the country. Most of the judges of the Parlement were Jansenists and Gallicans and, consequently, bitter enemies of the Jesuits. In 1762, during a trial that involved them, the Parlement of Paris declared the constitutions of the Jesuits contrary to the laws of France. Two years later, after much hesitation, Louis XV expelled the Jesuit order from the country. In the matter of finances, the judges of Parlement opposed systematically the imposition of new taxes and the registration of financial edicts. The king overruled them again and again by holding so-called beds of justice by which he compelled the registration of the unpopular laws dealing with finances. The judges combatted the king by refusing to function as a court and even by resigning en masse. They took this action five times between 1750 and 1770. The king retaliated by exiling the Parlement but soon gave way to public opinion and permitted the judges to return to Paris. In 1771, the government exiled the judges again and replaced the Parlement of Paris and some of the provincial parlements by new bodies.

In the final years of his reign, the unpopularity of the king, if possible, increased. In 1770, a new favorite, a former milliner's apprentice and more detested even than Madame Pompadour, rose to power. In 1772, the French nation was shocked almost as much as by a defeat by the first partition of its ally, Poland, without the slightest regard to French interests or French feelings. In 1774, the aging Louis XV finally died. A king had seldom been so unpopular. The authorities in charge of the funeral arrangements did not dare attempt to have the funeral cortege pass through Paris in the daytime. Even at night, the procession passed through the outskirts of the city very rapidly and was followed by the taunts of the spectators. Only a miracle could save France from a revolution.

The Failure of Louis XVI To Become a Benevolent Despot

The death of Louis XV brought two very young people to power in France. Louis XVI was twenty and his Austrian-born queen, Marie Antoinette, was only nineteen. Neither had the qualities needed to save France. The new king was large, heavy, a big eater, fond of physical exercise and working with his hands, inclined to be influenced by those around him, and entirely ignorant of government. The young queen was ignorant, frivolous, impatient of restraint, passionately fond of pleasure, and easily influenced by her companions. Neither had the ability needed to ward off the threatened revolution.

In spite of his lack of the qualities required by the times, Louis XVI made a good beginning. He seemed anxious to placate public opinion. He started his reign by recalling the parlements which had been suppressed in 1771, by dismissing some of the most unpopular ministers, and by putting able men in their places. Among the latter should be mentioned Maurepas, an old courtier, who became first minister; Vergennes, a skillful diplomat and the new minister of foreign affairs; Malesherbes, one of the most enlightened men of the time; and Turgot, the new controller general of finances.

The appointment of Turgot was a promise of reform. For a long time, he had been a student of economics, had made contributions to the *Encyclopedia,* had written an important book on economics, and had had practical and successful experience as an administrator in Limousin. Upon taking office, Turgot presented to the king a definite program in which he advocated a policy of no bankruptcy, no increase of taxes, and no loans. He hoped by economy and development of the public resources to improve the financial situation of the state and to develop the wealth of the country by establishing a regime of liberty in agriculture, industry, and commerce.

Immediately after taking office, Turgot began to put his program into operation. He effected important economies in the management of the royal household. In 1774, he freed the grain trade from the restrictions that had hampered it. Until this time, merchants dealing in grain were carefully supervised by the police; and, under threat of heavy fines, they were permitted to buy and sell grain only on certain days and at fixed hours and in definitely stated markets. The passage of grain from one province to another was prevented by the existing customs barriers. As a result of these regulations, each year some provinces had more grain than they needed, while the inhabitants of other provinces died of hunger. As a result, the peasants had no incentive to increase production. In 1776, an edict abolished the trade gilds which restricted industry. Hitherto, the regulations had limited the number of workshops and had designated the methods that must be employed in manufacture. Finally, in the same year, an edict was issued which put an end to the royal *corvée.* Previously, the peasants had had to work for nothing at inconvenient times for an uncertain length of time in maintaining and constructing roads. In place of the *corvée,* Turgot imposed a tax that both the privileged and the unprivileged were required to pay.

The reforms of Turgot aroused great opposition. They exasperated the dealers in grain, the masters of gilds who feared competition, and all those whose incomes had been reduced or whose taxes had been increased. The discontented found spokesmen in the parlements and among the courtiers. The Parlement of Paris declared that every system, which under the appearance of humanity and benevolence tended to establish in a well-ordered monarchy an equality of duties among men and to destroy the necessary distinctions, would soon lead to disorder and produce a revolution of society. At court, the courtiers, led by Queen Marie Antoinette herself, gave the unhappy king no peace. "Only Turgot and I," he said plaintively and weakly, "love the people." In the end, the king yielded to pressure, and in May, 1776, dismissed Turgot and authorized the repeal of his measures.

This dismissal of Turgot forestalled a trial of his most interesting proposal. He had drawn up a plan for a hierarchy of assemblies. At the bottom of the hierarchy, he proposed to organize in each city and rural community an elective assembly. These, in turn, were to elect assemblies for the *arrondissement*. These latter bodies finally were to elect provincial assemblies. The system was to have been completed by a national assembly.

After an interval of several months, Louis XVI entrusted the management of the finances of the kingdom to a well-known retired banker, Jacques Necker (1732–1804), a native of Geneva. After coming to Paris, he had made a large fortune in a few years and had gained some reputation as a publicist. He had been aided in this by the *salon,* one of the most famous of the period, which his wife maintained in the French capital. As he was a Protestant, he was given the duties but not the title of controller general. After taking office, he found himself confronted by an almost impossible task. He had to solve not only the same difficult problems as Turgot but to finance a war, the American Revolution, in which France had become involved.

Events soon proved that Necker hardly deserved his great reputation. Like Turgot, he believed in economy and the wisdom of imposing no new taxes. Unlike his predecessor, he borrowed large amounts of money to meet the mounting deficits and to finance the war against England. His prestige as a banker helped him to float the new loans. Unfortunately for the treasury, however, in order to insure their success, he made the new loans profitable to the investor and expensive for the treasury. He paid the interest on earlier loans out of the proceeds of later loans. At the moment, this enhanced his reputation but made the administration of the financial affairs of France still more difficult.

In 1781, Necker committed a still more serious blunder. He published a work entitled *Compte Rendu au Roi,* which pretended to penetrate the secrecy which had hitherto surrounded the finances of France. He had come to believe that the foundation of British credit was the publicity which surrounded British financial affairs. In his account of French finances, however, he did not tell the truth. He did not reveal how much the expenditures really exceeded the income of the state and said nothing about the war expenditures. Such admissions would have irrevocably damaged his popularity and reputation. Instead, he presented the finances of an imaginary "normal year" and omitted all extraordinary expenditures and unusual receipts. In this way, he created the impression that the state had a favorable balance. His imaginary account of the finances of France so increased his popularity that he ventured to ask for admission to the council of state. When his request was refused through the jealousy of other ministers, Necker resigned. By his publication of the supposed finances of the state, however, he had acknowledged that they were an affair of the nation as well as the king.

The resignation of Necker made the situation still more difficult for the French government. For two more years, the demands of the war continued. The financiers who had assisted Necker looked coldly at the proposals of his successor. Reassured by Necker's misleading statistics, the general public thought the government had a surplus. As the government could not borrow, it took the unpopular course of increasing taxes.

After two years, Calonne (1734–1802) took charge of the finances. He knew the grave situation of the treasury, but he had unbounded faith in the resources of France. Accordingly, he adopted the dangerous policy of giving the impression that the state was prosperous. He won the favor of the courtiers by paying the debts of the king's brothers and giving pensions to many others belonging to the court. He paid for a new royal chateau and, at the wish of the queen, bought still another. He made some useful public improvements. For a time, the new financial policy seemed successful. Confidence was restored. The public again eagerly subscribed for government loans. The country seemed to be prosperous.

The policy of Calonne, however, was unsound. After the lapse of two years (1785), criticisms began again to be heard. Necker attacked the policy of his successor in a substantial book entitled *Administration of the Finances of France*. The judges of the Parlement of Paris seized the opportunity to gain popularity and remonstrated against successive edicts authorizing public loans. Calonne himself at last realized that his policy could not go on indefinitely. It had merely increased the difficulties of the state. Accordingly, Calonne suddenly inaugurated a new policy. In the main, it took up again the ideas of Turgot. He advocated the removal of restrictions on the grain trade, the abolition of the royal *corvée,* and the organization of local assemblies. He proposed a new direct tax from which even the privileged classes were not to be exempt. As he knew the Parlement of Paris would oppose his proposals, he persuaded the king to lay the new projects before an Assembly of Notables.

This body met in February, 1787. In convening it, Calonne made the mistake of inviting many, like judges of parlement, who were certain to continue their opposition to his policies. He thought that by a vigorous denunciation of the existing financial system he could persuade those who profited by it to aid him in introducing the new policy. He naturally failed completely. Instead of agreeing with Calonne, the Notables discovered serious objections against all his proposals. They objected to the establishment of provincial assemblies, composed of representatives of the three estates, as a breaking down of the hierarchy of orders which they considered the foundation of the monarchy. The nobles feared his project for the sale of ground rents and feudal dues as a step toward the abolition of all feudal dues. As a result of his failure, Calonne resigned from office.

In the meantime, an event had occurred which greatly discredited the monarchy. As an Austrian, the queen, Marie Antoinette, had been unpopular from the first. In the succeeding years, she had done nothing to win the affections of her subjects. On the contrary, she had been unwise in her friendships and foolish in matters of public policy. In 1785, she was the innocent victim of a sordid plot that greatly increased her unpopularity and further damaged her reputation. Cardinal de Rohan, a dignitary of the Church but a notorious character, was duped into thinking that if he assisted the queen in obtaining a certain diamond necklace, she would favor him. The loose-living cardinal, accordingly, was persuaded to obtain the necklace and hand it over to one of the intriguers, who posed as the queen's *valet de chambre*. He obtained the expensive piece of jewelry by giving the jewelers a contract for payment bearing the queen's forged endorsement. Soon after the necklace had been handed over, the plot was discovered and Rohan was sent to the Bastille. When the cardinal was brought to trial before the Parlement of Paris, he was acquitted. The trial aroused the greatest interest, and the verdict was loudly applauded. The people of Paris asserted by their attitude that they thought the queen quite capable of engaging in such an intrigue.

A few weeks after the resignation of Calonne, the king entrusted the direction of the government to a distinguished member of the Assembly of Notables, the Archbishop of Toulouse, Lomenie de Brienne. Although he had opposed his predecessor's ideas, he now adopted the plan of Calonne and added to it a stamp tax. He had no more success than Calonne with the Assembly of Notables and finally dissolved that body. He then made an attempt to conciliate the Parlement of Paris. As a matter of fact, he succeeded in having registered without difficulty a series of decrees abolishing the grain trade and the royal *corvée* and instituting assemblies in the twenty-three provinces that had no provincial estates. He had to force the stamp and land taxes through against the opposition of parlement. The day following this arbitrary act, the parlement declared the registration of the two acts void and asserted that the consent of the almost forgotten States-General must be obtained for new taxes. The reply of the government to this revolutionary action was to exile the judges of parlement to Troyes. This measure did not end the resistance, since the provincial parlements took the same stand as the Parlement of Paris, and the spirit of revolt spread throughout France. By autumn, both the government and the Parlement of Paris were ready for compromise. The government abandoned its efforts to reform taxation, and the parlement agreed to prolong the collection of two existing taxes and to abolish exemptions.

The government and the parlement did not long remain at peace. Two months later, the government proposed a series of large loans as a means of meeting its financial obligations. To make the proposal more acceptable, the king promised to convene the States-General within five years. As the struggle between the government and the parlement became more bitter, the king, like his grandfather, Louis XV, tried to reorganize the parlement. To make the change more acceptable, he promised to codify and improve the laws, to abolish torture, and to reduce the costs of justice. By this time, public opinion was badly confused. The general public regarded the resistance of the highly privileged judges of parlement as a brave defence of liberty against oppression.

Resistance to the measures of the government was as strong in the provinces as at Paris. Some of the provincial parlements refused to register decrees accepted by the Parlement of Paris. The decrees of May, 1788, reorganizing the courts aroused even stronger opposition, particularly in Brittany, Béarn, and Dauphiné. In the last province, the ancient provincial estates were restored. Meanwhile, the financial situation was growing steadily worse. It became impossible to continue to borrow, because those who had money would not lend it without the sanction of parlement for the loans. The absolute government had managed its finances so badly there seemed no recourse but to call on the nation for help. As a consequence, the government reluctantly announced it would convene the almost forgotten States-General on May 1, 1789.

In his perplexity, Louis XVI turned to Necker, the minister whom he had once dismissed. Although events were soon to show his incapacity for a statesmanlike policy, his appointment temporarily restored public confidence. The securities of the state rose thirty points on the stock exchange, and Necker again succeeded in getting money from the bank of discount, loans for the most pressing needs of the government. He even advanced a large sum from his personal fortune. This enabled the government to continue to function.

Next to that of finance, the most pressing problem was the preparation for the promised States-General. Little was really known about the organization and working of that body. It had not met for one hundred and seventy-five years. By a decree issued in July, 1788, officials and others were urged to search for documents and to present memoirs which might aid in the task. The work of the government, of course, was made more difficult by the economic situation and the state of public opinion.

The economic situation was unusually bad. An industrial revolution which created a demand for more markets was taking place in England. The proposal to introduce the new machinery in France aroused even greater unrest and opposition than in England. It was under these conditions that the two powers negotiated a commercial treaty (1787). Great Britain agreed to admit the importation of French wines on the same terms as Portuguese wines, and, in return, the French promised to impose a relatively low duty on English cutlery and hardware. There were also other provisions of less importance. On the whole, the treaty was more favorable to England than to France. It was popular in the wine districts of France, but the French manufacturers, with their obsolete methods, complained bitterly at the competition to which the treaty subjected them.

The industrial crisis was accompanied by a partial failure of the wheat crop. Bread was an even more basic food in France than in English-speaking countries. For thirty years, its price had been steadily rising, and, by the early part of 1789, famine prices prevailed. In order to relieve this condition, Necker attempted to regulate the grain trade again. In one of his decrees, he seemed to confirm the popular suspicion that speculators were at the bottom of the trouble. In many towns, mobs attempted to force traders to sell grain below the market price. Parlements and local officers forbade the shipment of grain to other localities. In large cities like Paris, consequently, the supply of flour and bread was meagre and uncertain. So the whole economic situation was calculated to stir up a revolutionary spirit and mob action.

In the intellectual sphere, the invitation to investigate the organization and working of the States-General had the practical effect of abolishing censorship of the press. The politically ambitious rushed into print, and pamphlets poured from the presses of France. Their writers were, in the main, champions of the third estate and were quick to point out the disparity between the privileged and unprivileged classes in regard to numbers. They showed that the third estate practically constituted the nation. They tried to demonstrate the absurdity of belief in the historic organization of the States-General. They pointed out that the third estate had a right to expect to be something more than it had been. This was the thesis of the most famous of the pamphlets, the one written by the Abbé Sieyès. The pamphlets formed the staple of the conversation of the cafés of Paris and the *salons* of France.

Surrounded by such conditions, Necker was in doubt as to the course he should pursue. In December, 1788, he announced his conclusion that the third estate should have twice as many representatives as either of the other two orders, but he left unsettled the fundamental question of the relations that should exist among the three orders. At the same time, he made a number of other proposals. He advocated that no taxes should be levied without the consent of the States-General, a civil list should be established for the court, arbitrary arrest by *lettres de cachet* should be regulated, and freedom of the press should be established. The voters were to be permitted to present their grievances and wishes in *cahiers* which were to be brought to the attention of the government when the States-General was convened.

The elections to the States-General were complicated. The electoral district was the bailiwick or *senechaussée,* ancient administrative districts of the monarchy. In each electoral district, the three orders voted separately. The nobles voted directly for the representatives of their order. The bishops and parish priests did the same thing. The regular clergy, on the contrary, were given only one vote for each monastery. This arrangement gave the parish priests a preponderance among the deputies of the clerical order, and they obtained about two thirds of the seats assigned to their order. The third estate voted only indirectly for their representatives. The voters in each bailiwick chose an electoral assembly, which elected the representatives of the third estate. In most towns and cities, the voting was even more indirect than in rural France. There, they had electoral assemblies which chose representatives to the electoral assemblies of the bailiwicks. Five of the largest cities had special electoral assemblies which sent representatives directly to the States-General. In all electoral districts, the suffrage for the election of deputies to the third estate was nearly universal. The elections resulted in the choice of a large number of obscure country lawyers as representatives of the third estate.

As the representatives of France made their way by private carriages and public conveyances toward Versailles in the latter part of April and the opening days of May, 1789, they carried with them *cahiers* which were supposed to embody the wishes of the three orders of voters. These *cahiers* had been drawn up by all three orders and by the assemblies of voters as well as the electoral assemblies. In some cases, they embodied the ideas of some ambitious pamphleteer or politician. In other instances, they contained only the naive grievances of the peasants of some locality. The *cahiers* of all three orders asked for the liberties promised by Necker. All wanted a constitution. The clergy and nobles expressed a willingness to give up their exemption from taxation, but they wished to retain their other privileges. Many of the *cahiers* of the third estate complained of the vestiges of the seignioral system. All desired liberty.

The rulers of France in the eighteenth century failed to become benevolent despots. Louis XIV left behind him because of his extravagance and his wars a dangerous situation. The regency, Louis XV, and Louis XVI failed in turn to remedy the situation. Through indifference, carelessness, or weakness, they allowed the finances of the kingdom to grow steadily worse. At the same time, the nation was increasingly shocked at the frivolity of the court, the mismanagement of the finances, and the ineptness of the diplomats. The dissatisfaction mounted steadily. Enlightened nobles wished to play a part in the state like that taken by the English nobility. The third estate had come to realize that many of its members were equal or even superior to the nobles in ability, education, and wealth. There was great danger of a revolution against a framework of society that no longer fitted the French people. Just at the culmination of this unrest and disaffection, the absolute monarchy broke down because of its inability to manage its finances and was compelled to call on the discontented nation for help.

CHAPTER 27

Slavic Europe

During the greater part of the modern period, Slavic Europe had little or no connection with the civilization developing in Western Europe. Geography and differences in language and culture tended to keep separate the peoples of Eastern and Western Europe. Not until the eighteenth century did the greater part of the Slavs play any appreciable part in the affairs of Western Europe.

The Early History of the Slavs

At first, the Slavs were neither numerous nor powerful. When Western Europe first heard of them, they were a comparatively small body of people living in the valley of the Pripet River, a branch of the Dnieper. In the years that followed, however, they multiplied rapidly and spread over most of Eastern Europe. Some migrated westward until they occupied a region bounded by the Elbe, the Danube, and the Vistula rivers and the Baltic Sea. Others moved southward until they settled much of the Balkan Peninsula. Still others occupied the Great Russian Plain and finally pushed eastward until they had overrun the vast stretches of Siberia. In time, the Slavs began to form kingdoms and principalities. In Southern Europe, we hear of such medieval states as Bulgaria, Serbia, and Croatia. Among the Slavs who moved westward, we find the Poles, the Czechs, and the Slovaks being mentioned. In the rest of Slavic Europe, there were at first many Slavic principalities.

In the end, social and political forces led to the separation of the Slavs into three great divisions. For this result, many factors were responsible. In the ninth century it seemed likely that all the Slavs would be converted by Byzantine missionaries. If this had taken place, it might have altered greatly all subsequent history. Instead, they became divided, as has been mentioned, into three divisions. In the ninth century, Slavs of Southern Europe were cut off from the rest of their Slavic kinsmen by the eastward expansion of the Germans of the Danube Valley and the settlement of the Magyars farther down the same valley. The Western Slavs (the Czechs, the Poles, and the Slovaks) ultimately accepted Christianity from missionaries from Rome instead of Constantinople. This had an important effect on their culture and tended to cut off the Western Slavs from those farther east. The remaining Slavs became known as Eastern Slavs. It is customary to divide them into Great, White, and Little Russians. Each of the great divisions of the Slavs tended, until recently, to go its own way.

The Southern Slavs

It was the fate of the Southern Slavs to be in bondage throughout the greater part of the modern period of history. Shortly before 1492, the medieval kingdoms of Servia and Bulgaria fell under the control of the Turks. At first, the Southern Slavs were comparatively well governed by their Turkish masters. They were taxed more heavily than the Moslems and were forced to give up some of their children to be trained as Janissaries, but they retained their Eastern Orthodox religion and their local self-government. Later, when the Turkish government became corrupt and inefficient, they were shamefully mistreated and exploited. By 1800, they began to take advantage of the weakness of the Turkish government and commenced a struggle to gain their independence. By this time, the Southern Slavs under Turkish rule were called not only Serbs and Bulgars but by names derived from the provinces in which they lived. Thus, the various branches of the Serbs are often called Montenegrins, Dalmatians, Bosnians, and Herzegovinians as well as Serbs.

In addition, it must be remembered that many Southern Slavs fell under the rule of the Habsburgs. Some of them were included in Hungary and the rest were kept in other provinces ruled by the Habsburgs. These Southern Slavs were dominated either by the Germans or the Magyars. They are known as Croats and Slovenes. Most of the Croats were subject to Hungary. The Slovenes were to be found in the region north of the Adriatic Sea which was under German rule.

It is difficult to distinguish definitely among the three branches of the Southern Slavs. The Croats and Slovenes, it should be remembered, tended to be associated with the Habsburgs and Western civilization. They were Roman Catholics and used the Latin alphabet. The Serbs tended to be associated with Turkish rule. They were communicants of the Eastern Orthodox Church and used an alphabet derived from the Greeks. The situation was further complicated by the fact that some of the Serbian nobles turned Moslem to save their position and property, and that many Serbs ultimately emigrated into territories under Habsburg rule. As for the Croats and Slovenes, they were distinguished by differences in geography and culture.

The Western Slavs

The Western Slavs have never had political unity. Quite early, they became divided into Poles, Czechs, and Slovaks. After the tenth century, the Czechs built up a great state that occupied the three provinces of Bohemia, Moravia, and Silesia. From the first, the Czech state had to struggle against Germanizing influences. The rulers married German princesses. German merchants and colonists pushed into the country and settled there. Silesia was inhabited mainly by Germans and Poles. Bohemia and Moravia were Czech islands, dotted by German cities and surrounded by German border districts. The German colonists brought their culture with them.

Throughout the period from 1492 to 1918, the Czech state was closely associated with German or Austrian political institutions. In time, the native line of rulers died out and German sovereigns took its place. The kingdom of Bohemia, as it was known, became an integral part of the Holy Roman Empire. After 1526, it fell under the control of the Habsburgs and became one of the kingdoms in their hereditary state. It continued to have this status until 1918.

At first, the Poles were a comparatively small group in the valleys of the Vistula and the Warta rivers. After the latter part of the tenth century, however, they began to develop into a strong state. Under able and strong rulers, they extended their boundaries and established a prosperous state. By 1386, they had definitely lost Silesia to the Czechs and two Baltic provinces to the Teutonic Knights but had formed a union with the large and important principality of Lithuania. This was brought about by the marriage of Hedwig, queen of Poland, to Ladislas Jagellon, the heathen and uncultured Duke of Lithuania. Thenceforth, Lithuania was considered a Christian state, and the two states (Poland and Lithuania) cooperated until 1589, when they became united in an organic union. This made the kingdom of Poland a great state, able to compete on an equal footing with the Germans in the west, the Russians in the east, and the Swedes in the north.

The Slovaks did not become a political force until recent times. They occupied northern Hungary. They were closely related to the Czechs. The Czechs, however, were less loyal to the Roman Catholic faith, more industrialized, and in closer contact with Western civilizations. The Slovaks continued to be an agricultural and pastoral group.

438

The Rise of the Duchy of Muscovy

Throughout the greater part of the medieval period, the Eastern Slavs remained divided into numerous principalities. In the thirteenth century, this made them an easy prey to the invading Mongols. For two centuries, the petty Russian princes remained tributary to the Mongols. They groveled before their conquerors and sought the support of the Mongol Khan against their rivals. The situation bred in them the qualities of intrigue, treachery, cunning, and cruelty.

One Russian prince was particularly successful in profiting by the situation. The ruler of Muscovy secured for himself the odious right to collect the annual tribute for the invaders. This gave him authority in financial matters over his rivals and assured him the support of the Mongol conquerors. Muscovy became the most powerful principality in the region and, by the middle of the fifteenth century, it included a territory as large as modern Germany. One of the rewards of this policy was the transfer of the chief bishop of the Russian church to Moscow. This continued to be the situation until 1480.

By this date, an exceedingly able ruler, Ivan III (1462–1505), had come to the Muscovite throne. He laid the foundations of the later Russian Empire. During his reign, he made conquests that trebled the area of his principality. Toward the Mongols, he followed a very shrewd policy. In 1474, he secretly incited the Tatar Khan of Crimea to attack the Mongols. Six years later, he ventured to oppose them openly. A little later, the Mongols were destroyed as a political power by the Nogai Tartars. From 1480 onward, Ivan III began to assume the style of a great king. He inaugurated a policy of expansion at the expense of Poland that culminated in the eighteenth century in partition and extinction of that country. He contracted a marriage with the niece of the last emperor of Constantinople. Thenceforward, he adopted many of the customs and symbols of that court and styled himself Tsar, Autocrat, and Lord of All the Russias.

In spite of an occasional alliance with one of the Western powers, Russia remained aloof from Western Europe until the reign of Peter the Great. Under a succession of rulers, she continued her unique development. She suffered much from disputes in regard to the succession and in struggles to control the state. Russia continued to make important additions of territory. The most important development of these years, however, was the decline in status of the peasants, who constituted the bulk of the population. Until the sixteenth century, the vast majority of the peasants had been free. About that

439

time, however, the government followed a policy that led to the development of a nobility of service. The new nobles received lands occupied by the peasants and became intermediaries between them and the state. These masters came to regard themselves as guardians of the peasants and began to exploit them as well as to collect from them taxes for the state. As their lands were of value only when cultivated, the nobles did everything they could to attach the peasants to their holdings. The more docile protested but submitted. The bolder peasants escaped from their would-be masters and became liberty-loving Cossacks in the valleys of the Don and the Dnieper. Later, this decline of the peasants into serfdom was confirmed by legislation.

Peter the Great

By the latter part of the seventeenth century, outside influences were beginning to make themselves felt in Russian life. For a long time, foreign traders and adventurers had been making their way into Russia. They brought with them evidences of a different and, in many ways, a superior civilization. Finally, with the accession of Peter the Great, these influences reached the Russian government itself and resulted in fundamental changes in Russian life.

The story of his accession to power illustrates very clearly conditions that surrounded the Russian throne. Tsar Alexis, father of Peter the Great, was married twice. After the second marriage, the Russian court was divided into two parties headed by the two families into which he had married. Each family struggled to gain the support of the Streltzy—the military forces constituting the Moscow garrison. Upon the death of Tsar Alexis' eldest son, the sickly Feodor, the Naryshkins (the family of Peter's mother), passing by the claims of Ivan, a seventeen-year-old son of the first marriage, persuaded the population of Moscow to proclaim ten-year-old Peter as Tsar. Two weeks later, the rival family, the Miloslavskys, stirred the Streltzy into mutiny and forced the Naryshkins to compromise by setting up the two boys as co-tsars. As neither of the half brothers was yet capable of ruling, this put the actual control of the state for seven years in the hands of Peter's half sister, Sophia, a woman of great force and intelligence.

As a result of this situation, Tsar Peter, the younger of the two co-tsars, had a strange bringing up. During the period of his half sister's rule, he lived in a village near Moscow and grew up without any formal education. He was endowed by nature, however, with a lively temperament, extraordinary energy, and great intellectual curiosity. These qualities brought him into contact with the inhabitants of the

440

foreign quarter of Moscow. From them, he learned about the arts and skills of Western Europe. They taught him something about arithmetic, engineering, boats, and various other crafts. He organized the sons of the palace attendants into play regiments that ultimately grew up into a serious military force. These activities laid the foundation of his later policies.

In the meantime, the half sister of Peter, who was acting as regent, was becoming more and more unpopular because of the failure of her foreign policy. It was inevitable that there should be a struggle for power between the ambitious Sophia and the vigorous young Peter. In 1689, the situation reached a climax. Peter's play regiments, some of the regular troops, and members of the gentry and officialdom rallied round the young Tsar. His sister was forced to sue for peace. After her defeat, she was arrested and shut up in a convent.

After this *coup d'état,* the direction of affairs for a while fell mainly into the hands of Peter's mother and her followers. Peter himself devoted his attention largely to military and naval matters. In 1695, the outbreak of war with Turkey gave him an opportunity to test his new military and technical knowledge. In that year, he attacked unsuccessfully a fortress at Azov, at the mouth of the Don River. In the following year, he succeeded in taking this stronghold.

From this time onward, he took the administration of the government into his own hands. His ruling idea seems to have been not so much the good of the Russian people as the good of the Russian state. With this end in view, he conceived the idea of forming alliances with the principal states of Western Europe for a continuation of the war against Turkey. This was the reason for his famous embassy to the chief courts of Western Europe.

In the spring of 1697, a large embassy left Moscow. It included Peter himself, who traveled incognito. It went by way of Riga, Brandenburg, Holland, England, and back through Holland to Vienna. Everywhere he went, Peter attracted attention by his great height, convulsive features, ceaseless movement, and barbaric habits. In Holland, he first stayed a few days at Zaandam, where he lived in a cottage and worked as a common shipwright. When the attentions of the street boys drove him from there, he went to Amsterdam where he visited factories, picture galleries, anatomical theatres, and various other institutions. He seems to have been fascinated by the art of pulling teeth and to have insisted on practicing it on some members of his embassy. In England, too, he saw everything of interest that he could.

When he finally reached Vienna, he learned that the Streltzy had revolted and hurried home instead of going to Venice as he had planned. Upon his arrival at Moscow, he punished the Streltzy in a fearful manner. Peter himself executed five of the guilty soldiers and compelled his principal lieutenants to execute others. He followed this with a series of executions that killed hundreds of the Streltzy. He regarded them not only as traitors but as obstacles to the carrying out of his plans for Westernizing his country.

The embassy failed in its avowed object of obtaining alliances against Turkey but had other important results. It brought the Tsar and some of the leading Russians into contact with a civilization that had hitherto been known only by hearsay. The Tsar hired hundreds of experts who returned to Russia with him. The Tsar and his followers returned with a determination to introduce Western arts and skills into their own country. While Peter found Europe too busy with its own problems to aid him in his fight against Turkey, he did have his attention called to the Swedes who held the eastern share of the Baltic Sea and cut Russia off from direct contact with Western Europe through that body of water. He came back, accordingly, ready to take part in the great alliance forming against the young Charles XII of Sweden.

Peter the Great and Charles XII

Charles XI, the able father of Charles XII, had just died and left to his fifteen-year-old son the task of ruling Sweden. The whole situation invited attacks. The father of Charles XII had taken steps to have much of the land that had fallen into the hands of his nobles restored to the crown. This action understandably caused great dissatisfaction among the nobles. The leader of the discontented nobility, Patkul, a Livonian, set himself to the task of organizing an alliance against Sweden. He found Denmark, the Elector of Saxony, (who was also king of Poland) and, finally, after the ending of a war with Turkey in 1700, Russia, willing to listen to his proposals. Charles XII, supposedly, was hardly able to defend himself and Sweden; and yet, by making the Baltic a Swedish lake, held lands coveted by most of its neighbors.

The opening events of the ensuing war astonished the powers allied against Sweden. With great speed, the young Charles XII invaded Denmark and advanced to Copenhagen. There, he forced the astonished Danish authorities to make peace. Next, he moved into Livonia, where the Russians proved no match for the Swedish forces. Peter's plans for an army of European standards were just being put into force. The Russians had as yet no supply, transport, or medical services. Consequently, the well-organized Swedish army of 8,000 men ignominiously routed some 40,000 Russians in the battle of

Narva. Instead of finishing the work of crushing the Russians, however, Charles XII gave Peter the Great a chance to recuperate while the Swedish ruler attacked his remaining enemy, Augustus II, Elector of Saxony and king of Poland. Without much difficulty, Charles XII defeated his last enemy in Poland and followed him into Saxony. For a moment, he seemed to be master of Northern Europe. In Poland, he set his own candidate, Stanislas Leszczinsky, on the throne. In Saxony, the greatest general of Western Europe, the brilliant Marlborough, came to seek his aid.

In the meantime, the patient and persistent Peter the Great had taken advantage of the situation. He continued the training of his army according to European standards and attacked with increasing success the Baltic provinces of Sweden—Livonia, Estonia, and Ingria. He was determined to gain an outlet to the Baltic Sea. In 1703, on the conquered Neva River, he began the construction of a new capital, St. Petersburg, and, for its protection, the neighboring fortress of Cronstadt. Their construction in the swamps around the Gulf of Finland caused great loss of life.

By 1708, Charles XII was ready to turn his attention again to Russia. Leaving a garrison in Poland, he advanced with an army of 33,000 men toward the heart of Russia. His opponent, Peter the Great, who was in serious difficulties because of revolts, tried without avail to get the Swedish ruler to treat for peace. Checked finally in his march on Moscow, Charles XII made the fateful decision to turn eastward and join the Cossack leader, Mazeppa. From this point onward, Charles XII was most unfortunate. His principal lieutenant was completely defeated. He himself was disappointed by Mazeppa who joined him with only a handful of men instead of with the effective aid which he had promised to bring. The winter, furthermore, proved to be one of the severest in history. By 1709, Charles XII's army was ill-fed, short of supplies, and small in numbers. In the ensuing battle of Poltava, consequently, Peter the Great had little difficulty in defeating and dispersing the Swedish army. Its commander managed to escape to Turkey.

While Charles XII tarried in Turkey in the hope of stirring the Turks into a war with Russia, the war between Russia and Sweden dragged on for a number of years. In 1710, Peter the Great conquered Estonia and Livonia and gained his long-sought outlet to the sea. In 1711, through mismanagement, he lost his first conquest, the port of Azov. Three years later, the new Russian fleet, with the Tsar on board, won a naval victory over the Swedes that gave Russia possession of the Aland Islands. In 1718, Charles XII was killed while attempting to invade Norway. After three more years of fighting and negotiating, the combatants finally signed a series of treaties which gave Russia title to the much desired provinces of Livonia, Estonia, Ingria, and part of Finland.

The Reforms of Peter the Great

Throughout the war with Sweden, and in the years that followed, Peter the Great was busy with measures of domestic reform. He aimed to imitate in Russia the civilization which he had seen during his travels in Western Europe. In carrying out his plans, he often failed to distinguish between the important and the trivial. He considered the long beards and the longer kaftans worn by his subjects symbols of all which he wished to reform. He insisted that the former should be shaved off and the latter abandoned. He succeeded in persuading his nobles, civil servants, and military officers, but not the mass of the nation, to wear European clothes instead of the old Russian dress.

Up to this time, Russian women had been kept in oriental seclusion. After his return from Western Europe, Peter the Great was determined they should take part in social affairs as Western women did. Accordingly, he compelled the somewhat reluctant women of the upper classes to appear at public social affairs.

From the beginning of his reign, the reforming tsar tried to create a modern army. In his earlier engagements, he had found his Russian troops almost worthless against trained European forces. They had no system of provisioning, no adequate artillery, and no medical service. Using his play regiments as a beginning, he had gradually created an army trebled in size and trained in modern methods of warfare. He made every province recruit, clothe, quarter, and pay the military units assigned to it. The people found the new army a heavy burden. In time, as a result of being called on to preserve order, the local commanders came to have authority over local affairs. In spite of epidemics and desertions, Peter the Great finally molded his troops into a professional army.

Peter the Great reorganized those engaged in military, civil, and court service. He tried to make efficiency instead of birth the basis of rank. A table of ranks was drawn up. He made the first eight grades of the table members of the gentry. He made service compulsory for all members of this class. He expected them to train themselves for public service. For this purpose, he established schools in the chief provincial towns. He, likewise, sent many young Russians abroad to acquire the arts and skills of Western Europe.

The tsar also greatly changed the organization of the state. He tried without much success to have the gentry participate in local government. In an effort to relieve Moscow of work, he divided

Russia into eight, later into ten, gubernii, each with a governor or governor general over it. He created a senate of ten members, a consultative body which was often entrusted with the task of drafting and formulating legislation. For the central administration, in imitation of the Swedes, he set up ministerial colleges composed of a president, two vice-presidents, four councillors, and four assessors. In these colleges, foreigners who had come to Russia took a prominent part.

The tsar, likewise, completely reorganized the Russian church. At this time, with the approval of the Patriarch of Constantinople, the Russian church was subject to a patriarch resident at Moscow. The incumbents of the office had in the past been among the principal advisers of the tsars. Under Peter the Great, however, the Patriarch of Moscow and his subordinate clergy tended to oppose and denounce the reforms of the tsar. As a result, after 1700, Peter the Great simply failed to appoint a new patriarch to take the place of the one who had died in that year. In 1721, he entrusted the functions of the patriarch to a Holy Synod which proved to be more docile. This made the Russian church virtually a branch of the state, a development which, in time, had fatal results for religion in Russia.

Peter the Great, in addition, tried to make Russia an industrial state. He found Russian industry in the handicraft stage. Russia did not produce many things which it needed. The tsar tried to make Russia produce what it required. If he found the country lacked something, light cloth for uniforms, for instance, he would form a company, grant its promoters a subsidy, and give them a government loan or exemption from taxation for a number of years. He solved the problem of supplying a labor force by making the company masters of all the peasants in a given area. Many of the industries thus started declined after the death of the tsar.

The reforms of Peter the Great tremendously increased the burden borne by the peasants. They furnished the recruits for the new army. The new institutions made necessary increased taxation and more vigilance in the collection of taxes. Peter carefully supervised the movement of the peasants. They could not leave the landlords' estates without written permission or a passport. This had the practical effect of making the peasants completely dependent on their masters or of turning them into fugitives. They were constantly vexed with the visits of officials and punitive expeditions.

The Successors of Peter the Great

In 1725, Peter the Great died very suddenly without naming his successor. He had had, by his first wife, a son, Alexis, who showed no interest in affairs of government and, as a result of his mother's influence, opposed his father's reforms. Peter the Great finally put an end to this opposition by putting to death his own son. During the next thirty-seven years after the death of Peter the Great, there was a succession of incompetent sovereigns. Peter was succeeded in turn by his second wife, Catherine, a foreigner and ex-servant, who had come to have great influence over him; the son of the unfortunate Alexis; a daughter of Peter's stepbrother; her one-year-old grandnephew; the greataunt of the latter, Elizabeth, a daughter of Peter the Great; and, finally, the son of the daughter of Peter's stepbrother. To modern eyes, it seems almost incredible that a great nation should have tolerated such a group of figureheads and incompetent persons.

For the most part, however, their personal fortunes were of no consequence except as symbols of the victory or defeat of deeper forces. Throughout the period, two factions were really contending: those who favored the reforms of Peter the Great and those who opposed them. The partisans of each side wanted to stay in power and enjoy the perquisites of office. So they had to find, put in office, and then manipulate puppet sovereigns. Occasionally, the tool of the scheming courtiers was strong enough to enforce his own whims. The determining factor in each case was the garrison at the capital. The intriguer who gained its support was, for the time, master of the situation.

In spite of the degradation that usually prevailed at the top of the administrative machine, the country made some progress during these years. In 1727, the academy of science which Peter the Great had planned was actually set up. While engaged in establishing the relations of Asia and America, Behring, a Dane in Russian service, discovered the island and straits which bear his name. Under Elizabeth, the ablest ruler of the period, notable improvements were made in the field of education. These included the establishment in 1755 of the first Russian university, the one at Moscow. Up to this time, Russia had looked to Germany for inspiration. In Elizabeth's reign, the upper classes began to turn to French literature and thought.

Catherine the Great

In 1762, by another *coup d'état*, Catherine II became ruler of Russia. She proved to be a worthy successor of Peter the Great. She was the daughter of the ruling family of the petty German principality of Anhalt-Zerbst. Her father was an officer of high rank in the army of Frederick the Great. At the suggestion of that ruler, her marriage to Peter, the nephew and heir of Tsarina Elizabeth had been arranged. At the age of fourteen, she had been brought to Rus-

446

sia by her mother and, in due time, had been married to the heir of Elizabeth.

The course of events had placed the young foreigner in a most difficult position. She was married to a boy of feeble intellect and no character. He was, according to the reports of his contemporaries, childish, brainless, obstinate, and deceitful. From the first, he neglected his ambitious and intelligent wife. This created an almost impossible situation.

In 1762, this boy known in history as Peter III came to the throne. He promptly displayed his unfitness to rule. He relieved the nobles of the obligation of state service, imposed upon them by Peter the Great, but left them all their privileges. For the rest, he followed a policy that ran counter to every instinct of the Russian people. Brought up in the petty German principality of Holstein, he made almost a cult of Frederick the Great. While heir to the throne, he had made himself almost a spy in the interest of Prussia. Upon his accession, he publicly kissed a bust of Frederick II and knelt before his portrait. He selected natives of Holstein for his bodyguard. He clothed his troops in Prussian uniforms and drilled them in the Prussian manner. As has been explained in Chapter 23, he saved Frederick the Great from defeat by changing sides in the Seven Years' War. Besides this, he tampered with the religious prejudices of his subjects. He ordered the removal of the revered icons from the churches, made the Russian clergy dress like German pastors, and showed them a striking lack of respect. Finally, he treatened his wife with divorce and imprisonment in a nunnery.

These policies alienated both his wife and his subjects. The young Catherine had many friends among the bodyguards of the tsar. When Peter III decreed equal privileges for all forms of religion in Russia and that fasts should be voluntary, the conspirators decided the time had come for them to act. When one of their number was arrested, the others presented Catherine to the bodyguards and forced her weak and irresolute husband to abdicate. Within a few days, he was killed in a tavern brawl. In the meantime, Catherine had decided to accept the throne on the pretext of saving the country. The new ruler was, in many ways, an extraordinary woman. She had many talents. She read the best works of the day—the works of Voltaire, Blackstone's *Commentaries,* Buffon's *Natural History,* and many other books of similar character. She was interested in cameos and engravings and did some sculpture and painting. Her efforts at literary work are not of great merit, but her letters are of a high order. Throughout her reign, she corresponded with sovereigns like Joseph II and Frederick the Great and with literary men like Voltaire and Grimm. She worked hard at her task of ruling Russia. She rose at five in the morning and spent often as much as fifteen hours a day in the task of governing Russia. She traveled much around her immense realm. She had a long list of lovers, but her love affairs never dominated her judgment.

Her first measures aroused the enthusiasm of her friends among the French philosophers. After a year and a half of work on the document, she issued an instruction designed for the guidance of the delegates to a great national commission to which she proposed to give the task of laying down the principles of a much needed new law code for her empire. Even after it had been toned down, upon the advice of her advisers, it was a striking document. Half of its paragraphs came from *The Spirit of Laws* of Montesquieu. Many others came from Beccaria's *Crimes and Punishments*. Upon the completion of her instruction, Catherine summoned to Moscow a commission representing her whole empire, elected by all classes and nationalities. Its members sat for two years and debated the great problems of the Russian state. After its sessions were interrupted by war, several large subcommissions continued to discuss reform measures for six years longer.

It is usually asserted that the commission accomplished nothing of consequence. This is not altogether true. Though Catherine II made far too little use of them, its discussions supplied her with invaluable data about conditions in her empire. Then too, she made some changes in the central institutions of her government, particularly in the senate, which she divided into six departments. In local government, she also made some important changes. By this time, most of the administrative changes effected by Peter the Great had died out. Catherine II renewed, modified, and extended the local institutions which her predecessor had started. She divided the empire into some fifty provinces and the provinces into districts. These measures had the general tendency to subdivide local authority and introduced the principle of local initiative, particularly in matters affecting the Russian gentry. She made a beginning, too, toward self-government for the towns of Russia.

There was a fundamental and irremediable obstacle to any further success for the national commission. That was the basis of the empress's power. She owed her position, in the first place, to the troops and, in the second place, to the Russian nobility from which its officers were recruited. Their rights and privileges must at all costs be respected. Their economic and social position, however, was based on the institution of serfdom. Instead of improving the position of the serfs, she increased the privileges and power of their masters. By her gifts to favorites, she greatly increased the number of private serfs. She virtually relieved all the landlords of the empire of the restrictions, imposed by Peter the Great, on the sale and exploitation of their estates. Circumstances led her to be more Russian than the Russians and more aristocratic than the nobles.

Throughout her reign, Catherine was plagued by plots and risings. She had no real title to the throne. Throughout her period of rule, two persons, at least, had a far better claim to the Russian throne. This situation led to numerous attempts to obtain power. Other risings were due to the discontent of the peasants. The largest and most celebrated of the peasant risings occurred in 1773. It was headed by a Don Cossack, Pugachev, who posed as Peter III, set up a court, recruited a large force, and for a time carried on a campaign against the Russian nobility that caused widespread devastation and inspired great terror. As it progressed, it took on more and more the character of a peasant war. In the end, however, the resources of the empire and the discipline of her troops enabled Catherine II to triumph over the rebel chieftain.

The Decline of Poland

Throughout the reign of Catherine II, the area under her rule steadily expanded. Much of this territorial enlargement was at the expense of Poland. There were two causes for differences with the Polish state. To round out her Baltic lands, Russia needed Kurland, a province originally in the possession of the Teutonic Knights and later held by the family of the last grand master of the order. Furthermore, in the eastern provinces of Poland there also lived a large body of dissidents, communicants of the Russian church. To bring these two regions under Russian rule was a natural Russian ambition. In the eyes of the Russians, the two regions rightly belonged to Russia.

Catherine first devoted her attention to Kurland. This detached duchy was nominally under the suzerainty of Poland but, for some time, had been falling under Russian influence. The empress was determined to have undisputed hold on the territory. For this purpose, she bribed members of the Polish diet, threatened the Polish ministers, and finally marched her troops into the duchy. While in the very act of seizing Kurland, she brazenly pretended to be defending the Polish constitution and the rights of the Polish diet.

The story of the tsarina's seizure of Poland proper is longer and more complicated. Poland had once been one of the great states of Europe, but in the course of the years it had undergone a very different development from its neighbors. While they grew into absolute governments responsive to the will of their rulers, political conditions in Poland had grown more and more anarchical. This development left Poland finally at the mercy of its neighbors.

The anarchy in Poland was owing to the growth of certain peculiar institutions. While her neighbors were becoming absolutisms responsive to a single will, Poland was turning into a republic governed by an elective king and a diet composed of nobles and dignitaries. The royal power was being increasingly limited by the agreements extorted from the candidates for the Polish throne as the price of their election. The nobles, however, were becoming almost completely ineffective through the development of the "liberum veto." This institution gave a single noble the right to block any change in the constitution, any measure of reform, or any other legislation. The only way reforms could be effected was through the organization of a "confederation." If successful, its organizers could make changes in the state; if not, they were rebels. In any case, they precipitated civil war. The whole situation invited outside interference. France, Austria, Prussia, and Russia usually had their candidates for the vacant throne. They spent money freely in the bribery of venal Polish nobles. Although they often cloaked their intervention under a mantle of virtue by pretending to intervene in the interest of religious minorities, of a "confederation," or of defence of the Polish constitution, they steadily weakened the Polish state.

The decline of Poland is well illustrated by its last royal election. Superficially, it was a victory for the Polish faction led by the powerful Czartoryski family. In reality, it was a victory for Catherine II. In the election, intrigues, bribes, and promises were freely used. When these failed, thugs were brought in to intimidate opponents. All was carried on in the presence of Russian troops who had been marched into the country. The successful candidate was, it is true, a relative of the Czartoryski family. He owed his success, however, to the fact that at one time he had been the lover of the great empress and that she still thought she could control him.

The new king did not prove to be as docile as had been anticipated. Under the illusion that he could improve conditions in Poland with Russian support, he inaugurated a number of reform measures. A limit was at last placed on the "liberum veto." Some beginning was made toward administrative, economic, and social reforms. The budget was balanced. An excellent military school was founded. When, however, the Polish puppet king refused to sign a defensive and offensive treaty of alliance, the empress came to the support of a "confederation" composed of opponents of the reform policy. The advocates of reform, on the other hand, organized a

450

"confederation" which carried on a struggle for Polish freedom. It was evident that either the king or his opponents would have to give way.

Russo-Turkish Relations

Catherine could not devote her attention exclusively to Poland. Other neighboring states demanded her attention and resources. Her relations with the Turkish Empire, for example, were equally important. On the south, Russia had not reached its natural boundary. Economic, political, and social considerations caused Russia to seek to extend her boundaries to the Black Sea. Her trade demanded an outlet on the south, and she had to put a stop to the incursion of Tatar Khans. The growing population of Russia looked eagerly toward the steppes of southern Russia as a place of settlement.

The predecessors of Catherine II had already made considerable progress toward the defence and extension of the southern frontier. In 1768, war broke out again between Russia and Turkey. It lasted for six years. The Treaty of Kuchuk Kainardji, which terminated it, was one of the most important diplomatic documents ever signed by a Russian diplomat. Russia gave back Moldavia and Wallachia, which she had conquered during the course of the war. On the other hand, she reached the shore of the Black Sea between the Bug and the Dnieper rivers and at points on the Don River and the Straits of Kerch. The Turks recognized the independence of the Tatars of the region. The Sultan promised protection to his Christian subjects and their churches, a provision which Russia interpreted as giving her the right to interfere in their behalf.

After the conclusion of the Treaty of Kuchuk Kainardji, Russia established her authority firmly on the Black Sea. Catherine II appointed one of her ablest subjects, Potemkin, as administrator of the newly acquired region. He displayed unusual energy in its settlement and organization. He captured the stronghold of an important body of Cossacks. In 1783, Crimea was conquered. This led in 1788 to a new war with Turkey which resulted in the advance of the Russian frontier to the Dniester River.

After the annexation of Crimea, Potemkin staged a triumphal tour of her new conquests for his mistress. She invited Joseph II to meet her and took with her all the foreign ambassadors. Everything possible was done to impress them. Each foreign envoy was assigned a separate palace and provided with the best in furniture, porcelain, and wines. There were innumerable feasts, public welcomes, deputations, and reviews. It was a great piece of pageantry.

RUSSIA IN 1676

ACQUISITIONS UNDER PETER THE GREAT (1682-1725)

ACQUISITIONS UNDER ANNA (1730-40)

ACQUISITIONS UNDER ELIZABETH (1741-62)

ACQUISITIONS UNDER CATHERINE II (1762-96)

SCALE OF MILES

100   0   100   200   300   400

Territorial Growth of Russia in Europe to 1795

Though supposedly an ally of the empress, Frederick II watched with growing alarm the strengthening of Catherine II's hold on Poland and the expansion of Russia at the expense of Turkey. His anxiety finally led him to propose the partition of Poland for the benefit of the three neighboring powers—Russia, Prussia, and Austria. Though it was one of the most unprincipled proposals in history, it had the advantage of compensating Russia for her victories without despoiling Turkey and of maintaining intact the principle of the balance of power in Europe.

In 1772, accordingly, the three powers—Russia, Prussia, and Austria—brazenly proceeded to partition Poland. Before its spoliation, Poland had an area of 729,000 square kilometers and a population of 12,000,000. The conspiring powers deprived her of two-sevenths of her territory and five-twelfths of her population. Russia took as her share a region of Polish landlords and White Russian peasants beyond the Dwina and Dnieper rivers. Austria acquired the province of Galicia inhabited for the most part by Poles and Ruthenes. Prussia obtained West Prussia, an acquisition which at last linked up East Prussia with Brandenburg and Pomerania. The conspirators crowned their work by extorting from Poland a formal renunciation of the seized territories.

The division of their country rudely awoke even the most selfish of the Polish nobles to the need of doing something. As it happened, almost simultaneously with the partition of Poland the Pope dissolved the Jesuit order. After some discussion, the Poles decided to comply with the papal decision. This action placed the property of the order at the disposal of the Polish government. The Polish authorities decided to use it for education. They appointed for this purpose an educational commission. Although much of the property at its disposal was stolen, enough was left to do considerable for Polish education. Schools of all types were organized or modernized. The universities were provided with scientific equipment. In spite of many difficulties, the Polish authorities did much for Polish education.

An effort was made to give Poland a new constitution. In May, 1791, the new constitution was adopted. It strengthened the hereditary monarchy and abolished the pernicious "liberum veto." The king's decrees had to have the approval of his council and the ministers were to be responsible to the diet. The document was received with great popular rejoicing.

As was to be expected, a small minority wanted to cling to the old, bad ways of doing things. Catherine II made their opposition an ex-

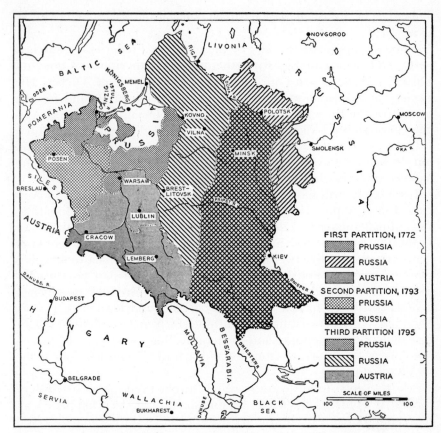

The Partitions of Poland, 1772, 1793, and 1795

cuse for Russian intervention in Poland. The helpless Polish diet was convened to sanction a second partition of Poland. As Austria was deeply involved in war with France, only Russia and Prussia participated in this division of Polish territory. Russia took 208,000 square kilometers of territory, occupied mainly by White Russians and Lithuanians. Prussia got 60,000 square kilometers situated in the heart of Poland.

The partition of 1793 stirred the Poles to a hopeless revolt. Thaddaeus Kosciuszko, a member of the minor nobility, who had fought for American independence, assumed the leadership. He appealed not only to the Polish nobility but to the forgotten peasants. As a result, recruits from all classes of society took part in the insurrection. They had no real chance of victory. Russian and Prussian troops poured into the country and crushed the rising. The suppression of the revolt led to negotiations that resulted in 1795 in the final partition of

Poland. The Polish nation lived on, but the Polish state ceased to exist.

The Slavs thus grew from small beginnings until they occupied most of Eastern and Northern Europe. As a result of history and geography, they never achieved political unity and became divided into three great branches and into many principalities. Among these latter, the duchy of Muscovy proved to be the most important and grew in time into the great Russian Empire. At first, it was almost entirely cut off from Western Europe. Under Peter the Great, however, the Westernizing influences reached the throne and led to an attempt to Westernize Russian society forcibly. Thenceforth, the Russian upper classes were increasingly Western in their outlook, and Russia took more and more part in the affairs of Western Europe. These tendencies culminated in the reign of Catherine II. During her long reign, she enjoyed a mistaken reputation of enlightened despotism, took part in the extinction of the rival Slavic state of Poland as an independent state, and carried the southern boundary of Russia to the Black Sea at the expense of Turkey, which for a long time had been declining politically and losing its hold on the Southern Slavs.

CHAPTER 28

Literary Movements of the Eighteenth Century

The eighteenth century witnessed an increasing amount of writing for popular consumption. In England and France, particularly, the upper and middle classes provided a considerable market of readers. This increase in demand led to more writing for the general public.

Literary Movements in Italy

In the eighteenth century, Italian writers were more productive than they had been for some time. There were several reasons for this increase in literary activity. Italy was free from Spanish rule and the times were more favorable to freedom of thought. In response to these improved conditions, a number of writers of a high order appeared in Italy.

A sign of this intellectual awakening was the appearance in 1725 of Vico's *Principles of a New Science*. Its author had been a professor of rhetoric at the University of Naples since 1697. In his book he set himself the task of investigating the laws governing the progress of the human race. From a psychological study of man, he tried to infer the nature of nations and the universal laws of history by which civilizations rise, flourish, and fall. He came to the conclusion that law emanates from the conscience of mankind into which God has infused a sentiment of justice. At first, it is wrapped in religious forms and consists of usages consecrated by religion. In time, these give way to rational philosophical principles. In his later years, his mind gave way and he was almost forgotten until he was rediscovered by the great French historian, Michelet.

In the meantime, Muratori (1672–1750) was reviving the study of Italian history. Although he was of humble parentage, he attracted the attention of the librarian of the Duke of Modena and through his influence finally became his patron's successor. He spent his life in preparing and publishing works dealing with Italian history. From 1723 to 1738, he was busy with a great work in twenty-five volumes entitled *Writers of Italian Affairs*. Subsequently, he published *Antiquities of Medieval Italy* in six volumes and a work on Latin inscrip-

456

tions in four volumes. The last years of his life were spent in writing a monumental work in many volumes entitled *Annals of Italy*.

The founder of Italian comedy was Carlo Goldoni (1707–1793). He was born in Venice and spent his early life there. As a natural result of these early influences, he drew his stage characters from Venetian life and wrote in the Venetian dialect. In 1761, he went to Paris. In France, he wrote comedies for the company of Italian players stationed in the city, taught the Italian language to the royal princesses, and wrote plays for the entertainment of the French court. He wrote too much to reach the highest level of excellence. His characters were often superficial and he did not take time to correct, polish, and perfect his plays. His career was cut short by the outbreak of the French Revolution, a movement which put an end to his pension and reduced him to actual misery.

In the latter half of the century, Italian writers were affected by the same currents as their French contemporaries. They fell under the influence of patriotism and classicism. The first Italian writer to show these tendencies in his work was Alfieri (1749–1803). He was a Piedmontese noble and early in life inherited a large fortune. This good fortune enabled him to indulge his taste for travel. A chance reading of Plutarch is said to have inspired him with a passion for freedom and independence. About 1775, he decided to seek theatrical fame and started to write plays. His works breathe a love for freedom and independence and they inveigh against tyrants. For this reason, he is looked upon as one of the forerunners of the Italian national movement. He was too much the aristocrat, however, to take the side of the French Revolutionists. He was swayed more by passion than by reason. He was generous and disinterested, impetuous and ungovernable.

English Literature

During the first half of the eighteenth century, English literature was largely under the influence of Joseph Addison (1672–1719). After being educated at English secondary schools and at Oxford, he was fortunate enough to attract the attention of two English lords. Through their influence he obtained a pension which enabled him to travel on the continent. After 1706, he usually held public office and was a member of Parliament. His fame as a literary man rests largely on his essays which he wrote for the *Tatler* and the *Spectator*. These publications had been started by his friend, Richard Steele (1672–1729), and were designed to interest the new reading public. For this circle of readers, Addison created a Spectators' club, the principal figure of which was Sir Roger de Coverley. His satirical pen sketched human character, social eccentricities, and the symptoms of corruption in public taste. These essays inspired many imitators.

A contemporary of Addison who wrote with a very different pen was Jonathan Swift (1667–1745), the greatest of pamphleteers. He was born in Ireland but was of English origin. After struggling through the University of Dublin with the aid of the authorities, he took in 1689 the position of secretary of Sir William Temple, a prominent figure of the day. Failing to obtain the expected preferment from his employer, he left this position, was ordained as a clergyman, and obtained a small clerical post in Ireland. After two years, he returned to his old position as secretary. In 1699, upon the death of his patron, he again went to Ireland where he received some minor clerical appointments. During these years he began to attract attention by his satirical *Battle of the Books* and *Tale of a Tub* and became a favorite of the fashionable society of Dublin. Gradually, he came to know the leading literary men of England and became a power in Tory circles. In 1713, he was made dean of St. Patrick's Cathedral. During these years he contributed to the *Tatler* and the *Spectator* and wrote much on political subjects. In 1724, he wrote his famous *Drapier Letters* which dealt with the coinage. Two years later, he published his *Gullivers Travels,* a work which satirized courts, parties, and statesmen. As he grew older, he became more and more capricious, parsimonious, and helpless. Upon his death, it was found that he had left his money for the founding of a hospital for idiots and lunatics. Unlike many Englishmen, he was always sympathetic with the Irish point of view. He sneered at most things but defended the church and the squirearchy against the conventicle and the court.

An English writer who impressed his contemporaries far more than his later critics was Henry St. John, Viscount Bolingbroke (1678–1751). After receiving the education of an English aristocrat of the time, he entered (1701) political life. His extraordinary eloquence soon gave him an important position in the House of Commons and in the state. After the accession of George I in 1715, he lost his office and fled to Paris. He then became secretary of the Stuart Pretender to the English throne but broke with him when the young prince failed to heed the advice given to him. Bolingbroke then married a Frenchwoman and settled near Orleans. Later, he was pardoned by the English government, but his hopes of further political preferment were never realized. In his younger years, he amazed his contemporaries by his dissipation; in later life, by his conversation, wit, good looks, and eloquence. He failed to obtain high rank as a writer because his character was superficial and his aims ephemeral. These qualities made his political writings rhetorical and his so-called philosophical works of little permanent interest. He is remembered by historians for his *Letters on the Study of History*. He is also credited with having had an influence on the political ideas of George III.

Eighteenth century England also produced some poets of importance. The first place among them is held by Alexander Pope (1688–1744), the son of a retired linen draper. In early life, he was looked upon as something of a prodigy and, through friends, gained a place in London society. Taking Dryden as his model, he made poetry his business. In this capacity he wrote such works as his *Rape of the Lock* (1712), his translation of Homer, the satire, *Dunciad* (1728), and his famous *Essay on Man*.

Two poets, quite different from Pope in character and in their verse, were James Thomson (1700–1748), and Thomas Gray (1716–1771). In 1726 the former, a modest tutor, began to publish his *The Seasons*. Later, he wrote a number of plays. Although he probably did not entirely realize the significance of his work, he was a forerunner of Cowper and Wordsworth. Thomas Gray, a shy, reserved poet in comfortable circumstances, is remembered for his *Elegy in a Country Churchyard*. William Cowper (1731–1800), between fits of insanity, wrote such charming descriptions of rural life as *The Task* and as rollicking a poem as *John Gilpin's Ride*.

The century also saw the beginning of the modern English novel. First in point of time came Daniel Defoe. In his earlier years, he was in business in London, first as a sort of commission merchant in Spanish and Portuguese goods and later as manager of a tile works. After failing in business, he was employed in a public office for a time and wrote many pamphlets in behalf of the government. Later, he turned to literature. In this capacity he wrote the imaginary adventures of *Robinson Crusoe,* which quickly became popular. It was founded on Dampier's *Voyage Round the World* and the adventures of a certain Alexander Selkirk. This work was followed by many others. They include *The Life and Adventures of Mr. Duncan Campbell; The Memoirs of a Cavalier; Captain Singleton,* the hero of an imaginary trip across Africa; *Moll Flanders* and *Roxana, or The Fortunate Mistress,* both accounts of fictitious adventuresses; an extraordinary *The Journal of the Plague Year;* and *The History of Colonel Jack,* a pickpocket. He owed his position as a novelist to his correct estimate of the popular taste, his plain, direct language, and his skillful use of details and illustrations.

The first English novelist to analyze the sentiment of love was Samuel Richardson. Literary success, however, did not come to him until he was fifty. He was early apprenticed to a printer and became, in time, printer of the journals of the House of Commons. He seems to have always been a moralist and adviser to women. Finally, two booksellers suggested that he write a model letter writer for country readers. While engaged on this task, he seems to have thought of telling a story through letters. The result was the appearance about 1741 of both the model letter writer and the novel, *Pamela*. In 1748, his novel, *Clarissa*, was published. In 1753, Richardson tried his hand at depicting in a work entitled *Sir Charles Grandison* a perfect model of manly character but only succeeded in drawing the outline of a prig. His works enjoyed great popularity and reveal the manners of the time.

The success of Richardson stimulated others to write. His first rival was Henry Fielding. He appealed to a different class in society. While Richardson belonged to middle-class and dissenting stock, Fielding sprang from a cavalier family and lived the life of a young man about town. He first tried his hand at the writing of plays. After he saw the success of Richardson, he turned to the novel. In 1742, he published *Joseph Andrews* and, seven years later, his masterpiece, *Tom Jones*. In contrast to Richardson, he exposed the frailty and the failures of mankind.

His contemporary, Tobias Smollet (1721–1771), introduced the English reading public to rougher phases of life. To some extent, he used his own experiences as a basis for his novels. After being apprenticed to a surgeon in Scotland, he went to England. After that, he became a ship's doctor and finally set up as a surgeon in London. Meeting with none too great success in his profession, he turned to literature. In 1748, he published his *Roderick Random* which embodied many of his own adventures and experiences. The work introduced the English public to the seaman. Later, he published *Peregrine Pickle,* a loosely connected string of episodes; *Ferdinand Count Fathom,* a work with somewhat more plot; and *Sir Humphrey Clinker.* He often obtained his episodes from other writers. Finally, he lost his sanity as a result of the death of a daughter.

Another famous novelist of the period was Laurence Sterne (1713–1768). The son of an officer and born in Ireland, he moved much around England and Ireland until he finally obtained a curacy. His *Tristam Shandy,* which began to appear in 1746, attracted considerable attention. Though his work is characterized by much indefensible indecency and overstrained sentimentality, he is one of the great literary artists of the eighteenth century.

The strangest literary figure of the century, however, was Dr. Samuel Johnson (1709–1784), the son of a bookseller. A good student, he received a thorough education which included two years at Oxford.

The decline of the family fortune and the death of his father forced Johnson to engage in a hard grinding struggle with poverty that lasted for thirty years. He was handicapped for such a struggle by his physical and mental inheritance. Though he possessed great strength, he was ungainly, awkward, and plagued by many infirmities. His face was distorted by scrofula. He was extremely eccentric. He was morbidly slothful, absentminded, given to strange gestures and grimaces, and was an incurable hypochondriac. After trying to make a living without much success in rural England, he went up to London where he found some employment on the famous *Gentleman's Magazine*. In 1738, he attracted some attention by his poem, *London,* an imitation of Juvenal. In 1747, several booksellers united and employed Johnson to compile a dictionary of the English language, which he finally finished in 1755. In the meantime, there had appeared *The Rambler,* an imitation of the *Spectator.* Both were hailed with enthusiasm by the reading public. The dictionary was characterized by acute definitions, apt quotations, and bad etymology. After this, the fortunes of Johnson began to improve. He was given a pension by the government and a doctorate by Oxford. He even had an interview with the king.

Dr. Johnson, however, talked better than he wrote. Much of his influence was due to his conversations. Much of his conversation took place in a literary club composed of some of the most noted men in England. In this body was a comparatively unknown Scottish lawyer, James Boswell, who was so impressed by the privilege of being in the presence of the famous doctor that he noted down the smallest details of his actions and conversation and embodied them in the famous biography of Dr. Johnson. The judgments of the club soon became known throughout literary circles in London and exercised a great influence.

The last years of Dr. Johnson were marked by the appearance of other works but were not particularly happy. In 1765 he finally brought out a long-promised edition of Shakespeare that added nothing to his literary fame but saved his reputation for honesty. In 1775 he published an account of his *Journey to the Hebrides.* Two years later, he finished his *Lives of the Poets,* which is generally considered the best thing that he did. His last years, though, were plagued by sickness, the loss of friends, and the complaints of one of the strangest households that was ever assembled.

Another member of Dr. Johnson's club who achieved literary fame was Oliver Goldsmith (1728–1774). He was the son of an Irish, Protestant curate. His ugliness and tendency to blunder appear to have made his early years very unhappy. He seems to have neglected his studies and to have studied law and medicine without much profit. Finally, at the age of thirty, he began to write. He wrote with a pure, easy, energetic, humorous style but knew little concerning the subjects about which he wrote. He first attracted attention by his poem, *The Traveller,* in which an English wanderer sits on a crag of the Alps and recalls his observations in the course of a long pilgrimage through three surrounding countries. In 1766 he published his only novel, *The Vicar of Wakefield,* a popular work that lacked probability and consistency. In 1770 appeared his famous *Deserted Village* that mixed up the one-time felicity of the typical English village with the steady poverty of the usual Irish village. In 1773 he successfully tried the writing of drama and produced *She Stoops to Conquer,* a farce that drew roars from both the pit and the gallery. He finally was able to live in some comfort and to be received in the best society, but he always lacked many of the qualities needed for both financial and social success.

Eighteenth-century England also produced at least two notable letter writers. A member of the aristocracy, the Earl of Chesterfield (1694–1773), wrote letters designed to form his natural son, Philip, into a man of the world. They contain much shrewd and solid observation and were well fitted to prepare the young man for adapting himself to the minute code of etiquette which then governed polite society. Another famous letter writer of the period was Lady Mary Wortley Montagu. Endowed with beauty, wit, and position, she corresponded with many people. While her husband was British ambassador to Constantinople, she described in graphic fashion life in the Near East. Upon her return, she brought back to England the practice of inoculation for smallpox. Later letters describe vividly a somewhat wandering life on the continent.

England, too, had some notable writers of memoirs during the reigns of George II and George III. Horace Walpole (1717–1797), a son of Sir Robert Walpole, portrayed very fully the chief character of the political stage in a diary covering the years 1750–1783, two memoirs, and his reminiscences. Baron Hervey treated in his memoirs a shorter period but gave a brutally frank account of George II, the Prince of Wales, and their family squabbles. Both writers throw interesting sidelights on the period of which they write.

In this century, Great Britain produced three historians who made their mark. The most prolific of the three was William Robertson, a Scottish minister, who attained fame both as a churchman and an historian. His works include *History of Scotland* (1753–1759), *History of the Reign of Charles V* (1769), and *History of America* (1777). They were based on scanty sources and have been superseded, but they were written in a clear, correct style and showed sagacity and power of generalization. The Scottish philosopher, David Hume (1711–1776), also tried his hand at historical writing. He wrote a *History of England* that was long read and quoted by the general public. The most famous historian of the three was Edward Gibbon (1737–1794). He had sufficient resources to enable him to live a life devoted to study and writing. After ranging widely in many fields of knowledge, he settled down to a systematic study of the decline and fall of the Roman Empire. He embodied the results of his study in a magnificent history with that title. The earlier part of the work is fuller and better than the later parts. The history is characterized by a bias against religion. This can be sampled by reading the fifteenth and sixteenth chapters, the two most famous chapters in the work. The whole history reveals historical accuracy, acute judgments, and the skillful use of irony and epigrams.

The century also produced one of the most famous writers on political economy of all time, Adam Smith (1723–1790), a Scottish professor. Up to his time, the nations of Europe had been trying to grow wealthy and strong by applying to their economy the mercantile system. Adam Smith wrote a devastating criticism of that system entitled *The Wealth of Nations* (1776). He pointed out that manual labor was the source from which a nation derives the necessities and conveniences of life, that improvement of productivity depends on a division of labor, and that this principle is more applicable to industry than to agriculture. He likewise asserted that a certain accumulation of capital is necessary and depends on the extent of the market. Exchange of goods gives rise to money and the idea of value. Prices depend on wages, profits, and rent and vary, also, with the demand. These in turn give rise to the landlord, the laboring, and the capitalist classes. He next discusses the nature, accumulation, and improvement of stock or capital. Then follows a history of the development of industry and commerce in Europe. Finally, he closes with an attack on the mercantile system which contains his theory of noninterference by the government in economic affairs or, in other words, the principle of *laissez faire*.

The northern part of the island of Great Britain, Scotland, has given the world one incomparable poet, Robert Burns (1759–1796). His father was a small farmer and was exceptionally poor even for infertile Scotland. As a result, Robert Burns had very little formal schooling. He spent his youth at hard physical labor which overtaxed his strength. He did, however, find some time for independent study and reading.

In 1786 he published a modest collection of poems. The small book contained some of his best poems and took Scotland by storm. The rustic, callow youth suddenly found himself invited to Edinburgh, feasted by the great in literary and social circles, and admired by the whole nation. His admirers, however, did little to improve his financial situation beyond obtaining for him an appointment in 1789 as an excise officer.

His last years were far from happy. A new venture in farming turned out badly and caused the loss of the little he had derived from his poems. He aged prematurely and lost much of his popularity. In the years of the French Revolution, sturdy independence and revolutionary views such as his were frowned upon by the leaders of society. Finally, he was a poor business man. The greater part of his poems were published only posthumously.

In a very real sense, though, Robert Burns is the national poet of Scotland. He expressed better than anyone else its melodies, its moods, and its memories. He wrote with great sincerity and deep sympathy of common things and experiences. His satirical poems struck a responsive chord in Scottish hearts. His moralizing coincided with the popular mind. He, therefore, is Scotland's unofficial poet laureate.

French Literature and Thought

The dominating figure in French literature and thought in the eighteenth century is best known under his adopted name of Voltaire (1694–1778). He, like most educated people of the time, was trained by the Jesuits. Early in life he showed talent in versification and a love for the stage. These qualities gained for him a place in Parisian society by 1725 and soon won for him recognition as a successful playwright.

At this point in his career, he was forced to leave France and go to England because he had ventured to challenge the right of the Duke of Rohan to have his lackeys beat the unfortunate but witty commoner. Voltaire stayed in England nearly four years. During his residence there, he met some of the chief figures of English life, observed with great profit English conditions, prepared himself to be the interpreter to his countrymen of English thought, and acquired a solid stock of money. The results of his sojourn in England were embodied in two books—his *Philosophic Letters* on the English, which attacked everything in France under the guise of describing English conditions, and his long treatise on the new Newtonian system, a popularization of the theories of Newton. These publications made it unsafe for Voltaire to stay in Paris, and he took refuge in Loraine with the Marquise of Chatelet. In this retreat, he continued to write the poetry, tales, plays, essays, histories, and letters that for the rest of his life came in an unending stream from his pen.

For a time, he attempted to be a courtier. Through the influence of Madame de Pompadour, he was appointed royal historiographer. During this time, he received a medal from the Pope and dedicated *Mahomet*, one of his best plays, to the head of the Church. In 1746 he was elected a member of the French Academy. On the whole, however, he did not make a very good courtier. His satiric tales, like *Zadig*, tended to get him into trouble with the court.

In 1741 he left France and went to Prussia as a guest of Frederick II. He was treated for a while as a favored guest and was given an order and a pension. He stayed in Prussia three years. Before he left the Prussian court, he quarreled with his host Frederick II. Voltaire was not humble enough to be the butt of Frederick the Great's jokes or gentleman enough to assert his dignity. The inevitable result was a series of controversies which finally ended in the return of Voltaire to France.

He then established himself as a country gentleman on French soil, but near enough to Geneva and the Swiss border to enable him to elude the French authorities if the occasion should arise. Here, as a man of wealth, he kept open house, was visited by many noted people, set up a theatre, and continued to write. In 1778, just before he died, he made a memorable visit to Paris.

It is difficult to estimate the place of Voltaire in the thought and literature of the time. He never uttered a great original thought; yet he dominated his contemporaries by his cleverness, his intensity, and the volume of his writings. He is remembered for his skill in many types of literature rather than for any one work. He was valued as a poet by the people of his period, but his poetry is now read only as a task by reluctant students. His poems display only wit and a command of meter and language. There is no realization of the beauty of nature or insight into human passions. The most characteristic of his writings were his romances and tales. They were, in reality, ironic pamphlets directed against the things he hated. As examples of his method, *Candide* and *Zadig* might be read for his attitude toward religion and *L'homme aux quarante ecus* for his criticism of the political and social ways of the time. Voltaire wrote in the neighborhood of a half hundred pieces for the stage. Some of his tragedies like *Zaire* and *Merope* are excellent, but his attempts to write of comedy were not very successful. One of his historical works, his *Age of Louis XIV*, is a landmark in historiography. For the first time, a historian treated all the aspects of a period in a simple work. There is nothing particularly distinctive about his *Charles XII, Essai sur les moeurs,* or his *Annals of the Empire.*

In fact, Voltaire was a critic rather than a constructive force. He hated bigotry and religious tyranny and attacked them with every weapon at his command. In his attacks, however, he was inclined to cut down the whole tree rather than to prune it. He undoubtedly considered the remedy for the social and political ills of the time to be benevolent despotism. He was not a democrat in either practice or theory. Although he is known as a philosopher, he had no right to the title. His so-called *Philosophic Dictionary* consists of the articles which he contributed to the famous *Encyclopedia* of Diderot and some other pieces. They are clever but superficial common sense and commonplace ethical and social criticism. Voltaire was more of a journalist than a philosopher.

His pictures and contemporary descriptions reveal a distinctive personality. He was very thin and had a long nose and very bright eyes. He took very little exercise and thought himself sick most of the time. For his day, he was moderate in eating and drinking. He was quite vain, good-natured when not opposed, and generous to those dependent on him. He was energetic, versatile, sarcastic, and flattering. He was unscrupulous in money matters or in attacking opponents. These various qualities made him the dominant literary figure of his age.

The claims of Montesquieu (1689–1755) to fame have a very different basis. Born near Bordeaux and well educated, he obtained the title of baron and an important judicial office from an uncle. For twelve years, he exercised the functions of a judge. After that, he usually spent half the year in Paris and then traveled in central Europe. He also spent eighteen months in England.

In 1721 he published anonymously his *Persian Letters*. They were supposedly written by two Persians of distinction. They satirized the social, political, ecclesiastical, and literary conditions of contemporary France. They interspersed criticism and pictures of oriental life in a manner that appealed to the reading public. The letters met with great success, but, for a time, they kept their author out of the French Academy.

In 1734 appeared the most widely read of Montesquieu's works in France, his *Considerations on the Causes of the Grandeur and Decadence of the Romans*. The work is a philosophy of history and is important for its views rather than its facts. It is written in irritating style which breaks up its two hundred pages into short paragraphs.

In 1748 Montesquieu published the work for which he is particularly remembered. It is probably the greatest book of the eighteenth century. It embodied the work of forty years. It is not quotable and

466

its facts are often inaccurate, but it founded the science of comparative politics and made an important contribution to the philosophy of history. It deals with law in general and the forms of government, with military arrangements and taxation, with manners and customs, economic conditions, religion, and Roman, French, and feudal law. It is notable for its handling of the effects of climate. Although even the followers of Montesquieu now think that they have outgrown him, the *Spirit of Laws* was for a whole generation the model of the advocates of moderate reform in France.

Denis Diderot (1713–1784) is more famous as an editor than as a writer. He was well educated but became a hack writer for publishers instead of the sober professional man his father wished him to be. After translating a number of works in this capacity, he was given the task of putting into French the English *Chamber's Encyclopedia*. In 1746 he persuaded the booksellers of Paris to make a new French encyclopedia instead of a translation. Diderot persuaded all sorts of people to contribute articles and information to the enterprise. The first volume appeared in 1751, the last volume of plates in 1772, only after the most unremitting toil and overcoming wellnigh unsurmountable obstacles at the hands of the conservative ecclesiastical party.

The enterprise was generally acclaimed as an extraordinary achievement by the reforming party in France. While there was no suggestion of atheism or even antipathy for the Church in the whole work, it was a mine of information for the curious and exalted toleration, the right of speculative freedom, the importance of scientific knowledge, and the interests of common people. From its articles and illustrations, one could broaden his knowledge indefinitely. The conservatives in the government, the Church, and the army opposed its publication and forced the editor and his publisher to do the work on the later volumes in the greatest secrecy. As a result of this opposition, the bookseller who was financing the enterprise censored the work drastically without Diderot knowing about it.

During these years, Diderot found time to do considerable other writing. While none of it can be classed as great literature, it attracted considerable attention from his contemporaries. In one of his writings he suggested the possibility of teaching the blind to read through the sense of touch. One of his plays was translated by Goethe. His contemporaries thought he was at his best in conversation. He was never elected to the French Academy or given either an office or a pension by the government. Toward the end of his career, he was forced even to sell his library. It was bought by the Empress Catherine II, who left it at Paris and appointed Diderot librarian at a yearly salary. In his correspondence are some of the most graphic pictures of the life led by the so-called "philosophic circle" at Paris.

At the time, Jean Jacques Rousseau (1712–1778) was counted a member of the Philosophic group, but, in reality, he was a sort of heretic. No one can be sure just how much we really know of his early life, as our only source for this period is his *Confessions*. He was born at Geneva. He was brought up in a haphazard fashion, first by his dissipated, violent, and foolish father, who was a watchmaker, and then by his mother's relatives. In 1728, after having been apprenticed in turn to a notary and an engraver, he ran away and led a vagabond existence. During this period, his fortunes fluctuated considerably. He seems to have received some formal education and to have tried his hand at teaching music, acting as a secretary, and living on the bounty of a lady of some wealth.

In 1741 he went to Paris. For some years he seems to have had a hard time. Through Diderot, whom he had met through a letter of introduction, he was introduced to the Philosophic circle and to many people of rank. In 1749, he began to attract attention as a writer. He wrote in competition for a prize, a work entitled *Discourse on the Arts and Sciences* in which he asserted the superiority of the savage state over civilization. His bizarre contention made him famous and won for him a more comfortable life. It also gained for him a post in the government and an invitation to the court, which through shyness or perverseness he did not take advantage of. In 1752 he brought out a successful opera.

After 1756 Rousseau usually found a patron who looked out for his material needs. It was under such conditions that he wrote his longer and more famous books. In 1760 appeared *Julie or The New Heloise*. In this work, in a series of letters, Rousseau describes the love of a man of low position and a girl of rank who finally marries a respectable man of her own station in life. It depicts the mental agonies of the lover whose distress is ultimately appeased in part by his noble sentiments. Two years later, Rousseau brought out his *Social Contact* and his *Emile*. The first tries to prove that all government is based on the consent of the governed. The second describes a system of education by natural development. The first came to be regarded by the Republican leaders of France in the days of the French Revolution as a sort of democratic bible. The second contained many new ideas concerning education that have now become commonplaces. His writings succeeded in irritating both the philosophers and the supporters of the Church, and Rousseau was forced to leave the country.

In 1765 the Scottish historian and philosopher Hume offered Rousseau a refuge in Great Britain. He was lionized by London society.

As repeatedly happened, however, Rousseau got into a controversy with his patron and returned to France where he quarreled with most of his friends. Probably he was not wholly sane during the last ten or fifteen years of his life.

The writers just described were the most outstanding members of the Philosophic group. Many others belonged to their circle who in that day were conspicuous but now are known only to the erudite. There was Baron Holbach (1723–1789), who in his writings attacked Christianity as the source of all human ills and at his table entertained the various philosophers. There was Condillac (1715–1780) the psychologist, who established in France the principles of Locke and Condorcet (1743–1794), who contributed to the *Encyclopedia,* whose wife maintained a *salon,* and who lived on into the period of the Revolution. There was Raynal (1713–1796), the author of several popular but superficial works of history, who became famous through his *Philosophic and Political History of the European Establishments of Commerce in the Two Indies.* In their day they were all considered prominent and important people.

In addition to the Philosophers there were French writers who did not write from the philosophic point of view. Le Sage (1668–1747) published in 1715 *Gil Blas,* an imitation of the Spanish picaresque romances of the sixteenth and seventeenth centuries. It records the adventures of a knavish valet who tries to supplant his master in love and gain. In 1731 Prevost d'Exiles (1697–1763) published his famous novel, *Manon Lescaut,* the story of the life of·a young woman who was drawn at the same time by her affection for her lover and her love of comfort and luxury.

In 1789 Bernadine de Saint Pierre (1737–1814) expressed the sensibility of the period and its appreciation of the beauties of nature in his *Paul and Virginia.* Marivaux (1688–1763) is remembered for the large number of plays which he wrote. Madame de Stael (1766–1817), the daughter of Necker, began toward the end of the century to publish her novels. These writers, too, have a permanent place in the history of French literature.

The period also produced a large number of memoir writers. Among these, only a few can be mentioned in a work of this sort. The memoirs of Madame d'Epinay (1726–1783) give a picture of some members of the philosophic group. Those of Marais (1664–1737) throw light on the period of the Regency and Louis XV. Bachanmont (1690–1771) gave his name to some famous memoirs which he did not write. Morellet (1727–1819) also wrote memoirs that are considered valuable. These memoirs can be found in most large libraries.

Eighteenth-century France produced a group of important writers on economic affairs. They are known as the Physiocrats. Although their principles were first put forward by R. Cantillon, a French merchant of Irish extraction, Francois Quenay (1694–1774), one of the royal physicians, and Vincent de Gournay (1712–1759) are considered the founders of the school. The term *physiocrat* means rule of nature. According to their doctrine, society is composed of individuals having the same natural rights. Each understands his own interest and is led by nature to follow it. Society is really united by a contract between its individual members that limits natural freedom as far as it is inconsistent with the rights of others. Government is a necessary evil and should be limited to the amount necessary to enforce the contract. In the sphere of economics, the individual has a right to such natural enjoyments as he can acquire by his labor. Property should be sacred, and exchange and competition should be freely maintained. Only such labors are really productive as add to the quantity of raw materials. Only agricultural products and metals increase wealth. The manufacturer simply gives a new form to the materials which he uses, and commerce merely moves goods from one place to another. The Physiocrats were never particularly popular in France. Turgot was their principal practical representative. Their ideas tended to establish economic freedom but pushed the doctrine of *laissez faire* too far.

German Literature

For a long time the Germans were thought to be of little consequence as producers of literature. The Thirty Years' War seemed to destroy the intellectual life of the people. This continued to be true until about 1740. After that date, Germany suddenly became one of the literary centers of Europe.

Among the early German writers of this period, the name of Lessing (1729–1781) takes first place. During the greater part of his life he made a living as a literary critic. In his writing he attacked the inaccurate scholarship of his time. He emphasized the importance of Greek literature and enthroned Aristotle as the arbiter of dramatic taste. In defiance of French critics, he championed Shakespeare and called the attention of the German people to his importance.

Lessing was also Germany's first great dramatist. In 1755 he published a play, *Miss Sara Sampson*. While it was not very original, it was noteworthy as the first German tragedy of common life, a form of literature on which the German people soon came to pride themselves. Twelve years later, he published *Mina von Barnhelm,* which portrayed the Fredrician era in a striking way. It is considered by many critics the best German comedy of the eighteenth century. A few years later, he published *Emilia Galotti,* a domestic tragedy. Finally, he summed up his religious ideas in *Nathan der Weise,* a noble plea for religious tolerance. After 1770, Lessing settled down at Wolfenbüttel, where the ruler of Brunswick offered him a post as librarian. In these last years of his life, much of his energy was expended in religious controversy.

After 1773, the central figure of German literature is Johann Wolfgang von Goethe (1749–1832). He was the son of prosperous parents who lived at Frankfort on the Main. A charming literary record of these first years can be found in his autobiography, *Dichtung und Wahrheit.* After a somewhat careless and carefree youth spent at various educational institutions, Goethe, at the age of twenty-four, published a play, *Götz von Berlichingen,* a character drama that tells the story of a strong man in the declining years of feudalism who repudiates his class, does brave deeds, and finally dies heroically. It was one of the first plays of the so-called "Storm and Stress" period and served as a model for a vast literature. In the following year, Goethe gave the same movement its chief novel, *Werther's Leiden,* an autobiographical work which reveals the influence of Rousseau. During this period of his life, Goethe also started work on some of his other productions.

Two years after the publication of his first play, Goethe went, at the invitation of the ruling prince, to Weimar. There he was entrusted with political responsibility. During this period of his life, he was interested in many kinds of activity—agriculture, horticulture, mining, and the natural sciences. These activities did not leave him much time for literary production.

In 1786 he started for Italy. The voyage was one of the moulding influences of his life. He visited the principal cities. The trip put an end to the Storm and Stress period and gave him something to put in its place. Some of his best works date from this time and show the Italian influence.

Goethe was neither greatly disturbed nor much influenced by the French Revolution and the Napoleonic period. As an aristocrat, he naturally opposed the revolutionary movement. He accompanied his master to Valmy and to Erfurt where he met Napoleon. In the main, he was busy with his own and his master's affairs. After 1791 he directed the ducal theatre. He was also interested in scientific studies and wrote a novel, *Wilhelm Meisters Lehrjahre,* which for thirty years was a model for German fiction. From 1794 to 1805, he was intimately associated with Schiller. From these years date his *Hermann und Dorathea,* one of his best poems, and the first part of *Faust,* which became the national poem of the German people.

471

In 1805 Goethe lost his friend Schiller. The works of this later period gave Goethe an indisputable ascendancy in the field of letters. They include two novels, his autobiography, his account of his travels in Italy, and the second part of *Faust*. The last work started as a specific story but came to be an allegory of human life.

Time has changed the judgments of the critics concerning Goethe's writings. Now, he is considered greatest as a lyric poet. As a dramatist he is judged inferior to Schiller; and as a novelist his fame has greatly declined. In spite of these changes in public opinion, however, he remains the greatest figure in German literature.

Schiller (1759–1805), for eleven years the intimate friend of Goethe, found more obstacles in his path. His father was an army doctor and he himself for a time practiced the same profession. Although he tried his hand as a lyric poet, it was as a dramatist that he first attracted attention. In 1781 he published *Die Räuber,* which was a typical play of the Storm and Stress period and expressed the ideas and feelings of the time. This was followed by his *Fiesco, Kabale und Liebe,* and *Don Carlos.*

His studies for the last of these plays aroused his interest in history. In 1788 he published the first volume of his *Revolt of the United Netherlands from the Spanish Government.* In 1789, through the influence of Goethe, he became professor of history at Jena. In the following year, he edited a collection of historical memoirs. Shortly afterwards, his most important historical work, *History of the Thirty Years' War,* began to appear.

For the last eleven years of his life, as has been mentioned, he was intimately associated with Goethe. This turned his attention again to literature. From this period spring such great plays as his *Wallenstein, Maria Stuart, The Maid of Orleans, The Bride of Messina,* and *William Tell.* As a reward for his literary achievements he was finally ennobled, three years before his death.

The eighteenth century was thus prolific in writers. Italy produced the philosopher, Vicco; the historian, Muratori; the dramatist, Goldoni; and the forerunner of Italian nationalism, Alfieri. Great Britain gave to the world an incomparable group of novelists, some famous essayists and pamphleteers, the unique Dr. Johnson, a group of charming poets, some famous letter and memoir writers, three historians, and an economist of first rank. France produced the group of writers inaccurately called the Philosophers. Germany gave the world Lessing, Goethe, and Schiller.

CHAPTER 29

Achievements in Science, Military Science, Painting, Music, Philosophy, and Education

At the opening of the eighteenth century, hardly a beginning had been made in many sciences toward the development of a systematic body of knowledge. In the course of the century, however, Western Europe experienced a veritable scientific renaissance. Particularly in chemistry, geology, botany, zoology, physics, mathematics, and astronomy, great advances were made.

Advances in the Field of Medicine

One of the earliest contributors to this scientific advance was Hermann Boerhave (1668–1738). In 1701 he was appointed a lecturer in medicine at the University of Leyden. Later, he served the same institution as professor of chemistry and botany and as rector of the university. He made the medical school at Leyden famous all over the world and had the best medical men of Europe as his students. He greatly improved the botanical garden at Leyden. He introduced modern clinical instruction in the university. He was the founder of organic chemistry, the chemistry of living substances. He tried to tell by means of chemistry the composition of the organs of the body and to discover from where these materials came. His researches proved that plants took material both from the earth and the air. This led him to a study of the juices of plants and to the decomposition of such substances as milk, blood, and bile.

Almost equal in fame was one of his students, Albrecht von Haller (1708–1777), of Berne. Reports of his botanical and anatomical researches led George II of England to offer him the chair of medicine, anatomy, surgery, and botany in his new Hanoverian University at Göttingen. During his seventeen years at that institution, Haller made it as famous as Leyden in the field of medicine. He conducted a monthly journal to which he is said to have contributed twelve thousand articles. In addition, he put out with the aid of students some one hundred and eighty books. He is credited, consequently, with many contributions to medicine. These include a recognition of the mechanism of respiration, and the automatism of the heart, the use of bile in digestion, and the power of muscles to contract. He made drawings of parts of the body that constituted an improvement on those previously made by Vesalius.

One of the men who took surgery out of the hands of barbers was John Hunter (1728–1783). He showed such great skill in dissecting in the anatomical school run by his brother in London that he was soon given charge of a practical class. He finally practiced as a surgeon in London. He devoted his spare time to the study of comparative anatomy. He obtained animal specimens from various menageries and is said to have dissected more than five hundred animals.

Advances in Botany

Meanwhile, considerable progress was being made in botany. The greatest botanist of the period is best known by his Latin name of Linnaeus (1707–1778). After a hard struggle to get through the University of Upsala, he began to lecture in that institution. Very early, he became convinced of the importance of stamens and pistils of flowers and hit upon the idea of basing a system of plant classification upon them. His system forms the foundation of the arrangement in use at the present time. He also supervised the remodelling of the garden of the university and is said to have added finally some eleven hundred plants to the collection. In 1732 he conducted for the Academy of Sciences at Upsala an exploratory expedition for the discovery and examination of the flora of Sweden. Three years later, Linnaeus went to Holland in order to study medicine and found friends who greatly aided him. Upon his return to Sweden, he soon was appointed professor of botany at the University of Upsala. His lectures drew hearers from all over Europe. As a result, the attendance at the university rose from five to fifteen hundred. As a recognition of his achievements, he was first knighted, the first Swedish scientist to be so honored, and later he was ennobled.

Progress in Geology

In the early part of the eighteenth century people still believed the earth had been created in just the form that we now know it. This view made it hard to understand the strata or layers of rock and the fossil shells, plants, and bones which were revealed by the digging of wells and mines. People were loathe to believe that the strata had slowly developed and that the fossils had once been alive.

The first geologist to give a real explanation of these phenomena was Lazzaro Moro, an Italian from Lombardy. He pointed out that the strata lie in a definite order and that the fossil fishes, shells, and plants are imprisoned in them in all countries and at all heights above the sea. He came to the conclusion that the rocks must have been soft when the fossils were buried in them. In addition, he believed that some of the fossils must have been near rivers, since they contain fresh water plants and animals and others contain only fossils derived from the sea. He came, therefore, to the conclusion that all must have been formed in lakes or seas and then raised by earthquakes or thrown out by volcanoes.

In Germany, the founder of modern geology was Abraham Werner (1750–1817). In 1775, he was appointed to a professorship at the school of mines, at Freiburg, in Silesia. As a professor in this institution, he pointed out that the study of rocks was more than a study of minerals and that the crust of the earth was full of wonderful stories. Like Lazzaro Moro, he called attention to the fact that rocks follow each other in a definite order, and he thought that all rocks were precipitated in the bed of a primeval ocean. He considered volcanoes abnormal phenomena. His teaching inaugurated a protracted quarrel over the origin of rocks.

In England, the pioneer geologist was James Hutton (1726–1797). He studied to be a doctor; then turned to agriculture; and, after his retirement, devoted his attention to geology. After years of study, he published his views on the history of the earth. He asserted that rocks were formed out of the waste of older rocks and that these materials were laid down under the sea under great pressure. Subsequently, they were upheaved by great heat. In this way, these two scholars laid the foundation of modern geology.

Determination of the Density of the Earth

In 1774 a British scientist found out the approximate density of the earth. The determination of this would be easy if the earth was made of one material. This, however, was not the case. The earth, in fact, is made up of rocks of different weights, and the material at its center is unknown. By a simple experiment with a plumb line, the scientist showed the difference between the pull of the earth and the pull of a mountain. Then the size and weight of the different rocks in the mountain were measured. When this was known, it was comparatively easy to estimate the density of the earth.

Advances in Chemistry

In spite of the work of Boyle and other early chemists, the science of chemistry was yet in its infancy. Its progress was hindered by the belief in the phlogiston theory. According to this theory, a substance called phlogiston was contained in all combustible matter, and the act of combustion was regarded as the escape of phlogiston from the burning substance. It took years to convince even skilled chemists of the erroneousness of this theory.

In the latter half of the eighteenth century, however, great advances were made in chemical knowledge. Old theories were discarded. New elements and gases were discovered. So that by the end of the century, the foundations of modern chemistry had been laid.

One of the most important contributors to this advance in chemistry was Joseph Black (1728–1799). He was born in Scotland and became a lecturer in chemistry at the University of Glasgow. In that same year, he discovered what he called fixed air, now known as carbonic acid. He also taught in his lectures the doctrine of latent heat. This explained two interesting phenomena. It showed why the thermometer stays at zero centigrade if a lump of ice is put in a sauce pan, set over a fire, and melted while it is stirred. It likewise explained why water never becomes any hotter than 100° centigrade if it is boiled on a stove. He proved by simple experiments that the heat is employed in changing the condition of the water. Recognition of his achievements came tardily, because he never took the trouble to publish the results of his experiments.

Another important contributor to modern chemistry was Joseph Priestley (1733–1804), a nonconformist minister. In 1774 he discovered oxygen. Later, he also made known ammonia. After his home and his chapel had been sacked by a mob, he moved to America where he spent the last ten years of his life.

Another famous chemist of the period was Henry Cavendish, a very strange individual. Sprung from a famous family and in later life rich in his own right, his main aim in life seemed to be to avoid attention. His work covered a wide range, but he is particularly noteworthy as the first to recognize hydrogen. Much of his work only became known after his death.

The most noted chemist of the period was the Frenchman, Lavoisier (1743–1794). He is regarded as the founder of modern chemistry. He discovered nitrogen and the fact that water is composed of hydrogen and oxygen. He also reformed the system of chemical terminology. He emphasized the importance of the balance in chemistry. Unfortunately for Lavoisier, however, chemistry was only one of his activities. In addition to being a chemist, he was one of the unpopular farmers-general. In spite of all his great contributions to science and to France, this activity finally cost him his life. The Revolutionary mob had no understanding of the importance of his work.

In the main, however, the story of chemistry in the eighteenth century is the story of the discovery and isolation of various elements. In

1742 Brandt isolated cobalt. In 1750 Cronstadt discovered nickel. In 1772 Daniel Rutherford found nitrogen. Scheele isolated chlorine and quite independently discovered oxygen. Other important discoveries of the period include molybdenum, tungsten, carbon disulphide, chromium, tellurium, and platinum.

Discoveries in Electricity

Very early, the discovery was made that some bodies have the power of attracting objects. The first person known to have studied this phenomena was a physician of Queen Elizabeth. In 1650 the term *electricity* was coined as a name for this property. About 1700 frictional electric machines were invented. Later, it was discovered that electricity could be transmitted from one body to another and that there were two kinds of electricity.

A number of persons discussed the possibility of electricity and lightning being the same thing, but the first man to demonstrate this fact was the famous American printer, diplomat, and man of affairs, Benjamin Franklin (1706–1790). He was born in Boston, was apprenticed to his brother, a printer, and subsequently ran away to Philadelphia. After winning in this city fame and wealth as a printer and man of affairs, he turned his attention about 1746 to the study of electricity. He discovered that every body contains electricity and that if it is distributed unequally, those that have more give up electricity to those that have less. Those with more electricity are said to be positively electrified; those with less, negatively electrified.

In 1749 he demonstrated the identity of lightning and electricity. After being laughed at by the members of the Royal Society, he proceeded to prove his contention by a simple experiment. He sent up into the sky during a storm a kite with a sharp wire projecting from the top and with a silk thread, a bad conductor, tied to the end of a string. He then tied a key between the string and the silk thread. When the string became wet, it was easy to demonstrate that lightning was an electric phenomenon. After 1751, however, he was compelled to give up his experiments in science and to turn his attention to political matters. In his later years, he added to his fame by representing the colony of Pennsylvania at London and his freed country at Paris.

Two other scientists made notable contributions to our knowledge of electricity. Galvani (1737–1798), an Italian physiologist, who attained great fame as a comparative anatomist at the University of Bologna, demonstrated the relationship of animal muscle to electricity. Volta (1745–1827), on the other hand, demonstrated the presence of electricity in metallic bodies, a discovery that led to the invention of an electric battery. The names of both investigators have been embodied in the vocabulary of modern electricity.

Progress of Mathematics and Astronomy

During the latter half of the eighteenth century, progress continued to be made in the field of astronomy. In 1739 James Bradley, a professor of astronomy at Oxford, explained the aberation of the fixed stars, the apparent movement of the fixed stars in a small circle. He showed that this apparent movement was really a combination of the yearly motion of the earth and of the time taken by light in coming from the stars. In 1742 he became Astronomer Royal. With the new apparatus that he was able to obtain in this position, he discovered the mutation or slight oscillation of the axis of the earth.

At the same time, France produced two mathematicians and astronomers of note. Though born and educated in Turin, Lagrange (1736–1813) was of French stock. By 1761 he was generally recognized as the greatest living mathematician. At the age of nineteen he sent a memoir to a fellow mathematician, Euler, from which grew the calculus of variations. In 1764 he wrote an essay which explained the libration of the moon. In it, he showed why, although the moon spins like a top, it turns only one side toward the earth and gives only glimpses of its other side. A decade later, he was invited to Berlin by Frederick the Great and stayed there for twenty years. After the death of his German patron, he was invited to Paris by Louis XVI and was lodged in the palace of the Louvre. During the French Revolution, he served as president of a commission for reform of weights and measures. When he died, he was honored by burial in the Pantheon, the place of burial for many illustrious Frenchmen.

Closely associated with Lagrange was Laplace (1749–1827). Sprung from humble stock, he was educated by the aid of more prosperous neighbors. In 1767 he went to Paris where he soon became professor of mathematics at the Military School. He applied himself especially to astronomy. In this position, he systematized the work of three generations of mathematicians and established the fact that the principle of gravitation applied to the solar system as well as to the earth. He embodied his findings in his famous *Celestial Mechanics* and his more popular exposition of *The System of the World*. Laplace was finally ennobled for his achievements.

The greatest English astronomer of the period was Sir William Herschel (1738–1822). For some time he had a hard struggle as a music teacher in Germany and England. After seeing the stars through a small telescope, he became interested in astronomy. As he could not afford to buy a good telescope, he made one. With the aid of this larger telescope, he was able to find the planet Uranus and discovered some five hundred double stars. He proved that the laws of gravitation held good for the stars as well as the earth and the solar system. He also suggested that star clusters and nebulae might be the beginning of new worlds.

The Popularization of Science

In 1749 Buffon (1708–1788) published the first volumes of a work that did much to popularize science. The author came from a good French family and was well educated. Early in life, he inherited enough property to free himself from financial worries. In 1739 he was made keeper of the royal garden and museum. About that time, he began making collections for his *Natural History,* a work that was almost an encyclopedia of the sciences. Upon its completion in 1804, it filled forty-four quarto volumes. In his great task, he had the help of some competent assistants. He was a member of the French Academy and of most of the learned societies of Europe. His great work made science popular and intelligible.

Advances in Military Science

About 1700 a number of important changes were made in the arms used by the infantry. Up to that date, the infantry had been armed as a usual thing with the heavy, cumbersome matchlock, which as an offensive weapon was more annoying than dangerous. About 1700 the matchlock was supplanted by a lighter weapon, the flintlock. The new firearm could be reloaded in half the time required by the older matchlock.

About the same time, the bayonet displaced the pike. As early as 1646, bayonets in the form of daggers inserted in the muzzles of muskets had been used in Flanders. About 1671, the new weapon was adopted in France. It had the disadvantage that the musket and the bayonet could not be used at the same time. This was overcome about the turn of the century by the invention of the socket bayonet. This enabled a musketeer to fire his flintlock without removing his bayonet. This greatly increased the fire power of the infantry without lessening its ability to charge with the bayonet.

The change in arms brought about a change in tactics. The old formation with files ten men deep gave place to two long lines of battalions three or four rows deep. Henceforth, tactical perfection consisted in precise marching, accurate wheeling, mastery of the manual of arms, and the delivery of successive volleys by groups of from twelve to thirty soldiers. At all costs, the line had to be maintained. The objective of the commander became the breaking or beating down of the opposing line, in the shortest possible time, by the use of fire power or the bayonet. These tactics, however, were only effective at from fifty to three hundred yards.

Thereafter, the chief problem was whether to close with the enemy as quickly as possible or stop to fire one or more volleys which would give the enemy time to reload. The solution of this problem was found by Frederick William I of Prussia and his commander, Leopold of Dessau. In place of alternating fire and movement, they combined them into one action. This required a more perfect drill than had ever before been attained. Upon approaching the enemy, the marching columns of companies four deep wheeled at a distance of eight hundred to twelve hundred yards from the enemy to the right or left, marched along the front of the enemy until the rear companies had wheeled into line, and then faced the enemy.

The first person to put the new principles into practice was Frederick the Great. The Prussian king made no innovations. He merely developed to the extreme limit what he found in the Prussian army. This was attained by perfection of execution which was the result of rigid discipline and remorseless drill. With this training, the Prussian infantry with their muzzle loading muskets could deliver five to their opponents' two volleys a minute. The companies successively fired volleys until every company had fired. By the time the last company had fired, the first company had reloaded.

The new weapons and new tactics, however, do not entirely explain the success of Frederick II. This was owing in part to the fact that he was his own master. He was responsible to no superior. There was, consequently, less friction in his army. He could put more energy in his leadership and take greater risks.

The cavalry as well as the infantry was improved during the course of the eighteenth century. Frederick the Great found the cavalry at a low point. In his first battle of the War of the Austrian Succession, the Prussian army was only saved from defeat by the rapid fire of the infantry. The Prussian king set to work at the task of improving his cavalry. He finally trained it to a point where it was the decisive factor in some of the most important battles of the Seven Years' War. During the century, the cavalry threw aside the lance and the heavy musket for the lighter musketoon.

In the eighteenth century the artillery continued to have a subordinate part. Battles were still decided by the infantry and the cavalry. In the first half of the century, the artillery continued to lack mobility. In 1759 Frederick II introduced horse artillery in order to enable it to keep up with the cavalry and discarded the heavier types of cannon in the field.

The most important military innovation of the century, however, was in the method of feeding and supplying the troops. In contrast to the horrors of the Thirty Years' War, the wars of the next century hardly touched the mass of the peoples engaged in the struggles. Wars were the affair only of the professional soldiers. The individual soldier was kept rigidly in hand and was hanged or flogged if he showed any tendency to revert to plunder or murder.

Eighteenth century armies were supplied instead from fixed magazines. These were kept filled either by contract from the home country or by inducing the surrounding peasantry, by good conduct and by cash payments, to bring in their produce to the magazines. Such magazines were located in a strong place. If one was not available, a stronghold had to be captured by siege operations. Soldiers had to be fed and housed well enough to prevent desertions, the great plague of the armies of the time. As a consequence, an army was not supposed to go more than seven marches from the nearest fortress or more than two days' march from the nearest field bakery. These practices made wars of the period mainly an affair of princes.

Painting in the Eighteenth Century

The eighteenth century witnessed some changes in painting. Great Britain, for the first time, produced a group of talented painters. France continued to be an artistic center. Spain had only one artist of the first rank. Germany witnessed some revival of artistic activity. Italy and Holland produced no painters of lasting fame. So painting reached a high level in a number of European countries.

In point of time, the first painter of the new British school, was Godfrey Kneller (1648–1723), who was born in Germany and did not go to England until 1674. He was invited there by the Duke of Monmouth and was soon introduced to Charles II. During five reigns, he held the post of court painter. He is said to have painted portraits of ten sovereigns. He was finally knighted and made a baronet by his royal patrons. His drawing and coloring are considered good, but his portraits are somewhat monotonous.

The second member of the British group, William Hogarth (1697–1764), probably thought of himself as an author rather than a painter. As a result of his apparent talent for drawing, he was apprenticed to an engraver. In 1720 he set up in business as an engraver and furnished illustrations for such well-known books as Butler's *Hudibras*. About 1731, he produced pictures which had a moral to them. One of the most famous was a series of six pictures which traced a harlot's progress from its facile beginning to its degraded end. Later, he painted a series of eight pictures which portrayed a rake's progress in a way to teach a lesson. In doing so, he depicted life in such institutions as a gaming house, Fleet prison, and Bedlam. His masterpiece was a satire on high life called *Marriage à la mode*. He was more appreciated by his contemporaries for his portraits than for his engravings. Later generations, though, have given him a place beside the great masters.

The generally recognized leader of the British school of painters was Sir Joshua Reynolds (1723–1792). After he had received a good education in a grammar school conducted by his father, he was apprenticed to a popular but mediocre portrait painter at London. In 1749 he went to Italy, where he studied the old masters. Upon his return to London, he quickly became the fashionable portrait painter of the day. In this, he was aided by his success in the social life of the capital. He numbered among his friends such important persons as Johnson, Burke, Goldsmith, Garrick, and Sterne. At Reynolds' suggestion, this group formed itself into a literary club. After the organization of the Royal Academy in 1768, Reynolds became its first president, a position which he continued to hold until the time of his death. In 1784 he was painter to the king. He aroused to some extent the jealousy of his contemporaries, and at times he lacked in generosity toward his competitors. He just missed by a small margin taking rank with Rubens, Rembrandt, Velasquez, and the great Venetians.

Almost equal to Reynolds as a painter was Thomas Gainsborough (1727–1788). By the age of fourteen, he is said to have sketched every fine tree and picturesque cottage near his home. He then persuaded his father to let him go up to London where he could study etching and painting. In 1759 he went to Bath, where people of wealth and fashion were accustomed to congregate. His studio was soon thronged with visitors. In 1774 he went back to London, where he painted various members of the royal family and many of the famous men and women of the day. Gainsborough was more independent of the older masters than most painters. He preferred to paint landscapes but found portrait painting more profitable. He initiated the custom of using in his pictures English instead of Italian landscapes. Critics consider the pictures of his Bath period his finest work. His *The Blue Boy*, probably his most famous picture, belongs to this period.

A worthy rival of Reynolds and Gainsborough was George Romney (1734–1802). In his youth his sketches attracted attention, and, at the age of nineteen, he was apprenticed to an itinerant portrait painter. At the age of twenty-seven he started for London, where in time he divided the admiration of the town with Reynolds. He was much helped by his famous model, Emma Hart, the later Lady Hamilton.

482

The successor to Reynolds was Thomas Lawrence (1769–1830). Early in life he was forced to support his family by painting. Like Gainsborough, he settled in Bath and found many patrons. Later, he, too, went to London, where he succeeeded Reynolds as painter to the king. This made him the fashionable portrait painter of the closing years of the eighteenth century and of the opening years of the nineteenth century. In 1815 he was knighted.

Scotland produced one painter of note during this period, Raeburn (1756–1823). He spent most of his life in Edinburgh. His marriage to a wealthy widow gave him financial independence but did not abate his ambition or industry. This marriage enabled him to visit Italy. Like so many of his British contemporaries, he was primarily a portrait painter.

The French painters of the eighteenth century hardly equal their British contemporaries. The French revolt against the pompous classicism of Louis XIV was led by Watteau (1684–1721). For him, life proved a hard struggle. He went to Paris almost penniless and worked for a time in a factory that turned out devotional pictures wholesale. Eventually, he found friends and patrons who made life somewhat easier for his tubercular body. In his paintings he portrayed the gay life of the Regency. He was not really appreciated as a painter until late in the nineteenth century.

Somewhat later in time was Chardin (1699–1779). Himself of humble origin, he chose simple subjects from daily life. He is famous for his still life, domestic interiors, and figure painting. He was, too, one of the greatest French colorists.

Another important French painter of the period was Fragonard (1732–1806), once a student of Chardin. He hesitated as to the type of pictures to which he should devote himself, but in the end surrendered to the taste of the art patrons of Louis XV's court and turned to the scenes of love and voluptousness that are always associated with his name. Late in the reign of Louis XV, he was assigned the task of decorating the apartments of the notorious Madame du Barry. His surrender to popular taste injured somewhat his permanent reputation.

A French painter of note more for his subjects than his skill was Greuze (1725–1805). To a large extent he was self-taught. At Paris he found patronage and reached the height of his fame about 1765. The subjects of his painting seem to exude freshness and vigor, health and youth. He finally died in poverty.

In this period Spain produced only one painter of note, the artist Goya (1746–1828). His father followed a profession which put him in touch with artists, and Goya early enrolled in a school of art. He led

483

a turbulent, tempestuous life. He is said to have earned his way to Italy by serving as a bullfighter. About 1775 he returned to Madrid where he made designs for a tapestry factory. His talent and originality were soon recognized, and he became the royal painter and intimately connected with the court. In this position, such famous personages sat for him as four kings of Spain, the infamous Godoy, the Duke of Wellington, and many titled ladies of the Spanish court. His portraits became the rage. In his etchings he revealed himself as a moralist and a caricaturist.

Music

The eighteenth century is a notable one in the history of music. One of the greatest musicians of the period was Johann Sebastian Bach (1685–1750). He came from a family that had given many organists to central Germany. The greatest musician of the family was taught to play the organ by a brother. He then served as organist in a number of places in Germany. For nine years, 1708 to 1717, he was employed at the cultivated court of Weimar; and, for six years more, by the Duke of Cöthen. After that he went to Leipsic. From the time of his stay at Weimar onward, he composed music and attracted many pupils. He brought to completion the development of music for the organ and the choir. Although he gained a measure of recognition in his lifetime, he had to wait for many years for a full realization by students of music of his true greatness.

Contemporary with Bach was George Frederick Handel (1685–1759). Though his father was only a barber-surgeon, he came to the notice of the Duke of Weissenfels through a brother who served the duke as a valet. As a result of this recognition, he was trained on the organ at the cathedral at Halle and finally became organist there. From Halle, he soon went to Hamburg, the only center in Germany where operas were being produced. From 1705 to 1741, he produced in all forty-one operas. During these years, he spent more or less time in Italy, in Hanover, and finally in England. After 1712, he made England his permanent home and finally became a naturalized subject. In later life, he turned from the writing of operas to the composition of oratorios. Though his operas are no longer popular, many of his oratorios are still sung and highly valued. As a musician, Handel overshadows all who preceded him except Bach.

About 1730, a new form of entertainment appeared in Western Europe. For some time, it had been the custom to fill up the time between the acts of serious operas with comic pieces. About this time, the comic pieces were expanded into a complete entertainment that began to compete with opera proper.

In the latter half of the eighteenth century, Europe continued to produce great musicians. First in point of time was Haydn (1732–1809), an Austrian subject of Croatian stock. He started his musical career as a choir boy in the Cathedral of St. Stephen's in Vienna. After he became too old for that, he had a hard struggle until he gained a patron among the Austrian nobility. In 1760 he found employment with a member of the Esterhazy family and continued in its employ for the next thirty years. He can hardly be said to have invented anything, but there came from his pen during this time a continuous stream of musical compositions in every known form. In time, his work gained for him a European reputation and was played in all the capitals of Europe. In 1797 he wrote the Austrian national anthem.

The most precocious musician of the period was Mozart (1756–1791). At the age of six, he made a tour under the supervision of his father, a musician in the employ of the Archbishop of Salzburg. This journey attracted the attention of many of the sovereigns of Germany and took him as far as Versailles and London. He is said to have written his first symphony at the age of eight and his first opera when he was only twelve. He lacked steadiness and, as a result, struggled with poverty most of his short life. He finally obtained an appointment in 1787 as a private musician to the Emperor. He was versatile in composition and a master of melody. His tendency to play for aristocratic audiences music that was regarded as breathing a revolutionary spirit made him much trouble.

An artist who left his mark on the music of the period was Gluck (1714–1787). Born in Germany, he finally became a Frenchman in art. He led a hand-to-mouth existence until he found an Austrian patron who introduced him to the nobility. In 1756 he settled at Vienna as master of the court chapel. Finally, he was called to Paris. He is credited with having rescued opera from its low estate. Under Italian leadership, it had finally become a mere display of vocal technique.

In the latter half of the eighteenth century, too, a new musical instrument was developed. In 1760 the piano was little more than a curiosity. By 1790 competent instructors became fairly plentiful. By the end of the decade, the supremacy of the harpsichord had ceased and the piano had taken its place.

Philosophy in the Eighteenth Century

In addition to the so-called French philosophers, there were a number of important real philosophers in the eighteenth century. They included Berkeley, Hume, Kant, and Fichte.

First in point of time was George Berkeley (1685–1753), who became toward the end of his life a bishop of the Irish church. He was born and grew to manhood in Ireland. In 1712 he visited England and was presented at court by Swift. In this circle he soon became a universal favorite. Still later, he traveled on the continent in the capacity of chaplain and tutor and then became preacher at the University of Dublin. He published his philosophic ideas in a treatise concerning *The Principles of Human Understanding* and in *Three Dialogues,* which set forth his new theory in more popular form. These two works, judged from the point of view of style, are among the finest philosophic writings produced in England. Berkeley was afraid materialism and atheism would take root and grow in English soil and set himself the difficult task of opposing the mechanistic explanation of things which was generally accepted in his day. Locke had maintained that ideas resemble external objects. Berkeley asserted that ideas are dependent on the mind. He maintained that it was absurd to suppose an idea can resemble anything that is not an idea. He declared it was not necessary to assume the independent existence of a material substance external to the mind. As long as it was not actually perceived by me or does not exist in my mind or in that of some other created person, it does not exist at all or only subsists in the mind of External Spirit. He rejected both the substantiality of matter and mechanistic explanations of the universe. In Berkeley's idealistic philosophy, the only realities are God, other spirits or minds created by him, and the innumerable ideas which he has produced or arranged.

The successor to Berkeley was Hume (1711–1776). He was, it will be remembered, a historian as well as a philosopher. Born in Scotland, he was opposed all his life to England and the English. At the age of twenty-eight, he published his most important philosophic work, his *Treatise of Human Nature* (1739). Subsequently, he published a number of other philosophic works. After the close of the Seven Years' War, he went to Paris as a member of the British embassy in the French capital and became for a time a popular figure in its society. He spent most of his later life, however, in Edinburgh. He was generous in his attitude toward other writers. This trait is well illustrated by his attitude toward Rousseau.

In his philosophical writings Hume tried to construct a theory of knowledge. He rejected Berkeley's arguments because in his opinion they caused no conviction but only confusion. He contended that the reasons which led Berkeley to disregard material substances and causes were equally valid against mental substances and causes. He even denied the certainty of mathematical knowledge and reduced all knowledge to mere probability. Thus, Hume's philosophy ended in scepticism.

A unique character among the philosophical thinkers of the eighteenth century was Immanuel Kant (1724–1804), of Königsberg. He had an unusually hard struggle to obtain an education and subsequently a post as professor in the university of his native city. In time, he became a popular lecturer in spite of a weak voice, an extraordinarily small stature, and a feeble constitution. Students flocked to his lecture room and regarded Kant as a sort of oracle. In spite of this adulation, he remained a modest man, guided by an almost spartan regime.

In his lectures and books, Kant attempted to explain the universe without leaving the limits of his native city. His philosophical predecessors had made a distinction between ideas and the external world. Kant attempted to bring once more thought and reality in touch with each other. According to Kant, known objects are sense materials which the apprehending mind synthesizes or combines in accordance with certain forms of intuition; in space and time; and certain categories of thought, like substance, attribute, and cause and effect. Men cannot know what these sense materials are before the mind has combined them. They are merely apprehended by the mind and molded by it. Kant called these forms a priori because they were not derived from experience. They were not peculiarities of individual minds but expressed the unity of consciousness in general. Human knowledge extended only to the appearance of things, not to their ultimate reality. Some things such as the existence of God, the immortality of the soul, and freedom of the will were not within the realm of possible human experience. Such things man might believe as a matter of faith. Kant believed in what he called the categorical imperative, or sense of duty. In his closing years, his teachings in regard to the field of religion involved him in a protracted dispute with the more orthodox Prussian government.

Fichte (1762–1814) attracted attention at first as a critic of Kant. He came of peasant stock but found a patron in a neighboring landlord. He attended several schools and visited Kant. As a result of his growing fame, he was invited to become a member of the faculty at Jena. While there, he produced a succession of philosophical works but was finally dismissed from the university on a charge of atheism. He then took a post in the new University of Berlin where he did much to raise the morale of the Prussian people by his *Addresses to the German Nation*. In spite of his great service, he was soon forced to resign at Berlin. The fundamental doctrine of Fichte was that there was nothing in the ego which was not a product of its activity.

Education in the Eighteenth Century

At the opening of the eighteenth century, education was still for the most part in a deplorable state. This was particularly true of the lower schools. Most of the teachers were unfitted for the task of educating the coming generation. Often, they had no buildings in which to teach. With the exception of Scotland and some parts of Germany, not much attempt was made to educate the common people. In the grammar schools the classical curriculum had lost its power to inspire, and even the universities were little esteemed.

During the course of the century, much was done to change this situation. In England, first the Dissenters and later the Anglicans began to open schools for the common people. By their efforts, some 2,000 schools were opened which extended some educational opportunity to 40,000 students. In Germany, under the leadership of August Hermann Francke (1663–1727), a Pietist, much was done for the education of commoners. His elementary school, orphan asylum, boarding school, and seminary for the training of teachers caught the attention of Frederick William of Prussia. In 1716–1717, this churlish sovereign made attendance at the elementary schools of his state compulsory. His grandson, Frederick II, even in the midst of his desperate struggle for survival, arranged for the support of the village schools of Prussia and, after peace was finally established, made school attendance compulsory under penalty of a fine for all children between the ages of five and fourteen. In 1747 the first *Realschule* designed to prepare boys to be good artisans was established at Berlin.

Fundamental changes, too, were made in higher education. A number of new universities were established. The subjects of study and the methods of teaching them were radically changed. The principles of freedom in research and teaching were proclaimed and to a certain extent accepted.

Three important changes took place in the methods of teaching. The old method of interpreting standard textbooks, inherited from medieval times, was abandoned and was replaced by the lecture in which a subject was systematically presented. Disputations were superseded by seminars which fostered independent pursuit of academic subjects. Lastly, the study of the classics no longer aimed at literary production. Armed with these new methods, the professors of Germany turned the attention of their students to the new subjects of science and philosophy.

The French contribution to education mainly took the form of new theories which have dominated recent educational thought. The chief creator of the new ideals was Rousseau. This French man of letters discovered the worth of the individual and emphasized the necessity of education for manhood and citizenship. He maintained, like many a schoolboy since, that education was contrary to nature but admitted the possibility of a good education in conformity to nature. He asserted that at the core of every institution there must be a natural instinct. Social ideas have to become personal. The educator must begin by studying the child. Each age and condition has a maturity of its own. Accordingly, he divided education into four periods: infancy, childhood, preadolescence, and adolescence. This recognition of the differences in age constitute at the same time the greatest significance and the chief exaggeration of his work. He thought it vain to teach ordinary school subjects before adolescence. In those earlier years, the child should be trained in physical activities.

The works of Rousseau dealing with education aroused great interest. His *Émile* was translated into other languages. Fashionable women began to nurse their own babies. Parents tried to bring up Sophies and Émiles. Some nobles, especially in Germany, installed workshops for the use of their sons. Everyone tried to be natural. The work of Rousseau thus created a widespread desire for reform.

In his day, Chatolais (1701–1785) was almost as noted as Rousseau. In 1763, he published his *Essay on National Education*. In an important report on Jesuit education, he condemned a number of features of the education of his day. He urged the setting up of a secular system of education to take the place of that of the Jesuits. He asserted that they were inefficient, taught little but Latin, and turned out students who could not write a letter or tell a good argument from a bad one. He maintained, however, that the education of the common people should not extend beyond studies which would fit them for their future occupations.

The eighteenth century was thus a period of achievement in many lines. It witnessed the growth of many sciences, important developments in military science, and some great achievements in painting, music, philosophy, and education. Contemporaries felt they had been privileged to live in the greatest of centuries.

CHAPTER 30

Social and Economic Developments

The men and women of the eighteenth century thought they were living in an exciting world. In their opinion it was a period of new ideas and reform measures. It is the purpose of this chapter to describe some of the changes which seemed important to the people of that day.

Dress in the Eighteenth Century

During most of the eighteenth century, elegant men and women still dressed quite differently from their descendants of today. In the main, they continued to wear clothes of the same cut and material as in the preceding century, and the changes in style were less frequent and less important than nowadays. For the most part, fashion dictated only minor changes. Until the middle of the century wigs were worn, but after 1730 they were considered old-fashioned. Men powdered their hair, wore three-cornered hats, knee breeches, and gay-colored coats and donned a sword and two watches. Women adopted hoop skirts, which in time became so large that the wearers had to go through doorways sideways, and wore tight and heavily boned bodices which were cut so as to emphasize the slender waist which was the mark of fashion. The dresses of the period were made of brocades and satin and trimmed with rich lace. Fashionable women, too, wore their hair piled high on their heads. These fashions held their ground until the days of the French Revolution.

Adoption of Potatoes as a Food

In the course of the years Europeans discovered many new foods. A few of the new edible plants came from America. One of the most important of these was the potato.

Europeans, however, seem to have adopted the potato as a food very slowly. Apparently, it was not described by a European until the middle of the sixteenth century. It seems then to have been carried to Italy by some member of one of the monastic orders and, toward the end of the sixteenth century, was sent from there to Vienna. A well-known work on agriculture, printed in 1600, did have a chapter which described potatoes, but they did not become an important food crop until a century later.

The details about the adoption of the potato as a food crop are not well known. More is known about its introduction into France than in most of the other countries of Europe. In France, early in the eighteenth century, some people began to eat potatoes. For a long time, however, they were eaten only by the lower classes in certain provinces. The potato was not yet a popular vegetable.

The popularization of potatoes as a food for the French people is inseparably connected with the name of a French chemist, Parmentier (1737–1813). During the Seven Years' War, he had been attached as a pharmacist to one of the French armies operating in Germany and, in this way, had learned about potatoes and their value as a food. After his return to France, a country chronically threatened by food shortages and famine, the Academy of Besançon offered a prize to the person who suggested the best substitute for bread. Parmentier entered the contest and proposed the potato.

Most people considered the suggestion a foolish if not a pernicious one. The great majority of Frenchmen actually believed potatoes were positively harmful. The popular attitude, however, did not deter Parmentier from waging a campaign in behalf of the potato. He kept up the agitation until he caught the attention and enlisted the support of the court. With the assistance of the court, Parmentier gradually conquered public opinion and eventually made the potato a popular food with all classes of Frenchmen.

The Contest between Snuff and Smoking

By the eighteenth century, the use of tobacco was firmly established in the social life of Europe. As at the present time, there was no agreement as to the most desirable form of using it. The various social classes differed decidedly in their ideas about the matter. The upper classes favored the taking of snuff, and etiquette prescribed very carefully the rules to be followed in its use. The lower classes, on the contrary, remained faithful smokers and clung to their pipes. The contest between the two methods was not decided in favor of smoking until the introduction of cigars late in the eighteenth century ended the struggle.

Development of the Newspaper

In the eighteenth century the newspaper, even in the most advanced countries, was far from being what it is today. It continued to be a small and jejeune affair. It remained a publication of from four to eight not very large pages, printed on an old-fashioned hand press. The newspapers of that day were filled to a large extent with advertisements, government announcements of various sorts, and pious but harmless admonitions. In the columns devoted to current events, they published considerable foreign news, but they had no sources of information beyond the reports of ship captains and travelers. The newspapers of the time scarcely ventured to express an opinion concerning domestic affairs.

Only in England, Holland, and France did the press show signs of developing some of the features of the modern newspaper. In Great Britain, the first provincial newspaper apparently dates from 1690. In the first two decades of the eighteenth century, a number of other provincial newspapers were started. In 1710, in a journal known as the *Examiner*, Jonathan Swift commenced to write what are now known as editorials. In 1772 the first British daily newspaper was started. Thirteen years later, the most famous of European journals in the nineteenth and twentieth centuries, the publication which soon became known as the *London Times*, made its appearance. After that date, journals multiplied rapidly in Great Britain. By the end of the century, in London alone, there were fifty-three newspapers.

This rapid increase in the number and the circulation of newspapers alarmed the British government. It feared that the new institution would lead to social unrest and even changes in the organization of society. In 1712, accordingly, in the hope of keeping the newspapers out of the hands of the lower classes, the government imposed a tax on all journals. By raising their price, it hoped to reduce or at least prevent further increases in their circulation.

For a long time, the newspaper did without one of the most striking features of the modern press. It had no illustrations. Like the newspaper itself, the illustrations started with the broadside, a single sheet of paper with a lone illustration on one side. One early example of such a broadside attempted to depict the exploits of Sir Francis Drake. Another vividly pictured the execution of Charles I, the unfortunate king of England. Not until 1731 were illustrations and news merged in a single journal.

The newspaper developed even more slowly in France than in England. Until almost the time of the outbreak of the French Revolution, French journals were carefully censored. This made them far less interesting than Dutch and English journals. As a consequence, fewer people took the trouble to buy or to read them. Not until 1777 did France have a daily newspaper. Just on the eve of the French Revolution, the censorship of the press broke down. This resulted in the starting of many new journals which soon boldly discussed current events and issues. By that time there were some ninety-three newspapers in France.

In Holland the press was much freer than in France. For the times, Dutch journalists were relatively unrestricted. This freedom, however, was not always understood. According to Saint Simon, the author of the famous memoirs, the Dutch newspapers greatly irritated Louis XIV. The distinguished French historian, Michelet, even makes their freedom in discussing Louis XIV himself and the affairs of his state one of the causes of the Dutch War which broke out in 1672. From the French point of view, the situation became worse after the revocation of the Edict of Nantes. Refugees from France poured into the United Netherlands and used their newly acquired freedom in criticizing their former ruler and existing conditions in France. Newspapers multiplied. Many of them were printed in the French language and reached the subjects of Louis XIV.

Development of Other Periodicals

About the middle of the century, specialized journals began to be published. In 1754, a journal devoted to medicine and surgery appeared. Five years later, journals which confined their columns exclusively to the interests of commerce or women commenced publication. Toward the end of the century, a number of other specialized journals were started.

Early in the eighteenth century, a type of periodical quite different from those hitherto published made its appearance. The new publications bore such names as the *Tatler* (1709), the *Spectator* (1711), and the *Guardian*. They contained essays which were a mixture of politics and literature. In these publications, authors often made personal attacks on each other and on prominent political figures of the time. After 1712, however, they were somewhat hampered and checked by the passage of a Stamp Act, which made them more expensive. In France attempts were made to found similar publications, but they did not prove to be very successful.

In 1731, another new type of periodical was started. In that year the first number of the *Gentleman's Magazine* was published. This periodical contained summaries of important or interesting events at home and abroad, scraps of news about art and antiquities, and informing obituary notices concerning people of importance. In form and content it was the forerunner in the English-speaking world of the modern magazine.

In other countries, periodicals which resembled to some extent the modern magazines appeared at some time during the eighteenth century. In one case such a publication was started as early as 1684. It was called the *Republic of Letters* and its editor was the famous French philosopher, Bayle. Forerunners of the modern magazine appeared in the Swiss cantons in 1703, in Sweden in 1733, in Spain in 1743, in Russia in 1755, in Portugal in 1779, and in Poland in 1782.

In 1758, still another type of publication was started. It was called the *Annual Register* and was put out by an English bookseller. From that time onward to the present day, it has come out once a year. It was designed to be an authority on the literary, artistic, scientific, and current political events of the preceding year. It has been used as a source of information by many students and historians and has been the model for many later annual publications. It made it easier for the ordinary reader to be up to date.

The Growth of the Slave Trade

In Chapter 13, the story of the origin of the European traffic in Negro slaves has been told. By the eighteenth century, the business had developed into one of the largest and most important in Europe. By that time, most of maritime nations participated in it. The British, the French, the Dutch, the Portuguese, and the Danes had all established factories or trading posts on the west Coast of Africa which carried on a thriving trade with America in Negro slaves. In 1776, it was estimated that Great Britain alone had one hundred and ninety-two ships engaged in the traffic. A few years later, it was thought that the British were exporting annually some 38,000 Negroes; France, 20,000; Portugal, 10,000; the Dutch, 4,000; and the Danes, 2,000. All were lured into the traffic by its great profits.

The passage of the years had done nothing to lessen the cruelty of the slave trade. The inhumane traffic had grown as the settlement and exploitation of America had progressed. In 1790, at the time of the first American census, Virginia had two hundred thousand Negro slaves. In Jamaica, in 1690, there were forty thousand Negro slaves. A hundred years later there were three hundred and forty thousand. In order to achieve this growth in numbers, however, eight hundred thousand had to be imported.

From an early date, there were some people who recognized the inhumanity and injustice which characterized the slave trade. As early as 1671, George Fox, the founder of the Society of Friends, spoke against the trade in Negro slaves. In 1727, his followers openly declared against it. After 1761, the Society of Friends debarred from their membership all engaged in the slave trade. By the end of the eighteenth century, it was evident that public opinion was slowly being aroused against the business. In 1783, for example, an association was formed for the relief and liberation of slaves in the West Indies and for the discouragement of the African slave trade. In 1786, Thomas Clarkson, a young Cambridge student, wrote a prize essay on *The Slavery and Commerce of the Human Species.* This essay set in motion an agitation which finally aroused Parliament against the trade in Negro slaves. In addition to writing this essay, Clarkson spoke against the traffic in the chief English towns and at Paris and wrote numerous pamphlets on the same subject. The agitation finally resulted in the formation of a committee which worked against the slave trade.

The Development of Stock Exchanges

Another modern institution which dates back to the eighteenth century is the stock exchange. It is difficult to say just when stock exchanges assumed their modern form. There was an almost imperceptible shift in some of the world markets from trade in goods to trade in the shares of the companies which owned the goods. At any rate, with the growth of public debts and the organization of such companies as the Dutch East India and the English East India Companies, people began to buy and sell the bonds of the various governments and the shares of the different companies. About 1720 the speculation in the stock of the Mississippi and the South Sea companies carried the trade in stocks to hitherto unheard of heights. In London these financial transactions were carried on at first by unorganized stock brokers who met at one of the coffee houses of Change Alley. They acquired Stock Exchange buildings only in 1801 at London and in 1826 at Paris.

The Beginning of Man's Conquest of the Air

For thousands of years men generally thought the proper place for man was on the ground. They believed that travel through the air was impossible. From early times a few brave spirits dreamed of the possibility of man's conquest of the air. Until the eighteenth century, however, these dreams remained vague and unrealized. No actual recorded experiments with travel through the air were attempted.

The first serious attempts to conquer the air took place in France. In 1782 two brothers, named Montgolfier, started to experiment with balloons. In the following year, in the presence of a considerable number of spectators, they inflated a linen globe, one hundred and five feet in circumference, by building a fire of chopped straw under it. Their balloon actually ascended to a great height and then descended to the ground. The experiment attracted much attention.

As a consequence of this public interest, a subscription was started for the purpose of repeating the experiment at Paris. This made possible a second trial of flight in the air. Later in the year, before a great concourse of people, assembled at the Champs de Mars in Paris, a balloon filled with hydrogen gas rose three thousand feet into the air and remained there about three quarters of an hour. About two months later, a Frenchman went up in a captive balloon. Finally, in November of the same year, two Frenchmen ventured to go up in a free balloon. They rose to a height of five hundred feet and remained in the air for nearly half an hour before they safely descended to the earth.

The news of these successful ascents spread rapidly. In 1783, successful balloon ascensions took place also in Italy and Great Britain. Two years later, some balloonists succeeded in crossing the English Channel.

Developments in Transportation

The development of coaches for the transportation of private persons led almost imperceptibly to the evolution of public stagecoaches for the conveyance of passengers. About the middle of the seventeenth century, vehicles for this purpose seem to have been used both in England and in France, but this means of travel did not reach its heyday until the eighteenth century. In some countries this means of transportation did not make its appearance until the early years of the nineteenth century. In Spain, for example, public coaches are said to have been introduced only in 1816. The stagecoach had a considerable development. The early vehicles of this type held only six to eight people and were drawn by from six to eight horses. Because of the bad roads and the dangers of travel, the first stagecoaches traveled only in daylight. As a usual thing they did not travel more than forty or fifty miles a day. Modern students will be interested to know that because of their "speed" they were known as "flying coaches."

In the course of time, stagecoaches were considerably improved. As the eighteenth century progressed, more and more effort was made to follow a regular schedule. The stagecoaches, too, were enlarged to a point where they could carry, inside and outside, sixteen passengers. Some of the stagecoaches finally reached a speed of six miles an hour. Toward the end of the century, contemporaries thought that the ultimate had been obtained in both speed and comfort. While Turgot was in charge of the finances of France, he inaugurated a service characterized by a more regular schedule, larger vehicles, and greater speed. The public, however, was not grateful. It only heaped ridicule on the man responsible for the improvements. In the meantime, in 1784, in England, the so-called mail coaches were introduced which reached at times a speed of seven miles per hour. In 1789 springs were installed in the clumsy, jolting stagecoaches. This innovation made travel more comfortable.

A trip in an eighteenth-century stagecoach was a trying, arduous, and even hazardous experience. The prospective traveler was expected to arrive at the starting point at least a half hour before the announced time of departure, but he might have to wait a much longer time for his stagecoach. Like modern trains and buses, stagecoaches were often crowded and quarrels frequently took place over the occupancy of the best seats. These were settled by the conductor, who was quite conscious of his own importance and was something of a tyrant. In summer the traveler had to contend with either clouds of dust or muddy, rough, and almost bottomless roads. At other seasons of the year, he was likely to suffer from the rain and the cold. At all times, traveling was tedious and expensive. When the traveler stopped for the night, he often found the inns poor and uncomfortable.

As has been hinted, those who undertook to travel in the eighteenth century frequently found the roads almost impassable. They had been very much neglected in the Middle Ages, and not much was done for their improvement until the nineteenth century. The problem of keeping up the roads was left to the localities, which were little interested in their maintenance.

The principal exception to the general situation was France. From the time of the Renaissance onward, the French state recognized its need of better roads. In 1599, Sully, the great minister of Henry IV, was entrusted with the task of keeping up the French roads. In the latter half of the seventeeth century, Colbert, the famous minister of Louis XIV, took charge of the roads of France. As a result of his efforts, the French highways were somewhat improved, but most of the improvements occurred in the vicinity of Paris and principally benefited the court.

The eighteenth century witnessed a further improvement of French roads. In 1705 it was decreed by the authorities that roads were to be as straight as possible even if they encroached on the lands of private persons. In 1720 a decree provided that drainage ditches should be dug for all roads, that the main roads should have a breadth of sixty feet and the lesser roads of thirty-six feet. In 1747 a decree provided for the creation of a school for the training of those engaged in the making of roads and the building of bridges. By the end of the century, as a result of the efforts made for their improvement, the highways of France aroused the admiration of as acute an observer as Arthur Young.

More is known about the history of English roads than of those on the continent. In England, for a long time, the roads grew worse rather than better. In the fifteenth and sixteenth centuries, the decline and dissolution of the monasteries contributed to the deterioration of the roads. The monks had felt the necessity for making travel safe and easy. Those who despoiled them did not have any such feeling. Another cause for the deterioration of the roads was the increase in the number and the weight of vehicles. With the advent of the coach, vehicles became more numerous and weighed more. The soft earth roads could not stand the heavier traffic and became full of deep ruts and chuck holes.

The letters and memoirs which have come down to us from the sixteenth and seventeenth centuries are filled with harrowing tales about travel over the roads of England and Scotland. In 1703, for example, Queen Anne sent her consort, Prince George, to greet Charles III of Spain, who was coming to visit the English court. At one stage of the trip, his coach made only nine miles in six hours. The journey of only fifty-one miles from Edinburgh to Glasgow regularly took six days. The important need of travelers in the eighteenth century was a large supply of patience. From time to time, many suggestions were made concerning the improvement of English roads. The old-fashioned advocated the banning of all wagons and coaches from the highways. Others proposed broader tires for heavy vehicles. Finally, the more practical solution was tried of creating trusts authorized to assume the management of portions of the main turnpikes and to establish tollgates for the collection of tolls. In return for this concession, the trust was supposed to maintain and improve the roads. Ultimately, most of the main roads of Great Britain came under the control of such trusts. In practice, however, the trusts collected the tolls but did little or nothing for the roads. For a general improvement of her roads, England had to wait until the nineteenth century.

The Attempt to Use Steam as a Motive Power

The success of Watt in using steam as a motive force for machinery set men to thinking of the possibility of using steam for the propulsion of vehicles. In 1765, Cugnot (1725–1804), a French military engineer, tried to use steam for the movement of heavy cannon. For this purpose he constructed a sort of locomotive. Its great defect was the rapidity with which its supply of steam was exhausted. It had to stop every quarter of an hour in order to give the machine an opportunity to renew its supply of steam. As a consequence, his loco-motive could travel only about four kilometers per hour. In 1770, Cugnot constructed a more powerful machine, a three-wheeled ve-hicle with a small boiler in front. It proved to be too violent in its movements to be practical. As a consequence, the problem of apply-ing steam for the movement of vehicles was not solved until the early years of the nineteenth century.

The Role of Porters in the Eighteenth Century

People of today have little conception of the role played in trans-portation in the eighteenth century and still earlier times by human beings. The porter with a great pack on his back was a familiar figure on the narrow streets of European cities. For his sake, porters' rests, horizontal shelves supported by two uprights, were constructed. They gave the porter a few moments respite from his heavy load.

PART 5

The Revolutionary Period

CHAPTER 31

The French Revolution

By the first of May, 1789, most of the deputies elected to be members of the States-General had arrived at Versailles. For many it was their first close view of the court and its life. Versailles had been chosen as a meeting place rather than Paris because of the king's desire to continue his hunting. The choice was an unfortunate one for the monarchy. Many of the deputies were soon unfavorably impressed by their difficulties in finding lodging and by the frivolity and extravagance of the court.

The States-General

The opening ceremony for the States-General took place on May 2. The king received in his palace some 1,700 deputies and alternates. The affair made an unfavorable impression. The large, heavy, and comparatively young king (he was only thirty-five) proved awkward, cold, and diffident and made a marked distinction in his treatment of the privileged and the unprivileged orders. In so doing, he ran counter to the rising demand for equality.

Two days later the deputies took part in a solemn religious service. Assembling at one of the two principal churches of the town, they marched two by two and by orders to the other large church in Versailles. Most of the townsmen and many from Paris filled the windows, the balconies, and the roofs along the route of the procession. The spectators acclaimed the king and the third estate but received the two privileged orders in silence. At the church the Bishop of Nancy spoke at length on the plans of the king for his people.

On May 5, the opening session of the States-General took place. It was held in a building that had been designed as a place of amusement for the court. It provided space for the approximately 1,200 deputies and some 2,000 spectators. The deputies began to assemble as early as 11:45 A.M., but the king did not arrive at the meeting place until 1:00 P.M. The deputies listened to three speeches. The king spoke briefly of the debt, the desire for innovations, and the retrenchments which he had already effected but said nothing about the constitution which a majority of the deputies had come to draw up. Next, the keeper of the seals spoke at length on the desires and sacri-

Plan of Versailles—1789

1, Chateau; 2, Chateau; 3, P^te Venise; 4, Garde Meuble; 5, Notre Dame; 6, Écuries de la Reine; 7, Theatre; 8, King's Chamber; 9, Marble Court; 10, Royal Court; 11, Court of the Ministers; 12, G^es Écuries; 13, Manége; 14, Garde du Corps; 15, Reservoir; 16, Place d'Armes; 17, Chenil; 18, P^tes Écuries; 19, Orangerie; 20, Tennis Court; 21, Hotel du G^d Maitre; 22, Royal entrance; 23, Hotel des Menus Plaisirs; 24, Salle des Menus Plaisirs (Meeting Place of the National Assembly); 25, Entrance for the Deputies.

fices of the king, the history of the clergy and nobles, and the purpose of the deliberations. Finally, Necker, the still popular director of the finances, spoke at even greater length on the financial affairs of the kingdom but said nothing about the question of how the States-General should be organized.

As a result, when the three orders met on the following day, they found themselves confronted by this pressing question. The defenders of privilege, who for the time being dominated the orders of the clergy and nobles, saw to it that the two privileged orders met separately and voted by orders. This method of organization would enable them to veto measures of reform which they did not favor. The advocates of reform, who included substantial minorities among the clergy and the nobles and practically all the 600 deputies of the third estate, stood for a union of the three orders and voting by heads. This organization would enable them to put through the reform measures which they desired.

As a result of this situation, the deputies of the third estate refused to organize for the transaction of business until they were joined by the deputies of the other two orders. The ensuing deadlock continued through May and much of June. Finally, on June 17, after the protracted negotiations had failed completely, the deputies of the third estate took decisive action. They assumed the title of the National Assembly, took an oath to proceed with the task of reforming the government of France, declared illegal all taxes not approved by the nation, and took a stand against relief of the treasury by bankruptcy.

The defenders of the privileges of the two upper orders persuaded the king to try to settle the question of organizing the States-General by royal action. On June 20, when the deputies tried to assemble, they found their place of meeting closed and guarded by royal troops on the pretext that the hall must be prepared for a royal session. The excluded deputies promptly repaired to a nearby, enclosed tennis court. There they dramatically took an oath never to separate until they had given France a constitution. On the following day, a majority of the clergy joined the National Assembly.

On June 23, the royal session took place. Under the influence of the queen, the courtiers, and the partisans of privilege, the king solemnly announced his annulment of the decision taken by the deputies of the third estate on June 17 and ordered the deputies to organize by orders. The Royal party and the defenders of privilege filed out of the place of meeting. The deputies of the third estate hesitated. The master of ceremonies, the Marquis of Dreux-Brezé, stepped forward and said, "Gentlemen, you have heard the king's orders." Every deputy realized that it was a decisive moment. Only one, the somewhat discredited Count Mirabeau, who had been rejected by his own order but had been elected a member of the third estate, acted decisively. Rising to his full height, he is reported to have thundered to the astonished master of ceremonies, "Go tell your master that we are here by the will of the people and that we will not leave here except at the point of the bayonet." In amazement, the royal lackey withdrew before the representative of the new sovereign of France, the French people. Four days later, the king gave way and ordered the deputies of three orders to conform to the wishes of the third estate and join the National Assembly, which on July 9 took the name of the Constituent Assembly.

The Constituent Assembly

The defenders of privilege were not yet ready, however, to acknowledge their defeat. They decided, therefore, to use force against the victorious deputies. Soon, reports began to circulate concerning the movements of troops stationed on the frontiers, particularly the regiments, composed of foreigners, toward Versailles. On July 11, the meaning of the military movements was made quite clear. On that day, the king dismissed from office Necker, the popular minister and the partisan of reforms. It was obvious that the defenders of privilege were making a serious effort to save themselves by force.

They were thwarted by the people of Paris. As soon as the news of Necker's dismissal became generally known, the Parisians were agitated and disturbed. The middle class foresaw the bankruptcy of the state and the ruin of their personal fortunes; the lower classes feared the defeat of the Revolution. The center of the agitation was the Palais Royal, a palace with shops on the ground floor arranged around an interior court. In the midst of the excitement a young journalist, Camille Desmoulins, seems to have touched off a popular explosion by a vibrant call to the milling throng to arm themselves. This stirring speech started a search for arms. In spite of futile efforts by the cavalry to stop them, the gathering mob pillaged the shops of the dealers in arms and searched for those stored away by the authorities.

The arming of the Paris mob had a number of results. For one thing, the electors of Paris, who had chosen the deputies to represent the city in the States-General, took vigorous action. They established a permanent commission to replace the old royal government and organized a civic militia of some 12,000 men for the protection of property. In the meantime, popular anger turned against the Bastille, an ancient fortress and prison which had become a

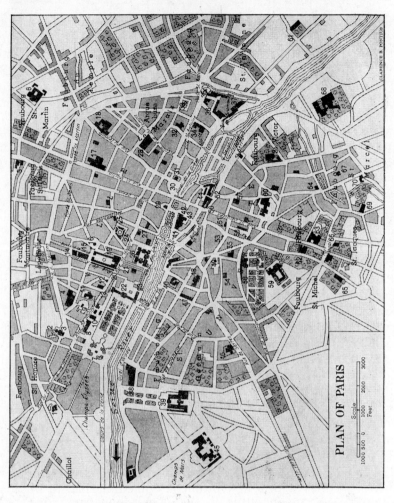

Plan of Paris—1789

1, The Colisée; 2, Cemetery; 3, The Madeleine; 4, The Capuchins; 5, St. Lazare; 6, Hospital St. Louis; 7, Place de Louis XV; 8, Garde Meuble; 9, Place Vendôme; 10, The Feuillants; 11, The Jacobins; 12, St. Roch; 13, Écuries; 14, Filles St. Thomas; 15, Bibliothéque; 16, Place des Victoires; 17, St. Martin; 18, The Temple; 19, Palais Royal; 20, Place de l'Opéra; 21, The Tuileries; 22, Place du Carrousel; 23, Guichet de Marigny; 24, Halles; 25, St. Eustache; 26, The Louvre; 27, Mairie St. Germain l'Auxerrois; 28, Hôtel Soubise; 29, Chatelet; 30, Place de Grève; 31, Hôtel de Ville; 32, La Force; 33, Place Royale; 34, St. Louis; 35, The Bastile; 36, The Celestins; 37, Grand Arsenal; 38, Palais Bourbon; 39, Hôtel des Invalides; 40, College des Quatre Nations (Mazarin); 41, Place du Dauphin; 42, Conciergerie; 43, Palais; 44, Notre Dame; 45, École Militaire; 46, The Incurables; 47, LaCharité; 48, Abbey of St. Germain des Prés; 49, The Cordeliers; 50, Hôtel Dieu; 51, Hôtel de Cluny; 52, Archevêché; 53, Café Corazza; 54, St. Sulpice; 55, Odéon; 56, The Sorbonne; 57, The Carmelites; 58, Luxembourg; 59, The Carthusians; 60, Ste. Geneviève (Panthéon); 61, Hôtel Rambouillet; 62, The Carmelites; 63, Val de Grâce; 64, St. Medard; 65, Institute de l'Oratoire; 66, The Capuchins; 67, St. Marcel; 68, Hôpital de la Salpétrière; 69, The Cordeliers; 70, The Gobelins.

symbol of tyranny. The attack on the Bastille took place July 14 and lasted about four hours. The assailants lost in all some 200 in killed and wounded. At the end of that time, the frightened and feeble garrison forced its commander to surrender.

The capture of the Bastille was followed by the capitulation of the king. The deputies of the Constituent Assembly had been in permanent session since July 13 and had been sleeping on the benches of their meeting place. On the day after the fall of the Bastille, the king himself came to announce to the weary deputies the removal of the royal troops. On the following day, he recalled Necker. The next day he went to Paris and by his presence there tacitly sanctioned what the Parisians had done. He was received by the head of the new revolutionary government of the municipality and by Lafayette, the commander of the recently organized militia or National Guard. From the latter, the king received the emblem of the newly won liberty: the red, white, and blue made by the union of the colors of Paris and those of the king. In despair, the defenders of privilege began to emigrate from the country.

France still celebrates the fall of the Bastille as its national holiday, because the capture of the famous fortress and prison was the signal for similar attacks on the institutions of absolutism all over France. The royal intendants lost their authority. The provincial cities imitated Paris and elected municipal governments and established units of the National Guard. In the country districts, rumors circulated that bands of brigands were pillaging and killing throughout rural France. In alarm, the peasants armed themselves. When the "Great Fear" did not actually materialize, the peasants attacked the chateaux and burned the records of their seigniorial dues.

The news from the provinces confronted the deputies of the Constituent Assembly with a new problem. Something had to be done to restore order. Nearly all finally saw that the privileges of the few at the expense of the many was at the root of the trouble. The general realization of this fact gave rise to one of the most dramatic episodes of the French Revolution. On the night of August 4, an impecunious noble, the Viscount of Noailles, who had nothing to lose, started a veritable orgy of renunciations by a declaration that the sole remedy for the ills of France was the abolition of seigniorial dues. Until two o'clock in the morning, amid scenes of wild enthusiasm, the deputies vied with each other in surrendering individual and provincial privileges, redeeming tithes and *banalités,* suppressing seigniorial dues, abolishing the sale of offices, and establishing free justice and the right of all Frenchmen to hold office. In brief, they inaugurated, seemingly, a régime of equality.

In the calmer light of the days which followed the tempestuous session, however, the deputies were inclined to regret their rash generosity. Accordingly, when, on August 11, they embodied their enthusiastic renunciations into formal decrees, they tended to moderate the legislation. The law of land tenure did destroy the feudal system. Serfdom and all dues of a servile origin were abolished without indemnity. Other land dues were to be extinguished by purchase. Such privileges as the right of keeping pigeons, maintaining warrens, and hunting were annulled. A new system of justice and its gratuitous administration were promised. All citizens were made eligible to office. Tithes and other church dues were to be suppressed with the understanding that the church and the clergy were to be provided for in another manner.

These decrees proved to be a general program rather than specific legislation. The peasants waited for months hoping to be told which dues were actually suppressed without indemnity and which were to be extinguished by purchase. Finally, in March, 1790, another law was really passed. It abolished without compensation rights over milling, baking, ferries, bridges, and markets and freed local industry. The management of roads, bridges, and markets was transferred to the community. In the case of feudal dues, the lord lost his right to collect them if the peasant offered to pay their money value. Men ceased to be the proprietors of other men. The peasants, however, had to wait two years for complete legal freedom from seigniorial dues.

The Reforms of the Constituent Assembly

For some time, the deputies had been debating the philosophic principles upon which they hoped to found the new social order. On August 27, consequently, they adopted the now famous Declaration of the Rights of Man and of the Citizen. It consisted of a preamble and seventeen articles. It maintained that men are free and equal in rights; that these natural and imprescriptible rights are liberty, property, security, and resistance to oppression; that sovereignty resides in the nation; that the natural rights of men should be determined by law; and that law is the expression of the general will. It declared that no one should be accused, arrested, or detained except in the cases determined by the law, that the law should establish only necessary punishments, that everyone should be presumed to be innocent until proved guilty, and that no one should be disturbed for his opinions unless they troubled the public order. It asserted the right to communicate thoughts and opinions and to maintain a public force for the benefit of all, that taxes for the support of the public

509

force ought to be determined by the representatives of the people, that all public officials should give an accounting of their administration, and that people should be indemnified for the seizure of their property. The declaration fills the same place in the life of the French nation that the Declaration of Independence and the Bill of Rights does in the political life of the United States.

For about two months after the session of August 4, then, the country appeared to be calm. Below the surface, however, there were signs of approaching disturbances. The king had not ratified either the decree of August 11 or The Declaration of the Rights of Man and of Citizen. Food was scarce in Paris and people feared a veritable famine. Any untoward event might precipitate trouble.

On October 4, 1789, another exciting rumor circulated around Paris. Report said that at a banquet given at Versailles by the officers of the royal bodyguard to the officers of the recently arrived Flanders regiment, the tipsy banqueteers had in the presence of the queen trampled under foot the new national colors. The news set all Paris in motion. Some thousands of Parisian women set out for Versailles to demand bread of the king. Soon, the National Guard followed the marching women.

Upon its arrival at Versailles, the mob surrounded the royal palace. On the morning of October 6, the rough throng actually broke into the palace. The rabble demanded bread, ratification of the unsigned decrees, and the removal of the king to Paris. The situation was so dangerous that Louis XVI decided to conform to the popular will. Accordingly, he and the royal family, surrounded by a great throng, some of whom bore on their pikes the heads of members of the royal bodyguard, left Versailles, rode amid the marching crowd to Paris, and installed themselves in the long unoccupied palace of the Tuilleries. A few days later, the deputies of the National Assembly followed the king and established themselves in a nearby building. The days of October 5 and 6 made the people of Paris masters of the situation.

For nearly two years after the tempestuous October days, the Constituent Assembly worked at the task of giving France a constitution. It held daily sessions, and the results of its work were put into effect piece by piece. The debates upon the constitution revealed the alignments of the Constituent body. There was a reactionary group made up of nobles and higher clergy; a moderate party, led by Mounier and Malouet, which admired and wished to imitate British institutions; a group that voted sometimes one way and sometimes another; and a radical group, led by such men as Sieyès, Talleyrand, and Lafayette, which included many of the young nobles who had fought

510

in the American Revolution and wished to give France distinctly French institutions. Lastly, there was Mirabeau who belonged to no party but whose disregard of the laws of morality partially destroyed the influence which his political wisdom should have given him. These parties debated amid the hisses and plaudits of three galleries, filled with excitable crowds, and with frequent interruptions from visitors and petitioners.

These divisions in the assembly first clearly appeared in the debates over the king's veto powers. Mirabeau and some of the wiser heads among the deputies wished to give the king a right to veto acts of the assembly, but the majority feared that to grant him such a right might enslave the people of France again. The debate finally resulted in a compromise. The king was given only a suspensive veto. This enabled him to block the enactment of measures temporarily but not permanently. If they were passed by three legislatures within a period of more than two years, they were to become law. As one author has put it, the suspensive veto could postpone everything but settle nothing.

When it took up the question of the suffrage under the new constitution, the Constituent Assembly displayed its real conservatism. It decreed that all male Frenchmen over twenty-five years of age were to be regarded as citizens. Citizens, however, were to be divided into two classes. Those who paid direct taxes of the value of three days' wages of unskilled labor were to be regarded as active citizens and were to have the vote in the primary assemblies. Those who did not pay such an amount, or were servants or were bankrupt, were to be considered passive citizens and were not to have the vote. To be eligible for membership in the secondary electoral assemblies which elected the deputies or to be eligible for local offices, citizens had to pay direct taxes to a value of ten days' wages. To sit in the legislative assembly, citizens were required to pay a tax equivalent to fifty days' wages and to possess landed property. In practice, these provisions excluded some two million persons from voting, or one-third of the adult male population.

In providing for the legislative branch of the new government, the deputies created a legislative assembly of a single chamber. It was composed of 745 members elected for a term of two years. Its extensive authority was destined to make it the dominant organ of the new constitution. It controlled war and peace, taxation and expenditure, the approval of treaties, the drafting of legislation, and the acts of royal ministers.

One of the fundamental desires of the French people was for civil equality. The Constituent Assembly, accordingly, gradually gave

Protestants and Jews the same rights as Catholics. In 1787 the Protestants had been given again the right to live in France. A decree of December, 1789, declared them eligible to civil and military offices. A later decree restored to Protestant heirs property still in the hands of the state which had been confiscated during the persecutions of Louis XIV. The improvement in the position of Jews came more slowly. As early as 1790, those of France received full rights of citizenship; but those of Alsace, who were little better than serfs, did not obtain a similar status until 1791. In the French colonies, due to the influence of the French planters, slavery was not abolished.

In the meantime, nothing had been done about the financial crisis that had led to the summoning of the States-General. The Constituent Assembly had tried, in turn, collection of the old taxes, loans, a new income tax, and gifts. Few paid the old taxes. The loans failed. The gifts helped only temporarily. Bankruptcy was at the door of the government.

In November, 1789, the Constituent Assembly turned to a dangerous expedient. To meet the crisis, Talleyrand proposed that the property of the Church should be nationalized. Accordingly, Church lands worth $80,000,000 in American money were ordered sold. In March, 1790, it was voted to issue scrip under the name of assignats, which were to bear interest, to be used in payment for the Church lands. The plan was perfectly sound but opened the door to dangerous practices. The assignats did not long circulate at par. More and more assignats were issued, and their value steadily declined. On top of this, there were all sorts of dishonest practices that cheated the state, such as making a first payment and then cutting all the timber off a piece of land. So the expedient of issuing paper money failed to help the financial crisis and inflicted a hardship on cautious investors but benefited the speculators.

The uprising of July, 1789, had largely destroyed the old machinery of local government. Rooted as it was in feudalism and the seigniorial system, its abolition by the revolution was inevitable. The Constituent Assembly, therefore, formally abolished the old, irregular, administrative divisions and replaced them with a simple, rational hierarchy of administrative districts. The whole country was divided into 83 departments named from rivers, mountains, or some other natural feature; and any point in a department could be reached from the chief place of a department in one day's travel. These departments, in turn, were divided into five or six districts and then into cantons and communes. These administrative subdivisions were given almost autonomous self-government. The communes were provided with municipal councils, *procureurs,* and

512

mayors; the districts with councils, an executive directory, and *pro-cureurs* general syndics; and the departments with councils, directories, and *procureurs* general syndics. The cantons were less important political units. The *procureurs* were presidents of their councils and sort of solicitors general for their administrative divisions. By creating these artificial units to take the place of the historic administrative districts of France, the assembly probably hoped to break down local patriotism and replace it with national feeling. In practice, each administrative unit did what seemed right in its own eyes without much regard for the authority or the wishes of their administrative superiors.

The seizure of the Church lands entailed important changes in the organization of the Church, which had depended largely on the lands for the support of both the regular and secular clergy. On February 13, 1790, accordingly, the Constituent Assembly simply abolished the monastic orders in France and forbade the establishment of such orders in the future. The inmates of the monasteries and convents were permitted to leave them if they chose to do so, but provision was made for the care and pensioning of those who did not wish to give up the monastic life.

The new organization of the secular clergy was regulated by a law known as the Civil Constitution of the Clergy. On July 12, 1790, the Constituent Assembly adopted a decree governing the relations of Church and state in France. It recognized the headship of the Pope over the French church but deprived him of most of his powers. It abolished the old dioceses, reduced the number of bishops and archbishops, and made each department of the new administrative system a diocese. It provided for the election of priests and bishops by the electoral assemblies of the districts and departments respectively. It reduced incomes of the higher clergy and increased the pay of the parish priests.

The adoption of the Civil Constitution of the Clergy had disastrous results for France and the Revolution. The conscientious king hesitated to sign such a document and negotiated with the Pope. In November, 1790, the impatient Constituent Assembly decided to exact from every public servant, a move that embraced the clergy, an oath of fidelity to the constitution, which included the Civil Constitution of Clergy. As a consequence, when the Pope finally condemned this latter piece of legislation, the king, a majority of the clergy, and a large part of the French people became hostile to the Revolution. The legislation finally lost the king his throne, divided the priests of France into "Constitutional" or "juring" and "refractory" or "non-juring" clergy, drove many of them into exile to join the *émigrés* among the nobility, and divided families and parishes into warring factions.

With a passionate longing for social equality, it was inevitable that the Constituent Assembly would do away with class distinctions. On June 19, 1790, accordingly, it abolished hereditary nobility. Henceforth, titles, liveries, and armorial bearings were suppressed, and Frenchmen were thereafter to be simply citizens.

The judicial system of the old régime had been even more complex and confusing than the administrative system. The right to administer justice had been inherited from seigniorial ancestors or purchased from the king. As early as the fall of 1789, the National Assembly began to modify the old system. By August, 1790, the new organic law was ready. It aimed to reduce the number of suits, to bring justice within the reach of all, and to establish a hierarchy of criminal and civil courts. The judges were to be elected. Juries were to be employed in criminal but not in civil cases. The death penalty was to be inflicted by decapitation, a method hitherto reserved for nobles. France still lacked a simple, rational civil code.

A year after it had taken steps to free agricultural labor, the Constituent Assembly freed trade and industry. It abolished the gilds or corporations which for so long had restricted capital, invention, and labor. Their abolition did away with the minute regulation of the processes of manufacture which had been in effect since the days of Colbert. Henceforth, industry and commerce merely paid a moderate tax called the *patente*. Citizens engaged in trade or industry, however, were not yet allowed to organize to promote their interests.

Commerce was still further freed by the removal of tariff barriers to the frontiers. France had been divided into "the five great farms" of central France, the reputed foreign provinces, and the provinces effectively foreign. These interior customs lines were now suppressed.

The revolution seriously interfered with the collection of the old taxes. In some cities, mobs destroyed the offices for the levying of the tax known as the octroi and the warehouses for the storing of salt. Everywhere there was a tendency to evade the old taxes. In an effort to establish equality, the Constituent Assembly reduced or abolished some taxes like the salt tax, the monopoly on tobacco, and the excise on wines and liquors. These developments, though, increased the gravity of the already serious financial crisis.

Only late in 1790 and in the early part of 1791, did the Constituent Assembly fulfill its promise to create a new system of taxation. It finally imposed a land tax, a personal property tax, the *patente* or tax on mercantile or industrial establishments which has already been mentioned, and a tariff on imports and exports. For some time, the collection of the new land tax was hampered by the impractical and complex system employed in appraising the value of the various pieces of land. The tax on personal property was estimated by such external signs of wealth as the rental value of houses or apartments. The estimated income from the two taxes was divided among the departments and then subdivided among the districts, communes, and individuals. The preparation of the tax lists was left to the local authorities, a fact that gave the new system a bad start, for the local authorities either were bewildered by the complexity of the regulations or hesitated to tax themselves and their neighbors. The tariff law finally adopted was in part a revenue measure and in part a device for the protection of French products.

The Flight of the King

As the time approached for putting the Constitution into effect, Louis XVI felt more and more ill at ease. Although he was the first functionary of the state, the king, like many of his subjects, felt unable to accept the ministrations of the constitutional clergy or to approve many features of the constitution which was taking shape. The king and queen, therefore, became more and more determined to get away from Paris and finally formulated a plan for escape. They planned to leave the palace in disguise, drive northeastward to the Luxemburg border, and take refuge in Montmédy, a town under the protection of regiments, composed mainly of foreigners, upon whom they could rely. The arrangements for the carrying out of the plan were entrusted to a confidant of the queen, Count Fersen, a Swedish noble who lived at the French court.

On June 20, 1791, the royal family succeeded in stealing away from the closely guarded palace and almost reached the waiting soldiers. Unfortunately for the royal family, the mistake had been made outside of Paris of changing to a large carriage which attracted attention, and the king was recognized and finally stopped at Varennes. The royal family, henceforth virtually prisoners, were brought back to Paris. In the capital, the royal party passed through silent throngs of spectators. As he passed the crowds of Parisians, no one saluted the king.

The flight of the king had serious consequences. The Constituent Assembly at first was alarmed lest the liberties which had been achieved should be lost by the king's escape. Later, they were angered by the royal desertion and deprived the king for the time being of his authority. Some, like Danton, took the view that the king had abdicated and advocated the organization of a republic. Others thought the Constituent Assembly had gone too far and were inclined

515

to undo some of the measures which had pushed the king too far. In general, however, his flight did much to destroy the king's influence and to start a movement which ended in the establishment of a republic.

For two years, those who disapproved the course of events in France, the so-called *émigrés*, had been leaving the country. They began to go after the fall of the Bastille. They had gone in greater numbers after the adoption of the Civil Constitution and the resulting denial of religious liberty. By the time the king was brought back to Paris from Varennes, it had become the fashion for members of the upper classes to emigrate. The movement tended especially to disrupt the army. More than 2,000 officers are said to have emigrated between September and December, 1791. Before the movement ended, two-thirds of the officers of the army had resigned. Many of them joined a small army, collected on the Rhine by the Prince of Condé, which did much to compromise the monarchy.

In September, steps were taken by the Constitutional Assembly to put the whole constitution into force. On the 14th, the king promised to accept and defend the constitution and was restored to his rights as sovereign. On the 30th, the Constituent Assembly held its last session. Very unwisely, it decreed that none of its members could sit in the Legislative Assembly which took its place.

The Legislative Assembly

The Legislative Assembly, which replaced the Constituent Assembly, met on October 1, 1791. In general, during the year of its existence, it followed a policy quite similar to that of the body which it had replaced. The extreme right of the Constituent Assembly, made up of nobles and upper clergy, was not represented in the new body. By this time, however, the so-called "Patriots" of 1789 were divided into distinct factions. A new right, which might be called the Constitutional Royalists and which included some 250 deputies, was the most influential group. A large number of the 745 deputies were unorganized and voted at times with the right and at other times with the left. The left, or more radical section of the deputies, numbered about 130. In time, it was to divide into two parties known as the Girondins and the Mountain.

Each faction of the Legislative Assembly had its political club which met outside the Legislative Assembly, usually in an empty monastery, and debated the questions of the day. The Constitutional Monarchists were known from their meeting place as Fenillants. Some radicals belonged to the Cordeliers. The most famous of the political clubs, however, was the Jacobins. It had been organized soon after the convening of the Constituent Assembly. At first, it was composed of men of very moderate opinions, but as time passed it became more and more radical. In the end the society at Paris was affiliated with some two thousand branch clubs in the villages and provincial cities.

The Legislative Assembly promptly set to work. One of the first problems which it attacked was the question of the *émigrés*. On November 9, 1791, the assembly decreed that *émigrés* who remained in arms on the frontier after the following January should be considered guilty of revolt, and if they appeared in France and were found culpable after trial they should be put to death. Two months later, the assembly decreed that the property of such *émigrés* should be confiscated.

Another pressing problem concerned the part of the French people that for religious reasons had not taken an oath to support the constitution. They had been authorized to lease property and to hold religious services provided they made no attacks on the new régime. At times, attempts to hold such services caused grave disorders. Finally, on November 29, 1791, the Legislative Assembly decreed that nonjuring priests must take an oath of allegiance or be subject to expulsion from their places of residence.

The most pressing problem confronting the Legislative Assembly, however, concerned foreign affairs. At first, the revolution taking place in France was widely acclaimed in England, in Germany, and in Italy. In time, public opinion outside of France shifted, and revolutionary France found herself confronted by a hostile Europe. For this change in public opinion, the French treatment of their sovereign and the French disregard for the rights of other states were largely to blame. In their enthusiasm for change, the French reformers abolished tithes, confiscated Church property, destroyed ecclesiastical jurisdictions, and suppressed serfdom, particularly in Alsace, in entire disregard of the rights of important German princes and prelates. In September, 1791, France even calmly annexed Avignon and the Comtat of Venaissin, which belonged to the Pope. To powers like Austria and Prussia, the revolution in France seemed to be becoming a grave menace.

With good will, war might have been averted, as Austria and Prussia were really more interested in Poland than in the fate of the French king. Unfortunately for the peace of Europe, however, the question of war became a political issue. The king, who had refused to sign the decrees concerning the *émigrés* and religion, hoped that war would extricate him from his humiliating position. The Constitutional Monarchists cherished the hope that a successful

517

war would make the king popular again. The future Girondins, on the contrary, thought that a war would rouse the French people and unmask the suspected disloyalty of the king. Only the deputies later known as the Mountain saw the danger of war and sought to avert it. As a result of this situation, the Legislative Assembly, on April 20, 1792, declared war on Austria. This declaration involved France in war with both Austria and her ally, Prussia.

The entrance of France into war had unexpected consequences. France proved to be unprepared to wage a military campaign. The revolution undermined discipline in the army, caused the resignation of a majority of the officers, and disrupted the French military forces. Equipment and supplies were inadequate. In the first encounters, the French troops were defeated. Only the unreadiness of Austria and Prussia seemed to save France from invasion and defeat.

These military events had disastrous consequences for the monarchy. The king was already unpopular because of his vetoes of the decrees concerning the *émigrés* and the refractory priests, and the French people now held him responsible for the defeats suffered by the French army. Then the discrediting of the king was completed by a manifesto, issued by the Duke of Brunswick, commander of the forces invading France, which ordered the French people to restore to Louis XVI his liberty of action and to refrain from every sort of opposition to the invading armies. To the radicals, the only solution of the problem was the overthrow of the king. France, they argued, could not hope to defend herself with a monarch who was secretly hostile to the revolution and in league with the invaders of the country. As early as June 20, 1792, there was a great popular demonstration against the king. In an effort to force him to approve the legislation against the *émigrés* and the non-juring priests, a mob stormed the Tuilleries palace, broke open the doors, invaded the royal apartment, and for three hours filed past the king, who sought to appease the demonstrators by coifing himself with the red cap of liberty, one of the symbols of the revolution.

On August 10, 1792, the radicals of Paris executed a carefully prepared plot against the king. They were aided by a detachment of Revolutionists who had come up from Marseille singing the new song hit of the day (written by a young officer, Rouget de Lisle), the revolutionary "Marseillaise." During the preceding night, under the leadership of Danton (1759–1794), a new municipal government installed itself in power. Then from all the towers of the city the bells summoned the workers of Paris to storm the royal palace. The king and the royal family made no attempt to resist but took refuge with the Legislative Assembly.

518

The episode marked the end of the monarchy. The Legislative Assembly, under pressure from the leaders of the insurrection, suspended the king, created an executive council, and voted the convocation of a constitutional convention. For the rest of August and most of September, however, the real power was in the hands of the new Commune of Paris. One of its first acts was, in defiance of the Legislative Assembly, to imprison the whole royal family in the Temple. Another was to tolerate early in September a bloody uprising, marked by lynchings and jail deliveries, known as the September Massacres.

In the meantime, the war took an unexpected turn. The army, commanded by the Duke of Brunswick, finally crossed the French frontier nine days after the fall of the monarchy. By the time of the September Massacres, these troops had taken a number of important border fortresses. One of these strongholds was the fortified city of Verdun. The invaders hoped to be in Paris by the middle of October. Without the French knowing it, hunger, disease, and heavy rains were fighting on their side. So when the advance of the invading Prussians was stopped at Valmy on September 20, 1792, the discouraged invaders quickly retreated. The unexpected victory enabled the leaders of France to continue the revolutionary experiment.

The Convention

When on September 21, 1792, the 783 deputies elected to the Conventions assembled, they formed a more radical body than the Legislative Assembly. At Paris, the new Commune largely influenced the election, and the people of Paris sent to the Convention the party which soon came to be known as the Mountain. Outside of Paris, the party which came to be known as Girondins was largely returned. To define these terms is difficult. Personal differences as well as real issues divided these two parties. Besides the Girondins and the Mountain, it must be remembered, there was a third and rather neutral group.

At its first session, the Convention abolished the monarchy. It said nothing about what should take its place until the Parisian populace began to shout for the republic. On the following day, September 22, consequently, the Convention used the word *republic*. It decreed that acts of the Convention should henceforth be dated as Year I of the Republic. Thus was imposed on France a new calendar.

The abolition of the monarchy raised the question of the future of the king. While the Convention hesitated to act, the discovery of a secret receptacle revealed the proofs of the king's treasonable rela-

519

tions with the *émigrés*. The Convention, therefore, decided to try the king. The trial lasted more than a month. In this ordeal, the king made a very bad showing. He pretended to have forgotten much that he must have known. On January 20, 1793, the Convention, by a close vote, found the king guilty of treason. On the following day, before a large throng, the king was publicly executed in the great square now known as the Place de la Concorde. The king, as was to be expected from one of his fatalistic disposition, met his end with calm courage.

Following the execution of the king, the situation grew steadily worse. The defeat of the Prussians at Valmy, it is true, was followed by some military successes. The Rhineland, the Austrian Netherlands, and Savoy were temporarily overrun and the latter territory was annexed to France, but these victories were soon followed by reverses. The execution of the king was the signal for the entrance of England, the United Netherlands, and Spain into the war against France. In their efforts to defend French soil from invasion, the Girondins adopted conscription, an expedient which stirred up revolts in a number of provinces, particularly in the Vendée, a province just south of the lower Loire River. The scarcity of food and the rising prices made the problem of feeding Paris and the larger cities of France very difficult. The whole situation was aggravated by the growing intensity of the political quarrel between the Girondins and the Mountain. The former were determined to control France but displayed no capacity for leadership. The members of the Mountain, supported by the Paris mob and the Jacobin clubs, constantly attacked their opponents. Menaces and insults were interchanged daily between the two parties. On every question that came before the Convention, the two parties took opposite sides. Each sought to discredit the other.

By the end of May, 1793, the political struggle had reached a crisis. It could no longer be settled by a parliamentary decision. On the last day of the month, a huge crowd surrounded the Convention and demanded the arrest of the Girondin leaders, cheaper bread, taxes on the rich, and some changes in the institutions of France. Two days later, a better-organized mob again surrounded the Tuilleries palace, the meeting place of the Convention, and insisted once more on the arrest of the Girondin leaders. The Convention tried to evade a decision by withdrawing from the place of meeting but found every egress blocked by the determined mob. Among the cries of the crowd, the helpless legislators returned to their place of meeting and voted the arrest of twenty-nine Girondins. Their action brought to an end, for the time being, the democratic experiment in France and established in its place a dictatorship of the Mountain. Their period of rule is usually designated as "the Terror."

The Mountain party found itself confronted by a dangerous situation. If the powers allied against France could have cooperated better, they might have had little difficulty in conquering her. French troops lacked nearly everything that was needed for a campaign. The military staffs had been discouraged by arrests and desertions. The Prussians and Austrians were taking French fortresses on the north and northeast boundaries of France. The French advance in the Alps was checked. At both ends of the Pyrenees Mountains, the southern frontier was broken by invading forces. It looked as if only a miracle could save the French state from utter defeat.

The domestic situation was equally bad. Some of the Girondins escaped to the provinces where they led uprisings against the new government that enlisted more or less popular support. Throughout the state, the people suffered from economic disorders, and there was an increasing amount of industrial distress. The collection of taxes was greatly in arrears. The assignats were decreasing in value. The government attempted to impose on the country a forced loan and fixed prices. People of moderate incomes found them inadequate. Holders of government securities were in distress. The whole situation was of a nature likely to make trouble for the government in power.

The Terror

The answer of the Mountain to these difficulties was the Terror. With the greatest energy and determination, the new leaders of France combatted their domestic and foreign enemies. For the execution of their will, they devised a group of institutions that characterized the period. Taking over old institutions or inventing new ones, they created a terrible machine that destroyed, for the time being, political liberty. These institutions included two great committees chosen from the members of the Convention (the Committee of Public Safety and the Committee of General Security), as well as the Revolutionary Tribunal at Paris, the Deputies on Mission, and the Revolutionary Army.

The Committee of Public Safety exercised a sort of dictatorship. It was composed first of nine and later of twelve men. At first, Danton and, later, Robespierre (1758–1794) was the leading figure in it. The Convention entrusted to it complete administrative power. Practically, it exercised a general supervision over policy. Each member had charge of a field or department of government, but a single member might sign for the whole committee. It made its power felt in the provinces by acting through deputies on mission and national agents. Chosen by the Committee of Public Safety and approved by the Convention, the deputies on mission were sent out to perform such tasks as the organization of government in the provinces, the supervision of the conscription of men and supplies, the insurance of the loyalty of generals, and similar tasks. In practice, they sometimes displayed almost complete independence. The national agents were permanent appointive agents of the central government in the local administrative districts and were charged with the execution of the laws. The deputies on mission usually had a more temporary appointment and carried out some special assignment.

The Committee of General Security was the central organ of the police power. It supervised the police of France, issued warrants of arrest, which were often arbitrary, supervised prisons, and administered so-called "justice" in the various departments. None of its twelve members enjoyed the personal distinction of some of the members of the Committee of Public Safety, but it held itself to be coordinate with that body. This claim was not always recognized by others and, as a consequence, the revolutionary government was apt to lack unity.

For such an arbitrary government, even the new courts were too slow and uncertain. For the trial of political offences, the Mountain created a distinct system of revolutionary justice. At the top of the system was the Revolutionary Tribunal of Paris. It was designed to deal expeditiously with the enemies of the Revolution and to insure swift punishment. The court was divided into four sections. It executed the terrible Law of Suspects of September 17, 1793, which treated everyone, particularly former nobles and relatives of *émigrés*, as suspected persons until they proved their innocence. Trials lasted only until the jury had made up its mind and usually ended in conviction. Conviction entailed a promptly executed sentence of death.

With this terrible machinery under their control, the Mountain set to work at the task of saving France. In their haste and zeal to suppress revolt and counterrevolution, however, their agents often acted with great and unnecessary cruelty. The victims of the Revolutionary Tribunal at Paris are estimated to have numbered 2,627. The greater number of the victims were put to death in the closing months of the Mountain's period of power. Some of the greatest outrages occurred in towns that had revolted against the dictatorship of the Mountain. At Lyons, two thousand were killed with the greatest cruelty. Toulon was similarly punished. Thousands were executed in the Vendée. There, the notorious Carrier, in his capacity as deputy on mission, shot some and drowned others. In all, there were probably 16,000 to 18,000 victims of the Terror outside of Paris.

Whatever one may think of their methods, the Mountain did repel the invaders of France. Under the leadership of two members of the Committee of Public Safety, Carnot and Prieur, the nation mobilized for victory. In the words of the famous decree of August 23, 1793, young men went to the front; married men forged arms and transported supplies; women made tents and clothes; children made lint; and scientists improved the manufacture of iron and steel and produced gunpowder. The military forces of the nation were gradually forged into an efficient machine. Armed with this weapon, the French rolled back the armies threatening France and in turn invaded the Netherlands and Germany.

As long as the danger was acute, those in control of France succeeded in maintaining something like unity. After the tide of battle turned, factions began to appear. They may be described as the followers of Robespierre, Danton, and Hébert. The first group had control of the government machinery. The second included a mixture of journalists, business men, middle-class politicians, and some very corrupt men. The followers of Hébert were extremists. Those in control of the government machinery wanted to use the Terror to set up a political and social order that was never very clearly defined. The followers of Danton thought the Terror had served its purpose and could be relaxed. The followers of Hébert likewise had no clear-cut program but controlled the Commune of Paris, posed as friends of the common man, and were responsible for a movement against Christianity that culminated in the absurd ceremonies known as the Worship of Reason, in which a handsome actress of doubtful reputation took a leading part.

In the end, these factions destroyed themselves. The government played one against the other. First, the Dantonists acquiesced in the elimination of Hébertist extremists. Then in a few weeks, they themselves were indicted as corruptionists and were destroyed. The government, however, did not long survive its triumph. The plans of Robespierre threatened and alarmed too many persons. As the Terror grew more terrible, their alarm increased. Those threatened by it began to plot the overthrow of Robespierre and his chief aides. When, on July 26, 1794, Robespierre made a long speech in which he seemed to threaten the security of many persons in the Convention, the conspirators took steps to put their plans into effect. The Commune of Paris, as it had done many times before, tried to organize an uprising. The attempt was thwarted by the failure of Robespierre to put himself at the head of the rising and by the success of the conspirators in raising troops from the richer sections of the city. Instead, Robespierre's enemies penetrated to the interior of the municipal building, seized Robespierre and some of his followers, and executed them without even the semblance of a trial.

The Reorganization of France

The fall of Robespierre (July 27, 1794) proved to be a turning point in the history of France. It was achieved by the union of certain members of the Mountain and the hitherto neutral center of the Convention. This move put the previously disregarded center in power. Under the pressure of public opinion the attempt to set up a republic of virtue was given up. Newspapers again enjoyed a virtual freedom. Attacks were made on the Jacobins. Social life began again. Fashions reflected the change in opinion. Prisoners suddenly and unexpectedly found themselves released. The machinery of the Terror was abandoned. The Jacobin Club at Paris was closed. Some of the worst Terrorists were prosecuted.

By 1795 the Convention was prepared to take up the task for which it had been summoned originally, to formulate a new constitution. Its members provided for the establishment of a middle-class republic. By the constitution which was drawn up, the suffrage was restricted again in such a way as to give property owners control of the government. The execution of the laws was entrusted to a directory of five members who could neither initiate nor veto legislation and had no voice in the administration of the treasury. Legislation was given to two bodies, a Council of Five Hundred which was to initiate legislation and a Council of Elders, composed of two hundred and fifty members, which was to accept or reject measures sent to it by the lower body.

The members of the Convention, however, were reluctant to let go the power which they had held for three years. They had a real fear of the Royalists. They identified their own supremacy and the safety of the republic. They enjoyed power. So they adopted a special decree along with the constitution which insured a perpetuation of their power. By its terms, the electoral assemblies were required to select two-thirds of the new councillors from members of the Convention. This confronted the French people with the prospect of the indefinite prolongation of a regime of which they were heartily tired.

While the vast majority of the voters stayed home when the new constitution and the accompanying decree were submitted to a plebiscite or referendum, Paris rejected the new regime. An armed force, composed largely of National Guards from the more conservative sections of the city, marched against the Tuilleries palace. This time, in contrast to some former occasions, the Convention had made preparations to defend itself. Barras, to whom the problem of defending the

Convention had been entrusted, called to his assistance General Napoleon Bonaparte, an artillery officer from the island of Corsica, who had distinguished himself in 1793 at the siege of Toulon. The young commander repelled the attack on the Convention by a resolute use of the cannon at his disposal. The attackers recoiled and the Convention and its work were saved.

The Reforms of the Convention

In spite of the war and the strife of factions, the Convention was responsible for many reforms. Some of its measures dealt with the subject of religion. The defeat of the Girondins virtually completed the discrediting of their friends, the constitutional clergy. In its place, the members of the Mountain made almost a religion of the revolution. In October, 1793, the Convention forbade the wearing of religious costumes and the observance of religious ceremonies outside of the churches. The Hébertist faction seized the Cathedral of Notre Dame at Paris and worshipped with elaborate ceremonies liberty represented by a handsome actress, but the state never approved of their follies. Under the leadership of Robespierre, the state even attempted to institute a sort of civic religion that recognized the existence of God and the immortality of the soul. In its closing months, the Convention formally separated Church and state. The state ceased to pay salaries to the clergy or to furnish a place of worship. The religious legislation of the Convention thus was largely destructive and left France in a chaotic condition in regard to religion.

The revolutionary authorities were much concerned with the problem of education. They realized the advantage of indoctrinating the youth of France and the impossibility of achieving political equality without equality of opportunity. Accordingly, they did away with the educational system of monarchical France controlled by the Church which had in the main been limited to the nobility and the middle class. In its place, in theory at least, they established a system of general education controlled by the state. In practice, they never found the time or the resources to carry out fully the plan of general education drawn up by the recently executed Condorcet. In place of the little colleges of the old regime, they did actually establish central schools in each department and broadened the curriculum to some extent. For higher education they set up the school which became the *École Polytechnique,* the important *École Normale Superieure,* and three medical schools. They planned a number of others.

Many of the famous institutions of France owe their present form to the Convention. A school of oriental languages was established. The royal gardens were transformed into the public botanical garden

525

known as the *Jardin des Plantes*. The royal library became the National Library, and libraries were started in each department. For the housing of models and useful machines and apparatus, a great museum of the arts and sciences (*Conservatoire des Artes et Metiers*) was created. A national museum for the preservation of pictures, statues, and other artistic objects was established at the Louvre. In place of the old royal academies, an institute was started.

Under the old regime, there had been a confused system of weights and measures. For this, the Convention substituted the more scientific metric system. Standard units of length, area, volume, and mass were established. Each unit was a decimal part of the unit above or a multiple of ten of the unit below it. The metric system is now used in most countries and by all scientific men.

A less important measure of the Convention was the creation of the Republican calendar. Time was dated from the establishment of the Republic. The year was divided into twelve months, each thirty days in length, and five complementary days. Each month was divided into three periods of ten days called "decades." The months were named after the natural phenomena that characterized them. The days were divided into ten hours. The new calendar was used until the end of 1805. It was a result of the effort to rationalize and dechristianize France.

In July, 1793, the Convention made legal the transformation (which had already actually taken place) of the French peasant into a free proprietor. It suppressed all the former seigniorial dues without any indemnity. In practice, the peasants had not been paying the dues for a long time.

The French Revolution was the attempt of the French nation to remedy the evils of the old regime. It profoundly modified the political, social, religious, and economic organization of France. In the political sphere, it set up first a limited monarchy and later a middle-class republic. It created new administrative and judicial systems. In the religious sphere, it first modified the relations of Church and state and ultimately separated the two institutions. It secularized the property of the Church, suppressed monastic institutions, and established, in theory, religious toleration. In the social sphere, as far as it could be done by legislation, it established social equality. In the economic sphere, it abolished seigniorial dues, shifted the ownership of much of the land, suppressed interior customs lines and tolls, did away with the gilds, and equalized the burden of taxation. In reality, however, it must be remembered, the Revolution fell far short of its professed ideals.

CHAPTER 32

The Rise of a Dictator in France (1795–1804)

The middle-class republic created by the Convention in 1795 did not prove to be permanent. The leaders of the French Revolution involved their country in a foreign war through their brusque reforms and disregard of the rights and feelings of neighboring states. The ensuing tension led to war, and the war eventually bred a dictator.

The Course of the War

As was explained in the previous chapter, the fortunes of war swayed back and forth during the French Revolution. The struggle opened in 1792 with an invasion of France. This was stopped in September, 1792, at Valmy. This victory was followed in turn by the retreat of the invaders, a temporary advance of the French armies into the Netherlands and Germany, the entrance of additional powers into the conflict, a new invasion of France, and a second repulse of the invaders. By the end of 1793, France, with the exception of the province of Roussillon in southeastern France, was free from foreign troops. During the Terror, French arms continued to be successful. In June, 1794, the French gained in the Austrian Netherlands the stunning victory of Fleurus. After this, the march of French troops to the Rhine was made easy by the dissensions of the allies and their concern over the partition of Poland. By October, 1794, nearly the whole left bank of the Rhine was in the hands of the French. They professed to be bringing peace to the cottages and war on the chateaux. In reality, the Austrian Netherlands and the Rhineland were indiscriminately plundered by the French invaders.

In the following winter, the victorious French pressed on and invaded the United Netherlands. Their invasion of the country was made easy by the policy of the so-called Patriots. In view of the widespread defection of his Dutch subjects, the prince of Orange concluded that resistance was useless and withdrew to England. Thereupon the body known as the States-General disbanded. When the Patriots tried to come to terms with the invaders, however, they received a rude shock. The negotiations dragged on for some time. Finally, under the threat of force, the Dutch and their conquerors reached a settlement. By a treaty signed May 16, 1795, the United Netherlands ceded to France the three border districts of Dutch Flanders, Venloo, and Maestricht; and they agreed to accept a French garrison in the port of Flushing, to pay a large indemnity, and to maintain an army of 25,000 men during the war with Great Britain. In actual practice, the French were even more severe than the terms of the treaty stipulated. In addition, the Dutch were dragged, as a consequence of the treaty, into all the wars of France. Within a year after its conclusion, they had lost to the British the Dutch colonial possessions in the West and the East Indies.

By 1795, Prussia, too, was tired of the war. Even before the French invasion of the United Netherlands, the Prussian authorities had begun negotiating with the rulers of France. The whole situation was complicated further by the ambitions of the three powers which had already participated in the partitioning of Poland and hoped for additional gains. On April 5, 1795, the Prussian negotiators finally concluded the Treaty of Basel. This document gave French troops the right to occupy the Prussian possessions west of the Rhine until the conclusion of peace between France and the Holy Roman Empire. A secret article stipulated that in case these territories were actually ceded to France, Prussia should be indemnified with other German lands. Since there were no vacant lands in the Empire, this foreshadowed the seizure of the city-states and the secularization of the ecclesiastical principalities of the Holy Roman Empire. A line of demarcation was also drawn which limited the French advance and neutralized most of the German states north of the Rhine and Main rivers. The example of Prussia was soon followed by Spain. The withdrawal of Prussia and Spain from the war left Austria, Great Britain, and the Kingdom of Sardinia as the principal opponents of France in the coming campaign.

The Campaign of 1796–1797

In the campaign of 1796, France, as a land power, directed her attack against Austria and Sardinia. The French authorities expected to attack simultaneously southern Germany and Italy. They planned to make their principal effort in Germany. Into this region, accordingly, they sent two large armies. In alarm, the south German states began to negotiate peace treaties with France. Baden and Württemberg actually signed treaties by which they gave up their territories west of the Rhine upon the promise of territorial compensation. The campaign in Germany, however, ended disastrously, and the French were saved from complete defeat only by the skill of General Moreau

528

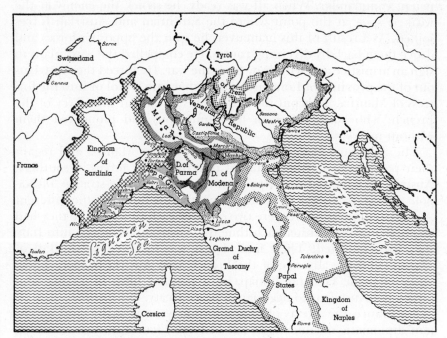

Northern Italy on the Eve of the First Italian Campaign

and the failure of subordinate officers to carry out the plans of the Austrian commander.

Quite unexpectedly, the campaign in Italy turned out to be the principal military operation. The French authorities entrusted their forces in the peninsula to the command of General Bonaparte. To most people, the appointment seemed merely a reward for his defense of the Convention. They did not expect much from such a political appointee. The new commander, however, soon won the respect of his army and his foes.

At the time that the young general took command, the military situation did not seem particularly favorable. After several years of fighting, the French army operating in the region had penetrated only a few miles into the peninsula along the Riviera. The discouraged forces placed under his command were unpaid and lacked supplies. In front of them, along the crest of the Alps and the Appenines, lay strong Sardinian and Austrian armies. The states of Italy were either at war with France or at least hostile to her.

The young general conducted the ensuing campaign with unexpected skill and speed. By a series of short, clear-cut orders he quickly convinced his subordinate officers and his troops that they had a com-

529

petent commander. When all was ready, he struck the enemy at the weakest spot, at the point where the Sardinian and Austrian forces joined. As a result of this maneuver, he split the opposing forces and drove them back by diverging routes. He compelled the Sardinians to sign an armistice and withdraw from the war. He forced the Austrians out of the province of Lombardy and either into Tyrol or into the fortress of Mantua. This put the little states of Italy at the mercy of the French, who harrassed them by requisitions and plundered them without mercy.

The Austrians made four attempts to relieve Mantua and regain their position in northern Italy. Collecting their forces in southern Austria, they crossed the Alps by various passes. The strategy of Napoleon Bonaparte was to attack with superior numbers the different Austrian columns (there were two or three each time) before they had an opportunity to unite. Each time the Austrians advanced into Italy they were defeated. Their final defeat was followed by the fall of Mantua and the advance of the French into Austria proper. These victories made General Bonaparte a popular hero in France and forced the Austrians to negotiate a peace treaty.

For France, the Treaty of Campoformio was one of the most important diplomatic documents in her history. Thanks to their victories, all northern Italy came under the control of the French. From the Austrian province of Lombardy, the duchy of Modena, three legations from the Papal States, and Venetian territory west of the Adige River, General Bonaparte had created a satellite state known as the Cisalpine Republic. By a series of highhanded measures, he had destroyed and dismembered the Republic of Venice. In the Treaty of Campoformio (signed October 17, 1797), accordingly, Austria recognized these changes, abandoned her claims to the Austrian Netherlands, received in compensation for her territorial losses the greater part of the lands of the Republic of Venice, and promised to assist France to obtain the left bank of the Rhine from the Holy Roman Empire. The Treaty of Campoformio thus gave France what she considered as her natural boundaries and footholds beyond the Rhine and in Italy.

General Bonaparte then proceeded to introduce French institutions into the newly formed Cisalpine Republic. He abolished feudal dues and primogeniture. He gave the new state a constitution based on that of the French Directory, a flag (green, white, and red), and a national guard composed of Italian partisans of the French regime. In January, 1798, the French government summoned the Directors of the Cisalpine Republic to Paris and forced them to sign a defensive and offensive alliance by the terms of which the new Italian state agreed to support a French army of twenty-five thousand men, to give

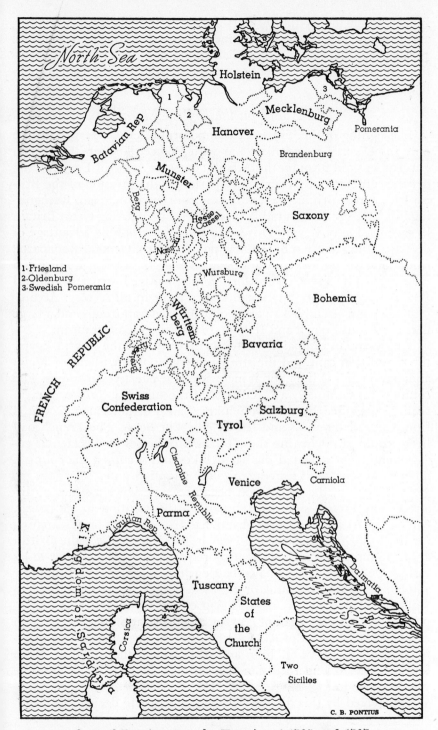

Central Europe after the Treaties of 1795 and 1797

North Sea

Holstein

Mecklenburg

Pomerania

Batavian Rep

Hanover

Brandenburg

Munster

Berg

Hesse Cassel

Saxony

Nassau

1·Friesland
2·Oldenburg
3·Swedish Pomerania

Wursburg

Bohemia

Württemberg

FRENCH REPUBLIC

Baden

Bavaria

Swiss Confederation

Salzburg

Tyrol

Cisalpine Republic

Venice

Carniola

Parma

Ligurian Rep

Kingdom of Sardinia

Corsica

Tuscany

States
of
the
Church

Adriatic Sea

Dalmatia

Two
Sicilies

C. B. PONTIUS

France command of the military forces of the Cisalpine Republic, and to grant France special commercial privileges in her territories. In the preceding year, in somewhat similar fashion, France had transformed the Republic of Genoa into the dependent Ligurian Republic.

The Attack on the British Empire

The signing of the Treaty of Campoformio left Great Britain the only important power still at war with France. Though the French government did form on the Atlantic coast an Army of England, under the command of General Bonaparte, for the invasion of the British Isles, Great Britain was really safe from such an attack. Recognizing this fact, a plan was gradually matured for attacking Great Britain by an invasion of Egypt. This proposal had the double advantage of diverting the attention of the new popular hero, General Bonaparte, from domestic politics in France and striking the British Empire at a vital spot. The French Directors, consequently, instructed General Bonaparte to prepare an expeditionary force in all secrecy. Accordingly, he soon assembled an army of 35,000 veteran troops and a large fleet at various French and Italian ports in the Mediterranean.

The Egyptian campaign started brilliantly. On the way to Egypt, the expedition captured the strategically important island of Malta and, upon landing in Egypt, it met with little effective resistance. The country was nominally a vassal state of the sultan of Turkey but, in reality, was ruled by the Mamelukes (bands of horsemen recruited from Circassian youths and led by chiefs or beys). The French had little trouble in defeating these forces. In a series of spectacular engagements, they defeated the Mamelukes and occupied the country. They then proceeded to reorganize the Egyptian state.

At this point, the expedition began to experience a series of disasters. The French seem to have paid little attention to sea power, while the British, on the other hand, had from the first been searching for the French fleet. After the French had disembarked, the British at last found the French ships anchored at Aboukir Bay, a few miles east of Alexandria. In the naval battle which followed, practically the whole French fleet was sunk or disabled. This defeat had serious consequences. It left the French in Egypt cut off from their base of supplies. It nerved the sultan of Turkey to a declaration of war. This, in turn, enabled the tsar of Russia, who by a curious chance was Protector of the Knights of St. John and still claimed the island of Malta for the order, to send a Russian fleet through the Dardanelles into the Mediterranean.

Undeterred by this disaster, General Bonaparte decided to attack

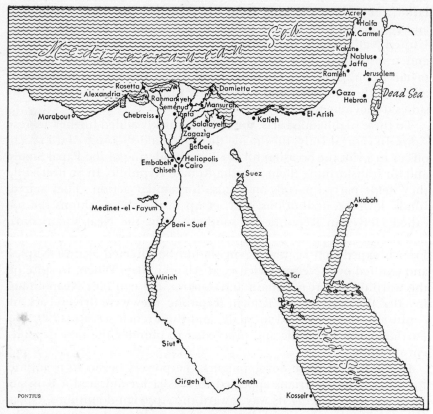

The Egyptian Campaign

the Pasha of Acre. Leaving a force to hold Egypt, he set out for Syria. At Acre, he encountered stubborn resistance. While the French gained local successes, the Turkish defenders of the town, encouraged by the English fleet, succeeded in holding the city. Thwarted by this defense and not daring to risk further losses, General Bonaparte finally retreated to Egypt.

The War of the Second Coalition, 1798–1801

In Europe, in the meantime, a new war had been brewing. The French, on the one hand, were more aggressive than they had been even in the days of Louis XIV. At the Congress of Rastadt, convened for the purpose of concluding peace with the Empire, France demanded the left bank of the Rhine. In Italy the French were constantly interfering in the affairs of both the Cisalpine Republic and the Kingdom of Sardinia. In the former state, they changed the make-up of the Council three times and levied heavy requisitions; in the latter, they drove the king from his principal province, Piedmont, and compelled him to take refuge in the island of Sardinia. In the United Netherlands, they forced a new constitution upon the Dutch and transformed their state, the United Netherlands, into the Batavian Republic (1798). On other hand, Great Britain was anxious for allies on the continent and stood ready to pay them substantial subsidies if they renewed the war.

To these highhanded acts, the French quickly added further aggressions. In central Italy, they made the accidental shooting of a French officer in a riot the occasion for further plundering of the Papal States and for transforming them into the Roman Republic. In Switzerland, they made party quarrels an excuse for similar action. They seized funds, levied contributions, and set up in the Swiss cantons the so-called Helvetian Republic. In southern Italy, the Neapolitan court had itself to thank for its misfortunes. It had been in terror lest the French expedition against Egypt should be directed against Naples and exulted over Nelson's victory at Aboukir Bay. When, in spite of the warning of Great Britain and Austria, the exultant Neapolitans invaded the newly set up Roman Republic, they were driven back in confusion, the court fled to Sicily, and the French set up (1799) the Parthenopean Republic and proceeded to plunder the new dependent republic.

In the face of these developments, the powers began to negotiate for allies. The Austrians appealed to Russia for aid, and a Russian force was soon making its way toward the Austrian dominions. Great Britain signed a treaty with Russia which promised that country subsidies for a large army. At this point, the French precipitated an armed struggle. When the Russian military forces reached Austria, the French issued an ultimatum. Their action led (March 1, 1799) to the war of the Second Coalition in which France was ranged against Great Britain, Russia, and Austria.

At first, the powers allied against France seemed to be victorious everywhere. In Germany, the French were severely defeated at Stockach. In Italy, the Russian general, Suvorov, overran the northern part of the peninsula and destroyed the work of the French in that region; and the former Bourbon rulers returned to Naples, put an end to the Parthenopean Republic, and instituted in their recovered state a reign of terror and vengeance. At this point, France was saved by the dissensions of the allies. Once in possession of Piedmont, the Austrians refused to recall the king of Sardinia. The British and the Russians, on the other hand, were in no mood to sacrifice men and resources for the benefit of Austria. The Russians, consequently, withdrew from Italy into Switzerland. If the Austrians in Germany had only cooperated with them, the French might have been driven from the Helvetian Republic. Instead of working with the Russians, however, the Austrians moved toward the Rhine in an effort to thwart the Prussians. This enabled the French to defeat the Russians in a terrible campaign in the Alps. About the same time, they defeated a British-Russian army which had debarked in the Netherlands.

French Politics, 1795–1799

In other ways besides its conduct of the foreign war, the Directory had failed to win public opinion and establish itself firmly in power. For one thing, its members had maintained themselves in office by the most highhanded methods. In the election of 1797, by which one-third of the members of the two legislative councils were to be renewed, scarcely a dozen former members of the Convention out of two hundred and sixteen who stood for re-election were chosen again. As soon as the new members took their places in the legislative councils, they attacked the laws against *émigrés* and priests and reorganized the National Guard along more conservative lines. These attacks alarmed the partisans of the existing regime. Some thought there was danger of a Royalist restoration, others feared for their titles to confiscated lands, and still others thought their own positions were endangered. These developments led in September, 1797, to a *coup d'état*. The majority of the Directors caused the arrest of the proprietors of opposition newspapers, editors, opposing councillors, and the newly elected director. Carnot, another hostile director, succeeded in escaping. Later, the majority of the directors caused the deportation of fifty-three deputies and forty-two newspaper editors and proprietors and annulled the elections in forty-nine departments. The three directors really in power were aided in the *coup d'état* by an army sent from Italy by General Bonaparte. A year later, they executed a similar *coup d'état* and annulled sixty-four elections to keep themselves in power. In 1799, however, when the elections were again unfavorable to the former members of the Convention, the directorial party did not dare to annul the elections and so lost control of the machinery of government.

These repeated *coup d'états* were accompanied by a practical declaration of bankruptcy. The Directors decreed that two-thirds of the public debt should be paid in bonds. At first, they could be used in the purchase of public lands; later, only for the construction of buildings upon such lands. The bonds, consequently, rapidly fell in value and were finally virtually repudiated. This was followed by a similar treatment of the assignats. This method of handling the public debt naturally alienated the investors in the state securities.

The government of the Directory was also corrupt. This may be illustrated by their treatment of the United States in 1797. For a number of reasons, the relations of France and the United States had grown worse, and the Directors had finally threatened the American minister with arrest and had forced him to leave the country. In an effort to preserve peace, the United States sent three commissioners to France. Upon their arrival in Europe, however, they found they could make no progress in their proposed negotiations. Finally, though, three French agents, designated in the report of the commissioners as X, Y, and Z, approached the American representatives and suggested that progress could be made if the latter would bribe Talleyrand, the French foreign minister. In this, the agents were merely following a well-established custom in the treatment of the small European states. The American commissioners indignantly refused to bribe the French authorities. The incident helped to lead to an undeclared war between France and the United States.

After the former members of the Convention had been checked in their efforts to maintain themselves in power, the victorious faction (headed by Sieyès), which had succeeded in gaining control of the machinery of government, began to plan for a revision of the constitution. They felt, though, the need of enlisting the support of some general who enjoyed popular support and could overawe opponents. They had already made tentative advances to one or two generals when surprising news reached them of the arrival in France on October 9, 1799, of a still more popular general, Napoleon Bonaparte, the hero of Italy, who had abandoned his army in Egypt and returned secretly to France. At once, the conspirators realized that he must be persuaded to cooperate with them.

The conspirators could count on some political support. They had a majority in the Senate, but they expected serious opposition in the Council of Five Hundred. In the latter body, however, they could rely on Lucien Bonaparte, a younger brother of the famous general, who had just been elected presiding officer of that body as a compliment to the general. They believed that a majority of the Directors could be persuaded or intimidated into resigning.

After considering the whole situation, General Bonaparte finally decided to cooperate with the conspirators. Assured of his support, the plotters drew up a plan of action. Using its constitutional powers, the Senate was to decree the removal of the two legislative councils to St. Cloud where they would be out of reach of a Parisian mob. General Bonaparte was to be put in command of the troops in the capital. Three of the Directors were to be persuaded or compelled to resign.

On November 9, 1799, the conspirators began to execute their plan. The decree transferring the councils was issued. General Bonaparte was put in command of the troops. Three of the Directors resigned. At St. Cloud on the next day, however, some of the deputies began to ask embarrassing questions. General Bonaparte, without success, tried to intervene. The two legislative bodies, consequently, were in an uproar. Finally, Lucien Bonaparte persuaded the troops to drive the deputies out of their place of meeting. During the night, a few of the deputies reassembled and appointed a consular commission of three members, which included General Bonaparte and Sieyès, and two legislative commissions, one from each council. They were entrusted with the task of setting up a new government. Most of the men who had taken part in the *coup d'etat* thought that they had saved the republic. Events were soon to show that they had set up a dictator.

The Successful Conclusion of the War

The most pressing problem facing the new government of France was the war. If it did not regain what had been lost in northern Italy and bring the war to a successful conclusion, it would be discredited. Austria and Great Britain must be defeated. Russia, embittered by the policy of Austria in Italy, had already withdrawn from the war.

Most of the fighting took place in Italy. After collecting a reserve army at a point where it could operate in either Italy or southern Germany, General Bonaparte led his troops across the Alps by way of the Great St. Bernard Pass. On June 2, 1800, he entered Milan, the capital of the former Cisalpine Republic. After checking an Austrian attempt to escape, he advanced into the plain of Allessandria. On June 14, 1800, in the vicinity of the little town of Marengo, the decisive battle took place. There, the French commander failed to display his usual military skill. In the face of the enemy, he divided his forces and the Austrians attacked the main part of the French army and drove it back in disorder. Fortunately, General Bonaparte's remaining forces returned in time to win the battle by a famous cavalry charge. In his bulletin of victory, however, the French commander took all the credit for his success. The battle of Marengo, with an important victory of the French at Hohenlinden in southern Germany late in the year, compelled the Austrians to make peace.

The treaty which brought hostilities to an end was signed February 9, 1801, at Lunéville. In the main, it repeated the terms of the Treaty of Campoformio. In addition, it forced the Emperor to agree, without consulting the German diet, that the west bank of the Rhine should be annexed to France and that the Grand Duke of Tuscany should give up his Italian principality (which became the kingdom of Etruria) and take German territory in compensation. Austria further recognized the Batavian and Helvetian republics. The French made no effort to restore the short-lived Parthenopean Republic.

After the conclusion of the Treaty of Lunéville, a continuance of the war between France and Great Britain seemed futile. Neither power could destroy the other. France was a land power, Great Britain, a sea power. The French did do considerable damage to British trade by privateers. The British seized the French, the Dutch, and the Spanish colonies. Neither power could force the other to surrender. The continuance of the conflict was costly and prevented the French from carrying out their colonial plans. So the two powers finally concluded the Treaty of Amiens on March 27, 1802. By its terms Great Britain returned all her colonial conquests except Ceylon and Trinidad, and promised to restore Egypt to the Turks and the island of Malta to the Knights of St. John. The British negotiators assumed that the Treaty of Lunéville would mark the limits of French aggression.

The Beneficent Dictatorship

Meanwhile, the temporary government set up in France after the *coup d'état* had been replaced by the Consulate. General Bonaparte promptly shoved aside his civilian colleagues like Sieyès and seized control of the machinery of government. To the temporary commissions which had been charged with revising the government, he dictated the main features of the new constitution. The document provided for the establishment of three consuls as head of the executive branch of the government but gave most of the authority to General Bonaparte as First Consul. He was to appoint most of the officials, to select the members of the Council of State (the body that was to initiate legislation), and to direct the armies in the field. A tribunate was entrusted with the right of discussing legislation; a legislative corps was then to accept or reject the conclusions of the Tribunate, and a senate was to pass on the constitutionality of the measures approved by the legislative body. The constitution established universal suffrage, but most of those elected were selected by a very complicated and indirect system of voting. Upon the completion of the constitution, it was submitted to a plebiscite and, according to official statistics, was ratified by an overwhelming majority.

Immediately after it assumed power, the new consular government inaugurated a number of policies calculated to conciliate public opinion. One of the new measures concerned the *émigrés* who had left the country voluntarily. The First Consul at first tried to deal with each case individually, but this method opened the way to too much intrigue and corruption. After abandoning this plan, he began to admit whole classes of the proscribed. By 1802 he had authorized the return of all but about 1,000 militant Royalists.

Another early measure of the Consulate dealt with the problem of local government. The Constituent Assembly had broken with the traditions of France and had decentralized local administration. The Consulate returned to a policy of centralization. The First Consul entrusted local administration to prefects, who had the departments as their administrative districts. They were the successors of the pre-revolutionary intendants. By the side of the prefect sat a council of prefecture which considered questions arising between the administration and the individual citizen. In addition, the district known as the commune was restored to its old place in the administrative hierarchy. The mayors of the communes were appointed either by the First Consul or by the prefects.

The most difficult task confronting the Consulate was the improvement of the finances. In 1799 the French government was on the brink of bankruptcy. The new government set up by the *coup d'état* sought to instill in the French people the idea that the payment of taxes was a public duty. The collection of taxes was pushed more vigorously. The budget was reduced. The news of the victory of Marengo tended to establish the credit of the government more firmly. This enabled the administration to begin to pay in coin the holders of annuities and pensions. Within a short time, as a result of its measures, the treasury was able to report a slight surplus.

In January, 1800, the First Consul authorized the establishment of the Bank of France. It was hoped that the new institution would accomplish for France what the Bank of England had been doing for that country for the last century. The success of the Bank of France was immediate. In 1803 it was given the exclusive right to issue bank notes. The government refrained from subordinating its administration to the financial necessities of the state. As a result, its shares soon doubled in value. Ever since its founding it has been the center of the French financial world.

The Consulate also found the religious affairs of France in a state approaching chaos. The Civil Constitution of the Clergy had alienated the supporters of the old church, who were found especially in rural France, and had driven most of its bishops and many of its priests into exile. The fall of the Girondins had discredited even the constitutional clergy. The Convention had then separated Church and state and sought to dechristianize France. The First Consul naturally wished to enlist the support of all forces in the state. Consequently, he promptly began to reverse the policy of the government toward the ancient church. In contrast with the Constituent Assembly, he demanded of the clergy only a declaration of submission and permitted the churches to be opened again.

The victory of Marengo enabled the First Consul to go further. In defiance of his principal advisers he made advances to the Pope and the old church. The result was the conclusion in 1801 of a concordat. In this document both parties made concessions. The Concordat recognized the Roman Catholic Church as the faith of the Consuls and the majority of Frenchmen without abolishing religious toleration. The French government, having done away with tithes, assumed the task of paying the clergy. The First Consul was to nominate the bishops, who were then to be consecrated by the Pope. The Church promised not to disturb the purchasers of confiscated Church property. In return for these concessions, the Church put an end to schism in France and was assured of possession of the greater part of the Papal States. There was considerable opposition to the Concordat on the part of the legislators, but the great majority of Frenchmen heartily approved it.

In place of the old nobility, the First Consul tried to create an aristocracy of achievement. For this purpose he established in 1802 the Legion of Honor. Its members were to be chosen by a council for distinguished civil or military service. They were to receive, as a reward for their deeds, decorations and annuities. In establishing the Legion of Honor, the First Consul encountered considerable opposition.

The chaos existing in the laws of France had been one of the chief complaints against the old regime. The leaders of the revolution, however, had been too engrossed with war and constitutional changes to take up the problem of codifying French laws. Immediately after his accession to office, Napoleon Bonaparte appointed a committee to push forward the codifying of the laws of France. Upon its completion in 1801, the project of the committee was sent to the law courts and finally to the Council of State for criticism. The First Consul himself is credited with having made important contributions to the new code. He presided at thirty-five of the eighty-seven sessions of the Council of State and often took part in the discussions. Under the name of the Napoleonic Code, a name adopted in 1807, the new code exercised an immense influence not only in France but in many other countries.

Immediately after assuming power, General Bonaparte took steps toward control of the press. Within three weeks he suppressed all but thirteen of the seventy-three Parisian journals. One of the thirteen, the *Moniteur,* was made the official journal. Three of the remaining twelve journals disappeared before the end of the year. The others survived only by using the greatest caution in the expression of views.

Colonial Plans of the First Consul

The First Consul could not take any steps toward the creation of a colonial empire until peace had been signed with Great Britain, and the former French colonies had been returned. Upon the conclusion of peace in 1802, he attempted to regain control of Santo Domingo and to acquire Louisiana.

In neither region was he successful in permanently establishing his authority. In Santo Domingo, the French Revolution had been the signal for slave insurrections. Out of this turmoil had risen to power Toussaint L'Ouverture. At first, he was in the service of France as a general and prevented the island from falling into the hands of the British and the Spanish. Later, he expelled the representatives of France and followed an independent policy. He took steps to attract the return of the planters and drew up a constitution which made him almost completely independent of the French government. This situation was intolerable to the First Consul. Consequently, he replied to the appeal of Toussaint L'Ouverture for recognition by sending to the island an expedition of 35,000 men under his brother-in-law, General Leclerc. The expedition had little difficulty in crushing the military opposition but was unable to cope with the yellow fever. L'Ouverture was tricked into boarding a French vessel and was sent as a prisoner to France where he died. Yellow fever, however, made casualties of all but 4,000 of the French troops.

As early as 1795 the French had tried to acquire control of Louisiana from Spain. After the great victory of Marengo, the Spaniards did not dare to oppose any longer the plans of the First Consul and secretly agreed to return Louisiana to France. As compensation, the First Consul agreed to transform the grand duchy of Tuscany into the kingdom of Etruria for the infanta of Spain and her husband, the Duke of Parma. In the spring of 1801, reports of the transfer of Louisiana to France began to appear. The news caused great excitement in the United States, and President Jefferson immediately took steps to avert the danger. Although naturally sympathetic with France, he made it very clear to the French authorities that in case France should acquire Louisiana the United States would ally itself with the British, and he began to sound out the French on the possibility of the United States acquiring New Orleans and West Florida. Without the American president knowing it, the situation in Europe favored his plan. War was again imminent. The French, unable to defend their colony, therefore surprised the American negotiators by offering them the entire territory of Louisiana. Their offer was gladly accepted and a treaty, providing for its transfer, was signed May 2, 1803.

The Reward of Success

The French people felt grateful to the First Consul for his achievements. In foreign affairs he had brought the war to a successful conclusion. In domestic affairs he was conferring many benefits on France. The general skillfully used this feeling of gratitude to increase his power. On the very day peace with Great Britain was announced, steps were taken toward increasing his authority. As a result of the activity of his supporters, the question of giving the First Consul office for life was submitted to a popular vote. The French people, according to official figures at least, approved the proposal by an overwhelming majority. Emboldened by this show of support, the First Consul then modified the constitution in a way that removed every obstacle to his will. Thereafter, he conducted himself as a sovereign.

In 1804 the First Consul was given the trappings as well as the substance of power. The Tribunate voted to declare Napoleon Bonaparte emperor of the French and to vest the succession to the new dignity in his family. The Senate thereupon modified the Constitution in such a way as to make France an empire. The Tribunate and the Legislative Corps were reorganized so as to make them less responsive to public opinion. The government was put completely under the control of the emperor. After this, a court was organized which imitated in many ways the one which had been overthrown by the French Revolution.

New French Aggressions

The signing of the treaties of Lunéville and Amiens did not put an end to the spread of French influence. In Germany, Italy, and Switzerland the French continued their aggressive policy.

The intervention of France in German affairs grew out of the treaties of Basel, Campoformio and Lunéville with Prussia and Austria. In these and other treaties with the minor secular princes of Germany, it had been agreed that the secular states which had lost territories as a result of the wars with France should be compensated for their losses. After the signing of the Treaty of Lunéville, negotiations were resumed. Since there was no free land in the Empire, this was a threat to the ecclesiastical and city-states of Germany.

Nominally, Germany reorganized itself but, in reality, the French authorities dictated the territorial changes. The *salon* of Talleyrand,

French minister of Foreign Affairs, became the center of the negotiations. The princes of Germany paid huge sums to Talleyrand and his agents in the hope of retaining their territories and acquiring new lands. In March, 1803, the so-called "Conclusion of the Empire" was adopted. By its provisions, most of the ecclesiastical and city-states disappeared from the map, while many of the secular princes—especially Prussia, Austria, Bavaria, Württemberg, Baden, Hesse-Darmstadt, and Hesse-Cassel—made important additions to their territories.

The effect of the reorganization of Germany is well illustrated by Bavaria. In 1799 the Elector of Bavaria was ruler of a compact, contiguous group of territories in the Upper Danube Valley and some detached territories in the Rhine Valley. The former included Upper and Lower Bavaria, Neuburg, Sulzbach, and the Upper Palatinate; the latter included the Rhine Palatinate and the duchies of Zweibrücken, Jülich, and Berg. By the Treaty of Lunéville, the Elector of Bavaria lost the larger part of the Rhine Palatinate, the duchies of Jülich and Zweibrücken, and several small lordships. As a result of the reorganization of Germany, he gave up most of the remaining detached territories but received in compensation either all or the greater parts of five former bishoprics, seventeen free imperial cities, twelve abbeys, and the provostship of Kempten. These changes consolidated and enlarged the Bavarian state.

In Italy, after the victory at Marengo, the Cisalpine Republic was re-established under the name of the Italian Republic (1801–1805). Disregarding the former constitution, it was given a new one largely copied after the French Constitution of 1800. After some delay, the First Consul took the presidency of the revived republic. He gave the vice-presidency to Melzi, a prominent Italian. After its re-establishment, Napoleon Bonaparte levied on the country without mercy and harassed it with an army of occupation. At the same time, however, he did confer some positive benefits on the revived republic. He introduced universal military service, founded military schools, put down brigandage, restored order to the finances, and established freedom of worship.

The First Consul also wished to annex Piedmont, the most important province of the Kingdom of Sardinia. He saw, however, that he must act with caution. Tsar Paul of Russia, in particular, took a deep interest in the fate of this territory. As a consequence, at first the First Consul merely occupied Piedmont. In 1801, after the death of the Russian ruler, he took the first step toward annexation. He divided the province into military districts about the size of French departments and began to collect taxes and administer justice. Finally, in September, 1802, several months after the conclusion of the Treaty of Amiens, he formally annexed the province.

The First Consul took several other measures to strengthen his hold on northern Italy. He gave the Ligurian Republic a new constitution more in keeping with the times, and appointed the doge, the nominal head of the transformed state. This gave the ruler of France control of the valuable port of Genoa. At the same time, he took the canton of Valais from the Swiss and put it under the protection of the French and Italian republics. This gave him control of the important Simplon Pass. These measures, with the establishment of the puppet state of Etruria, made the First Consul master of northern Italy.

In 1803 the French likewise intervened in Swiss affairs. The constitution imposed on the Swiss by the directors had never been popular. The partisans of the old aristocratic constitution had never abandoned hope of its restoration. They were opposed by partisans of the new order now taking root in Europe. The First Consul, however, had no intention of allowing the Swiss to settle their differences themselves. At first, his intervention threw the cantons into turmoil. In February, 1803, though, he succeeded in imposing the so-called Act of Mediation. It proved one of the shrewdest political acts of his career. It adapted itself to the habits and aspirations of the Swiss and so rallied them to the side of the First Consul.

Renewal of the War

To the British, the developments in Italy, Germany, and Switzerland seemed to be dangerous aggressions. Then the handing back of the Dutch colony of the Cape of Good Hope appeared to be about the same as handing it over to the French and thus endangered the important route to India. On top of this came a report of a French agent, who had been sent to study the situation in Egypt, in which he asserted that a force of 6,000 Frenchmen could easily conquer that country. All these developments caused Great Britain to take countermeasures. The British authorities refused to surrender the strategically important island of Malta and began to arm for a possible struggle. This breach of the Treaty of Amiens threw the First Consul into a rage and caused him to order the arrest of all British subjects traveling in France. This brusque action precipitated war.

The French Revolution thus led to dictatorship and war. The brusque introduction of reforms and the disregard of long-established rights led to the outbreak of war between revolutionary France and reactionary Europe. The war produced a popular hero and en-

544

abled him to seize power. At first, his rule seemed to confer many benefits on France. He brought the war to a successful conclusion and introduced needed reforms. In the end, however, dictatorship led to a renewal of the war. In his efforts to justify his rule, Napoleon Bonaparte adopted an aggressive policy that led to war, first with Great Britain and a little later with Austria and Russia.

CHAPTER 33

The Conquest and Loss of the Continent

For some time, the war which broke out in 1803 was like the struggle of a whale and an elephant. Great Britain was a sea power; France was a land power. They could not attack each other directly; so they had to resort to indirect measures.

The War between Great Britain and France, 1803–1805

With the aim of weakening Great Britain, France took a number of measures. The First Consul ordered the exclusion of all British merchandise and colonial products from the ports of France and her allies. He occupied the free cities of Bremen and Hamburg and the coast of Hanover. He marched troops into three of the principal Neapolitan ports. He coerced Holland, Spain, and Portugal into closing, nominally at least, their ports to British goods. These measures gave him apparent control of the whole coast of Europe from the Elbe River to the heel of Italy.

At the same time, the First Consul made it appear that he was planning a descent on Great Britain although the English Channel and the British fleet were in his path. For this avowed purpose, he gathered along the coast from the Elbe River to the port of Brest 100,000 men and a great fleet of barges and small vessels. A few days of fog or calm might make possible a crossing of the channel. At any rate, the presence of French troops on the coast kept Great Britain in a constant state of alarm and put a great strain on her resources.

The British took such defensive measures as they could. They strengthened the defences of the British Isles. They blockaded the coast of the continent. They seized a Spanish treasure fleet, an act which drove Spain into the war on the side of France. Neither France nor Great Britain, however, was able to bring the conflict to a decision.

The War of the Third Coalition

For two years this continued to be the situation. By 1805, however, the aggressive policies of France in Germany, the Swiss cantons, and Italy had produced a continental war. The powers of Europe, as well as Great Britain, had become increasingly alarmed at the exten-

546

sion of French influence. Austria disliked Napoleon's assumption of the Imperial dignity and the encroachment of France in Italy. Russia feared the French emperor's designs against the Turkish Empire and his occupation of territories beyond the Alps and the Rhine. Prussia disliked the French occupation of Bremen, Hamburg, and Hanover. Great Britain found that peace did not bring a reopening of its old markets. The powers gradually came to the conclusion that the French emperor must be pushed back toward the limits of France, either by diplomacy or force.

Out of this situation gradually developed a third coalition of the powers against Napoleon Bonaparte. As early as November, 1804, Austria and Russia signed a defensive alliance. Upon Napoleon's refusal to heed the tsar's request for an evacuation by the French of all territories beyond the Alps and the Rhine, Russia proposed that Russia and Great Britain should cooperate in freeing the conquered provinces from French rule and France from the yoke of Napoleon and that the two powers should promote a league of European states which would guarantee to all states the right of self-government. This proposal coincided with the more practical plans of Great Britain. In April, 1805, accordingly, the two powers concluded an alliance. Austria was easily persuaded to endorse this pact. Only Prussia held back and tried to maintain a neutral position. According to the terms of the various agreements, Great Britain was to assist Austria and Russia with large subsidies.

In the meantime, Napoleon gave every appearance of being intent on his project for a direct attack on Great Britain. He needed command of the English Channel only for a few days. His plan, apparently, was to delude the British naval authorities into dispersing their fleet which was concentrated in the English Channel. That would enable the units of the French and Spanish fleets, scattered along the Atlantic coast, to unite, to outwit the British seamen, and to appear in the English Channel at the proper time.

The plan ended in a great naval disaster. Admiral Villeneuve did manage to escape from the harbor of Toulon, to unite with a Spanish squadron at Cadiz, and to sail for the West Indies. When Nelson, the famous British admiral, followed him, Villeneuve returned to Europe. Thereupon, Nelson, too, returned and warned the British authorities by a swift dispatch boat of the new developments. Using his discretionary powers, Villeneuve first attempted to proceed toward the region of the proposed attack on Great Britain and then, baffled by strong head winds, turned toward Cadiz.

Even if he had carried out his original intention, Villeneuve would not have found the army of Napoleon. Having learned of the steps taken against him, the French emperor undoubtedly welcomed the opportunity to abandon the unworkable plan for an attack on Great Britain and to launch an attack on Austria. In carrying out his attack, the French emperor was greatly aided by the folly of General Mack, the Austrian commander. According to the Austrian plan, the main Austrian attack was to take place in Italy while General Mack saved the resources of southern Germany for the allies and waited for the oncoming Russians. Instead of carrying out this plan, General Mack recklessly advanced to Ulm on the Danube. There, before he realized what was happening, he was surrounded by French troops. With astonishing rapidity, they had withdrawn from stations along the Atlantic coast and closed like the fingers of a great hand on the Austrian army. As a result, on October 20, 1805, Mack and most of his army surrendered to the French. This left the road open to Vienna.

This great French victory on land was followed the next day by a crushing defeat at sea in the battle of Trafalgar. At Cadiz, Villeneuve, goaded by the reproaches of Napoleon and lured by the British from his place of refuge, again ventured out to sea. On October 21, 1805, the two fleets met each other. The French were drawn up in a long line which was pierced by the British, who were arranged in two columns. After some fighting, the French and Spanish began to surrender. During the struggle, Nelson was mortally wounded by a French sharpshooter. The naval battle ended in the complete defeat of the French and Spanish and gave Great Britain an almost uncontested command of the sea.

From Ulm, the French emperor marched into Vienna and on to Moravia. There, he found himself in a precarious position. His long line of communication could be easily threatened by Prussia; and it seemed highly probable that Prussia, angered at violation of Prussian territory by French troops advancing on Ulm, would intervene. Napoleon was saved by the rashness of Tsar Alexander and the hesitancy of Prussia to take decisive action. Instead of waiting for a second Russian army to arrive in Moravia, the Tsar decided to attack the French with his first army and the remnants of the Austrian forces. As a result of this resolve, the decisive battle of Austerlitz was fought (December 2, 1805). It was a great victory for Napoleon and his army. It was due in large measure to the skillful planning of the French emperor. The French were drawn up along a line seven miles in length. Napoleon left his right wing isolated and exposed and encouraged the allies to weaken their center in an effort to outflank the French. This enabled Napoleon to pierce the Russian center and then to destroy the opposing troops on the two wings. Napoleon himself always counted the battle of Austerlitz as one of his greatest victories.

This battle had important consequences. The Russian army withdrew from Austrian territory. Hesitant Prussia found that it had waited too long. Relieved from his anxiety about his communications, the French emperor forced Prussia to abandon all idea of an attack on the French and to sign instead a treaty of alliance with France. By its terms Prussia gained Hanover, which it had long coveted, but gave up the three important territories of Neuchatel, Ansbach, and Cleves, and agreed to close the ports of northern Germany to British trade. By a treaty signed at Pressburg, (December 26, 1805) Austria lost much territory. She surrendered to France all the Venetian territory which she had acquired by the treaties of Campoformio and Lunéville and gave up other territories in southern Germany to the three South German states of Bavaria, Württemberg, and Baden. Napoleon handed over most of the former Venetian territory to the kingdom of Italy, the former Italian Republic. He gave the rulers of the three South German states higher titles and freed them from their allegiance to the Holy Roman Empire. By a simple army order, Napoleon deposed the rulers of Naples and occupied the Neapolitan kingdom with his own troops.

These additions to what he called the "Grand Empire" enabled Napoleon to provide well for the members of his large and grasping family. He made his brother Joseph king of Naples. He created Italian principalities for two of his sisters. He appointed his brother Louis, who had reluctantly married the emperor's step-daughter, Hortense Beauharnais, king of Holland. He assumed the title of King of the Italian Kingdom and made his step-son, Eugene, viceroy of his Italian state. He created his dashing brother-in-law, Murat, Duke of Berg, a Rhenish principality formed out of former Prussian territory. He found, however, that even his relatives were difficult to manage.

The victory of Austerlitz made it possible, too, for Napoleon to reorganize Germany. Ever since the days of Henry II, it had been the policy of French rulers to control a greater or smaller number of the German states. Napoleon now carried out this policy to its logical conclusion. After considerable negotiation, he finally (July 17, 1806), organized sixteen of the remaining German states into what he called the Confederation of the Rhine. He gave them the alternative of joining the new confederation or taking the risk of being absorbed by some more fortunate state or at least losing all hope of further territorial gains. In most instances, states like Bavaria, Württemberg, and Baden, that joined the new Confederation, received substantial increases in territory. On the other hand, some sixty-seven petty German states disappeared. As the sixteen states which joined the new confederation withdrew from the old Holy Roman Empire, the organization of the new Confederation of the Rhine gave that ancient institution its death blow. There was nothing left for the Holy Roman Emperor to do but to renounce his titles. Henceforth, he was simply the emperor of Austria, a title which he had assumed two years earlier.

Napoleon's treatment of Prussia was not calculated to make that state a dependable ally. The most that she had to show for her policy of neutrality was the acquisition of Hanover. When she learned through a British diplomat that the French emperor had offered this hard-won territory to Great Britain in the hope of persuading that country to make peace, the resentment of Prussia flared openly and the Prussian king mobilized his army. Even yet, however, Napoleon refused to take the situation seriously. To him, it seemed unlikely that Prussia would venture to wage war against France. He did not know that about the same time that Prussia openly signed a treaty of alliance with France, it signed a secret agreement with Russia. As a result, Prussia counted on Russian help in the approaching struggle.

In September, 1806, the king of Prussia, Frederick William III, sent an ultimatum to Napoleon demanding the withdrawal of French troops across the Rhine and approval of the idea of the organization of a North German confederation. The ultimatum found the French already moving toward Berlin. Having the resources and the recruits from France, Italy, and the Confederation of the Rhine, the French emperor planned with his superior forces to threaten the communications of the Prussians moving toward the Rhine. In three great columns, the French reached the plains of Saxony and sought contact with the Prussians.

The Prussians offered a striking contrast to the French and their allies. The king of Prussia felt that it was his duty to be near his troops. This hampered the Duke of Brunswick, his commander-in-chief, who naturally deferred military decisions to his sovereign. One of the Prussian generals insisted on acting independently. Instead of acting decisively, the Prussians debated indefinitely. They changed their plans a number of times and wore out their soldiers in useless marches. On October 14, 1806, the French finally came into contact with the Prussians at Jena and Auerstadt, two towns about twelve miles distant from each other. At both points, the Prussians were decisively defeated.

The defeat of the Prussians at Jena and Auerstadt was followed by a complete collapse of the Prussian state. The defeated army retreated in great disorder closely followed by the victorious French and their allies. Berlin was occupied by the French without a struggle. Fortress after fortress fell with scarcely a blow being struck in self-defence. The Prussian court took refuge in Memel, beyond the Vistula, at the extreme eastern limit of the Prussian kingdom. Prussia seemed on the verge of complete disintegration. A crowning humiliation was the French seizure and removal to Paris of the sword and insignia of Frederick the Great from his tomb in Potsdam.

The Campaign of 1807

The approach of the French roused in the Poles the hope that Napoleon would undo the partitioning of Poland and restore their independence to the Polish people. Accordingly, the Poles sent a delegation to the conqueror of Prussia. Napoleon, however, was extremely cautious. In reply, he only stated that the Poles must show themselves worthy of independence. By that, he meant they must come to his assistance with men and supplies in the approaching campaign against Russia. He knew that his lines of communication were nearly as long as in 1805 and that his action in Poland might stir Austria to another war. In addition, he was still at war with Russia.

In the months that followed, Napoleon found that waging war in Poland was very different from campaigning in central Europe. In November, the French did occupy Warsaw, but the roads seemed bottomless and the desolate plains offered little in the way of supplies. The troops of Napoleon suffered from cold, hunger, and disease and grumbled at being employed in schemes of conquest that had no real relation to the interests of France. In February, 1807, the French suffered a serious check at Eylau near Konigsberg, but in June, 1807, after reorganizing and strengthening his army, Napoleon did win a crushing victory at Friedland, in East Prussia.

The Treaty of Tilsit

The victory at Friedland was followed by a startling diplomatic revolution. Thwarted in his efforts to liberate Europe from French domination by the failure of Austria and Great Britain to support him energetically and by the defeat of Prussia, the tsar gave a willing ear to the surprising proposals of Napoleon. The negotiations between Napoleon and the Russian tsar were conducted dramatically on a raft moored in the middle of the Niemen River near Tilsit. As the two men met alone, no one knows exactly the course of the conversations. It is certain, however, that instead of demanding concessions, the French emperor astonished the tsar by seeming to offer him many advantages and a share in the control of Europe. The offer tempted the tsar and turned him into an ally.

One of the most important questions decided by the two men was the fate of Poland. The tsar refused the crown of a restored Poland for himself but opposed the idea of placing it on the head of Napoleon's youngest brother, Jerome. The two rulers finally reached a compromise. They agreed to the creation of a smaller state, the duchy of Warsaw, which was composed mainly of territory acquired by Prussia in the Polish partitions of 1793 and 1795. The new state was to be under the nominal rule of the king of Saxony and was to join the Confederation of the Rhine.

The two sovereigns were more indefinite about the Balkans. The tsar really wanted Constantinople, but the French emperor had no intention of letting him have it. They agreed instead that France should mediate between Russia and Turkey. In case mediation failed, the Turks were to be deprived of all their European provinces except Constantinople and Rumelia. The two negotiators did not reach a definite agreement as to what territory should go to Russia. After the conclusion of the Treaty of Tilsit, Napoleon showed an unwillingness to come to more definite terms.

Out of deference to Tsar Alexander, Prussia was saved from complete ruin. Although the king of Prussia was forced to submit to the humiliation of having no part in the negotiations, Napoleon promised to restore to him most of his provinces east of the Elbe River upon payment of an unspecified indemnity. After the treaty between Napoleon and the tsar was signed (July 7, 1807), a treaty embodying these provisions was concluded by the French emperor and the king of Prussia. A personal plea of Queen Louise of Prussia to Napoleon failed to persuade him to soften the terms of the treaty.

Alexander recognized all the new states created by Napoleon. These included the new state of Westphalia, composed of lands that formerly belonged to Hesse-Cassel, Brunswick, Hanover, and Prussia. The French emperor appointed Jerome, his youngest brother, ruler of the new state.

The Continental System

In some ways, the most important clauses of the Treaty of Tilsit were those dealing with commerce. As far back as 1793, the French authorities had tried to injure British trade by excluding British merchandise from the continent and arresting all British subjects found on French soil. As French power spread, the ban on the purchase of British goods was extended. The French sought by these

552

measures to destroy the trade of Great Britain and thereby to weaken its navy, prevent the payment of subsidies to continental powers, and stop plots against the French government. This policy, if successful, would enable the French to replace the British in their former markets.

In 1806 the conquest of Prussia enabled Napoleon to apply his policy on a grander scale. From Berlin as a dramatic setting, he now promulgated his so-called Berlin decree which set in motion the Continental system. By its terms the British Isles were declared to be in a state of blockade. All trade or correspondence with them was forbidden. If it had been carried out, the decree would have destroyed all British trade.

In the following year, the Treaty of Tilsit enabled Napoleon to make an attempt to extend his commercial system to the whole continent. Prussia was forced to apply the system. The tsar agreed to help Napoleon impose it on such states as Portugal, Denmark, and Sweden. If they refused to cooperate, they were to be treated as enemies. The Continental system seemed on the verge of completion.

The effort to impose the Continental system on some of the minor states of Europe had important consequences. In Denmark the British tried to forestall French action. They sent an agent to Copenhagen with an offer of alliance and a request that the Danish fleet be surrendered to the British as a pledge. When the demand was refused, the British sent a large naval force to Danish waters. They supposed the Danes would see the uselessness of resistance. On the contrary, the Danes felt compelled to resist. The British, therefore, bombarded Copenhagen for three days and forced the Danes to surrender their fleet. This action drove the Danes into an alliance with Napoleon and caused neutrals to overlook the highhanded methods of the French emperor.

In order to impose the Continental system on Portugal, Napoleon needed the cooperation of Spain. He gained it by taking advantage of the scandalous situation existing in the royal family. Through appealing to the cupidity of Godoy, the chief Spanish minister and royal favorite, and threatening to reveal to the king, Charles IV, the disgraceful relations of his queen and his minister, Napoleon succeeded in gaining permission to send troops through Spain into Portugal. He held out the hope that the Portuguese state was to be divided into three parts: one to be assigned to Godoy, another to the king of Etruria, and a third to Napoleon. In accordance with the treaty signed October 27, 1807, a French army reached Lisbon in November but found that the court, the treasure, and the archives of Portugal had sailed for Brazil under the protection of a British fleet.

Sweden, too, refused to accede to the demand of Napoleon. In accordance with the agreement made at Tilsit, therefore, the tsar invaded the Swedish province of Finland and drove out the troops of Sweden. In order to avert a rising on the part of the Finns, the tsar made important concessions to them. He allowed the province to retain its identity as a grand duchy. He assumed the title of grand duke and conceded his new subjects a constitution which gave them a considerable amount of self government.

The Berlin decree was only the first of a series of measures taken by the French and British governments in an effort to destroy the other's trade. Great Britain replied to the Berlin decree by two orders in council. An order of January, 1807, forbade all trade between ports which excluded British ships.

In November of the same year, another order in council declared a blockade against all ports which barred British ships and made trade in the products of such countries unlawful. Neutral vessels wishing to trade with the continent were to stop at a British port and to pay certain specified duties. In the same year, Napoleon replied to these orders in council by the Milan decree, which declared any neutral ship that complied with the British orders in council to be a lawful prize of war.

The measures announced by France and Great Britain put the ships of neutral powers in an almost impossible position. At first, they had reaped a rich harvest by taking the place of French and British ships. Later, they found it impossible to obey both France and Great Britain. Compliance with the orders of one power meant the infraction of the rules of the other. This made the neutral ships liable to seizure by either one or both of the powers.

By 1806, as a result of the extension of French influence, the United States was the principal neutral. Both France and Great Britain were determined to enforce their restrictions, and the United States was not strong enough to win respect for its rights as a neutral. The French confiscated American ships. The British searched American vessels on the high seas, practically blockaded the American coast, and impressed American seamen on the pretext that they were fugitives from the British navy. In an effort to procure better treatment, the United States first enacted a nonimportation act and later declared war against Great Britain.

On the continent, meanwhile, Napoleon was having difficulty in enforcing the Continental system. In theory, the system gave French producers a monopoly of the continental market, but, in practice, it led to widespread smuggling. As a result of the Industrial Revolution, British manufactured goods were cheap in comparison with

554

French goods which were still produced by antiquated methods. The general public on the continent, too, was eager for such colonial products as coffee and sugar. So there was a prospect of large profits for the successful smugglers. Such islands as Helgoland, Jersey, Sardinia, Sicily, and Malta became centers for their activities. All sorts of methods were employed to get the merchandise past the French custom officials. Many of the French officials were open to bribery by the determined smugglers. The states conquered by Napoleon enforced his system only as rigorously as they were compelled to do so. Then, too, it was possible for Prussian, Russian, and Swedish vessels to obtain British licences to trade. So the Continental system was never completely enforced.

One remedy for this situation, employed by Napoleon, was the annexation of coastal territories. In 1808 the emperor occupied both Rome and Spain. Two years later, he annexed the whole coast along the North Sea from southern Holland to the port of Lübeck. In 1806 he had tried to accomplish the same purpose by making his younger brother Louis the king of Holland. The new king of Holland had found himself caught in the conflict between the orders of Napoleon with regard to the Continental system and the desire of the Dutch people to continue their commerce, and he had finally abdicated from the Dutch throne. Thereupon, Napoleon annexed the whole coast of the North Sea. This series of annexations gave him nominal control of the coast of Europe from the Baltic to the Adriatic Sea.

The National Uprising in Spain

For some time, Napoleon had been dissatisfied with the situation in Spain. The Spanish authorities showed no eagerness to enforce the Continental system. Before the battle of Jena, Godoy persuaded his sovereign to issue a call to arms, an action that showed very plainly the desire of Spain to free herself from the burdensome alliance with France. The Spanish minister maintained after the Prussian defeat that he had mobilized Spanish forces only against Portugal; but Napoleon knew quite well from dispatches found by his agents at Berlin that this was not true. For the time being, Napoleon merely demanded the services of 1,500 Spanish troops at the mouth of the Elbe River, the cooperation of the Spanish fleet, and a real application of the Continental system.

After the conclusion of the agreement with Russia at Tilsit, the French emperor felt that he was in a position to take more vigorous action against Spain. Before his forces reached Portugal, he sent a reserve army into Spain without notice or Spanish permission. He explained his highhanded action as an attempt to conquer Gibraltar.

As Murat, the French commander, approached Madrid, a Spanish mob, enraged at the subservient policy toward France, frightened the weak and deluded sovereign of Spain, Charles IV, into abdicating in favor of his son, Prince Ferdinand.

Upon his arrival at Madrid, however, Murat refused to recognize Ferdinand as king of Spain. On the contrary, he persuaded the Spanish royal family and Godoy to meet Napoleon on French soil at Bayonne. Charles IV promptly placed all his rights in the hands of Napoleon as the only one capable of restoring order. Finally Ferdinand, who had no desire to be a martyr, was intimidated into renouncing the Spanish throne. The Spanish royal family and Godoy thereupon became pensioners of Napoleon.

This action left the Spanish throne vacant. The humiliation of the Spanish people, however, was not yet at an end. The French authorities intimidated some ninety-one Spanish notables into taking the road to Bayonne. Upon their arrival, they requested Napoleon to place his oldest brother, Joseph, king of Naples, on the Spanish throne. Napoleon then formally ceded his rights over Spain to his brother and appointed his brother-in-law, Murat, to the vacant Neapolitan throne.

The French emperor, however, had failed to take into consideration the proud Spanish people. They bitterly resented the humiliating intervention of the French in their domestic affairs. They looked upon Napoleon as nothing more than an atheist because of his treatment of the Pope and matters of religion. For these reasons, long before Joseph reached his new kingdom, the Spanish people spontaneously rose in revolt all over Spain. The movement began on May 2, 1808, a date since celebrated in Spain as the national holiday, and soon spread to all parts of the country. At first, the revolt was directed by local committees. Later, a central committee was established which gave the uprising a semblance of unity.

At first, Napoleon made the mistake of underestimating the strength of the revolt. He wished to keep the bulk of his seasoned troops in Germany where they would be maintained by the Germans and would exercise an important influence on affairs in Northern Europe. So in order to quell the revolt in Spain, he sent mainly raw conscripts, many of them raised in Italy, the Swiss cantons, and Germany. The mistake caused the expedition to end in disaster. A force of 20,000 men marching toward Seville, commanded by General Dupont, was surrounded and forced to surrender. Later, a French army was repulsed at Saragossa. For the first time, the rule of Napoleon was being seriously challenged.

The British promptly realized Napoleon's blunder and prepared to profit by it. In an effort to gain control of the Iberian Peninsula, they debarked in Portugal an army commanded by Sir Arthur Wellesley. This British force repulsed the French army in Portugal and, if superior officers had not intervened, might have compelled it to surrender. As it was, the French agreed in the convention of Cintra (1808) to return to France in British ships. Within a short time, King Joseph had been forced to abandon Madrid, and the French had lost all of Spain south of the Ebro River.

The misfortunes of the French in Spain enhanced the importance of Russia. Napoleon needed the cooperation of the tsar more than ever to enforce the Continental system and to hold Austria and Germany in check. Otherwise, he would not dare to withdraw troops from Central Europe to put down the revolt in Spain. It became necessary for the French emperor to have an interview with Tsar Alexander and assure himself of the Russian ruler's support. The tsar, for his part, realized the situation but thought the time had not yet come to break with Napoleon. Accordingly, Alexander agreed to meet his ally at Erfurt in central Germany.

The two world figures met in September, 1808, for two weeks. Everything possible was done to make the meeting a dramatic occasion and to impress the tsar with the power of his French ally. The kings and princes of Europe formed the court of the French emperor. The members of the *Comedie Française* played the classical pieces of the French stage for their amusement. Interspersed through the festivities, however, were serious interviews between the two emperors. Both men made concessions. It was finally agreed that the Russians were to have Finland and the Danubian principalities and that the French reorganization of Spain should be recognized. In case Austria should attack France, Russia was to come to the aid of the French.

From Erfurt, Napoleon hurried south to lead an army of veterans into Spain. The Spanish volunteers, inferior in numbers and training, were no match for the seasoned troops of France, and their principal armies were defeated. By December, 1808, Napoleon was in Madrid. From the Spanish capital he issued a series of revolutionary decrees. In them, he decreed the abolition of the Inquisition and the remains of feudalism, removed provincial customs lines, and reduced the number of monasteries by two-thirds. Without waiting for the decree to be actually applied, Napoleon then set out to attack the British commander, Sir John Moore. Upon the retreat of the British toward Corunna, the French emperor handed over the pursuit to Marshal Soult and returned to Paris.

Spain, however, was far from being subdued. While unsuccessful in the open field, the Spaniards made admirable guerilla warriors and constantly harrassed the French armies. Meanwhile, the British forces had become strong enough to offer serious resistance in both Spain and Portugal. In the meantime, Napoleon was hampered by the necessity of devoting most of his attention during 1809 to the campaign against Austria. So it was not until 1810 that the French were able to take Andalusia and drive the Spaniards back on that province. In Portugal, the British, again under the command of Wellesley with the new title of Viscount Wellington, constructed from the Tagus River to the sea a remarkable defense line, "the lines of Torres Vedras," that the French found impregnable. Finally, in 1811, after being repulsed and almost starved to death, the French abandoned Portugal entirely.

The War of 1809

The Spanish uprising was bound to affect public opinion in other countries. The people of Spain had shown that successful resistance to Napoleon was possible. Other peoples could not be expected to accept much longer the humiliating rule of Napoleon. Sooner or later, they would be likely to take advantage of his difficulties in Spain to rise against him.

Nowhere had events in Spain been watched with more interest than in Austria. Before the rise of Napoleon, Austria had been one of the great states of Europe. After he came to power, she had been repeatedly humiliated. In 1805 she had been shorn of important provinces, and a year later she had been forced to renounce her position of primacy in Germany. In 1807 she had been ignored at Tilsit, and in the following year she had been compelled to join in the enforcement of the Continental system. By 1809 Austrian leaders even feared that Austria might be entirely destroyed.

The situation caused the leaders of Austria to advocate a renewal of war. They counted on the resistance of the Spaniards and the presence of the British in Portugal to prevent Napoleon from employing all the forces at his disposal against Austria. They hoped Prussia, too, would rise against French rule. They believed that financial aid could be obtained from Great Britain. They even hoped that misunderstandings would arise between Napoleon and Tsar Alexander. These features of the situation made them inclined to risk a renewal of war.

In 1809, the cautious preparations of Austria finally led to an armed conflict. The struggle began with an Austrian invasion of Bavaria. After some preliminary successes, the Austrian forces were defeated and driven back into the Bohemian Mountains, and the French and their allies pressed on toward Vienna. When they tried to cross to the northern bank of the Danube, however, their efforts to establish a bridgehead failed at first, and it took them six weeks to force their way across the river. Once across, the French won a great victory at Wagram not far from Vienna, an event which practically ended the war.

A striking incident of the campaign was a rising of the peasants in the former Austrian province of Tyrol. In 1805, their province had been ceded to Bavaria, but its inhabitants remained loyal to their old dynasty and objected to the political and religious reforms introduced into their province. Encouraged to rise by Austrian agents, and aided by their mountain fastnesses, they defeated several Bavarian and French armies sent against them. In the end, they were subdued by the superior forces of their opponents. The chief result of the rising was the division of Tyrol in 1810 between the kingdom of Bavaria and the kingdom of Italy.

After waiting some weeks in vain for the British or the Prussians to intervene, the Austrian emperor signed the disastrous treaty of Schönbrunn. The terms of the peace were very severe. Besides paying a large indemnity, the Austrian authorities were compelled to cede most of Galicia to the duchy of Warsaw, a small portion of East Galicia to Russia, another western district to Bavaria, and provinces and parts of provinces in the south to the French emperor. They also agreed to reduce the Austrian army to 150,000 men. Austria ceased for the time being to be a great power and felt that her very existence was threatened.

Napoleon at the Height of his Power

Napoleon was now at the height of his power and seemed able to do whatever he pleased. He made numerous temporary changes in the map of Europe and in the organization of states. In reality, his position was precarious. He never completely conquered Spain nor was he ever able to carry out fully his Continental system. He never had the wholehearted cooperation of Russia, and his arbitrary rule steadily increased the hostility of the peoples under his rule. Any shock might destroy his empire.

One of the questions that perplexed both him and those who had risen to power with him was the problem of the succession. His wife, Josephine, had borne him no children. As matters stood, some member of his grasping family would succeed him. He naturally wanted to hand his power over to a direct heir. The solution of the problem seemed to be a divorce from Josephine and a marriage with a European princess. Finally, he opened negotiations with both Russia and Austria in the hope of obtaining the hand of a princess.

In 1810, the negotiations led to the divorce of Josephine and a marriage with an Austrian archduchess, Marie Louise, daughter of the Austrian emperor. Questions of age, religion, and personal differences prevented a marriage with one of the sisters of the tsar, while Metternich, who had recently come to power in Austria, saw advantages for his master in a marriage alliance of the French emperor with a daughter of the Austrian emperor. So finally a marriage was arranged. In 1811, the marriage resulted in the birth of the hoped for heir to the French throne.

From the lands along the eastern coast of the Adriatic Sea, which had been taken from Venice and Austria, Napoleon created in 1809 what he called the Illyrian Provinces. They were composed of Dalmatia, Carniola, Croatia, and a part of Carinthia. During the four short years of their existence, they shared all the advantages and disadvantages of French rule. On the one hand, they benefited from the just administration, the introduction of the Napoleonic Code, and the construction of public works. On the other, they suffered from the enforcement of the Continental system, heavy taxation, and conscription. After the downfall of Napoleon, however, the coming of the French into the Illyrian Provinces was generally regarded as the starting point of the national movement among the Yugoslavs.

The Treaty of Tilsit had a strange effect on Sweden. Tsar Alexander, it will be remembered, agreed in that document to compel Sweden to comply with the Continental system. When Sweden refused, he forced the Swedes to join the powers opposed to Great Britain and to surrender Finland. This turn of affairs led in 1809 to an insurrection and the deposition of the Swedish sovereign. As his successor had no direct heir, the Swedes, uninformed as to his relations with Napoleon, proposed to make Bernadotte, one of the latter's marshals, crown prince of Sweden and heir to the Swedish throne because he had created a favorable impression by his conduct of affairs in northern Germany. Quite reluctantly, Napoleon finally consented to Bernadotte becoming Prince Royal of Sweden.

The harmony supposedly created by the adoption of the Concordat did not last. Immediately after its adoption, Napoleon had in a sense modified it to the detriment of the Church by the publication of what he called the Organic Articles. As his power increased, it became obvious that Napoleon looked upon the Pope as an ally and a subordinate. He pretended, at least, not to see the obligation of the Pope to remain neutral. At the time of his coronation, he had pub-

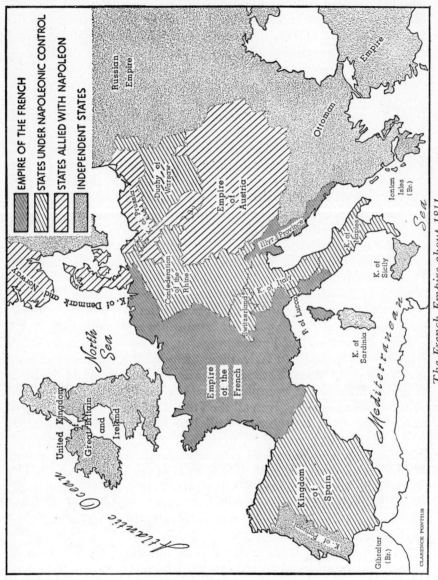

The French Empire about 1811

CLARENCE PONTIUS

Legend:
- EMPIRE OF THE FRENCH
- STATES UNDER NAPOLEONIC CONTROL
- STATES ALLIED WITH NAPOLEON
- INDEPENDENT STATES

Russian Empire

Ottoman Empire

Duchy of Warsaw

Empire of Austria

Prussia

Confederation of the Rhine

K. of Denmark and Norway

Illyr. Provinces

Ionian Isles (Br.)

K. of Naples

K. of Sicily

Switzerland

K. of Italy

P. of Lucca

Mediterranean Sea

North Sea

United Kingdom of Great Britain and Ireland

Empire of the French

K. of Sardinia

Atlantic Ocean

Kingdom of Spain

K. of Portugal

Gibraltar (Br.)

licly humiliated the Pope by placing the crown on his own head. In Italy, he had introduced his civil code which modified the Concordat adopted for the Cisalpine Republic. In 1808 Napoleon took the step of occupying Rome and annexing some of the papal territory to the kingdom of Italy. During the campaign of 1809, he formally annexed Rome and the remaining territory of the Pope. When the Pope in self-defense excommunicated all who had a hand in the proceedings, Napoleon had the Pope arrested and imprisoned. This action did not solve the problem. For the remainder of his reign, Napoleon found himself hampered and embarrassed by the consequences of his high-handed action.

By 1810 French influence was at its height. From Gibraltar to the Vistula and from the English Channel to beyond the Adriatic Sea, Napoleon was seemingly supreme and imposed on the newly con-quered regions French institutions to a greater or less extent.

Under his rule, it must be remembered, the boundaries of France proper were greatly extended. At its greatest extent it included not only the territory within the so-called natural boundaries of France (the Ocean, the Rhine, the Alps, the Mediterranean Sea, and the Pyrenees) but about a third of Italy and Holland and the German coast as far north as Lübeck. For the time being, Rome, Cologne, Amsterdam, and Hamburg were French cities. Within these limits were imposed all the Napoleonic institutions and conditions.

Beyond the limits of France proper was a circle of puppet states created by Napoleon. In Italy, these included the kingdoms of Italy and Naples; in Central Europe, the Swiss cantons, the grand duchy of Berg, the kingdom of Westphalia, and the duchy of Warsaw. In the main, these states were given all the French reforms. With the excep-tion of the Swiss cantons, they all had monarchical governments which were entirely responsive to the will of Napoleon. In ecclesiasti-cal affairs, French rule meant religious toleration, the secularization of Church property, and the modification of the relations of Church and state in favor of the state. Serfdom as well as the seigniorial sys-tem was abolished. The Napoleonic Code was introduced. Interior customs lines were suppressed. For good or ill these territories were modernized.

In the remaining lands under French influence, the adoption of French institutions and conditions varied widely. All the rulers of the different German states were quite responsive to the will of Na-poleon. Some of them, like the king of Bavaria, introduced sweeping reforms that modernized the political machinery, changed the rela-tions of Church and state, introduced religious toleration, secularized Church property, and wiped out monasticism, abolished serfdom, and swept away long-established social customs. Others, like the rulers of the two Mecklenburgs and the Thuringian duchies, clung tenaciously to the inheritance from the past. Nevertheless, in Germany, many states and the Imperial knights disappeared; many central governments were modernized and the feudal estates were abolished; in some places, serfdom was done away with; many monastic institutions were suppressed and much Church property was secularized; many tolls and customs lines were swept away; the Napoleonic Code was widely introduced; and local government was in many cases made more modern. The Napoleonic period thus made an important contribution to the unification of Germany.

Developments in Spain

Meanwhile, important developments had been taking place in Spain. As we have seen, the leaders of the Spanish Revolt, organized into a central committee, finally took refuge in Cadiz. Early in 1810, they took the step of summoning a Cortes to represent Spain and its American colonies. It was to be made up of representatives of the towns, provincial committees, and the American colonies. In practice, districts and colonies, because of geography or the military situation, were represented by persons who happened to be in Cadiz. As a result, the Cortes which finally assembled was far more liberal in tone than the public it supposedly represented.

Upon convening, the Cortes established a regency, declared all acts of Prince Ferdinand invalid during his captivity, and assumed for itself the double role of legislative body and constitutional assembly. It then proceeded to draw up the Constitution of 1812, which drastically reorganized the state. This document greatly reduced the power of the king and vested sovereignty in the Spanish people. The latter were defined so as to include the population of the Spanish colonies. Complicated machinery was designed for the election of members of the Cortes. The Catholic faith was declared to be the religion of Spain, but the Inquisition was abolished and monastic bodies were reduced in numbers. The Cortes thus tried to give Spain the political reforms that it had refused to accept from the hands of Napoleon.

These events in Spain had an important effect on the Spanish colonies in America. Although they had many causes of complaint against the Spanish government, they had refused to recognize Joseph Bonaparte as their sovereign after the seizure of Spain by Napoleon and professed their loyalty to the fallen regime. This made them practically independent. For the first time, they openly traded with the outside world, particularly with Great Britain.

The Reorganization of Prussia

Meanwhile, Prussia had been attempting to solve the many problems left unsolved by the Treaty of Tilsit. The Prussian state had been deprived of half of its territory. The remaining provinces were occupied by French troops. The French demanded as an indemnity a sum larger than the annual Prussian revenue. Other sums were extracted from the hapless Prussian people for the support of the French army, for the benefit of Napoleon, and for French officials. Defeat had made necessary a change of councillors. The future of the state depended on the protection of Russia. The existence of the state was at stake.

In the emergency, upon the advice of Hardenberg, his retiring chief minister, and against his own prejudices, the king summoned to power Baron Stein, who had long been urging upon his sovereign the need of reform. As early as October, 1807, the new minister took the responsibility of issuing an edict which revolutionized Prussian society. It removed restrictions on the holding of land and upon the choice of occupation. It laid down the principle that, henceforth, peasant, townsman, or noble might acquire, without authorization, any land that he wished to acquire or engage in any occupation which attracted him. It permitted the noble to go into business and the townsman to invest in agricultural land. The edict also abolished serfdom but did not free the peasant from such seigniorial dues as work, products, or money. In other words, the edict left the Prussian peasant in about the position occupied by the French peasant before the French Revolution.

In November, 1808, Stein caused an edict to be issued which restored the right of self-government to Prussian towns. The towns were divided into three classes according to the size of their population, and the inhabitants of the towns were classified as citizens and residents. Citizens included those who possessed a house in a town or paid taxes of a certain amount. Citizens could not instruct their representatives how to vote. The central government retained control of police matters. In a sense, the burgomasters, the chief officials, were selected by the state. Stein hoped by the measure to train a body of citizens capable of conducting public affairs. Limited as were the provisions for self-government, the measure provided the only democratic political machinery Prussia was to have for forty years.

Stein likewise initiated significant changes in the army. The first task was the punishment of those responsible for the debacle during the campaign of 1806. All but eight of 143 generals on the roster in that year were dismissed from the service. The next task was the adoption of the lessons learned during the French Revolution. Armies could no longer be recruited from the vagabonds of Europe. The peasants could no longer be subjected to cruel and humiliating punishments. Under the leadership of Scharnhorst and Gneisenau, a new military system was introduced. The practice of hiring mercenaries was abandoned. Citizens were given some chance to become officers. Methods for supplying the army were changed. A system was devised for evading the restrictions on the number of soldiers that might be retained. In a few years these reform measures gave Prussia an efficient military force.

As a result of an indiscreet letter, written by Stein, which fell into the hands of Napoleon, that minister was soon forced to resign. In 1810, his place was taken by Hardenberg. Upon assuming office, this minister took up the problem of seigniorial dues. He proposed that peasants with a life tenure should become proprietors of their lands and that a system should be worked out by which the loser by the transaction should be indemnified. The project was materially changed by the assembly of notables who discussed it, and the renewal of the war prevented the application of the measure. So the status of the peasants was not actually very much improved.

The Downfall of Napoleon

Meanwhile, forces were at work which tended to terminate the alliance of the tsar and Napoleon. Russia found the application of the Continental system according to the agreement reached at Tilsit very injurious to her real interests. War with Great Britain interfered seriously with the usual Russian export trade in such raw materials as wheat, timber, and shipping supplies. In 1810, consequently, as a measure of self-protection, Russia adopted a new tariff that either prohibited importation entirely or levied a high duty on such typical French products as wines, brandies, and silks. Besides the economic differences between the two countries, there were other causes of conflict. The annexation of the North Sea coast involved Oldenburg, a petty German principality ruled by a relative of the tsar. The moves of Napoleon in Poland caused Alexander to fear a restoration of a Polish kingdom. The tsar likewise resented the secret efforts of French agents to prolong the war in progress between Russia and Turkey. As a result, the two powers steadily drifted apart, and each began to make preparations which were almost sure to end in an armed struggle.

By 1812 the two powers were ready for war. For the approaching conflict, Napoleon had collected along the banks of the Niemen River a force of nearly a half million men. Only about half his troops were

Frenchmen. The rest, furnished by the states Napoleon had made dependent on his will, consisted of German, Italian, Dutch, and Polish conscripts and volunteers. Even Prussia and Austria were forced to send contingents to the motley army gathered by Napoleon.

Late in June, Napoleon began the actual invasion of Russia. He started from a point 700 miles distant from France, his real base of operations. On either flank he had Prussia and Austria, two questionable allies that might threaten his communications. He entered a region sparsely settled and poor in supplies of all kinds. Moscow, the goal of the invasion, lay six hundred miles to the east. The opposing Russian forces steadily retreated. As a result of this policy, Napoleon soon found himself in difficulties. His men and beasts were worn out by the endless marches. Fatigue, disease, and hunger steadily depleted his forces. Finally, after fighting a serious battle at Borodino, a point two-thirds of the way to Moscow, Napoleon entered the great Russian city.

Entrance into Moscow brought only disillusionment. Napoleon found the city practically abandoned by its usual population. No municipal deputation met him. No overtures of peace from the defeated tsar reached him. Instead, fires soon broke out which quickly destroyed the wooden buildings that made up the greater part of the city. This deprived him of the winter quarters that he had counted on for the approaching Russian winter.

The situation left Napoleon no alternative but to retreat. On October 18, 1812, the army of Napoleon, greatly reduced in numbers but laden with booty, left Moscow. The military situation compelled it to take the same route by which it had come. The retreat was a tragedy for the French. The already devastated route yielded little in the way of supplies. The peasants, infuriated by their losses and inspired by national feeling, harried the retreating army during the whole march. Early in November, winter set in and added to the horrors of the retreat. By the time the French army reached Poland, all semblance of military discipline was gone.

The great defeat called in question the whole Napoleonic system. Abandoning the remnants of his once vast army, Napoleon hurried back across Germany to France to raise new forces for the campaign of 1813. Much depended on the course adopted by the European powers, particularly by Russia. Raised suddenly from defeat to victory, the tsar, satisfied with the clearing of Russia from her enemies, could stop at the boundaries of his state or continue the struggle until the complete defeat of Napoleon.

While the tsar hesitated, an event took place which forced him to make a decision. The governor of Riga had been trying to convince the commander of the Prussian auxiliary troops, General Yorck, that Prussia should desert Napoleon and join Russia against the French emperor. The Prussian general, however, wanted assurances of what he might expect if he cooperated with Russia. Late in December, he received the promise of the tsar that he would not lay down his arms until he had restored Prussia to the place she held before the battle of Jena. A convention embodying this promise was finally signed at Tauroggen. The desertion of 18,000 Prussian troops was a great blow to Napoleon and did much to encourage the people of Prussia to rise against him. In March, 1813, the Prussian state finally followed Yorck's example. The action of Prussia forced Napoleon to evacuate Poland.

Meanwhile, Napoleon had been straining every nerve to raise troops for the campaign of 1813. On April 15th he put himself at the head of his new army. For the most part, as a result of the defection of Prussia and the refusal of Austria to help him, Napoleon found himself again at the head of an army that was mainly French. The campaign opened with two victories for the French emperor, but they were not decisive. On June 4 Napoleon agreed to sign an armistice, but he derived no benefit from the ensuing negotiations. When the French emperor refused to give up most of his conquests beyond the Rhine, Austria joined the alliance against him. The action of his former Austrian ally forced Napoleon back into Saxony. In September his efforts to hold central Germany in a great four-day battle at Leipzig ended in his defeat, the retreat of his remaining troops behind the Rhine, and the desertion of his cause by his remaining German allies. At the same time, his troops were being driven out of Spain and were being defeated in Italy. Thus, at the end of the campaign of 1813, Napoleon found his armies forced back to French soil.

It took four months of fighting to complete the defeat of Napoleon. Early in January, 1814, the allies crossed the French border and began to close in on all sides. With the slender resources at his command, Napoleon fought one of his most brilliant campaigns. In the end, all his efforts terminated in defeat. At the end of March, news came that the allies had occupied Paris. Napoleon wanted to continue his hopeless struggle, but his marshals insisted on his surrender. Finally, on April 11, 1814, he reluctantly signed a treaty of abdication. By its terms he retained his Imperial title and remained sovereign of the tiny island of Elba. Provision was also made for his support and that of various members of his family. It seemed as though Europe could devote its attention to the problem of establishing peace.

The effort of Napoleon to establish a European empire thus ended in defeat. For many reasons, the short peace established by the treaties of Lunéville and Amiens could not last. Ambition and personal interests of the new dictator of France called for a vigorous foreign policy. The intervention of France in Italy, the Swiss cantons, Germany, and the Netherlands convinced first Great Britain and ultimately Austria, Russia, and Prussia that war was preferable to such a peace. At first, Napoleon won a series of brilliant successes that placed most of Europe in his power and made Russia an ally. For the time being, he was able to organize Europe as he pleased. In the end his tyranny, his plundering, his constant changing of governments and shifting of boundaries aroused the nations of Europe against him. When disaster overtook him in Spain and Russia, they rose in revolt and finally overthrew his regime.

CHAPTER 34

The Settlement of 1813–1815

The collapse of the empire of Napoleon under the pressure of the peoples of Europe put in question every territorial and institutional change which had taken place between 1789 and 1814 from the Adriatic Sea to the English Channel and from the Straits of Gibraltar to beyond the Vistula River. As the tide of victory rolled on toward Paris, displaced rulers and privileged classes began to hope, intrigue, and take what action they could for the recovery of their old rights and possessions, defeated states commenced to work for the restoration of their former boundaries and position, the allies of Napoleon began to fear for their new acquisitions, the victorious states strove to acquire long-coveted provinces, and all, rulers and subjects, looked forward with hope for the realization of their ideas about a reorganization of Europe.

Restorations in the Wake of the Allied Armies

As the armies struggling against Napoleon fought their way from Spain toward the Pyrenees and into southern France, into the valley of the Po in Italy, and across Poland and Germany into northern France, the states created by the French emperor fell to pieces and the former rulers of the territories composing these artificial political creations began to return. In December, 1813, Napoleon abandoned the idea of maintaining his brother Joseph on the Spanish throne and recognized the right of the imprisoned Ferdinand VII to the Spanish kingdom. In 1813 and 1814, the Illyrian Provinces and the kingdom of Italy went to pieces as a result of the advance of the military forces of Austria, and the Austrian government again established itself firmly on the eastern shore of the Adriatic Sea and in northern Italy; the French withdrew beyond the Alps; and the Sardinian government came back from its island refuge and re-established itself in Piedmont. For the time being, Murat, the brother-in-law of Napoleon, was allowed to retain Naples as a reward for his desertion of Napoleon. In the valley of the Vistula, as a consequence of the disastrous campaign of 1812 in Russia, the new attitude of Austria, and the uprising in Prussia, the French duchy of Warsaw disappeared, and the allied powers suddenly found themselves confronted by the problem of the future of Poland. In the campaign of 1813 in Germany, the delay of the king of Saxony in deserting Napoleon raised the question of punishing him for his slowness by confiscating his kingdom. As the French emperor retreated from the battlefield of Leipsig toward the Rhine, his former German allies, one by one, changed to the winning side, his dependent states of Westphalia and the grand duchy of Berg dissolved, and the old rulers of Brunswick, Hesse-Cassel, Hanover, Oldenburg, the Hanseatic cities, and the Dutch Netherlands returned to their former capitals and set up governments. These events, however, left unsolved the future organization of Germany and the ultimate fate of many German territories and institutions. As a consequence, the allied powers set up a temporary civil and military administration for the control of Germany.

The First Restoration

In France, the defeat and abdication of Napoleon raised many problems which demanded immediate solution. On April 11, 1814, the question of the future of the fallen emperor was settled, supposedly, by the Treaty of Fontainebleau. This agreement provided for the payment to Napoleon himself of the sum of two million francs annually from the revenues of France and an additional two and one-half million francs to various members of his family. It likewise assigned the duchies of Parma, Piacenza, and Guastalla to his empress, Marie Louise, and the island of Elba to himself. It also permitted him to retain the title of Emperor. In accordance with the terms of this treaty, the allied powers promptly transported Napoleon to his petty principality off the western coast of central Italy.

In solving the question of the future government of France, the famous French politician and diplomat, Talleyrand, Prince of Benevento, played the leading part. Convinced that his defeated country could obtain more lenient terms from the victorious allies if the almost forgotten Bourbons were recalled to France, he skillfully brought about the restoration of Louis XVIII, a brother of the Louis XVI guillotined in 1793, to the French throne. He first manipulated the populace of Paris in such a way as to create the impression that there was a demand for the restoration of the Bourbons and induced the allied sovereigns to announce that they would make no peace with Napoleon. Then he persuaded the pliant Imperial senate to decree the abdication of the Emperor, to establish a provisional government, and to recall Louis XVIII. As a guarantee against a return to the *ancien régime,* however, the Senate stipulated that the restored king must give his adhesion to a constitutional charter which preserved for the French people most of the fundamental gains of the French Revolution. On his way to Paris, Louis XVIII rejected the charter of the Senate on the ground that it had been drawn up in too great haste. In its place he finally issued, on June 4, 1814, a charter of his own which provided for a chamber of hereditary peers chosen by the king, a chamber of deputies elected by a very restricted suffrage, a definite civil list, religious toleration for all creeds, protection for the purchasers of national property, the retention of the jury system, and an independent judiciary.

The first task of the new French government was the negotiation of a treaty of peace. As Talleyrand had foreseen, the allied powers treated France in the Treaty of Paris (May 30, 1814) with great consideration. They imposed no indemnity on a state which had been levying heavy requisitions of all sorts on the rest of Europe since 1793, and they permitted her to have the boundary which she had on January 1, 1792. This gave France certain territories like Avignon and part of Savoy which she had not had under the *ancien régime*. They compelled France to surrender, on the other hand, her claims to all territory beyond these boundaries which she had held temporarily during the Napoleonic regime.

In the Treaty of Paris the allied powers made a number of other important decisions concerning the reorganization of Europe. They decided to extend the boundaries of the kingdom of Holland, which had just been re-established as an independent state, so as to include the Belgian provinces; to unite the states of Germany again by a federative bond; to establish Switzerland as an independent state; to recognize the claim of Great Britain to the strategically important island of Malta; to restore to the king of Sardinia his territories on the mainland with the exception of a part of Savoy and to cede to him the former Republic of Genoa; and to return Lombardy and Venetia to the emperor of Austria. They decided to leave the remaining problems concerning the reorganization of Europe to the decision of a general European congress to be held at Vienna.

The Congress of Vienna

The people of Europe looked forward to the assembling of this congress with high hopes. During the Revolutionary period they had caught visions of better things. All anticipated a respite from the long, exhausting war and a distribution of the Polish, German, and Italian territories taken from Napoleon which would restore a balance of power in Europe. The liberals of Europe hoped for the creation of an effective international court, the abolition of the African slave trade, the suppression of piracy in the Mediterranean, the freeing of the American colonies of Spain, and the establishment of freedom of the seas. German patriots desired a centralized Germany with liberal institutions. The Jews of Europe began to work for an amelioration of their lot. Before the congress finally opened, a hundred thousand visitors, sovereigns, ministers, subordinate officials, servants, petitioners, and observers, are said to have crowded into Vienna.

The final decision in the questions confronting Europe, however, lay with the sovereigns of the four great allied powers (Russia, Prussia, Austria, and Great Britain) and their chief ministers. They had grown to manhood in the closing years of the *ancien régime* and had inherited the prejudices and point of view of the classes which benefited by that organization of society. They neither sympathized with nor understood the ideals of the French Revolution. They had the contempt for vague idealism customary with men of long experience in practical problems. They still trembled at the thought of Napoleon. They feared at any moment a new revolutionary movement which would carry the armies of France again over Europe. They were more anxious for peace than the liberals of Europe. They understood, however, the vital interests of their dynasties, their class in society, and their states, and came to Vienna determined to advance these interests by every means in their power.

Austria was represented by two typical products of the *ancien régime*. The emperor, Francis I, was egotistic, jealous, petty, procrastinating, and afraid of revolution, but he shrewdly kept in the background. He found in Metternich a man well suited to his purpose. In ordinary times his chancellor would have been a polished, skeptical, aristocratic man of the world, of moderately liberal opinions, but with slight sympathy for people outside his own class. His own experiences with the excesses of the French Revolution and the problem of holding together the diverse peoples of the Austrian Empire made him a thoroughgoing conservative. His qualities as a courtier made him subordinate his own opinions to those of his master. His diplomatic skill enabled him to achieve a great measure of temporary success. In Frederick Gentz he had an able assistant for the carrying out of the details of his policies.

Russia was represented above all by its own powerful tsar, Alexander I. He had started life endowed with good looks, a pleasing manner, personal vanity, and a fondness for playing a conspicuous role. His tutor, the Swiss republican, Laharpe, had imparted to the tsar a superficial veneer of liberalism which wore off as he grew older and his troubles with dissatisfied subjects increased. His experiences had tended to make him morbid and religious. He knew too much about the tragic events which had brought him to the throne to have an entirely easy conscience. His success in the campaign of 1812 seemed to him a divine miracle and made him somewhat of a mystic. His position as the all-powerful head of the vast Russian Empire made him an influential figure in European politics. His early training made him the most liberal among the influential figures at the congress. His instability made him a somewhat incalculable force.

The British government sent as its chief representative Lord Castlereagh. He was naturally inclined to find practical solutions for the complex problems confronting the congress. He saw that British interests demanded a limited degree of participation on the part of his government in the affairs of the continent. Backed up by a powerful navy which had played a conspicuous role in defeating Napoleon, a victorious army which had just driven the French out of Spain, and great financial, industrial, and commercial resources, he stood in a position to speak with a decisive voice in his efforts to reconcile the conflicting interests of the continental states.

Prussia, on the other hand, did not play so important a role at Vienna as her three allies. The Prussian sovereign, Frederick William III, was by nature hesitant and afraid to assume responsibility. Neither the king nor his advisers were certain about the restoration of Prussia as a great power. They had been forced by Napoleon to cede half the area of their state. They desired to be compensated for these losses. They were inclined to depend on the traditional friendship of Prussia and Russia, but they hesitated to take an independent and decisive stand.

These leaders of the four allied powers intended to arrogate to themselves control of the Congress of Vienna. They failed to take into consideration the consummate diplomatic skill of Talleyrand, the principal French representative at the Congress. Born a member of the old French nobility and crippled by an accident early in life, he had served as a dignitary of the Church under the *ancien régime,* a member of the National Assembly, a diplomatic agent of the Legislative Assembly, and foreign minister of the Directory, the Consulate, and the Empire. His long experience in affairs made him indispensable for the time being to the restored Bourbons. Louis XVIII, accordingly, had given him the difficult task of representing France at Vienna. Upon his arrival at the Austrian capital, he found his country feared and hated and himself socially and politically isolated. The story of how he temporarily gained for himself and France an influential place again in the councils of Europe is one of the most interesting chapters in the history of the period. In accordance with instructions which he had drawn up for himself he persuaded the representatives of the great allied powers to admit him to their deliberations, convinced the smaller powers that France stood for the principles of public law in Europe and asked nothing for herself, and finally for a moment restored his country to a position of equality by concluding an alliance with Austria and Great Britain over the Polish-Saxon question.

In a sense, the Congress never really organized. The representatives of the four great allied powers met in the middle of September, 1814, with the intention of dictating the decisions of the congress. Upon his arrival, Talleyrand quickly convinced them that he was less dangerous within their councils than outside of them. They expanded their directing committee, in consequence, to include Spain and France. Later they included Sweden and Portugal, the other two signers of the Treaty of Paris, in the directing committee. Metternich served as president and Gentz as secretary of this body. Most of the work of the congress was done by committees. These committees submitted their decisions to the directing committee for ratification. Finally, the decisions of the committees were embodied in many special treaties.

Before this stage of the work could be reached, however, months of negotiating had to be done to reconcile the innumerable clashing interests of the states of Europe. The most serious of these differences of opinion developed over the questions of the future of Poland and the restoration of Prussia to her rank as a great power. The Polish problem went back to the partition of the former kingdom of Poland in 1772, 1793, and 1795 by its three powerful neighbors—Russia, Prussia, and Austria. From that time onward, each of the three states had been extremely sensitive not only concerning the question of the restoration of the kingdom of Poland but about every political and diplomatic move which affected the status of the Poles. In 1807 Napoleon had greatly complicated the Polish problem and raised the hopes of the Poles for a revival of their former kingdom by creating the duchy of Warsaw from territory taken away from Prussia by the Treaty of Tilsit. In 1812 the defeat of Napoleon led to the fall of this French dependency and raised again the question of the future of the Poles. The tsar came to the Congress of Vienna determined to form from the territories ceded by Prussia to Napoleon a kingdom of Poland with himself as sovereign. His proposal alarmed Austria (which held the former Polish province of Galicia), foreshadowed an advance of the powerful Russian Empire further into Central Europe, and raised the question of compensating Prussia for the loss of these territories.

The Prussian representatives were willing to surrender their claims to most of their former Polish provinces provided they were given German territory which would be equivalent in population and resources. They proposed, therefore, as a solution of this problem, the assignment of Saxony to Prussia on the grounds that the Saxon sovereign had been too slow in deserting Napoleon. The interrelation of the two problems—the future of Poland and the compensation of Prussia—caused the whole dispute to be known as the Polish-Saxon question and caused Prussia and Russia to stand together in the congress.

The two questions brought the directing powers of the congress to the verge of war. Through weeks of heated dispute, Russia and Prussia insisted on their own point of view, while Austria and Great Britain refused to accept the Prusso-Russian solution of the two problems. This situation gave the skillful Talleyrand an opportunity to form an alliance with the two opponents of Russia and Prussia and to re-establish France momentarily as a great power. After a few days of great tension, however, the four directing powers receded from their extreme demands and settled down to the business of parceling out peoples and territories in such a way as to satisfy the more powerful states and still maintain a balance of power in Europe.

The Return of Napoleon

In March, 1815, however, the leisurely diplomats who had been interspersing a large number of social affairs with business were suddenly thrown into consternation by the news that Napoleon, the man who for years had dominated Europe and had seemed for so long invincible, had left Elba and landed on the southern coast of France. The news imposed on them the task of scotching this new danger.

For a time, the former French emperor seemed to bury himself in the petty affairs of his miniature principality. In reality, however, he had been observing events on the continent with a watchful eye. From France he heard tales of profound dissatisfaction with the restored Bourbons. From Vienna he heard stories of the serious dissensions of the directing powers over the Polish-Saxon and other questions.

Upon his return to France after twenty-five years of exile, Louis XVIII had found himself in a difficult position. He assumed rule over a people which had grown up under the freer conditions and wider opportunities offered by revolutionary France. They could not be forced back into the social and political framework which had characterized the *ancien régime*. Marshals of Napoleon continued to command the armies of France. Former functionaries and dignitaries of the Napoleonic régime controlled its administrative machinery. The mass of the French nation desired, at least, the enforcement of the Charter of 1814. Many wished for even a greater approach to the political, social, religious, and economic conditions which they had enjoyed for a brief time during the French Revolution. Others remembered with respect and admiration the fallen French emperor who had been banished to the island of Elba.

Unfortunately for the success of the restored government, there came back to France in the train of the restored Bourbons a much smaller but very influential group of people whose ideals differed radically from those of the mass of the nation. They had left France during the troublous years of the Revolution. During their years of exile, they had suffered the loss of the positions in state and Church which they considered their exclusive privilege and the confiscation of all their property. They came back, with the Count of Artois, the brother of the king, at their head, determined to re-establish as far as possible the *ancien régime*. They advocated an absolutist rather than a liberal government. They favored re-establishment of the Church in its old position. They desired to monopolize again the lucrative posts in state and Church and to regain the estates which had been taken from them. The demands of these representatives of old France alarmed the adherents of the new France.

Louis XVIII did very little to conciliate these two conflicting points of view. On the contrary, the initial measures of the government and the policy of the returned nobles tended to widen the gap between the two Frances and to deepen the discontent with the restored monarchy. The returned aristorcrats, the so-called Ultra-royalists, insolently inflicted slights on some of the greatest names in French history, tried to regain their lost estates without compensating the new holders, attempted to oust the royal advisers, and opposed even the Charter of 1814. The government, meanwhile, found itself unable to reduce taxes as it had promised to do and sent home thousands of veteran officers and soldiers. At the same time, the government re-established the military household of the *ancien régime* (composed of *émigré* nobles, who had never seen service) at a great cost, and attempted to remove the high prohibitive duties of the Continental system, an action which threatened French manufacturers with ruin. As a result of this situation, the resentment of the old soldiers and officials of Napoleon steadily mounted, the hatred of the peasants for the priests and nobles revived, and the opposition of the liberals to the restored Bourbons steadily grew.

After careful consideration of his own position on the island of Elba, the situation in France, and conditions at the Congress of Vienna, Napoleon decided to attempt to regain the French throne. Setting sail with 1,100 men of his guard, he landed on March 1, 1815, at a little bay near Nice. From there he hurried toward Paris. The troops sent to capture him deserted and swelled the ranks of his followers. His old soldiers flocked to his standard. The peasants and working-men welcomed his return. Nearly all abandoned the Bourbons. Napoleon, on the contrary, entered Paris without firing a shot or shedding a drop of blood. Upon arriving at the capital, he set up a government and did his best to reassure France and Europe that his return did not mean war.

Although the French people accepted the returned emperor as their ruler without protest, except for some slight resistance in the Vendée and southern France, the representatives of the directing powers at Vienna refused to receive his assurance of peaceful inten-tions and decided to treat him as an enemy of Europe. Their decision forced Napoleon to renew the war. He decided, in consequence, to attack the allied forces in Belgium before reinforcements could reach them. His campaign ended in his defeat at the Battle of Waterloo (June 18, 1815). His army fled from the field in wild disorder. The recently elected deputies at Paris decided against the making of any further sacrifices in behalf of the defeated emperor and warned him of their inability to protect him. Napoleon, consequently, fled to the coast and, finding it impossible to escape, surrendered to the British authorities. The French nation, on the contrary, turned to the vic-torious allies to learn its fate.

Results of the Congress of Vienna

The landing of Napoleon on French soil galvanized the Congress of Vienna into action. Faced by the danger of a revival of the Napo-leonic Empire, the representatives of the powers found solutions for the various questions at issue and embodied their agreements into many treaties. On June 9, 1815, they signed the Final Act of the Con-gress of Vienna, a document which embodied the main points of the various special agreements.

In the final settlement, both sides made concessions in regard to the Polish question. In the end, Tsar Alexander I agreed to leave in the possession of Prussia and Austria some of the territory of the grand duchy of Warsaw which he originally wanted. The powers in return then permitted him to assume the title, king of Poland, and to form from the rest of the grand duchy of Warsaw a kingdom which was to have a distinct constitution and administration. In addition, the directing powers promised the Polish subjects of Prussia and Aus-tria as well as Russia such representation and national institutions as each of the governments to which they belonged should judge ex-pedient and proper to grant them.

In accordance with the promise of the tsar, Prussia was re-established as a great power. Of her former Polish provinces, she retained West Prussia, Posen, and the fortress of Thorn. From Sweden, she obtained Swedish Pomerania and the island of Rugen. As compensation for giving up the larger part of her former Polish provinces, she acquired her former lands in western Germany and additional territories in Westphalia, Saxony, and the valley of the Rhine.

In the Treaty of Paris, the powers had agreed that Germany should again become a confederation of independent states. At the Congress of Vienna, the views of Austria and the German Conservatives triumphed over the hopes of the German liberals for a strong central government. Austria knew that she could neither bring into such a confederation all her non-German peoples nor dominate it. The governing classes in the various German states had no wish to give up their position of power or their independence. As a result, the Congress organized from thirty-eight of the surviving states the German Confederation, a loose union of states with the same boundaries and approximately the same defective political machinery as the former Holy Roman Empire. Hanover was restored to the king of England and became a kingdom. The king of Saxony recovered about three-fifths of his former state. Bavaria had to give up the Austrian territory which she had acquired and take in compensation a smaller and noncontiguous area.

In the Netherlands, the directing powers carried out the plan foreshadowed in the Treaty of Paris. They recognized the sovereignty of the House of Orange over the kingdom of Holland, a state composed of the former United Provinces and set up by the Dutch people at the time of the collapse of the Napoleonic Empire, and added to the restored state the former Austrian Netherlands. They left in the hands of Great Britain, however, the island of Ceylon and the Cape of Good Hope, territories which she had conquered while fighting Napoleon.

The Congress of Vienna recognized, also, the measures already taken by the Habsburgs to re-establish their power. After the battle of Leipzig in the campaign of 1813, they forced Bavaria to return the acquisitions she had made at the expense of Austria. In 1814 they had re-occupied the Illyrian Provinces and the territories of Lombardy and Venetia in northern Italy. They made no attempt to regain the Austrian Netherlands or the Polish lands lost in 1809.

The directing powers made few changes in the map of Italy and left the peninsula still a geographical expression. Only Venetia and Genoa disappeared from the map. Republics, the former ruling oligarchies were told, were no longer in style. Venetia, as we have seen, was assigned to Austria. Genoa was given to the Kingdom of Sardinia with the idea of making it a stronger bulwark against possible French

United Kingdom
of Great Britain
and Ireland

North
Sea

Atlantic
Ocean

K. of
Denma

London

K. of Netherlands

Paris

Kingdom

Hano

Hessen

P

Bader

W

F

K. of France

Switz.

Kingdom of Sardinia

Lucca

Pap

Tuscan

Corsica
(To France)

Rome

Sardinia

K. of Portugal

Lisbon

K. of Spain

Madrid

Balearic Islands

Mediterranean

Eur

hristiania

Stockholm

St. Petersburg

K. of Sweden

openhagen

BOUNDARY OF THE GERMAN CONFEDERATION
P= Palatinate   T= Thuringian States
W= Württemberg

r u s s i a

erlin

R u s s i a

K. of
Poland

ny

E m p i r e   o f

Vienna

A u s t r i a

Moldavia

Serbia

Wallachia

Black Sea

Montenegro

O t t o m a n

Constantinople

Empire

the

Sicilies

Sea

C. B. PONTIUS

1815

expansion. Members of the House of Habsburg became rulers of the duchies of Parma and Modena and the grand duchy of Tuscany. The Pope regained the Papal States. For a few months Murat, the brother-in-law of Napoleon, was allowed to retain his place on the Neapolitan throne, but within a short time he lost his throne by his effort to gain all Italy by a surprise attack. The kingdom of Naples was thereupon restored to its former Bourbon rulers.

The Second Restoration of the Bourbons in France

On the 22 of June, four days after his defeat at Waterloo, Napoleon, discouraged and powerless to control the political situation in France, abdicated the second time. Warned by the provisional government that it could not guarantee his safety, he made his way to Rochefort in the hope of escaping to America. Finding his way blocked by the British navy, he surrendered himself to the commander of the Bellerophon and demanded an asylum for himself in Great Britain.

In the meantime, the armies of the European powers crossed the French frontiers and pushed on toward the defenseless capital. In this situation the provisional French government saw in the return of Louis XVIII the best guarantee against the punishment of France for her defection to Napoleon. When, therefore, their former Bourbon ruler re-entered the country upon the advice of Wellington, the allied commander, they recognized the authority of their former sovereign at the same time that they arranged for the capitulation of Paris. On July 8, accordingly, Louis XVIII returned to his capital and established himself in the Tuilleries palace.

For four months, France waited to know her fate while her people endured the exactions of invaders who had suffered for two decades from the requisitions and plundering of the French. Finally, however, on November 20, 1815, the powers signed with France the second Treaty of Paris. This document reduced France to the limits she had had in 1790 and took from her Nice and Savoy and several fortresses on the northern frontier. On the plea of guaranteeing the security of neighboring states, they imposed an indemnity of 700,000 francs on France and required her to submit to occupation of her northern provinces by not more than 150,000 allied troops for a period not longer than five years. These terms forced on the powers the necessity of continuing to a certain extent their cooperation.

After the defeat of Napoleon, the political leaders of the victorious states took two years to make peace. There were four major steps in the making of peace. As the allied armies followed Napoleon from Moscow to northern France, some rulers came back to their old capitals and some provinces changed hands. After the defeat of Napoleon in northern France, the Bourbons were restored to the throne of France, and some questions were definitely settled. The rest of the peacemaking was left to a congress which assembled at Vienna. Its deliberations were accelerated by the return of Napoleon from Elba. His favorable reception by the French people made necessary a reconsideration of the peace terms offered to the French people after his final defeat.

The outbreak of the French Revolution affected the economic and social life of Europe as well as its political institutions and conditions. It stopped all development in some lines of endeavor. It stimulated important changes in other cases. It is the purpose of this chapter to describe some of the more significant developments in the economic and social life of European society during the Revolutionary period.

Effect of the French Revolution on Dress

The French Revolution affected styles of dress as well as political institutions. The former extravagant eccentricities of dress were abandoned in favor of new and plainer styles more in keeping with the spirit of the age. After the fall of the Bastille, the uniform of the new National Guard was for a time generally adopted by men. Merchants in their shops, lawyers at the courts, the members of the *bourgeoisie* out for a promenade, and even the servants of the king wore the new uniform. Three-cornered hats, shoe buckles, and many other former features of dress, likewise, disappeared. The women of the time, too, were quick to adopt fashions supposed to display their patriotism. They wore Bastille and citizeness hats, medallions made of stone from the Bastille, and tricolored rings in place of the jewelry they had contributed to the state.

The Revolution changed styles of wearing the hair even more than dress. Patriots, at least, began to denounce the use of powder on the hair when food was so scarce. Soon, only the bolder partisans of the *ancien régime* continued the custom of powdering their hair. Instead of wearing the wigs which had been worn for over a century, the male partisans of the Revolution cut their hair short and round in imitation of the Puritans of the preceding century.

These changes affected profoundly one of the most important businesses of France. For a long time, the wigmakers had been one of the most powerful gilds. They owned, according to contemporary calculations, about one-sixth of all the capital invested in French industry. Even Turgot, for lack of money to compensate its members, had not disturbed the wigmakers' gild when he abolished the gilds of other crafts. The Revolution, however, ended their prosperity. They were ruined by the emigration of some of their more important patrons and the economies forced on others. A fortunate few emigrated to places like London and opened shops. The remainder did not survive the monarchy.

The greatest innovation in dress, though, was the abandonment of short knee trousers for long pantaloons which came down to the ankle. This new article of clothing seems to have been worn first by French sailors. From the sailors its use appears to have spread to the boys. A short time before the outbreak of the French Revolution, the pantaloon apparently was adopted as the daily dress of the urban artisans. Above it, they wore a round jacket called a carmagnole. When the common people of France rose to power, the pantaloon and the jacket became popular with all members of French society.

This, therefore, was the dress of the defenders of the Revolution, of those who captured the Bastille and intimidated the monarchy. In derision, their opponents called them sans-culotte. They proudly accepted the title. The cautious *bourgeoisie* followed their example. Soon, the mark of a true patriot was the pantaloon, the carmagnole, and a loose-fitting riding coat. After August 10, 1792, wooden shoes were added to this outfit. So the pantaloon triumphed along with the Revolution.

Origin of the French and Italian Flags

During the Revolutionary period, the French and Italian flags took their present form. Before the French Revolution the monarchy, but not the people of France, had a flag. When at the time of Necker's dismissal, the French people took control and established their sovereignty in place of the monarchy, they felt for the first time the need of colors. At the suggestion of someone, it may have been Camille Desmoulins, the people chose green, the color of hope. At any rate, as soon as the suggestion was made, the crowd assembled in the Palais Royal quickly stripped the trees in the courtyard of their leaves.

Upon reflection, however, someone remembered that green was the color of the livery of the Count of Artois, the leader of the most reactionary faction in France. So in place of green the committee of electors, then sitting at the Hotel de Ville, adopted blue and red as the colors of Paris. After the capture of the Bastille the, for the moment, all-powerful Lafayette, commander of the new National Guard, demanded that white, the color of the Bourbons, should be added as a sign of the supposed reconciliation between the king and his people.

Ever since, the French tricolor has always been the flag of republican France.

The Italian tricolor has a different origin. Since the days of Dante, green, white, and red (colors emblematical of the three cardinal virtues, faith, hope, and charity) had been popular in Italy. So it was not surprising in 1795 that students demonstrating at Bologna should have chosen the three colors for their own or that in 1796 they should be adopted as the flag of the Cisalpine Republic. They continued to be the colors of the Italian Republic and the kingdom of Italy until the downfall of Napoleon for the time being put an end to that Italian state.

Abolition of the Slave Trade

By the last decade of the eighteenth century, the agitation against the slave trade was strong enough to enlist the support of some of the politicians. Although Denmark was the first European state to abolish the traffic, Great Britain was the leader in putting an end to the trade in Negro slaves.

As early as 1772 a judicial opinion was handed down in Great Britain that a Negro slave was free as soon as he set foot on British soil. Four years later, the first motion to abolish the slave trade was introduced in the House of Commons. From that date onward, many petitions about the subject were sent to Parliament. In the nineties, the colony of Sierra Leone was established with the threefold aim of settling the west coast of Africa, discouraging the slave trade, and creating a center for the civilization of Africa. These hopes were never fulfilled. In 1796 a bill to abolish the slave trade passed in the House of Commons but failed in the House of Lords.

In 1806 the opposition to this reform began to crumble. In that year a bill passed both houses of Parliament which put an end to the British slave trade for foreign supply. In the following year, a bill carried in both houses which provided that no vessel should clear out for slaves from any port within the British dominions and that no slave should be landed in the colonies after May 1, 1808.

This law was frequently violated. The slave traders knew that if one voyage in three was successful they would still make money. If they were caught they suffered only pecuniary penalties. In 1811, in order to abolish the traffic, persons engaging in it were punished by transportation to a penal colony. A little later, engaging in the slave trade was made a capital offence. This legislation proved to be effective and put an end to the traffic in Negro slaves.

The name of William Wilberforce (1759–1833) is inseparably connected with the abolition of the British slave trade. As a young man, he attended Cambridge, where he became a friend of the Younger Pitt. Later, he inherited a considerable fortune. Early in life he became converted to evangelical Christianity and henceforth suffered from remorse because of his wasted opportunities.

In 1780 he was elected to Parliament. There, he again came in contact with Pitt. In 1787 he met Thomas Clarkson, the agitator, an event which caused him to take up the struggle against the slave trade. At the suggestion of Pitt, he took the lead in the parliamentary struggle against the slave traffic. Later, he supported such reforms as extension of the suffrage and the emancipation of Catholics.

For a moment it looked as if France, too, was going to put an end to the trade in Negro slaves. In 1788 a society was formed at Paris for the abolition of both the slave trade and slavery. Condorcet was president of the organization and Lafayette was one of its members. In the following year, the Declaration of the Rights of Man seemed to apply to black as well as white men. The advocates of the abolition of the traffic, however, soon encountered some very practical opposition.

The territory especially affected by the policy of the government was the island of Santo Domingo, or Haiti. In the seventeenth century the western part of the island had been occupied by French buccaneers, and in 1677 this territory had been formally ceded to France. The planters of Santo Domingo had no intention of giving up their labor force for the sake of an abstract theory, and soon well-founded rumors of their dissatisfaction began to reach the French National Assembly. Finding themselves confronted by this very dangerous situation, the members of the National Assembly hastily passed in 1790 a resolution excluding the colonies from the benefits of the Rights of Man. The Negro population of the island refused to remain slaves and rose in revolt. Finally, in 1794, the National Assembly decreed the abolition of slavery. Thereupon, the planters offered the island to Great Britain, but the British were unable to maintain themselves in Santo Domingo. In the following year, the French acquired the rest of the island from Spain by the Treaty of Basel. This confused situation continued to characterize the island until the accession of Napoleon to power.

The subject of traffic in Negro slaves was brought to the attention of the Congress of Vienna. This body condemned the trade in principle but left the time and method of abolishing it to negotiations between the individual states. Within the next few years, most of the states of Europe did put an end to the cruel traffic.

The Beginning of Great Exhibitions

The national and international exhibitions which have played such an important part in recent times really started in the Revolutionary period. A display designed to show the industrial progress which was being made was held in 1791 at Prague. This suggested to François de Neufchateau, minister of interior under the Directory, the idea of holding annual industrial expositions to stir up the French industrialists.

His first exhibition was held in 1799 on the anniversary of the founding of the French Republic and lasted a week. One hundred and thirty exhibitors, most of them from Paris and its vicinity, displayed their products in a temporary gallery of sixty-eight arcades built around an open court. Twelve prizes were awarded by a jury of nine, and the exhibition, in spite of its hasty organization and the war that was in progress, met with general approval.

Three other exhibitions were held during the rule of Napoleon. The number of the exhibitors and of the departments represented steadily increased. In the exhibition held in 1806, there were 1,422 exhibitors, from one hundred and four departments. After this date, the war prevented the holding of other exhibitions until after the restoration of peace.

The Invention of Gas Lighting

During this troubled period, some men searched for new ways of doing things, while others fought and destroyed the civilization which had been bequeathed to them by the past. Among the problems taken up by the inventors of the time was the illumination of houses and factories by some sort of gas.

Two men are yet remembered for their work in this field. In France, Philippe Lebon (1767–1804) worked at the problem. He obtained gas by burning wood in a closed vessel and passing the resulting gas through water. As early as 1786, he began to experiment with what he called thermolamps. In 1799 he patented his invention, and three years later he publicly demonstrated its use. Death intervened, however, and prevented the practical application of his discovery.

In the meantime William Murdock, a trusted employee of Watt and Boulton, had been experimenting with gas obtained from coal. This dependable but singularly unambitious Scot began his experiments about 1795. A few years later, he actually lighted a factory by gas, but his achievement did not attract a great deal of attention. The demonstration was a part of the celebration of the conclusion of peace at Amiens in 1802. In 1804 one of the cotton manufacturers ordered the installation in his house of one of the new illuminating machines and toward the end of the same year decided to light his mills with gas. In 1808 Murdock was induced to read a paper before the Royal Society telling of his experiments and was awarded a medal for his achievements. He received little else for his discoveries, as his ideas fell into the hands of promoters who exploited them for their own benefit.

The Attempt to Use the New Balloons in War

The military men quickly attempted to use the new balloons in warfare. In 1793 a commission was appointed for the purpose of utilizing the new scientific discoveries for military purposes. The commission promptly recommended the use of captive balloons for observation and charged a physician named Coutelle with the carrying out of the idea. He had to find the necessary hydrogen gas, to develop an impermeable cover for the balloon, and to organize and train a company of military balloonists.

Such balloons were used to some extent in the ensuing campaigns in Belgium and Germany. They were kept under control by cables and rose to a height of five hundred meters. This enabled an observer to see the enemy lines. In 1796 the equipment fell into the hands of the enemy. In the meantime, a second company of military balloonists had been organized.

General Bonaparte thought enough of the new military balloons to take a company of balloonists with him to Egypt. There the equipment again fell into the hands of the enemy. After this disaster, the General dismissed the military balloonists, closed their school, and never made another attempt to employ balloons in warfare.

The Invention of Canning

The war brought to the fore the problems of feeding the army and the preservation of food. The problem had long been partially solved by drying, salting, or smoking the foods, but these processes destroyed much of their value. As a consequence, the French government offered a prize of 12,000 francs for the discovery of the best practical method of food preservation.

The prize was won by Nicolas Affert, a Parisian confectioner. In 1809 he succeeded in preserving certain foods in especially made glass bottles which had been kept in boiling water for varying lengths of time. In the following year, he announced his discovery in a book entitled *The Book of All Households, or the Art of Preserving Animal Substances for Many Years.* Notwithstanding his success, however, like many other discoverers and inventors, he finally died in poverty.

The Adoption of the Principle of Universal Military Service

During the eighteenth century, as we have seen, wars were usually the concern of only a small part of the nation. The upper classes furnished the officers, the peasants provided the rank and file of the armies. The rest of the nation took little or no part in military affairs.

These relatively small armies were highly trained. They lived under an iron discipline. They were taught all the tricks of the parade ground. They depended for success on the steadiness, speed, and precision of their evolutions. They attained almost mechanical perfection.

In France, the Revolution destroyed the old royal army. The officers, for the most part, emigrated. The common soldier deserted or at least ceased to be well disciplined. These developments forced upon the Revolutionary government the problem of reorganizing the army on a new basis.

Logic pointed to the adoption of the principle of universal conscription. The French people had adopted the idea of equality as a slogan. This implied compulsory enlistment for all and, finally, after considerable experimentation, they organized the army on this basis.

At first, the French authorities only partially adopted the principle of universal conscription. They proposed voluntary enlistment for the line, the organization of those between the ages of eighteen and forty into a militia, and the formation of the remaining men into a national guard. The result of the experiment was disappointing. Although the Convention in 1792 declared every able-bodied citizen liable to military service, the majority of Frenchmen showed no anxiety to put themselves in a position where they might get shot. The authorities recruited only some thirty thousand men to fill the depleted ranks of the army, and many of the new recruits deserted after a few days or months of service. The next year a similar attempt brought similar results.

Later in the same year, Carnot, in charge of military matters, introduced a different system. The new plan made liable for military service only those between the ages of eighteen and twenty-five. As they were not strong enough politically to resist coercion, the French people, in the main, accepted the new scheme. By 1794 the new plan brought 770,000 men under arms.

In 1798, the prospect of a renewal of the European war turned the attention of the French authorities again to the problem of raising an army. In that year, Jourdan, the minister of war, proposed that the young men of France from twenty to twenty-five should be registered in five classes, that each year the youngest class should be called out first, and that the other classes should only be drawn into active service if they were needed. The new law was a failure under the Directory but made the conquests of Napoleon possible.

On the basis of the law of 1798, Napoleon raised very large armies.

Each year France was compelled to furnish thousands of recruits to the armies. The number varied from 30,000 in 1800 to 1,140,000 in 1813. All told, France is estimated to have furnished during the Napoleonic period 2,613,000 men as cannon fodder.

The Revolutionary armies, however, did not have the time to learn the tricks of the parade ground or the discipline and precision of eighteenth-century armies. They had to find officers where they could and evolve new tactics for the raw but numerous recruits. The search for new methods resulted in the rapid promotion of capable officers, regardless of their origin, and the development of tactics that were effective in gaining desired objectives though wasteful in human lives.

The victories gained by the Revolutionary and Napoleonic armies by the new methods of recruiting and different tactics called into question every military system that was defeated. Sooner or later, the defeated powers abandoned their old military systems and adopted those of the victorious French. They hoped by their adoption of the new methods to avert defeats in the future.

The first power to apply the new principles was Prussia. As early as 1808 it approved of the new methods. In 1814, under the leadership of its war minister, Herman von Boyen (1771–1848) it applied the principle of universal military service to the Prussian army. Ultimately, it was adopted by all the European powers.

The Invention of the Steamboat

One of the most important events of the so-called Revolutionary period was the invention of the steamboat. As soon as the problem had been solved of applying steam power as a motive force for machinery, men of an inventive type of mind turned their attention to the problem of the steamboat. In the closing years of the eighteenth century, many men were at work on the problem of propelling boats by steam. Austria points to a successful experiment in 1778; France advances the claims of Denis Papin and the Marquis of Jouffroy; Great Britain, those of Henry Bell and William Symington; and the United States, those of Fitch, Rumsey, and Fulton. While it is impossible to divide fairly the credit among these various claimants, it is certain that Fulton and Bell solved more completely the mechanical, economic, and political problems confronting the aspirants for the honor of having invented the steamboat than did any of their competitors.

Robert Fulton (1765–1815) was the son of a Pennsylvania farmer. Quite early, he showed ability in drawing and had training as a mechanic at Lancaster, a center for gun making during the Revolutionary War. At the age of seventeen, he went to Philadelphia where he supported himself by painting. After four years he went to Europe in the hope of improving his health. He stayed there twenty years and again supported himself by painting. During these years, he carefully observed the progress of mechanical inventions and busied himself with mechanical devices of his own. As early as 1794 he was in correspondence with Boulton and Watt about an engine suitable for installation in a boat. Later, he invented a dredging machine which was much used in cutting channels for canals, and he also worked on submarine mines and torpedoes. In 1800, after having gone to Paris, he invented a diving boat capable of submerging itself to a depth of twenty-five feet for four hours and a half. During his efforts to interest Napoleon in the device, the First Consul suggested that Fulton be paid in proportion to the damage that he inflicted on the British fleet. Unfortunately for Fulton, the American inventor failed to overtake any British vessel, and the French authorities lost interest in the scheme. In 1804 his efforts to interest the British in his invention failed because of the use of defective torpedoes which did no damage to the French fleet.

Having failed to find a market for his diving boat through French skepticism and British conservatism, Fulton turned to steamboats. He was fortunate enough to find a financial backer in Robert R. Livingston, the wealthy American ambassador to France, who had been interested in the problem of steamboats and had had the foresight to obtain for himself for twenty years a monopoly in the waters of the state of New York. In 1803 an experimental boat on the Seine River broke in two and sank because of the weight of the machinery. After this failure, Fulton sailed for America where he built the *Clermont,* a ship 133 feet long, 18 feet broad, and 7 feet deep, propelled by paddle wheels 15 feet in diameter and driven by an engine constructed by the firm of Boulton and Watt.

The success of this steamboat is a matter of general knowledge. In 1807, to the astonishment of most of the onlookers, the *Clermont* slowly moved up the Hudson River at a speed of nearly five miles per hour. The trip from New York to Albany and back took sixty-two hours. Until Fulton's death eight years later, the two partners were busy with the management and establishment of steamboat lines and the defense of their monopoly.

In the meantime, Henry Bell (1767–1830), a Scottish millwright, was solving the same problem in Great Britain. After going to work for a firm of shipbuilders, he conceived, about 1786, the idea of applying steam power to navigation. A few years later, he commenced to experiment with an engine in a small boat. Still later, he built a vessel called the *Comet* that had an engine of three horsepower and plied between Glasgow and Greenock for the next eight years. It was the first steamer to ply regularly on European waters. By 1815 steamers were sailing regularly between London and Glasgow.

The Development of Vaccination

Down to the end of the century, smallpox continued to take a heavy toll of lives. In 1721, it is true, Lady Mary Wortley Montague had introduced into England the practice of inoculation, and from England it had spread to the continent. Inoculation, as a means of securing immunity from the disease, had a number of disadvantages. The smallpox virus used might cause death rather than free the individual from the disease. Besides, the person inoculated had to be segregated for several days. Then the patient was usually ill for a number of days. Finally, inoculation was a somewhat expensive process.

These facts, therefore, made the discovery of vaccination as a preventive against smallpox very welcome. About 1775 Edward Jenner, a practicing physician of Gloucestershire, ran across the popular belief that cowpox was a preventive against smallpox. He had no opportunity of studying the subject until 1796 when he inoculated an eight-year-old boy with matter from the cowpox vesicles on the hands of a milkmaid. After repeating the experiment two years later, he announced his discovery to the world. This brought his method to the attention of the British medical profession. The new preventive soon reduced the annual average of deaths from smallpox from 2,018 to 622. In his zeal for the new method, Jenner often vaccinated patients free of charge.

In spite of the state of war which existed between Great Britain and France, news of the British conquest of smallpox reached France quickly. The French doctors who wished to try the experiment labored under a serious handicap. It was difficult to obtain good vaccine. They tried three times without success to vaccinate patients. It was not until they had sent a French doctor from Geneva to London to observe and learn at first hand the new techniques that they succeeded in vaccinating patients.

In spite of the war, not only vaccine but medical men crossed the English Channel. By 1800 the practice of vaccination was thoroughly established in France. Various committees were set up. Institutions for the preparation of vaccine and for the care of patients were established. A veritable campaign, backed by Napoleon Bonaparte, was started. Soon the movement was making headway among the more enlightened not only in France but in neighboring countries.

The Adoption of the Optical Telegraph

The outbreak of foreign war brought home to the French authorities the desirability of developing some quicker means of communicating between distant points. At the time, a number of individuals were engaged in attempts to solve the problem. The man who succeeded in attracting the support of the French authorities was Claude Chappe (1763–1805), a French physician and engineer. While his invention was superior to its rivals, he was undoubtedly aided by a brother who was something of a politician and not without influence.

Chappe seems to have been at work for some years on the problem of transmitting messages through space. In 1791 he demonstrated his device before a group of officials in his own locality. In the following year, he presented his proposals to the Legislative Assembly which merely referred them to a committee and never took further action. Undaunted by this failure, he presented a petition to the Convention. This time, the French authorities acted. The Convention appropriated 6,000 francs from the funds of the war department to build a number of experimental stations.

In due time three experimental stations were built. Each station consisted of a post thirty feet high with a moveable crosspiece fourteen feet long. At each end of the latter was an indicator six feet long and one foot wide. The indicators could be moved by a system of pulleys to any position desired. The crosspiece could be moved to four different positions and the indicators to seven. So the optical telegraph was capable of transmitting one hundred and ninety-six different signals. The messages were sent a word at a time. In clear weather, about three signals a minute could be transmitted. On dark days and in time of storms, of course, the new telegraph could not be used.

The trial with the three experimental stations was successful. On July 12, 1793, before representatives of the Convention, scholars, and artists, dispatches were quickly and accurately transmitted. The Convention, consequently, appropriated money for the construction of a line from Paris to Lille, a city near the frontier of the Austrian Netherlands. Upon its completion in 1794 the line had sixteen stations.

After the success of this line had been demonstrated, the country became enthusiastic over the new invention. In 1795 the construction of a line from Paris to London was begun. Two years later communications were established with Strasbourg. Soon, Paris could send messages to Dunkerque, Brest, Brussels, Flushing, and Amsterdam. Finally, late in Napoleon's reign, lines were constructed to Milan and Venice.

Improvements in Printing

Toward the close of the Napoleonic period a notable improvement in the printing of newspapers took place. The first printing presses had been constructed of wood and were operated on the screw principle. No radical changes were made in the printing process until 1800. In that year a press made entirely of iron was developed. Shortly afterwards, the screw was abandoned. After 1811, two Germans, Koenig (1774–1833) and Bauer (1783–1860), devised a power-driven press. It consisted of a flat bed and a cylinder that continuously revolved. Later, the machine was built to permit both sides of the paper to be printed at once. The new printing press could produce 1,000 impressions an hour, four times as many as the former hand presses could print. On November 29, 1814, the *London Times* announced that it had installed two of the new machines. The ultimate effect of the invention was to reduce the cost of newspapers and broaden their influence.

The Development of Beet Sugar

Until the Napoleonic period, cane sugar was the principal source of sweetening for food. By 1500 its use seems to have spread from Arab lands to Europe. By 1600 it had been introduced into America, particularly in the West Indies. In the seventeenth and eighteenth centuries, these islands were considered among the most valuable of the colonial possessions of the European states.

The wars of the French Revolution and the Napoleonic wars cut Europe off not only from its usual supplies of sugar but from such commodities as coffee, tobacco, and cotton. The French government made great efforts to encourage the production of these commodities in Europe or to find substitutes for them. Its efforts resulted in the use of chicory in place of coffee, the growth of a considerable amount of European tobacco, unsuccessful attempts to grow cotton, and the substitution of beets for cane in the production of sugar.

The possibility of using beets as a source of sugar was suggested as early as 1605 in a well-known work on agriculture. The extraction of sugar from beets proved to be a difficult problem. It was finally solved by a German scientist in 1799. The cutting off of Europe from the usual supplies of cane sugar stimulated interest in the subject of beet sugar. Napoleon allotted a large sum of money for the encouragement of the new industry. By the end of 1811, forty factories for the production of beet sugar had been established. The new industry continued to grow until the re-establishment of peace. The war was thus responsible for the development of a new and important industry.

BIBLIOGRAPHIES

Readings on the Period from 1492–1815

An important function of a textbook is to introduce the student to the literature of the subject. That is the purpose of the following lists of books. For the most part, the readings are secondary works in the English language, the only language most students read easily, that throw additional light on the period. It is subdivided into lists of works covering the whole period such as political histories, economic histories, works on painting, architecture, music, literature, philosophy, commerce, colonies, exploration, military science, and other subjects. These are followed by works on the histories of countries and regions. Then come lists that throw light on the different chapters of the book.

The list of works in the English language should be followed by a list of works in foreign languages. The best books on the history of most European countries have been written by citizens of those countries who wrote in their own languages. In many cases, the works in the English language do not adequately cover the topics treated in the text. This is particularly true in England, France, Germany, Italy, Spain, and Holland. For the histories of other countries besides these listed, the writers of France and Germany must usually be consulted. Printing difficulties, however, have made it inadvisable to give a list of works in foreign languages.

The secondary works in any language, however, are based on *sources*. This is the name applied by historians to the reports of eye-witnesses. These take the form of diaries, autobiographies, letters, and memoirs; of such documents as decrees, laws, and treaties; and of pictures of persons and places that have played a part in history. Again, however, conditions have made it necessary to give only a list of sources in the English language.

Most readers, however, understand events and conditions better if they have the aid of pictures. For the benefit of eye-minded students, a small list of works that give especially good pictures have been inserted. It is the hope of the author that this list will help to stimulate the imaginations of students. History must be visualized to be understood.

GENERAL WORKS COVERING ALL OR A CONSIDERABLE PART OF THE PERIOD

POLITICAL AND DIPLOMATIC HISTORIES

Abbott, W. C., *The Expansion of Europe*, New York, 1918.

Acton, Lord, *Lectures on Modern History*, London, 1921.

Baron, S. W., *A Social and Religious History of the Jews*, New York, 1939.

Birkhead, A., *Heroes of Modern Europe*, New York, 1923.

Cambridge Modern History, Vols. 1–7, New York, 1907–1912.

East, G., *Historical Geography of Europe*, New York, 1944.

Eyre, E., *European Civilization*, Vols. 4–6, London, 1935–1937.

Fisher, H. A. L., *The Republican Tradition in Europe*, New York, 1911.

———, *A History of Europe*, Vols. 2–3, Boston, 1939.

Freeman, E. A., *The Historical Geography of Europe*, London, 1882.

Geise, J., *Man and the Western World*, New York, 1940.

Gettel, R. G., *History of Political Thought*, London, 1924.

Gooch, G. P., *Annals of Politics and Culture, 1492–1899*, Cambridge, 1901.

———, *Courts and Cabinets*, New York, 1946.

Grant, A. J., *A History of Europe*, New York, 1932.

Hill, D. J., *A History of Diplomacy in the International Development of Europe*, Vols. 2–3, New York, 1905–1906.

Lavisse, E., *General View of the Political History of Europe*, New York, 1902.

Lodge, R., *A History of Modern Europe*, New York, 1886.

Marriott, J. A. R., *The Evolution of Modern Europe*, New York, 1933.

Mowat, R. B., *The European State System*, London, 1926.

Randall, J. H., *The Making of the Modern Mind*, Boston, 1926.

Stubbs, W., *Lectures on European History*, New York, 1904.

ECONOMIC HISTORIES OF EUROPE

Barnes, H. E., *An Economic History of the Western World*, New York, 1937.

Beard, M., *A History of the Business Man*, New York, 1938.

Birnie, A., *An Economic History of Europe, 1760–1930*, New York, 1930.

Bogart, E. L., *Economic History of Europe, 1760–1939*, New York, 1942.

Bowden, W., Karpovich, M., and Usher, A. P., *An Economic History of Europe Since 1750*, New York, 1937.

Clough, S. B., and Cole, C. W., *Economic History of Europe*, Boston, 1941.

Gras, N. S. B., *An Introduction to Economic History*, New York, 1922.

Heaton, H., *An Economic History of Europe*, New York, 1936.

Knight, M. M., Barnes, H. E., and Flügel, F., *Economic History of Europe in Modern Times*, Boston, 1928.

Nussbaum, F. L., *A History of the Economic Institutions of Modern Europe*, New York, 1934.

See, H., *Modern Capitalism*, New York, 1928.

Soltau, R. H., *An Outline of European Economic Development*, New York, 1935.

ECONOMIC HISTORIES OF ENGLAND

Ashley, W. J., *The Economic Organization of England*, London, 1915.

Cheyney, E. P., *An Introduction to the Industrial and Social History of England*, New York, 1930.

Cunningham, W., *The Growth of English Industry and Commerce*, 2 vols., Cambridge, 1890–92.

Milner, F., *Economic Evolution in England*, London, 1931.

HISTORIES OF AGRICULTURE

Curtler, W. H. R., *The Enclosure and Redistribution of Our Land,* Oxford, 1920.

Emmison, F. G., *Types of Open Field Parishes in the Midlands,* London, 1937.

Ernle, (R. P. Prothero) Baron, *English Farming, Past and Present,* New York, 1936.

————, *The Pioneers and Progress of English Farming,* London, 1888.

Garnier, R. M., *History of the English Landed Interest,* New York, 1908.

Gonner, E. C. K., *Common Land and Enclosure,* London, 1912.

Gras, N. S. B., *A History of Agriculture in Europe and America,* New York, 1925.

Marriott, J. A. R., *The English Land System,* London, 1914.

Marshall, W., *The Rural Economy of Norfolk,* London, 1787.

————, *The Rural Economy of Yorkshire,* London, 1796.

————, *The Rural Economy of the Midland Counties,* London, 1796.

Slater, G., *The English Peasantry and the Enclosure of Common Fields,* London, 1907.

HISTORIES OF COMMERCE

Biggar, H. P., *The Early Trading Companies of New France,* Toronto, 1901.

Bourne, H. R. F., *The Romance of Trade,* London.

Day, C., *A History of Commerce,* New York, 1907.

Haring, C. H., *Trade and Navigation between Spain and the Indies,* Cambridge, 1918.

Jeudwine, J. W., *Studies in Empire and Trade,* New York, 1923.

Khan, S. A., *The East India Trade in the Seventeenth Century,* London, 1923.

Oakeshott, W. F., *Commerce and Society,* Oxford, 1936.

Packard, L. B., *The Commercial Revolution, 1400–1776,* New York, 1927.

Rooseboom, M. P., *The Scottish Staple in the Netherlands,* The Hague, 1910.

Selfridge, H. G., *The Romance of Commerce,* London, 1923.

HISTORIES OF INDUSTRY

Johnston, T., *The History of the Working Classes in Scotland,* Glasgow.

Renard, G. F., and Weulersse, G., *Life and Work in Modern Europe,* London, 1926.

Unwin, G., *Industrial Organization in the Sixteenth and Seventeenth Centuries,* Oxford, 1904.

Usher, A. P., *The Industrial History of England,* Boston, 1920.

HISTORIES OF BANKING

Clapham, Sir J. H., *The Bank of England,* New York, 1945.

Conant, C. A., *A History of Modern Banks of Issue,* New York, 1927.

Dillen, J. G. von, *History of the Principal Public Banks,* The Hague, 1934.

A History of Banking in All the Leading Nations, Vols. 1–2, New York, 1926.

Usher, A. P., *Early History of Deposit Banking in the Mediterranean Europe,* Vol. 1., Cambridge, 1943.

HISTORIES OF FINANCE

Ehrenberg, R., *Capital and Finance in the Age of Renaissance,* London, 1928.

Flynn, J. T., *Men of Wealth,* New York, 1941.

Mottram, R. H., *A History of Financial Speculation,* Boston, 1929.

Wantoch, H., *Magnificent Money Makers,* London, 1932.

HISTORIES OF TRANSPORTATION

Duncan, H. O., *The World on Wheels,* Paris, 1927.

Gregory, J. W., *The Story of the Road,* New York, 1931.

Hawks, E., *The Romance of Transportation,* New York, 1931.

Jackson, G., *From Track to Highway,* London, 1935.

Mitman, C. W., *An Outline of Development of Highway Travel*, Washington, 1935.

Pratt, E. A., *A History of Inland Transport and Communication in England*, London, 1912.

Webb, S., *English Local Government*, 2 vols. in 3, London, 1827–29.

Wilkindon, T. W., *From Track to Bypass*, London, 1934.

HISTORIES OF COLONIZATION

Andrews, C. M., *The Colonial Period of American History*, New Haven, 1937.

Becker, C. L., *Beginnings of the American People*, Boston, 1915.

Bolton, H. E., and Marshall, T. M., *The Colonization of North America*, New York, 1925.

Chapman, C. E., *Colonial Hispanic America*, New York, 1933.

Chitwood, O. P., Colonial America, New York, 1931.

Clark, C., *The Crown Colonies and Their History*. London, 1939.

Doyle, J. A., *English Colonies in America*, 5 vols., New York, 1889–1907.

Egerton, H. E., *A Short History of British Colonial Policy*, London, 1913.

Hertz, G. B., *The Old Colonial System*, Manchester, 1905.

Keller, A. G., *Colonization*, Boston, 1908.

Laboree, L. W., *Royal Government in America*, New Haven, 1930.

Means, P. A., *The Spanish Main, 1492–1700*, New York, 1935.

Mulvey, M. D., *French Catholic Missionaries in the Present United States*, Washington, 1936.

Nettles, C. P., *The Roots of American Civilization*, New York, 1938.

Newton, A. P., *The European Nations in the West Indies, 1493–1688* London, 1933.

Priestley, H. E., *The Coming of the White Man, 1492–1848*, New York, 1929.

Priestley, H. E., *France Overseas through the Old Regime,* New York, 1939.

Roberts, S. H., *History of French Colonial Policy*, 2 vols., London 1929.

Thwaites, R. G., *The Colonies, 1492–1750,* New York, 1910.

Tilby, A., *The English People Overseas,* 6 vols., Boston, 1914–16.

Wertenbaker, T. J., *The Founding of the American Civilization,* New York, 1938.

Woodward, W. H., *The Expansion of the British Empire, 1500–1902,* Cambridge, 1911.

Williamson, J. A., *A Short History of British Expansion*, New York, 1931.

HISTORIES OF ARCHITECTURE

Briggs, M. S., *The Architect in History,* Oxford, 1927.

Ferguson, J., *History of Modern Architecture,* 2 vols., London, 1891.

Hamlin, A. D. F., *A Textbook of the History of Architecture,* New York, 1922.

Kimball, S. F., and Edgell, G. H., *A History of Architecture,* New York, 1918.

Moore, C. H., *Character of Renaissance Architecture,* New York, 1905.

Russel, A. L. N., *Architecture,* London, 1927.

Simpson, F. M., *A History of Architectural Development,* New York, 1913.

Stathan, H. H., *A Short Critical History of Architecture,* London, 1912.

Sturgis, R., *A Short History of Architecture,* New York, 1908.

HISTORIES OF PAINTING

Abbot, E. R., *The Great Painters,* New York, 1927.

Bell, C., *An Account of French Painting,* London, 1932.

Blum, A., *The Origins of Printing and Engraving,* New York, 1940.

Caffin, C. H., *The Story of French Painting,* New York, 1911.

Clutton-Brock, A., *An Introduction to French Painting,* London, 1932.

596

Cole, T., *Old English Masters*, New York, 1902.
———, *Old Spanish Masters*, New York, 1907.
Cox, K., *Old Masters and New*, New York, 1905.
Craven, T., *Men of Art*, New York, 1931.
Crowe, J. A., *The German, Flemish and Dutch Schools of Painting*, London, 1911.
———, and Cavalcaselle, G. B., *A History of Painting in North Italy*, 6 vols., London, 1912.
Davidson, M., *Understanding Modern Art*, New York, 1931.
Lafarge, J., *Great Masters*, New York, 1915.
Macfall, H., *A History of Painting*, 8 vols., Boston, 1911.
Mather, F. J., *Venetian Painters*, New York, 1936.
Muther, R., *The History of Painting*, 2 vols., New York, 1907.
Tonks, O. S., *A History of Italian Painting*, New York, 1927.
Turner, W., *Great Schools of Painting*, Philadelphia, 1915.
Van Marle, R., *The Development of the Italian Schools of Painting*, Vols. 10–19, The Hague, 1923.
Ward, J., *History and Methods of Ancient and Modern Painting*, Vols. 3 and 4, New York, 1921.
Wilenski, R. H., *An Introduction to Dutch Art*, London, 1929.

HISTORIES OF MUSIC

Bauer, M., and Peyser, E. R., *Music Through the Ages*, New York, 1932.
Dickinson, E., *The Study of the History of Music*, New York, 1914.
Ferguson, D. N., *A Short History of Music*, New York, 1943.
———, *A History of Musical Thought*, New York, 1935.
Finney, T. M., *A History of Music*, New York, 1935.
Gray, C., *The History of Music*, New York, 1928.
Lang, P. H., *Music in Western Civilization*, New York, 1941.

McKinney, H. D., and Anderson, W. K., *Music in History*, New York, 1940.
Pratt, W. S., *History of Music*, New York, 1935.
———, *The History of Music*, New York, 1930.
Prunières, H., *A New History of Music*, New York, 1943.

HISTORIES OF EXPLORATION AND DISCOVERY

Baker, J. L. N., *A History of Geographical Discovery and Exploration*, London, 1931.
Dickinson, R. E., and Howarth, O. J. R., *The Making of Geography*, Oxford, 1933.
East, W. G., *An Historical Geography of Europe*, London, 1935.
Gillespie, J. E., *A History of Geographical Discovery, 1400–1800*, New York, 1933.
Sykes, P., *A History of Exploration*, London, 1935.
Synge, M. B., *A Book of Discovery*, New York, 1912.
Taylor, E. G. R., *Tudor Geography*, London, 1930.

HISTORIES OF SLAVERY AND THE SLAVE TRADE

Ballagh, J. C., *A History of Slavery in Virginia*, Baltimore, 1902.
Flanders, R. B., *Plantation Slavery in Georgia*, Chapel Hill, 1933.
Jernegan, M. W., *Laboring and Dependent Classes in Colonial America, 1607–1783*, Chicago, 1931.
Seeber, E. D., *Anti-Slavery Opinion in France during the Second Half of the 18th Century*, Baltimore, 1937.
Williams, E., *Capitalism and Slavery*, Chapel Hill, 1944.

HISTORIES OF NEWSPAPERS

Morison, S., *The English Newspaper*, Cambridge, 1932.
Shaaber, M. A. *Some Forerunners of the Newspapers in England, 1476–1622*, Philadelphia, 1929.

SOCIAL AND CULTURAL HISTORIES

Apperson, G. L., *The Social History of Smoking*, New York, 1916.

Clendening, L., *Source Book of Medical History*, New York, 1942.

Crane, T. F., *Italian Social Customs of the Sixteenth Century and Their Influence on the Literatures of Europe*, New Haven, 1920.

Eyre, E., *European Civilization*, Vols. 5 and 6, Oxford, 1939.

Friedel, E., *A Cultural History of the Modern Age*, 5 vols., New York, 1933.

Gosse, P., *The History of Piracy*, New York, 1932.

Larwood, J., and Hotten, J. C., *History of Signboards*, London, 1908.

Robins, F. W., *The Story of the Lamp*, Oxford, 1939.

Roth, C., *The Jewish Contribution to Civilization*, New York, 1940.

Smith, P., *A History of Modern Culture*, 2 vols., New York, 1930–34.

Vincent, J. M., *Costume and Conduct*, Baltimore, 1935.

Winslow, C. E. A., *The Conquest of Epidemic Disease*, Princeton, 1943.

HISTORIES OF THE POSTAL SERVICE

Crutchley, E. T., *G. P. O.*, Cambridge, 1938.

Harlow, A. F., *Old Post Bags*, New York, 1928.

Hemmeon, J. C., *The History of the British Post Office*, Cambridge, 1912.

Hyde, J. W., *The Royal Mail*, London, 1899.

Joyce, H., *The History of the Post Office*, London, 1893.

Marshall, C. F. D., *The British Post Office*, London, 1926.

Smith, A. D., *The Development of Rates of Postage*, London, 1917.

HISTORIES OF COSTUME

Barton, L., *Historic Costume for the Stage*, Boston, 1935.

Chalmers, H., *Clothes On and Off the Stage*, New York, 1928.

Evans, M., *Costume throughout the Ages*, Philadelphia, 1930.

Kelley, F. M., and Schwabe, R., *Historic Costume*, London, 1925.

——, *A Short History of Costume and Armour*, New York, 1931.

Köhler, C., and Sichart, E. von, *A History of Costume*, London, 1928.

Leeming, J., *The Costume Book*, New York, 1938.

Parsons, F. A., *Psychology of Dress*, New York, 1921.

Varagnac, A., and Lepage-Medvey, E., *French Costumes*, London, 1939.

Wingfield, L. S., *Notes on Civil Costume in England*, London, 1891.

HISTORIES OF EDUCATION

Adamson, J. W., *A Short History of Education*, Cambridge, 1922.

Boyd, W., *History of Western Education*, London, 1921.

Ebby, F., and Arrowood, C. F., *Development of Modern Education*, New York, 1945.

Graves, F. P., *Great Educators of Three Centuries*, New York, 1912.

Hobhouse, C., *History of Oxford*, New York, 1946.

HISTORIES OF MILITARY SCIENCE

Colby, E., *Masters of Mobile Warfare*, Princeton, 1943.

Dodge, T. A., *Great Captains*, Boston, 1931.

——, *Gustavus Adolphus*, Boston, 1895.

Earle, E. M., *Makers of Modern Strategy*, Princeton, 1943.

Grancsay, S. V., *Historical Armor*, New York, 1945.

Hart, L., and Henry, B., *Great Captains Unveiled*, Boston, 1927.

Mahan, A. T., *The Influence of Sea Power, 1660–1783*, Boston, 1925.

Spaulding, A. L., Nickerson, H., and Wright, J. W., *Warfare*, New York, 1925.

HISTORIES OF SCIENCE

Barnouw, A. J., and Landheer, B., *The Contribution of Holland to the Sciences*, New York, 1943.

Buckley, A. B., *Short History of Natural Science*, New York, 1881.

Dampier, Sir W. C., *A Shorter History of Science*, New York, 1944.

———, *Science and the Human Mind*, New York, 1912.

———, *Cambridge Readings in the Literature of Science*, Cambridge, 1924.

———, *A History of Science and Its Relation with Philosophy and Religion*, Cambridge, 1929.

Duncan, C. S., *The New Science and English Literature in the Classical Period*, Menasha, 1913.

Gibson, C. R., *Heroes of the Scientific World*, London, 1916.

Gumpert, M., *Trailblazers of Science*, New York, 1936.

Gunther, R. W. T., *Early Science in Cambridge*, Oxford, 1937.

———, *Early Science in Oxford*, 13 vols., Oxford, 1923–45.

Hammond, D. B., *Stories of Scientific Discovery*, Cambridge, 1924.

Hart, J. B., *Makers of Science*, London, 1924.

Harvey-Gibson, R. J., *Two Thousand Years of Science*, 1931.

Jastrow, J., *The Story of Human Error*, New York, 1936.

Lenard, P., *Great Men of Science*, New York, 1933.

Libby, W., *An Introduction to the History of Science*, Boston, 1917.

Marmery, J. V., *Progress of Science*, London, 1895.

Pledge, H. T., *Science Since 1500*, London, 1939.

Riley, I. W., *From Myth to Reason*, New York, 1926.

Schuster, A., and Shipley, A. E., *Britain's Heritage of Science*, London, 1917.

Sedgwick, W. T., and Tyler, H. W., *History of Science*, New York, 1917.

Shorr, P., *Science and Superstition in the 18th Century*, New York, 1932.

Speiser, E. A., and others, *Studies in the History of Science*, Philadelphia, 1941.

Taylor, F. S., *The March of Mind*, New York, 1939.

Trattner, E. R., *Architect of Ideas*, New York, 1938.

Turner, D. M., *History of Science Teaching in England*, London, 1927.

Walsh, J. J., *The Popes and Science*, New York, 1908.

Warshaw, J., *Spanish Science and Invention*, New York, 1933.

Wilson, G., *The Human Side of Science*, New York, 1929.

Wolf, A., *A History of Science, Technology, and Philosophy in the 16th and 17th Centuries*, London, 1935.

Woodruff, L. L., *The Development of the Sciences*, New Haven, 1923.

HISTORIES OF ASTRONOMY

Forbes, G., *History of Astronomy*, New York, 1909.

Lodge, Sir O., *Pioneers of Science*, London, 1893.

Macpherson, H., *Modern Astronomy*, London, 1926.

HISTORIES OF BOTANY

Arber, A., *Herbals, Their Origin and Evolution*, Cambridge, 1938.

Greene, E. L., *Landmarks of Botanical History*, Washington, 1907.

Harvey-Gibson, R. J., *Outlines of the History of Botany*, London, 1919.

Hawks, E., *Pioneers of Plant Study*, London, 1928.

Locy, W. A., *The Growth of Biology*, New York, 1925.

Oliver, F. W., *Makers of British Botany*, Cambridge, 1913.

Reed, H. S., *A Short History of the Plant Sciences*, Waltham, 1942.

Rhode, E. S., *The Old English Herbals*, London, 1922.

HISTORIES OF GEOLOGY

Adams, F. D., *The Birth and Development of the Geological Sciences*, Baltimore, 1938.

Geikie, A., *The Founders of Geology*, London, 1897.

Woodward, H. B., *History of Geology*, London, 1911.

599

Zittel, K. A. von, *History of Geology and Paleontology*, London, 1901.

HISTORIES OF LITERATURE

France

Duclaux, A. M. F., *The French Procession*, New York, 1909.

Guyer, F. E., *The Main Stream of French Literature*, Boston, 1932.

Jones, P. M., *French Introspectives from Montaigne to Andre Gide*, Cambridge, 1937.

Mornet, D., *A Short History of French Literature*, New York, 1935.

Nitze, W. A., *A History of French Literature from Earliest Times to the Great War*, New York, 1922.

Saintsbury, G. E. B., *French Literature and Its Masters*, New York, 1946.

———, *A Short History of French Literature*, Oxford, 1928.

Strachey, G. L., *Landmarks in French Literature*, New York, 1912.

Wright, C. H. C., *A History of French Literature*, New York, 1925.

Germany

Francke, K., *A History of German Literature Determined by Social Forces*, New York, 1921.

Holzworth, F. J., *German Students Manual of the Literature, Land, and People of Germany*, New York, 1910.

Moore, R. W., *History of German Literature*, Hamilton, 1901.

Priest, G. M., *A Brief History of German Literature*, New York, 1909.

Robertson, J. G., *A History of German Literature*, New York, 1931.

Thomas, C., *A History of German Literature*, New York, 1914.

Waterhouse, G., *A Short History of German Literature*, London, 1942.

Italy

Collison-Morley, L., *Modern Italian Literature*, London, 1911.

Everett, W., *The Italian Poets Since Dante*, New York, 1904.

Foligno, C., *Epochs of Italian Literature*, Oxford, 1920.

Gardner, E. G., *The Story of Italian Literature*, New York, 1927.

Kennard, J., *A Literary History of the Italian People*, New York, 1941.

Sanctis, F. de, *History of Italian Literature*, New York, 1931.

Trail, F., *A History of Italian Literature*, New York, 1903–04.

England

De Vries, T., *Holland's Influence on the English Language and Literature*, Chicago, 1916.

Garnett, R., and Gosse E., *English Literature*, 4 vols., New York, 1903–04.

George, R. E. G., *India in English Literature*, London, 1925.

Long, W. J., *English Literature*, Boston, 1919.

Mair, G. H., *English Literature*, New York, 1911.

Marshall, R., *Italy in English Literature*, New York, 1934.

Neilson, W. A., *A History of English Literature*, New York, 1920.

Osgood, C. G., *The Voice of England*, New York, 1935.

Price, L. M., *The Reception of English Literature in Germany*, Berkeley, 1932.

Sampson, G., *The Concise Cambridge History of English Literature*, New York, 1941.

Ward, A. W., and Walker, A. R., *The Cambridge History of English Literature*, 15 vols., Cambridge, 1907–27.

The Netherlands

Persyn, J., *A Glance at the Soul of the Low Countries*, Leiden, 1916.

Portugal

Bell, A. F. G., *Portuguese Literature*, Oxford, 1922.

Spain

Clarke, H. B., *Spanish Literature*, New York, 1921.

Fitzmaurice-Kelly, J., *Chapters on Spanish Literature*, London, 1908.

Laborde, E. D., *A History of Spanish Literature*, London, 1931.

Merimee, E., *A History of Spanish Literature,* New York, 1930.

Northrup, G. T., *An Introduction to Spanish Literature,* Chicago, 1925.

HISTORIES OF COUNTRIES AND REGIONS

AUSTRIA

Coxe, W., *History of the House of Austria,* Vol. IV, London, 1864.

Leger, L., *History of Austria-Hungary,* New York, 1889.

Whitman, W. S., *Austria,* New York, 1906.

THE BALKANS

Forbes, N., Mitrany, D., Toynbee, A. J., and Hogarth, D. G., *The Balkans,* Oxford, 1915.

Leger, L., *Serbs, Croats, and Bulgars,* Paris, 1913.

Marriott, J. A. R., *The Eastern Question,* Oxford, 1924.

Miller, W., *The Balkans,* New York, 1908.

Schevill, F., *The Balkan Peninsula,* New York, 1922.

ALBANIA

Chekrezi, C. A., *Albania, Past and Present,* New York, 1919.

BULGARIA

Mischeiv, D., *The Bulgarians in the Past,* Lausanne, 1919.

MONTENEGRO

Stevenson, F. S., *A History of Montenegro,* London, 1912.

ROUMANIA

Jorga, N., *A History of Roumania,* London, 1925.

Seton-Watson, R. W., *A History of the Roumanians,* Cambridge, 1934.

SERBIA

Lazarovich-Hrbelianovich, Prince and Princess, *The Servian People,* 2 vols., New York, 1911.

Temperley, H. W. V., *History of Serbia,* London, 1917.

TURKEY

Lybyer, A. H., *The Government of the Ottoman Empire in the Time of Suleiman, the Magnificent,* London, 1913.

BELGIUM

Essen, L. van der, *A Short History of Belgium,* Chicago, 1916.

Linden, H. van der, and Hamelius, P., *Anglo-Belgian Relations, Past and Present,* London, 1918.

FRANCE

Adams, G. B., *The Growth of the French Nation,* New York, 1905.

Bainville, J., *History of France,* New York, 1926.

Bridge, J. S. C., *A History of France,* 5 vols., Oxford, 1921.

Creighton, L., *A First History of France,* London, 1893.

Davis, W. S., *A History of France,* Boston, 1919.

Duruy, V., *A History of France,* New York, 1889.

Grant, A. J., *The French Monarchy,* Cambridge, 1925.

Guerard, A., *The Life and Death of an Ideal,* New York, 1928.

Guignebert, C., *A Short History of the French People,* 2 vols., New York, 1930.

Hassall, A., *The French People,* New York, 1912.

Haught, F. A., *A History of French Commercial Policy,* New York, 1941.

Kitchen, G. W., *A History of France to 1793,* 3 vols., Oxford, 1896–1903.

Macdonald, J. Moreton, *A History of France,* 3 vols., New York, 1915.

Mackinnon, J., *Growth and Decline of the French Monarchy,* London, 1902.

601

Marriott, J. A. R., *A Short History of France*, London, 1942.

Sedgwick, H. D., *France, A Short History*, Boston, 1929.

Seignobos, C., *The Evolution of the French People*, New York, 1933.

Tilley, A., *Modern France*, Cambridge, 1922.

Van Dyke, P., *The Story of France*, New York, 1929.

GREAT BRITAIN

Adams, J. T., *Building the British Empire*, New York, 1939.

Andrews, C. M., *A History of England*, Boston, 1903.

Beard, C. A., *Introduction to the English Historians*, New York, 1908.

Bright, J. F., *History of England*, Vols. 1–3, New York, 1905.

Cheyney, E. P., *A Short History of England*, New York, 1904.

———, *A Social and Industrial History of England*, New York, 1905.

Clark, G. N., ed., *Oxford History of England*, Vols. 7–12, Oxford, 1934–43.

Cross, A. L., *A History of England and Greater Britain*, New York, 1914.

———, *A Shorter History of England and Greater Britain*, New York, 1929.

Dietz, F. C., *A Political and Social History of England*, New York, 1927.

Dunham, W. H., *Complaint and Reform in England, 1436–1714*, New Haven, 1938.

Fisher, H. A. L., *An Introductory History of England*, London, 1935.

Fletcher, C. R. L., *An Introductory History of England*, 2 vols., New York, 1910.

Gardiner, S. R., *A Student's History of England*, London, 1929.

Gipson, L. H., *The British Empire*, 6 vols., Caldwell, Idaho, 1936–42.

Hassall, A., *The History of British Foreign Policy*, Edinburgh, 1912.

Hunt, W., and Poole, R. L., eds., Vols. 5–11, *The Political History of England*, New York, 1906–07.

Hulme, E. M., *A History of the British People*, New York, 1924.

Innes, A. D., *A History of England and the British Empire*, 4 vols., London, 1927.

Jordan, W. K., *The Development of Religious Toleration in England*, Cambridge, 1933.

Jose, A. W., *The Growth of the Empire*, London, 1913.

Larson, L. M., *History of England and the British Commonwealth*, New York, 1924.

Lunt, W. E., *A History of England*, New York, 1928.

Mowat, R. B., and Slosson, P., *History of the English Speaking Peoples*, New York, 1943.

———, *A History of Great Britain*, Oxford, 1922.

Muir, R., *Short History of The British Commonwealth*, 2 vols., New York, 1922.

Mullett, C. F., *The British Empire*, New York, 1938.

Newton, A. P., *The British Empire to 1783*, London, 1935.

Notestein, W., *English Folk*, New York, 1938.

Oman, C., ed., *A History of England*, Vols. 4–6, New York, 1913.

Pollard, A. F., *The History of England*, New York, 1922.

———, *The British Empire*, London, 1909.

———, *Factors in Modern History*, London, 1932.

Powell, F. Y., and Tout, T. F., *History of England*, New York, 1910.

Robinson, H., *History of England*, Boston, 1927.

———, *Development of the British Empire*, Boston, 1922.

Rose, J. H., Newton, A. P., and Benians, E. A., eds., *History of the British Empire*, Vols. 1–2. New York, 1929.

Seeley, J. R., *The Growth of British Policy*, Cambridge, 1930.

Tickner, F. W., *Social and Industrial History of England*, New York, 1915.

Trevelyan, G. M., *History of England,* New York, 1927.

———, *English Social History,* New York, 1942.

Tout, T. F., *An Advanced History of Great Britain,* New York, 1919.

Usher, A. P., *The Industrial History of England,* Boston, 1920.

Ward, A. W., and Gooch, G. P., *Cambridge History of British Foreign Policy,* Vol. 14, Cambridge, 1923–39.

Williams, B., *The British Empire,* New York, 1928.

Williamson, J. A., *The Evolution of England,* Oxford, 1931.

Wingfield-Stratford, E., *The History of British Civilization,* New York, 1927.

Woodward, W. H., *A Short History of the Expansion of the British Empire,* Cambridge, 1931.

SCOTLAND

Brown, P. H., *History of Scotland,* Cambridge, 1902.

Mackenzie, A. M., *Scotland in Modern Times,* 6 vols., New York, 1942.

Mackie, R. L., *A Short History of Scotland,* Oxford.

Mackintosh, J., *The Story of Scotland,* New York, 1894.

Rait, R., and Pryde, G. S., *Scotland,* London, 1934.

Terry, C. S., *A History of Scotland,* Cambridge, 1920.

HOLY ROMAN EMPIRE

Brachmann, *Germany and Poland,* Munich, 1934.

Bryce, J., *The Holy Roman Empire,* New York, 1901.

Henderson, E. F., *A Short History of Germany,* New York, 1916.

Holland, A. W., *Germany,* London, 1914.

Lowenstein, Prince H. zu, *The Germans in History,* New York, 1946.

Phillips, W. A., Headlam, J. W., and Holland, A. W., *A Short History of Germany and Her Colonies,* London, 1914.

Pinnow, H., *History of Germany,* New York, 1923.

Priest, G. M., *Germany Since 1740,* New York, 1915.

Schevill, F., *The Making of Modern Germany,* Chicago, 1916.

Schuster, G. N., and Bergstrasser, A., *Germany, A Short History,* New York, 1944.

Valentine, V., *The German People,* New York, 1946.

PRUSSIA

Marriott, J. A. R., and Robertson, C. G., *The Evolution of Prussia,* Oxford, 1915.

HUNGARY

Andrassy, G., *The Development of Hungarian Constitutional Liberty,* London, 1908.

Horvath, E., *The Banat,* Budapest, 1931.

Knatchbull-Huegessen, C. M., *The Political Evolution of the Hungarian Nation,* London, 1908.

Sassu, C., *Rumanians and Hungarians, Historical Premises,* Bucharest, 1940.

Teleki, *The Evolution of Hungary and Its Place in History,* New York, 1923.

Vamberry, A., *The Story of Hungary,* New York, 1894.

IRELAND

Colles, R., *The History of Ulster,* London, 1919.

Curtis, E., *A History of Ireland,* London, 1942.

D'Alton, E. A., *History of Ireland,* 8 vols., London, 1910.

Dudley, E., *Church and State in Tudor Ireland,* Dublin, 1935.

Dunlop, R., *Ireland from the Earliest Times to the Present Day,* Oxford, 1922.

Gwynn, D., *The Struggle for Catholic Emancipation, 1750–1829,* New York, 1928.

Gwynn, S., *The History of Ireland,* New York, 1923.

Johnston, C., and Spencer, C., *Ireland's Story,* Boston, 1905.

McManus, S., *The Story of the Irish Race,* New York, 1944.

603

Macbeth, J., *The Story of Ireland and Her Church*, Dublin, 1899.

Phillips, W. A., *History of the Church of Ireland*, London, 1933.

Turner, E. R., *Ireland and England*, New York, 1920.

ITALY

Gardner, E. G., *Italy*, London, 1934.

Gifford, A., *Italy, Her People and Their Story*, Boston, 1905.

Jamison, E. M., *Italy, Medieval and Modern*, Oxford, 1917.

Okey, T., *Venice and Its Story*, New York, 1930.

Savatorelli, L., *A Concise History of Italy*, New York, 1940.

Sedgwick, H. D., *Short History of Italy*, New York, 1905.

Thayer, W. R., *History of Venice*, New York, 1905.

Trevelyan, J. P., *Short History of the Italian People*, New York, 1920.

THE NETHERLANDS

Barker, J., *The Rise and Decline of the Netherlands*, London, 1906.

Barnouw, A. J., *The Making of Modern Holland*, New York, 1944.

Bense, J. F., *Anglo-Dutch Relations*, The Hague, 1924.

Blok, P. J., *History of the Netherlands*, 5 vols., New York, 1898–1912.

Edmundson, G., *History of Holland*, Cambridge, 1922.

Kitchin, G. W., *Holland*, London, 1883.

Riemens, H., *The Netherlands*, New York, 1939.

Van Loon, W., *The Fall of the Dutch Republic*, Boston, 1913.

Veraart, J. A., *Holland*, London, 1944.

Vlekke, B. H., *Evolution of the Dutch Nation*, New York, 1945.

NORWAY

Gjerset, K., *History of the Norwegian People*, 2 vols., New York, 1915.

Keary, C. F., *Norway and the Norwegians*, New York, 1892.

Koht, H., *The Voice of Norway*, New York, 1944.

Sorensen, S., *Norway*, New York, 1899.

POLAND

Gorka, O., *Outline of Polish History*, London, 1942.

Halecki, O., *A History of Poland*, London, 1942.

Lewinski-Corwin, *Political History of Poland*, New York, 1917.

Morfil, W. R., *Story of Poland*, New York, 1895.

Newman, B., *The Story of Poland*, London, 1940.

Orvis, J. S., *A Brief History of Poland*, London, 1919.

Phillips, W. A., *Poland*, New York, 1915.

Reddaway, W. F., *The Cambridge History of Poland*, Cambridge, 1941.

Rose, W. J., *Poland*, Middlesex, 1939.

Whitton, F. E., *A History of Poland*, London, 1917.

PORTUGAL

Prestage, E., *The Diplomatic Relations of Portugal*, Watford, 1925.

Stephens, H. M., *Portugal*, New York, 1903.

Young, G., *Portugal, Old and Young*, Oxford, 1917.

RUSSIA

Alexinsky, G., *Russia and Europe*, London, 1917.

Allen, W. E. D., *The Ukraine*, Cambridge, 1940.

Bain, R. N., *The First Romanoffs*, London, 1905.

Bain, R. N., *Slavonic Europe*, Cambridge, 1908.

Beazley, R., Forbes, N., and Birkett, G. A., *Russia from the Vorangians to the Bolshevics*, Oxford, 1918.

Box, P. H., *Russia*, Bristol, 1933.

Brianchaninov, *A History of Russia*, London, 1930.

Chaninov, N. B., *A History of Russia*, New York, 1930.

Eckardt, H. von, *Russia*, New York, 1932.

Hrushevsky, M., *A History of the Ukraine*, London, 1941.

Kerner, R. J., *The Urge to the Sea*, Berkeley, 1942.

604

Kliuchevsky, V. O., *History of Russia,* New York, 1911.

Kornilov, A., *Modern Russian History,* 2 vols., New York, 1917.

——, *History of Russia,* New York, 1933.

Mavor, J., *Economic History of Russia,* 2 vols., London, 1925.

Mirsky, D. S., *Russia,* London, 1931.

Platonov, S. E., *History of Russia,* New York, 1925.

Pokrovsky, M. N., *History of Russia,* New York, 1931.

Rambaud, A., *History of Russia,* 2 vols., Boston, 1880.

Robinson, G. T., *Rural Russia under the Old Regime,* New York, 1932.

Morfil, W. R., *Russia,* New York, 1908.

Munro, H., *The Rise of the Russian Empire,* London, 1900.

Nowak, F., *Medieval Slavdom and the Rise of Russia,* New York, 1930.

Pares, Sir B., *A History of Russia,* New York, 1928.

Segal, L., *Russia, A Concise History,* London, 1944.

Summers, B. H., *A Short History of Russia,* New York, 1943.

Tompkins, S. R., *Russia Through the Ages,* New York, 1940.

Vernadsky, G., *A History of Russia,* New Haven, 1929.

——, *A Political and Diplomatic History of Russia,* Boston, 1936.

Wallace, D. M., Kropotkin, Prince, Mijatovich, C., and Bourchier, J. D., *A Short History of Russian and the Balkan States,* London, 1914.

Wolkonsky, S. M., *Pictures of Russian History and Literature,* Boston, 1897.

SCANDINAVIA

Bain, R. N., *Scandinavia,* Cambridge, 1905.

Hovde, B. J., *The Scandinavian Countries, 1720–1865,* Boston, 1944.

SPAIN

Altamira, R., *A History of Spanish Civilization,* London, 1930.

Bertrand, L., and Petrie, Sir C., *The History of Spain, 1711–1931,* London, 1931.

Chapman, C., *A History of Spain,* New York, 1918.

Hume, M. A. S., *The Spanish People,* London, 1901.

——, *Spain, Its Greatness and Decay, 1479–1788,* Cambridge, 1898.

Klein, J., *The Mesta, 1273–1836,* Cambridge, 1920.

Martins, O., *A History of Iberian Civilization,* London, 1930.

Merriman, R. B., *Rise of the Spanish Empire in the Old World and the New, 1918–1925,* 3 vols., 1918–1925.

Moran, C., *Spain,* Boston, 1932.

Salmon, E. D., *Imperial Spain,* New York, 1931.

Sedgwick, H. D., *Spain,* Boston, 1926.

SWEDEN

Cronholm, N. M., *A History of Sweden,* Chicago, 1902.

Grimberg, C. G., *A History of Sweden,* Rock Island, 1935.

Hallendorf, C. J. H., and Schück, A., *History of Sweden,* Stockholm, 1929.

Stomberg, A. A., *A History of Sweden,* New York, 1931.

Svanström, R., and Palmstierna, C. F., *A Short History of Sweden,* Oxford, 1934.

SWITZERLAND

Dandliker, K., *History of Switzerland,* London, 1899.

Hug, L., and Stead, R., *Switzerland,* New York, 1890.

Oechsli, W., *History of Switzerland,* Cambridge, 1922.

TURKEY

Creasy, E. S., *History of the Ottoman Turks,* London, 1877.

Davis, W. S., *A Short History of the Near East,* New York, 1933.

Eversley, (G. J. Shaw-Lefevre) Baron, *The Turkish Empire,* New York, 1917.

Freeman, E. A., *The Ottoman Power in Europe,* London, 1877.

605

Luke, Sir H. C. J., *The Making of Modern Turkey*, London, 1936.
Marriott, J. A. R., *The Eastern Question*, Oxford, 1940.

Merriman, R. B., *Suleiman the Magnificent, 1520–1566*, Cambridge, 1944.

PART 1. EUROPEAN SOCIETY ABOUT 1492

CHAPTER 1. THE BACKGROUND OF MODERN EUROPEAN HISTORY

General

Bax, E. B., *German Society at the Close of the Middle Ages*, London, 1894.
Brown, W. E., *The Achievements of the Middle Ages*, London, 1928.
Crump, C. G., and Jacob, E. F., *The Legacy of the Middle Ages*, Oxford, 1926.
Janssen, J., *History of the German People at the Close of the Middle Ages*, 16 vols., Freiburg, 1892–94.
Pirenne, H., *Economic and Social History of Medieval Europe*, London, 1936.
Salzman, L. F., *English Life in the Middle Ages*, London, 1926.
Sitwell, Sir G. P., *The Hurts of Holdworth and Their Descendants*, Oxford, 1930.

Geographical Background

Cornish, V., *The Great Capitals*, London, 1923.
Darby, H. C., *An Historical Geography of England before 1800*, Cambridge, 1936.
East, W. G., *An Historical Geography of Europe*, London, 1935.
Huntington, E., *Economic and Social Geography*, New York, 1933.
Johnston, K., *A Physical, Historical, Political and Descriptive Geography*, London, 1896.
Newbigin, M., *Geographical Aspects of Balkan Problems*, London, 1915.
Wright, J. K., *The Geographical Basis of European History*, London, 1928.

Printing

Butler, P., *The Origin of Printing in Europe*, Chicago, 1940.

Carter, T. F., *The Invention of Printing in China and Its Spread Westward*, New York, 1925.
Haynes, *The Student's History of Printing*, New York, 1930.
Hunter, D., *Papermaking*, New York, 1913.
McMurtie, D. C., *The Book*, New York, 1937.
Orcutt, W. D., *Master Makers of Books*, Garden City, New York, 1928.
Winship, G. P., *Gutenberg to Plantin*, Cambridge, 1926.
Wroth, L. C., *A History of the Printed Book*, New York, 1938.

Art

Crane, W., *The Decorative Illustrations of Books*, Boston, 1905.
Simon, H., *500 Years of Illustration*, New York, 1942.
Wright, T., *History of Caricature and the Grotesque in Art*, London, 1835.

CHAPTER 2. THE ECONOMIC AND SOCIAL ORGANIZATION OF EUROPE

Agriculture

Andrews, C. M., *The Old English Manor*, Baltimore, 1892.
Ashley, W. J., *The Bread of Our Forefathers*, Oxford, 1928.
Bennett, H. S., *Life on the English Manor*, Cambridge, 1938.
The Cambridge Economic History of Europe, Vol. I., New York, 1942.
Denholm-Young, N., *Seigniorial Administration in England*, London, 1937.
Fedden, K. W., *Manor Life in Old France*, New York, 1933.
Gras, N. S. B., *The Economic and Social History of an English Village*, Crawley Manor, Cambridge, 1930.

Gray, H. L., *English Field Systems,* Cambridge, 1915.

Homans, G. C., *English Villagers of the 13th Century,* Cambridge, 1941.

Hone, N. J., *The Manor and Manorial Records,* London, 1906.

Jessop, A. J., *The Coming of the Friars,* London, 1917.

Lennard, R. V., *Rural Northamptonshire under the Commonwealth,* Oxford, 1916.

Levett, A. E., *Studies in Manorial History,* Oxford, 1938.

Muhlfield, H. E., *A Survey of Manor of Wye,* New York, 1933.

Neilson, N., *Agrarian Life in the Middle Ages,* New York, 1936.

————, *Economic Conditions on the Manors of Ramsey Abbey,* Philadelphia, 1899.

Page, F. M., *The Estates of Crowley Abbey,* Cambridge, 1934.

Ruston, A. G., and Witney, D., *Hooton Pagnell,* New York, 1936.

Seebohn, F., *The English Village Community,* London, 1890.

Spiegel, H. W., *Land Tenure Policies at Home and Abroad,* Chapel Hill, 1941.

Stenton, F. M., *Types of Manorial Structure in the Northern Danelaw,* Oxford, 1910.

Waldo, K., *Manor Life in Old France,* New York, 1933.

See also works listed under Agriculture and Peasants.

Cities

Clark, M. V., *The Medieval City State,* London, 1926.

Green, J. R., *Town Life in the 15th Century,* London, 1894.

Lane, F. C., *Andrea Barbarigo, Merchant of Venice,* Baltimore, 1944.

Letts, M., *Bruges and Its Past,* London, 1926.

Scaife, W. B., *Florentine Life during the Renaissance,* Baltimore, 1893.

Schevill, F., *History of Florence,* New York, 1936.

Thorndike, L., *The History of Medieval Europe,* Boston, 1917.

Gilds

Franklin, A. L. A., *Les Corporations Ouvrieres de Paris du XII au XVIII siècle,* Paris, 1889.

Staley, E., *The Guilds of Florence,* Chicago, 1906.

Unwin, G., *The Gild Companies of London,* London, 1908.

Fuggers

Ehrenberg, R., *Capital and Finance in the Age of the Renaissance,* London, 1928.

Strieder, J., *Jacob Fugger, the Rich,* New York, 1931.

Medici

Armstrong, E., *Lorenzo de Medici and Florence in the Fifteenth Century,* London, 1896.

Booth, C., *Cosimo I,* Cambridge, 1931.

Brinton, S. J. C., *The Golden Age of the Medici,* Boston, 1926.

Vaughn, H. M., *The Medici Popes,* New York, 1908.

Young, G. F., *The Medici,* 2 vols., New York, 1923.

CHAPTER 3. EUROPEAN STATES AND GOVERNMENTS

Feudalism

Seignobos, C., *The Feudal Regime,* New York, 1902.

Governments and States

Beuf, C., *Cesare Borgia,* New York, 1942.

Carlyly, R. W., and A. J., *A History of Medieval Political Theory in the West,* 5 vols., London, 1903–28.

Cheyney, E. P., *The Dawn of a New Era, 1250–1453,* New York, 1935.

————, *European Background of American History,* New York, 1904.

Collins, R. W., *A History of Medieval Civilization,* New York, 1936.

Ferguson, W. K., *The Renaissance,* New York, 1940.

Garner, J. L., *Caesar Borgia,* New York, 1912.

Gierke, O., *Political Theories of the Middle Ages,* Cambridge, 1900.

Huizinga, J., *The Waning of the Middle Ages,* London, 1924.
Stephenson, C., *Medieval History,* New York, 1935.
Thompson, J. W., *The Middle Ages,* New York, 1931.
See also works under General Histories and Histories of Countries and Regions.

CHAPTER 4. EUROPEAN CULTURE

Allen, P. S., *The Age of Erasmus,* Oxford, 1914.
Benesch, O., *The Art of the Renaissance in Northern Europe,* Cambridge, 1945.
Berenson, B., *The Central Italian Painters of the Renaissance,* New York, 1897.
———, *North Italian Painters of the Renaissance,* New York, 1907.
———, *The Venetian Painters of the Renaissance,* New York, 1897.
Brinton, E., *The Renaissance in Italian Art,* 9 vols., London, 1907–8.
Burckhardt, J., *The Civilization of the Period of the Renaissance in Italy,* 2 vols., London, 1878.
Bush, D., *The Renaissance and English Humanism,* Toronto, 1939.
Cambridge Modern History, Vol. I, Chapters 16 and 17, New York, 1902–12.
Coulton, G. G., *Medieval Panorama,* Cambridge, 1939.
Cox, T., *The Renaissance in Europe,* London, 1933.
Dennistoun, J., *Memoirs of the Dukes of Urbino,* London, 1909.
Einstein, L. D., *The Italian Renaissance in England,* New York, 1913.
Elliot-Binns, L. E., *England and the New Learning,* London, 1937.
Ferguson, W. K., *The Renaissance,* New York, 1940.
Field, L. F., *An Introduction to the Study of the Renaissance,* New York, 1898.
Funck-Brentano, F., *The Renaissance,* New York, 1930.
Gardner, E. G., *Dukes and Poets of Ferrara,* New York, 1904.

Gobineau, J., *The Renaissance,* New York, 1913.
Hare, C., *Courts and Camps of the Italian Renaissance,* London, 1908.
Jerrold, M. F., *Italy in the Renaissance,* London, 1927.
Keyser, C. J., *Humanism and Science,* New York, 1931.
Lanciani, R., *The Golden Days of the Renaissance in Rome,* Boston, 1906.
Lynn, C., *A College Professor of the Renaissance,* Chicago, 1937.
Marcus, J. R., *The Jews in the Medieval World,* Cincinnati, 1928.
Martin, A. W. O. von, *Sociology of the Renaissance,* New York, 1944.
McCaffery, E., *History of Astrology,* New York, 1942.
Mead, W. E., *The English Medieval Feast,* Boston, 1931.
Miller, B., *Beyond the Sublime Porte,* New Haven, 1931.
Paschang, J. L., *The Popes and the Revival of Learning,* Washington, 1927.
Schevill, F., *History of Florence,* New York, 1936.
Symonds, J. A., *Renaissance in Italy,* 7 vols., London, 1875–1904.
———, *A Short History of the Renaissance in Italy,* London, 1893.
Taylor, R. A., *Aspects of the Italian Renaissance,* Boston, 1923.
Thompson, J. W., Rowley, G., and Schevill, F., *The Civilization of the Renaissance,* Chicago, 1929.
———, *The Medieval Library,* Chicago, 1939.
Thorndike, L., *Science and Thought in the Fifteenth Century,* New York, 1929.
Van Dyke, P., *The Age of the Renascence,* Edinburgh, 1897.
Ward, W. H., *The Architecture of the Renaissance in France,* London, 1911.
Wedel, T. O., *The Medieval Attitude toward Astrology,* New Haven, 1920.
Weiss, R., *Humanism in England during the Fifteenth Century,* Oxford, 1941.
Whitlesey, A., *The Renaissance Archi-*

tecture of Central and Northern Spain, New York, 1920.

See also works under Architecture and Painting.

PART 2. THE SIXTEENTH CENTURY

CHAPTER 5. THE BEGINNINGS OF EUROPEAN EXPANSION, 1492-1598

Ships and Sailors

Bowen, F. C., Conquest of the Seas, New York, 1940.

Culver, H. B., The Book of Old Ships, Garden City, 1924.

Lane, F. C., Venetian Ships and Shipbuilders of the Renaissance, Baltimore, 1934.

Meigs, I. F., The Story of the Seaman, Philadelphia, 1924.

Portuguese Explorations

Beazley, O., Prince Henry the Navigator, New York, 1895.

Bell, A. F. G., Portuguese Portraits, Oxford, 1917.

Morison, S. E., Portuguese Voyages to America in the Fifteenth Century, Cambridge, 1940.

Prestage, E., The Portuguese Pioneers, London, 1933.

Sanceau, E., The Land of Prester John, New York, 1944.

Synge, M. B., A Book of Discovery, New York, 1912.

Discovery of America

Beazley, C. R., John and Sebastian Cabot, New York, 1898.

Bolton, H. E., Spanish Exploration in the Southwest, New York, 1916.

Bourne, E. G., Spain in America, New York, 1904.

——, The Demarcation Line of Alexander VI, Yale Review, 1892.

Harisse, H., Americus Vespucius, London, 1895.

——, The Diplomatic History of America, London, 1897.

Harisse, J., The Discovery of North America, London, 1892.

Keane, J., The Evolution of Geography, London, 1899.

Kirkpatrick, F. A., Latin America, New York, 1939.

——, The Spanish Conquistadores, London, 1934.

Mirsky, J., The Westward Crossings, New York, 1946.

Moore, D. R., A History of Latin America, New York, 1939.

Pohn, F. J., Amerigo Vespucci, Pilot Major, New York, 1944.

Richman, J. B., The Spanish Conquerors, New Haven, 1919.

Rippy, J. F., Historical Evolution of Hispanic America, New York, 1932.

Robertson, W. S., History of the Latin-American Nations, New York, 1922.

Wilgus, A. C., Colonial Hispanic America, Washington, 1936.

Columbus

Madariaga, S. de, Christopher Columbus, New York, 1940.

Marius, A., Columbus, New York, 1928.

Morrison, S. E., Admiral of the Ocean Sea, 2 vols., Boston, 1942.

Nunn, G. E., The Geographical Conceptions of Columbus, New York, 1924.

Wassermann, J., Columbus, Boston, 1930.

Magellan

Benson, E. F., Ferdinand Magellan, New York, 1930.

Guillermard, F. H. H., Life of Ferdinand Magellan and the First Circumnavigation of the Globe, New York, 1891.

Hildebrand, A. S., Magellan, New York, 1924.

Ober, F. A., Ferdinand Magellan, New York, 1907.

Mexico

Braden, C. S., Religious Aspects of the Conquest of Mexico, Durham, 1930.

MacNutt, Ferdinand, *Cortez and the Conquest of Mexico,* New York, 1909.

Madariaga, S. de, *Hernan Cortez,* New York, 1941.

Priestley, H. I., *The Mexican Nation,* New York, 1923.

Wagner, H. R., *The Discovery of New Spain in 1518 by Juan de Grijalva,* Berkeley, 1942.

——, *The Rise of Fernando Cortez,* Berkeley, 1944.

Pizarro

Means, P. A., *Fall of the Inca Empire and the Spanish Rule in Peru,* New York, 1932.

Smyth, C., *Francisco Pizarro and the Conquest of Peru,* New York, 1931.

Portugal in the Far East

Chang, Tien-tse, *Sino-Portuguese Trade from 1514 to 1644,* Leyden, 1934.

Danvers, F. C., *The Portuguese in India,* 2 vols., London, 1894.

Jayne, K. G., *Vasco da Gama and His Successors, 1460–1580,* London, 1910.

Prestage, E., *The Portuguese Pioneers,* London, 1933.

Stephens, H. M., *Albuquerque and the Portuguese Settlements in India,* Oxford, 1897.

Whiteway, R. S., *The Rise of Portuguese Power in India, 1497–1550,* Westminster, 1899.

Portuguese in Brazil

Calogeras, J. P., *A History of Brazil,* Chapel Hill, 1939.

Spanish Colonization

Bolton, H. E., and Marshall, T. M., *The Colonization of North America, 1492–1783,* New York, 1925.

——, *The Spanish Borderlands,* New Haven, 1921.

Chapman, C. E., *Colonial Hispanic America,* New York, 1933.

Hamilton, E. J., *American Treasure and the Price Revolution in Spain, 1501–1650,* Cambridge, 1934.

Hanke, L., *The First Social Experi-ments in America,* Cambridge, 1935.

Haring, C. H., *Trade and Navigation between Spain and the Indies in the Time of the Habsburgs,* Cambridge, 1918.

Lea, H. C., *The Inquisition in the Spanish Dependencies,* New York, 1908.

Parry, J. H., *The Spanish Theory of Empire in the Sixteenth Century,* Cambridge, 1940.

Roscher, W. G. F., *The Spanish Colonial System,* New York, 1904.

Simpson, L. B., *Studies in the Administration of the Indians in New Spain,* Berkeley, 1934.

Zavala, S. A., *New Viewpoints on the Spanish Colonization of America,* Philadelphia, 1943.

Philippines

Barrows, D. P., *History of the Philippines,* New York, 1924.

Blair, *The Philippine Islands, 1493–1803,* 55 vols., Cleveland, 1903–09.

McCarthy, E. J., *Spanish Beginnings in the Philippines, 1564–1572,* Washington, 1943.

Schurz, W. L., *The Manila Galleon,* New York, 1939.

Effects

Gillespie, J. E., *The Influence of Overseas Expansion on England to 1700,* New York, 1920.

Hamilton, E. J., *American Treasure and the Price Revolution in Spain,* Cambridge, 1934.

CHAPTER 6. EUROPEAN POLITICS, 1494–1559

Henry VII

Conway, A. E., *Henry VII's Relations with Scotland and Ireland, 1485–1498,* Cambridge, 1932.

Gairdner, J., *Henry VII,* London, 1926.

Temperley, G., *Henry VII,* Boston, 1914.

Isabella

Plunket, I. L., *Isabel of Castile and the Making of the Spanish Nation,* New York, 1919.

Walsh, W. T., *Isabella of Spain,* London, 1933.

Maximilian I

Hare, C., *Maximilian, the Dreamer, 1459–1519,* London, 1913.

Seton Watson, R. W., *Maximilian I,* Westminster, 1902.

Waas, G. E., *The Legendary Character of Kaiser Maximilian,* New York, 1941.

Henry VIII

Crabites, P., *Clement VII and Henry VIII,* London, 1936.

Gasquet, F. A., *Henry VIII and the English Monasteries,* 2 vols., London, 1888–93.

Hume, M. A. S., *The Wives of Henry the Eighth,* New York, 1905.

Pollard, A. F., *Henry VIII,* New York, 1905.

Suleiman, the Magnificent

Merriman, R. B., *Suleiman the Magnificent, 1520–1566,* Cambridge, 1944.

Charles V

Armstrong, E., *The Emperor Charles V,* 2 vols., London, 1902.

Brandi, K., *The Emperor Charles V,* New York, 1939.

Lewis, D. B. W., *Charles of Europe,* Hartford, 1931.

McElwee, W. L., *The Reign of Charles V, 1516–1558,* New York, 1936.

Julius II

Gobineau, J. A., Comte de, *The Golden Flower,* New York, 1924.

Klaczko, J., *Rome and the Renaissance,* New York, 1903.

Charles the Bold

Haggard, A. C. P., *Louis XI and Charles the Bold,* London, 1913.

France

Bridge, J. S. C., *A History of France, 1483–1515,* 5 vols., Oxford, 1921–1936.

Palm, F. C., *Politics and Religion in Sixteenth Century France,* Boston, 1927.

Spain

Lea, H. C., *The Moriscos of Spain,* Philadelphia, 1901.

Merton, R., *Cardinal Ximenes and the Making of Spain,* London, 1934.

Prawdin, M., *The Mad Queen of Spain,* London, 1938.

Prescott, W. H., *History of the Reign of Ferdinand and Isabella the Catholic,* 3 vols., Philadelphia, 1875.

Roth, C., *A History of the Marranos,* Philadelphia, 1932.

Seaver, H. L., *The Great Revolt in Castile,* Boston, 1928.

England

Cheyney, E. P., *Social Changes in England in the Sixteenth Century as Reflected in Contemporary Literature,* Boston, 1895.

Dietz, F. C., *English Government Finance, 1485–1558,* Urbana, 1921.

——, *English Public Finance, 1558–1641,* New York, 1932.

——, *Finances of Edward VII and Mary,* Northampton, 1918.

Einstein, L. D., *Tudor Ideals,* New York, 1921.

Feiling, K. G., *England under the Tudors and the Stuarts,* New York, 1927.

Fisher, H. A. L., *The History of England, 1485–1547,* New York, 1924.

Harbison, E. H., *Rival Ambassadors at the Court of Queen Mary,* Princeton, 1940.

Jameson, S., *The Decline of Merrie England,* Indianapolis, 1930.

Jones, P. V., *The Household of a Tudor Nobleman,* Urbana, 1918.

Innes, A. D., *England under the Tudors,* London, 1921.

Lee, S., *Great Englishmen of the Sixteenth Century,* New York, 1904.

Lumsden, C. B., *The Dawn of Modern England,* New York, 1910.

Palmer, R. L., *English Social History in the Making,* London, 1934.

611

Pollard, A. F., *England under Protector Somerset*, London, 1900.

Powers, G. W., *England and the Reformation, 1485–1603*, New York, 1898.

Prescott, H. M., *A Spanish Tudor*, New York, 1940.

Read, C., *The Tudors*, New York, 1936.

Reese, M. M., *The Tudors and the Stuarts*, New York, 1940.

Salzman, L. F., *England in Tudor Times*, New York, 1926.

Smith, A. G., *The Babington Plot*, London, 1936.

Smith, H. M., *Pre-Reformation England*, New York, 1938.

Stafford, H. G., *James VI of Scotland and the Throne of England*, New York, 1940.

Wilding, P., *Thomas Cromwell*, London, 1935.

Williams, C. H., *The Making of Tudor Despotism*, London, 1928.

CHAPTER 7. RELIGIOUS REVOLT AND REFORM IN GERMAN AND SCANDINAVIAN LANDS

General Works on the Reformation or Protestant Revolt

Baldwin, S., *The Organization of Medieval Christianity*, New York, 1929.

Beard, C., *The Reformation in the Sixteenth Century*, London, 1896.

Belloc, H., *Characters of the Reformation*, London, 1937.

———, *How the Reformation Happened*, London, 1928.

Coulton, G. G., *Art and the Reformation*, Oxford, 1928.

Church, F. C., *The Italian Reformers, 1534–1564*, New York, 1922.

Fisher, G. P., *The Reformation*, New York, 1906.

Hulme, E. M., *The Renaissance, the Protestant Revolution, and the Catholic Reformation*, New York, 1917.

Hyma, A., *Christianity, Capitalism, and Communism*, Ann Arbor, 1937.

Lindsay, T. M., *A History of the Reformation*, 2 vols., New York, 1906–7.

Lucas, H. S., *The Renaissance and the Reformation*, New York, 1924.

McSorley, J., *An Outline History of the Church by Centuries*, St. Louis, 1943.

Messenger, E. C., *The Reformation, the Mass and the Priesthood*, London, 1936.

McGiffert, A. C., *Protestant Thought before Kant*, New York, 1911.

Murray, R. H., *The Political Consequences of the Reformation*, Boston, 1926.

O'Brien, G. A. T., *An Essay on the Economic Effects of the Reformation*, London, 1923.

Powers, G. W., *England and the Reformation, 1485–1603*, New York, 1898.

Seebohm, F., *The Era of the Protestant Revolution*, London, 1920.

Smith, P., *The Age of the Reformation*, New York, 1920.

Walker, W., *The Reformation*, New York, 1901.

Erasmus

Allen, P. S., *Erasmus, Lectures and Wayfaring Sketches*, Oxford, 1936.

Elliott-Binns, L. E., *Erasmus the Reformer*, London, 1928.

Emerton, E., *Desiderius Erasmus*, New York, 1899.

Fronde, J. A., *Life and Letters of Erasmus*, New York, 1911.

Hollis, C., *Erasmus*, London, 1933.

Huizinga, J., *Erasmus*, New York, 1924.

Hyma, A., *Erasmus and the Humanists*, New York, 1930.

———, *The Youth of Erasmus*, Ann Arbor, 1930.

Mangan, J. J., *Life, Character, and Influence of Desiderius Erasmus*, 2 vols., New York, 1927.

Smith, P., *Erasmus*, New York, 1923.

Lutheran Movement

Bax, E. B., *The Peasants' War in Germany, 1525–1526*, London, 1897.

Bergendoff, C., *Olavus Petri and the Ecclesiastical Transformation in Sweden*, New York, 1928.

Wordsworth, J., *The National Church of Sweden*, London, 1911.

Luther

Boehmer, H., *Luther in Light of Recent Research*, New York, 1916.

Booth, E. P., *Martin Luther, Oak of Saxony*, New York, 1933.

Fife, R. H., *Young Luther*, New York, 1928.

Hyma, A., *Luther's Theological Development from Erfurt to Augusburg*, New York, 1928.

Jacobs, H. E., *Martin Luther*, New York, 1898.

McGiffert, A. C., *Martin Luther*, New York, 1911.

Waring, L. H., *The Political Theories of Martin Luther*, New York, 1910.

Anabaptists

Bax, E. B., *Rise and Fall of the Anabaptists*, London, 1903.

Horsch, J., *Mennonites in Europe*, Scottdale, 1942.

Smithson, R. J., *The Anabaptists*, London, 1935.

Vedder, H. C., *Balthasar Hubmaier*, New York, 1905.

Zwingli

Jackson, S. M., *Huldreich Zwingli*, New York, 1900.

Simpson, S., *Life of Ulrich Zwingli*, New York, 1902.

Bucer

Eells, H., *Martin Bucer*, New Haven, 1932.

CHAPTER 8. THE CALVINIST AND ANGLICAN REVOLTS AGAINST THE MEDIEVAL CHURCH

Calvin

Hyma, A., *John Calvin*, Grand Rapids, 1943.

Mackinnon, J., *Calvin and the Reformation*, New York, 1936.

Moura, J., *Calvin*, Garden City, 1932.

Palm, F. C., *Politics and Religion in Sixteenth Century France*, Boston, 1927.

Will, J. S., *Protestantism in France*, Toronto, 1921.

Knox and Scotland

Balfour of Burleigh, A. H. B., Baron, *An Historical Account of the Rise and Development of Presbyterianism in Scotland*, Cambridge, 1911.

Brown, P. H., *John Knox*, 2 vols., London, 1895.

Cowan, H., *John Knox*, New York, 1905.

Fleming, D. H., *The Reformation in Scotland*, London, 1910.

Glasse, J., *John Knox*, London, 1905.

Stalker, J., *John Knox*, London, 1905.

Anglican Movement

Birt, H. N., *The Elizabethan Religious Settlement*, London, 1907.

Black, J. B., *The Reign of Elizabeth*, Oxford, 1936.

Fronde, J. A., *The Divorce of Catherine of Aragon*, London, 1897.

Gairdner, J., *Lollardy and the Reformation in England*, 4 vols., London, 1908.

Garrett, C. H., *The Marian Exiles*, Cambridge, 1938.

Hughes, P., *Rome and the Counter-Reformation in England*, London, 1944.

Innes, A. D., *Cranmer and the Reformation in England*, New York, 1910.

Jordan, W. K., *The Development of Religious Toleration in England*, Cambridge, 1940.

Mattingly, G., *Catherine of Aragon*, Boston, 1941.

Patterson, M. W., *A History of the Church of England*, New York, 1933.

Pollard, A. F., *Thomas Cranmer and the English Reformation*, New York, 1904.

Powers, G. W., *England and the Reformation, 1485–1603*, New York, 1898.

Prescott, H. F. M., *A Spanish Tudor*, New York, 1940.

Savin, A. N., *English Monasteries on the Eve of the Dissolution*, Oxford, 1909.

White, H. C., *Social Criticism in Popular Religious Literature of the Sixteenth Century*, New York, 1944.

Reform in Poland

Fox, P., *The Reformation in Poland,* Baltimore, 1924.

Krausinski, Count V., *The Reformation in Poland,* 2 vols., London, 1938.

Hungary

Craig, J., *A History of the Protestant Church in Hungary,* Boston, 1854.

CHAPTER 9. THE CATHOLIC REFORMATION AND SPANISH IMPERIALISM

General

Church, F. C., *The Italian Reformers,* New York, 1932.

Kidd, B. J., *The Counter-Reformation,* London, 1933.

Jesuits

Bolton, H. E., *Wider Horizons of American History,* New York, 1939.

Campbell, T. J., *The Jesuits, 1534–1921,* New York, 1921.

Harney, M. P., *The Jesuits in History,* New York, 1941.

Parkman, F., *The Jesuits in North America,* Boston, 1910.

Fulop-Miller, R., *The Power and Secret of the Jesuits,* New York, 1932.

Loyola

Harvey, R., *Ignatius Loyola,* Milwaukee, 1936.

Marcuse, L., *Soldier of the Church,* London, 1939.

O'Connor, J. F. X., *Autobiography of Ignatius Loyola,* New York, 1900.

Sedgwick, H. D., *Ignatius Loyola,* New York, 1923.

Thompson, F., *St. Ignatius Loyola,* New York, 1900.

Van Dyke, P., *Ignatius Loyola,* New York, 1926.

Other Jesuits

Fichter, J. H., *Man of Spain, Francis Suarez,* New York, 1940.

Gowen, H. H., *Five Foreigners in Japan,* New York, 1936.

The Theatines

Kunkel, P. A., *The Theatines in the History of Catholic Reform before the Establishment of Lutheranism,* Washington, 1941.

Inquisition

Cardew, A. G., *A Short History of the Inquisition,* London, 1933.

Carvablo e Aramjo, A. H. de, *History of the Inquisition in Portugal,* Stanford, 1926.

Coulton, G. G., *Inquisition and Liberty,* London, 1938.

Lea, H. C., *A History of the Inquisition of Spain,* 4 vols., New York, 1906–1907.

Tuberville, A. S., *The Spanish Inquisition,* London, 1932.

Walsh, W. T., *Character of the Inquisition,* New York, 1940.

Philip II

Hume, M. A. S., *Philip II of Spain,* London, 1897.

Loth, D., *Philip of Spain,* London, 1933.

Mariejol, J. H., *Philip II, the First Modern King,* New York, 1933.

Prescott, W. H., *Philip the Second,* 3 vols., Philadelphia, 1874.

Rachfal, F., *Don Carlos,* Freiburg, 1921.

Walsh, W. T., *Philip II,* London, 1938.

CHAPTER 10. THE PROTESTANT RESISTANCE TO THE CATHOLIC REFORMATION AND THE IMPERIALISM OF PHILIP II

Wars of Religion

Armstrong, E., *The French Wars of Religion,* Oxford, 1904.

Besant, W., *Gaspard de Coligny,* London, 1894.

Elliot, F., *Old Court Life in France,* New York, 1893.

England, S. L., *The Massacre of Saint Bartholomew,* London, 1938.

Kelly, C. G., *French Protestantism, 1559–1562,* Baltimore, 1918.

Marlowe, C., *The Massacre at Paris*, London, 1929.

Neale, J. E., *The Age of Catherine de Medici*, London, 1943.

Palm, F. C., *Calvinism and the Religious Wars*, New York, 1932.

———, *The Establishment of French Absolutism*, New York, 1928.

———, *Politics and Religion in Sixteenth Century France*, Boston, 1927.

Roeder, R., *Catherine de Medici and the Lost Revolution*, New York, 1937.

Sedgwick, H. D., *Henry of Navarre*, Indianapolis, 1930.

———, *The House of Guise*, Indianapolis, 1938.

Thompson, J. W., *The Wars of Religion in France, 1559–1576*, Chicago, 1909.

Waldman, M., *Biography of a Family*, Boston, 1936.

Willert, P. F., *Henry Navarre and the Huguenots in France*, New York, 1893.

Revolt of the Netherlands

Geyl, P., *The Revolt of the Netherlands*, London, 1932.

Harrison, F., *William the Silent*, London, 1897.

Slocombe, G., *Don Juan of Austria*, London, 1935.

Stirling-Maxwell, W., 2 vols., *Don Juan of Austria*, London, 1883.

Wedgwood, C. V., *William the Silent*, New Haven, 1944.

Wegg, J., *The Decline of Antwerp under Philip II of Spain*, London, 1924.

English Resistance

Browning, A., *The Age of Elizabeth*, New York, 1935.

Campbell, M., *The English Yeoman under Elizabeth and the Early Stuarts*, New Haven, 1942.

Chamberlain, J., *A Jacobean Letter Writer*, New York, 1920.

Cheyney, E. P., *A History of England*, 2 vols., New York, 1914–1926.

Creighton, M., *The Age of Elizabeth*, New York, 1886.

Hinds, A. B., *The Making of the England of Elizabeth*, New York, 1895.

Pollard, A. F., *The History of England, 1547–1603*, London, 1934.

Powers, G. W., *England and the Reformation*, New York, 1898.

Raleigh, Sir W. A., *Shakespeare's England*, Oxford, 1926.

Tough, D. L. W., *The Last Years of a Frontier*, Oxford, 1928.

Elizabethan Seamen

Bell, D. H., *Elizabethan Seamen*, Philadelphia, 1936.

Froude, J. A., *English Seamen in the Sixteenth Century*, New York, 1896.

Oakeshott, W. F., *Founded Upon the Seas*, Cambridge, 1942.

Raleigh, Sir W. A., *The English Voyages of the Sixteenth Century*, Glasgow, 1928.

Wood, W. C. H., *Elizabethan Sea Dogs*, New Haven, 1921.

Elizabeth

Beesley, E. S., *Queen Elizabeth*, New York, 1916.

Black, J. B., *The Reign of Elizabeth*, Oxford, 1936.

———, *Elizabeth and Henry IV*, Oxford, 1914.

Creighton, M., *Queen Elizabeth*, London, 1906.

———, *The Age of Elizabeth*, New York, 1917.

Hume, M. A. S., *Two English Queens and Philip*, New York, 1908.

———, *The Courtship of Queen Elizabeth*, London, 1904.

———, *Treason and Plot*, London, 1901.

Klein, A. J., *Intolerance in the Reign of Elizabeth*, Boston, 1917.

Meyer, A. O., *England and the Catholic Church under Queen Elizabeth*, London, 1916.

Mumby, F. A., *Elizabeth and Mary Stuart*, London, 1914.

Neale, J. E., *Queen Elizabeth*, New York, 1934.

Pollen, J. H., *The English Catholics in*

the Reign of Elizabeth, London, 1920.

Williams, F. B., Jr., *Elizabethan England*, Boston, 1939.

Elizabethan Englishmen

Anthony, J., *Raleigh and His World*, New York, 1934.

Corbett, J. S., *Drake and the Tudor Navy*, London, 1898.

Hume, M. A. S., *The Great Lord Burghley*, London, 1898.

Read, C., *Mr. Secretary Walsingham and the Policy of Queen Elizabeth*, Oxford, 1925.

Smith, A. G., *William Cecil*, New York, 1935.

Williamson, J. A., *The Age of Drake*, London, 1938.

CHAPTER 11. SCIENTIFIC AND MILITARY DEVELOPMENTS

Johnson, F. R., *Astronomical Thought in Renaissance England, 1500–1645*, Baltimore, 1935.

Kepler, *1571–1630*, Baltimore, 1931.

Miziva, S. P., *Nicholas Copernicus, 1543–1943*, New York, 1943.

Piersol, G. A., *Andreas Vesalius and his Times*, University of Pennsylvania Lectures, Vol. 3, pp. 39–416, Philadelphia, 1916.

Stimson, D., *The Gradual Acceptance of the Copernican Theory of the Universe*, Hanover, 1917.

CHAPTER 12. ADVANCES IN EDUCATION, ART, AND LITERATURE

General

Beck, N. W., *The Political Science of Nicolo Machiavelli*, Chicago, 1944.

Beuf, C., *Cesare Borgia*, New York, 1942.

Boulting, W., *Tasso and His Times*, New York, 1907.

Butterfield, H., *The Statecraft of Machiavelli*, London, 1940.

Craig, H., *The Enchanted Glass*, New York, 1936.

Crane, T. F., *Italian Social Customs of the Sixteenth Century and Their Influence on the Literatures of Europe*, New Haven, 1920.

Gardner, E. G., *The King of Court Poets*, New York, 1906.

Gilbert, A. H., *Machiavelli's Prince and Its Forerunners*, Durham, 1938.

Grillo, G., *Poets at the Court of Ferrara*, Boston, 1943.

Edwards, L., *The Orlando Furioso and Its Predecessor*, Cambridge, 1924.

Elliott-Binns, L. E., *England and the New Learning*, London, 1937.

Fletcher, J. B., *Literature of the Italian Renaissance*, New York, 1934.

Hearnshaw, F. J. C., *The Social and Political Ideas of Some Great Thinkers of the Renaissance and Reformation*, London, 1925.

Keating, L. C., *Studies on the Literary Salon in France, 1550–1615*, Cambridge, 1941.

Muir, D. E., *Machiavelli and His Times*, New York, 1936.

Pulver, J., *Machiavelli*, London, 1937.

Taylor, H. O., *Thought and Expression in the Sixteenth Century*, New York, 1920.

Tilley, A. A., *The Dawn of the French Renaissance*, Cambridge, 1918.

————, *From Montaigne to Moliere*, London, 1908.

————, *The Literature of the French Renaissance*, Cambridge, 1904.

————, *Studies in the French Renaissance*, Cambridge, 1922.

Woodberry, G. E., *The Inspiration of Poetry*, New York, 1910.

General Biographical Works

Cox, K., *Old Masters and New*, New York, 1905.

Lafarge, J., *Great Masters*, Garden City, 1915.

Stearns, F. P., *The Midsummer of Italian Art*, Boston, 1914.

Leonardo da Vinci

Clark, K. M., *Leonardo da Vinci*, New York, 1939.

Cottler, J., *Man with Wings*, Boston, 1942.

Douglas, R. L., *Leonardo da Vinci*, Chicago, 1944.
Hart, J. B., *The Mechanical Investigations of Leonardo da Vinci*, London, 1925.
Leonardo da Vinci's Notebooks, New York, 1938.
The Literary Works of Leonardo da Vinci, New York, 1939.
Popham, A. E., *The Drawings of Leonardo da Vinci*, New York, 1945.

Raphael

Armstrong, Sir W., *Raphael*, London, 1888.
Fraprie, F. R., *The Raphael Book*, Boston, 1923.
Oppé, A. P., *Raphael*, London, 1909.

Michelangelo

De Tolnay, C., *The Youth of Michelangelo*, Princeton, 1943.
Finlayson, D. L., *Michelangelo*, New York, 1936.
The Paintings of Michelangelo, New York, 1940.
The Sculptures of Michelangelo, New York, 1940.

Titian

Gronau, G., *Titian*, New York, 1904.
Titian's Drawings, London, 1927.

Dürer

Hind, A. M., *Albrecht Dürer, His Engravings and Woodcuts*, New York.
Moore, T. S., *Abert Dürer*, New York, 1911.
Panofsky, E., *Albrecht Dürer*, Princeton, 1943.

CHAPTER 13. SOCIAL AND ECONOMIC DEVELOPMENTS

Jews

Bloom, H. I., *The Economic Activities of the Jews of Amsterdam in the 17th and 18th Centuries*, Williamsport, 1937.
Browne, L., *Stranger than Fiction*, New York, 1930.
Emden, P. H., *Jews of Great Britain*, London, 1943.

Goodman, P., *A History of the Jews*, New York, 1930.
Gratz, H. H., *History of the Jews*, Vols. 4 and 5, Philadelphia, 1891–98.
Hosmer, J. K., *The Story of the Jews*, New York, 1891.
Hyamson, A. M., *A History of the Jews in England*, London, 1908.
Lowenthal, M., *The Jews of Germany*, New York, 1931.
Sachar, A. L., *A History of the Jews*, New York, 1945.
Sanders, F. K., *History of the Jews*, New York, 1914.
Vogelstein, H., *History of the Jews in Rome*, Philadelphia, 1941.
There are many regional studies on the Jews.

English Commerce

Gerson, A. J., Vaughn, E. V., and Deardorff, N. R., *Studies in the History of English Commerce in the Tudor Period*, New York, 1912.
Guiseppi, M. S., *Alien Merchants in England in the 15th Century*, Royal Historical Society Transactions, N. S. 9, pp. 75–99.
Lingebach, W. E., *The Merchant Adventurers of England*, Philadelphia, 1902.
Power, E. E., *Studies in English Trade in the Fifteenth Century*, New York, 1933.
Rowland, A. L., and Manhart, G. B., *Studies in English Commerce and Exploration in the Reign of Elizabeth*, Philadelphia, 1924.

Mercantilism

Buck, P. W., *The Politics of Mercantilism*, New York, 1942.
Castillo, A. V., *Spanish Mercantilism*, New York, 1930.
Harrocks, J. W., *A Short History of Mercantilism*, London, 1924.
Heckscher, E. F., *Mercantilism*, London, 1935.
Packard, L. B., *The Commercial Revolution, 1400–1776*, New York, 1927.
Schmoller, G., *The Mercantile System*, New York, 1884.

Thomas, P. J., *Mercantilism and the East India Trade,* London, 1926.

Miscellaneous

Howard, C. M., *English Travellers of the Renaissance,* London, 1914.

Penrose, B., *Urbane Travellers, 1591–1635,* Philadelphia, 1942.

Trotter, E., *Sixteenth Century Life in the Country Parish,* Cambridge, 1919.

PART 3. THE SEVENTEENTH CENTURY

GENERAL HISTORIES OF THE SEVENTEENTH CENTURY

Boulenger, J., *The Seventeenth Century,* London, 1920.

Clark, A., *Working Life of Women in the Seventeenth Century,* New York, 1919.

Clarke, G. N., *The Seventeenth Century,* Oxford, 1929.

Ogg, D., *Europe in the Seventeenth Century,* London, 1925.

Routh, E. M., *The Attempt to Establish a Balance of Power in Europe in the Second Half of the 17th Century,* London, 1904.

Sacret, J. H., *Bourbon and Vasa,* Oxford, 1914.

Smith, D. N., *Characters from the Histories and Memoirs of the 17th Century,* Oxford, 1920.

Wakeman, H. O., *Europe, 1598–1715,* New York, 1929.

CHAPTER 14. DEVELOPMENT OF FRENCH ABSOLUTISM, 1598–1661

General

Doolin, P., *The Fronde,* Cambridge, 1935.

Palm, F. C., *The Establishment of French Absolutism,* New York, 1928.

Will, J. S., *Protestantism, in France,* Toronto, 1920.

Henry IV

Black, J. B. *Elizabeth and Henry IV,* Oxford, 1914.

Bloundelle-Burton, J. E., *The Fate of Henry of Navarre,* New York, 1911.

Hurst, I., *Henry of Navarre,* New York, 1938.

Perefixe, H. de B. de, *History of Henry IV,* New York, 1903.

Sedgwick, H. D., *Henry of Navarre,* Indianapolis, 1930.

Willert, P. E., *Henry of Navarre and the Hugenots in France,* New York, 1893.

Richelieu

Bailly, A., *The Cardinal Dictator,* London, 1939.

Belloc, H., *Richelieu,* Philadelphia, 1929.

Bridges, J. H., *France under Richelieu and Colbert,* London, 1912.

Burckhardt, *Richelieu,* New York, 1940.

Federn, K., *Richelieu,* London, 1938.

Lodge, R., *Richelieu,* London, 1896.

McCabe, J., *The Iron Cardinal,* London, 1909.

Palm, F. C., *The Economic Policies of Richelieu,* Urbana, 1922.

Mazarin

Hassal, A., *Mazarin,* London, 1903.

Perkins, J. B., *France under Mazarine,* 2 vols., New York, 1902.

CHAPTER 15. FRANCE IN THE AGE OF LOUIS XIV

Abercrombie, N., *The Origins of Jansenism,* Oxford, 1936.

Airy, O., *The English Restoration and Louis XIV,* London, 1888.

Baird, C. W., *History of the Huguenot Emigration to America,* 2 vols., New York, 1885.

Bradby, G. F., *The Great Days of Versailles,* New York, 1927.

Belloc, H., *Louis XIV,* New York, 1938.

Bourgeois, E., *The Century of Louis XIV*, London, 1896.

Churchill, W., *Marlborough, His Life and Times*, New York, 1933.

Clark, R., *Strangers and Sojourners at Port Royal*, Cambridge, 1932.

Cole, C. W., *French Mercantilist Doctrines before Colbert*, New York, 1931.

——, *French Mercantilism, 1663–1780*, New York, 1943.

——, *Colbert and a Century of French Mercantilism*, New York, 1939.

Duclaux, A. M. F., *The French Procession*, New York, 1909.

Geikie, R., and Montgomery, I. A., *The Dutch Barrier, 1705–1729*, Cambridge, 1930.

Hassall, A., *Louis XIV and the Zenith of the French Monarchy*, New York, 1895.

Packard, L. B., *The Age of Louis XIV*, New York, 1929.

Tilley, A., *The Decline of the Age of Louis XIV*, Cambridge, 1929.

CHAPTER 16. DEVELOPMENT OF PARLIAMENTARY GOVERNMENT AND RELIGIOUS TOLERATION IN ENGLAND

General

Airy, O., *The English Restoration and Louis XIV*, London, 1888.

Albion, R. G., *Forests and Sea Power*, Cambridge, 1926.

Ashley, M. P., *Financial and Commercial Policy under the Cromwellian Protectorate*, Oxford, 1934.

Bedford, J., *Home Life under the Stuarts, 1603–1649*, New York, 1903.

Biloff, M., *Public Order and Popular Disturbances, 1660–1714*, London, 1938.

Campbell, D., *The Puritan in Holland, England, and America*, 2 vols., New York, 1893.

Clark, G. N., *The Later Stuarts, 1660–1714*, Oxford, 1934.

Davies, G., *The Early Stuarts, 1603–1660*, Oxford, 1937.

Dietz, F. C., *English Public Finance, 1558–1641*, New York, 1932.

Figgis, J. N., *The Theory of the Divine Right of Kings*, Cambridge, 1896.

Firth, Sir C. H., *Notes on the Diplomatic Relations of England and France*, Oxford, 1906.

——, *Oliver Cromwell and the Rule of the Puritans in England*, New York, 1900.

——, *A Commentary on Macauley's History of England*, London, 1938.

Gardiner, S. R., *History of the Great Civil War, 1642–49*, London, 1910.

——, *History of the Commonwealth and the Protectorate, 1649–1660*, 4 vols., London, 1894–1903.

——, *History of England from the Accession of James I to the Outbreak of the Civil War, 1603–1642*, 10 vols., London, 1884–91.

——, *The First Two Stuarts and the Puritan Revolution, 1603–1660*, Boston, 1876.

Griffiths, O. M., *Religion and Learning*, Cambridge, 1935.

Innes, A. D., *The Maritime and Colonial Expansion of England under the Stuarts*, London, 1932.

Jones, J. D., *The English Revolution, 1603–1714*, London, 1931.

Jordan, W. K., *The Development of Religious Toleration in England, 1603–1640*, London, 1936.

——, *The Development of Religious Toleration in England, 1640–1660*, Cambridge, 1938.

Lodge, R., *The History of England from the Restoration to the Death of William III*, London, 1918.

Lyons, T., *The Theory of Religious Liberty in England, 1603–1639*, Cambridge, 1937.

Mackenzie, A. N., *The Passing of the Stuarts*, New York, 1937.

Marriott, J. A. R., *The Crisis of English Liberty*, Oxford, 1930.

Mathew, D., *The Jacobean Age*, London, 1938.

McCarthy, J., *The Reign of Queen Anne*, New York, 1902.

619

Montague, F. C., *The History of England from the Accession of James I to the Restoration*, New York, 1929.

Morgan, W. T., *English Political Parties and Leaders in the Reign of Queen Anne*, New Haven, 1920.

Newton, A. P., *The Colonial Activtiy of the English Puritans*, New Haven, 1914.

Ogg, D., *England in the Reign of Charles II*, Oxford, 1934.

Petrie, Sir C. A., *The Stuarts*, Boston, 1937.

Petergorsky, D. W., *Left-Wing Democracy in the English Civil War*, London, 1940.

Reese, M. M., *The Tudors and the Stuarts*, New York, 1940.

Relf, F. H., *The Petition of Right*, Minneapolis, 1907.

Schlatter, R. B., *The Social Ideas of Religious Leaders, 1660–1688*, London, 1940.

Thompson, G. S., *Life in a Noble Household, 1641–1700*, London, 1937.

Trevelyan, G. M., *England under the Stuarts*, New York, 1933.

———, *The English Revolution, 1688–1689*, New York, 1939.

———, *England under Queen Anne*, New York, 1930–1934.

Charles I

Belloc, H., *Charles I*, Phildelphia, 1933.

Coffin, R. P. T., *The Dukes of Buckingham*, New York, 1931.

Cooke, H. P., *Charles I and His Earlier Parliaments*, New York, 1939.

Gibbs, M. A., *Buckingham, 1592–1628*, London, 1935.

Higham, F. M. G., *Charles I*, London, 1932.

Pichel, M. B., *Charles I as Patron of Poetry and Drama*, London, 1936.

Skelton, Sir J., *Charles I*, London, 1898.

Wedgewood, C. V., *Strafford, 1593–1641*, London, 1935.

Land

Bell, H., *Archbishop Land and Priestly Government*, London, 1905.

Benson, A. C., *William Land*, New York, 1897.

Trevor-Roper, H. R., *Archbishop Land*, London, 1940.

Pym

Brett, S. R., *John Pym, 1583–1643*, London, 1940.

Hexter, J. H., *The Reign of King Pym*, London, 1941.

Wade, C., *John Pym*, London, 1912.

Cromwell

Ashely, M. P., *Oliver Cromwell*, London, 1937.

Belloc, H., *Cromwell*, Philadelphia, 1934.

Blauvelt, M. T., *Oliver Cromwell*, New York, 1937.

Buchan, J., *Oliver Cromwell*, Boston, 1934.

Clark, G. H., *Oliver Cromwell*, Boston, 1893.

Firth, C. H., *Oliver Cromwell and the Rule of the Puritans in England*, New York, 1900.

Gardiner, S. R., *Cromwell's Place in History*, London, 1897.

———, *Oliver Cromwell*, New York, 1901.

Hayward, F. H., *The Unknown Cromwell*, London, 1934.

Ramsey, R. W., *Richard Cromwell*, New York, 1935.

Wolfe, D. M., *Milton in the Puritan Revolution*, New York, 1941.

Charles II

Barbour, V., *Henry Bennet, Earl of Arlington*, Washington, 1914.

Belloc, *Charles II*, London, 1939.

Bryant, A., *King Charles II*, New York, 1939.

Craik, Sir H., *The Life of Edward, Earl of Clarendon, Lord High Chancellor of England*, 2 vols., London, 1911.

———, *The Life of Edward, Earl of Clarendon*, London, 1911.

Davies, J. D. G., *Honest George Monck*, London, 1936.

Hartman, C. H., *Charles II and Madame*, London, 1934.

William III

Renier, G. J., *William of Orange,* New York, 1933.

Scott, E., *The Travels of the King,* London, 1907.

Traill, H. D., *William III,* London, 1888.

Warner, O., *Hero of the Restoration,* London, 1940.

Anne

Adams, W. H. D., *Good Queen Anne,* 2 vols., London, 1886.

Ashton, J., *Social Life in the Reign of Queen Anne,* London, 1883.

Connel, N., *Anne, the Last Stuart Monarch,* London, 1938.

McCarthy, J., *The Reign of Queen Anne,* 2 vols., New York, 1902.

Marlborough

Atkinson, C. P., *Marlborough and the Life of the British Army,* New York, 1921.

Belloc, H., *The Tactics and Strategy of the Great Duke of Marlborough,* London, 1933.

Campbell, K. W., *Sarah, Dutchess of Marlborough,* Boston, 1933.

Chidsey, D. B., *Marlborough,* New York, 1929.

Churchill, W., *Marlborough,* New York, 1933–38.

Colby, E., *Masters of Mobile Warfare,* Princeton, 1943.

Fortescue, J. W., *Marlborough,* New York, 1932.

Saintsbury, G. E. B., *Marlborough,* New York, 1886.

Thomas, E., *The Life of the Duke of Marlborough,* London, 1915.

Wolseley, G. J. W., *Viscount, The Life of John Churchill,* London, 1894.

Non-Conformists

Bebb, E. D., *Nonconformity and Social and Economic Life,* London, 1935.

Hall, T. C., *The Religious Background of American Culture,* Boston, 1930.

Scheffer, J. G. de H., *History of the Free Churchmen Called Brownists,* *Pilgrim Fathers, and Baptists in the Dutch Republic, 1587–1701,* Ithaca, 1921.

Vedder, H. C., *The Baptists,* New York, 1902.

Friends

Belasco, P. S., *Authority in Church and State,* London, 1928.

King, R. H., *George Fox and the Light Within,* Philadelphia, 1940.

Knight, R., *The Founder of Quakerism,* London, 1922.

Russel, E., *The History of Quakerism,* New York, 1943.

Wright, L. M., *The Literary Life of the Early Friends, 1650–1725,* New York, 1932.

CHAPTER 17. DEVELOPMENT OVERSEAS IN THE SEVENTEENTH CENTURY: THE RISE AND DECLINE OF DUTCH PREDOMINANCE

General

Beer, G. L., *The Origins of the British Colonial System, 1578–1660,* New York, 1908.

Bowman, F. L., and Roper, E. J., *Traders in East and West,* New York, 1924.

Hewins, W. A. S., *English Trade and Finance Chiefly in the Seventeenth Century,* London, 1892.

Dutch Colonial and Commercial Activity

Edmundson, G., *Anglo-Dutch Rivalries during the First Half of the Seventeenth Century,* Oxford, 1911.

Furinvall, J. S., *Netherlands India,* New York, 1939.

Harper, L. A., *The English Navigation Laws,* New York, 1939.

Hyma, A., *The Dutch in the Far East,* Ann Arbor, 1942.

Klerck, E. S. de, *History of the Netherlands East Indies,* 2 vols., Rotterdam, 1938.

Riemens, H., *The Netherlands,* New York, 1944.

Van Loon, H. W., *The Fall of the Dutch Republic,* Boston, 1913.

Vlekke, B. H. M., *Nusantaria,* Cambridge, 1943.

Vlekke, B. H. M., *The Story of the Dutch East Indies*, Cambridge, 1945.

Wilson, C. H., *Anglo-Dutch Commerce and Finance in the Eighteenth Century*, Cambridge, 1941.

England in India

Anderson, J., *English Intercourse with Siam in the Seventeenth Century*, London, 1890.

Banarjea, P., *Indian Finance in the Days of the Company*, London, 1928.

Fawcett, Sir C., *The English Factories in India*, Oxford, 1936.

Hall, D. G. E., *Early English Intercourse with Burma*, London, 1928.

Jeudwine, J. W., *Studies in Empire and Trade*, New York, 1923.

Morse, H. B., *The Chronicles of the East India Company Trading to China, 1635–1834*, 5 vols., Cambridge, 1926–29.

Mottram, R. H., *Traders' Dream*, New York, 1939.

Wright, A., *Early English Adventurers in the East*, London, 1917.

America

Andrews, C. M., *Colonial Self-government, 1652–89*, New York, 1904.

———, *The Fathers of New England*, New Haven, 1919.

Osgood, H. L., *The American Colonies in the Seventeenth Century*, 3 vols., New York, 1907–30.

Tyler, L. G., *England in America*, New York, 1904.

Wertenbaker, T. J., *The First Americans, 1607–1690*, New York, 1929.

CHAPTER 18. CENTRAL EUROPE IN THE SEVENTEENTH CENTURY

The Thirty Years' War

Cobb, S. H., *The Story of the Palatines*, New York, 1897.

Gardiner, S. R., *The Thirty Years' War*, London, 1875.

Reade, H. G. R., *Sidelights on the Thirty Years' War*, 3 vols., London, 1924.

Wedgwood, C. V., *The Thirty Years' War*, New Haven, 1939.

Gustavus Adolphus

Almlund, N. G., *Gustav Adolf*, Princeton, 1940.

Fletcher, C. R. L., *Gustavus Adolphus*, New York, 1892.

McMunn, Lt. Gen. Sir G., *Gustavus Adolphus*, New York, 1931.

Trench, R. C., *Gustavus Adolphus in in Germany*, London, 1892.

Wallenstein

Watson, F., *Wallenstein*, New York, 1938.

Prussia in the Seventeenth Century

Fay, S. B., *The Rise of Brandenburg-Prussia to 1786*, New York, 1937.

Marriott, J. A. R., and Robertson, C. G., *The Evolution of Prussia*, Oxford, 1915.

Muir, D. E., *Prussian Eagle*, London, 1940.

The Teutonic Order

Krollmann, C. A. C., *The Teutonic Order in Prussia*, Elbing, 1938.

Olins, P. S., *The Teutonic Knights in Latvia*, Riga, 1928.

Plum, H. G., *The Teutonic Order and Its Secularization*, Iowa City, 1906.

CHAPTER 19. CULTURAL ACHIEVEMENTS OF THE SEVENTEENTH CENTURY

Velasquez

Armstrong, W., *The Life of Velasquez*, London, 1896.

Stevenson, R. A. M., *Velasquez*, London, 1900.

Van Dyck

Lucas, E. V., *Van Dyck*, New York, 1926.

Rubens

Calvert, G. H., *The Life of Rubens*, New York, 1878.

Cammaerts, E., *Rubens, Painter and Diplomat*, London, 1932.

Frans Hals

Davies, G. S., *Frans Hals*, London, 1904.

Rembrandt

Bell, M., *Rembrandt van Ryn*, London, 1901.

Hammerton, P. G., *The Etchings of Rembrandt*, London, 1904.

Hind, A. M., *Rembrandt*, Cambridge, 1932.

The Unseen Rembrandt, New York, 1942.

Van Dyke, J. C., *Rembrandt and His School*, New York, 1923.

Architecture

Loftie, W. J., *Irigo Jones and Wren*, New York, 1893.

Weaver, Sir L., *Sir Christopher Wren, Scientist, Scholar, Architect*, New York, 1923.

Opera

Brockway, W., *The Opera*, New York, 1941.

Elson, A., *A History of Opera*, Boston, 1912.

Jell, G. C., *Master Builders of Opera*, New York, 1933.

Lee, E. M., *The Story of Opera*, London, 1909.

Streatfeild, R. A., *The Opera*, London, 1925.

General Philosophy

Mellone, S. H., *The Dawn of Modern Thought*, London, 1930.

Descartes

Haldane, E. S., *Descartes, His Life and Times*, New York, 1905.

Keeling, S. V., *Descartes*, London, 1934.

Maritian, J., *The Dream of Descartes*, London, 1934.

Hobbes

Brandt, F., *Thomas Hobbes' Mechanical Conception of Nature*, Copenhagen, 1928.

Laird, J., *Hobbes*, London, 1934.

Robertson, G. C., *Hobbes*, Edinburgh, 1910.

Stephen, L., *Hobbes*, New York, 1904.

———, *The Political Philosophy of Hobbes*, Oxford, 1936.

Woodbridge, F. J. E., *The Philosophy of Hobbes*, Minneapolis, 1903.

Locke

Fowler, T., *Locke*, New York, 1906.

Maclean, K., *John Locke and English Literature of the Seventeenth Century*, London, 1936.

Morris, C. R., *Locke, Berkeley, Hume*, Oxford, 1931.

Spinoza

Roth, L., *Spinoza*, Boston, 1929.

Wolfson, H. A., *The Philosophy of Spinoza*, Cambridge, 1934.

Leibnitz

Merz, J. T., *Leibnitz*, Edinburgh, 1907.

Grotius

Knight, W. S. M., *The Life and Works of Hugo Grotius*, London, 1925.

Vreeland, H., *Hugo Grotius*, New York, 1917.

CHAPTER 20. SCIENTIFIC AND MILITARY DEVELOPMENTS

Brown, H., *Scientific Organizations in Seventeenth Century France (1620–1680)*, Baltimore, 1934.

Ornstein, M., *The Role of Scientific Societies in the Seventeenth Century*, Chicago, 1928.

See works listed under Science.

CHAPTER 21. LITERATURE IN THE SEVENTEENTH CENTURY

General

Dowden, E., *Puritan and Anglican*, London, 1900.

Wright, C. H. C., *French Classicism*, Cambridge, 1920.

Lope de Vega

Fitzmaurice-Kelly, J., *Lope de Vega and the Spanish Drama*, London, 1902.

Rennert, H. A., *The Life of Lope de Vega*, Philadelphia, 1904.

Calderon

Parker, A. A., *The Allegorical Drama of Calderon*, Oxford, 1943.

Jonson

Bentley, G. E., *Shakespeare and Jonson,* Chicago, 1945.

Dun, E. C., *Ben Jonson's Art,* Northampton, 1925.

Johnston, G. B., *Ben Jonson,* New York, 1945.

Kerr, M., *Influence of Ben Jonson on English Comedy, 1598–1642,* Philadelphia, 1912.

Noyes, R. G., *Ben Jonson on the English Stage,* Cambridge, 1935.

Palmer, J., *Ben Jonson,* New York, 1928.

Smith, G. G., *Ben Jonson,* London, 1919.

Francis Bacon

Levine, I., *Francis Bacon,* Boston, 1925.

Nichol, J., *Francis Bacon,* 2 vols., Edinburgh, 1907.

Penrose, S. B. L., *The Reputation and Influence of Francis Bacon in the Seventeenth Century,* New York, 1934.

Steeves, G. W., *Francis Bacon,* London, 1910.

Stuart, M., *Francis Bacon,* New York, 1932.

Wallace, K. R., *Francis Bacon on Communication and Rhetoric,* Chapel Hill, 1943.

Williams, C., *Bacon,* New York, 1933.

Milton

Brooke, S. A., *Milton,* London, 1879.

Cawley, R. R., *A Study of Milton's Literary Craftmanship,* Princeton, 1941.

French, J. M., *Milton in Chancery,* New York, 1939.

Dryden

Baumgartner, M. D., *On Dryden's Relation to Germany in the Eighteenth Century,* Chicago, 1913.

Bredwold, L. I., *The Intellectual Milieu of John Dryden,* Ann Arbor, 1934.

Osborn, J. M., *John Dryden,* New York, 1940.

Van Doren, M., *John Dryden,* New York, 1946.

Bunyan

Buckland, A. R., *John Bunyan,* Chicago, 1921.

De Blois, A. K., *John Bunyan,* Philadelphia, 1928.

Griffith, G. D., *John Bunyan,* London, 1928.

Harding, R. W., *John Bunyan,* London, 1928.

Hutton, W. H., *John Bunyan,* London, 1928.

Knox, E. A., *John Bunyan in Relation to His Times,* New York, 1928.

Nelson, W. H., *Tinker and Thinker,* Chicago, 1928.

Tindall, W. Y., *John Bunyan,* New York, 1934.

Pepys and Evelyn

Bryant, A., *Samuel Pepys,* New York, 1933.

Marburg, C., *Mr. Pepys and Mr. Evelyn,* Philadelphia, 1935.

Morhouse, E., *Samuel Pepys,* London, 1922.

Ponsonby, A., *Samuel Pepys,* London, 1928.

Tanner, J. R., *Mr. Pepys,* London, 1925.

French Academy

Robertson, D. M., *A History of the French Academy,* New York, 1910.

Vincent, L. H., *The French Academy,* Boston, 1901.

Bossuet

Simpson, W. J. S., *A Study of Bossuet,* New York, 1937.

Fénelon

Ramsay, A. M., *History of the Life of Fénelon,* Paisley, 1897.

Pascal

Bishop, M., *Pascal,* New York, 1936.

Calliet, E., *The Clue to Pascal,* Philadelphia, 1943.

Clark, W., *Pascal and the Port Royalists,* Edinburgh, 1902.

Eastwood, D. M., *The Revival of Pascal*, Oxford, 1936.

Sevigné

Tilley, A. A., *Madame de Sevigné*, Cambridge, 1936.

La Fontaine

Hamel, F., *Jean La Fontaine*, London, 1911.

Molière

Oliphant, M. O., and Tarver, F., *Molière*, Edinburgh, 1938.
Tilley, A. A., *Molière, Cambridge*, 1921.
Trollope, H. M., *The Life of Molière*, London, 1905.
Vincent, L. H., *Molière*, Boston, 1902.

Racine

Clark, A. F. B., *Jean Racine*, Cambridge, 1939.
Fisher, D. F., *Corneille and Racine in England*, New York, 1904.
Giraudoux, J., *Racine*, Cambridge, 1938.

CHAPTER 22. SOCIAL AND ECONOMIC DEVELOPMENT

General

Bate, E. S., *Touring in 1600*, Boston, 1911.

Crump, L., *Nursery Life 300 Years Ago*, New York, 1930.
Howard, C., *English Travellers of the Renaissance*, London, 1913.
Jameson, J. F., *Privateering and Piracy in the Colonial Period*, New York, 1923.
Lambert, R. S., *Grand Tour*, New York, 1937.
Lennard, R., *Englishmen at Rest and Play*, Oxford, 1931.

Coffee

Ukers, W. H., *All About Coffee*, New York, 1935.

Tea

Ukers, W. H., *All About Tea*, 2 vols., New York, 1935.
———, *The Romance of Tea*, New York, 1936.

Smoking

Apperson, G. L., *The Social History of Smoking*, New York, 1916.
Corti, E. C., Count, *A History of Smoking*, New York, 1932.

Piracy

Gosse, *The History of Piracy*, London, 1932.
Means, P. A., *The Spanish Main*, New York, 1935.

PART 4. THE EIGHTEENTH CENTURY

GENERAL HISTORIES OF THE EIGHTEENTH CENTURY

Atkinson, C. T., *A History of Germany, 1715–1815*, London, 1908.
Cheke, M., *Dictator of Portugal*, London, 1938.
Gershoy, L., *From Despotism to Revolution, 1763–1789*, New York, 1946.
Hassal, A., *The Balance of Power, 1715–1789*, New York, 1896.
Kerner, R. J., *Bohemia in the Eighteenth Century*, New York, 1932.

Marcazali, H., *Hungary in the 18th Century*, Cambridge, 1910.
Strienskie, C., *The Eighteenth Century*, London, 1916.

CHAPTER 23. CENTRAL EUROPE IN THE EIGHTEENTH CENTURY

General

Bruford, W. H., *Germany in the Eighteenth Century*, Cambridge, 1935.

Corbett, J. S., *England in the Seven Years' War*, 2 vols., New York, 1907.

Dorn, W. L., *Competition for Empire, 1740–1763*, New York, 1940.

Eldon, C. W., *England's Subsidy Policy Toward the Continent during the Seven Years' War*, Philadelphia, 1938.

Longman, F. W., *Frederick the Great and the Seven Years' War*, London, 1917.

Maria Theresa

Bright, J. F., *Maria Theresa*, London, 1920.

Mahan, J. A., *Maria Theresa*, New York, 1932.

Moffat, M. M., *Maria Theresa*, London, 1911.

Joseph II

Padover, S. K., *The Revolutionary Emperor*, New York, 1934.

Frederick William I

Ergang, R., *Frederick William I*, New York, 1941.

———, *The Potsdam Fuehrer*, New York, 1941.

Frederick the Great

Carlyle, T., *Carlyle's Frederick the Great*, Oxford, 1916.

Gaxotte, *Frederick the Great*, New Haven, 1942.

Gooch, G. P., *Frederick the Great*, New York, 1947.

Hamilton, R., *Frederick the Great*, Cambridge, 1936.

Hanns, F., *Church and State in Silesia under Frederick II*, Washington, 1944.

Hegemann, W., *Frederick the Great*, New York, 1929.

Kugler, F. T., *Life of Frederick the Great*, New York, 1902.

Reddaway, W. F., *Frederick the Great and the Rise of Prussia*, New York, 1904.

Veale, F. J. P., *Frederick the Great*, London, 1935.

Young, N., *The Life of Frederick the Great*, New York, 1919.

Prince Henry of Prussia

Easum, C. V., *Prince Henry of Prussia*, Madison, 1942.

Wilhelmina Margravine of Baireuth

Cuthel, E. E., *Wilhelmina Margravine of Baireuth*, 2 vols., London, 1905.

Pietism

Pinson, K. S., *Pietism as a Factor in the Rise of German Nationalism*, New York, 1934.

CHAPTER 24. THE STRUGGLE FOR COLONIAL AND COMMERCIAL SUPREMACY

Histories of the British Struggle for Colonies and Commerce

Gipson, L. H., *The British Empire before the American Revolution*, Caldwell, Idaho, 1936–46.

Innes, A. D., *Britain and Her Rivals in the Eighteenth Century*, London, 1895.

Muir, R., *A Short History of the British Commonwealth*, 2 vols., Yonkers, 1922.

Sutherland, L. S., *A London Merchant, 1695–1774*, London, 1933.

Westerfield, R., *Middlemen in English Business*, New Haven, 1915.

Willan, T. S., *The English Coasting Trade, 1600–1750*, Manchester, 1938.

Wilson, C. H., *Anglo-Dutch Commerce and Finance in the Eighteenth Century*, Cambridge, 1941.

India

Allan, J., Haig, T. W., Dodwell, H. H., *The Cambridge Shorter History of India*, Cambridge, 1943.

Dalgliesh, W. H., *The Perpetual Company of the Indies, 1722–1734*, Philadelphia, 1933.

Dodwell, H. H., *The Cambridge History of India*, Vol. 5, New York, 1929.

Dunbar, G., *A History of India*, London, 1936.

Hoskins, H. L., *British Routes to India*, Philadelphia, 1928.

Hunter, W. W., *A History of British India*, 2 vols., New York, 1899–1900.

Jackson, A. V. W., *History of India*, London, 1906.

Keene, H. G., *History of India*, 2 vols., Edinburgh, 1900.

Locke, J. C., *The First Englishmen in India*, London, 1930.

Philips, C. H., *The East India Co., 1784–1834*, Manchester, 1940.

Robinson, F. P., *Trade of the East India Company, 1709–1813*, Cambridge, 1912.

Smith, V. A., *The Oxford History of India*, Oxford, 1919.

Wheeler, J. T., *A Short History of India*, London, 1899.

Wright, A., *Early English Adventurers in the East*, London, 1917.

Dupleix

Thompson, V. M., *Dupleix and His Letters, 1742–1754*, New York, 1935.

Clive

Davies, A. M., *Clive of Plassey*, New York, 1939.

Forest, G. W., *The Life of Lord Clive*, New York, 1918.

Malleson, G. B., *Lord Clive and Establishment of the English in India*, Oxford, 1907.

Wilson, C. W., *Lord Clive*, London, 1890.

The Struggle for Colonies and Commerce in America

Andrews, C. M., *The Colonial Period of American History*, 4 vols., New Haven, 1934–38.

———, *The Colonial Background of the American Revolution*, New Haven, 1939.

Bassett, J. S., *A Short History of the United States*, New York, 1913.

Becker, C. L., *Beginnings of the American People*, Boston, 1915.

Beer, G. L., *British Colonial Policy, 1754–1765*, New York, 1922.

———, *The Commercial Policy of England toward the American Colonies*, New York, 1893.

Channing, E., *A History of the United States*, Vols. 1, 2, and 3, New York, 1905–25.

Doyle, J. A., *English Colonies in America*, 5 vols., New York, 1882–1907.

Greene, E. B., *The Revolutionary Generation, 1763–1790*, New York, 1943.

———, *Provincial America, 1680–1740*, New York, 1905.

Hackett, H. C., *Political and Social History of the United States*, New York, 1925.

Jernegan, M. W., *The American Colonies, 1492–1750*, New York, 1931.

Jones, R. M., *The Quakers in the American Colonies*, London, 1911.

McLachlan, J. O., *Trade and Peace with Old Spain, 1667–1750*, Cambridge, 1940.

Morison, S. E., and Commager, H. S., *The Growth of the American Republic*, New York, 1930.

Nettels, C. P., *The Roots of American Civilization*, New York, 1938.

Osgood, H. L., *The American Colonies in the Eighteenth Century*, 4 vols., New York, 1924–5.

Spector, M. M., *The American Department of the British Government, 1768–1782*, New York, 1940.

Thwaites, R. G., *France in America, 1497–1763*, New York, 1905.

Canada

Bourinot, J., *Canada*, New York, 1898.

Burt, A. L., *A Short History of Canada for Americans*, Minneapolis, 1942.

Wittke, C. F., *A History of Canada*, New York, 1941.

Wood, W. C. H., *The Winning of Canada*, Toronto, 1914.

Wrong, G. M., *The Fall of Canada*, Oxford, 1914.

———, *The Conquest of New France*, New Haven, 1898.

Wolfe

Bradley, A. G., *Wolfe*, London, 1895.

Casgrain, H. R., *Wolfe and Montcalm*, London, 1926.

Whitton, F. E., *Wolfe and North America*, Boston, 1929.

West Indies

Crouse, N. M., *Pioneers in the West Indies*, New York, 1940.

Crouse, N. M., *The French Struggle for the West Indies*, New York, 1943.

CHAPTER 25. GREAT BRITAIN IN THE EIGHTEENTH CENTURY (1714–1789)

General

Dubois, A. B., *The English Business Man after the Bubble Act, 1720–1800*, New York, 1939.

Erleigh, G. R. I., Viscount, *The South Sea Bubble*, New York, 1933.

Head, F. W., *The Fallen Stuarts*, Cambridge, 1901.

Hunt, W., *The History of England from the Accession of George III to the Close of Pitt's First Administration*, New York, 1930.

Lawson, M. G., *Fur*, Toronto, 1943.

Lecky, W. E. H., *A History of England in the Eighteenth Century*, London, 1878–1890.

Quisilan, M. J., *Victorian Prelude*, New York, 1941.

Robertson, C. G., *England under the Hanoverians*, New York, 1927.

Thiers, A., *The Mississippi Bubble*, New York, 1933.

Walpole

Ewald, A. C., *Sir Robert Walpole*, London, 1878.

Industrial Revolution

Allsop, H., *An Introduction to English Industrial History*, London, 1912.

Ashton, T. S., *The Eighteenth Century Industrialist, Peter Stubs of Warrington, 1756–1806*, Manchester, 1939.

——, *Iron and Steel in the Industrial Revolution*, Manchester, 1924.

Baines, Sir Edward, *History of the Cotton Manufactures in Great Britain*, London, 1835.

Beard, C., *The Industrial Revolution*, London, 1902.

Bowden, W., *Industrial Society in England towards the End of the Eighteenth Century*, New York, 1925.

Buer, M. C., *Health, Wealth, and Population in the Early Days of the Industrial Revolution, 1760–1815*, London, 1926.

Burn, D. L., *The Economic History of Steelmaking*, New York, 1940.

Cantrill, T. C., *Coal Mining*, New York, 1914.

Chapman, S. J., *Lancashire Cotton Industry*, Manchester, 1904.

Clapham, J. H., *The Woolen and Worsted Industries*, New York, 1907.

Cunningham, W., *The Growth of English Industry and Commerce in Modern Times*, 3 vols., Cambridge, 1892.

Daniels, G. W., *The Early English Cotton Industry*, Manchester, 1920.

Dietz, F. C., *The Industrial Revolution*, New York, 1927.

Dunlop, O. J., and Denman, R. D., *English Apprenticeship and Child Labour*, London, 1912.

French, G. J., *Life and Times of Samuel Crompton*, Manchester, 1860.

Hamilton, H., *The Economic Evolution of Scotland in the Eighteenth and Nineteenth Centuries*, London, 1933.

——, *The English Brass and Copper Industries*, New York, 1926.

Hammond, J. L. and B., *The Rise of Modern Industry*, New York, 1926.

——, *The Town Labourer, 1760–1832*, New York, 1917.

——, *The Skilled Labourer, 1760–1832*, New York, 1920.

——, *The Village Labourer, 1760–1832*, New York, 1913.

Heaton, H., *Yorkshire Woolen and Worsted Industries*, Oxford, 1920.

Kirkaldy, A. W., and Evans, A. D., *The History and Economics of Transport*, London, 1915.

Kirkaldy, A. W., *British Shipping*, New York, 1914.

Lipson, E., *History of the Woolen and Worsted Industries*, London, 1921.

Leopold, R. W., *Robert Dale Owen*, Cambridge, 1940.

Lloyd, G. I. H., *The Cutlery Trades*, London, 1913.

Lord, J., *Capital and Steam-power, 1750–1800*, London, 1923.

Mantoux, P., *The Industrial Revolution in the Eighteenth Century*, New York, 1927.

Moffit, L. W., *England on the Eve of the Industrial Revolution*, London, 1925.

Pinchbeck, I., *Women Workers and the Industrial Revolution*, New York, 1930.

Pratt, E. A., *A History of Inland Transport and Communication in England*, London, 1912.

Preble, G. H., *A Chronological History of the Origin and Development of Steam Navigation*, Philadelphia, 1883.

Roberts, D. W., *An Outline of the Economic History of England*, London, 1932.

Roll, E., *An Early Experiment in Industrial Organization*, New York, 1930.

Smiles, S., *Lives of the Engineers*, 5 vols., London, 1874.

Thurston, R. H., *History of the Growth of the Steam Engine*, New York, 1907.

Toynbee, A., *Lectures on the Industrial Revolution of the Eighteenth Century in England*, London, 1812.

Unwin, G., Hulme, A., and Taylor, G., *Samuel Oldnow and the Arkwrights*, New York, 1924.

Usher, A. P., *An Introduction to the Industrial History of England*, Boston, 1920.

———, *A History of Mechanical Inventions*, New York, 1929.

Wadsworth, A. P., and Mann, J. de L., *The Cotton Trade and Industrial Lancashire, 1600–1780*, Manchester, 1931.

Wood, H. T., *Industrial England in the Middle of the Eighteenth Century*, London, 1910.

The Agricultural Revolution in England

Curtler, W. H. R., *The Enclosure and Redistribution of Our Land*, Oxford, 1920.

Garnier, R. M., *Annals of the British Peasantry*, London, 1895.

———, *History of the English Landed Gentry*, New York, 1893, 1908.

Gonner, E. C. K., *Common Land Enclosure*, London, 1912.

Hasbach, W., *History of the English Agricultural Labourer*, London, 1908.

Johnson, A. H., *The Disappearance of the Small Landowner*, Oxford, 1909.

Slater, G., *The English Peasantry and the Enclosure of the Common Fields*, London, 1907.

Wesleyan Movement

Bready, J. W., *England Before and After Wesley*, London, 1938.

Edwards, M., *After Wesley*, London, 1935.

Laver, J., *Wesley*, New York, 1933.

MacArthur, K. W., *The Economic Ethics of John Wesley*, New York, 1936.

Taylor, E. R., *Methodism and Politics*, Cambridge, 1935.

Warner, W. J., *The Wesleyan Movement and the Industrial Revolution*, New York, 1930.

Wearmouth, R. F., *Methodism and the Working Class Movements of England*, London, 1937.

———, *Methodism and the Common People of the Eighteenth Century*, London, 1945.

George III

Farrer, J. A., *The Monarchy in Politics*, New York, 1917.

Noble, G., *The North Briton*, New York, 1939.

Pemberton, W. Baring, *Lord North*, New York, 1939.

Lord Chatham

Green, W. D., *William Pitt*, New York, 1901.

Harrison, F., *Chatham*, New York, 1905.

Hotblack, K., *Chatham's Colonial Policy*, New York, 1917.

Long, J. C., *Mr. Pitt and America's Birthright*, New York, 1940.

McDowall, A. S., *Chatham*, New York, 1903.

Roseberry, A. P. P., Earl of, *Lord Chatham*, New York, 1910.

Ruville, A. von, *William Pitt*, New York, 1907.

Pitt the Younger

Barnes, D. G., *George III and William Pitt, 1783–1806*, Stanford University, 1939.

Chatterton, E. K., *England's Greatest Statesman, A Life of William Pitt*, Indianapolis, 1930.

Petrie, Sir C. A., *William Pitt*, London, 1935.

Rose, J. H., *William Pitt and National Revival*, London, 1911.

Wilson, P. W., *William Pitt*, Garden City, 1930.

Williams, B., *The Life of William Pitt*, 2 vols., New York, 1914.

Winstanley, D. A., *Personal and Party Government*, Cambridge, 1910.

———, *Lord Chatham and the Whig Opposition*, Cambridge, 1912.

CHAPTER 26. THE HISTORY OF FRANCE IN THE EIGHTEENTH CENTURY

The Ancien Regime

Johnson, A., *The Intendant as a Political Agent under Louis XIV*, Lowell, 1899.

Lowell, E. J., *Eve of the French Revolution*, Boston, 1922.

Taine, H., *The Ancient Regime*, New York, 1896.

Toqueville, A. de., *The State of Society in France before the Revolution of 1789*, London, 1883.

The Eighteenth Century

Brunn, G., *The Enlightened Despots*, New York, 1929.

Green, F. C., *Eighteenth Century France*, New York, 1931.

Hassal, A., *The Balance of Power*, London, 1929.

Johnson, A. H., *The Age of the Enlightened Despot, 1660–1789*, London, 1911.

Lowell, E. J., *Eve of the French Revolution*, Boston, 1922.

Jeudwine, J. W., *Religion, Commerce, Liberty*, New York, 1925.

Mowat, R. B., *The Age of Reason*, London, 1934.

Palmer, R. R., *Catholics and Unbelievers in the 18th Century France*, Princeton, 1930.

Reddaway, W. F., *A History of Europe 1715–1814*, London, 1936.

Russell, P., *The Glittering Century*, London, 1936.

See, H., *Economic and Social Conditions in France during the Eighteenth Century*, New York, 1927.

Stryienski, C., *The Eighteenth Century*, London, 1916.

The Regency

Perkins, J. B., *France under the Regency*, New York, 1920.

Wiston-Glynn, A., *John Law of Lauriston*, Edinburgh, 1907.

Louis XV

Perkins, J. B., *France under Louis XV*, Boston, 1897.

Allison, J. M. S., *Malesherbes*, New Haven, 1938.

Louis XVI

Fay, B., *Revolutionary Spirit in France and America*, New York, 1927.

Funck-Bretano, F., *The Diamond Necklace*, Philadelphia, 1901.

Garrett, M. B., *The States General of 1789*, New York, 1935.

Gaxotte, P., *Louis XV and His Times*, Philadelphia, 1934.

Gershoy, L., *From Despotism to Revolution, 1763–1789*, New York, 1944.

Gottschalk, L., *Lafayette and the Close of the American Revolution*, Chicago, 1942.

Haggard, A. C. P., *Louis XVI and Marie Antoinette*, 2 vols., New York, 1909.

Hyslop, B. V., *French Nationalism in 1789*, New York, 1934.

Lockitt, H., *The Relations of French and English Society*, London, 1920.

Mac Lehose, S. H., *The Last Days of the French Monarchy*, Glasgow, 1901.

Padover, S. K., *The Life and Death of Louis XVI*, New York, 1939.

Rocquain, F., *The Revolutionary Spirit Preceding the French Revolution*, London, 1891.

Marie Antoinette

Belloc, H., *Marie Antoinette*, New York, 1928.

Bicknell, A. L., *The Story of Marie Antoinette*, London, 1897.

Turgot

Dakin, D., *Turgot*, London, 1939.

Say, L., *Turgot*, Chicago, 1888.

Shepherd, R. P., *Turgot and the Six Edicts*, Lincoln, 1903.

Stephens, W., *The Life and Writing of Turgot*, London, 1895.

CHAPTER 27. SLAVIC EUROPE

Russia

Curtin, J., *The Mongols in Russia*, London, 1908.

Fisher, R. H., *The Russian Fur Trade*, Berkeley, 1944.

Lantzeff, G. V., *Siberia in the Seventeenth Century*, Berkeley, 1943.

Marriott, Sir J. A. R., *Anglo-Russian Relations, 1689–1943*, London, 1944.

Nowak, F., *Medieval Slavdom and the Rise of Russia*, New York, 1930.

Ivan IV

Walizewski, K., *Ivan the Terrible*, London, 1904.

The Early Romanoffs

Bain, R. N., *The First Romanoffs*, London, 1905.

Peter the Great

Browning, O., *Peter the Great*, London, 1898.

Graham, S., *Peter the Great*, New York, 1929.

Oudard, G., *Peter the Great*, New York, 1929.

Walizewski, K., *Peter the Great*, London, 1898.

The Successors of Peter the Great

Bain, R. N., *The Pupils of Peter the Great*, Westminster, 1897.

———, *The Daughter of Peter the Great*, New York, 1899.

———, *Peter III*, Westminster, 1902.

Catherine II

Hodgetts, E. A. B., *The Life of Catherine II*, London, 1914.

Waliszewski, K., *The Romance of an Empress*, New York, 1894.

Poland

Eversley, G. J. S., Baron, *The Partitions of Poland*, London, 1915.

Hainau, M., *The Fall of Poland in Contemporary American Opinion*, Chicago, 1935.

Lord, R. H., *The Second Partition of Poland*, Cambridge, 1915.

Czechoslovakia

Seton-Watson, R. W., *A History of the Czechs and Slovaks*, New York, 1943.

Thompson, S. H., *Czechoslovakia in European History*, Princeton, 1942.

Charles XII

Bain, R. N., *Charles XII and the Collapse of the Swedish Empire, (1682–1719)*, London, 1895.

CHAPTER 28. LITERARY MOVEMENTS OF THE EIGHTEENTH CENTURY

General

Becker, C. L., *The Heavenly City of the Eighteenth Century Philosophers*, New York, 1932.

Collins, J. C., *Voltaire, Montesquieu, and Rousseau in England*, London, 1908.

Gide, C., and Rist, C., *A History of Economic Doctrines from the Time of the Physiocrats*, New York, 1915.

Kelly, J. A., *England and the Englishman in German Literature of the Eighteenth Century*, New York, 1921.

631

Jensen, E. M., *The Influence of French Literature on Europe*, Boston, 1919.

Mornet, D., *French Thought in the Eighteenth Century*, New York, 1929.

Robertson, J. M., *A Short History of Free Thought*, 2 vols., London, 1915.

Singer, E. A., *Modern Thinkers and Present Problems*, New York, 1923.

Wade, I. O., *The Clandestine Organization and Diffusion of Philosophic Ideas from 1700 to 1750*, Princeton, 1938.

Vico

Croce, B., *The Philosophy of Giambattista Vico*, London, 1913.

Goldoni

Chatfield-Taylor, H. C., *Goldoni*, New York, 1913.

Kennard, J. S., *Goldoni and the Venice of His Time*, New York, 1920.

Alfieri

Megaro, G., *Vittorio Alfieri*, New York, 1930.

Addison

Carritt, E. F., *Addison, Kant, and Wordsworth*, Oxford, 1937.

Courthope, W. J., *Addison*, New York, 1884.

Swift

Goodwin, F. S., *Jonathan Swift*, New York, 1940.

Gwynn, S. L., *The Life and Friendships of Dean Swift*, New York, 1933.

Jackson, R. W., *Jonathan Swift*, New York, 1939.

Newman, B., *Jonathan Swift*, Boston, 1937.

Quintana, R., *The Mind and Art of Jonathan Swift*, London, 1936.

Taylor, W. D., *Jonathan Swift*, London, 1933.

Defoe

Dottin, P., *The Life and Strange and Surprising Adventures of Daniel Defoe*, New York, 1929.

Jackson, H., *Great English Novelists*, London, 1908.

Secord, A. W., *Studies in the Narrative Method of Defoe*, Urbana, 1924.

Sutherland, J. R., *Defoe*, London, 1937.

Trent, W. P., *Daniel Defoe*, Indianapolis, 1916.

Samuel Richardson

Downs, B. W., *Richardson*, New York, 1928.

McKillop, A. D., *Samuel Richardson*, Chapel Hill, 1936.

Sale, W. M., *Samuel Richardson*, New Haven, 1936.

Fielding

Banerji, H. K., *Henry Fielding*, Oxford, 1929.

Bissel, F. O., *Fielding's Theory of the Novel*, Ithaca, 1933.

Blanchard, F. T., *Fielding*, New Haven, 1926.

Cross, W. L., *The History of Henry Fielding*, New Haven, 1918.

Digeon, A., *The Novels of Fielding*, London, 1925.

Smollet

Benjamin, L. S., *The Life and Letters of Tobias Smollet*, Boston, 1927.

Kahrl, G. M., *Tobias Smollet*, Chicago, 1945.

Martz, L. L., *The Later Career of Tobias Smollet*, New Haven, 1942.

Sterne

Benjamin, L. S., *The Life and Letters of Laurence Sterne*, London, 1911.

Cross, W. L., *The Life and Times of Laurence Sterne*, 2 vols., New Haven, 1925.

Dr. Johnson

Bailey, J. C., *Dr. Johnson, and His Circle*, New York, 1913.

Boswell, J., *The Life of Samuel Johnson*, 2 vols., London, 1907.

Carlson, C. L., *The First Magazine*, Providence, 1938.

Hollis, C., *Dr. Johnson*, London, 1928.

Houston, P. H., *Doctor Johnson*, Cambridge, 1923.

Lynd, R., *Dr. Johnson and Company*, London, 1927.

Roberts, S. C., *The Story of Doctor Johnson,* Cambridge, 1919.

Tuberville, A. S., *Johnson's England,* 2 vols., Oxford, 1933.

Robert Burns

Carswell, C., *The Life of Robert Burns,* New York, 1931.

Ferguson, J. De, *Pride and Passion, Robert Burns,* New York, 1939.

Snyder, F. B., *The Life of Robert Burns,* New York, 1932.

Horace Walpole

Chase, I. W. U., *Horace Walpole,* Princeton, 1943.

Kelton-Cremer, R. W., *Horace Walpole,* New York, 1940.

Stuart, D. M., *Horace Walpole,* New York, 1927.

Gibbon

Low, D. M., *Edward Gibbon, 1737–1794,* New York, 1937.

Morison, J. C., *Gibbon,* New York, 1878.

Mowat, R. B., *Gibbon,* London, 1936.

Young, G. M., *Gibbon,* London, 1932.

Adam Smith

Hasek, C. W., *The Introduction of Adam Smith's Doctrines in Germany,* New York, 1925.

Hirst, F. W., *Adam Smith,* New York, 1904.

Johnson, E. A. J., *Predecessors of Adam Smith,* New York, 1937.

Nicholson, J. S., *A Project of Empire,* London, 1909.

Scott, W. R., *Adam Smith as Student and Professor,* Glasgow, 1937.

Small, A. W., *Adam Smith and Modern Sociology,* Chicago, 1907.

Goldsmith

Dobson, A., *Life of Oliver Goldsmith,* London, 1888.

Gwynn, S. L., *Oliver Goldsmith,* London, 1937.

Kent, E. E., *Goldsmith and His Booksellers,* London, 1933.

Moore, F. F., *The Life of Oliver Goldsmith,* London, 1910.

Lord Chesterfield

Craig, W. H., *Life of Lord Chesterfield,* New York, 1907.

Connely, W., *The True Chesterfield,* London, 1939.

Coxon, R., *Chesterfield and His Critics,* London, 1925.

Shellabarger, S., *Lord Chesterfield,* London, 1935.

Rousseau

Babbitt, I., *Rousseau and Romanticism,* New York, 1919.

Charpentier, J., *Rousseau,* New York, 1931.

Cobban, A., *Rousseau and the Modern State,* London, 1934.

Morley, J., *Rousseau,* New York, 1898.

Mowat, R. B., *Jean Jacques Rousseau,* Bristol, 1938.

Spell, J. R., *Rousseau in the Spanish World before 1833,* Austin, 1938.

The Physiocrats

Higgs, H., *The Physiocrats,* London, 1897.

Diderot

Cru, R. L., *Diderot as a Disciple of English Thought,* New York, 1913.

Montesquieu

Fletcher, F. T. H., *Montesquieu and English Politics, 1750–1800,* London, 1939.

Levin, L. M., *The Political Doctrine of Montesquieu's Esprit des Lois,* New York, 1936.

Spurlin, P. M., *Montesquieu in America, 1760–1801,* University of Louisiana, 1940.

Voltaire

Ballantyne, A., *Voltaire's Visit to England, 1726–1729,* London, 1893.

Barr, M. M. H., *Voltaire in America, 1744–1800,* Baltimore, 1941.

Bruce, H. L., *Voltaire on the English State,* Berkeley, 1918.

Espinasse, F., *Life of Voltaire*, London, 1892.

Maestro, M. T., *Voltaire and Beccaria as Reformers of Criminal Law*, New York, 1942.

Meyer, A., *Voltaire, Man of Justice*, New York, 1945.

Morley, John, *Viscount, Voltaire*, London, 1923.

Noyes, A., *Voltaire*, London, 1936.

Torrey, N. L., *The Spirit of Voltaire*, New York, 1938.

Lessing

Rolleston, T. W. H., *Life of Gotthold Ephraim Lessing*, London, 1889.

Goethe

Düntzer, J. H. J., *Life of Goethe*, London, 1908.

Mulloy, W. J., *The German Catholic Estimate of Goethe, 1790–1939*, Berkeley, 1944.

Schiller

Ewen, F., *The Prestige of Schiller in England, 1788–1859*, New York, 1932.

Hudson, W. H., *Schiller and His Poetry*, London, 1914.

Meakin, A. M. B., *Goethe and Schiller, 1785–1805*, London, 1932.

Nevinson, H. W., *Life of Friedrich Schiller*, London, 1889.

Thomas, C., *The Life and Works of Friedrich Schiller*, New York, 1901.

CHAPTER 29. ACHIEVEMENTS IN SCIENCE, MILITARY SCIENCE, PAINTING, MUSIC, PHILOSOPHY AND EDUCATION

General

Lodge, Sir O., *Pioneers of Science*, London, 1893.

Linnaeus

Greene, E. L., *Carolus Linnaeus*, Philadelphia, 1912.

Jackson, B. B., *Linnaeus*, London, 1923.

Cavendish

Wilson, G., *The Life of the Honorable Henry Cavendish*, London, 1851.

Franklin

Cohen, I. B., *Benjamin Franklin's Experiments*, Cambridge, 1941.

Reynolds

Gower, Lord R. C. S., *Sir Joshua Reynolds*, London, 1902.

Hilles, F. W., *The Literary Career of Sir Joshua Reynolds*, New York, 1936.

Gainsborough

Armstrong, W., *Thomas Gainsborough*, London, 1894.

Gower, Lord R. S., *Thomas Gainsborough*, London, 1903.

Watteau

Manclair, C., *Antoine Watteau*, London, 1905.

Goya

Flitch, J. E. C., *An Idler in Spain*, New York, 1914.

Gudiol i Ricart, J., *Goya*, New York, 1941.

Poore, C. G., *Goya*, London, 1935.

Stokes, H., *Francisco Goya*, London, 1914.

Bach

Boughton, R., *Bach, the Master*, New York, 1930.

Forkel, J. N., *Johann Sebastien Bach*, London, 1920.

Parry, Sir C. H. H., *Johann Sebastien Bach*, New York, 1901.

Terry, C. S., *Bach*, London, 1933.

Haydn

Fox, D. G. A., *Joseph Haydn*, London, 1927.

Hadden, J. C., *Haydn*, New York, 1911.

Mozart

Breakspeare, E. J., *Mozart*, New York, 1913.

Davenport, M., *Mozart*, New York, 1932.

Einstein, A., *Mozart,* New York, 1945.
Holmes, E., *The Life of Mozart,* New York, 1939.
Sitwell, S., *Mozart,* New York, 1938.

Gluck

Newman, E., *Gluck and the Opera,* London, 1895.

Berkeley

Fraser, A. G., *Berkeley,* Philadelphia, 1888.
Hone, J. M., *Bishop Berkeley,* New York, 1931.
Johnston, G. A., *The Development of Berkeley's Philosophy,* London, 1923.
Morris, C. R., *Locke, Berkeley, Hume,* Oxford, 1931.
Wild, J., *George Berkeley,* Cambridge, 1936.

Hume

Anderson, W., *An Orientation of Hume's Moral Philosophy,* Chicago, 1935.
Greig, J. Y. T., *David Hume,* London, 1931.
Hendel, C. W., *Studies in the Philosophy of David Hume,* Princeton, 1925.
Hume and Present Day Problems, London, 1939.
Huxley, T. H., *Hume,* New York, 1902.
Knight, W. A., *Hume,* Edinburgh, 1905.
Mossner, E. C., *The Forgotten Hume,* New York, 1943.
Smith, N. K., *The Philosophy of David Hume,* London, 1941.

Kant

Lindsay, A. D., *Kant,* London, 1934.
Singer, E. A., *Modern Thinkers and Present Problems,* New York, 1923.
Ward, J., *A Study of Kant,* Cambridge, 1922.
Wellek, R., *Immanuel Kant in England,* Princeton, 1931.

Fichte

Engebrecht, H. C., *Johann Gottlieb Fichte,* New York, 1933.
Talbot, E. B., *The Fundamental Principle of Fichte's Philosophy,* New York, 1906.

Rousseau

Charpentier, J., *Rousseau,* Toronto, 1931.
Cobban, A., *Rousseau and the Modern State,* London, 1934.
Mowat, R. B., *Jean Jacques Rousseau,* Bristol, 1938.

CHAPTER 30. SOCIAL AND ECONOMIC DEVELOPMENTS

Slave Trade

Coupland, R., *East Africa and Its Invaders,* Oxford, 1938.

Travel

Andrews, C. M., and E. W., *Journal of a Lady of Quality,* New Haven, 1923.

Newspapers

Bowman, W. D., *The Story of the Times,* New York, 1931.
Hindle, W., *The Morning Post, 1772–1937,* London, 1937.

PART 5. THE REVOLUTIONARY PERIOD

GENERAL WORK ON THE REVOLUTIONARY PERIOD

Bourne, *The Revolutionary Period in Europe,* New York, 1916.
Fortescue, I. W., *British Statesmen of the Great War, 1793–1814,* Oxford, 1911.

Gershoy, L., *The French Revolution and Napoleon,* New York, 1933.
Gottschalk, L. R., *The Era of the French Revolution,* Boston, 1929.
Lokke, C. L., *France and the Colonial Question,* New York, 1932.
Parkinson, C. N., *Trade in Eastern*

Seas, 1793–1813, Cambridge, 1937.

Phillips, C. S., The Church in France, 1789–1848, London, 1929.

Rose, J. H., The Revolutionary and Napoleonic Period, 1789–1815, New York, 1913.

CHAPTER 31. THE FRENCH REVOLUTION

Acton, J. E. E. D., Baron, Lectures on the French Revolution, London, 1920.

Alger, J. G., Paris in 1789–1794, London, 1902.

———, Glimpses of the French Revolution, London, 1894.

Aulard, F. V. A., Christianity and the French Revolution, Boston, 1927.

———, The French Revolution, 4 vols., London, 1910.

Bax, E. B., The Story of the French Revolution, New York, 1934.

———, The Last Episode of the French Revolution, Boston, 1911.

Belloc, H., The French Revolution, London, 1911.

Bishop, M. C., Prison Life of Marie Antoinette, London, 1894.

Bradby, E. D., The French Revolution, Oxford, 1932.

Brinton, C. C., The Jacobins, New York, 1930.

———, A Decade of Revolution, 1789–1799, New York, 1934.

Browning, O., The Flight to Varennes, London, 1893.

Correspondence of Jean Baptiste Carrier, New York, 1920.

Childs, F. S., French Refugee Life in the United States, 1790–1800, Baltimore, 1940.

Clapham, J. H., The Causes of the War of 1792, Cambridge, 1899.

Clery, E. J., The Royal Family in the Temple Prison, New York, 1909.

Dunoyer, A., The Public Prosecutor of the Terror, New York, 1913.

Eagan, J. M., Maximilian Robespierre, New York, 1938.

Elton, L., Locks, Bolts, and Bars, London, 1945.

Farmer, P., France Reviews Its Revolutionary Origins, New York, 1944.

Gaxotte, P., The French Revolution, New York, 1932.

Gershoy, L., The French Revolution, 1789–99, New York, 1932.

Gibbs, Sir P. H., Men and Women of the French Revolution, London, 1926.

Gooch, G. P., Germany and the French Revolution, London, 1920.

Greer, D., The Incidence of the Terror during the French Revolution, Cambridge, 1935.

Hazen, C. D., The French Revolution, 2 vols., New York, 1932.

———, Contemporary American Opinion of the French Revolution, Baltimore, 1897.

Henderson, E. F., Symbol and Satire in the French Revolution, New York, 1912.

Herbert, S., The Fall of Feudalism in France, London, 1921.

Johnston, R. M., The French Revolution, New York, 1909.

Kerr, W. B., The Reign of Terror, 1793–94, Toronto, 1927.

Kropotkin, P. A., Prince, The Great French Revolution, 1789–1793, London, 1909.

Lokke, C. L., France and the Colonial Question, New York, 1932.

Laprade, W. T., England and the French Revolution, Baltimore, 1909.

Madelin, L., The French Revolution, New York, 1926.

———, Figures of the French Revolution, London, 1922.

Mahan, A. T., Influence of Sea Power upon the French Revolution and Empire, 2 vols., Boston, 1894.

Mathews, S., The French Revolution, New York, 1928.

Mathiez, A., The French Revolution, New York, 1929.

———, The Fall of Robespierre and Other Essays, New York, 1927.

Palmer, R. R., Twelve Who Ruled, Princeton, 1941.

Phipps, Col. R. W., The Armies of the

First French Republic, 5 vols. London, 1926.

Stephens, H. M., *The French Revolution,* 2 vols., London, 1886.

Sirich, J. B., *The Revolutionary Committees in the Departments of France,* Cambridge, 1943.

Thompson, J. M., *The French Revolution,* Oxford, 1943.

Personalities of the French Revolution (General)

Beraud, H., *Twelve Portraits of the French Revolution,* Boston, 1928.

Gibbs, P., *Men and Women of the French Revolution,* London, 1906.

Madelin, L., *Figures of the French Revolution,* New York, 1934.

Witham, J. M., *Men and Women of the French Revolution,* New York, 1933.

Babeuf

Bax, E. B., *The Last Episode of the French Revolution,* Boston, 1911.

Buonarrotte, F. M., *History of Babeuf's Conspiracy for Equality,* London, 1936.

Carnot

Dupre, H., *Lazare Carnot,* Oxford, Ohio, 1940.

Charlotte Corday

Cher, M., *Charlotte Corday and Certain Men of the Revolutionary Torment,* New York, 1929.

Dobson, A., *Four French Women,* New York, 1890.

Danton

Beesley, A. H., *Life of Danton,* New York, 1899.

Belloc, H., *Danton,* London, 1899.

Wendel, H., *Danton,* New Haven, 1935.

Fourquier-Tinville

Dunoyer, A., *The Public Prosecutor of the Terror, Fourquier-Tinville,* New York, 1913.

Lafayette

Gottschalk, L. R., *Lafayette and the Close of the American Revolution,* Chicago, 1942.

Jackson, S. W., *Lafayette,* New York, 1930.

Tuckerman, B., *Life of General Lafayette,* 2 vols., New York, 1889.

Marat

Bax, E. B., *Jean Paul Marat, the People's Friend,* London, 1901.

Gottschalk, L. R., *Jean Paul Marat,* New York, 1927.

Mirabeau

Fling, F. M., *Mirabeaux and the French Revolution,* New York, 1908.

Tallentyre, S. G., *The Life of Mirabeau,* New York, 1909.

Trowbridge, W. R. H., *Mirabeau,* London, 1907.

Willert, P. F., *Mirabeau,* London, 1898.

Robespierre

Belloc, H., *Robespierre,* London, 1930.

Egan, J. M., *Maximilien Robespierre,* New York, 1938.

Lewes, G. H., *The Life of Maximilien Robespierre,* London, 1899.

Mathiez, A., *The Fall of Robespierre and Other Essays,* New York, 1927.

Mme. Roland

Young, C., *A Lady Who Loved Herself,* New York, 1930.

Saint-Just

Brunn, G., *Saint-Just, Apostle of the Terror,* Boston, 1932.

Curtis, E. N., *Saint-Just,* New York, 1935.

Morton, J. B., *Saint-Just,* New York, 1939.

Sieyès

Deusen, G. G., *Sieyès,* New York, 1932.

Neton, A., *Sieyès, 1748–1836,* Paris, 1901.

Condorcet

Burlingame, A. E., *Condorcet,* Boston, 1933.

Schapiro, J. S., *Condorcet and the Rise of Liberalism*, New York, 1933.

CHAPTER 32. THE RISE OF A DICTATOR IN FRANCE (1795–1804)

The Directory

Allinson, A., *The Days of the Directoire*, London, 1910.

Sargent, H. H., *Napoleon Bonaparte's First Campaign*, Chicago, 1896.

———, *The Campaign of Marengo*, Chicago, 1897.

Wheeler, H. F. B., and Broadley, *Napoleon and the Invasion of England*, 2 vols., New York, 1908.

Histories of the Napoleonic Period

Brunn, G., *Europe and the French Imperium, 1799–1814*, New York, 1938.

Deutsch, H. C., *The Genesis of Napoleonic Imperialism*, Cambridge, 1938.

Dunn-Pattison, R. P., *Napoleon's Marshals*, Boston, 1909.

Frischauer, P., *England's Years of Danger*, New York, 1938.

Fyffe, C. A., *A History of Modern Europe*, Vol. I, London, 1880.

Hall, R. A., *Studies in Napoleonic Strategy*, London, 1918.

Madelin, L., *The Consulate and the Empire*, New York, 1936.

Lokke, C. L., *France and the Colonial Question*, New York, 1932.

Mowat, R. B., *Europe in the Age of Napoleon*, New York, 1928.

———, *The Diplomacy of Napoleon*, London, 1924.

Rose, J. H., *William Pitt and the Great War*, London, 1911.

Strupp, P. F., *The European Powers and the Near Eastern Question*, New York, 1932.

Biographies of Napoleon I

Bainville, J., *Napoleon*, Boston, 1933.

Brice, R., *The Riddle of Napoleon*, New York, 1937.

Butterfield, H., *Napoleon*, London, 1940.

Clark, P., *Napoleon Self Destroyed*, New York, 1929.

Dodge, T. A., *Napoleon*, 4 vols., Boston, 1904–7.

Driault, E., *The True Visage of Napoleon*, Paris, 1929.

Fisher, H. A. L., *Napoleon I*, New York, 1924.

———, *Bonapartism*, Oxford, 1914.

Fournier, *Napoleon I*, New York, 1903.

Hassall, *Life of Napoleon*, London, 1911.

Johnston, R. M., *Napoleon*, New York, 1904.

———, *The Corsican*, Boston, 1910.

Kircheisen, F. M., *Napoleon I*, Berlin, 1927–29, 2 vols.; Munich, 1913–1934, 9 vols.

Lenz, M., *Napoleon*, New York, 1907.

Masson, F., *Napoleon at Home*, Philadelphia, 1894.

———, *Napoleon, Lover and Husband*, New York, 1894.

Merezhkovsky, D., *The Life of Napoleon*, New York, 1929.

Ropes, J. C., *The First Napoleon*, Boston, 1896.

Rose, J. H., *The Life of Napoleon I*, New York, 1902.

———, *Napoleonic Studies*, London, 1906.

Roseberry, A. P. P., Earl of, *Napoleon, the Last Phase*, New York, 1900.

Sloane, W. M., *Life of Napoleon Bonaparte*, 4 vols., New York, 1910.

Sokoloff, B., *Napoleon, A Doctor's Biography*, New York, 1937.

Tarlé, E., *Bonaparte*, New York, 1937.

CHAPTER 33. THE CONQUEST AND LOSS OF THE CONTINENT

Broadley, A. M., *Napoleon in Caricature, 1795–1821*, New York, 1911.

Coquelle, P., *Napoleon and England*, London, 1904.

Espitalier, A., *Napoleon and King Murat*, New York, 1912.

Fisher, H. A. L., *Bonapartism*, Oxford, 1908.

Haight, F. A., *A History of French Commercial Policy*, New York, 1941.

Masson, F., *Napoleon and His Coronation*, Philadelphia, 1911.

Parker, H. T., *Three Napoleonic Battles*, Durham, 1944.

Nicolay, F., *Napoleon at the Boulogne Camp*, New York, 1907.

Rose, J. H., *Napoleonic Studies*, London, 1906.

Tarlé, E., *Napoleon's Invasion of Russia, 1812*, New York, 1945.

Naples

Colletta, P., *History of the Kingdom of Naples, 1734–1825*, 2 vols., London, 1858.

Johnston, R. M., *The Napoleonic Empire in Southern Italy*, 2 vols., New York, 1904.

Germany

Fisher, H. A. L., *Studies in Napoleonic Statesmanship: Germany*, Oxford, 1903.

Prussia

Anderson, E. N., *Nationalism and the Cultural Crisis in Prussia, 1806–1815*, New York, 1939.

Ford, G. S., *Stein and the Era of Reform in Prussia, 1807–1815*, Princeton, 1922.

Grunuvald, (de), *Baron Stein*, London, 1936.

Henderson, E. F., *Blücher and the Uprising of Prussia against Napoleon, 1806–1815*, New York, 1911.

Seeley, J. R., *Life and Times of Stein*, 3 vols., Cambridge, 1878.

Shanahan, W. O., *Prussian Military Reforms, 1786–1815*, New York, 1945.

Austria

Langsam, W. C., *The Napoleonic Wars and German Nationalism in Austria*, New York, 1930.

Trevelyan, G. M., *British History in the 19th Century, 1782–1901*, New York, 1928.

Turberville, A. S., *Great Britain in the Latest Age*, London, 1921.

Great Britain

Brodrick, G. C., *The History of England, 1801–1837*, New York, 1928.

Brown, P. A., *The French Revolution in English History*, London, 1918.

Maxwell, Sir H. E., *A Century of Empire*, 3 vols., London, 1909–1911.

Quinlan, M. J., *Victorian Prelude, 1700–1830*, New York, 1941.

Temperley, H., and Penson, L. M., *Foundations of British Foreign Policy, 1792–1902*, New York, 1939.

Italy

McClellan, G. B., *Venice and Bonaparte*, Princeton, 1931.

Personalities of the Napoleonic Period (General)

Atterbridge, A. H., *Napoleon's Brothers*, New York, 1909.

Geer, W., *Napoleon and His Family*, New York, 1927–1930.

Bernadotte

Barton, D. P., *The Amazing Career of Bernadotte*, Boston, 1929.

———, *Bernadotte, the First Phase*, New York, 1914.

———, *Bernadotte and Napoleon, 1763–1810*, London, 1927.

Scott, F. D., *Bernadotte and the Fall of Napoleon*, Cambridge, 1935.

Charles James Fox

Hammond, J. L., *Charles James Fox*, London, 1903.

Lascelles, E., *The Life of Charles James Fox*, Oxford, 1936.

Fouché

Forssell, N., *Fouché, the Man Napoleon Feared*, New York, 1928.

Josephine

Forester, C. S., *Josephine, Napoleon's Empress*, London, 1925.

Masson, F., *Josephine, Empress and Queen*, New York, 1899.

Sergeant, P. W., *The Empress Josephine*, 2 vols., New York, 1909.

Letitia Bonaparte

Richardson, N., *Mother of Kings*, New York, 1928.

Louis Bonaparte

John, K., *The Prince Imperial,* New York, 1939.

Marie Louise

Geer, W., *Napoleon and Marie Louise,* New York, 1925.

Nelson

Beresford, C. W. de la P., Baron, *Nelson and His Times,* London, 1898.
Corbett-Smith, A., *Nelson,* Boston, 1926.
Edinger, G. A., *Nelson,* Boston, 1926.
Kircheisen, F. M., *Nelson,* New York, 1931.
Mahan, A. T., *The Life of Nelson,* Boston, 1897.
Moorhouse, E., *Nelson in England,* London, 1913.
Thursfield, J. R., *Nelson and Other Naval Studies,* London, 1909.
Wikinson, C., *Nelson,* New York, 1931.

William Pitt

Petrie, C. A., *William Pitt,* London, 1935.
Rose, J. H., *Pitt and Napoleon,* London, 1912.
Roseberry, A. P. P., Earl of, *Pitt,* London, 1892.

Talleyrand

Cooper, D., *Talleyrand-Perigord,* New York, 1932.
Dodd, A. B., *Talleyrand,* New York, 1927.
Fleury, S., *Talleyrand,* Montreal, 1942.
Huth, H., and Pugh, W. J., *Talleyrand in America as a Financial Promoter,* Washington, 1942.
McCabe, *Talleyrand,* London, 1906.
Saint-Aulaire, A. F. C., Count de, *Talleyrand,* New York, 1937.

Sir Robert Wilson

Costigan, G., *Sir Robert Wilson,* Madison, 1932.
See Histories of the Napoleonic Period and Biographies of Napoleon listed under preceding chapter.

CHAPTER 34. THE SETTLEMENT OF 1813–1815

The First Restoration in France

Hall, J., *The Bourbon Restoration,* Boston, 1909.
Henderson, E. F., *Blücher,* New York, 1911.
Lucas-Dubreton, J., *The Restoration and the July Monarchy,* New York, 1929.

The Settlement of 1813 to 1815

Cecil, A., *British Foreign Secretaries, 1807–1916,* London, 1927.
Debidour, A., *Histoire diplomatique de l'Europe,* Vol. 1, Paris, 1919–1920.
Hazen, C. D., Thayer, W. R., and Lord, R. H., *Three Peace Congresses of the 19th Century,* Cambridge, 1917.
Lockhart, J. G., *The Peacemakers, 1814–15,* London, 1932.
May, A., *The Age of Metternich,* New York, 1933.
Nicolson, H., *The Congress of Vienna,* New York, 1946.
Renier, G., *Great Britain and the Establishment of the Kingdom of the Netherlands, 1813–1815,* The Hague, 1930.
Webster, C. K., *The Congress of Vienna, 1814–1815,* New York, 1919.
———, *British Diplomacy, 1813–1815,* London, 1921.

Alexander I

Cresson, W. P., *Diplomatic Portraits,* New York, 1923.
Joyneville, C., *Life and Times of Alexander I,* London, 1875.
Paleologue, M., *The Enigmatic Czar,* New York, 1938.

Castlereagh

Hassall, A., *Viscount Castlereagh,* London, 1908.
Hyde, H. M., *The Rise of Castlereagh,* London, 1833.
Marriott, J. A. R., *Castlereagh,* London, 1936.
Webster, C. K., *The Foreign Policy of Castlereagh, 1812–1815,* New York, 1931.

Gentz

Sweet, P., *Friedrich von Gentz*, Madison, 1941.

Metternich

Buckland, C. S. B., *Metternich and the British Government from 1809–1813*, London, 1932.

Cecil, A., *Metternich*, London, 1933.

Coudray, H. du, *Metternich*, New Haven, 1936.

Cresson, *Diplomatic Portraits*, New York, 1923.

Herman, A., *Metternich*, New York, 1932.

Malleson, G. B., *Life of Prince Metternich*, Philadelphia, 1888.

Sandeman, G. A. C., *Metternich*, London, 1911.

Woodward, E. L., *Three Studies in European Conservatism*, London, 1929.

Duke of Wellington

Addington, R., *The Duke*, New York, 1943.

Brett, O., *Wellington*, London, 1928.

Fortescue, J. W., *Wellington*, New York, 1925.

Maxwell, Sir H. E., *The Life of Wellington*, London, 1899.

One Hundred Days

Chesney, C. C., Lt. Col., *Waterloo Lectures*, London, 1868.

Guerard, A., *Reflections on the Napoleonic Legend*, New York, 1924.

CHAPTER 35. ECONOMIC AND SOCIAL DEVELOPMENTS

The Steamboat

Chatterton, F. F., *Steamships and Their Story*, London, 1910.

Fletcher, R., *Steamships*, Philadelphia, 1910.

Livingston, R. R., *The Invention of the Steamboat*, Old South Leaflets, Boston, 1900.

Preble, G. H., *A Chronological History of the Origin and Development of Navigation*, Philadelphia, 1883.

Thurston, R. H., *Robert Fulton*, New York, 1891.

SOME AVAILABLE PRINTED PRIMARY SOURCES

GENERAL WORKS

Reddaway, W. F., *Select Documents of European History, 1492–1715*, New York, 1931.

Robinson, J. H., *Readings in European History*, Vol. 2, Boston, 1905.

Robinson, J. H., and Beard, C. A., *Readings in Modern European History*, Vol. 1, Boston, 1908–09.

ENGLISH ECONOMIC SOURCES

Bland, A. E., Brown, P. D., and Tawney, R. H., *English Economic History, Select Documents*, London, 1914.

Young, A., *A Six Weeks' Tour Through the Southern Counties of England and Wales*, London, 1769.

Young, A., *A Six Months' Tour Through the North of England*, 4 vols., London, 1770.

COLONIES

Commager, H. S., *Documents of American History*, New York, 1934.

Hakluyt, R., *The Principal Navigations, voyages . . . of the English Nation*, London, 1927.

Hart, A. B., *American History Told by Contemporaries*, 4 vols., New York, 1898.

Jameson, J. F., *Original Narratives of Early American History*, 20 vols., New York, 1906–17.

Purchas, S., *Hakluytus Posthumus or Purchas, His Pilgrims*, 29 vols., Glasgow, 1905–07.

SOURCES ON COUNTRIES AND REGIONS

France

Hawkins, R. L., *Newly Discovered French Letters of the 17th, 18th, and 19th Centuries,* Cambridge, 1933.

Great Britain

Bell, K., and Winbolt, S. E., *Bell's English History Source Books,* 14 vols., London, 1913–14.

British Diplomatic Instructions, 16 vols., Royal Historical Publications, 1922–1934.

Adams, G. B., and Stephens, N. M., *Select Documents of English Constitutional History,* New York, 1937.

Medley, D. J., *Original Illustrations of English Constitutional History,* London, 1910.

Cheyney, E. P., *Readings in English History,* Boston, 1908.

Colby, W. C., *Selections from the Sources of English History,* New York, 1899.

Gee, H., and Hardy, W. J., *Documents Illustrative of English Church History,* London, 1910.

Dykes, D. O., *Source Book of Constitutional History,* New York, 1930.

Robertson, G., *Select Statutes, Cases, and Documents to Illustrate English Constitutional History,* New York, 1904.

Stephenson, C., and Marcham, F. C., *Sources of English Constitutional History,* New York, 1938.

Warner, G. T., ed., *English History Illustrated from Original Sources,* London, 1901.

Prothero, G. W., *Select Statutes and Other Constitutional Documents Illustrative of the Reigns of Elizabeth and James I,* London, 1894.

Wernham, R. B., *England under Elizabeth,* New York, 1932.

Ireland

Curtis, E., and McDowell, B. B., *Irish Historical Documents, 1172–1922,* London, 1943.

PART I. EUROPEAN SOCIETY ABOUT 1492

Chapter 4. European Culture

The Fugger News-Letters, London, 1924.

Klarwell, V., *The Fugger News-Letters,* New York, 1926.

McMurtrie, D. C., *The Guttenberg Documents,* New York, 1941.

Richards, G. R. B., *Florentine Merchants in the Age of the Medici,* Cambridge, 1932.

Whitcomb, M., *A Literary Source Book of the German Renaissance,* Philadelphia, 1899.

PART 2. THE SIXTEENTH CENTURY

Chapter 5. The Beginnings of European Expansion, 1492–1598

Cleven, N. A. N., *Readings in Hispanic American History,* New York, 1929.

Ford, P. L., *Writings of Christopher Columbus,* New York, 1892.

Jane, L. C., *Select Documents Illustrating the Four Voyages of Columbus,* London, 1930.

The Journal of Christopher Columbus, London, 1893.

Major, R. H., *Select Letters of Christopher Columbus,* London, 1870.

Ravenstein, E. G., *A Journal of the First Voyage of Vasco da Gama, 1497–1499,* London, 1898.

Wilgus, A. C., *Readings in Hispanic American Colonial History, 1492–1824,* Washington, 1937.

See also volumes in J. F. Jameson, *Original Narratives of Early American History,* under Colonies.

Chapter 6. European Politics, 1494–1559

Gairdner, J., *Letters and Papers Illustrative of the Reigns of Richard III and Henry VII,* London, 1861–63.

Gairdner, J., and Brodie, R. H., *Letters and Papers Foreign and Domestic of the Region of Henry VIII,* 21 vols., London, 1862–1910.

Gomara, F. L. de, *Annals of the Emperor Charles V,* Oxford, 1912.

Pollard, A. F., *The Reign of Henry VII from Contemporary Sources,* New York, 1913–14.

Tanner, J. R., *Tudor Constitutional Documents, 1485–1603,* Cambridge, 1922.

Tawney, R. H., and Power, E., *Tudor Economic Documents,* 3 vols., London, 1924.

Williams, C. H., *England under the Early Tudors,* New York, 1925.

Chapter 7. Religious Revolt and Reform in German and Scandinavian Lands

Allen, P. S., *Selections from Erasmus,* Oxford, 1908.

Erasmus, D., *The Education of a Christian Prince,* New York, 1936.

———, *The Epistles of Erasmus,* 3 vols., New York, 1901–18.

———, *The Praise of Folly,* Oxford, 1913, and Princeton, 1941.

Jacobs, H., *The Book of Concord,* Philadelphia, 1882–1883.

Kidd, B. J., *Documents Illustrative of the Continental Reformation,* Oxford, 1911.

Smith, P., *Luther's Correspondence and Other Contemporary Letters,* 2 vols., Philadelphia, 1913–18.

———, *Luther's Table Talk,* New York, 1907.

Wace, H., and Buckhein, C. A., *Luther's Primary Works,* London, 1896.

Works of Martin Luther, 2 vols., Philadelphia, 1915–16.

Chapter 8. The Calvinist and Anglican Revolts against the Medieval Church

Calvin, J., *Institutes of the Christian Religion,* Philadelphia, 1921.

Châteillon, S., *Concerning Heretics . . . ,* New York, 1935.

Jackson, S. M., *Selected Works of Huldreich Zwingli,* Philadelphia, 1901.

Chapter 9. The Catholic Reformation and Spanish Imperialism

Loyola, Ignatius, *The Spiritual Exercises of St. Ignatius of Loyola,* New York, 1914.

Loyola Ignatius, *The Autobiography of St. Ignatius,* New York, 1900.

Waterworth, J., *The Canons and Decrees of the Council of Trent,* London, n.d.

Chapter 10. The Protestant Resistance to the Catholic Reformation and the Imperialism of Philip II.

Consult memoirs in the Petitot and Michaud and Poujoulat series.

Biron, A. de, Baron, *The Letters and Documents of,* Berkeley, 1936.

Chapter 12. Advances in Education, Art, and Literature

The Literary Works of Leonardo da Vinci, New York, 1939.

The Notebooks of Leonardo da Vinci, New York, 1938.

Hulton, E., ed., *Memoirs of the Dukes of Urbino, 1440–1630,* New York, 1909.

Machiavelli, N., *The Prince,* London, 1908.

The Autobiography of Michel de Montaigne, Boston, 1935.

Essays of Montaigne, New York, 1907.

More, Sir Thomas, *Utopia,* Oxford, 1904, and New York, 1931.

Chapter 16. Development of Parliamentary Government and Religious Toleration in England

Abbott, W. C., *The Writings and Speeches of Oliver Cromwell,* 3 vols., Cambridge, 1945.

Brown, B. C., *The Letters and Diplomatic Instructions of Queen Anne,* London, 1935.

Chamberlain, J., *A Jacobean Letter Writer,* New York, 1920.

Evelyn, John, *Diary and Correspondence of John Evelyn,* 4 vols., London, 1870–72.

Foot, I., *A Selection from the Letters and Speeches of Oliver Cromwell,* London, 1941.

Fox, George, *The Short Journal and*

Itinerary Journals of George Fox, Cambridge, 1925.

Gardiner, S. R., *The Constitutional Documents of the Puritan Revolution,* Oxford, 1889.

Haller, Wm., and Davies, G., *The Leveller Tracts,* New York, 1944.

James, M., *England during the Interregnum,* London, 1935.

Ludlow, E., *The Memoirs of Edmund Ludlow,* Oxford, 1894.

Pepys, Samuel, *Diary and Correspondence,* 2 vols., London, 1914–17.

Tanner, J. R., *Constitutional Documents of the Reign of James I,* Cambridge, 1930.

———, *English Constitutional Conflicts of the Seventeenth Century, 1603–1689,* Cambridge, 1928.

Trevelyan, G. M., *Select Documents for Queen Anne's Reign,* Cambridge, 1929.

Williams, B., *The Edinburgh Source Book for British History, 1603–1707,* London, 1933.

Chapter 17. Development Overseas in the Seventeenth Century: The Rise and Decline of Dutch Predominance

Consult J. F. Jameson, *Original Narratives of Early American History,* under Colonies.

Chapter 23. Central Europe in the Eighteenth Century

Memoirs of Frederica Sophia Wilhelmina, London, 1828.

Philips, T. R., *Frederick the Great: Instructions for His Generals,* Harrisburg, 1944.

Chapter 25. Great Britain in the Eighteenth Century (1714–1789)

Young, A., *Autobiography,* London, 1898.

———, *A Six Weeks' Tour through the North of England,* 4 vols., London, 1770.

———, *A Six Weeks' Tour through the Southern Counties of England and Wales,* 4 vols., London, 1769.

Young, A., *The Farmer's Tour through the East of England,* 4 vols., London, 1771.

Wesley, J., *The Letters of John Wesley,* London, 1915.

Parker, P. L., *The Heart of John Wesley's Journal,* New York, 1903.

Chapter 26. The History of France in the Eighteenth Century

Young, A., *Travels in France during the Years, 1787–89,* London, 1909.

Chapter 27. Slavic Europe

Reddaway, W. F., *Documents of Catherine the Great,* New York, 1931.

Chapter 31. The French Revolution

Anderson, F. M., *Constitutions and Other Select Documents,* France, 1908.

Legg, L. G. W., *Select Documents Illustrative of the History of the French Revolution,* Oxford, 1905.

Higgins, E. L., *The French Revolution as Told by Contemporaries,* Boston, 1939.

Thompson, J. M., *English Witnesses of the French Revolution,* Oxford, 1938.

Morris, Gouveneur, *Diary and Letters,* 2 vols., Boston, 1939.

Andrews, G. G., *The Constitution in the Early French Revolution,* New York, 1927.

Chinard, G., *The Letters of Lafayette and Jefferson,* Baltimore, 1929.

Stephens, H. M., *The Principal Speeches of the Statesmen and Orators of the French Revolution, 1789–1795,* London, 1892.

Rigby, Dr., *Letters from France,* London, 1880.

Fox, C. J., *Speeches during the French Revolutionary Period,* New York, 1924.

Chapter 32. The Rise of a Dictator

Thompson, J. M., *Napoleon Self-Revealed,* Boston, 1934.

Lloyd, Lady Mary, *New Letters of Napoleon I,* London, 1898.

Masson, F., *The Private Diaries of the Empress Marie Louise*, New York, 1922.

Saint-Amand, I. de, *The Memoirs of the Empress Marie Louise*, London, 1886.

Chapter 33. The Conquest and Loss of the Continent

Bourrienne, L. A. F., de, *Memoirs of Napoleon Bonaparte*, 4 vols., New York, 1891.

Memoirs Illustrating the History of Napoleon I, 3 vols., New York, 1894.

Memoirs of Queen Hortense, 2 vols., New York, 1927.

Memoirs of Caulincourt, 2 vols., New York, 1935–36.

The Memoirs of Joseph Fouché, duc d'Otranto, 2 vols., London, 1896.

Memoirs of Marshal Oudinot, New York, 1897.

Memoires de duc de Raguse, 9 vols., Paris, 1857.

Memoirs of C. M. de Talleyrand-Perigord, 5 vols., New York, 1891–1892.

Chapter 34. The Settlement of 1813–1815

British and Foreign State Papers, 1812–16, London, 1841.

Webster, C. K., *British Diplomacy, 1813–1815*, London, 1921.

Supplementary Despatches and Memoranda of Field Marshall, Arthur, Duke of Wellington, 15 vols., London, 1858–72.

SOME WORKS CONTAINING ILLUSTRATIONS

For pictures of European landscapes consult the fine pictures to be found in the *Enciclopedia Italiana*.

GENERAL

Barbagallo, C., *Storia Universale*, Vols., 4 and 5, Turin, 1931–1940.

Hirth, G., *Kulturgeschichtliches Bilderbuch aus drei Jahrhunderts*, 6 vols., Leipzig, 1881–90.

La Farge, H., ed., *Lost Treasures of Europe*, New York, 1946.

Parmentier, A., *Album Historique*, Vols., 2, 3, and 4, Paris, 1896–1907.

Propylaen Weltgeschichte, 10 vols., Berlin, 1929–33.

PEASANT HOUSES

Consult Der Grosse Brockhaus article on Bauernhäusser; and other German encyclopedias:

Bartels, A., *Der Bauer in der deutschen Vergengenheit*, Leipzig, 1900.

Ekkehart, K., *Deutsche Bauerngeschichte*, Gotha, 1934.

Mielke, R., *Der Deutsche Bauer und sein Dorf*, Weimar, 1935.

PAINTING

Abbott, E. R., *The Great Painters*, New York, 1927.

Cole, T., *Old English Masters*, New York, 1902.

Cole, T., *Old Spanish Masters*, New York, 1907.

Craven, T., *A Treasury of Art Masterpieces*, New York, 1939.

Kent, R., *World Famous Paintings*, New York, 1939.

Lafenestre, G., and Richtenberger, E., *La peinture en Europe*, 7 vols., Paris, 1905.

MacFall, H., *A History of Painting*, Boston.

Raffael, des Meisters Gemälde in 203 Abbildungen, Stuttgart, 1906.

The French Renaissance, Boston, 1940.

Most of the biographies of painters are well illustrated.

MUSIC

Kinsky, G., Haas, R., and Schnock, H., *A History of Music in Pictures*, London, 1930.

COSTUME

Most of the histories of costume are profusely illustrated. See Costume in *A List of Histories in English*. Pictures illustrating the Histories of Countries and Regions.

FRANCE

Histoire de France Illustree, Vol. 1 and 2, Paris.

GREAT BRITAIN

Historical Portraits, 4 vols., Oxford, 1911.
Roberts, *A Picture Book of British History*, New York, 1941.
Recording Britain, 4 vols., London, 1947.

HOLY ROMAN EMPIRE

Hofman, A., *Politische Geschichte der Deutschen*, Berlin, 1922–28. (Consult Bilderatlas.)
Deutsche Kulturatlas, 5 vols., Berlin, 1928–1938.

RUSSIA

Loukomski, G. K., *Les Russes*, Paris, 1919.
Howard, A., *Pictorial History of Russia* . . . , New York, 1943.

PROTESTANT REVOLT

Luther Album, St. Louis, 1910.

AGE OF LOUIS XIV

Bourgeois, E., *Le Grand Siécle*, Paris, 1896.
Dayot, A., *Louis XIV*, Paris, 1909.

WALLENSTEIN

Wallenstein und die zeit des dreissigjahrigen Krieges, Leipzig, 1898.

THIRTY YEARS' WAR

Beller, E. A., *Caricatures of the Winter King of Bohemia*, Oxford, 1928.

GOYA

Gomez de la Serma, R., *Don Francisco de Goya y Leicientes*, Buenos Aires, 1942.

FREDERICK WILLIAM I

In Tormentis finxit, Briefe and Belder des Soldatinkonigs, Sluttgart, 1938.

THE FRENCH REVOLUTION

Gibbs, Sir P. H., *Men and Women of the French Revolution*, London, 1926.
Henderson, E. F., *Symbol and Satire in the French Revolution*, New York, 1912.
Lacrois, D., *Histoire de Napoleon*, Paris, 1928.
Vatel, C., *Recueil de gravures de Corday et les Girondins*, Paris, 1864–1872.

NAPOLEON

Broadley, A. M., *Napoleon in Caricature*, New York, 1911.
Dayot, A., *Napoleon raconte par l'image*, Paris, 1902.
Thompson, J. M., *Napoleon Self-Revealed*, London, 1933.

INDEX

Chesterfield, Lord, 462
Chile, 63
Christian Church, origin of, 4
Christians, enslavement of, 84; differences between, 90
Christian union, 107
Church, the Christian, 4–5; Medieval, 13–16; Eastern Orthodox, 90–95; Roman Catholic, 90–95; services of, 94; criticism of, 95–97; differences in beliefs and practices, 130; in Hungary, 138–139; Russian, 445; and state, 417–418
Cinqu-Mars, 205
Cintra, Convention of, 557
Cisalpine Republic, 530, 533
Cities and towns, organization of, 13–18; political organization of French, 422
Civil Code, 540
Civil constitution of clergy, 513–514
Clarendon, Code, 252; Lord, 252, 343
Claude of Lorraine, 308
Clergy, secular, 90–92; regular, 92; higher, 418; lower, 418; regular, 418
Clive, Robert, 385–386
Code, civil, 540; Napoleonic, 540
Coffee, 348–349
Colbert, 213–217, 321
Colet, John, 96, 97
Coligny, Admiral, 153
Columbus, 53–56, 57–58
Comenius, John Amos, 303
Commerce, 18–20, 215, 419–420, 514
Committee of General Security, 522
Committee of Public Safety, 521–522
Commonwealth, the, 247–248
Communications, 189, 350–351
Conception of the Universe, 37–38
Concordat (1576), 417; (1800), 539–540
Condé, 208, 209, 210, 211, 213, 219
Condillac, 469
Condorcet, 469, 584
Coen, 265–266
Coke of Holkam, Lord, 403
Colonial plans of First Consul, 541–542
Confederation of the Rhine, 549–550
Conscription, 586–588
Conservatoire des Arts et Metiers, 526
Constituent assembly, 506–509; reforms of, 509–515
Constitution of 1812, 563
Contagious diseases, 187
Continental system, 552–555
Convention, the, 519–521; reforms of, 525–526
Cop, Nicolas, 112
Copenhagen, bombardment of, 553
Copernican theory, acceptance of, 160
Copernicus, Nicolaus, 157–158

Corneille, 334
Cornwallis, Lord, 390
Coronada, 61
Cortez, Hernando, 59–61
Council of state, 538
Coup d'Etat, 535, 536–537
Court life, 166
Courts (French), 416–417
Covenant, National, 243
Cowper, William, 459
Cranach, Lucas, 175
Cranmer, Archbishop, 123; Book of Common Prayer, 183
Crompton, Samuel, 397
Cromwell, Oliver, 246, 247, 248–249, 328; Richard, 249; Thomas, 123
Cromwell's Ironsides, 246
Cugnot, 498–499
Czartoryski family, 450

Danton, 523
Deccan, Nizam of, 383
Declaration of independence, 389
Defoe, Daniel, 459
Denmark, 36, 285–286; spread of Lutheranism to, 110
Descartes, René, 316–317, 325
De Soto, 61
Devolution, war of, 219–220
Diaz, 67
Diaz de Solis, 56–57
Diderot, Denis, 467–468
Diemen, Anthonie von, 266
Dinwiddie, 379–380
Diplomatic revolution, 364–365
Directory, the, 535–537
Diu, 382
Donatello, 45
Douay, 129
Drake, Sir Francis, 70, 150–151
Dress, in the sixteenth century, 185–187; in the seventeenth century, 347–348; in the eighteenth century, 490; effect of French Revolution on, 581–582
Dreux-Brezé, Marquis of, 505
Dryden, John, 342–343
Dunes, Battle of, 211
Dupes, Day of, 205
Dupleix, 382–384
Dupont, surrender of General, 556
Duquesne, Fort, 380; Marquis of, 379
Dürer, Albrecht, 175
Dutch colonial empire, establishment of, 264–267
Dutch East India Company, 265–266
Dutch success, 263–264

649

Gallican Liberties, Declaration of, 224
Galvani, 477
Gas, 326
Gas lighting, 585–586
Gaston of Orleans, 203
General Security, Committee of, 522
Geneva, Calvin at, 113–115
Gentz, Frederich von, 572
Geographical knowledge, the new, 160
Geology, 474–475
Geometry, analytical, 325
George I, 391, 394
George II, 394
George III, 396, 405–407
German literature, 181–182, 470–472
German princes, 85
German problem, 84–85
Germans of Bohemia, 109
Germany, status of Jews, 190–191
Ghetto, 191
Ghiberti, 45
Gibraltar, 235, 390
Gilbert, Sir Humphrey, 70
Gilds, 16–17; French craft, 419; abolished, 514
Girondins, 516, 520
Goa, 382
Godoy, 555, 556
Goethe, 471–472
Goldoni, Carlo, 457
Goldsmith, Oliver, 461–462
Good Hope, Cape, 67
Goya, 483–484
Governments, some generalizations about, 23–25
Grand Remonstrance, 245
Gray, Thomas, 459
Great Britain, and France, early colonial conflicts of, 376–377
Greuze, 483
Grimmelshausen, 346
Grocyn, 97
Grotius, Hugo, 319
Guiana, Dutch, 273
Guise, Duke of, 88, 116; Mary of, 118, 152–153, 154
Gustavus Adolphus, 207, 289–292, 328, 346

Habeas Corpus Act, 254
Habsburg lands, 80
Habsburg state, development of, 80–82; in the seventeenth century, 300–302; in the eighteenth century, 361–367, 370–374
Haiti, 70
Hakluyt, Richard, 184
Hals, Frans, 307

Haller, Albrecht von, 473–474
Hampden's case, 243
Hampton Court, 238
Hanover, 364–365; Prussia gains, 549
Hanseatic League, 19, 194, 286
Hardenberg, 564
Hargreaves, James, 397
Harvey, William, 323–324
Hawkins, Sir John, 70, 149–150
Hébert, 523
Hedwig, 438
Heinsius, 232
Helmont, 326
Helvetian republic, 534
Henry the Navigator, Prince, 31
Henry II, 85, 88, 105
Henry III, 152–153, 154
Henry IV, 153, 154; and the restoration of order, 197–200
Henry VII, 31–32, 74, 121, 122
Henry VIII, 77–80, 121–125; and parliament, 123–124; Ireland in the time of, 125; death of, 125
Heritage, from ancient times, 4; from medieval times, 5–7
Hertford, 125
Hobbes, Thomas, 313–314
Hogarth, William, 481–482
Hohenlinden, Battle of, 537
Holbach, Baron, 469
Holbein, Hans, 175
Holy League, 83
Hooch, 308
Hooker, Rev. Thomas, 270
Hospitals, 187–188
Houtman, Cornelius, 264
Hubertusburg, Treaty of, 367
Hudson, Henry, 267
Hudson's Bay Company, 277
Hudson's Bay region, 235
Huguenots, 115, 116–117, 203–204
Human body, discovery of, 161–162
Humanism, Italian, 43–44; German, 44
Humanists, patrons of, 44, 96, 111; and education, 167
Hume, 486–487
Hungary, 34, 81–82; division of, 121
Hunter, John, 474
Huntsman, Benjamin, 398
Hus, John, 100–281
Hutten, Ulrich von, 101–102
Huyghen van Liuschoten, 264
Huyghens, 327

Illyrian provinces, 560, 569
Inca empire, conquest of, 61–63